Whereas, We have noticed with pleasure the action taken in different parts of our Confederacy in response to the call of the President for the Soldiers to reenlist for the war, and whereas we feel with pride the interests that bind us together in a common brotherhood struggling for the same common rights and liberties, and earnestly desiring to emulate the example of those who have resolved to serve their Country until the last armed foe shall be driven beyond the borders of our land,

Therefore be it:

Resolved that having already enlisted unconditionally for the war, we take this method of renewing our pledge to stand by our brethren in the field, until we have achieved an honourable independence among the nations of the world, and have avenged the death of our gallant commanders, who have sealed their devotion to our Country's cause, and enriched the soil of every State in the Confederacy by their blood.

Captain L.A. Whilden
Company E, 5th Regiment, South Carolina Cavalry
1864

South Carolina's Military Organizations During the War Between the States

Volume I: The Lowcountry & Pee Dee
Volume II: The Midlands
Volume III: The Upstate
Volume IV: Statewide Units, Militia and Reserves

South Carolina's
Military Organizations During the
War Between the States

The Midlands

Robert S. Seigler

Charleston   London
The History Press

Published by The History Press
Charleston, SC 29403
www.historypress.net

Cover image: The Burning of Columbia. *Courtesy Library of Congress.*
Cover design by Marshall Hudson

First published 2008

Manufactured in the United States

ISBN 978.1.59629.193.5

Library of Congress Cataloging-in-Publication Data

Seigler, Robert S.
South Carolina's military organizations during the War between the States / Robert S. Seigler.
p. cm.
Includes bibliographical references and index.
ISBN 978-1-59629-193-5 (alk. paper)
1. South Carolina--History--Civil War, 1861-1865--Regimental histories. 2. United States--History--Civil War, 1861-1865--Regimental histories. 3. Confederate States of America--Armed Forces. I. Title.
E577.4.S45 2008
973.7'457--dc22

2007049670

In memory of:
Milledge Rivers Gunter
Company F
Palmetto Sharpshooters
Bratton's Brigade
Field's Division
Longstreet's Corps
A.N.V.

Joseph O'Hear Sanders
The Citadel Cadets, and
The Stono Scouts

Andrew Altman Seigler
Percival's Company
Colcock's Regiment
South Carolina State Troops

A.J. Bulkley
Company A, 17th Battalion, South Carolina Cavalry
Company D, 5th Regiment, South Carolina Cavalry

Contents

ACKNOWLEDGEMENTS

The following people offered invaluable assistance in the production of this work: John Mills Bigham, Curator of Education, South Carolina Confederate Relic Room and Museum, Columbia, South Carolina; Beth Bilderbeck, Visual Materials Archivist, South Caroliniana Library, University of South Carolina, Columbia, South Carolina; Suzanne Case, Supervisor, South Carolina Room, Greenville County Library System, Greenville, South Carolina; Doris Gandy, Director, Darlington County Historical Society, Darlington, South Carolina; Carl Hill, Director, The War Between The States Museum, Florence, South Carolina; Stephen L. Johnson, President, The State Printing Company, Columbia, South Carolina; Webster Jones, The 16th Regiment Museum, Greenville, South Carolina; Ola Jean Kelly, Director, Union County Museum, Union, South Carolina; Sidney R. Thompson, Executive Director, Greenville County Historical Society, Greenville, South Carolina; Jane Yates, Director, Archives and Museum, The Citadel, Charleston, South Carolina.

I deeply appreciate the expert editorial assistance of Ann Bowen of Greenwood, South Carolina, whose knowledge and guidance handmolded this work.

Finally and most importantly, I would like to thank my wife, Patti, and my children, Carrie and Robert, for their remarkable patience and encouragement throughout the fifteen or so years that I researched and wrote this book. I dedicate it to them.

INTRODUCTION

More than a century has passed since a comprehensive account of the organization of South Carolinians for military service in the War Between the States has appeared in print. In 1899 Professor William J. Rivers published *Rivers's Account of the Raising of Troops in South Carolina for State and Confederate Service 1861–1865*, and in the same year, Rivers's collaborator and then-state historian of Confederate records, John Peyre Thomas, issued an augmented version of Rivers's work as a report to the South Carolina legislature entitled *Annual Report of the State Historian of Confederate Records For The Year 1899.*[1] Since that time, a great many historical works dealing with South Carolina's Confederate history have been published. None, however, has attempted to update or expand upon Rivers's and Thomas's seminal works. This book attempts to do just that. It records the history of the infantry, cavalry, artillery and reserve units organized in South Carolina immediately before and during the War Between the States.

OVERVIEW

On November 13, 1860, the South Carolina General Assembly authorized the creation of a convention of the people to be called the South Carolina Secession Convention. In late 1860 and early 1861, both the General Assembly and the Secession Convention approved several acts and resolutions creating a significant state military force. The South Carolina General Assembly passed its first act related to the raising of troops for possible armed conflict on December 17, 1860, just three days before the Ordinance of Secession passed the Convention. In a precautionary move designed to arm ten thousand men, the legislature authorized the governor to call up troops for the defense of the state by "engrafting a volunteer system on the existing militia" thus creating an "Armed Military Force."[1] The act directed "that whenever it shall appear that an armed force is about to be employed against the State, or in opposition to its authority, the Governor be, and he is hereby, authorized to repel the same; and for that purpose to call into the service of the State...such a portion of the militia as he may deem necessary and proper."[2] It also directed the governor to call at once for one volunteer company of infantry from each militia infantry battalion, two rifle companies from each militia infantry brigade, one or more cavalry companies from each militia cavalry regiment and one regiment of artillery from Charleston. In addition, he was allowed to call for three artillery companies, one each from Columbia, Georgetown and Beaufort.[3]

This act also authorized the governor to receive into service any volunteer organization that had a full complement of officers and men and to draft men from any militia battalion that did not furnish its quota within thirty days.[4] These volunteer units were to be organized into battalions or regiments, which, in turn, were to be organized into four brigades. Then the entire organization was to be incorporated into a single division under the command of a major general. The men in ranks were to elect officers up to and including the rank of colonel. The governor, with the advice and consent of the Senate, was to appoint the four brigadier generals and the sole major general. The governor could call any or all elements of this organization into service for no more than twelve months. Governor Pickens duly appointed Milledge L. Bonham of Edgefield as major general; Patrick H. Nelson of Sumter, T.G. Rhett and Samuel McGowan of Abbeville and Albert C. Garlington of Newberry would be the four brigadier generals.

On December 26, 1860, Major Robert Anderson of the United States Army withdrew his troops from Fort Moultrie to Fort Sumter. On December 29, Governor Pickens responded by issuing the call to begin raising troops as authorized by the act of December 17.[5] The first regiments to be raised were called "South Carolina Volunteers." Initially there were to be ten of these volunteer regiments. They were given numeric designations—2nd Regiment Infantry, South Carolina Volunteers, for example—and were usually abbreviated "SCV." In 1860 South Carolina was divided into thirty districts.[6] These thirty districts were further divided into ten "regions" for the purpose of raising the ten regiments created by the December 17 act.[7] It is possible the first ten regiments were numbered based on their geographical origin. It is also possible that they were based on the dates of elections for field officers. In fact, Johnson Hagood said his regiment was the first to volunteer and for that reason was designated the 1st Regiment, SCV.[8]

While these volunteer regiments were being organized, the South Carolina legislature and the Secession Convention realized that the state militia, as it existed, was unable to meet the immediate needs of the state to defend itself. On January 1, 1861, the Secession Convention passed two resolutions. One created a Board of Ordnance and a Corps of Military Engineers. The other authorized the immediate enlistment of volunteer companies to be formed into a single regiment to serve for six months[9] and allowed the governor to accept volunteer companies attached to the South Carolina Militia to serve until they could be replaced by the forces raised under the legislature's December 17 act.[10] Acting on this resolution, the governor, on January 8, accepted Maxcy Gregg's regiment, known as the 1st Regiment Infantry, SCV, for six months' service as infantry support for Sullivan's Island and Fort Moultrie in the event of a Federal land attack.[11] He also employed the 4th Brigade, South Carolina Militia, as the primary military force in and around Charleston during the first few months of 1861.

The preceding day the Secession Convention had passed a resolution authorizing the creation of one or two regiments that would soon become known as the Regular Army of South Carolina. The first regiment was to have eight companies whose 640 privates who would enlist for twelve months. Company officers and field officers were to be appointed by the governor and confirmed by the Senate. The governor could enlist a second regiment following the same guidelines "whenever the public interest, in his opinion, may require it."[12] Originally, these "regular troops" were created to relieve the volunteers who were then in possession of the forts in the state, primarily in and around Charleston Harbor. On January 19, 23 and 28 the Senate confirmed Governor Pickens's recommendations for many of the field-grade and company-grade officers.

On January 28 the South Carolina legislature passed an act entitled "An act for creating a military establishment for the State of South Carolina, and for other purposes." This act modified the Secession Convention's resolution of December 31, 1860.[13] It created a state military establishment to be known as the Regular Army of South Carolina, and it extended the men's term of service to three years unless they were discharged earlier. All officers were to be approved by the governor and confirmed by the Senate. The organization was modified to comprise one infantry regiment, one artillery battalion and one cavalry squadron. Between them, the resolution of December 31 and the act of January 28 created the following units: the 1st Regiment, South Carolina Infantry, Regulars; the 1st Battalion, South Carolina Artillery, Regulars; and DeSaussure's Squadron, South Carolina Cavalry, Regulars. Brigadier General R.G.M. Dunovant commanded the Regular Army of South Carolina. Colonel R.H. Anderson commanded the infantry regiment, Lieutenant Colonel Roswell Ripley commanded the artillery battalion and Major W.D. DeSaussure commanded the cavalry squadron.[14]

In March 1861 the Secession Convention passed a resolution allowing the South Carolina Regular Army to be transferred to Confederate service for the remainder of its three-year term.[15] The intention was to have these troops form the nucleus of the Confederate Regular Army. Although these men enlisted in Confederate service as state volunteers, not regulars, they remained in and around Charleston Harbor until February 1865.[16] In December 1861, the legislature passed an amendment that augmented the artillery battalion to a regiment of eight companies and the cavalry to four squadrons.[17] Consequently, the 1st Battalion Artillery, South Carolina Regulars, was redesignated the 1st Regiment Artillery, South Carolina Regulars, on March 25, 1862. Although four cavalry squadrons were allowed, DeSaussure's Squadron was the only cavalry organization accepted into the South Carolina Regular Army, and it was converted to artillery within a few months of its organization. In fact, all three branches of the South Carolina Regular Army—infantry, artillery and cavalry—served as artillery units from shortly after their creation in 1861 until February 1865.

Meanwhile, South Carolinians were volunteering for twelve months' service under the act of December 17, 1860. By March 6, 1861, nearly nine thousand volunteers had enlisted in 104 companies. These companies of twelve-month volunteers were organized into the mandated ten regiments, four brigades and one division, with the ten regiments numbered one through ten.[18] The organization of the South Carolina volunteer infantry regiments numbered two through eight and ten was fairly straightforward. But it is easy to confuse some of the other regiments, especially the 1st, 9th and 11th. Johnson Hagood, for example, commanded one of the original regiments called the 1st Regiment, SCV. But Hagood's regiment should not be confused with either Colonel Maxcy Gregg's 1st Regiment (six-month), SCV; Colonel Butler's 1st Regiment, South Carolina Regulars; or Colonel Orr's 1st Regiment of Rifles, SCV. Colonel Nathaniel Heyward commanded the 9th Regiment, SCV, which was later redesignated the 11th Regiment, SCV, and it is usually referred to as such. Colonel J.D. Blanding's 9th Regiment, SCV, was not one of the original ten volunteer regiments, even though most of the companies of Blanding's regiment were among the initial 104 companies. The nucleus of Blanding's 9th Regiment was created by the consolidation of some of the original companies of the 2nd Regiment that refused to volunteer for service in Virginia in the spring of 1861 and some additional companies. In addition to these regiments, the 2nd Battalion, South Carolina Artillery, enlisted under the South Carolina General Assembly's act of December 17, 1860.[19]

On February 28, 1861, the Confederate Congress passed an act creating the Confederate States Provisional Army, usually abbreviated P.A.C.S. or C.S.P.A. After the bombardment of Fort Sumter in April 1861, President Davis called for eight thousand volunteers from South Carolina to enlist in the P.A.C.S., and Governor Pickens urged existing state troops to volunteer for Confederate service.[20] Though the response was generally positive, Davis's and Pickens's actions caused a great deal of disruption and confusion among South Carolina organizations. John Peyre Thomas wrote:

> *The Act of the Confederate States to raise provisional forces conferred upon the President the appointment of officers above the rank of Colonel. In transferring the enlisted troops of the state to the Confederate Government, the Governor was instructed by the Convention to endeavor to preserve the rank of State officers and obtain for them commissions of the same grade for at least the period of their enlistment. But many officers, natives of Southern states, were now resigning from the United States Army and seeking commissions in the Army of the Confederacy; and it was the policy of the government to hold in its own hands the appointment of all superior*

> *officers. Indeed, it was their desire to accept volunteers only by companies, and such alone as volunteered for the whole war; although, through the necessity of bringing large forces rapidly forward, it was accorded to the volunteer troops to retain their regimental organizations.*[21]

Every one of the original eleven regiments ultimately enlisted in part or in whole in Confederate service. Many of the men and companies who had enlisted for twelve months of state service, however, refused to enter Confederate service with their original regiments in the spring of 1861. Many South Carolina regiments were affected by this switch from state to Confederate service. Severely affected were Maxcy Gregg's reorganized 1st Regiment, Johnson Hagood's 1st Regiment, J.B. Kershaw's 2nd Regiment and J.D. Blanding's 9th Regiment. Moderately affected were the 3rd, 4th, 5th, 6th, 10th and 11th Regiments. Least affected were the 7th and 8th Regiments. On April 25, 1861, Governor Pickens, who believed the troops should be transferred under certain conditions, wrote: "Hardly any full regiment with all its companies was prepared to go suddenly [to Virginia]."[22] William W. East, a corporal in the 5th Regiment who wrote to the *Yorkville Enquirer* under the sobriquet "Our Corporal," explained the feelings of the men in May 1861: "Some think there is no danger and therefore, no need of us here [in South Carolina]; others wish to go to Virginia; others shrink from encountering the yellow fever or other disease during the idle garrison life…; and others still, feeling that the state is secure, are desirous of returning to their work-shops, their farms, or their merchandise."[23] At that time, many of the twelve-month volunteer companies, which had been in existence for only a few months, refused to enter Confederate service and were disbanded altogether, but the regiments quickly enlisted new companies to replace them. The 2nd Regiment, SCV, was split into two regiments—the 2nd Regiment, SCV, and Blanding's 9th Regiment, SCV. Another regiment, Johnson Hagood's 1st, SCV, was temporarily disbanded until the men and the governor could settle their differences. John Peyre Thomas wrote that in the summer of 1861, "the Governor exhorted the lately formed regiments from the upcountry to re-volunteer for Virginia. It was understood that such volunteering for Confederate service among the twelve months State troops would not bind them to the new service beyond the term of their first enlistment."[24] In June and July 1861, the 3rd, 4th, 5th, 6th, 7th and 8th Regiments, SCV, mustered in Confederate service and were sent to Virginia, where Maxcy Gregg's reorganized 1st Regiment and J.B. Kershaw's 2nd Regiment had been since April. The men of Johnson Hagood's 1st Regiment were still uncommitted and remained in South Carolina. Blanding's 9th Regiment, Manigault's 10th Regiment and Heyward's 11th Regiment also remained in the state. When the dust settled in the late spring and summer of 1861, the original ten regiments were intact. They had recruited back to full strength and had spawned one new regiment, Blanding's 9th. All eleven regiments had mustered in Confederate service. The eleven South Carolina Volunteer regiments, however, contained many new companies, which had replaced those that had refused to enter Confederate service.

Another organization, the Hampton Legion, mustered in Confederate service in 1861. In April, President Davis authorized its creation as a combined force of infantry, cavalry and artillery, which had originally enlisted for twelve months' service in the Provisional Army of the Confederate States.

On June 30, 1861, President Davis called for the creation of a thirty-thousand-man reserve army corps. This new call-up included an additional three thousand South Carolinians, who would enlist "for the duration of the war."[25] Under the plan, the three thousand men were to be organized into companies at two camps of instruction, and President Davis was to appoint the field officers for the new regiments. As the sites for the camps of instruction, Governor Pickens chose Lightwood Knot Springs, located about seven miles north of Columbia, and Camp Butler, near Polecat (now Montmorenci) in Barnwell District. A later modification of the terms of the call-up said a combination of ten companies could form a regiment, men could elect their field officers, and the regiment could enter service with this organizational structure.[26] In early September, there were forty-two infantry companies, three cavalry companies and two artillery companies at Lightwood Knot Springs. Except for one cavalry company, this contingent completed South Carolina's quota.[27] President Davis's call for three thousand new troops resulted in the creation of the 12th, 13th, 14th and 15th Regiments, SCV.

On July 1, 1861, President Davis called for two additional regiments to enlist for the duration of the war. This call resulted in the organization of two infantry regiments and one infantry battalion. The two regiments were Maxcy Gregg's 1st Regiment, SCV, which had reorganized for the duration after its initial six-month term of enlistment expired in early July 1861, and James L. Orr's 1st Regiment, South Carolina Rifles, the first South Carolina regiment to enlist for the duration of the war. Sixteen companies offered their services to Colonel Orr. He accepted ten; the remaining six were organized into the 5th Battalion Rifles, SCV, which was later augmented to become the 2nd Regiment Rifles, SCV.

By November 1, 1861, nineteen volunteer infantry regiments and one volunteer infantry battalion had been raised. One—Maxcy Gregg's 1st (six-month) Regiment—disbanded at the end of its term of enlistment in

July 1861, and it reorganized shortly thereafter. Gregg's regiment, along with five others and the 2nd Battalion, had enlisted for the duration of the war. Eleven regiments and the Hampton Legion signed on for twelve months. In addition, the South Carolina Regular Army, consisting of one infantry regiment, one artillery battalion and one cavalry squadron, had enlisted for three years. Several artillery batteries and about twenty-one independent companies of cavalry and mounted infantry were also organized during this period. Some of the cavalry companies were raised under a special resolution of the Secession Convention, with their terms of service limited to ten days after the adjournment of the regular session of the legislature.[28] It is difficult to determine exactly which company was which, but most likely they were the undersized companies of Martin's 1st Regiment Cavalry, South Carolina Militia. These troops were stationed along the South Carolina coast.

In November 1861, the South Carolina legislature met in special session to appoint electors for president and vice-president under the permanent Confederate Constitution. In response to the fall of Port Royal in early November and the subsequent threat to Charleston, the legislators passed a resolution authorizing the governor to call for volunteers to defend the state either against an actual invasion or against one he believed to be imminent.[29] Acting under a Confederate act entitled "an act to provide for local defense and special service" passed on August 21, 1861, the governor, on November 11, called for volunteers to enter Confederate service in special defense of the state. The response was slow.[30] As a result, the General Assembly amended the South Carolina Militia Law of 1841 on December 7, 1861, by passing an "Act to amend and suspend certain portions of the Militia and Patrol laws of the State."[31] This act stated that unless exempt, all free white males between the ages of sixteen and sixty years were liable to perform ordinary military duty during the war. In addition, it made eighteen- to forty-five-year-old men liable to be called for twelve months' service either in South Carolina or in any other Confederate state instead of the previously allowed three months' service inside and two months' service outside the state. The governor was authorized to call out these troops at any time.[32] If the South Carolina Militia did not furnish the allotted number of men, a draft would follow.[33] The law also tried to revitalize the South Carolina militia system by calling for new elections of officers and more frequent drilling. On December 9, 1861, Governor Pickens called for twelve thousand volunteers to enlist for twelve months' service, unless they were discharged before that time.[34] As a result, the 16th and 17th Infantry Regiments, SCV, and the 3rd Infantry Battalion, SCV, were organized. The 18th, 19th, 20th, 21st, 22nd, 23rd and 24th Infantry Regiments, SCV, were also organized under this call.

By the end of 1861, more than 7,000 men had enlisted "for and during the war" and 20,251 for shorter terms, usually either twelve or thirty-six months. A total of 27,362 men were in uniform, and an additional sixty-four companies were either in camp or under marching orders.[35] In 1861, a number of organizations enlisted for the duration of the war. These were the infantry regiments of Gregg's 1st SCV, the 12th SCV, 13th SCV, 14th SCV, 15th SCV and Orr's regiment of rifles; the 5th Battalion Rifles Infantry, Edward Manigault's Battalion, four companies of Hatch's Battalion of Coast Rangers and the 1st Battalion Cavalry; the artillery organizations of the 2nd Battalion, the 3rd Battalion (Palmetto Battalion) Light Artillery and the Chesterfield Light Artillery. Captain Boyce's Company, Captain Mangum's Company, Captain Boykin's Cavalry Company and Captain Shannon's Cavalry Company also signed on for the duration in 1861.

Many units enlisted in 1861 for shorter terms of service, usually for twelve months. Infantry regiments included Hagood's 1st SCV, the 2nd through the 11th SCV, the 16th SCV, the 17th SCV, the Hampton Legion and the Holcombe Legion. Infantry battalions were the 3rd (James's) Battalion and six companies of Hatch's Battalion of Coast Rangers. Artillery organizations were Bachman's Battery, the Beaufort Volunteer Artillery, Bonneau's Artillery, the Calhoun Light Artillery, the Santee Light Artillery, the Macbeth Artillery, the Marion Artillery and the Washington (Hart's) Artillery. Cavalry units were Boykin's Cavalry Troop, J.G. Harlan's Company, Lipscomb's Cavalry Troop, St. James Mounted Riflemen, Tucker's Squadron and Trenholm's Squadron. In addition, the 18th, 19th, 20th, 21st, 22nd, 23rd and 24th Regiments, SCV, along with some companies of Hatch's Battalion of Coast Rangers, were raised late in 1861 and early in 1862 for twelve months' service.

The South Carolina Regular Army, consisting of the 1st Regiment, South Carolina Infantry (Regulars), the 1st Battalion, South Carolina Artillery (Regulars) and the 15th Battalion, South Carolina Artillery (Regulars), also enlisted for three years in 1861. Other organizations enlisting for three years were the Pee Dee Legion Militia, Martin's Cavalry Regiment Militia, the 4th Brigade Militia, the Battalion of South Carolina Cadets and several independent cavalry companies.[36]

After the close of 1861, the record of the raising of troops for service in South Carolina is less clear. The accounts of both Professor Rivers and J.P. Thomas become ever more vague about which organizations were created under which act, resolution, law or authority in 1862.

On December 11, 1861, the Confederate Congress passed the first Confederate Conscription Act, also called the Bounty and Furlough Act. On February 19, 1862, the *Mercury* reprinted that act, along with subsequent orders from the War Department dated January 1, 1862.[37] The Conscription Act dictated a reorganization of existing Confederate military forces and provided for the following: (1) a bounty of fifty dollars would be paid to all privates, musicians and non-commissioned officers who would enlist in the Confederate States Provisional Army for three years, or for those men already enlisted for twelve months who would re-enlist for two additional years; (2) a furlough, not to exceed sixty days, would be granted "to all twelve months men now in service, who shall, prior to the expiration of their present term of service, volunteer or enlist for the next two ensuing years subsequent to the expiration of their present term of service, or for three years, or the war." The secretary of war would issue the furloughs at such times and in such number as he deemed most compatible with the public interest; (3) the act applied to any man who had already enlisted for twelve months or more in the service of any Confederate state; (4) all men who re-enlisted would be allowed, at the expiration of their original terms of service, to reorganize themselves into new companies and to elect new company officers. The new companies would be allowed to organize into new battalions or regiments, and the men would elect new field officers. Subsequent vacancies among the officer corps would be filled by promotion within the ranks of the existing officers of the unit. If the lowest ranking officer in a company had to be replaced, an election would be held to fill that vacancy. When a vacancy arose within the units of any state's Regular Army, new officers would be appointed and not elected; (5) further provisions were made for the reorganization of new companies into battalions and regiments.[38]

On February 2, 1862, the secretary of war called on Governor Pickens for South Carolina to fill its quota of troops to be furnished "for and during the war."[39] This quota—6 percent of the white male population of the state—translated to about 18,000 men.[40] An estimated 6,000 South Carolinians had already enlisted for the duration of the war. To meet the requisition of an additional 12,590 men, the secretary of war projected the need to enlist at least five new regiments and to re-enlist enough of the twelve months' troops whose terms were about to expire to make up the difference.[41] On February 20, 1862, the South Carolina adjutant and inspector general provided more accurate figures. His report showed that, of 30,670 South Carolinians currently in uniform, 9,349 had enlisted for the duration of the war and 21,321 had signed on for twelve months. At about the same time, by contrast, the secretary of war counted 6,260 South Carolinians enlisted for the duration and 23,975 enlisted for twelve months.[42] James Chesnut Jr., a member of the South Carolina Executive Council, urged the twelve months' troops to re-enlist for the duration to meet the quota of 18,000 men.

As a part of this call for additional troops, the *Mercury* reported on February 21, 1862, that President Davis had issued a call for 5,000 more men—approximately five regiments—from South Carolina. Another call for 5,000 men went out on March 5, 1862, with a notice that said until five regiments were raised, no man could enter any organization then in service for less than the duration of the war.[43] On March 6, 1862, the *Mercury* reprinted a proclamation from Governor Pickens stating that President Davis called for an additional 12,590 men from the state, a number that included the two previous calls for 5,000 men each.[44] To meet the state's quota, including the five new regiments called for, the governor and Executive Council, on March 5, 1862, adopted a system of conscription.[45] They also directed South Carolina Adjutant and Inspector General States Rights Gist to issue a statement in early March. Gist's proclamation, issued on March 7, declared a reorganization of the South Carolina Military System to bring it into compliance with the Executive Council's decision.[46] The statement contained several major points, among them: the system of volunteering by individuals or by companies would be in place until March 20, 1862, when all volunteering would be discarded and a system of conscription, as provided for by law, would be instituted; all male citizens between the ages of eighteen and forty-five would be required to enroll for active duty and would not be allowed to serve in the reserves; all eligible men must report for duty within ten days of being called or be liable for the draft; volunteer companies already in service would be required to re-enlist ten days before their term of service expired; any individuals who refused to re-enlist would be eligible for the draft; and the governor would appoint all field officers in new regiments and company-grade officers in new companies.[47] In addition, boards of exemption were to be created throughout the state, a system of conscription was to be established and a method for substitution was to be set in place.[48] Troops were to be received at Lightwood Knot Springs, north of Columbia.[49]

Even before the cutoff date of March 20, 1862, more than 22,000 South Carolinians had volunteered for the duration of the war, and an additional 17,210 men had enrolled for twelve months.[50] On March 21, the governor and Executive Council responded to this positive news by extending the deadline to April 15 and allowing the men to elect their officers, subject to approval by the Executive Council.[51] Under this proclamation, the 24th Regiment, SCV, was accepted for the duration of the war, and Lamar's 2nd Artillery Battalion was increased to regiment strength.

The Confederate Congress passed a new conscription law, entitled "An Act to further provide for the public defense," on April 16, 1862.[52] It contained even more details concerning re-enlistment of soldiers and distribution of conscripted men than had the law passed the previous December. And it authorized the president to call into service all white male residents of the Confederate States between the ages of eighteen and thirty-five years who were not legally exempted from duty. The term of service would be "three years, unless the war shall have been sooner ended."[53] In addition, all the twelve-month volunteers were to serve two additional years from the expiration of their original terms. Any men younger than eighteen and older than thirty-five were required to remain in service for ninety days unless their places were filled by recruits. Bounties were granted to the twelve-month men, and furloughs would be granted at the discretion of the secretary of war. Transfers from one organization to another and the creation of new organizations were cancelled unless they could be completed within thirty days. All the twelve-month men who re-enlisted were allowed to hold elections for their officers within forty days of April 16.[54] This act had little effect on the creation of new units in South Carolina because most eligible men were already in the service. About five thousand South Carolinians enlisted or re-enlisted in existing units in response.

According to estimates of the state's adjutant and inspector general, 39,274 South Carolinians were in the field by April 28, 1862. Of this number, 22,064—some 4,000 more than required—had enlisted for the duration and 17,210 had enlisted for twelve months.[55] By August 30, the number of men enlisted for service in all South Carolina military organizations had grown to 42,973. At that time, the infantry comprised twenty-eight regiments, two legions, eight battalions and two unattached companies. The artillery comprised two regiments, one battalion and eighteen unattached companies; the cavalry units numbered two regiments, five battalions and seven unattached companies.[56]

The conscription laws, especially the Conscription Act of April 16, set the stage for significant reorganization of the entire Confederate army in the spring of 1862; the laws greatly affected the organization of South Carolina troops as well. D.A. Dickert, captain of Company H of the 3rd Regiment, wrote of the Conscript Laws:

> *The Conscript Act was condemned in unmeasured terms in many places at the South, but its necessity and expediency was never doubted. To have allowed so great a number to absent themselves from the army at this time, in the face of an overwhelming enemy, and that enemy advancing upon our Capitol, was more than the morale of the army would admit. Not altogether would the absence of the soldiers themselves effect the army, but in the breaking up of organizations, for in some companies all had re-enlisted,*

> *while in others one-half, and in many cases none. New regiments would have to be formed out of the re-enlisted companies, and new companies out of the large number of recruits, now in camps of instruction. So by keeping up the old organizations, and filling up the ranks by the conscripts at home, the army would be greatly benefited.*[57]

The term of enlistment for most of the men who originally signed up for twelve months was set to expire in the spring of 1862. Twelve-month men not otherwise exempt were required to re-enlist "for three years or the duration of the war," meaning three years from their initial date of enlistment. Most men of eligible age who were exempt from re-enlistment in the spring of 1862 were those who had originally signed on for a term greater than twelve months; all new recruits were required to enlist "for three years or the duration of the war." This phrase caused some confusion. Some men interpreted it to mean three years, or for the duration of the war, whichever was shorter. Others interpreted it to mean the opposite—three years, or for the duration of the war, whichever was longer. In his discussion of the re-enlistment for "three years or the war," Douglas Southall Freeman wrote in *Lee's Lieutenants* that the soldiers took the phrase to mean a maximum of three years. This position is supported by the original wording, "three years, unless the war shall have been sooner ended."[58] D.A. Dickert, captain of Company H of the 3rd Regiment, held a similar view: "It was during our stay in winter quarters, March 1864, that the term of our second enlistment expired." Dickert explained that the troops who had originally enlisted for twelve months in the spring of 1861 and who had then re-enlisted for "three years" in the spring of 1862 were due to re-enlist a third time in the spring of 1864. He held that the men had re-enlisted in the spring of 1862 for three years, or for the duration of the war, whichever was the shorter of the two terms. Dickert wrote further that the re-enlistment in March 1864 was "only a form, no change in officers or organization."[59]

All but a few men voluntarily re-enlisted in March 1864, but because of the conscription laws, no one was allowed to leave the army or change his branch of service. An interesting example of the effect on the ranks lies in the 1st Regiment, South Carolina Infantry (Regulars). The men in that regiment clearly believed that their original term of service expired in early 1864, and they were right. On February 8, 1864, P.G.T. Beauregard published the following statement: "Soldiers of the Department of South Carolina, Georgia and Florida. The term of service of some of you is about to expire. You must have observed from the newspapers of your city that your brothers in arms of the veteran armies of Northern Virginia and of Tennessee have re-enlisted as was to be expected of such men, by entire companies, battalions, regiments and brigades, proudly retaining the organizations intact under which they have won renown. Will the men who have defended Forts Sumter and Moultrie, and Battery Wagner fail to follow these examples of soldierly patriotism?"[60] Beauregard's goal, of course, was to preserve the integrity of the 1st Regiment, and his method was to appeal to honor and patriotism. Left unsaid was the stark fact that, under the law, if the men did not re-enlist in the 1st Regiment, they would not be allowed to leave the service.[61]

Lieutenant J.F.J. Caldwell, historian of McGowan's Brigade, also discussed the issue of "three years or the duration of the war" and arrived at a different conclusion:

> *In February* [1864], *there was a general call for re-enlistment in the Confederate armies. It will be remembered that almost all the regiments organized in the summer of 1861 enlisted for "three years or the war." I always held the expression to mean a consent to serve three years, whether the war lasted so long or not; and to serve for the war, should it last for even longer than three years. But as there was doubt about it; as there were many originally twelve-month regiments, who reenlisted, it is said, for two years from the expiration of their first year, so making their term expire in the spring of 1864; and as, above all things, the weary citizens at home needed encouragement; a renewal of enlistment and of allegiance to the Confederacy was invited. The army adopted the suggestion most cordially, and declared afresh their determination never to lay down their arms until the independence of the South should be achieved.*[62]

To avoid a catastrophe of disorganization in early 1864 when the three-year terms would expire, and perhaps also to clarify the issue, the Confederate Congress, in early 1864, passed "A Bill to Organize Forces to Serve During the War."[63] This bill required all white males between seventeen and fifty years of age to serve during the war. All men between eighteen and forty-five currently in service were to remain in their units. Men between seventeen and eighteen and between forty-five and fifty would form companies and regiments of reserves, which would serve within the borders of their states. Consequently, in the first few months of 1864, most South Carolinians then in service either re-enlisted if their three-year term had expired or reaffirmed their commitment to the Confederacy if it had not; there were no major changes in organizational structure.

As a part of the reorganization in the spring of 1862, a Confederate soldier between eighteen and thirty-five years of age whose twelve-month term of enlistment had expired was required to re-enlist in the service. In the process, however, he could change to a different company or regiment, enlist in a new unit entirely, change to a unit from another state or even select a different branch of service. Men were also allowed to form new companies and regiments and re-elect both company-grade (lieutenants and captains) and field-grade (colonels, lieutenant colonels and majors) officers.[64] J.P. Thomas wrote: "The State Adjutant General reported that 'entire companies and even regiments were lost, and new companies and regiments formed; in most instances retaining their names, but the regiments in all instances were composed to a great extent of new company organizations. The original 9th [Blanding's] Regiment was, in this way, wholly lost; and the old 4th [Regiment] was reduced to a mere battalion.'"[65]

When the men were allowed to choose their own officers, many were not re-elected because they were judged either too old or too incompetent to perform their duties. It should be noted, however, that many efficient officers were not re-elected simply because they were unpopular. Thomas wrote that the reorganization act of February 1862 should have been named the disorganization act since it caused the loss of many of the Confederacy's best officers, the disciplinarian being turned out by the politician.[66]

Many new organizations were created in South Carolina during the first half of 1862. Infantry regiments created in early 1862 and not already mentioned were the 2nd (Moore's) Regiment of Rifles and the Palmetto Sharpshooters. Several infantry battalions were raised in the first half of 1862 as well, including the 1st (Charleston), the 1st Battalion Sharpshooters, the 13th (4th), the 6th (Byrd's), the 7th, the 9th (Pee Dee), the 11th (Eutaw) and Dunlop's Battalion of Sharpshooters. The only cavalry regiment created in the first half of 1862 was the 1st Regiment. Cavalry battalions created were the 1st (14th), the 2nd (10th), the 3rd (4th), the 6th (17th), the 8th (2nd Battalion Reserves) and the 12th (4th Squadron). Independent cavalry units created during this time were the German Hussars, the Rebel Troop, the Charleston Light Dragoons, Harlan's Company, the Yeadon Rangers, Whitner's Troop, Hough's Company, the Ripley Rangers, A.C. Earle's Company, M.J. Kirk's Squadron, Keitt's Mounted Riflemen and E.M. Boykin's Squadron. Two artillery regiments were created in early 1862: the 1st Regulars, an augmentation of the 1st Battalion, and the 2nd (Lamar's) Regiment. The 18th Artillery Battalion and several other batteries were also created, including the Brooks Guard Artillery, the Inglis Artillery, the Palmetto Light Battery, the German Artillery, the Gist Guards Battery and the McQueen Light Artillery. Still other batteries were the Lafayette Artillery, the Pee Dee Artillery, the Washington (Walter's) Artillery, the Waccamaw Light Artillery, Ferguson's Light Artillery, the Edisto Artillery, B.E. Dickson's Battery, the Carolina Artillery, the Silverton Artillery, Willis's Battery and S.D. Lee's

Battery. Thomas wrote, "In addition to these organizations, under the call for all arms-bearing men between eighteen and thirty-five years of age for Confederate service, many separate companies of infantry, artillery and cavalry were raised, most of which became merged into regiments or other organizations."[67]

Organizations created in the second half of 1862 or later were the 25th, 26th and 27th Regiments, SCV; Brooks's Partisan Rifles, later designated Company H of the 7th Battalion; and the 2nd Battalion Sharpshooters. Six of the seven South Carolina cavalry regiments, the 2nd–7th, as well as the 19th Cavalry Battalion, were created in July 1862 or were created later in the war.

The South Carolina militia played an important role in the organization of troops for military service. As an effective fighting force, the militia's role was limited to the first few months of 1861 when the 4th Brigade, South Carolina Militia, supplied most of the manpower around Charleston Harbor. Several militia regiments remained in active service until early 1862, but by that time the militia no longer existed as a fighting force. Its major contribution between late 1862 and late 1864 lay in providing an organizational structure upon which the governor could call for reserve troops as needed. The South Carolina Militia Law of 1841 had created forty-six regiments organized into ten brigades and five divisions, with the governor as commander-in-chief. Men between sixteen and sixty years of age were eligible for service, while those between eighteen and forty-five were liable to serve for three months in South Carolina and two months outside the state. Men elected their company and field officers, brigade officers elected brigadier generals and division officers elected major generals.[68]

The first Conscription Act of April 16, 1862, which claimed for active duty all white males between eighteen and thirty-five years of age, significantly depleted the ranks of the South Carolina militia.[69] The second Conscription Act, passed on September 27, 1862, further depleted the militia. The new law allowed the president to call up men between the ages of thirty-five and forty-five for three years unless the war ended sooner, an option that he implemented in stages.[70] These acts took "all the material of armies between the ages mentioned, from the control of the state."[71] The South Carolina Executive Council wrote: "To meet this new condition of things, it becomes necessary that the State shall adopt further measures to organize its forces and provide for its defence."[72] Soon after the passage of the conscription laws, the Executive Council decided to separate the remainder of the men between thirty-five and fifty from the militia and organize them into companies and regiments to be held in reserve for defense of the state or other service at the discretion of the governor.[73]

Consequently, on April 23, 1862, the Executive Council of South Carolina passed resolutions creating two corps of state reserves.[74] The 1st Corps was composed of thirty-five-year-old to fifty-year-old men conscripted from within the existing South Carolina militia regiments and battalions to be held for active service anywhere the state required, as the occasion dictated.[75] They were also subject to patrol and police duty until called to active service.[76] Men of the 1st Corps were allowed to elect their company officers—the lieutenants and captains. The governor and the Executive Council were to appoint field officers—the colonels, lieutenant colonels and majors.[77] When not on active duty, men of the 1st Corps of reserves were to perform patrol duty under the command of the officers of the 2nd Corps.[78]

On May 13, 1862, the governor and the Executive Council called for the organization of five regiments, each to consist of men between thirty-five and fifty years of age in one set of companies and men between sixteen and eighteen years of age in a second set. Each company would elect its own officers, and the Executive Council would appoint the field officers of any battalions or regiments formed from the companies.[79] These regiments were to be held in reserve until ordered into active service. At all times, one company was to remain in each regiment's camp of instruction without pay, with this duty rotating among companies every two weeks.[80] Unfortunately, whether these five regiments were ever actually organized is unclear. By August 30, 1862, the 1st Corps comprised ten regiments called regiments of reserves; these regiments consisted of about eight thousand men with elected company-grade officers. Each of the ten regiments was assigned a numeric designation of two through eleven.[81] To avoid confusion with the 1st Regiment, Charleston Reserves, which was organized in October 1861, none of these new regiments was designated the "1st Regiment." Originally, the Executive Council's resolution creating the reserve corps did not apply to the 1st Regiment of Charleston Reserves. By August 22, 1862, however, the Charleston unit was officially designated the 1st Regiment of the 1st Corps of Reserves, a modification that gave the 1st Corps of Reserves eleven regiments.[82]

Between October 4, 1862, and October 31, 1862, Governor Pickens reviewed nine of the eleven reserve regiments. On October 25, Secretary of War G.W. Randolph wrote James Chesnut that the Confederate States Government would accept four regiments—the 2nd, 3rd, 8th and 11th—for local service and that the remaining seven would be disbanded. Randolph also wrote that he would accept men over forty years of age for service in the reserve regiments, and that the men between thirty-five and forty, along with conscripts from the seven disbanded regiments, would be placed in existing South Carolina regiments. These four regiments, consisting of about three thousand men, were expected to be in camp in about twenty days.[83] On November 11, President Davis modified the plan to accept eight of the reserve regiments into service, with the result that, on November 18, eight of the ten new regiments of the 1st Corps Reserves entered Confederate service for state defense for ninety days.[84] These were the 2nd, 3rd, 5th, 6th, 7th, 8th, 9th and 11th. At least four of these regiments were ordered to report to Lightwood Knot Springs, north of Columbia, and then on to Charleston.[85] The 4th and the 10th Regiments were disbanded on November 7 because of disaffection among the men.[86]

The Secession Convention expired by its own ordinance on December 12, 1862. The very next day, the South Carolina General Assembly declared many of the Executive Council's decisions invalid.[87] In one action it revoked the Council's order to disband the 4th and 10th Regiments. On December 18, it passed an act forbidding the reserve regiments to serve more than ninety days. It also called for the replacement of council-appointed field officers through elections to be held on January 1, 1863.[88] P.G.T. Beauregard criticized this provision, and Governor M.L. Bonham requested and received an appeal. As a result, new elections were never held.[89] On February 10, 1863, after ninety days' service, the reserve regiments of the 1st Corps were disbanded.[90] The thirty-five- to forty-year-old men of the 1st Corps who had not been called to active service because of their age, however, were now required by the second Conscription Act of September 27, 1862, to enter active service. On February 18, 1863, Governor Bonham ordered the 1st, 4th and 10th Regiments back into the field. He held the remainder in reserve in anticipation of an immediate Federal assault.[91] On March 9, 1863, the governor suspended his order, and the reserves stayed at home.[92]

The 2nd Corps of Reserves was composed of men between sixteen and eighteen years of age, men between fifty and sixty-five years of age, alien residents and all others exempt from ordinary military duty. After organization into companies and regiments, the 2nd Corps was placed under the command of South Carolina militia officers, who were already commissioned but who could not, for some reason, serve in the 1st Corps. The 2nd Corps was used for patrol and police duty and for internal defense as required by the state. Since the 2nd Corps did not enter Confederate service, virtually no information about it appears in the *Compiled Service Records* (CSR). Additionally, little information about its organizational structure exists. On July 21, 1862, the Executive Council amended resolutions that said if the 1st and 2nd Corps of Reserves were brought into active service at the same time, the 1st Corps was to act as regulars and the 2nd Corps as militia.[93] When not under orders, both the 1st and 2nd Corps would perform patrol duty.[94]

To further shore up the South Carolina militia, the Executive Council passed a resolution on November 7, 1862, that contained the following directive: "the public safety imperiously demands that all white male residents of the State of South Carolina capable of bearing arms should be immediately placed into military organizations and armed." The Executive Council ordered the formation of companies to include practically all males between sixteen and sixty-five. Drill under pain of court martial was required every two weeks. The order included members of the legislature, doctors, ministers, millers and others; it exempted only a few groups like the Executive Council, judges and state treasurers. The force as a whole was designed as a district police with access to arms deposited at each courthouse.[95] To have troops available to serve as "alarm men" for military service in the South Carolina militia,[96] the commanding officer of each beat was ordered to keep a separate roll of men between forty and fifty years of age. Subject to the call of the commander in chief, these men would constitute a reserve force for the defense of the state.[97]

In the summer of 1863, Federal assaults were anticipated along the South Carolina coast. On June 6, and again on July 31, President Davis called on the governor of South Carolina to provide 5,384 volunteers for local defense and special service.[98] On June 16, Governor Bonham ordered South Carolina militia regiments to respond to President Davis's 5,000-man quota.[99] The president's authority was based on two acts passed by the Confederate Congress: the first, passed on August 21, 1861, was entitled "An act to provide for local defense and special service"; the other, passed on October 13, 1862, was called "An act to authorize the formation of volunteer companies for local defense."[100] The 1861 act authorized the president to accept volunteers to serve in a capacity and for a duration prescribed by him for the defense of exposed places or for special service.[101] Under this act, the volunteers would be mustered in Confederate service, and the president would appoint the field officers. Men were to be between forty and forty-five years of age and, beginning August 1, 1863, would serve in South Carolina for six months.[102] The governor was instructed to ask for volunteers from this age group. If the quota of 5,384 men went unmet, then the governor was authorized to draft men between forty and fifty years of age. Sixteen- and seventeen-year-old-men in the South Carolina militia were not subject to the draft. South Carolina militia regiments were ordered to assemble at their muster grounds on July 7 and to organize new companies either by volunteering or, if necessary, by means of a draft.[103] Each company was to carry between 64 and 125 privates on its roster, and each regiment was to contain ten companies.[104] The men elected their company-grade officers in early July.[105] Since all the men were volunteers, President Davis agreed on July 23 to allow them to elect their field officers as well. He set a date of July 31 for elections in all five regiments,[106] and he required the regiments to be ready for immediate service after elections were held.

As a result of the presidential call-up, about five thousand South Carolinians volunteered for service in five new regiments, known as the "South Carolina State Troops (Six Months)." It was understood that the regiments were raised only for local defense and special service—most importantly, the defense of Charleston.[107] The five regiments, numbered one through five, were ready for service on August 1. Beauregard, however, did not call them to active duty until September 5.[108] At that time, one regiment was sent to Pocotaligo, the other four to Charleston and their six months' service began.[109] In December 1863, Governor Bonham argued successfully that the six-month service should date from August 1; consequently, the five regiments of South Carolina state troops were mustered out on February 3, 1864.[110] Men between forty and forty-five years of age who were mustered out, however, were almost immediately conscripted into service again.[111]

The Conscription Act passed on February 17, 1864, was entitled "An act to organize forces to serve during the war."[112] On March 1, 1864, Adjutant General Samuel Cooper implemented the new law.[113] Under it, all white male citizens of the Confederate States between seventeen and fifty years of age were liable for service within their respective states for the duration of the war.[114] Men between eighteen and forty-five were to remain with their respective organizations. Seventeen-year-old men and forty-five- to fifty-year-olds were required to form a reserve corps and were allowed to elect their own company and field officers. They were ordered to organize themselves first into companies and then into either battalions or regiments.[115] Within thirty days from March 15, the men were required either to enroll in an existing local defense company or to organize a new company. "Those between seventeen and eighteen and between forty-five and fifty were organized and commanded by General (James) Chesnut under an appointment by President Davis; some were called into active service at Charleston, of course, at Confederate expense."[116] Camps of instruction were established and provisions were made for exemptions.[117]

Eight new battalions, designated the "1st to 8th Battalions, South Carolina Reserves," were created under this law. These battalions were later referred to as the Battalions of Senior Reserves to distinguish them from the regiments of Junior Reserves. The *Yorkville Enquirer* reported in late March that the new battalions were not to be called into active service "unless a greater emergency occurs."[118] In early April 1864, the *Daily South Carolinian* reported that all eligible men were to enroll before April 16 and that the new battalions were to serve as a "reserve for state defense" within the boundaries of the state.[119] The *Yorkville Enquirer* reported on June 15 that eight new battalions had been organized.[120] On June 24, General Chesnut ordered each battalion to elect a major to command it.[121] On July 13, he issued another order calling the reserve battalions to active duty "at once" because infantry support of the artillery on John's Island and James Island was needed.[122] By July 20, several of the reserve battalions were in the field.[123] Throughout the summer of 1864, the reserve battalions continued to muster in state service, and in December, they became part of the Confederate forces. Though some of the reserve battalions were disbanded shortly before the end of the war, others were merged into nonreserve South Carolina regiments on April 9, 1865.

In August and early September 1864 South Carolina required all white males between sixteen and sixty years of age to be liable for service in the South Carolina Militia.[124] Each regiment of militia provided one new company toward the creation of four new regiments designated the "1st, 2nd, 3rd and 4th Regiments, Junior Reserves, South Carolina State Troops." They were also called "Regiments of South Carolina Militia" and "Regiments of State Troops" and might also have been known as Battalions of State Troops.[125] These new regiments should not be confused with the 1st, 2nd, 3rd and 4th Regiments, South Carolina Militia, all of which had existed before and continued during the war. The Junior Reserves consisted of sixteen-year-old men. Before this call-up, the militia was a strictly local force, on duty as home guards and in other capacities.[126] All regiments of South Carolina Militia were ordered to rendezvous on September 12, 1864, so each could raise one company of Junior Reserves.[127] The men then went home and reassembled at Hamburg in late November. On March 29, 1865, Governor Magrath ordered militiamen who were between sixteen and seventeen years of age to assemble by April 1 in Spartanburg for the defense of the state. The Citadel and Arsenal cadets were to be placed in command of the camp of instruction.[128] By early April, all four of the regiments of Junior Reserves had been disbanded.[129] Older men were allowed to go home, but the "boys," called "State Troops, First Class Militia," were required to remain in service.[130] In early April, about seven hundred sixteen-year-olds were being held for state service and drilling at Spartanburg.[131] On April 3, they were ordered to reorganize immediately and report to Captain J.P. Thomas at Greenville. This move never took place, and on April 8, the State Troops, First Class Militia, was disbanded.

John Peyre Thomas offered an in-depth enumeration of South Carolinians who served in the War Between the States.[132] He estimated that 64,903 men were enrolled in Confederate service; of those, some 56,661 were considered effective. Thomas also estimated that 6,180 men were enrolled in state service, and that all but 3 of these were effective. Thus, of the 71,083 South Carolinians enrolled, a full 62,838 were effective. This service population of 71,083 men was drawn from an 1860 voting population of only 60,000 men.[133] In 1899 Thomas estimated that 20,101 South Carolinians were killed or died in service during the war. He noted that because many rolls were missing or incomplete, this number could run as high as 21,146. In a further breakdown, he estimated infantry deaths at 17,918, cavalry at 1,467 and artillery at 716. In his book *Broken Fortunes*, B.F. Kirkland records the deaths of South Carolinians as 18,666, but he suggests that the actual number could have been as high as 21,166 because the records of 2,500 men were missing.[134]

Thomas records a total of thirty-four infantry regiments and four infantry battalions; seven cavalry regiments, one cavalry squadron and one cavalry company; and three artillery regiments, two artillery battalions and nineteen unattached artillery batteries.[135] The accounting is actually somewhat more complicated because of duplications and other ramifications. Many independent companies, for example, were subsequently attached to battalions or regiments, and many battalions eventually merged into regiments. Additionally, a number of companies, battalions and regiments ceased to exist before the end of the war. If all duplications are avoided, the following summarizes South Carolina units in Confederate service during the war: thirty-six infantry regiments, seven infantry battalions, two artillery regiments, three artillery battalions, twenty-seven independent artillery batteries, seven cavalry regiments and one cavalry battalion. This listing includes neither the militia nor the reserves.

The basic building block of all military units during the War Between the States was the company. Men mustered in service as part of a company, and it was at the company level that all official records of individuals were kept. In the infantry, companies were referred to as such; in the cavalry, they were usually called a troop; and in the artillery, the words company and battery were used interchangeably. At the start of the war, a company was composed of 80 to 104 officers and men. Under the first Conscription Act passed in the spring of 1862, an infantry company consisted of 125 men, rank and file; each cavalry company consisted of 80 men; and a field artillery battery was made up of 150 men.[136] A captain commanded each company, with lieutenants as his immediate subordinates. Numerous independent companies were raised for local defense purposes early on, but most were consolidated into battalions or regiments before the end of the war.

Usually ten companies formed a regiment, and each regiment was commanded by a colonel, whose immediate subordinates were the lieutenant colonel and major. Four to eight companies normally formed a battalion, which was commanded by a lieutenant colonel or a major. Some battalions maintained their integrity throughout the war, but often two battalions or one battalion and several independent companies were merged to create a new regiment. Such mergers or consolidations typically occurred in South Carolina's cavalry regiments, and sometimes with the infantry and artillery as well—the creation, for example, of the 23rd, 24th, 25th, 26th and 27th Regiments, SCV, and the 2nd Regiment, South Carolina Artillery. In one instance the 4th Regiment, SCV, was raised as a regiment, but was downsized to the 13th Battalion at the reorganization as a result of losses from combat and disease. Subsequently, the 13th Battalion was disbanded and the remaining companies consolidated into just two that merged into the Hampton Legion. The cavalry branch of the service had a subdivision called the squadron, which was usually made up of two companies or troops. As the war progressed, most South Carolina cavalry squadrons were incorporated into cavalry regiments. Three to five regiments or battalions usually formed a brigade, which was commanded by a brigadier general. Three to five brigades usually formed a division, which was commanded by a major general. Three to five divisions usually formed a corps, which was under the command of a lieutenant general. Two or three corps usually formed an army.

This work concentrates on the company, battalion and regimental levels of South Carolina military organizations during the War Between the States. Companies were usually designated alphabetically, though several exceptions to this rule arose early in the war, when some regiments designated their companies numerically. The letter *J* was eliminated from military nomenclature because of the difficulty in distinguishing between the letters *J* and *I* when written by hand. An exception was that of the 4th Regiment, SCV, which had a Company J—the Confederate Guards. This company was composed of men from Anderson whose backgrounds were not military. Because other letter designations were already in use when they enlisted, these men innocently chose the letter *J* and opted to retain it even after they discovered their error.[137]

Early in the war, before many companies were attached to regiments, companies were designated by the name of their first captain; Captain Bill Smith's Company, SCV, for example. When companies became attached to a regiment or battalion, they were given an alphabetic designation, such as Company B, 3rd Regiment, SCV. A common practice in most companies was to allow the men to choose a company nickname, often some brief and colorful term, in addition to its alphabetic designation or its captain's name. Many of these nicknames reflected upon the men's hometown or district, their desire to defend their rights or some person whom they wished to honor. Nicknames included the Enoree Mosquitoes, the Meeting Street Saludas, the Horry Rough and Readys, the Lancaster Invincibles and the Bozeman Guards. Some companies had more than one popular name. This practice of nicknames was common among infantry companies and almost universal among cavalry companies and independent artillery batteries, but it was virtually nonexistent among companies of the South Carolina Regular Army. A good deal of evidence suggests that most of South Carolina's volunteer companies had a popular name or nickname. Many such names have been recorded in various newspapers, books and other records. Unfortunately, others probably existed but were not preserved and thus are lost forever. Multiple sources exist for the 14th Regiment, SCV, for example, and most of its companies' popular names are well documented. None of the known regimental records for Company G of the 14th Regiment, SCV, however, contain the company nickname—the McGowan Greys; the only known source that documents this popular name is an obituary in the *Due West Times*.[138]

Keeping track of companies and individuals throughout their service is usually straightforward but can sometimes be quite confusing. Some men whose original enlistments were for the duration never re-enlisted because the companies they first joined managed to maintain their integrity throughout the war. Many companies, however, had at least one opportunity, and some even a second, to re-enlist. The first such opportunity for many South Carolina companies came in the spring and summer of 1861 when they voluntarily left state service and joined the Confederate forces. This change of service offered at least three possibilities: men and officers could transfer individually to a different company; a company could remain intact, but it could transfer to a different regiment; and some companies could disband altogether. The second opportunity for many companies to re-enlist came when the army reorganized in the spring of 1862 at the expiration of the initial twelve-month term of enlistment. This reorganization offered many of the same possibilities for individuals and companies as had the changes of the preceding year. An extreme example of change can be found in the records of the Wee Nee Volunteers, which served with four different regiments and one battalion between 1861 and 1865.

At the reorganization of the Confederate army in the spring of 1862, many companies and regiments remained intact; some companies remained relatively intact but transferred to a different regiment; others disbanded completely and the men re-enlisted elsewhere. In some cases, most of the men from one company re-enlisted together in a new company. The 9th Regiment, SCV, was completely disbanded, and the 4th Regiment, SCV, was converted to a battalion. Further confusion arose from the practice of allowing individuals to transfer to a different company, though this did not happen on a large scale after the 1862 reorganization. Occasionally, companies were granted special permission to transfer to a different battalion or regiment, and sometimes regiments were transferred to a different brigade.

Every South Carolina company, squadron, battalion and regiment was provided with an official designation. While companies in Confederate service received alphabetic designations, regiments, battalions and cavalry squadrons were usually given numeric designations—the 1st Regiment, SCV, for example. In addition, most regiments were referred to unofficially by the name of their colonel—Gregg's regiment, for instance. Some, like the Eutaw Regiment (25th SCV) or the Pee Dee Regiment (8th SCV), had unofficial names. Three South Carolina regiments and one battalion in Confederate service received no numeric designation: the Hampton Legion, the Holcombe Legion, the Palmetto Sharpshooters and Manigault's Battalion.

Regiments and battalions in each service—infantry, cavalry and artillery—were given sequential numerical designations in 1861. All three services duplicated the use of numbers for regiments throughout the war. Numbering of battalions, on the other hand, was different. There was some duplication in the use of numbers among the three services during the first year of the war, and gaps in available information suggest that other numbers were probably skipped over and not used at all. In 1861, for example, infantry battalions were numbered the 1st, 3rd and 5th; cavalry battalions were designated the 1st, 2nd, 3rd and 4th; and artillery battalions used the designations 1st, 2nd and 3rd. At or shortly after the reorganization of the armies in 1862, all battalions in the state, regardless of service branch, seem to have been incorporated into a system of numerical designation that both avoided duplication of numbering among the various branches and started the numbering sequence all over again. There is, however, no documentation for this theory; it is simply an observation. At the reorganization, some battalions became full regiments, others remained unchanged and a few ceased to exist altogether. After that, the infantry battalions, some old and others new, were the 1st, 2nd, 3rd, 5th, 6th, 7th, 9th, 11th and 13th. The cavalry used the 4th, 8th, 10th, 12th, 14th, 16th, 17th and 19th. Artillery had the 15th and 18th Battalions. The artillery also carried the 3rd Battalion, which appears to duplicate the 3rd Infantry Battalion, but the artillery battalion, which failed in an effort to become a regiment, probably retained its designation for that reason.

An officer could lose his commission in several ways. Many, some excellent and some downright incompetent, were simply not re-elected at the reorganization of the Confederate armies in the spring of 1862 and were consequently dropped from the rolls of their respective organizations.

Such officers were then required to serve elsewhere unless they were overage or otherwise exempt. An officer could resign his commission by tendering a letter of resignation to the secretary of war through his commanding officer, who would either recommend approval or, rarely, denial and forward the letter up the chain of command. Most officers who resigned did so because chronic or severe illness, advanced age or the effect of wounds left them unable to perform their duties. A few resigned because they realized they lacked the intellect or leadership ability needed for their position. Confederate law gave an officer the option of resigning his commission if he held certain offices in the civil government, and some individuals resigned on those grounds. A few officers were cashiered or discharged by court martial, usually for drunkenness on duty or some other crime. The Invalid Corps was created by the Confederate Congress on February 17, 1864, to retain competent officers who wished to remain in the service but who had been disabled for further duty in the field. Many officers were retired to the Invalid Corps after approval from a medical examiners' board upon documentation by means of a surgeon's certificate. These men were usually assigned to light duty as officers in camps of instruction, at military posts or as enrolling officers.

This work will emphasize the company, battalion and regimental organization of South Carolina troops during the War Between the States. To obtain proper perspective, however, it is also necessary to present a basic outline of the relationship of battalions and regiments to higher levels of organization—brigades, divisions, corps and armies, as well as departments and their sub-units of military districts and subdivisions. This work gives a cursory overview of this relationship so readers can relate regiments and battalions to each other in their respective higher levels of organization. An excellent, and quite exhaustive, review of these higher levels of organization can be found in *Compendium of the Confederate Armies, South Carolina and Georgia* by Stewart Sifakis.

This work presents a history of South Carolina's military organizations in the War Between the States in four volumes. Within each volume, the order of presentation is: first, infantry, followed by cavalry and artillery. Volume I discusses those organizations whose men came from the Lowcountry and the Pee Dee; Volume II discusses those whose men came from the Midlands; Volume III discusses those whose men came from the Upstate; and Volume IV discusses those units that drew from all over the state, militia, reserves and miscellaneous organizations. Within each volume, each organization is set forth and described in numeric order—the 1st Infantry Regiment, for example. This order generally follows that of the *Compiled Service Records*, but, for the sake of clarity, there are exceptions. In numeric order, regiments are listed first, followed by battalions, squadrons and, finally, independent companies. The presentation of each regiment and battalion follows the same pattern. First, it gives a history of the organization of each unit followed by a brief wartime biography of each field officer (colonels, lieutenant colonels and majors). Next, it presents a synopsis of the origins and commanders (captains) of each company. Finally, it summarizes the brigade affiliations and the major movements and engagements of each regiment or battalion.

Unit Designation	When Organized	Under What Authority	Initial Enlistment
1st Regiment, SCV (Gregg's 6-month Regiment)	01/08/61	2	6 months
1st Regiment, South Carolina Infantry, Regulars	01/28/61	3 and 4	3 years
1st Battalion, South Carolina Artillery, Regulars	01/28/61	3 and 4	3 years
DeSaussure's Cavalry Squadron, Regulars	01/28/61	3 and 4	3 years
1st SCV Infantry (Hagood's)	04/12/61	1	12 months
2nd SCV Infantry	04/09/61	1	12 months
3rd SCV Infantry	04/14/61	1	12 months
4th SCV Infantry	04/14/61	1	12 months
5th SCV Infantry	04/13/61	1	12 months
6th SCV Infantry	04/11/61	1	12 months
7th SCV Infantry	04/15/61	1	12 months
8th SCV Infantry	04/14/61	1	12 months
9th SCV Infantry	07/12/61 to date from 04/08/61	1	12 months
10th SCV Infantry	~05/31/61	1	12 months
11th SCV Infantry	05/20/61	1	12 months
12th SCV Infantry	08/30/61	7	war
13th SCV Infantry	09/04/61	7	war
14th SCV Infantry	09/10/61	7	war
15th SCV Infantry	09/10/61	7	war
Gregg's (reorganized) 1st SCV Infantry	08–09/61	8	war
Orr's Regiment Rifles	07/20/61	8	war
5th Battalion Infantry	12/10/61	8	war
1st Battalion Cavalry	10/31/61	25	war

Unit Designation	When Organized	Under What Authority	Initial Enlistment
2nd Battalion Artillery	10/61	1	war
3rd Battalion Artillery	07–12/61	7	war
Manigault's Battalion	12/61	17	war
Chesterfield Light Artillery	08/25/61	—	war
16th SCV Infantry	12/12/61	10	12 months
17th SCV Infantry	12/18/61	6	12 months
Holcombe Legion	11/21/61	22	12 months
Hatch's Battalion Coast Rangers	09/61	—	mixed
3rd Battalion Infantry	12/04/61	10	12 months
Pee Dee Legion, South Carolina Militia	12/60–01/61	—	12 months
1st (Martin's) Cavalry Regiment, South Carolina Militia	11/61	2	90 days
4th Brigade, South Carolina Militia	1861	2	—
Stono Scouts	11/10/61	—	—
W.F. Percival's Company	11/61	—	—
South Carolina College Cadets	01/19/61	—	—
German Light Artillery	08/22/61	—	5 years
Beaufort Volunteer Artillery	05/61	1	12 months
Bonneau's Artillery	10/01/61	—	—
Calhoun Light Artillery	~04/26/61	—	~90 days
Santee Light Artillery	10/30/61	prob. 17	war
Macbeth Artillery	09/16/61	—	war
Marion Artillery	09/61	—	—
Washington (Hart's) Artillery	05/18/61	6	12 months
1st Regiment Charleston Guards	—	—	—
1st Regiment Reserves, South Carolina Militia	11/11/61	—	—
A.H.Boykin's Cavalry Troop	06/26/61	—	war
J.G.Harlan's Company	12/30/61	—	—
Lipscomb's Cavalry Troop	12/61	—	—
St. James Mounted Riflemen, Company A	04/15/61	9	war
Marion Men of Winyah	05/05/61	—	—
Trenholm's Squadron	09/09/61	—	12 months
Battalion South Carolina Cadets	01/28/61	24	—
6th Battalion Infantry	05/29/62	prob. 18	war

Unit Designation	When Organized	Under What Authority	Initial Enlistment
18th SCV Infantry	01/02/62	10	12 months
19th SCV Infantry	01/03/62	10	12 months
20th SCV Infantry	01/11/62	10	12 months
21st SCV Infantry	11/12/61	10	12 months
22nd SCV Infantry	12/61	10	12 months
23rd SCV Infantry	11/15/61	10, 39	mixed
24th SCV Infantry	12/61–04/62	10, 11	war
25th SCV Infantry	07/22/62	11 and 38	war
26th SCV Infantry	09/09/62	20	mixed
27th SCV Infantry	09/30/63	21	war
2nd Regiment Rifles	04/27/62	35	war
2nd Battalion Sharpshooters	09/01/62	prob. 10	—
4th (13th) Battalion Infantry	04/21/62	36	3 years or war
15th Battalion Artillery Regulars	summer 1861	37	3 years
18th Battalion Artillery	05/01/62	—	war
Palmetto Sharpshooters	04/16/62	23	2 years or war
1st Regiment Artillery Regulars	03/25/62	5	war
2nd Regiment Artillery	04/12/62	34	war
1st Regiment Cavalry	06/25/62	26	war
2nd Regiment Cavalry	08/22/62	27	war
3rd Regiment Cavalry	08/62	29	war
4th Regiment Cavalry	12/16/62	30	war
5th Regiment Cavalry	01/18/63	31	war
6th Regiment Cavalry	11/01/62	32	war
7th Regiment Cavalry	03/18/64	33	war
7th Battalion Infantry	02/22/62	19	war
1st (Charleston) Battalion Infantry	02/17/62	15	12 months
1st Battalion Sharpshooters	06/62	16	—
11th Battalion Infantry	~02/22/62	10	12 months
9th Battalion Infantry	01–03/62	prob. 10	12 months
1st (14th) Battalion Cavalry	01/62	—	12 months
3rd (4th) Battalion Cavalry	01–02/62	prob. 10	12 months
2nd (10th) Battalion Cavalry	01/19/62	—	12 months
6th (17th) Battalion Cavalry	03/62	—	mixed
Brooks Guard Artillery	01/28/62	17	2 years and 3 months
Inglis Light Artillery	03/20/62	17	war

Unit Designation	When Organized	Under What Authority	Initial Enlistment
Palmetto Light Battery	~04/08/62	—	—
German Artillery	02/12/62	prob. 10	—
Gist Guards Artillery	02/62	prob. 10	3 years
McQueen Light Artillery	04/14/62	—	—
Lafayette Artillery	03/13/62	prob. 10	12 months
12th Battalion (4th Squadron Cavalry)	01/01/62	—	mixed
16th (6th) Battalion Cavalry	07/21/62	prob. 10 and 11	war
19th Battalion Cavalry	12/20/64	—	war
Pee Dee Artillery	03/62	—	war
Washington (Walter's) Artillery	02/20/62	prob. 10 or 11	3 years or war
Waccamaw Light Artillery	01/20/62	prob. 10	war
Ferguson's Light Battery	04/62	—	—
Edisto Artillery	03/19/62	—	war
B.E. Dickson's Battery	03/19/62	—	war
Carolina Artillery	04/12/62	—	war
Silverton Artillery	04/09/62	—	2 years or war
Willis's Battery	spring 1862	—	—
S.D. Lee's Battery	~05/12/61	—	—
South Carolina Reserve Regiments	11/62	12, 40	90 days
South Carolina State Troops	08/04/63	14	6 months
South Carolina Reserve Battalions	09/64	13	war
South Carolina Junior Reserves	summer 1864	41	—
Brooks Foreign Battalion	10/10/64	—	—
Dunlop's Battalion Sharpshooters	05/03/62	—	—
8th Battalion (2nd Battalion Reserves) Cavalry	05/30/62	28	war
St. Peters Guards	1861	9	—
German Hussars	1861	prob. 9	—
Rebel Troop	01/17/62	prob. 10	—
Charleston Light Dragoons	04/61	prob. 10	—
Yeadon Rangers	07/27/62	—	war
Whitner's Troop	—	—	—
Hough's Company	01/01/62	—	war

Unit Designation	When Organized	Under What Authority	Initial Enlistment
Ripley Rangers	04/03/62	—	war
A.C. Earle's Company	04/15/62	—	war
M.J. Kirk's Squadron	07/11/62	—	war
Keitt's Mounted Riflemen	06/10/63	—	—
E.M. Boykin's Squadron	11/05/62	—	—
Brooks Infantry Partisan Rangers	07/14/62	17	war

1. South Carolina legislature act of December 17, 1860.
2. South Carolina Convention resolution of January 1, 1861.
3. South Carolina Convention resolution of December 31, 1860.
4. South Carolina legislature act of January 28, 1861.
5. South Carolina legislature act of December 1861.
6. President Davis authorized the Hampton Legion on April 27, 1861.
7. President Davis called for three thousand men to enlist for the duration of the war on June 30, 1861.
8. President Davis called for two regiments to enlist for the duration of the war on July 1, 1861.
9. Special resolution of the South Carolina Convention in 1861 calling for twenty-one cavalry companies to serve until the end of the legislative session.
10. South Carolina legislature resolutions of November 1861 and December 7, 1861, and Governor Pickens's calls on November 11, 1861, and December 9, 1861, for special local defense troops.
11. Confederate Congress act of February 28, 1862.
12. South Carolina Executive Council created two corps of reserves in the summer of 1862.
13. Confederate Conscription Act of February 17, 1864.
14. Confederate Congress act of August 21 1861, and Confederate Congress act of October 13, 1862 and President Davis's call for troops.
15. Arose from a failed scheme of John Pemberton to raise a battalion of sharpshooters in late 1861 and early 1862.
16. Primarily compulsory draft and a few volunteers.
17. Special permission from the Confederate War Department.
18. A series of calls in 1862 (February 2, 21 and 28, 1862, and March 5, 1862) for eighteen thousand South Carolinians to enlist for the duration of the war.
19. Confederate Congress called for twenty-five hundred men for the duration of the war.

20. Consolidation of the 6th and 9th Infantry Battalions.
21. Consolidation of the 1st (Charleston) Battalion and the 1st Battalion Sharpshooters.
22. Governor Pickens authorized the Holcombe Legion in the fall of 1861.
23. Act of Congress and permission of the secretary of war.
24. South Carolina legislature created the South Carolina Military Academy (The Citadel and The Arsenal) as well as the Battalion State Cadets.
25. Governor Pickens called up the 1st Battalion in the fall of 1861.
26. Augmentation of the 1st Battalion Cavalry.
27. Alignment of the Hampton Legion Cavalry Battalion with the 4th (3rd) Cavalry Battalion, Lipscomb's Company and A.H. Boykin's Company.
28. Consolidation of eight independent companies.
29. Consolidation of the 8th cavalry Battalion (2nd Battalion Reserves) with three independent companies.
30. Augmentation of the 10th and 12th Cavalry Battalions with B.H. Rutledge's Company and Thomas Pinckney's Company.
31. Augmentation of the 14th and 17th Cavalry Battalions with Harlan's Company and Whilden's Company.
32. Augmentation of the 16th (6th) Cavalry Battalion with three companies.
33. Augmentation of the Holcombe Legion Cavalry Battalion with Tucker's Squadron, Trenholm's Squadron and E. Boykin's Squadron.
34. Augmentation of the 2nd (Lamar's) Artillery Battalion with six companies when the secretary of war called for additional troops on February 2, 1862.
35. Augmentation of the 5th Battalion Infantry.
36. Abatement of the 4th Regiment Infantry.
37. Formed from DeSaussure's Cavalry Squadron Regulars.
38. Augmentation of the 11th Battalion Infantry.
39. Augmentation of Hatch's Battalion Coast Rangers.
40. Confederate Conscription Act of September 17, 1862, and South Carolina Executive Council resolutions of April 23, 1862 and November 7, 1862.
41. South Carolina Militia Laws, not Confederate States troops.

1.

THE 1ST REGIMENT, SOUTH CAROLINA VOLUNTEERS

The 1st Regiment, SCV, was also called the 1st (Hagood's) Infantry and the 1st SCV. The public press occasionally referred to it as the 9th Regiment, SCV, probably because it was the ninth volunteer regiment to enter service and to avoid confusion with Maxcy Gregg's 1st Regiment.[1]

The South Carolina General Assembly passed an act on December 17, 1860, calling for the creation of an "Armed Military Force" from existing state militia. On December 20, South Carolina seceded from the Union, and on the twenty-ninth, Governor Pickens, under the terms of the act, issued a call for volunteers; his call resulted in the organization of ten regiments of volunteers for a twelve-month enlistment. Regiments were numbered according to the geographical area in which the men lived, not to the dates of acceptance into service. Johnson Hagood's regiment was designated the first of the ten, and its companies rendezvoused at various sites on January 3, 1861.[2] The 15th Militia Regiment of Orangeburg District assembled at Orangeburg Court House and furnished four companies—Companies A, B, C and D. The 11th and 43rd Regiments of Militia from Barnwell District assembled at Barnwell Village, where volunteers formed Companies E, F, G, H and I. The 15th Regiment from Colleton District gathered at Walterboro and furnished two companies. One became Company K, and the other did not enlist in Hagood's Regiment because of the ten-company limit. These ten companies were then organized into the 1st SCV; the regiment was completed on January 27, when elections were held for field officers.[3] The governor received the regiment into state service on March 6, just six days before it reached its full complement.[4] The regiment, consisting of 832 men, rank and file, mustered in state service for twelve months on April 12 in Charleston.[5]

Soon after the fall of Fort Sumter on April 13, the governor of Virginia asked for military assistance from South Carolina. James Hagood wrote that though Virginia had seceded from the Union, it was not at that time part of the Confederacy. "Supportive of the Virginia governor," Governor Pickens urged the South Carolina troops, including those on on Morris Island, to volunteer for service in Virginia.[6] This situation set off an unfortunate chain of events and caused much confusion and disaffection among the men, for many of them believed they had volunteered strictly for service in South Carolina. Even so, portions of the 2nd Regiment, along with part of Maxcy Gregg's 1st Regiment, complied with the governor's request.[7] Of the state's regiments, Hagood's 1st, Gregg's 1st, Kershaw's 2nd and Jenkins's 5th were the most seriously impacted. On April 16, Governor Pickens sent then-Colonel Johnson Hagood a copy of resolutions passed by the South Carolina Secession Convention. They said that if the government of the Confederate States called for a volunteer force, the governor of South Carolina could ask existing regiments of twelve-month volunteers to respond to the call. They also said that the troops must consent to their transfer to Confederate service and that if only some men in a regiment responded, the remaining vacancies could be filled by others. James Hagood wrote: "The 1st Regiment when called upon responded by Mangum's Company volunteering nearly unanimously; the other companies volunteered from ten to thirty men each, but coupled with the condition in each case that the whole company went. No special effort was made by the officers to induce their men to volunteer; for it was seen that it would disrupt the regiment, and it was thought more advisable, with a view of subsequently taking Confederate service, to keep it together."[8]

Within a few days of April 16, most of the men had rejected the governor's request. Pickens wrote, "the first regiment...under Colonel Hagood, declined to muster into Confederate service, and I immediately relieved them from duty and discharged them for the present."[9] Governor Pickens, supported by the adjutant general of South Carolina, then issued a proclamation saying that he had the "right to order the twelve months' volunteers to march or to serve wherever he deemed proper beyond the borders of the State."[10] The reaction was predictable. The men—most of whom had refused to serve in Virginia—saw the proclamation as coercion, and their "indignation was felt to such a degree that it required an exertion of authority to prevent its public expression."[11] For more than a month, Hagood's men discussed among themselves the issue of whether or not to enter Confederate service.[12] When they left Morris Island for Orangeburg on May 22, the question remained. Orangeburg had been chosen as a regimental campsite because it was considered a favorable spot from which to furlough and a good place to take up the discussion of Confederate service when the men returned. On May 23, the men were given a ten-day furlough, and that same day, "Governor Pickens's second proclamation arrived." A second proclamation. This one, dated May 16, which arrived in camp too late to be read to the men before they left, stated that the commander-in-chief—the governor—could direct the volunteer regiments to march wherever and whenever he wished.

The resolution of the Secession Convention had been less confrontational. It intended that the governor would give existing volunteer regiments the honor of volunteering for Confederate service and that those regiments would be allowed to enter Confederate service with their field officers intact. It also said a minimum of six companies would be required to maintain regimental integrity, and ten companies would constitute a complete regiment. "When these eight regiments are made up a portion of them will be retained by the Governor to defend the State of South Carolina, and if the regiments decline to be mustered into Confederate service, then still a sufficient number of them will be retained for seacoast defense in this state. In any case, however, a selection for this service will be made."[13] Until now, "the claims of home" had been "too strong for the calls of patriotism."[14] The men believed that just as they had defended South Carolina, so, too, should the other states defend themselves. Further, given what happened to Maxcy Gregg's six-month regiment—some of whose companies were disbanded because their men would not serve in Virginia—they also thought their choice boiled down to Confederate service or disbandment. Governor Pickens, on the other hand, saw the choice for the twelve-month volunteers as being between service in Virginia or service along the South Carolina coast. South Carolina Secretary of War General D.F. Jamison visited Hagood's regiment in Orangeburg and assured the officers that the choice was not between Confederate service and disbandment but between service in Virginia or along the coast.

When they returned from furlough in early June, the men considered their options and resumed the discussion. Toward the end of May, following Jamison's clarification, six skeleton companies were organized from the original companies. On June 2, Colonel Hagood requested a mustering officer to accept the six skeleton companies for immediate service in Virginia; he also requested that future recruits be allowed to follow the regiment to the new posting. Governor Pickens, however, refused to accept the companies, arguing that only a full and complete regiment—ten companies—could be sent to Virginia. On June 4, Pickens ordered Hagood to remove from the regiment those men who had not volunteered for Confederate service and to march them under the command of Major O'Cain to camp at Ridgeville. This new order spurred the organization of two additional skeleton companies from the original complement. Most likely, the eight skeleton companies, totaling about five hundred men, were A, B, C, D, E, F, G and H. Captain Collier's company refused to muster in Confederate service, but many of its members combined with Captain Kemmerlin's company and opted for Virginia duty. This arrangement was impermanent since both Collier and Kemmerlin commanded a company until the spring of 1862. The men of Captain White's Company I unanimously refused to enter Confederate service; as a result, Company I was exchanged with Captain Rice's Company from Colonel Heyward's 9th (11th) SCV, Regiment.[15] Rice's Company became the ninth company, and both Captain Steedman's Company from Lexington District and Captain Cantey's Company from Camden applied for the tenth position. Cantey's Company was rejected, and Steedman's Company was briefly added to the regiment as the tenth. Probably designated Company I, this unit remained with Hagood's regiment for only five or six weeks. On July 10, Steedman's Company mustered in as Company K of the 9th Regiment, SCV. In early June 1861, with these changes, the regiment had its full complement of companies. Within a few days, each skeleton company filled to an average of eighty men, and the ten companies prepared to muster in Confederate service. A.S. Salley wrote: "Just as the regiment was ready to be mustered into Confederate service, with the expectation of being sent to the scene of war in Virginia, Colonel Hagood received a communication from Governor Pickens, dated June 6, 1861, saying that the regiment would not be allowed to go to Virginia, but must serve on the coast of South Carolina. At that time there was no prospect of fighting on the coast of South Carolina and not a man of the regiment would muster in. On this report being made, orders were issued retaining the regiment in service for state defense. A few days later these orders were countermanded, and on June 15, 1861, the regiment was 'relieved from duty until further orders.'"[16] James Hagood wrote: "The men who had signed the Confederate rolls were exasperated to the last degree."[17] Shortly after June 15, Captain Mangum's Company E volunteered for Confederate service and mustered in a Mississippi regiment, leaving Hagood's regiment with only nine companies. James Hagood wrote:

> *To do his excellency justice, he seemed utterly dismayed at the result of his communication of the 6th of June and evinced every disposition to remedy the evil by acquiescing in the new scheme. The Secretary of War telegraphed his assent from Richmond, but the men failed entirely to respond. They had lost all confidence in the authorities—the delights of home loomed up in magnified proportions; the last spark of volunteering enthusiasm was extinguished; and they seemed bent on disbanding at whatever consequences to themselves or country. Desiring to disembarrass the question of every*

> *difficulty, the field officers issued a card pledging themselves to resign if so many as one-half of each of six companies wished to volunteer under other officers; but the same stubborn silence was maintained.*[18]*...During the time the first regiment was relieved from duty the authorities sometimes acted as if it was finally disbanded, and at other times as if it was only temporarily relieved and future service expected of it.*[19]

On July 13, 1861, Governor Pickens ordered the remaining nine companies to assemble on July 20 at Summerville under the command of Lieutenant Colonel Glover. None of the companies were full, and many were mere fragments. "The recruiting of the regiment had commenced and the question of taking Confederate service was again presented, accompanied with a communication from the Adjutant General setting forth that those refusing would be still kept on duty till their term expired. Still many doubted the *bona fide* character of the communication and (to anticipate somewhat) the sequel showed that they were well posted on the subject of executive vacillation. After keeping the recusants in service for some time his excellency on the 30th of September incontinently disbanded them."[20] By late July or early August 1861, the issues between the governor and Hagood's men were finally resolved, and the regiment reorganized, quickly filling its ranks.[21] Salley wrote that "two of the companies failed to obtain a basis to recruit upon Confederate service."[22] These two were Captain Frederick's Company G and Captain Brown's Company K, but a considerable number of the men enlisted in the remaining companies of the regiment. Companies A, B, C, D, F, H and K (Rice's Company) were with the regiment as of July 20. Company E (Mangum's Company) had left the regiment, and neither Frederick's Company G, nor the original Company K under Captain Brown, nor Steedman's Company mustered in Confederate service along with the regiment. Colonel Hagood returned from a three-month furlough on August 10 to resume command of the regiment. Three new companies—E under Captain Pressley, G under Captain Duncan, and I under Captain Brabham—were added, and a full ten companies of the newly organized 1st SCV Regiment mustered in Confederate service between August 20 and August 22 at Summerville.[23] The term of enlistment was twelve months, effective from April 12, 1861. The men signed on for Confederate service unconditionally, meaning with no pledge from the government as to where they would serve; still they regarded Virginia as the "field of honor" and wanted to serve there. James Hagood wrote that the regiment could not have been raised without the prospect of its being ordered to Virginia. Though Colonel Johnson Hagood requested immediate service for the regiment there, his request was denied.[24] James Hagood wrote: "A great deal has been said...on the difficulties which prevented the 1st Regiment from being mustered into the Confederate service at the time her sister regiments were, and official details have been dwelt upon, perhaps to too great an extent...but the writer has been persuaded to this step by the many reflections which invidious persons have attempted to cast upon the spirit and pluck of his regiment as evinced in the first months of the war, and his object has been merely to show the matter in its proper light."[25]

In the spring of 1862, the regiment was once again reorganized; this time the men re-enlisted for Confederate service "for the duration of the war."[26] At the reorganization, eleven new companies were formed from the ten existing companies of Hagood's regiment, and on re-enlistment they were briefly given numeric designations. Captain Martin's Company H ceased to exist when it chose not to re-enlist. Two other original companies, B and G, were each subdivided into two new companies, and three of the four new companies, B, K and E, remained with the regiment. Hagood's regiment lost five of its original companies—A, C, D, E and H—along with a number of men from the other five original companies. Five of the eleven reorganized companies mustered in other regiments or battalions. The 1st Company, under Captain W.H. Sellars, was previously Company D; the 10th, under Captain J.G. Pressley, had been Company E and the 11th, under Captain J.V. Glover, was previously Company A. These three companies mustered in the 11th Battalion. The 2nd Company, under Captain T.K. Legare, was previously Company C and the 6th, under Captain F. Sanders, was formerly part of Company G. These two companies mustered in the 2nd Regiment, South Carolina Artillery. James Hagood wrote that these five companies chose to leave the regiment not out of any disaffection but for the better possibility of promotion for company-grade officers in new organizations like the 11th Battalion or the 2nd Artillery Regiment. Six of the recently reorganized companies were left in Hagood's regiment. The original Companies B, F, part of G, I and K remained with the regiment, and Company B divided into two companies, the new B and the new K, both of which remained with the regiment. This reorganization left Hagood's regiment with five of its original companies when the regiment re-enlisted in April 1862. Company K, which was created from the original Company B, became the sixth. To preserve the old organization, the six companies decided to combine.[27] Four new companies—D, F, H and I—authorized by the Executive Council in early April were added to the regiment in late May.[28] Four of the original six companies received new letter designations at the reorganization: old Company B divided into new B and K, old Company F became new

Company G, old Company G was renamed E, old Company K became new Company A and old Company I became new Company C.

Thus, three sets of companies made up the 1st Regiment, SCV. The first set comprised those that originally enlisted in state service and served from April 12 to August 22, 1861. The second set was created when some original and some new companies volunteered for Confederate service on August 22, 1861, and served until April 12, 1862. The third set—ten in all—was created when the regiment was reorganized on April 12. James Hagood lists numeric designations for three companies when they re-enlisted in Confederate service in April 1862, but there is no indication that such designations were officially assigned. The 1st SCV Regiment was excellent when competent officers were in command, but it often suffered severely from inadequate leadership.

FIELD OFFICERS

Johnson Hagood of Barnwell, a brigadier general in the South Carolina Militia at the outbreak of the war, was elected the first colonel of the regiment on January 5, 1861.[29] A.S. Salley gives the date as January 8.[30] Hagood entered state service with the regiment on April 12. During the confusion surrounding volunteer forces entering Confederate service in the early summer, Hagood, "believing that his regiment wouldn't be again called into service (if at all) before the winter months," obtained a three-month furlough and went to Virginia as a private soldier. He was detailed to the Engineer Corps and supervised the construction of works near Fairfax Court House.[31] He also served as a volunteer in the Palmetto Guard of the 2nd Regiment, SCV, during the battle of First Manassas before returning to command the 1st Regiment on August 10. Hagood was re-elected colonel on April 12, 1862, when the regiment was reorganized.[32] He was assigned to command a new temporary brigade on James Island called the "Advanced Forces" on June 18.[33] Hagood was promoted to brigadier general July 12, 1862, (also shown as July 21) was detached from his regiment and was assigned to command the 2nd Military District of the Department of South Carolina, Georgia and Florida.[34] He was later given command of his own brigade and commanded it until the end of the war, though about March 30, 1865, he left his post in North Carolina and returned to South Carolina to round up absentees.[35] Hagood was still in his home state at the end of the war. Sergeant William V. Izlar wrote: "General Hagood was a dignified man, of rather retiring disposition; and while he did not wear his heart on his coat sleeve those who knew him best admired him most. He was a rigid disciplinarian, but always just. He was quiet and unpretentious in camp life, but in battle he was dashing and superbly brave. My admiration for him was unbounded."[36] After the war, Hagood served as comptroller general and governor of South Carolina as well as chairman of the Board of Vistors at The Citadel.

Thomas Jamison Glover of Orangeburg, the first captain of Company A, was elected the first lieutenant colonel of the regiment on January 5, 1861.[37] Salley records the date as January 8, 1861.[38] Glover entered Confederate service at this rank on July 20 and was re-elected at the reorganization on April 12, 1862.[39] Glover took over as colonel when Hagood was promoted to brigadier general on July 12.[40] Glover received a flesh wound below the right knee early on August 30 at Second Manassas but refused to leave the field. Later, near the end of the battle, he was struck in the right side by a Minié ball, which passed obliquely through his abdomen. Another struck his right calf as he was borne from the field. Glover lapsed into unconsciousness after about five hours and died about eighteen hours later on August 31.[41] Salley records incorrectly that Glover was wounded on the twenty-ninth.[42] A battery on the north side of James Island near the Ashley River was named in Glover's memory.[43] He is buried in the cemetery on Doyle Street in Orangeburg.[44] James Hagood wrote that Glover's death was "deeply regretted by his whole command" and "as an officer, Colonel Glover possessed the esteem and confidence of his superiors and the warm admiration of his men."[45] J.G. Pressley, captain of the Wee Nee Volunteers, wrote that Glover was "held in high esteem by all who knew him" as "an unselfish, noble, generous spirit."[46] According to W.H. Duncan, lieutenant colonel of the 1st Regiment, "when he [Glover] fell the regiment wept around him as though they had been deprived of a father. He was a brave and skilful soldier, a noble, courteous gentleman, his loss to the state is severe, to us irreparable."[47] He was also described as: "gifted, gallant, and full of fresh, generous and elevating impulses."[48]

Watson A. O'Cain of Orangeburg was elected the first major of the regiment in January 1861.[49] Though he entered Confederate service as major on July 20, he declined to offer himself for any office in the spring of 1862 and was dropped from the rolls on May 19.[50]

William Hansford Duncan of Barnwell was re-elected captain of Company E on April 12, 1862, and was elected major on May 16. He was promoted to lieutenant colonel on July 12, when Johnson Hagood was promoted to brigadier general.[51] From September 1, 1862, to January 10, 1863, Duncan held the rank of colonel of the 1st Regiment by order of Micah Jenkins. His fellow officers recognized him as such, and he drew colonel's pay.[52] The War Department, however, rejected the unorthodox promotion, and Duncan was absent without leave at home in South Carolina from September 15 to the following January. He failed to return to the regiment during this time and gave no reason for his inaction.[53] The case was referred to the War Department, and Duncan resigned his commission as lieutenant colonel on January 10, 1863. He was dropped from the rolls on January 16, a date also shown as January 15.[54] The *CSR* gives the year, incorrectly, as 1862 and also indicates that he held the rank of colonel at the time. Johnson Hagood writes that Duncan not only failed to distinguish himself personally, but also that at his hands, the regiment suffered in both discipline and usefulness.[55]

Daniel Livingston of Orangeburg was promoted from captain of Company B to major on July 12, 1862, replacing Duncan in that post when Hagood was named brigadier general. Livingston was promoted to lieutenant colonel on September 1 pursuant to an order from Micah Jenkins that was confirmed by the War Department.[56] Livingston was wounded at both Second Manassas and Sharpsburg. James R. Hagood writes that Livingston fainted from the heat at Sharpsburg, but Mixson contends that he was wounded while leading the regiment through a "furor of bursting shells."[57] Lieutenant Colonel Duncan, at the time acting colonel, resigned his commission in mid-January 1863. There was, however, no one to take his place since both Lieutenant Colonel Livingston and Major Grimes had "given no evidence of deserving further promotion," and the company officers were too inexperienced for elevation to field-grade.[58] Thus, F.W. Kilpatrick was appointed colonel of the 1st Regiment in late January. As Kilpatrick worked to restore discipline and morale in April and May, he came to regard as hopeless both Lieutenant Colonel Livingston and Major Grimes. Though permitted to remain in their quarters, neither officer shared in the work of the 1st Regiment's reorganization nor in the development of its newfound enthusiasm. In January 1864, when the regiment was relatively inactive, it addressed the matter of poor leadership. General Hagood ordered Livingston, who was at home, to either return to the regiment immediately or be considered absent without leave and dropped from the rolls.[59] James Hagood's view of Livingston then was stark: "This officer is of advanced age, limited education, lacks energy and decision of character, and in a word, is utterly unqualified for the position that he occupies. He is now under charges of incompetency." He adds: "In Livingston's case there was no alternative but to force him to resign or, in the event of his refusal to do this, to bring him before a Court-Martial."[60] Livingston finally resigned on March 17, 1864, a date also shown as March 19.[61] His letter of resignation reads in part: "It will be of no disadvantage to the service for me to resign and I can better serve my country in some other capacity." Perhaps he was right; after his resignation, Livingston served as quartermaster in Captain Fredericks's Company. Johnson Hagood's final assessment of Livingston mirrors his assessment of Duncan.[62]

Franklin Whitner "Whit" Kilpatrick from the Anderson/Pendleton/Pickens area was previously captain of Company E, 4th Regiment, SCV, and major in the Palmetto Sharpshooters. Having earlier declined the colonelcy in the Palmetto Sharpshooters, he accepted the application of the 1st Regiment's officers and was appointed colonel with rank from January 31, 1863.[63] Kilpatrick followed Colonel Glover, who had been killed the year before, and replaced acting Colonel Duncan, who resigned. According to Johnson Hagood, Kilpatrick "soon restored the discipline and esprit of the regiment," which had been hacked and cuffed about by inefficient officers since Glover's death at Second Manassas.[64] In command during the night battle at Wauhatchie Junction in Lookout Valley, Tennessee, on October 28 and 29, 1863, Kilpatrick was observing the enemy from a kneeling position when he was struck and killed instantly by a bullet that entered his left breast and passed out below the left shoulder blade.[65] John Bratton, then colonel of the 6th Regiment, SCV, wrote: "His loss is irremediable to his regiment"; Micah Jenkins wrote: "Never…could one's loss so completely desolate me."[66]

James Robert "Jim" Hagood of Barnwell, brother of Johnson Hagood, was promoted from captain of Company K to colonel on November 16, 1863, succeeding Kilpatrick.[67] Know affectionately as "our boy colonel," Hagood was just ten days shy of his nineteenth birthday.[68] He had been made adjutant for gallant conduct on the field, and his promotions to captain of Company K and to colonel recognized his distinguished valor and skill. He was made colonel over Lieutenant Colonel Livingston, Major Grimes and four senior captains. In 1868, R.E. Lee wrote of James Hagood: "It gives me pleasure to state that Colonel J.R. Hagood during the whole term of his connection with the Army of Northern Virginia was conspicuous for gallantry, efficiency and good conduct. By his merit constantly exhibited he rose from a private in his Regiment to its command, and showed by his actions that he was worthy of the position."[69] Paroled at Appomattox on April 9, 1865, Hagood wrote his memoirs, though they were never published. In 1868, Hagood decided to seek his fortunes abroad, and he solicited letters of recommendation from his former commanding officers. Brigadier General John Bratton responded:

> *In the most trying and eventful campaign* [of 1864],…*he was throughout conspicuous for his gallantry and indomitable energy. Whether storming the works of the enemy, or defending our own, he was equally energetic,*

> *judicious, and reliable. Whether his command was full or reduced by more than half, as it frequently was by casualties in battle, he managed to resist the disorganizing influences of heavy casualty lists, the sudden loss of valuable officers and men, and to maintain its efficiency. He not only fought his regiment well, but by his judicious and energetic management kept it always in condition to fight well. In a word, he is commended for his efficiency as an officer.*

Major General Charles Field wrote: "During our eventful service together in the bivouac, on the march, and in the shock of battle, your high-toned soldierly bearing at all times, your thorough handling of your regiment, and your distinguished gallantry in action, won my hearty admiration and praise." From James Longstreet came: "Colonel Hagood served with distinction as an officer of the 1st Corps of the Army of Northern Virginia and is highly esteemed as an accomplished gentleman." And from General P.G.T. Beauregard: "Colonel Hagood enjoyed in the late Confederate States Army the reputation of being a gallant and meritorious officer."[70] James Hagood, still under the age of thirty, died from injuries sustained in a railroad accident in 1870.[71]

George Martin Grimes of Bamberg was promoted from captain of Company G to acting major on September 1, 1862, by order of Micah Jenkins. Because Lieutenant Colonel Livingston was sick at home, Grimes actually commanded the regiment from the time Colonel Kilpatrick was killed in October 1863 until James R. Hagood's appointment as colonel on November 16, 1863.[72] Grimes's performance had, in the past, been utterly inadequate; Kilpatrick went so far as to confine the acting major to his quarters during the spring of 1863. Even so, Grimes managed to hold on to his rank until early 1864, when the War Department failed to confirm his promotion of more than a year earlier. James Hagood wrote:

> *It would be difficult to conceive of a person less fitted for this position* [command of the regiment] *than* [Grimes]. *Gifted by nature with a mind less than mediocre—slow and obtuse even under the circumstances—without one shadow of military esprit—this office was onerous to himself and intolerable, by his occupation of it, to those under him. Grimes did not want his position but his entire incapacity of resistance prevented his declining it when it was thrust upon him by his seniority of commission. Heretofore he had only held the usual sinecure of Major, with the Colonel or Lieutenant Colonel present in command, and his incompetency was not then so glaringly exhibited. Now that his responsibility was no longer withheld, his inadequacy to the burden imposed on him became mortifyingly*

> *apparent in the rapid degeneration to a state of almost worthlessness of a regiment which, a few weeks before, had been accounted one of the finest, in point of morale and discipline, in the service. These things were manifest to all who had eyes but where was the remedy? Lieutenant Colonel Livingston, now absent, who would, in the usual course of military elevation, succeed Kilpatrick, was less desirable than even Grimes; the latter was only passively hurtful to the command, the former would be actively so. Grimes had personal courage, though no faculty of inspiration—Livingston was utterly deficient in both. All the honesty which existed between the two belonged to Grimes. The condition of affairs had a profound influence on the troops. They saw no hope. They saw themselves sinking into disrepute amongst their sister regiments and their esprit fell.*[73]

In January 1864, Colonel James R. Hagood gave Grimes the choice of going before an examining board on charges of incompetence or resuming his old post as captain of Company G. Grimes chose the latter and returned to company command in less than a month. The *CSR* indicates that Grimes continued as acting major until September 7, 1864. That date, however, should probably read February 7 since Grimes's successor, B.B. Kirkland, was promoted to major on February 7 and to lieutenant colonel in July 1864. Grimes received a flesh wound in the right arm at the Wilderness on May 6, 1864, and he was mortally wounded—shot in the face and left side—during the assault on Fort Harrison on September 30; he died from the wounds the next day.[74]

Benjamin Brown Kirkland of the Buford's Bridge section in Barnwell District was promoted from captain of Company C to major on February 7, 1864.[75] Having acted as lieutenant colonel from February, he was officially awarded the promotion replacing Lieutenant Colonel Livingston on July 6, 1864, with rank from March 19. Kirkland's promotion left the regiment without a major. Kirkland was wounded at the battle of Second Manassas and paroled at Appomattox on April 9, 1865.[76] Kirkland was regarded as "a gallant soldier [who] had the respect and admiration of the whole regiment, both as a man and an officer." He survived the war.[77]

G.B. Lartigue served as assistant quartermaster of the regiment with the rank of major. He briefly commanded the regiment when Glover was killed, but he was never promoted to the rank of colonel.[78]

COMPANIES

The original companies—those that elected officers on January 27, 1861, and mustered in Confederate service on August 22, 1861—were:

Company A, the Edisto Rifles, was formed in Orangeburg in 1851.[79] In early 1861, all its commissioned officers, most of the noncommissioned officers and many of the privates were college graduates.[80] Captains of the company before the war included John J. Salley, John V. Glover and William L. Ehney. Thomas Jamison Glover was captain just before the company entered service in January 1861.[81] He is not listed as captain in the *CSR*, probably because he was elected lieutenant colonel on January 5. When the company reorganized for active duty on January 22, First Lieutenant John Vinyard Glover was promoted to captain. His commission was dated February 7, and he mustered in state service with the company on April 12, 1861. He re-enlisted for the duration of the war on July 20. The company was in state service until August 22, when the men and Captain J.V. Glover mustered in Confederate service. The company was stationed at Summerville when it entered Confederate service for twelve months from April 12, 1861. This company retained its designation as Company A when the regiment enlisted in Confederate service in August.

On April 12, 1862, most of the men re-enlisted for three years or for the duration of the war, and the Edisto Rifles was the eleventh company of Hagood's regiment to re-enlist then.[82] Both the *Memory Roll* and an article in the *Confederate Veteran* erroneously say the Edisto Rifles re-enlisted in the 25th Regiment in April 1862; the 25th Regiment, however, did not exist until July 22, 1862.[83] Another article in the *Confederate Veteran* correctly says the Edisto Rifles disbanded on April 12, 1862, re-enlisted in the Eutaw (11th) Battalion and then mustered in to the 25th Regiment on July 22, 1862.[84] Sergeant William Valimore Izlar records in his book, *A Sketch of the War Record of the Edisto Rifles*, that the company disbanded when its term of enlistment expired on April 12, 1862. He adds that most of the men immediately re-enlisted for three years or for the duration of the war under the same officers, joined the 11th (Eutaw) Battalion and shortly thereafter merged into the 25th Regiment as Company G.[85] Some of the men re-enlisted in other organizations in April 1862. J.V. Glover, dropped as captain of Company A of Hagood's regiment on April 11, was re-elected captain of the Edisto Rifles when it joined the Eutaw (11th) Battalion.

Company B, the Jamison Guards, was from Orangeburg District.[86] Daniel Livingston, elected captain on January 7, 1861, and the only captain of the company in state service, was reappointed on July 20, 1861, just before the company entered Confederate service. The company was in state service from April 12 to August 22, 1861. Also stationed at Summerville and mustered in Confederate service, effective for twelve months from April 12, 1861, the original Company B, Livingston's Company, divided into two companies in April 1862. Both remained in Hagood's regiment. One of the companies continued under Livingston's command; it became the 8th company to re-enlist in Confederate service and retained its designation of Company B. The other company fell under the command of Captain Joseph E. Knotts and became the 9th company to re-enlist in Confederate service, entering as Company K.

Company C, the Glover Guards, was from Orangeburg.[87] Samuel M. Kemmerlin, the only captain in state service, mustered in Confederate service at that rank on July 20, 1861. Companies C and D combined in May 1861 to form one company for Confederate service, but since the company was not accepted, C and D returned to their original status. Company C was in state service from April 12 to August 22, 1861. Stationed at Summerville at the time, the company mustered in Confederate service for twelve months from April 12, 1861, retaining its designation as Company C. In April 1862, most of the men re-enlisted in Company F, 2nd Regiment, South Carolina Artillery, and were the second company to re-enlist in Confederate service. A few men enlisted in the 25th Regiment, and some moved to other companies in Hagood's 1st Regiment.

The *Mercury* called Company D the St. Matthews Rifles on July 23, 1860, and it called the company the Keitt Guards on April 13, 1861. The men of Company D were from Orangeburg District and also from Bamberg in Barnwell District. The company was in state service from April 12 to August 22, 1861, and was stationed at Summerville, when it, too, mustered in Confederate service for twelve months from April 12, 1861. James Daniel Wesley Collier was a captain as early as July 1860; he was the only captain during state service, and he retained command of the company when he enlisted in Confederate service on July 20, 1861. He died on November 9 of fever contracted while still in camp, though the *Roll of the Dead* and Hagood give the date of his death as October, and Kirkland records that Collier died at home about December 15, 1861.[88] First Lieutenant John W. Sellers, who replaced Collier as captain on November 9, was dropped from the rolls on April 15, 1862. In April 1862, at the time of re-enlistment, most of the men of Company D re-enlisted in the 1st company in Confederate service, mustering in the 11th (Eutaw) Battalion; a few re-enlisted in the 2nd Regiment, South Carolina Artillery.

Company E, the Allen Guards, consisted mostly of members of the 11th and 43rd Regiments, South Carolina Militia, from Aiken, then part of Barnwell District.[89] The company, named in honor of Senator J. Duncan Allen of Barnwell District, was ready for service on January 8, 1861.[90] Though Thomas H. Mangum was captain, his name was not recorded with Hagood's Brigade in the *CSR* because he served only when the brigade was in state service.[91] The Allen Guards joined Hagood's regiment as twelve-month volunteers and participated in its movements on James Island and Morris Island in the spring of 1861. In late May, Mangum's company was the only one in the regiment to volunteer for service outside the state, an almost unanimous decision. Mangum tendered the services of his company to the secretary of war, and the Allen Guards mustered in Confederate service on July 15, 1861. The company became Company E in John D. Martin's regiment of volunteers, which was called both the 1st Mississippi Valley Regiment and the 25th Mississippi Regiment. Martin's regiment was called into service on August 10 and was attached to John S. Bowen's Brigade.[92] Mangum was appointed major of Martin's regiment on November 16 with rank from August 10, and James M. Day became captain of Company E. On January 31, 1862, Martin's regiment was redesignated the 2nd Confederate Regiment, with the Allen Guards in place as Company E, but a number of South Carolinians left that company to re-enlist in Company E of the 2nd Regiment, South Carolina Artillery, on March 19, 1862, while at Fort Johnson on James Island. Major Mangum remained with the 2nd Confederate Regiment and commanded it at the battle of Shiloh. The *CSR* does not contain complete records, but it appears that most of the South Carolinians in Company E of the 2nd Confederate Regiment were absent from the battle of Shiloh. Mangum's Company was one of the few South Carolina companies to serve in a regiment from another state.

A new company, the Wee Nee Volunteers, became Company E when it mustered in Confederate service at Fort Johnson on September 11, 1861, effective from April 12.[93] J.P. Thomas wrote, incorrectly, that the Wee Nee Volunteers enlisted for the duration of the war on that date, but in reality, the company enlisted for one year only, the period to date from April 12.[94] The Wee Nee Volunteers, also known as the Williamsburg Company, was raised in Kingstree in Williamsburg District. Its name came from the American Indian name for the Black River, which runs through Kingstree.[95] By the time it enlisted in Confederate service, the company had acquired a complicated history. Originally, it had served from January to April 1861 as Company F in Maxcy Gregg's regiment. From May to August 14, 1861, when most of its men had refused to enter Confederate service with that regiment, it had served as Company D, 10th Regiment, SCV. At that time, a nucleus of seventeen or eighteen Company D men, along with a number of new recruits, met at the courthouse in Kingstree and organized a new company for Confederate service in Hagood's regiment. They unanimously re-elected J.G. Pressley as captain.[96] Later in the same month, the original first lieutenant, Samuel Maurice, recruited more men from Company D of the 10th Regiment into a new company raised for state service in Harlee's Legion, South Carolina Militia, with himself as its captain.

Naturally, Maurice and Pressley argued over which group had the right to use the names "Wee Nee Volunteers" and "Wee Nee Riflemen." Maurice provided a statement published by the *Mercury* on October 24, 1861; it said that the official name of the Wee Nee Volunteers during its initial six-month enlistment was actually the Wee Nee Riflemen, a claim supported by the incorporation of the "Wee Nee Riflemen" by the South Carolina General Assembly on January 28, 1861.[97] Maurice added that Pressley had appropriated the name when he raised the new company in the summer of 1861, and that he (Maurice), a first lieutenant at the time, had gone on to recruit many more Company D, 10th Regiment, men than Pressley had attracted and to form yet another company which also claimed the name Wee Nee Riflemen.[98] On November 2, 1861, the *Mercury* printed Pressley's reply. Pressley "clarified" the issue and calmed the waters by claiming the original company in Gregg's regiment was the Wee Nee Volunteers, that Maurice's new company was the Wee Nee Riflemen and that Pressley's new company in Hagood's regiment was the Wee Nee Volunteers.[99] By late 1861, Maurice's Company was attached to Harlee's Legion, South Carolina Militia, also called the Pee Dee Legion. After Harlee's Legion was dissolved in January 1862, there is no record of Maurice's Wee Nee Riflemen; probably, it was also dissolved at that time. Two sources refer to Pressley's company as the Wee Nee Volunteers, Company B, implying that Maurice's company was the Wee Nee Volunteers, Company A.[100]

On August 27, 1861, Pressley's Company was ordered to Summerville to join Hagood's regiment. About September 1, the men took a train to Charleston and a steamboat to Fort Johnson, where they mustered in Confederate service on September 9. The company joined Hagood's regiment, then at Cole's Island, on September 18. John G. Pressley enlisted as captain of the company on September 5 or September 11, 1861.[101] Service records for the 11th (Eutaw) Battalion indicate that he was elected captain on September 5 and mustered in Confederate service the same day. The reorganization in the spring of 1862 brought another change for the Wee Nee Volunteers. Though the men were free to re-enlist in other companies, most of them remained with the Wee Nee Volunteers and about April 6, 1862, they re-elected Pressley captain.[102] Though it was the tenth company from Hagood's regiment to re-enlist in Confederate service, the Wee Nee Volunteers mustered out of the regiment on April 12, left Hagood's regiment at Cole's Island on the morning of the fourteenth, went to Charleston and then went home for two weeks.[103] The company reorganized and returned to service, not with Hagood's regiment, but as part of a new battalion, the 11th South Carolina Battalion.[104] The letter designation of the Wee Nee Volunteers in the 11th Battalion is unknown.

Company F, from Barnwell District, was in state service and stationed in Summerville from April 12 to August 22, 1861, when it mustered in Confederate service for twelve months, retroactive to April 12. The first captain was Winchester Graham.[105] Graham is not listed in the *CSR*, but James Hagood named him as captain.[106] First Lieutenant George Martin Grimes of Bamberg replaced Graham and entered Confederate service on July 20, 1861, as captain of the company, which retained its designation as Company F at that time. When the time for re-enlistment came in the spring of 1862, most of the men opted for Company G, Hagood's 1st SCV Regiment, though possibly a few chose the 2nd Regiment, South Carolina Artillery, instead. Company G became the fifth to re-enlist in Confederate service. Grimes was re-elected captain on April 12.

Company G was also from Barnwell District. Though Edward J. Frederick was the first captain, his name is not recorded in the *CSR*.[107] Frederick's Company mustered in state service with the regiment on April 12, 1861, but it failed to volunteer for Confederate service that summer, and William H. Duncan's Company, the Johnson Guards, replaced it in September. The Johnson Guards were from Barnwell District as well, primarily the area of Upper Three Runs.[108] The company was organized and its officers elected on August 24, 1861.[109] It was named for the Hampton Legion's Lieutenant Colonel Benjamin J. Johnson, who was killed at the battle of First Manassas.[110] Duncan and his company enlisted in Confederate service at Fort Johnson on September 18, 1861, for twelve months' service dating from April 12, and they were designated Company G.[111] Duncan's Company was subdivided at the reorganization in March or April 1862. Frederick Sanders, a first lieutenant who was dropped from Duncan's Company in April, raised a new company, which became the sixth company from Hagood's regiment to re-enlist in Confederate service and Company G of the 2nd Regiment, South Carolina Artillery, at the reorganization. A few men from Duncan's Company re-enlisted in the reorganized Company G, Hagood's regiment, but most went into Company E, Hagood's regiment, as the seventh company to re-enlist in Confederate service.

Company H from Barnwell District was in state service from April to August 22, 1861. It, too, was stationed at Summerville and entered Confederate service for twelve months from April 12. John Vincent Martin, the only captain in state service, entered Confederate service as captain of the company on July 20. An effort had been made in May to exchange Martin's Company with Rice's Company of Heyward's regiment, but this in unconfirmed, and the records indicate no swap took place. Company H ceased to exist when it failed to reorganize in April 1862, and its members re-enlisted in Company C, in other companies of Hagood's regiment, in the 11th Battalion and in the 2nd South Carolina Artillery Regiment. Martin was dropped as captain of Company H on April 12, 1862, and became a captain in the Commissary Department, a position he resigned on January 5, 1863.

Company I from Barnwell District was probably known as the Republican Blues. Its first captain, James White, is not mentioned in the *CSR*.[112] Izlar writes that White's Company was from Colleton District.[113] The company probably mustered in state service with the regiment on April 12, 1861. Its men unanimously refused to enter Confederate service in May and subsequently served for about four months as Company F in Heyward's 11th Regiment, SCV. Johnson Hagood writes that a Captain Steadman, probably John Marcellus Steedman, offered his Lexington District company, the Pickens Sentinels, as the tenth company of Hagood's regiment in May 1861. It appears that Steedman's Company, probably designated Company I, served with Hagood's regiment until late June or early July but was not accepted in Confederate service. On July 10, 1861, it mustered in the 9th Regiment, SCV, as Company K. J.J. Brabham raised a new company in Barnwell District; it enlisted at Cole's Island on September 5 for twelve months from April 12, 1861.[114] Brabham's Company, the Buford's Bridge Guards, was designated Company I.[115] In April 1862, most of the men of this company re-enlisted as Company C, Hagood's 1st SCV, and were the fourth company to re-enlist in Confederate service. Some men enlisted in other companies of Hagood's regiment, and a few went into Company G, 2nd Artillery Regiment.

Company K, the Bamberg Guards, was from Barnwell District.[116] On November 3, 1860, W.B. Rice and Joseph J. Brown, both of Barnwell, raised a company of minutemen called the Bamberg Guards and immediately offered its services to Governor W.H. Gist or to any other state that might secede before South Carolina.[117] Brown was elected captain either on January 7 or January 14, 1861.[118] He is not mentioned in the *CSR*, probably because he commanded the company only in state service. When Brown's Company failed to volunteer for Confederate service in the summer of 1861, many of its men went into Company A of Gregg's reorganized 1st SCV Regiment. Captain W.B. Rice had raised another company, also called the Bamberg Guards, which had served as Company F in Heyward's 11th Regiment until it was exchanged for White's Company in the summer of 1861. Rice's Company replaced Brown's Company as Company K in Hagood's regiment.[119] Rice enlisted in Confederate service with Hagood's regiment as captain on July 20, 1861.[120] While stationed at Summerville, Rice's Company mustered in Confederate service on August 22 for twelve months to date from April 12, 1861; it became Company K. Most of the men of Company K re-enlisted in Company A, Hagood's 1st SCV, at the reorganization in April 1862, and they were the third company to re-enlist in Confederate service. A few men went into the 2nd Regiment, South Carolina Artillery. Rice himself was dropped from the rolls on April 12, 1862.

Following are the companies of Hagood's regiment that were created at the reorganization on April 12, 1862:

Company A, the Bamberg Guards, was commanded by Isaac S. Bamberg, previously a second lieutenant in Company K; he was elected captain on April 12, 1862.[121] The men in this company were from Bamberg, in Barnwell District, and most had served in Company K of Hagood's regiment before the reorganization. A shell at the battle of Second Manassas wounded Bamberg and rendered him unfit for duty for six months. Chronic inflammation of the kidneys forced him to resign on June 16, 1863. Only one other captain, former First Lieutenant L.A. Wright, who replaced Bamberg on June 16, commanded Company A. Wright was slightly wounded at the Wilderness and Spotsylvania, was struck in the left thigh on July 29, 1864, near Petersburg, and while "gallantly leading his company," was seriously wounded in both legs at Fort Harrison on September 30, 1864.[122] Wright was listed as absent without leave on December 25 and failed to return to the company.[123]

Company B, from Orangeburg, was commanded by Daniel Livingston, who had led the company since its inception.[124] Most of the men had served in Company B, the Jamison Guards, of Hagood's regiment before the reorganization, and a few had previously served in Company C. When Livingston was promoted to major on July 12, 1862, First Lieutenant James A. Inabinet was made captain, effective July 10. At Fredericksburg on December 13, Inabinet was severely wounded in the ankle when either a ball or piece of shrapnel caused a compound fracture of the lower fibula.[125] Inabinet's wound was the only serious casualty the 1st Regiment sustained in the battle.[126] The projectile was extracted, but Inabinet developed stiffening in his ankle and failed to return to the company. He was dropped on March 24, 1864, because of a prolonged absence without leave. First Lieutenant J.C. Wannamaker commanded the company in 1864 but never officially as captain.[127] Because he had hidden behind a house and refused to move during the charge on Fort Harrison in September, Wannamaker was arrested in December and charged with misbehavior in the presence of the enemy. He was judged not guilty, but he could not deal with the contempt of the troops and resigned on January 31, 1865.[128] Samuel Boyd Clowney was promoted from adjutant to captain on February 20, 1865, in recognition of his valor and skill. Clowney, who had been wounded near Richmond on June 30, 1862, and again on May 10, 1864, was paroled at Appomattox on April 9, 1865.[129]

Company C, the Buford's Bridge Guards, was made up of men from Buford's Bridge in Barnwell District.[130] Most of these men had served in Company I of Hagood's regiment before the reorganization, though some were previously in Captain Martin's Company H. Benjamin Brown Kirkland, the company's original first lieutenant, was elected captain on April 12, 1862. Kirkland received a flesh wound from a Minié ball in the left thigh at Second Manassas on August 30, 1862.[131] He recovered from the wound and was promoted to major on February 7, 1864. First Lieutenant John Fletcher Brabham was promoted to captain on that date, also shown as March 19, 1864. Brown was wounded at Hanover Junction and paroled at Appomattox Court House on April 9, 1865.[132] He was "a gallant officer."[133]

Company D, the Waxhaw Guards, was new to Hagood's regiment in April 1862.[134] The *Memory Roll* records, incorrectly, that this company was from Spartanburg and Sumter, but the men were actually from Lancaster District.[135] Mixson gets it wrong as well; he says the company was from Marion.[136] Robert L. Crawford, a retired physician living in Lancaster District who had signed the South Carolina Ordinance of Secession in December 1860, enlisted as a private in Blanding's 9th Regiment, SCV, and subsequently served as its assistant surgeon.[137] It was Crawford who raised the Waxhaw Guards, organized on March 31, 1862.[138] The men unanimously elected Crawford as their captain on April 11.[139] According to Salley, Crawford began service at Lancaster on April 28.[140] Crawford was wounded on August 30, 1862, at the battle of Second Manassas.[141] He received a flesh wound in the right calf, and a shell fragment struck a Testament in his left breast pocket; the fragment left a severe contusion but the Testament saved his life.[142] The thirty-seven-year-old Crawford recovered from these wounds but was decapitated by a shell while relieving his pickets on April 20, 1863, near Suffolk, Virginia.[143] James Hagood wrote that during the siege of Suffolk, Crawford was leading a company of sharpshooters in an attack on a Federal gunboat on the Blackwater River when he was struck in the left side of the neck by a shell fragment and killed instantly.[144] Crawford "had served with distinction at the battle of Second Manassas, when he was wounded, and was regarded as one of the best officers in the regiment. His loss was, therefore, a public misfortune as well as a source of universal private bereavement."[145] Lieutenant James H. Kirk of Lancaster succeeded Crawford as captain, effective from April 20. The *Roll of the Dead* spells the name *Kirks*, and a typewritten list of the members of Company D gives the name as Kirke.[146] At Lookout Creek on October 28, 1863, Kirk received a severe contusion to the neck from a Minié ball.[147] On May 10, 1864, near Spotsylvania Court House, he was slightly wounded again, this time in the left side and face. Kirk was killed while leading his company at Fort Harrison on September 30, 1864.[148] He was not replaced as captain of Company D. James Hagood cites Kirk for his "conspicuous gallantry under trying circumstances."[149] After his death, the *Lancaster Ledger* wrote: "Kirk was a gallant officer and an upright and unselfish citizen. His death is a serious loss to the service and to this district."[150] First Lieutenant Francis "Frank" M. Welsh is shown as captain on both the *Memory Roll* and the author's list, but there is no record in the *CSR* that he was ever promoted to captain. Welsh was wounded at Second Manassas and was captured on January 22, 1864, on the French Broad River in Tennessee. He was sent first to Camp Chase, Ohio, and then to Louisville, Kentucky. He was imprisoned at Fort Delaware on March 25 and was held there until his release on June 15, 1865.

Company E, the color company, was commanded by William H. Duncan from September 1861—at the time it was designated Company G—to April 1862.[151] The men were from Upper Three Runs Creek in the part of Barnwell District that is now in Aiken County.[152] Most of these men had been in Company G, and a few had been in Companies H and I. Duncan was re-elected captain on April 12, 1862, and was made major on May 16. First Lieutenant John H. Thomson, also shown as Thompson, of Beaufort and Barnwell, was promoted to captain on that date.[153] While leading the company and holding the colors at Second Manassas on August 30, 1862, Thomson was killed instantly by a Minié ball that passed laterally through his head.[154] Hagood says Thomson "had conducted himself with marked bravery up to the time of his death."[155] Major Duncan wrote: "No man in America possessed a loftier courage, a higher patriotism, or a purer heart" than Thomson.[156] First Lieutenant Patrick H. Wood of Steel Creek was wounded at the battle of Second Manassas and was promoted to captain on August 30, 1862, a date also shown as September 1.[157] Wood was severely wounded at Fort Harrison on September 30, 1864, when a gunshot fractured the left side of his face in two places. Mixson describes the incident: "He was shot directly below the nose, knocking out his teeth and lodging them in his tongue. He was terribly disfigured at that time, but was operated on that night, they cutting out the ball from his neck, taking his teeth out of his tongue, etc. After the war he looked nearly as handsome as ever, and he was a handsome man."[158] Though Wood never returned to the company, he did survive the war.[159] James Hagood indicates that Wood retired to the Invalid Corps, but the *CSR* makes no such assertion.[160]

Company F, the Dixie Guards, was new to Hagood's regiment in April of 1862.[161] Most of the men were from Greenville District, but some were from Summerville and Cole's Island. Thomas D. Gwin was elected captain on April 24, 1862, but he declined to accept a promotion to major the following month.[162] He was wounded at the battle of Second Manassas. James Hagood suggests that Gwin might have failed an examination for captain in the fall of 1864.[163] He was appointed chaplain of the regiment on March 16, 1862, and he resigned the captaincy on January 7, 1863, to assume the post full-time.[164] He resigned the chaplaincy on February 15, 1864. First Lieutenant John Lewis Southern succeeded Gwin as captain on February 7, 1863. Southern was severely wounded in the left shoulder on May 6, 1864, at the Wilderness. He was paroled at Appomattox Court House on April 9, 1865.[165] The *Memory Roll* erroneously lists G.M. Grimes as a captain of Company F. Before the reorganization, Grimes was a captain in Company F, and after it, he was captain of Company G.

Company G was composed mostly of Bamberg men who had served in Company F of Hagood's regiment before the reorganization, along with a few recruits. George Martin Grimes of Barnwell District had been captain of Company F in Hagood's regiment before the reorganization and was re-elected on April 12, 1862.[166] He was wounded at Second Manassas. Micah Jenkins promoted Grimes to acting major on September 1, 1862, but on September 7, 1864, when the promotion was not confirmed, Grimes returned to his former post. He received a flesh wound in the right arm at the Wilderness on May 6, 1864, and was mortally wounded in the left side at Fort Harrison on September 30. He died on October 1, 1864.

George W. Grimes had served as second lieutenant in Company F from August 22, 1861, to April 11, 1862. He was elected first lieutenant on April 12 and was named acting captain on September 1, 1862, when G.M. Grimes was made acting major. On August 30, 1862, at Second Manassas, G.W. Grimes was struck in the head by a Minié ball, which caused a scalp wound and a concussion. He was delirious for six hours, but he recovered.[167] G.W. Grimes resigned on April 16, 1863. According to James Hagood, G.W. Grimes retired to the Invalid Corps because of the wound, but the *CSR* is silent as to whether he resigned or retired to the Invalid Corps.[168] First Lieutenant Lawrence J. Sweat of Barnwell was slightly wounded at Sharpsburg while temporarily in command of the regiment.[169] He was promoted to captain on April 16 and was wounded in a skirmish near Chattanooga on September 25, when a Minié ball caused a compound fracture of the upper third of the right arm. Ten days later, suffering a secondary hemorrhage, Sweat's arm was amputated at the shoulder joint. He died from the ordeal on October 15, 1863, a date also shown as October 17.[170] Sweat was called "a brave and skillful officer," and James Hagood wrote: "As a valuable officer, he proved a serious loss to the regiment, as a brave and honorable gentleman, he was universally regretted."[171]

George Martin Grimes was not confirmed as major of the regiment in February 1864, and he returned to Company G as its fourth captain on September 4. He was mortally wounded at Fort Harrison on September 30 and died on October 1.[172] James Hagood believed Grimes lacked the skills necessary for field-grade command but praised what he termed "conspicuous gallantry under trying circumstances."[173] Hagood also wrote that Grimes demonstrated "a devoted patriotism and plenty of personal courage" and that he was "warmly beloved by his old company."[174] First Lieutenant Richard J. Steedly, who was wounded in the right side at Fort Harrison on September 30, 1864, was promoted to captain on October 1, 1864. He was paroled at Appomattox Court House on April 9, 1865.[175]

Company H, the Winsmuth Guards, was a Spartanburg District company and new to Hagood's regiment in the spring of 1862. Company H mustered in Confederate service on May 3, 1862, at Charleston and was assigned to the regiment nine days later. J. Christopher Winsmuth was elected captain on April 15, 1862. Winsmuth was slightly wounded at Second Manassas and also sustained a contusion from a shell at Sharpsburg on September 17, 1862.[176] He was recommended for promotion to major of the regiment in January or February 1864. At Fort Harrison on September 30, he received a fracture of the clavicle and scapula when he was shot in the right shoulder.[177] According to James Hagood, Winsmuth was disabled by the wound.[178] He was still on leave as late as February 1865 and probably did not return to the company. His name does not appear on the list of those paroled at Appomattox Court House. He was "a meritorious office."[179]

James Nott Moore, a prominent Spartanburg surgeon, served as assistant surgeon of Hagood's regiment until the spring of 1862, when he was elected second lieutenant of Company H. He was promoted to first lieutenant on August 30, 1862. Moore received a contusion to the right thigh from a shell fragment at Campbell's Station, Tennessee, on November 16, 1863. He developed erysipelas but managed to survive and recover.[180] *The Confederate Military History* records that Moore was the last captain of Company H, but the *CSR* does not confirm a promotion to captain.[181] He was paroled at Appomattox Court House with the rank of first lieutenant.[182]

Company I from Marion, new to Hagood's regiment at the reorganization, mustered in Confederate service for three years on May 2, 1862, at Lightwood Knot Springs, north of Columbia. James H. Stafford was elected captain on April 24, 1862, with rank from April 29, 1862.[183] Stafford was wounded at the battle of Second Manassas and again at Spotsylvania on May 10, 1864. He was arrested on October 30, 1864, for misconduct before the enemy. James Hagood said that two years earlier, on September 17, 1862, he had "ingloriously abandoned his post" at the battle of Sharpsburg. In command of the regiment after Captain Knotts left the field and believing the battle was over, Stafford took his company and left to search for rations.[184] The specific action that prompted his arrest, however, occurred during the assault on Battery Harrison on September 30, 1864, when he hid behind a house and refused to move.[185] He was found not guilty, but he could not deal with the troops' contempt and resigned his post. James R. Hagood wrote, incorrectly, that Stafford was disqualified by an examining board and was dismissed in December 1864.[186] Stafford tendered his resignation without explanation, and it was accepted on March 18, 1865. The *Memory Roll* records that poor health forced him to resign in March 1865.[187] Hagood believed that Stafford was "unfit for any grade whatsoever—and it was necessary to get rid of him."[188] H. Bentivoglis Middleton was promoted from private to second lieutenant for valor and skill on December 24, 1864, and he replaced Stafford as captain, probably in March 1865. Captain Middleton was paroled at Appomattox Court House on April 9, 1865. He was a "gallant young man."[189]

Company K from Orangeburg District was also new to Hagood's regiment at the reorganization. Company B, the Jamison Guards, was subdivided at that time, its members reforming into both Company B under Captain Livingston and Company K under Captain Knotts. Most of the men of Company K had served in Company B before the reorganization, but some came from other companies. Joseph Evandiver Knotts was elected captain on April 12, 1862.[190] He was wounded at the battle of Second Manassas. Temporarily in command of the regiment at the battle of Sharpsburg, Knotts left the field during the action to help his wounded brother to a field hospital.[191] Hagood wrote that he "ingloriously abandoned his post" that day and was dismissed from the service.[192] Knotts resigned on November 19, 1862, stating that circumstances had dictated the propriety of the course he followed. Micah Jenkins wrote that Knotts was totally useless as an officer; he recommended accepting the resignation and allowing Knotts to join the ranks. James Robert Hagood, younger brother of Johnson Hagood, left The Citadel on June 9, 1862, with thirty-six other cadets who formed a company that eventually became Company F, 6th Regiment, South Carolina Cavalry.[193] Hagood enlisted as a private in his brother's regiment, the 1st Regiment, SCV, and served as sergeant major of the regiment from July 1, 1862. He was promoted to adjutant on November 5, 1862, though he recorded the date in his memoirs as November 16.[194] He was promoted to captain for gallant conduct on the field on January 2, 1863, and to colonel, by General Micah Jenkins, on November 16, 1863. This last promotion advanced him over both Lieutenant Colonel Livingston and Major Grimes and over four captains—Kirkland, Winsmuth, Stafford and Wood—all of whom wanted personal promotion except Stafford. First Lieutenant William B. Mack was promoted to captain as of November 16, 1863. Mack was slightly wounded by a Minié ball in the left leg at Fort Harrison on September 30, 1864, and was paroled at Appomattox Court House on April 9, 1865.[195]

BRIGADE AFFILIATIONS

Hagood's regiment was part of a brigade commanded successively by Simons, Bonham, Nelson, Anderson and Ripley while in South Carolina in 1861 and early 1862. From April 1861 to early August 1862, the regiment's assignments covered Charleston Harbor, the Department of South Carolina, the Department of South Carolina and Georgia and the Department of South Carolina, Georgia and Florida.[196] In June 1862, the regiment was placed in a temporary brigade called the "Advanced Forces" under Johnson Hagood; it comprised Hagood's regiment, the 24th SCV Regiment, the 11th (Eutaw) Battalion (soon to be designated the 25th Regiment) and McEnnery's Louisiana Battalion. In mid-August 1862, Hagood's regiment became part of Micah Jenkins's (later John Bratton's) Brigade in Longstreet's corps of the Army of Northern Virginia. The 2nd South Carolina Rifles joined Jenkins's Brigade, and the St. Paul (Louisiana) Battalion was detached after the battle of Seven Pines. Other regiments in Jenkins's Brigade were the 5th and 6th SCV, the Palmetto Sharpshooters, and from December 1862 to March 1864, the Infantry Regiment of the Hampton Legion. John Bratton took command of the brigade after Micah Jenkins was killed at the battle of the Wilderness on May 6, 1864.

MAJOR MOVEMENTS AND ENGAGEMENTS

Colonel Johnson Hagood received the order to move his regiment to Charleston on the afternoon of April 8, 1861.[197] The 1st Battalion of Hagood's regiment—Companies A, B, C and D—under the command of Lieutenant Colonel Glover left Orangeburg by rail on April 11. Arriving at Charleston about ten o'clock the same evening, the men marched to the Race Course, now Hampton Park.[198] The 2nd Battalion of the regiment, under the command of Major O'Cain, left Barnwell and arrived at the Race Course just before dawn the next day, and the entire regiment mustered in state service at the Race Track before eight o'clock on the morning of April 12.[199] In full view of the bombardment of Fort Sumter later that day, the regiment marched to the Battery, crossed the harbor to Dill's Landing on James Island and proceeded across James Island to Legare's Landing at Light House Inlet. On the evening of April 13 between ten and eleven o'clock, following the surrender of Fort Sumter about one o'clock in the afternoon, Hagood's regiment crossed over to Morris Island. It moved to Vinegar Hill Battery about April 29, and after four days, it moved farther south to Gadberry Hill.[200] The regiment remained on Morris Island until May 22, when the men left for Charleston.[201] Early in the morning of the twenty-third, the troops boarded a train in Charleston and passed through Summerville on their way to Orangeburg, arriving there later the same day and bivouacking in an old field about one mile east of the Orangeburg Female College.[202]

The regiment did not volunteer for Confederate service in the spring of 1861 and was relieved from duty and temporarily disbanded on June 15. Colonel Hagood obtained a three-month furlough and went to Virginia to serve as a private in Company I, 2nd Regiment, SCV. He fought at both Bull Run and the battle of First Manassas in July and returned to South Carolina in early August. A few other members of the regiment also fought at First Manassas.[203] Reorganization, with only nine companies, got underway at Summerville on July 20, and on August 22, the regiment mustered in Confederate service, ten companies strong, for one year dating from April 12. On August 28, the regiment moved through Charleston on its way to Cole's Island at the mouth of the Stono River.[204] While most of the companies drilled and performed fatigue duty at Cole's Island, Company A, under Captain Glover, manned two heavy artillery batteries nearby on Goat Island. On January 11, 1862, Company E moved about two miles upriver to Battery Island to staff the heavy artillery batteries at Fort Pickens. As planned, Hagood's regiment disbanded (and reorganized) on April 12. It was relieved the next day by the 24th Regiment, SCV, and marched to James Island. On furlough, the men of Hagood's regiment passed through Charleston on April 14 and deposited their arms at The Citadel Armory.[205] Those who re-enlisted in Hagood's regiment moved to Binnaker's Campground just below Bamberg, near the point where the South Carolina Railroad crossed over the Edisto River. Men who re-enlisted in other units joined those commands, and those who did not re-enlist were disbanded and became subject to the draft. Hagood's men were granted a thirty-day furlough, and their commander was appointed provost marshal for Charleston, which was then under martial law. Ten to twelve days into the furlough, however, Hagood's six remaining companies were called back into service by special order. After rendezvousing at Bamberg, the men were sent to Charleston for provost guard duty. Arriving on May 5, they camped first at the Charleston Race Track and then at Citadel Green.

They patrolled the streets and guarded the docks and wharves. Four new companies—D, F, H and I—were added to the regiment at this time, raising it to its full complement of ten.

Federal troops landed on James Island on June 2, 1862. Hagood's regiment was transferred to James Island the next day and Colonel Hagood followed on June 9. About that time, the regiment was attached to a new temporary brigade called the "Advanced Forces," along with the 24th Regiment, SCV, the Eutaw (11th) Battalion (soon to be designated the 25th Regiment) and McEnnery's Louisiana Battalion. The regiment was assigned to picket duty along most of the southern portion of the James Island lines, the exception being those immediately in front of Secessionville. Two companies under the command of Captain Kirkland skirmished at the Presbyterian church on June 6, and the 1st Regiment, the 47th Georgia Regiment and the Louisiana Battalion, along with two guns of Preston's Battery, were engaged in a skirmish at Grimball's plantation on James Island on the tenth.[206] During the battle of Secessionville on June 16, the regiment was primarily held in reserve, performing picket and skirmish duty on the right of the Confederate line near Secessionville. Colonel Hagood was relieved of command of his regiment and transferred to the 2nd South Carolina Military District on July 19. Promoted to brigadier general effective July 21, 1862, he was not associated with the 1st Regiment for the remainder of the war.

The 1st Regiment left James Island for Charleston on August 10, 1862, and left Charleston by rail for Virginia three days later. The regiment arrived in Richmond on August 14 and bivouacked at the Capitol Square. Soon afterwards it was attached to Micah Jenkins's Brigade, and "this intelligence when communicated to the men produced much satisfaction."[207] Jenkins's Brigade consisted of the 1st, 5th, 6th and 2nd Rifle Regiments, 13th (4th) Battalion and Palmetto Sharpshooters. The major movements and engagements of the brigade are discussed below. The 1st Regiment skirmished at Waterloo Bridge on August 18, and on the twenty-eighth, it marched with Jenkins's Brigade and Longstreet's corps through Thoroughfare Gap to the battlefield at Manassas.[208] The brigade was not engaged at Manassas that day. The first major engagement for the 1st Regiment came during the battle of Second Manassas when it was involved in a ten-minute skirmish at Groveton on August 29.[209] The other regiments of Jenkins's Brigade participated in light skirmishing and maneuvering but were not engaged at Groveton.[210] The brigade was also heavily engaged between the Henry House and the Chinn House and suffered heavy losses on the afternoon of August 30, when both Companies E and F of the 1st Regiment were nearly decimated.[211] The 1st Regiment's losses—25 men killed and 145 wounded—amounted to 54 percent of the men who went into battle that day. Colonel Moore, acting Major White and all but one captain of the 2nd Rifles were killed or wounded on the thirtieth. The brigade marched toward Centreville on August 31 and toward Germantown on September 1.[212] The 150-man 1st Regiment passed through Leesburg, Virginia, on September 3, crossed the Potomac River into Maryland the next day and rested at Frederick City for about four days.[213] On the move again, the brigade marched toward Hagerstown on September 13 but soon shifted direction for South Mountain, or Boonsboro Gap, where it was engaged on the fourteenth The P.S.S., 2nd Rifles and the 13th (4th) Battalion were lightly engaged late in the afternoon at Boonsboro Gap. The rest of the brigade—the 1st, 5th and 6th Regiments—was more heavily engaged, fighting from about five in the afternoon until after dark. The brigade withdrew toward Sharpsburg the next morning. Jenkins's Brigade endured two days of artillery fire on the field near Sharpsburg on September 15 and September 16 and was engaged there on the seventeenth. The 1st Regiment took only about eighty men into battle on September 17.[214] Jenkins's men remained; they took care of the wounded and dead until the next evening, and they withdrew from the battlefield that night.[215] The brigade crossed the Potomac three miles below Shepherdstown about dawn on September 19. It marched through Martinsburg on the twentieth and on to Big Spring near Winchester, Virginia, on September 27. After resting at Winchester for three to four weeks, the brigade moved on to Culpeper Court House, arriving on November 1 and leaving on the twelfth to march toward Fredericksburg.[216] The 1st Regiment boosted its strength through recruitment to about two hundred men during this time.

Meanwhile, during the autumn of 1862, "The incompetent officers of the First Regiment were overhauled and their names reported for examination. [The actual] examination did not take place until afterwards" because it was necessary for practical reasons to wait for the right moment to implement an earlier law affecting the issue at hand.[217] Captain Gwin of Company F, Lieutenant Kearse of Company G and Lieutenant Langford of Company H were eventually examined.

On November 11, the 13th (4th) Battalion merged with the Infantry Battalion, Hampton Legion, forming the Infantry Regiment, Hampton Legion, and remained in Jenkins's Brigade. The brigade arrived at Fredericksburg on November 24 and went into camp on the right of the Telegraph Road about two miles from town. The brigade was primarily held in reserve during the battle of Fredericksburg, first on the heights about 1.5 miles south of town and, after four in the afternoon, in the trenches on the Telegraph Road. Nevertheless, the men suffered heavy shelling from December 12 to December 14.[218] The P.S.S. was under heavy shelling while on advanced picket duty from the afternoon of December 13 until the afternoon of December 14, and the men acted as sharpshooters and skirmishers on December 14.[219] The 5th Regiment moved to the stone wall along the sunken road on Marye's Heights early in the morning of December 14 and remained there throughout the day. On December 16, Companies C and F of the 5th Regiment were sent into Fredericksburg to see if the Federal troops had evacuated the town. The two companies captured 155 Federal prisoners. The brigade performed picket duty along the Rappahannock River from mid-December to mid-January. At that time, the men camped near Hamilton's Cross Roads, about three miles below Fredericksburg, until February 14, 1863. Jenkins's Brigade marched with Longstreet's corps to Richmond. It arrived on February 18, and the next day, it marched through the city, crossed to the south side of the James River, and moved to Chester Station on the Richmond and Petersburg Railroad.[220] On March 1, the brigade was sent to Petersburg, and on the fifth it was transferred from Pickett's Division to S.G. French's Division in the Department of Southern Virginia. On March 9, Jenkins's Brigade was sent to the Blackwater area around Suffolk, Virginia.[221] On March 13, it went into camp in the vicinity of Franklin, where the Weldon and Suffolk Railroad crossed over the Blackwater River. The primary purpose of this move was to allow Jenkins's men to occupy the Federal forces at Suffolk while food and other supplies were gathered in southeastern Virginia and northeastern North Carolina.[222] The 1st Regiment, the 2nd Rifles and the 6th Regiment were held in reserve while the Palmetto Sharpshooters were based at Franklin Station; the Hampton Legion was sent several miles below Franklin to South Quay; and the 5th Regiment was based above Franklin. The P.S.S. skirmished with and repelled Federal cavalry at Franklin Station on March 17 and possibly on March 20.[223]

In late March or early April, five companies of the 1st Regiment, including Companies C and K, skirmished near Old Church about five miles below Franklin. Jenkins's Brigade left Franklin for Suffolk on April 10. It was joined there by Hood's, Pickett's and French's Divisions, and it participated in the siege of Suffolk from April 11 to April 30. The 5th, 6th and 2nd Rifle Regiments and Palmetto Sharpshooters skirmished there on April 11.[224] The 1st Regiment was on duty every third day of the siege and skirmished nearly every time. Twenty men of the 6th Regiment participated in an attack on two Federal gunboats on the Nansemond River on April 18. Hood's and Pickett's Divisions returned to northern Virginia on May 3, but Jenkins's Brigade returned to the Franklin area about that time and served under D.H. Hill; consequently, it was not present during the battle of Chancellorsville.

From May 3 to June 14, the brigade was stationed in the Blackwater area. The 1st Regiment was posted at Joiner's Bridge where it remained until June 14. The 5th and 6th Regiments marched to South Quay on the Blackwater River, arriving there on May 6. On May 15, the 5th Regiment, the 2nd Rifles and a portion of the 6th Regiment were sent to Carrsville, where they were exposed to shellfire. On May 16 and 17, they, along with the P.S.S., skirmished at Carrsville. On May 18 and 19, the P.S.S. performed picket duty at Beaverdam Church, on May 20 it marched to Blackwater Creek Church and on May 23 it returned to Franklin Station. From May 16 to May 21, the 5th Regiment occupied the trenches at Franklin. On May 22, the 2nd Rifles skirmished at the Blackwater Bridge, and the 5th Regiment was under shellfire at Windsor the next day. The Hampton Legion and the 6th Regiment were sent to Murfreesboro, North Carolina, in late May 1863 but were not engaged there.[225] In late May and early June, the P.S.S. guarded the workers on the Weldon Railroad. On June 5, the 5th Regiment was sent to the Nottoway River, on June 7 it was sent to Murfreesboro, North Carolina, and on June 22 it was sent back to Petersburg. On June 10, the P.S.S. marched to Smith's Ferry on the Nottoway River and returned to camp at Franklin on June 13.

Though most of the brigade was sent by rail to Petersburg on June 14, the 1st Regiment marched as guard to the artillery and wagon trains. For the next three months, the brigade marched and countermarched between Petersburg and Richmond, and some of the regiments returned to the Blackwater area. On June 14, the P.S.S. left camp at Franklin and marched to Murphy's Depot or Murphy's Station; it returned to Franklin the next day. The P.S.S. was divided about that time. Four companies were sent toward Weldon, North Carolina, on June 15 to prevent the enemy from crossing the Blackwater River, and they returned on June 18. The rest of the regiment was sent by rail to Garysburg, North Carolina, on June 16 and returned to Murphy's Station on June 18. On June 21, the P.S.S. was sent to Weldon, North Carolina. The 2nd Rifles was sent to City Point on June 15 and returned to Petersburg two days later. On June 18, the 2nd Rifles went to Franklin Station but was sent back to Petersburg on June 21. On June 15, the 6th Regiment marched toward Weldon, North Carolina, and returned to the Blackwater River on June 19. On June 21 or June 22, most of the brigade marched to Petersburg, and on June 28, it was ordered to Richmond. On June 30, the P.S.S. was engaged in repelling the vanguard of the commands of Major General John A. Dix and Major General John J. Peck. The brigade was engaged at Bottom's Bridge over the Chickahominy River below Richmond on July 2.[226] As a result of these orders and events, Jenkins's Brigade remained in or near Richmond during the entire Gettysburg campaign.

On September 11, Jenkins's Brigade was reassigned to John Bell Hood's Division and finally left Richmond by rail on September 14 to rejoin Longstreet's corps, which was already on its way to Tennessee. Passing through Atlanta at three o'clock in the morning on September 20 and arriving at Catoosa Station about eight o'clock that night, the brigade found itself within hearing distance of the cannons at Chickamauga.[227] It marched in double-quick time to nearby Ringgold, Georgia, the same day and bivouacked three miles farther north. Jenkins's Brigade was one of three in Longstreet's corps that was not engaged at the battle of Chickamauga.[228] After the battle, the brigade marched with the rest of the corps toward Chattanooga, and on September 23, it took up its new position on the extreme left of the Confederate lines at the base of Lookout Mountain. Companies L and M of the P.S.S. skirmished in a failed effort to capture a bridge over Chickamauga Creek near Lookout Mountain on September 23 and September 24.[229] The 1st and 5th Regiments skirmished on the night of September 25 in a second unsuccessful attempt to capture the same bridge, and the P.S.S. was shelled as the men marched to Lookout Mountain on September 26. The brigade skirmished along Chickamauga Creek when it captured Lookout Mountain about October 17.[230] The brigade performed picket duty at the base of Lookout Mountain until October 21. In an unsuccessful attempt to dislodge Federal troops from the Charleston to Memphis Railroad, Jenkins's Brigade, now under the command of Colonel Bratton, was heavily engaged during action at Lookout Valley (also called Wauhatchie Station) Lookout Creek and Will's Valley, on the night of October 28.[231] The 1st Regiment suffered heavy losses during that action; more than half its men were killed, wounded, or reported missing.[232] During that engagement, several companies were detached, including Company G of the 2nd Rifles, Companies E and F of the P.S.S., Companies D and H of the 5th Regiment and Companies B, C and G of the Hampton Legion.[233] The brigade left Chattanooga with Longstreet's corps on November 5 and November 6, thereby missing the battle of Missionary Ridge, which took place on November 25.[234] The brigade marched about thirty miles to Tyner's Station near Cleveland and boarded the train there for Sweetwater, where the men spent the next week before crossing the Tennessee River.[235]

On the evening of November 13, Companies B and D of the P.S.S. crossed the Tennessee River near Loudon and created a bridgehead on the opposite shore. The brigade skirmished while protecting its bridgehead near Loudon on November 13 and November 14, and the rest of the brigade crossed the river on the fourteenth.[236] The brigade pursued the enemy toward Knoxville on the morning of November 15. The Hampton Legion, 2nd Rifles, 5th and 6th Regiments and the P.S.S. were engaged at Lenoir Station on the Knoxville

Railroad on the fifteenth, and they were joined by the 1st Regiment in an engagement with the Federal rear guard at Campbell's Station the next day.[237] The brigade arrived at Knoxville on the seventeenth and was placed on the extreme left of the Confederate lines that invested the city. The siege of Knoxville took place from November 20 to November 29. On November 25, the P.S.S. attacked the Federal picket line at Knoxville. Jenkins's Brigade saw duty as skirmishers during the unsuccessful assault on Fort Loudon (also called Fort Sanders), near Knoxville, on November 29. Longstreet's corps withdrew from Knoxville on December 4 and camped at Rogersville about thirteen miles above Bean's Station until the fourteenth. The Knoxville campaign lasted from November 5 until Longstreet's corps withdrew northward toward Rogersville on December 4.[238] By that time, many of the troops were barefooted, poorly clad and scantily fed; in addition, winter was upon them and the weather was already extremely cold. The campaign was the most difficult the men had yet experienced.

The brigade marched back toward Bean's Station on December 14 but was not engaged until the next day, when it skirmished nearby.[239] On December 21, the men left Bean's Station. The brigade crossed the Holston River on December 23 and went into winter quarters on its east bank near Morristown, Tennessee, on December 24. On January 15, 1864, the brigade left Morristown and moved toward Dandridge. The Palmetto Sharpshooters, along with the 1st, 6th and 2nd Rifle Regiments and the Hampton Legion, skirmished at Dandridge, also called Strawberry Plains, on January 17.[240] The 5th Regiment was present but not engaged that day. The brigade returned to Morristown on January 19. On January 23, the brigade moved to New Market, Tennessee, and on February 13 or February 14, the men were sent back to Strawberry Plains. On February 22, the brigade left Strawberry Plains, and by the twenty-sixth, it was in camp at Bull's Gap in east Tennessee. The 1st Regiment participated in another small skirmish on March 1.[241] The Infantry Regiment, Hampton Legion, was permanently detached from the brigade in March. By mid-March, the 1st Regiment had increased its total to about four hundred men, and morale had improved greatly under the new, and very young, colonel—James R. Hagood. On March 28, the regiment left Bull's Gap. It arrived at Zollicoffer in east Tennessee on April 1, and it remained there until the seventeenth.

Two days later, the men arrived by rail at Charlottesville, Virginia, and moved on toward Gordonsville on the twenty-seventh.[242] On May 1, the brigade left Cobham Station on the Orange and Alexandria Railroad for Gordonsville, where it reunited with the Army of Northern Virginia. Jenkins's Brigade left the vicinity on May 4 and camped within twelve miles of the Wilderness on the evening of the fifth. Leaving camp about midnight, the brigade reached the Wilderness in the early morning of May 6, during the second day of action, and formed into a line of battle while under fire. The 1st and 5th Regiments were heavily engaged that day, while the 2nd Rifles, the 6th Regiment and the Palmetto Sharpshooters were primarily held in reserve. Following a day of heavy rifle fire, the brigade pulled out late in the evening of May 7 for a rapid march toward Spotsylvania Court House, arriving the next day about ten o'clock in the morning. A light engagement on Brock Road on the eighth and three straight days of skirmishes led to a heavy engagement at Spotsylvania Court House on May 12.[243] The brigade, now led by John Bratton, remained in the vicinity until May 21 when, acting as the rear guard of the army, it moved on to the North Anna River near Hanover Junction, crossing about sunset on May 22.[244] The 1st Regiment was engaged at Hanover Junction from May 23 to May 25.[245] The brigade left Hanover Junction on May 27 and was in the trenches near Cold Harbor from May 30 to June 13.[246] It was engaged at Cold Harbor lightly from June 1 to June 2 and heavily on the third. Longstreet's corps withdrew from the Cold Harbor lines on June 13, crossed over the Chickahominy River the same day and reached the south side of the James River at Drewry's Bluff on the sixteenth. The brigade was engaged on the Bermuda Neck at Clay's farm from June 16 to June 17. Bratton's Brigade marched to Petersburg on the night of June 17 and was placed in the trenches on the right of Jerusalem Plank Road and along Baxter Road, very near where the battle of the Crater would be fought the next month. From June 2 to June 28, the troops were given a respite, but then they returned to their trench positions on Baxter Road, where they remained almost continuously until July 28. The brigade left the trenches that day, crossed to the north side of the James River at Drewry's Bluff, and arrived at Deep Bottom on the twenty-ninth. The men were in the lines near Deep Bottom from July 30 to August 14. The entire Company F of the 1st Regiment was captured at New Market Hill, near Deep Bottom, during the brigade's engagement there on August 14, but the regiment continued to skirmish for two more days.[247]

Bratton's Brigade was divided on August 16. The 2nd Rifles and the 5th Regiment were engaged at Fussell's Mill (White's Tavern) on August 16, but the Palmetto Sharpshooters, along with the 1st and the 6th Regiments, was engaged along the defensive lines at New Market Hill that day.[248] The brigade left Deep Bottom for Petersburg on August 24; from the twenty-fifth to the thirty-first, its men supported the line at Halifax Road and constructed works along Indian Town Creek between Weldon Railroad and Boydton Plank Road on the extreme right of the Confederate lines, where trenches had not yet been dug. Bratton's Brigade was stationed at Cox's Cross Roads on the Squirrel Level Road from September 8 to September

28; it carried out some construction work and did a little marching, but it engaged in little fighting. On September 29, the brigade was again sent to the north side of the James River to help in the recapture of the recently lost Battery Harrison. The next day was devastating for the brigade. The 1st, 5th and 6th Regiments and the 2nd Rifles were engaged, but the Palmetto Sharpshooters had been sent to cover the left flank and did not participate directly in the poorly coordinated assault on Battery Harrison. The 1st Regiment suffered heavy losses. Five captains and 140 of its 238 men were either killed or wounded.[249] J.P. Thomas wrote that the engagement at Fort Harrison "seems to have been the only place during the whole war where the (6th) regiment was unable to perform what was expected of it. The difficulties to be overcome here were too much for human valor."[250] For the next four days, the brigade remained near Fort Harrison constructing earthworks while under fire. On October 6, it withdrew from the works and moved toward the left of the lines, about three or four miles north to Darbytown Road. Engagements along Darbytown and New Market Roads followed the next day.[251] The 2nd Rifles and the 5th Regiment were engaged again on Darbytown Road on October 13. On October 18, the brigade was sent to the Charles City Road and saw action on October 27 on the Williamsburg Road.

From early November 1864 to February 1865, the men erected breastworks, built winter quarters and performed picket duty between the Charles City and Williamsburg Roads. The regiment skirmished while on reconnaissance on Darbytown Road near Deep Bottom on December 10. The brigade was sent to Gordonsville via Richmond on the twenty-second to meet a Federal cavalry advance, but, except for light skirmishing on the twenty-third, the engagement never took place, and the men returned to their camp below Richmond on Christmas Day. In December 1864, Colonel Hagood sought permission to convert the 1st Regiment to a cavalry unit to make use of those men who could ride and fight as cavalry but who were too debilitated to continue as infantry. His application was denied. In January and February 1865, the brigade was stationed on the New Market Road near Richmond. On February 24, the brigade was sent down the line to Fort Gilmer. The 6th Regiment built Fort Stedman but was not engaged there on March 25. The brigade left Fort Gilmer, marched to Richmond and moved, by rail, on to Petersburg, arriving on April 1 about eight in the morning. As the men evacuated Petersburg the next day, they skirmished near Cox Road between the South Side and Weldon Railroads. The 5th Regiment acted as rear guard when the brigade evacuated Petersburg. The brigade also skirmished northwest of Petersburg on April 3 and at Amelia Court House on the fourth. It left Amelia Court House on April 5, ran into a skirmish at Jetersville the same day and clashed again at Rice's Station on the South Side Railroad on the sixth. The brigade arrived at Farmville on April 7, where it saw action for the last time.[252] Bratton's Brigade marched toward Appomattox Court House through the night of April 7 and all the next day and night, arriving near dawn on April 9 at a spot about two miles away. There, the men constructed fieldworks and prepared for an engagement even as General Lee was negotiating the terms of surrender at Appomattox Court House. Bratton's Brigade was the largest infantry brigade in the Army of Northern Virginia to surrender at that place.[253] The men rested on April 10 and April 11, and they laid down their arms, accoutrements and colors on the twelfth. Between April 13 and April 15, the regiments of the brigade started the long march home together, but the men soon broke up into smaller groups for the six-hundred-mile journey that lay before them.[254]

2.

The 1st Regiment, South Carolina Volunteers (six months), and the 1st Regiment, South Carolina Infantry, Provisional Army

Maxcy Gregg commanded two military units bearing the name 1st Regiment, South Carolina Infantry, a situation that came about this way: The South Carolina Secession Convention passed a resolution on January 1, 1861, authorizing Governor Pickens to enlist volunteer companies attached to the militia of the state for organization into battalions, regiments, brigades and divisions. These companies would enlist for six months' service to the state of South Carolina. Field officers appointed by the governor were officially confirmed by the Senate, and men elected their own company-grade officers. The *Confederate Veteran* incorrectly records that the 1st Regiment was raised by an act of the legislature dated December 20, 1860, but it was actually organized on January 7, 1861, under specific and well defined terms: service would be for six months effective from January 3, and duty would be in-state.[1] The governor accepted Gregg's regiment, the 1st SCV (six months) Regiment, into service on January 8. The regiment was composed of volunteers who understood that in general it was to defend Charleston Harbor from an anticipated invasion and in particular it was to prevent Federal troops from recapturing Fort Moultrie, which Major Anderson had evacuated on December 26, 1860.[2] Some of the companies were prewar, semi-military organizations known as minutemen, while others were raised specifically for service in the regiment. Twenty-seven physicians, thirty lawyers and many of the most eminent businessmen of the state signed on.[3] The regiment that assembled in Charleston comprised eleven companies, designated A through L. Gregg's regiment followed the military custom of not using the letter J.

After the bombardment of Fort Sumter in April 1861, the focus of the war shifted to Virginia. Because Gregg's regiment was raised for service within the state of South Carolina, it could not be sent elsewhere without the consent of the men. Soon after the fall of Fort Sumter, President Davis and Governor Pickens requested members of the first ten South Carolina regiments and Gregg's regiment to volunteer for Confederate service in Virginia. When Colonel Gregg asked for volunteers on April 19, about five hundred of the men volunteered for Confederate service.[4] These men were sent to Virginia for the remainder of their six-month term and mustered in Confederate service there on April 23. Three companies and many individuals from other companies, however, refused to go along with the plan. The men of Companies D, F and G maintained that they had enlisted strictly to defend their state and were not required under any law to serve outside its borders.[5] F.F. Warley, captain of Company B, was in command of the three companies until they were disbanded; he wrote an account of the episode on May 15. According to Warley, when Colonel Gregg showed up to drill the men on April 19—only the second time he had done so—he told the commissioned officers about the request from Virginia's Governor Letcher for South Carolina volunteers and added that he was authorized to pass the request directly on to the men. Understandably concerned, the officers asked Gregg for time to speak with their troops since such a move had never occurred to them. Warley said Gregg ignored this and, instead, presented the case to the men and asked for volunteers on the spot. Only about one hundred volunteered. The rest were confused because they had been told for a week that a Federal invasion was imminent and they were needed for defense of their positions. When a repeat request faired no better, Gregg pronounced the regiment's response a "disgrace." According to Warley, Gregg supplied the men with liquor on April 20 and April 21; on the twenty-second, about three hundred and fifty volunteers from his regiment left Charleston bound for Virginia.[6]

The Secession Convention had passed a resolution in early April allowing the governor to disband the companies of Gregg's regiment before their six-month term of enlistment was up. These companies would however, remain subject to the governor's authority until the term of enlistment expired.[7] Under this resolution, Companies D, F and G were disbanded on April 26, 1861, by order of the adjutant and inspector general.[8] During a parade and ceremony held in Charleston on the twenty-ninth, Governor Pickens thanked the companies for their service and released them from duty.[9] Three new companies—M, N and O—were added to the regiment in April to compensate for those that had disbanded early. At that point, the regiment comprised Companies A, B, C, E, H, I, K, L, M, N and O. The entire regiment mustered out of Confederate service on July 9, 1861, in Richmond.

When the initial six-month enlistment expired on July 9, President Davis and the Secession Convention quickly authorized Gregg to reorganize his regiment, using the same arms, equipment and regimental name and banner.[10] The understanding this time was that the companies would tender their services directly to the Confederate States, and that Davis would appoint field officers.[11] Many men of Gregg's original regiment re-enlisted in the new one, many others chose instead the 15th Regiment, SCV, and most of the men who had gone to Virginia insisted on returning home before re-enlisting at all.[12] On July 26, the *Edgefield Advertiser* reported that Gregg's new regiment comprised six companies from the old unit and four new ones.[13] By late August, seven companies consisted of men who were either totally or mostly carryovers from Gregg's former regiment, and five were entirely new. On September 1, Governor Pickens sent a special request to Secretary of War L.P. Walker, asking that Colonel Gregg be allowed to maintain twelve companies in his regiment instead of the usual ten.[14] Walker rejected the request on September 10. As a result, Companies D and M were eventually transferred out of the regiment.[15] The reorganization of Gregg's regiment, under the same field officers as before but with differently configured companies, took place partly in Richmond and partly at Lightwood Knot Springs north of Columbia between June and September 1861.

The new regiment was designated the 1st South Carolina Infantry Regiment, Provisional Army and, later, the 1st (McCreary's) Infantry (1st Provisional Army). The companies of the new regiment mustered in Confederate service between August 17 and September 7. The Provisional Army of the Confederate States, created by acts of the Confederate States Congress on February 28 and March 6, 1861, was to comprise six infantry regiments, one artillery corps and one cavalry unit. On July 1, 1861, President Davis called for two South Carolina regiments to enlist for the duration of the war.[16] At the reorganization of Gregg's regiment in the summer of 1861, the men responded to the president's call and enlisted "for the war." James L. Orr's 1st Regiment of Rifles was the other South Carolina regiment to do so at that time. Even though Gregg's men had enlisted for the duration of the war in the summer of 1861, they passed a resolution on February 6, 1864, to the effect that "we will never lay down our arms 'till independence is recognized."[17]

FIELD OFFICERS

Governor Pickens appointed Maxcy Gregg, a Columbia lawyer and member of the South Carolina Secession Convention, colonel of the regiment by a commission dated January 1, 1861. Gregg, in fact, was the only field and staff officer in the six month regiment listed by the *CSR*. On July 25, he was reappointed colonel of the reorganized regiment and was promoted to brigadier general on December 14, 1861. Gregg was bruised on the right hip at Sharpsburg on September 17, 1862, and sustained a mortal wound to the spine at Fredericksburg on December 13, 1862.[18] He died two days later and was brought home for burial in Elmwood Cemetery in Columbia.[19] Caldwell wrote that Gregg was "the bravest of the brave," adding that he was "unsurpassed in drill, and as a disciplinarian I have not known his equal."[20] A.C. Haskell, one of Gregg's staff officers and later colonel of the 7th Regiment, South Carolina Cavalry, wrote in 1861: "Colonel Gregg is a gentleman and a soldier, as kind as can be and as stern as Brutus."[21] F.F. Warley wrote in May 1861 that Gregg was "a man without feeling or sympathy."[22]

Adley Hogan Gladden was a native of Fairfield District who saw service during the Florida campaign with the Richland Rifle Company.[23] He was a field officer in the Palmetto Regiment during the Mexican War and was wounded at Mexico City.[24] Gladden had settled in New Orleans after the Mexican War, but when the governor named him lieutenant colonel of Gregg's regiment in an appointment that was met with "universal satisfaction," he agreed to accept it.[25] In February 1861, Gladden resigned his commission as lieutenant colonel to accept a seat in the Louisiana Secession Convention. On March 13, he became colonel of the 1st Regiment of Louisiana Regulars and was promoted to brigadier general on September 30, 1861. Gladden was wounded at Shiloh and died of his wounds on April 12, 1862.[26]

Daniel Heyward Hamilton Sr. of Orangeburg was formerly the United States marshal for the district of South Carolina. Governor Pickens appointed Hamilton the first major of Gregg's regiment. The *CSR* states, incorrectly, that he was named lieutenant colonel of the six-month regiment on January 1, 1861, but the *Mercury* got it right: Hamilton was the regiment's first major and was promoted to lieutenant colonel when Gladden resigned in February.[27] Hamilton was reappointed lieutenant colonel of the reorganized regiment on July 26, 1861. He was promoted to colonel on December 14, 1861, replacing Maxcy Gregg.[28] At his request, Hamilton was permanently detached from the regiment and left for the South Carolina coast on August 27, 1863. A.C. Haskell wrote of Hamilton: "The Brigade had no confidence in him, for he had never shown any capacity."[29] In Hamilton's defense, however, Roswell Ripley wrote in December 1863 that the regiment should be sent to South Carolina, that a new brigade should be created and that command of the new brigade should be given to Hamilton by virtue of his service and position. Hamilton subsequently held a command in Charleston. When the wounded Samuel McGowan did not return to command his brigade in September 1863, Abner Perrin, who was junior to Hamilton, was promoted to command the brigade. Hamilton, offended that he had not received the promotion, resigned from the army on January 4, 1864, though he gave no reason in his letter of resignation.[30] Caldwell wrote that Hamilton was a "gallant officer, an excellent disciplinarian, a careful manager of troops, and an honorable and accomplished gentleman. His regiment expressed great regret at his loss, and properly."[31]

Augustus Marshall Smith of Abbeville was the first lieutenant in Company D and the adjutant of Gregg's regiment in early 1861. Smith was made major when Lieutenant Colonel Gladden resigned. The *CSR* gives two dates for Smith's appointment to major: January 1 and July 26, 1861. The correct date was probably early February, when Gladden resigned, and Hamilton was promoted to lieutenant colonel—moves that left the office of major vacant. In the summer of 1861, when Gregg's regiment was reorganizing, Smith attempted to raise a cavalry company for service in Virginia. When that failed, he resumed the post of major in Gregg's new regiment.[32] Smith was promoted to lieutenant colonel on December 14, 1861, to replace Hamilton.[33] Though suffering from a "wasting disorder" that left him feeble, Smith was at the battle of Gaines's Mill on June 27 and was wounded in the left arm at the shoulder.[34] He remained on the battlefield because the wound seemed not serious. By the evening of the twenty-ninth, however, Smith's condition had deteriorated, and he died the next morning at Mrs. Allen's house in Richmond.[35] Lieutenant J.F.J. Caldwell wrote that Smith died on Sunday, June 29, adding that he was "an excellent drill officer, a thorough disciplinarian, a gallant leader. Although ill at our departure from camp, he persisted in going with us, and at last received his death stroke at the front. He was universally lamented, as an officer, a patriot, and a gentleman… Without disparagement of any others who fell that day…it is probable that he was the severest loss to the brigade."[36] J.P. Thomas incorrectly records Smith's name as Augustine.[37]

Edward E. McCrady Jr. of Charleston, previously captain of Company K, was promoted to major on December 14, 1861, replacing Major Smith.[38] McCrady was appointed lieutenant colonel, with rank from June 30, 1862, at Smith's death.[39] McCrady sustained a severe wound to the head at the battle of Second Manassas and did not return to duty until October 30, 1862.[40] While in camp at Moss Neck near Fredericksburg on January 27, 1863, McCrady was hit by a falling tree a soldier had cut for fuel. His right arm was paralyzed, and his face was lacerated in several places.[41] His recovery was slow. He tried to return to duty on several occasions that year, only to find himself unfit for the field. On October 16, 1863, McCrady received a twenty-day furlough because of a fractured scapula and concussion of the spine he had sustained earlier, probably in the January accident. Citing physical disability, McCrady resigned on March 17, 1864, effective January 1. He applied for appointment to a military court in February and received a number of letters of support. On February 11, 1864, he was assigned as an enrolling officer in the conscription bureau with the rank of major, and on the twenty-fifth, he sought, unsuccessfully, to be restored to his former rank of lieutenant colonel. He was assigned to the temporary command of the camp of instruction in Madison, Florida, on March 18, 1864, and was paroled there on May 18, 1865.[42]

Charles Wickliffe "Wick" McCreary of Barnwell was promoted to major on July 1, 1862, to replace Major McCrady.[43] McCreary's first name is uncertain. Krick wrote that, according to family records, his given name was Comillus; McCreary himself used the initials C.W.; the name Charles also appears in some sources.[44] McCreary was promoted from major to colonel, the regiment's last, effective January 4, 1864. This promotion filled voids left by the resignations of McCrady and Hamilton.[45] The *Memory Roll* records McCreary's promotion to colonel on March 18 or March 19, 1863. These dates not only conflict with the *CSR* but would have been impossible in any case since Hamilton was not relieved of his duties until August. McCreary was wounded three times in 1864: a severe wound in the shoulder and throat at Spotsylvania on May 12, a wound at Jones's Farm on September 30 and another wound at the Pegram house on October 10.[46] The next year, McCreary was shot through the lungs as the brigade was retiring near Gravelly Run on White Oak Road on March 31.[47] He was transported by litter back to the breastworks but died immediately afterward. Caldwell wrote that McCreary's "discipline was good, his drill better than almost any known to us, and his management in action as fine as I ever saw. Indeed, we had but two colonels during our whole service who effected as much in battle as he."[48] Sergeant B.F. Benson of Company L wrote that McCreary was "brilliant, fearless, and magnetic."[49]

Washington Pinckney Shooter, a lawyer from Marion District and a former captain of Company E, was appointed lieutenant colonel on January 4, 1864, on McCrady's resignation.[50] The *Memory Roll* erroneously records the date as March 18, 1864, probably indicating the date of promotion rather than the effective date of rank. Shooter was struck by a Minié ball just as the regiment reached the outer line of works at the "bloody angle" at Spotsylvania on May 12, 1864.[51] Though the *Charleston Daily Courier* reported that Shooter was killed instantly, he lived, according to Caldwell, long enough to say, "I know that I am a dead man; but I die with my eyes fixed on victory!"[52] Caldwell also wrote that Shooter "possessed a great quickness of perception, clearness of reasoning, and energy of action" and that he was "a most gallant and efficient officer. He drilled accurately, disciplined carefully, fought obstinately and coolly…His loss was felt deeply throughout the brigade."[53] Colonel J.N. Brown of the 14th Regiment wrote simply that Shooter's death was a great loss to the brigade.[54]

Thomas Pinckney Alston was promoted to major from captain of Company F with rank from January 4, 1864, when McCreary advanced from major to colonel.[55] The *Memory Roll* shows the date as March 19, 1864, and the *CSR* shows it as the sixteenth, both indicating the date of promotion, not the effective date of rank. Alston participated in every major battle of the Army of Northern Virginia from First Manassas until his death.[56] He was slightly wounded in the face at Fredericksburg in December 1863 and in the side on May 12, 1864, at Spotsylvania.[57] Alston's right arm was shattered at Jericho Ford on the North Anna River on May 23, 1864.[58] After enduring amputation of the arm above the elbow in a field hospital tent, he died on June 19, 1864, at Jackson Hospital in Richmond.[59] The *Daily South Carolinian* reported, incorrectly, that Alston was mortally wounded at Spotsylvania.[60] Nine days after his death, Alston was awarded a posthumous promotion to lieutenant colonel with rank from Shooter's death on May 12, 1864.[61] Both the *Mercury* and the *Roll of the Dead* record correctly that Alston died as major in command of the regiment, but both were incorrect in adding that he was never promoted to lieutenant colonel.[62]

Andrew Pickens Butler of Hamburg, captain of Company G, was promoted to major with rank from May 12, 1864, replacing Major Alston. He was named lieutenant colonel at Alston's death on June 19. Butler suffered a severe contusion to the right thigh at Deep Bottom on August 16, 1864.[63] In command of the regiment for the last ten days of the war, Butler was paroled at Appomattox Court House on April 9, 1865.[64]

Edward DuBose Brailsford of Clarendon District, captain of Company I, was promoted to major effective June 19, 1864, replacing Major Butler. Brailsford was wounded several times: first at Gaines's Mill, then severely in the right shoulder at Spotsylvania on May 12, 1864, and at Sutherland's Station on April 2, 1865.[65] He was paroled at Appomattox Court House on April 9, 1865.[66]

COMPANIES

Gregg's six-month Regiment comprised the companies listed below.

Company A, the Richland Rifles, was from Columbia, in Richland District.[67] The company celebrated its forty-sixth anniversary on August 8, 1861.[68] It was known by several other names, including the Richland

Volunteer Rifle Company, the Richland Volunteer Rifles and the Richland Riflemen.[69] On November 20, 1860, the Richland Volunteer Rifle Company was under the command of Captain Daniel B. Miller.[70] It mustered in state service for six months as the right company on January 3, 1861, and left for Charleston the same day.[71] John P. Thomas wrote that Company A entered state service on January 4 immediately after Company B.[72] According to the *Mercury*, Thomas W. Radcliffe was elected captain at that time, but the *CSR* indicates that Miller held the post.[73] We do know that Miller was captain of the company when it went with Colonel Gregg to Virginia on April 22.[74] Company A mustered out of service on July 9, 1861, and Miller turned up later as captain of Company F, 3rd South Carolina Battalion. Some men mustered in Company C, 1st (Gregg's) SCV, on August 30, 1861, under First Lieutenant John Cordero, while others joined Company A, 15th SCV, on September 5, 1861.[75]

Company B from Darlington District, the Darlington Guards (or Guard), was organized on June 28, 1859, and was incorporated by the General Assembly on January 28, 1861.[76] Frederick Fraser Warley, who had raised the company, tendered its services to the governor even before the Ordinance of Secession was passed.[77] On January 3, 1861, immediately following Warley's appointment as captain, Company B boarded the train for Charleston.[78] The Darlington Guard became the left company of Gregg's six-month Regiment. As noted above, Thomas wrote that Company B was the first to enter state service, mustering in on January 4 just before Company A, but Thomas's account conflicts with two other sources: official records indicate that the governor named Warley captain on January 3, and the *CSR* notes that Company A entered service that day as well.[79]

A sketch in *Recollections and Reminiscences* claims that most of the men of Company B would have volunteered for service in Virginia in April 1861 except for a disagreement between Warley and Gregg, which caused a rift within the company.[80] While Warley and many of his men refused to volunteer for service out of state, First Lieutenant David Gregg McIntosh, a Darlington lawyer, led a small contingent of the company to Virginia in April.[81] Warley remained in command of the three companies of Gregg's regiment that remained in South Carolina from April 22 until they disbanded on the twenty-sixth. In late April or early May, he also led home to Darlington the majority of the Darlington Guards who refused to go to Virginia.[82] Warley's men reorganized as the Darlington Guards and elected him captain on June 24, 1861.[83] This new company probably became the Inglis Light Artillery, ultimately designated Company D, 2nd Regiment, South Carolina Artillery. The *Mercury* reported that McIntosh's contingent of Company B appears on the roster of Gregg's regiment in Virginia in May

1861.[84] When the regiment was reorganized in July, McIntosh's contingent became the nucleus of Company D, the Pee Dee Rifles.

Company C from Edgefield District, the Edgefield Rifles (also called Edgefield Riflemen), was organized before September 1860.[85] Cicero Adams commanded the company in late 1860 and early 1861.[86] The General Assembly created another company called the Edgefield Riflemen on January 28, 1861. It was attached to the 7th Regiment, South Carolina Militia.[87] Whether or not the two companies shared a common origin is unclear. H. Rufus Dean was captain in late April 1861, but the status of Cicero Adams from late 1860 until then is unclear.[88] Adams tried, unsuccessfully, to raise a mounted light artillery battery in October 1861.[89] He was named captain of Company A of the 22nd Regiment in January 1862, and he advanced to major the following year.

Company C arrived in Charleston on January 7, 1861, and went with the regiment to Virginia in April.[90] The company disbanded as planned on July 9 and did not reorganize for Gregg's new regiment. About twenty of the men enlisted in Company D of the 14th Regiment, also called the Edgefield Rifles, in September 1861, while other Company C men chose Company A of the 22nd Regiment in December 1861 and January 1862. In the spring of 1862, Captain Dean enlisted as a private in another Edgefield company, Company C of the 19th Regiment, and was elected captain of that company at the reorganization in May 1862.

Company D from Abbeville District, the Abbeville Volunteers, was organized as the Abbeville Minute Men on October 29, 1860.[91] Though the *CSR* fails to mention this company, a sketch in *Recollections and Reminiscences* names it as one of two companies of minutemen organized in Abbeville on October 15, 1859, in anticipation of armed conflict between the North and the South.[92] The other company organized then was under the command of Patrick H. Bradley and ultimately became Company C of the 7th Regiment, SCV.[93] Abbeville District, which had been a hotbed of secession for many months, raised a whole regiment, the Abbeville Regiment of Minute Men, consisting of about six hundred and fifty troops under the command of Colonel Augustus M. Smith.[94] Company D was attached to the regiment, which offered its services to the state as early as December 4, 1860. The governor accepted, contingent upon legislative approval, but the legislature determined on January 4, 1861, that the governor was authorized to accept only companies, not regiments. As a result, the Abbeville Regiment disbanded on January 7.[95]

James Monroe Perrin, a veteran of Company E of the Palmetto Regiment in the Mexican War, was named captain of the Abbeville Volunteers, with A.M. Smith as the first lieutenant.[96] Perrin was elected captain of Company

B in Orr's Rifles in July 1861. Company D refused to volunteer for service out of state in April 1861, and only about ten men from the company went to Virginia.[97] Company D returned to Abbeville on April 30, 1861, and disbanded there.[98] Most of its men enlisted in Company B, Orr's 1st Rifle Regiment, in July 1861. Eight colonels came from the ranks of the Abbeville Volunteers.

Company E, the Union Volunteers, was a company of minutemen from Union District. It was also known as the Union District Volunteers.[99] James M. Gadberry was elected captain on January 12, 1861. The Union Volunteers went with the regiment to Virginia in April.[100] Company E mustered out of service on July 9, 1861; most of its men later served in Company C, 18th Regiment, SCV. Captain Gadberry eventually became colonel of the 18th Regiment. In addition, all the commissioned and most of the non-commissioned officers of the Macbeth Light Artillery originally served in Company E.[101]

Company F, the Wee Nee Volunteers, also known as the Williamsburg Company, was raised in Kingstree in Williamsburg District and was commanded by John Gotea Pressley.[102] The company's intriguing name, *Wee Nee*, comes from the American Indian word for the Black River running through Kingstree.[103] As early as November 5, 1860, Captain Pressley commanded a Kingstree company that was part of the 31st Regiment, South Carolina Militia.[104] Most of the men of this company had enlisted as Company E, the Black Mingo Guards of the 10th Regiment, SCV. On January 1, 1861, however, Pressley raised an entirely new company organized for state service.[105] The men of this company took the name Wee Nee Volunteers and left Kingstree for Charleston on January 3.[106] The next day the company mustered in for six months of service in South Carolina.[107] It was designated Company F in Maxcy Gregg's 1st Regiment, SCV (six months). Pressley was elected captain shortly afterward, and Samuel W. Maurice was elected first lieutenant.[108] Company F was one of three companies that did not go with Gregg's regiment to Virginia in April.[109] Even though the six-month term of enlistment still had more than a month to go, an order from the adjutant and inspector general on April 26 sent the Wee Nee Volunteers back to Kingstree to disband.[110] The company reorganized in May as the Wee Nee Volunteers under the command of Captain R.M. Gourdin and mustered in state service as Company D, 10th Regiment, SCV.[111]

Company G, the Hamburg Volunteers, was raised in Hamburg, Edgefield District. It was also called the Hamburg Company and the Hamburg Minute Men and had existed under the latter name even before the war.[112] The captain, William Spires, and his men left Hamburg for Charleston on January 8, 1861.[113] The Hamburg Volunteers, like Companies D and F, did not go with the regiment to Virginia in April.[114] The *CSR* indicates, incorrectly, that Company G was disbanded before Gregg's other companies entered Confederate service in April. In fact, the other companies mustered in Confederate service on April 22, and Companies D, F and G were ordered to disband on the twenty-sixth. Nineteen of the men of Company G, along with some from Company H, were consolidated into Company H, probably the Company H of Gregg's reorganized regiment. Eight men from the original Company G enlisted in Companies I and G of Gregg's new regiment.

Company H, the Cherokee Pond Volunteers, was also called the Cherokee Pond Guards and the Meriwether Guards.[115] Its men were from a part of Edgefield District now in Aiken County. Robert Meriwether enlisted as captain on January 7, 1861, and left with his men for Charleston the next day.[116] Though contemporary newspapers printed his name in a variety of ways, Meriwether is the correct spelling.[117] The Cherokee Pond Volunteers went with the regiment to Virginia in April, and the company mustered out of service there on July 9, 1861.[118] Some of the men joined Company G of Gregg's reorganized regiment later that summer. Robert Meriwether held the rank of major of the 6th Battalion Reserves in 1864 and 1865.

Company I, the Monticello Guards, was from Fairfield District and was also known as the Fairfield Volunteers and the Monticello Volunteers.[119] The *Mercury* referred to this company as Company J even though the letter *J* was rarely used in military alphabetic designation. Company J of the 4th Regiment, SCV, was one of the few to carry the designation. Under command of Captain John Bunyan Davis, the Monticello Guards went with the regiment to Virginia in April.[120] When Company I reorganized in August 1861, a few of its men mustered in Davis's Company E, 15th Regiment, SCV, on the thirtieth.[121] McCrady wrote that Company I transferred to the 15th Regiment, indicating that more than just a few of its men became part of that unit.[122]

Company K, the Marion Volunteers, was raised in Marion District and mustered in service on January 5, 1861. M.B. Stanley was the first captain, and Washington Pinckney Shooter the original first lieutenant.[123] The *CSR* claims that W.P. Shooter enlisted on January 5 as the only captain in the six-month regiment and mustered out of service on July 9. This is incorrect. Shooter's command was of Company E and was assumed after the regiment was reorganized in July 1861. M.B. Stanley was probably Mathew B. Stanley who later served as captain of the McQueen Light Artillery in the 18th Artillery Battalion. The Marion Volunteers went with the regiment to Virginia in April.[124] Company K does not appear on the regimental roster of May 1861, printed in the *Mercury*, but that was probably an oversight.[125] It mustered out of service in Richmond on July 9, 1861, along with the other six-month companies. Some Company K men enlisted in Company E, the Marion Rifles, in Gregg's reorganized regiment on August 19.

Company L, the Rhett Guards, was a company of minutemen drawn from the 39th Regiment, South Carolina Militia.[126] The company, also called the Rhett Guard, was composed of men primarily from Newberry District, though some came from Lexington District.[127] It was organized on January 5, 1861, and was named for Robert Barnwell Rhett.[128] The men of Company L mustered in state service on January 14 under the command of Captain Whitfield Walker.[129] According to the *Mercury*, Captain J. Elvin Knotts commanded the company in May 1861, but the *CSR* states that Knotts held the rank of first lieutenant.[130] The Rhett Guards went with the regiment to Virginia in April 1861 and appeared on the regimental roster in May.[131] The company disbanded with the regiment in early July, and many of the men mustered in Company B of Gregg's reorganized regiment on August 17.

Company M, the Richardson Guard, was from Charleston and was the right company of the regiment. It was originally made up of members of the Palmetto Fire Company, commanded by Captain John Symons.[132] The Richardson Guard was organized at the time of secession as part of the 17th Regiment, South Carolina Militia.[133] The first captain of the Richardson Guard was John M. Pundt.[134] Evidently Pundt resigned after a short time since John Symons was elected captain of the Richardson Guard about January 11.[135] The company was named for D.F. Richardson, who was elected captain on March 1.[136] In late April, the Richardson Guard was detached from the 17th Regiment, South Carolina Militia, and joined Gregg's regiment in Virginia as a replacement for one of the companies that refused to serve there.[137] Richardson himself resigned about April 23, and Charles "Charley" Henry Axson was elected captain in his place.[138] Company M mustered out of service with the regiment on July 9 and returned to Charleston two days later.[139] Later in July, Captain Axson and some of the men of Company M created a new company, which became Company I of Gregg's reorganized regiment.

Company N, the DeKalb Rifle Guards, was from Camden in Kershaw District.[140] It was also called the DeKalb Rifles and the DeKalb Guards.[141] The company came from a prewar organization, the Camden Rifle Guards, commanded by a Captain Parker, a detachment of which formed the DeKalb Rifle Guards and joined Kershaw's 2nd Regiment, SCV.[142] Thomas Lang Boykin commanded the company.[143] The company served in the 2nd Regiment until late April 1861, when its men refused to volunteer for service in Virginia under Colonel Kershaw. Instead, about May 1, they volunteered to serve under Colonel Gregg, also in Virginia.[144] On May 8, Company N was enroute by train for Virginia. There it replaced one of Gregg's three companies that had refused to serve there.[145] Company N mustered out of service as planned on July 9. A few of its men later served in Company D, 15th Regiment, SCV.

Company O, the Saluda Guard (or Guards), was from Lexington District.[146] It was organized at the Old Fair Grounds opposite the Lutheran Church in Lexington.[147] W. Moultrie Gibbes enlisted as captain on April 26, 1861.[148] The *Mercury* names A.B. Gibbes instead, but he is not listed in the *CSR*.[149] Company O was part of the regiment by May 10 as a replacement for one of the three companies that refused to go to Virginia.[150] Company O mustered out of service on July 9 and on the thirteenth arrived back in Columbia.[151] A few of its men enlisted in Company C of Gregg's reorganized regiment later the same month.

Gregg's regiment, after the reorganization in the summer of 1861, was made up of the following companies:

Company A, the Gregg Guards (or Gregg Guard), was new to the reorganized regiment. It left Williston on August 14, 1861, to join Gregg's regiment in Virginia.[152] Company A mustered in Confederate service at Richmond on August 19 for the duration of the war.[153] Most of the men were from Barnwell District, but a few came from Colleton, Spartanburg and Orangeburg Districts. Many had served previously in Company K of Hagood's 1st Regiment, SCV. According to the *Mercury*, Company A was the first to be raised in Barnwell District.[154] Charles Wickliffe "Wick" McCreary was the first captain. Krick wrote that McCreary's commission dated from July 13, 1861, but the *CSR* gives the date as August 19.[155] This discrepancy could have a simple explanation: the August date might indicate the time of his enlistment in Confederate service, and the earlier that of his election as captain before the company left South Carolina. We do know that McCreary was promoted to major on July 1, 1862, and First Lieutenant William D. Bush was made captain the same day.[156] Bush was wounded and captured on July 28, 1864, at Deep Bottom while acting as lieutenant colonel.[157] He was sent to Old Capitol Prison in Washington, D.C., on August 3 and then to Fort Delaware on the eleventh. He was released from Fort Delaware on June 17, 1865, and was not replaced as captain of Company A.[158]

Company B, the Rhett Guards, was originally Company L in Gregg's (six-month) Regiment. Its men, mostly from Newberry, mustered in Confederate service at Richmond on August 17, 1861, for the duration of the war.[159] A.S. Salley records that Company B mustered in service for the duration of the war at Newberry on July 27, 1861.[160] Whitfield Walker was elected captain on August 17, 1861, and resigned on February 11, 1862, but he saw service later as major of the 3rd Alabama Reserves.[161] Salley dates the resignation as February 8.[162] First Lieutenant Sampson Pope replaced Walker as captain on February 11, though once again Salley says February 8.[163] Pope resigned on July 10—a date also shown as July 12—and probably transferred to the Medical Department.[164] First Lieutenant John Caldwell McLemore was promoted to captain either on the tenth or twelfth. He received a wound to the head on August 29, 1862, at the battle of Second Manassas, and died from its effects on September 19 in Richmond.[165] The *CSR* gives the date of McLemore's death as September 9. Lieutenant J.F.J. Caldwell wrote that McLemore "combined such qualities, as man and soldier, as to place him easily among the first class of our dead."[166] Thomas H. Lyles, who was promoted to captain on September 9, 1862, was killed at the battle of Fredericksburg about three months later on December 13.[167] That same day, Basil Manly Blease was named captain—the company's fifth. Wounds to the left shoulder and left lung at Gaines's Mill on June 27, 1862, had caused a deformity of Blease's left shoulder and extreme atrophy of the left arm. His disability forced him to resign on a surgeon's certificate on August 6, 1863. Blease's death on January 2, 1877, was attributed to the long-term effects of wounds sustained nearly fifteen years earlier at Gaines's Mill.[168] First Lieutenant Daniel Pickens Goggans was promoted to captain on August 6, 1863. The *Mercury* reported Goggans as captain in July 1863, but he was probably commanding the company as first lieutenant then.[169] Wounds to Goggans's hands and the right arm sustained at Jericho Ford on May 23, 1864, resulted in amputation of the little finger of his left hand, and he lost his left leg at Gravelly Run on March 31, 1865.[170] Goggans was paroled at sometime between April 11 and April 21, 1865.

Company C, the Richland Rifles, was also called the Richland Volunteer Rifle Company.[171] The company, from Columbia in Richland District, volunteered for service there on July 29, 1861, and left Columbia for Richmond on August 6. Company C mustered in Confederate service for the duration of the war on August 30.[172] Some men of Company C had served previously in Company A of Gregg's six-month regiment, and a few had served in Company O; the rest were new recruits from Richland District. John Cordero was elected captain on July 29, 1861, but he resigned on November 5.[173] Under a surgeon's certificate saying he was unfit for duty due to hemorrhoids, Cordero entered another branch of the service.[174] First Lieutenant James S. McMahon replaced Cordero as captain of Company C on November 5. McMahon received a contusion to the left knee at Gettysburg and was also wounded at the Wilderness.[175] The *Memory Roll* says he was wounded a third time, but it does not say when and where.

McMahon was granted a leave of indulgence with an expiration date of February 28, 1865, but apparently never returned to the company. He was not paroled with the regiment at Appomattox Court House.[176] Salley spells the name McMahan, but his signature on documents in the *CSR* appears as McMahon.[177]

Company D, the Pee Dee Rifles, was formed by several men from Darlington District who had served in Company B, the Darlington Guards, of Gregg's six-month regiment. They were the same men who followed First Lieutenant David Gregg McIntosh to Virginia in April 1861.[178] McIntosh's group returned to South Carolina after the six-month regiment had disbanded in July, reorganized into a new company, and elected McIntosh captain. The men mustered in Confederate service as Company D in Gregg's regiment on July 21 and left Darlington on August 15. They joined Gregg's regiment in Richmond a few days later. Gregg's reorganized regiment had twelve companies, two more than authorized. For that reason, the Pee Dee Rifles converted to a light artillery battery in March 1862 and changed its name to the Pee Dee Light Artillery, also called McIntosh's Battery. The company was detached from Gregg's regiment then and served as an independent battery for the next twenty-seven months. McIntosh's Battery became Company C, 18th Battalion, South Carolina Artillery, on June 4, 1864.

Company E, the Marion Rifles, came from Marion District and was also called the Marion Volunteers.[179] Its men volunteered for the duration of the war in their home district on August 12, 1861, and left for Virginia soon after. The company mustered in Confederate service on August 19. Some of its members had previously served in Company K of Gregg's six-month regiment. Washington Pinckney Shooter was elected captain on August 1.[180] He was promoted to lieutenant colonel on January 4, 1864, and First Lieutenant George A. McIntyre replaced him as captain on that date.[181] McIntyre had lost his left arm at Chancellorsville on May 3, 1863, and had subsequently served as an enrolling officer in South Carolina. He was absent from the company for nearly a year—from May 1863 to April 1864—and in spite of his wound, he was promoted to captain. Unable to perform his duties because of the wound, McIntyre resigned on April 12, 1864. D.A. Smith, who had also been wounded at Chancellorsville the same day as McIntyre, was made captain on April 12 and was the last captain to command Company E.[182] Smith was paroled at Appomattox Court House on April 9, 1865.[183]

Company F, the Horry Rebels, or Horry Rifles, was new to Gregg's reorganized regiment in the summer of 1861.[184] Its men were from Conwayboro in Horry District, where they enlisted on August 12, 1861.

Company F mustered in Confederate service at Richmond on August 18 for the duration of the war. Thomas Pinckney Alston, who had been elected captain on August 7, mustered in service with the company on the twelfth. Alston was severely wounded in the face at Fredericksburg on December 13, 1862, and was promoted to major on January 4, 1864.[185] First Lieutenant Josiah Cox was made captain the same day. Cox had been wounded at Gaines's Mill on June 27, 1862, and was seriously wounded again, this time in the testicles, at Gettysburg on July 1, 1863. He sustained a severe wound to the hip, injuring the ischium, at the Wilderness on May 6, 1864.[186] The hip wound forced Cox to retire to the Invalid Corps nearly a year later, on March 6, 1865. He was paroled at the Academy General Hospital at Chester, South Carolina, on May 5, 1865.

Company G, the Butler Sentinels, was from Hamburg and Briar Patch (now Kirksey) in Edgefield District.[187] It was also called the Edgefield Company.[188] About half the men were from Hamburg and the rest were from Briar Patch.[189] Some had served in both Company H and Company G of Gregg's six-month regiment. Both Andrew Pickens Butler and Wiley H. Holloway raised companies in the summer of 1861.[190] Butler's was probably a reorganization of the Cherokee Pond Volunteers, formerly Company H in Gregg's six-month Regiment.[191] Holloway's Company might have come from the Mountain Creek Home Guards, which he had raised in May 1861.[192] At some point in August, these two companies were merged into the Butler Sentinels and volunteered for service at Hamburg on August 16. Butler was elected captain on the same day. The company mustered in service for the duration of the war on August 19, 1861, at Richmond. Butler was promoted to major, and First Lieutenant Holloway was promoted to captain, effective May 12, 1864. Holloway was severely wounded in the right shoulder at Deep Bottom on July 28, 1864.[193] He was paroled with the regiment at Appomattox Court House on April 9, 1865.[194]

Company H was called Haskell's Rifle Corps. Nineteen Edgefield District men in Company H had previously served in Company G, and others had served in Company H of Gregg's six-month regiment.[195] Most of the others came from Beaufort and Charleston, and a few came from Abbeville. The company was derisively called "The Models" because Captain Haskell was known as a stern disciplinarian.[196] The company mustered in on September 3, 1861, at Lightwood Knot Springs for the duration of the war. According to A.S. Salley, the company mustered in service at Richmond on September 7, 1861.[197] William "Willy" Thomson Haskell of Abbeville raised the company and was elected its captain on September 2, 1861.[198] While leading his battalion of sharpshooters at Gettysburg on July 2, 1863, Haskell was shot under the arm and killed instantly.[199] Caldwell wrote of Haskell: "In camp he was the most thorough, yet the most discriminating, disciplinarian, on the drill ground he was infallibly accurate, on the march he was indefatigable, in battle he was the very spirit of gallantry and self-possession. It was everywhere conceded that we could have sustained no heavier loss to those in the line, than in him."[200] There were other accolades as well: "The Brigade mourn his loss more than that of any man who has ever fallen in it, more even its seems than that of General Gregg."[201] Sergeant Berry Benson considered Haskell "the strictest officer in the regiment" and noted though the regiment hated him at first, Haskell soon won the men over.[202] He added that Haskell was "as cool and courageous as he was kind."[203]

First Lieutenant John Gibbes Barnwell was promoted to captain on Haskell's death. Barnwell had been wounded at Cold Harbor (Gaines's Mill) as a lieutenant. He was slightly wounded again at the Wilderness on May 5, 1864, but remained on the field and reported for duty the next morning.[204] Barnwell received a severe wound to the right knee at Deep Bottom on July 28, 1864.[205] According to Benson, Barnwell was also wounded at Spotsylvania.[206] On September 30, 1864, Barnwell sought examination by a medical board and retirement to the Invalid Corps. No further information on his retirement appears in the record, and he was paroled with the regiment at Appomattox Court House on April 9, 1865.[207] Benson wrote that though the men were slow to warm up to Barnwell, because "he outshone everyone else…at Falling Waters" the men "liked him very well and liked him better every day."[208] The *Mercury* reported that William Aiken Kelly, captain of Company L, commanded his own and Company H for a time in 1864.[209] The *CSR* shows Kelly on the muster roll for Company H from April 30 to August 31, 1864. These dates coincide with Barnwell's absence while recuperating from one of his wounds.

Company I was called the Richardson Guards.[210] Some of its men served previously in Company M of Gregg's six-month regiment. Most were from Charleston District, but a few came from Edgefield District and others from various parts of the state. Charles "Charley" Henry Axson, captain of Company M in Gregg's first regiment, returned to Charleston when the first enlistment expired to reorganize his company for further service in Virginia. The *Mercury* reported on July 26, 1861, that Axson was re-elected captain at the reorganization of the regiment, but he is not listed in that capacity in the *CSR*.[211]

A detachment of twenty-five men of the Richardson Guards left Charleston for Richmond by rail on July 25, 1861.[212] Axson and the rest of the company followed by train five days later. On the evening of Tuesday, July 30, on the Wilmington and Weldon Railroad while near Wilson, North Carolina, Axson got into a fight with an intoxicated soldier, Private

Arthur B. Davis, from Georgia. The fight was over some watermelons that Axson planned to present to Mrs. Jefferson Davis. Davis shot Axson to death.[213] Later in Richmond, some of Axson's men attacked Davis with guns and knives, but they failed to kill him.[214] Since Company I had not yet mustered in Confederate service at the time of Axson's death, this incident probably explains the omission of his rank in the *CSR* listing. A.C. Haskell, then adjutant of the regiment, wrote that Axson was the "most remarkable man for Captain and the most remarkable material in the line that I have ever seen."[215]

Company I mustered in Confederate service for the duration of the war at Richmond on September 7, 1861, with Charles Lawton Boag as its captain. The *CSR* says Boag was elected captain on July 20, 1861, a date that conflicts with Axson's time in the rank and his death.[216] Possibly this entry is a mistake and should have read July 30. Salley records that Boag was appointed captain in July 1861.[217] Boag served for about a year; he was killed at the battle of Gaines's Mill on June 27, 1862.[218] Boag was called "a brave, gallant officer, the life and soul of his company."[219] First Lieutenant Edward DuBose Brailsford replaced Boag as captain on June 27.[220] Brailsford was severely wounded in the right shoulder at Spotsylvania on May 12, 1864.[221] He was promoted to major, effective from June 19, 1864, and First Lieutenant Wallace Ioor Delph was named captain with rank from the same day.[222] Delph had been wounded at Fredericksburg on December 13, 1862, and also in May or June 1863. He was captured on April 3, 1865, near Petersburg and sent to Johnson's Island, where he was released on June 18, 1865.

Company K, the Irish Volunteers, was the regiment's color company.[223] The *Mercury* referred to this company as the "Irish Volunteers For The War."[224] A Charleston militia company called the Irish Volunteers was created about 1783, and in early 1861 was part of the 17th Regiment, South Carolina Militia.[225] The prewar Irish Volunteers raised two companies from its ranks for Confederate service, Company K of Gregg's reorganized regiment and Company C of the Charleston Battalion, which later became Company H, 27th Regiment, SCV. Both were called the Irish Volunteers. Company K was organized in Charleston for the duration of the war on June 25, 1861, and joined the regiment as a new company in July. Some of the Irishmen of Company K were members of another prewar Irish militia company called the Meagher Guards. Edward McCrady Jr., who was the first captain of Company K, had commanded the Meagher Guards in 1860.[226] A company in the 1st Regiment Rifles, South Carolina Militia, this unit was named for the Irish Patriot, Thomas Francis Meagher.[227] Unfortunately for the Charlestonians, however, Meagher himself raised a militia company in

New York to fight for the Union, and the Charleston Irishmen felt compelled to change their name to the Emerald Light Infantry in the spring of 1861.[228] The *Mercury* reported that the Emerald Light Infantry provided some men for Company K.[229]

In June 1861, Edward McCrady was authorized to raise "a Charleston Battalion for the war."[230] Company K was the second to be raised for McCrady's battalion, but evidently the battalion was never completed. The *Mercury* reported that Edward E. McCrady Jr. was elected captain on June 7, 1861, and the *CSR* records his commission dated from June 25.[231] According to Thomas, Company K mustered in Confederate service as an independent company on June 23, 1861; Salley writes that the men enlisted on the twenty-fifth.[232] The *Mercury* and the *Charleston Daily Courier* record the date as July 1, and the *CSR* indicates the company mustered in at Richmond on September 21.[233] The men elected to join Gregg's regiment in early July and left Charleston for Virginia on the twenty-second.[234] The company was in camp on July 24 and expecting to be joined by the Emmett Guards.[235] The *Daily Southern Guardian* reported on that day that the "second" company of the Irish Volunteers had reported to camp. This company was surely Company K of Gregg's regiment. The fact that it was referred to as the second company had to mean that the first was either the Emmett Guards or the Magrath Rangers of the 17th Regiment, South Carolina Militia.[236] Thomas records that the Irish Volunteers was the first company in South Carolina to volunteer for the duration of the war and the first to volunteer for Gregg's reorganized regiment.[237] Because this was the first company to enlist in Gregg's reorganized regiment, and because McCrady was the senior captain, it appears that the Irish Volunteers should have been designated Company A. Thomas notes that Gregg's companies were not given letter designations until after McCrady was promoted to major on December 14, 1861.[238] If the Irish Volunteers' enlistment date in Confederate service was actually September 21, however, its designation as Company K seems more consistent with the enlistment dates of the other companies in the regiment.

First Lieutenant Michael P. Parker was promoted to captain on January 23, 1862.[239] He was slightly wounded in the knee at Second Manassas later that year, on August 29, 1862. At Sharpsburg on September 17, he was disabled by a bullet that entered his mouth and came out his cheek.[240] Parker served as provost marshal in Augusta, Georgia, in September and October 1863. Because of disabilities caused by his wound, he retired to the Invalid Corps on November 2, 1864, retroactive to June 2.

James Armstrong Jr. was the last captain.[241] Armstrong, who signed his name as Jimmy, commanded Company K as acting captain with the rank of lieutenant from September 17, 1862, until he was actually promoted on November 2, 1864, with rank from June 2.[242] Armstrong was slightly wounded at Sharpsburg on September 17, 1862, and at Fredericksburg on December 13.[243] He was wounded again in the left forearm while carrying the colors on July 1, 1863, at Gettysburg. Though slightly wounded a fourth time at Spotsylvania on May 12, 1864, Armstrong was present for duty on the twenty-third.[244] The upper third of his right tibia was shattered by a Minié ball, and he was captured at Sutherland's Station on the South Side Railroad on April 2, 1865.[245] He developed necrosis of the shaft of the tibia and spent the next eleven months in several hospitals in Washington. Armstrong's leg wound seemed healed in 1871, but the leg had to be amputated nearly fifty years later, on March 23, 1920. For six decades following the war, he became a popular speaker, especially at dedication ceremonies of Confederate monuments across South Carolina. The dedication ceremonies of the Williston monument in September 1924 and of the Grace Memorial Bridge in Charleston in August 1929 were among his last. Armstrong died on August 15, 1930.[246]

Company L, the Carolina Light Infantry Volunteers, was also called the "Carolina Light Infantry for the War" and the Boy Company, the latter because most of its members were under twenty-one.[247] The name also reflects the fact that the men came from all parts of South Carolina. Most were from Charleston, but a few came from the Districts of Lexington, Laurens, Georgetown, Spartanburg, Sumter, York, Barnwell, Clarendon, Marion, Abbeville and Union; a scattering came from Marlboro, North Carolina and Virginia. Company L, another company new to Gregg's reorganized regiment, mustered in at Lightwood Knot Springs for the duration of the war on September 3, 1861. The Carolina Light Infantry, organized in 1858, had been part of the 1st Regiment Rifles, South Carolina Militia. Some of the men volunteered for Confederate service and applied to the Hampton Legion.[248] Like many companies, however, they were not accepted, and they enlisted as Company L of Gregg's regiment instead. Collyar Douglas Barksdale, born in Laurens District but a merchant in Charleston at the outbreak of the war, was elected captain on August 3, 1861.[249] He was wounded in early 1862 and was sent to the Institute Hospital at Richmond, where he recovered. Barksdale was mortally wounded in the shoulder at Second Manassas on August 29, 1862; he died on August 31.[250] The *Roll of the Dead* and the *Charleston Daily Courier* record the date of his death as September 1.[251] First Lieutenant John W. Chambers of Charleston was promoted to captain on August 31, 1862. He was killed while on picket duty at Hagerstown, Maryland, on July 13, 1863.[252] The *Confederate Veteran* notes, erroneously, that he was killed on July 11, 1863.[253] Abner Perrin wrote that Chambers was a most gallant and worthy officer.[254] First Lieutenant William Aiken Kelly succeeded Chambers as captain on July 13.[255] Kelly commanded both Company L and Company H from about April 30 to August 31, 1864.[256] He was wounded at Cold Harbor and slightly wounded in the breast above the clavicle on May 5, 1864, at the Wilderness, though he remained on the field and was present for duty the next morning.[257] Kelly received a flesh wound in the right shoulder on May 12 at Spotsylvania.[258] He was paroled at Appomattox Court House on April 9, 1865.[259]

Company M, the Furman Guards, also known as William Hans Campbell's Company, was new to the regiment in the summer of 1861.[260] It was named in honor of Dr. James C. Furman, a prominent Greenville citizen.[261] Company M, made up of men from Greenville, was organized on August 15, 1861. Salley records that the men enlisted for the duration of the war on August 27, 1861, in Greenville, but other sources indicate they mustered in for the duration on September 3, 1861, at Lightwood Knot Springs.[262] The company had become large enough to split into two by September 1861. Maxcy Gregg was aware that his regiment had too many companies. Because of the need for artillerists, he agreed to release Company M from his regiment.[263] On October 13, 1861, the company was transferred to the 3rd Battalion, South Carolina Artillery, and its name was changed to the Furman Artillery. The Reverend William Hans Campbell raised the company and transferred with it to the 3rd Artillery Battalion.[264]

Brigade Affiliations

In early 1861, Gregg's regiment and the 2nd Regiment, SCV, made up Brigadier General P.H. Nelson's Palmetto Brigade in Major General (both state militia ranks) M.L. Bonham's Division of the South Carolina Army.[265] Later that spring—in April, May and early June—the regiment served in South Carolina and Virginia as part of the Palmetto Brigade under Brigadier General (Confederate rank) Bonham, along with, at various times, the 2nd, 3rd, 4th, 5th, 6th, 7th, 8th and 9th Regiments, SCV.[266] From June 21 to July 21, Bonham's Brigade comprised the 1st, 2nd, 3rd, 7th and 8th Regiments, SCV, as well the 11th North Carolina Volunteer Regiment. The regiment was attached to J.R. Anderson's Brigade until late May 1862, when it was reassigned to Maxcy Gregg's new brigade. The brigade was known thereafter as Gregg's (later McGowan's) Brigade in A.P. Hill's Light Division of the Army of Northern Virginia. It comprised Gregg's 1st, SCV, Regiment; Orr's 1st Regiment of Rifles; and the 12th, 13th and 14th, SCV, Regiments. Abner Perrin commanded the brigade for a time in 1863, as did James

Conner in 1864. Wade Hampton was offered command after Gregg's death in December 1862, but he refused.[267]

Major Movements and Engagements

The companies of the six-month regiment began arriving in Charleston in early January 1861.[268] Companies A, B and F reached the Race Course about January 3; Company K arrived on the fifth, and Company C arrived on January 7.[269] Company D got in on the ninth, and Company I the next day.[270] Company L arrived at Sullivan's Island on the eleventh or twelfth, and Company E left Union for Charleston on January 12.[271] Some companies began the move to Sullivan's Island in early January; Companies A and B were there as early as the fourth.[272] Companies B and L had arrived at Fort Moultrie by January 8 and were able to observe the firing on the *Star of the West*, which took place the next day.[273] Companies G and H were based about a mile from Fort Moultrie by January 16.[274] Company F and most, if not all, of the other companies had reached Sullivan's Island by the twenty-sixth.[275] The entire regiment was in Charleston by February 1 and had moved on to Morris Island by the middle of the month. Company F transferred there on the fourteenth, and headquarters moved there on the eighteenth.[276] Duty on Morris Island meant erecting fortifications, mounting guns and manning batteries.[277] One detachment of Company B staffed the battery at Oyster Point at the south end of Morris Island, while another manned the Beach Battery there.[278] The regiment garrisoned the Morris Island channel batteries and took some shellfire during the engagement with Fort Sumter on April 12 and April 13. From April 13 to April 19, the troops slept in their clothes with accoutrements in place and guns loaded in anticipation of an attack.[279] Near the end of April when President Davis called for troops to volunteer for Confederate service in Virginia, about 500 of Gregg's men answered the call.[280] Some companies, parts of others and assorted individuals refused on the grounds that they had enlisted for service in South Carolina only. The *Mercury* reported, incorrectly, that only companies A, B, C, D, E, K, L and M went to Virginia.[281] The *CSR* listing of companies A, B, C, E, H, I, K and L is accurate. Companies D, F and G did not serve in Virginia; they were replaced with three new companies—M, N and O. The eight companies bound for Virginia left Morris Island for Charleston on April 21.[282] They left Charleston by rail on the afternoon of Monday, April 22, for Richmond and were among the first organized out-of-state troops to arrive.[283] By April 28, the regiment was at the Central Fair Grounds in

Richmond at a spot the men had named Camp Pickens.[284] Company O arrived in Virginia on May 4, bringing the regiment to a strength of about 580 men.[285] Meanwhile, those who had refused to serve in Virginia were relieved of duty at Morris Island on April 29. They went to Charleston for an official dismissal ceremony conducted by Governor Pickens.[286]

The regiment remained in Richmond for a few weeks before moving on to Centreville and, later, to Fairfax Court House.[287] On May 24, the regiment marched to Manassas Junction and then back to Fairfax.[288] Gregg's regiment, Captain Delaware Kemper's Alexandria Artillery and two cavalry troops were sent to the nearby village of Vienna Station to meet an anticipated Federal advance coming from the direction of Alexandria. Company B of Gregg's regiment provided support for the artillery, and Companies A and E acted as skirmishers when Kemper's Artillery ambushed Companies C, E, G and H of the 1st Ohio Volunteers aboard a Federal troop train near Vienna Station on June 17.[289] The regiment left Fairfax for Richmond on July 2 or July 3 and arrived there on the fourth.[290] When the regiment's term of enlistment expired on July 9, the men mustered out of service. Gregg and his men planned a trip home to South Carolina, where they would reorganize and return to Virginia in about two weeks.[291]

During this period, President Davis authorized Colonel Gregg either to raise a "new" 1st SCV Regiment or reorganize his old regiment under the original name. Field officers—Colonel Gregg, Lieutenant Colonel Hamilton and Major Smith—were to retain their commissions. Companies of the regiment began the return to Richmond in July; three were encamped near the city by mid-month.[292] Part of Company I left Charleston for Virginia on July 25.[293] Company H arrived at Richmond on August 4 and camped first at the Old Fair Grounds, later at the New Fair Grounds and finally at the Rocketts.[294] Detachments of Company L left Charleston for the training camp at Lightwood Knot Springs on August 26, August 29 and September 2; but most of the company remained in Charleston until October 3, when they left to join the regiment at Suffolk.[295] By August 12, most of the elements were in Virginia, and by the middle of the month the new regiment was ready. It comprised the original field officers and eleven of its twelve companies, some original and the rest new. Eight full and two partial companies were in camp at Fulton Hill, near Chimborazo just outside Richmond, by August 27.[296] About two weeks later, on September 15, the regiment left Richmond for Suffolk in the Tidewater area of Virginia, and it remained inactive at Camp Huger until February 1862.[297]

Gregg was promoted to brigadier general in December 1861, and he returned to South Carolina to organize a brigade. The 1st Regiment, now under the command of Colonel Hamilton, spent a brief period—February to April—at Goldsboro, North Carolina, before returning to Suffolk only to leave again in April or May.[298] The regiment moved to Guiney's Station near Fredericksburg, and by May 22, it was stationed at Massaponax Hills, about five miles from Fredericksburg. The 1st Regiment and Orr's regiment of rifles joined Maxcy Gregg's Brigade—the 12th, 13th and 14th Regiments—along the Nine Mile Road below Richmond in late May 1862. The brigade was present, though not engaged, at the battle of Seven Pines on May 31 and June 1. The brigade marched to the Meadow Bridge on the Chickahominy River on June 25, and it crossed the river the next day, just before the Seven Days battles. The brigade was under artillery and small arms fire while in reserve at Mechanicsville on Thursday, June 26.[299] On the twenty-fifth, the 14th Regiment remained behind on picket duty along the Chickahominy River and was not present with the rest of the brigade on the twenty-sixth.[300] On the twenty-seventh, Gregg's Brigade opened the battle of Gaines's Mill and suffered heavy casualties. The 14th Regiment arrived on the field late in the afternoon of the twenty-seventh after the brigade took the Federal works at Beaverdam Creek, but it was engaged at Gaines's Mill.[301] The 13th Regiment was only lightly engaged that day.[302] A marble marker, the Standard Bearers Tablet, was placed in the South Carolina statehouse rotunda in 1897 in memory of the four color bearers from the 1st Regiment who were shot down at Gaines's Mill. On Saturday, June 28, the men rested and took care of the brigade's 829 casualties from the day before. The next day, the brigade crossed the Chickahominy River but did not participate in the engagement at Savage's Station.[303] The troops did fight at Frayser's Farm on Monday, June 30, but only the 14th Regiment suffered significant casualties. Though not actually engaged at Malvern Hill on Tuesday, July 1, the brigade endured two hours of general shelling.[304] The brigade performed picket duty near Malvern Hill for the next week and then rested in camp near Laurel Church on the New Market Road seven miles below Richmond until late July. On August 1, the brigade moved via Richmond by rail to Gordonsville, and on the sixth, it marched northward toward Orange Court House. On August 9, the brigade was left to guard the wagon trains near Culpeper Court House and for that reason was not engaged at the battle of Cedar Mountain. The brigade left its bivouac on August 16 to begin the Maryland campaign, but it was not engaged during the artillery duel on August 21. It began the march toward the Rappahannock River on August 22, and on the twenty-fourth, it provided infantry support to artillery engaged in a duel with the Federals near Warrenton Springs Ford. Part of Jackson's flanking march on August 25, the brigade crossed through Thoroughfare Gap in the Bull Run Mountains on the twenty-sixth.

Gregg's Brigade arrived at Manassas Junction early in the morning of August 27 but was not engaged that day. It crossed Bull Run to Centreville in the early morning hours of the twenty-eighth, then it recrossed to take up its position in an unfinished railroad cut near the Warrenton Turnpike. The brigade was not engaged there on the twenty-eighth, but it moved farther to the right that evening. On August 29, at the battle of Second Manassas, the brigade was heavily engaged at its railroad cut position, but it was held in reserve on the thirtieth and suffered only a few casualties from stray shells and balls that day.[305] The brigade participated in the pursuit of Federal units the next day. Orr's Rifles and the 12th, 13th and 14th Regiments were engaged at Chantilly, or Ox Hill, on September 1. The 1st Regiment was also present and under fire, though not actively engaged, at Chantilly.[306]

Gregg's Brigade crossed the Potomac River into Maryland on September 5 and rested at Frederick City, Maryland, until the tenth. On September 11, the brigade recrossed the river into Virginia at Williamsport and arrived at Harpers Ferry on the thirteenth. On the night of September 14, the brigade was positioned at Bolivar Heights near Harpers Ferry. It was preparing to attack when the Federal garrison surrendered on the fifteenth. Gregg's Brigade lost no men in that affair. The brigade marched toward Shepherdstown the next day but countermarched to Harpers Ferry. It crossed the Potomac at Boteler's Ford about two in the afternoon of September 17 and was engaged at Sharpsburg later that afternoon. The 14th Regiment was posted behind a stone fence on the right of the brigade, but it was not actively engaged then.[307] Gregg's Brigade remained on the battlefield during the night of the seventeenth and all the next day. Late on the eighteenth, the brigade recrossed the river into Virginia at Boteler's Ford, arriving on the morning of the nineteenth. Two companies—E and G—of the 14th Regiment were engaged in rear guard action on the Maryland side of the Potomac River on September 19.[308] Gregg's Brigade was engaged in driving McLellan's army from the Virginia side of the river at Shepherdstown Ford, or Boteler's Ford, on the twentieth. The 14th Regiment suffered most of the brigade's casualties that day, while the 1st Regiment received only shellfire.[309] Caldwell's description is grim: "It is difficult to describe the condition of the troops at this time, so great and various was their wretchedness. They now stood, an emaciated, limping, ragged, filthy mass, whom no stranger to their valiant exploits could have believed capable of anything the least worthy."[310]

The brigade spent about a week at Martinsburg, Virginia, before moving on to Bunker Hill, a distance of about twelve miles. It was part of the force that destroyed the Baltimore and Ohio Railroad near Berryville in late October. The brigade might have skirmished at Snicker's Gap on October 30, and its men were present but not engaged during an artillery exchange at Castleman's Ferry on the Shenandoah River on November 2. On the twenty-second, the brigade left its camps near Berryville and Winchester and marched 175 miles over the next twelve days to Massaponax Hills near Fredericksburg, arriving on December 3.[311] At the battle of Fredericksburg on the thirteenth, Orr's Rifles held a position on the right of Gregg's Brigade but was routed during the assault that temporarily broke the lines of A.P. Hill's Division.[312] The 1st (McCreary's) Regiment stopped the Federal thrust pouring through the gap in Hill's lines.[313] Gregg himself was mortally wounded in this action. The brigade wintered at Camp Gregg near Moss Neck below Fredericksburg on the Rappahannock River until late April 1863. On April 29, the brigade left its camp and marched to Fredericksburg. It marched up the Rappahannock River toward Chancellorsville on May 1 and entered the lines under light artillery fire. Orr's Rifles and the 14th Regiment were the only regiments of the brigade engaged that day. The next day, the brigade participated in Jackson's march around Hooker's unprotected right flank. During Jackson's advance in the late afternoon and evening of May 2, McGowan's Brigade was exposed to artillery and small arms fire but was primarily held in reserve.[314] The 12th Regiment was detached to guard the ordnance trains and prisoners on May 2. The 12th Regiment remained detached while the rest of the brigade was heavily engaged at Chancellorsville on May 3.[315] It remained in the breastworks there until the sixth, when the men left to return to camp at Moss Neck. About a month later, the brigade left Moss Neck and returned to the old lines near Fredericksburg. It remained there until June 14. It moved up the Rappahannock River and started its westward march on the fifteenth. After crossing the Potomac into Maryland on June 25, the brigade moved into Pennsylvania, arriving in Cashtown on June 30. The men marched toward Gettysburg on July 1 and were heavily engaged there all day, finally occupying the town. Orr's Rifle Regiment was left behind to guard the wagon trains and prisoners at the mountain pass where the brigade had encamped the previous night.[316] For that reason, Orr's regiment was not present at Gettysburg on July 1 and 2. The Battalion of Sharpshooters and McCreary's 1st Regiment were engaged as skirmishers on the second, and two companies of the 12th Regiment were engaged in driving back a Federal line of battle on Seminary Ridge.[317] The rest of the brigade, except for Orr's Rifles, endured shellfire on the field but was not engaged that day. Orr's Rifles rejoined the brigade on July 3. The full brigade was on the battle line under shellfire and heavy skirmishing but was not otherwise engaged as it observed Pickett's Charge on July 3.[318] It remained on the field until about midnight on July 4 when it withdrew toward Hagerstown, Maryland. The brigade reached Hagerstown on July 7 and established a battle line. Light skirmishing followed from July 11 to July 13. The men were surprised by Federal cavalry at Falling Waters, Maryland, on July 14. Later that day, after engaging the enemy, the brigade crossed the Potomac River into Virginia.[319] For the next ten days, it marched by stages to Culpeper Court House, arriving there on July 25. On August 1, while on picket duty, the 14th Regiment skirmished with Federal cavalry near Culpeper. The brigade marched on to Orange Court House, where it arrived on the fourth. It was assigned to picket duty at Barnett's Ford on the Rapidan River about every twentieth day. Though the brigade provided support to the cavalry and the 12th Regiment skirmished some on September 25, the brigade was not generally engaged at Liberty Mills on the Rapidan River. It crossed the Rapidan on October 9, marched through Culpeper Court House, and lay in line of battle, but it was not engaged in the action that followed at Bristoe Station on the fourteenth. The brigade then marched back by stages and recrossed the Rappahannock on October 19. The men camped along the river, performed picket duty and tore up the Alexandria and Orange Railroad until November 1, when the 1st Regiment was sent to round up deserters in the Blue Ridge Mountains of Virginia. The brigade was not engaged on the Rappahannock River on either November 8 or November 9, but it did withdraw its camp to Orange Court House, where it remained until early December.

On November 27, the brigade left its camps and marched toward Fredericksburg, but it was not engaged that afternoon. Though it participated in skirmishes, including one involving the 12th Regiment about three miles from Verdiersville, and drew picket duty until December 2, the brigade was not generally engaged during the Mine Run campaign. On December 3, the men returned to winter quarters near Orange Court House. There they performed picket duty along the Rapidan River. The brigade was called out twice that winter in response to Federal cavalry raids—once on February 7 and again for Dahlgren's Raid in March—but it was not engaged either time. In February 1864, all five regiments of the brigade passed resolutions declaring they would never lay down their arms until the independence of the South was recognized. Leaving its encampment on May 4, 1864, the brigade began the march toward the Wilderness. It was heavily engaged the next day from about four in the afternoon until nightfall, and the 1st Regiment found itself fighting alone for part of that time. Orr's Rifles was detached from the brigade on May 6 and was engaged on the extreme left of the Confederate lines. Having fought hard from sunrise, the rest of the brigade was forced to give ground before Longstreet's corps arrived on the field. The brigade remained on the field all the next day. On the evening of the eighth, it marched for Spotsylvania Court House and bivouacked that night at Shady Grove Church.[320] McGowan's Brigade was not engaged at Brock's Crossroads on May 8. The brigade arrived at Spotsylvania Court House about noon on May 9; the men entrenched on the extreme right of the Confederate line but were not engaged that day. Light skirmishing and some shelling followed on May 10. The brigade moved to its left the next day, and there it was involved in a few skirmishes. On May 12, McGowan's Brigade quickly moved further to the left to help recapture Confederate trenches that had been overrun earlier that morning. The firing went on until after midnight. A large oak about twenty inches in diameter, weakened by incessant rifle fire throughout the day, fell on the 1st Regiment about ten that evening. Several men were hurt. Just after daylight on May 13, McGowan's Brigade was withdrawn to an inner line of works. The brigade remained in the lines around Spotsylvania Court House, where there was some skirmishing but no significant engagement until the twenty-second, when it marched toward the North Anna River. The brigade saw action at Jericho Ford on the North Anna River, part of the Overland campaign, on May 23.[321] That evening, the men marched to Hanover Junction, where they engaged in some light skirmishing. The brigade lay under artillery fire in the lines at Hanover Junction on the twenty-fourth and twenty-fifth, then it marched and skirmished from May 27 until it reached the vicinity of Cold Harbor on May 31. Though the brigade took the field, it was not actively engaged in the battle of Cold Harbor beyond a few minor skirmishes over the first three days of June. The brigade crossed the Chickahominy River on June 13, moved toward the old battlefield of Frayser's Farm, and was lightly engaged at Riddell's Shop.

On June 18, the brigade crossed the James River at Drewry's Bluff and moved by rail and by foot to Petersburg, where the men were deployed at the extreme right of the Confederate lines but not actually engaged that day. The brigade was lightly engaged near the Weldon Railroad on the twenty-first. The men were held in support the next day but lost about thirty men to shellfire while lying down on the field. The brigade continued to occupy the Petersburg lines and to deal with light skirmishing until the end of June. The brigade was withdrawn from the Petersburg lines after dark on June 29 or June 30 and marched all night, crossing to the north side of the James River at Chaffin's Bluff and entering the lines near Fort Harrison. The brigade was engaged at Deep Bottom on July 28.[322] During late July and early August, the brigade remained on the north side of the river in the fortifications near the fort. On August 11, the brigade moved toward Dutch Gap, where it was shelled the next day. Skirmishing and shelling continued for two days, August 13 and August 14, just before the brigade's active engagement at the battle of Fussell's Mill on August 16.[323] Skirmishing continued on the seventeenth. About August 20, the brigade crossed to the south side of the James River. There, the men were posted on the extreme right of the Confederate lines on the Weldon Railroad below Petersburg. The brigade marched down the Weldon Railroad on August 24 and was lightly engaged at Reams Station about nine miles below Petersburg on the twenty-fifth. The men returned to the trenches the next day for about a month of relative quiet, consisting mainly of picket duty and daily work on the entrenchments. After this respite, the brigade was withdrawn from the trenches on September 30 and marched through Petersburg toward Richmond. In a sudden course reversal, the men were sent to the Boydton Plank Road about four miles south of Petersburg. The brigade was engaged at Poplar Spring Church (also called Jones's Farm, Peebles's Farm and Pegram's Farm) on September 30, though only Dunlop's Sharpshooters skirmished there on October 1.[324] On October 2, the brigade entrenched near Jones's Farm and went into winter quarters. It was not engaged during the battle near Hatcher's Run on October 27, nor for the whole month of November, but on December 8, it marched down the Boydton Plank Road toward Dinwiddie Court House, where it unsuccessfully pursued a body of Federal infantry and cavalry. After about a week, the brigade returned to winter quarters, where the men were occupied with picket duty and improving the breastworks and field fortifications.

The brigade marched toward the right of the Confederate line on February 5, 1865, but was not engaged at Hatcher's Run from February 5 to February 7. While it did not participate in the attack on Fort Stedman on March 25, the brigade was engaged in the Petersburg lines that day. Some skirmishing and sharpshooting followed on March 26. Dunlop's Sharpshooter Battalion of the brigade was the only unit in the brigade to be engaged at McIlwaine's Hill the next day. The brigade marched toward Hatcher's Run on the evening of March 29. It skirmished about one and a half miles south of Hatcher's Run on the thirtieth, and it was heavily engaged at Gravelly Run the following day. The brigade left its fortified positions and marched toward Dinwiddie Court House on April 1, but it soon returned without engagement. The brigade dealt with light picket firing that grew in intensity as the afternoon and evening wore on. On April 2, the brigade was engaged in the trenches, and then it evacuated its fieldworks and marched across Hatcher's Run toward Sutherland's Station on the South Side Railroad. Later that day during the withdrawal from Petersburg, it saw action near the station. Overwhelming odds in favor of Federal forces forced the men to withdraw from the battlefield in a disorderly retreat. The brigade rested along the Appomattox River the night of April 2, and the next day it moved, still in a disorganized fashion, along the river toward Amelia Court House.

On the fourth and most of the fifth, with order somewhat restored, the brigade continued its march toward Amelia Court House. Marching toward Farmville on April 6, the brigade fell under artillery fire and intermittent skirmishing. After an all-night march, the brigade reached Farmville on April 7. The men were not engaged that day and were able to cross to the north side of the Appomattox River at Farmville. After marching most of the night toward Lynchburg, the brigade bivouacked about four to five miles east of Appomattox Court House on the morning of April 8. The following day, the brigade marched toward Appomattox Court House, where the Army of Northern Virginia surrendered. The men of the brigade laid down their arms and started the long journey back home on April 12, 1865.

3.

The 2nd Regiment, South Carolina Volunteers

The 2nd Regiment, SCV, also called the 2nd South Carolina Infantry and the 2nd Palmetto Regiment, was authorized under the Act of December 17, 1860, calling for ten regiments of volunteers for twelve months' service in the state. According to the *Mercury*, organization of the regiment was complete on March 12, 1861.[1] It was received into state service on April 9.[2] Soon after the fall of Fort Sumter on April 13, President Davis and Governor Pickens asked the men of the first ten South Carolina regiments, along with Gregg's six-month regiment, to volunteer for Confederate service in Virginia. Four companies of the 2nd Regiment—A, C, D and E—agreed to go and mustered in Confederate service in Virginia on May 22 and May 23.[3] The six remaining companies, numbering about 540 men, chose to stay in South Carolina under the command of Lieutenant Colonel Blanding, thus permanently dividing the regiment. Three of the six became the nucleus of Blanding's regiment, which was initially known as the 2nd Regiment but by August had been designated the 9th Regiment, SCV.[4] The last three companies were dispersed in various ways: one mustered in Gregg's regiment, another mustered in the Hampton Legion and the third became part of the 12th Regiment, SCV.

Meanwhile, Kershaw led four companies to Virginia, where he added six new companies for the full complement of ten to make up his regiment. At the expiration of the original term of service, about May 13, 1862, the men of Kershaw's 2nd Regiment, along with his entire brigade, re-enlisted for two more years. In March 1864, they re-enlisted again, this time for the duration of the war. On April 9, 1865, the 2nd Regiment was consolidated with the 20th Regiment, SCV, and elements of Blanchard's 1st, 2nd, 6th and 7th South Carolina Reserve Battalions to form the 2nd South Carolina Infantry Regiment, Consolidated, also called the (New) 2nd Regiment, South Carolina Infantry.[5] The new regiment was paroled as the 2nd South Carolina Infantry on May 2, 1865, at Greensboro, North Carolina.

FIELD OFFICERS

Joseph Brevard Kershaw of Camden in Kershaw District served as an officer in the Mexican War and was a member of the Secession Convention. Kershaw was elected colonel with no opposition on February 2, 1861, and was promoted to brigadier general with rank from February 15, 1862, when Brigadier General Milledge L. Bonham resigned.[6] Kershaw was dropped from the rolls of the 2nd Regiment at the reorganization on May 13, 1862, since he was no longer its colonel. He was promoted to major general on May 18, 1864. Kershaw played a distinguished role in the Army of Northern Virginia from Manassas until his capture at Sayler's Creek on April 6, 1865. He was taken to Fort Warren in Boston Harbor and released on July 24. His only war wound was a slight injury to the right arm sustained at Fredericksburg on December 13, 1862. Kershaw was popular among the troops. One of his men wrote: "There is not a man in [the regiment] who would not follow him to death."[7]

James Douglass Blanding of Sumter raised Company D, the Sumter Volunteers.[8] Blanding defeated William Wallace, captain of Company C, in the election for lieutenant colonel on February 2, 1861.[9] His commission dated from April 8, when the regiment entered state service. Blanding commanded the six companies of the 2nd Regiment, which chose not to go to Virginia in April 1861. When three of the six companies joined other organizations that summer, seven companies were recruited to make up the 9th Regiment, SCV, effective July 12, 1861. Lieutenant Colonel Blanding commanded this organization, also called the 2nd Regiment, SCV, and was elected colonel when it was redesignated the 9th Regiment, SCV.[10]

Dixon Barnes of Lancaster District defeated Artemas D. Goodwyn in the election for major of the regiment on February 2, 1861.[11] The original captain of the Lancaster Grays, Barnes remained in South Carolina when four companies went to Virginia in May 1861.[12] He was elected lieutenant colonel of the 9th Regiment, SCV, on July 5. When new elections for field officers were held on the twelfth, Companies A, B and D—those attached to the original 2nd Regiment—voted nearly unanimously for Barnes as colonel; the seven new companies, however, swung the vote to Blanding.[13] Barnes left the 9th Regiment that summer to raise Company I of the 12th Regiment, SCV, and was elected captain on August 28, 1861.[14]

Ervin P. Jones, a lawyer from Greenville and previously a private in the Butler Guards, was elected lieutenant colonel, replacing Blanding, who remained in South Carolina. The election was probably held on May 16, but dates of the fifteenth and twenty-first are also recorded.[15] The election was not unanimous, but Ervin's opponent is not known.[16] Other sources show his name as Erwin and Ervine.[17] Jones was promoted to colonel in February 1862, when Kershaw was promoted to brigadier general. Wyckoff gives Jones's date of promotion as the second, while Salley records February 15.[18] Jones himself noted on September 20, 1864, that he was lieutenant colonel in early 1862 and rose to the rank of colonel when Kershaw made brigadier general.[19] Krick incorrectly lists Jones as holding the rank of lieutenant colonel only, and Warner wrote, also incorrectly, that J.D. Kennedy was colonel of the 2nd Regiment as early as January 1861.[20] Jones was not re-elected at the reorganization in May 1862, and he resigned on May 13. He was offered the position of lieutenant colonel in the 3rd Regiment, South Carolina Reserves, but he refused it.

Artemas Darby Goodwyn of Gadsden in Richland District was colonel of a Volunteer Battalion in November 1860.[21] This battalion was composed of five Columbia companies: the Richland Rifle Company, the Cedar Creek Riflemen, the Governor's Guards, the Emmett Guards and the Columbia Artillery. Goodwyn served as adjutant of the 2nd Regiment from February 2, 1861, until he was elected major in May, replacing Dixon Barnes.[22] The election date was probably May 16, but dates of the fifteenth, twenty-first and twenty-second also appear in the records.[23] Goodwyn's election was not unanimous.[24] Known to his friends as "Cuty," Goodwyn was elected lieutenant colonel at the reorganization on May 13, a date also shown as May 14, 1862.[25] A.S. Salley wrote that Goodwyn was promoted to lieutenant colonel on February 15, 1862. He received a disabling wound when a Minié ball struck him in the left ankle at Savage's Station on June 29, 1862. Goodwyn submitted a letter of resignation on June 3, 1863; he claimed physical disability and requested assignment to other duty appropriate to his rank. The resignation was accepted on July 15. Goodwyn was elected colonel of the 3rd Regiment, South Carolina Junior Reserves, in the fall of 1864 and commanded the brigade to which it was assigned until the end of the war. Wyckoff spells his Christian name as Artemus.[26]

William H. Casson's record is interesting but confusing. Casson, of Richland District, was captain of Company A and, though the *CSR* does not record a date for promotion to major, two notes in the *CSR* refer to him as such.[27] Wyckoff indicates that Casson was promoted to major but gives no date.[28] He also records that First Lieutenant Malcolm A. Shelton of Company A was promoted to captain on March 11, 1862, implying that a vacancy existed because of Casson's promotion to major.[29] A.S. Salley says Casson was promoted on March 15, 1862.[30] Lieutenant Shelton appears on the muster rolls for March and April 1862 as captain, and there are several references in the *CSR* to him at that rank. Shelton, however, was dropped from the rolls on May 13, 1862, as first lieutenant of Company A. Gaillard wrote that the men refused to serve further under Captain Casson and did not re-elect him at the reorganization. Probably, Casson acted as major before the reorganization in 1862 but was never officially promoted to that rank. He later served in the 8th Regiment, SCV, and with the railroad service.[31] Franklin Gaillard wrote: "The men are very much dissatisfied with Capt. Casson, through duplicity and insincerity and other qualities, equally uncommendable, he has become very unpopular. I never was more disappointed in any man. The consequence is that they have signified to me that they will not serve again under him."[32] In a conflicting opinion, Ellison Capers wrote that Casson was a gallant survivor of the 2nd Regiment.[33]

John Doby Kennedy of Camden in Kershaw District was captain of Company E until May 14, 1862, when he was elected colonel of the 2nd Regiment. His commission was dated May 13. Wyckoff incorrectly records that Kennedy was promoted to colonel on February 2, 1862, replacing Kershaw.[34] Warner wrote, also incorrectly, that Kennedy was colonel as early as January 1861.[35] Kennedy was wounded six times. Initially, he was wounded at First Manassas, then at Harpers Ferry on September 13, 1862, and then in the instep and achilles tendon at Sharpsburg four days later; he also received a slight wound to the hip and a severe wound in the hand at Gettysburg, was seriously wounded in the shoulder at Knoxville and he sustained a severe wound to the right shoulder and nearly bled to death when he commanded the brigade at the battle of the Wilderness on May 6, 1864.[36] He was also struck by fifteen spent balls at various times during the war. Kennedy was promoted to brigadier general on December 22, 1864. Dickert wrote: "J.D. Kennedy was a very good officer, however his kindness of heart, his sympathetic nature, his indulgent disposition caused him to be rather lax in discipline." He had "the entire confidence of the troops, and was dearly loved by both officers and men."[37] Kennedy was paroled on May 2, 1865, at Greensboro.

Franklin Gaillard was born in Pineville but was living in Columbia and editing the *Carolinian* at the outbreak of the war. He was first lieutenant of Company A before the reorganization and was elected major on May 14, 1862.[38] A.S. Salley states that Gaillard was elected captain of Company A and major of the regiment on May 13 and accepted the office of major.[39] Gaillard was slightly wounded in the chin and severely in the foot at

Fredericksburg.[40] He was promoted to lieutenant colonel on June 3, 1863, when Goodwyn resigned. Gaillard often led the regiment when Colonel Kennedy was on furlough recovering from his wounds. When Kennedy was wounded at the Wilderness, Gaillard commanded the regiment briefly; after mounting the breastworks to get a better view of the enemy lines, he was shot in the forehead as he stepped back among the men in the trenches. Carried about two hundred yards to the rear by litter, Gaillard lingered for only a short while before he died.[41] Dickert wrote: "He was an accomplished gentleman, a brave soldier, a trusted and impartial officer, a peer of any in Kershaw's Brigade."[42]

William W. Wallace, a lawyer and planter in Columbia before the war, was promoted from captain of Company C to major on June 3, 1863, to replace Gaillard when Goodwyn resigned. Wallace was severely wounded in the arm the next month at Gettysburg. Wallace was promoted to lieutenant colonel on June 28, 1864, with rank from the date of Gaillard's death, May 6.[43] He was wounded in the right foot at Charlestown, Virginia, on September 13, 1864. Wallace was made colonel at the consolidation of the 2nd and 20th Regiments on April 8, 1865, and was paroled on May 2 at Greensboro. Dickert wrote: "Upon the battleline he was brave almost to rashness," and "Colonel Wallace was a soldier born and a leader of men."[44] William W. Wallace should not be confused with William Henry Wallace, colonel of the 18th Regiment, SCV, and later a brigadier general.

Benjamin R. Clyburn of Lancaster District was promoted to major on August 10, 1864, with rank from May 6. Clyburn was promoted from captain of Company H as the replacement for Wallace. He was elected to the General Assembly in the fall of 1864 while on active duty.[45] A Minié ball shattered the lower third of Clyburn's left femur at Cedar Creek on October 19, 1864. The *Lancaster Ledger* reported that his leg was amputated, and he was captured while waiting in an ambulance for removal to the rear.[46] The *CSR* indicates that Clyburn was captured and his leg was amputated later that day at the United States Army Depot Field Hospital in Winchester, Virginia. He was sent to the United States Army General Hospital in Baltimore on December 30 and was moved on January 10, 1865, to prison at Fort Delaware. He was paroled and exchanged at City Point, Virginia, on February 27. One veteran wrote that Clyburn's "bravery is beyond all praise."[47]

James Dupre Graham of Sumter was promoted from captain of Company D to lieutenant colonel of the Consolidated 2nd and 20th Regiments, SCV, on April 8, 1865. He was paroled at Greensboro on May 2.

Godfrey Leaphart of Lexington District was promoted from captain of Company C of the 20th Regiment to major of the Consolidated 2nd

Regiment about April 8, 1865. He was paroled as major of the (New) 2nd Regiment on May 2.

COMPANIES

Descriptions of the six companies that refused to go to Virginia in May 1861 follow. They were originally attached to the 2nd Regiment when it was in state service, and they all joined other regiments that summer. On April 11, 1861, the *Mercury* named five as belonging to the 2nd Regiment, the exception being the DeKalb Guards.[48] The six companies were designated B, F, G, H, I and K. The letter designations, however, cannot be matched to the individual companies.

The DeKalb Rifle Guards, commanded by Captain Thomas Lang Boykin, was made up of men from Camden in Kershaw District.[49] The company was also called the DeKalb Rifles and the DeKalb Guards.[50] A detachment of the Camden Rifle Guards, a prewar organization, formed the DeKalb Rifle Guards and joined Kershaw's 2nd Regiment early in the war.[51] After refusing to go to Virginia with Kershaw, the men mustered in Maxcy Gregg's 1st (six-month) Regiment as Company N about May 1, 1861. The fact that the company joined Maxcy Gregg's regiment, which, at the time, was recruiting companies for service in Virginia, suggests there was a strong sentiment among many of the guards to go to Virginia with Kershaw. Why, in the end, they refused to go to Virginia with Kershaw but went instead with Gregg is unclear.[52] The company left for Virginia on May 8, 1861.[53] Gregg's six-month Regiment disbanded on July 9, 1861, and many of the DeKalb Guards mustered in Company D, 15th Regiment, SCV.[54]

The Lancaster Grays of Lancaster District, organized from the Upper Battalion of the 21st Regiment, South Carolina Militia on November 11, 1860, was originally commanded by Dixon Barnes.[55] The *Mercury* gives the company name as the Lancaster Greys.[56] John D. Wylie commanded the company after Barnes was elected major in February 1861.[57] This company remained with Blanding and became Company A, 9th Regiment, SCV.

The Richland Guards was raised in the nullification days by the father of Edwin F. Bookter, who commanded the company in early 1861.[58] Most of the men were from Richland District. When the 2nd Regiment went to Virginia, Captain Bookter and his men returned home, reorganized the company and mustered in as Company D, 12th Regiment, SCV, on August 28, 1861.

The Salem Company, also called the Chicora Guards, was made up of men from Sumter, Clarendon and Williamsburg Districts and was commanded by S.D.M. LaCoste.[59] The company was organized on April 8, 1861.[60] After about five weeks on Morris Island near Charleston, the company was disbanded.[61] It must have been reorganized, however, since it remained with Blanding and became Company D, 9th Regiment, SCV, in the summer of 1861.

The States Rights Guards, also known as the Fork Troop, was made up of men from Richland District.[62] This company, commanded by Duncan William Ray, also remained with Blanding and became Company B of the 9th Regiment in July 1861.[63] According to a sketch in *Recollections and Reminiscences*, the men were from the lower part of Richland District.[64]

The Claremont Rifles, from Darlington and Sumter Districts, was commanded by James G. "Ransom" Spann.[65] This company mustered in the Hampton Legion as Company G shortly after July 29, 1861.[66]

The following ten companies made up the 2nd Regiment after it entered Confederate service in April 1861. They included the four original companies—A, C, D and E—which went to Virginia in April 1861, as well as the six new companies added to the regiment in late April and early May 1861. These ten companies did not change at the reorganization in the spring of 1862.

Company A, the Governor's Guards, was one of the four original companies in Kershaw's regiment. Its members came from Columbia in Richland District, and some later recruits came from Pickens District. The company was organized in 1843.[67] It was part of A.D. Goodwyn's Volunteer Battalion in Columbia in November 1860, and of the 23rd Regiment, South Carolina Militia, in January 1861.[68] The governor accepted the company in state service on January 5. William H. Casson, who commanded the company before the war, was re-elected captain on April 8, when the regiment was called into state service. About thirty-two men of the Governor's Guards refused to serve in Virginia and remained with Blanding's detachment of the regiment on Morris Island in April 1861.[69] The remainder mustered in Confederate service for twelve months at Richmond on May 22; Casson's commission as captain in Confederate service dated from the same day. There is some evidence that Casson was promoted to major in March 1862.[70] Wyckoff records that First Lieutenant Malcolm A. Shelton was promoted to captain on March 11, 1862, implying that a vacancy existed because of Casson's promotion to major.[71] Shelton's muster rolls for March and April 1862 listed him as captain, but he was dropped from the rolls of the 2nd Regiment on May 13, 1862, with the rank of first lieutenant. Lieutenant Sherod Luther Leaphart was elected captain on May 13, 1862.[72] The *CSR* gives the name also as Samuel and Sherard. Leaphart was wounded at Sharpsburg on September 17, 1862, and wounded and captured at Gettysburg on July 2, 1863; his right arm was amputated as a result of the Gettysburg wound.[73] Leaphart was moved from Pennsylvania to Fort McHenry, Maryland, on August 24 and to the federal prison at Johnson's Island, Ohio, on September 28.[74] He was sent to Point Lookout Prison in Maryland on March 14, 1865, and was probably exchanged from there.[75] Leaphart was paroled at Augusta, Georgia, on May 25. Moses M. Maddrey was the company's last captain. Wounded at Chickamauga, he was elected on March 7, 1864, and was promoted to captain later, probably after Leaphart was exchanged in March 1865. Maddrey was paroled on May 2, 1865, at Greensboro.

Company B, the Butler Guards, was from Greenville District and named for General Pierce Butler, a Mexican War hero.[76] It existed before the war as a volunteer corps attached to the South Carolina Militia and tendered its services to the state on December 4, 1860. It was called into state service on April 15, 1861, as Company A of the 4th Regiment, SCV. Though men of the Butler Guards wanted to serve in Virginia, the 4th Regiment was in camp in Columbia at the time. The Butler Guards requested and received a transfer into the 2nd Regiment and left to join it in Virginia on May 6, 1861.[77] Between May 16 and June 24, the Butler Guards was officially transferred out of the 4th Regiment, which did not get to Virginia until late June.[78] The company mustered in Confederate service at Richmond for twelve months on May 22, 1861. Augustus Dewitt "Gus" Hoke, a Greenville physician who had attended The Citadel, raised the company and served as its first captain.[79] Hoke might also have served as major of the 4th Regiment in the spring of 1861. Hoke sustained a severe wound when his right arm was fractured at First Manassas on July 21. He was briefly captured but escaped from Federal troops while still on the battlefield.[80] Because the wound rendered him unfit for field service, Hoke resigned at the reorganization on May 13, 1862, and returned to Greenville to resume his medical practice. Lieutenant Robert C. Pulliam was elected captain on May 13 and was shot in the head at Gettysburg on July 2, 1863, a wound that was not initially thought fatal. Pulliam deteriorated overnight, however, and died in a hospital near the battlefield the next day.[81] "[U]niversally beloved by all who knew him," Pulliam's death was "a severe and heavy blow upon the corps."[82] First Lieutenant William Robert Powell, also a Citadel man, was promoted to captain on July 4.[83] Powell was slightly wounded by spent grapeshot at Gettysburg and again in the face and neck by a Minié ball at the North Anna Bridge on May 23, 1864.[84] He was paroled on May 2, 1865, at Greensboro. Several sources say Jacob W. Cagle also commanded the company as captain.[85] Second Lieutenant Cagle had been severely wounded in the calf at Gettysburg and was captured during the withdrawal but managed to escape.[86] Cagle was still a second lieutenant in July 1864, and was paroled at Greensboro on May 2, 1865. It is possible, though not documented, that he was promoted to captain in the Consolidated 2nd Regiment on April 8, 1865.

Company C, the Columbia Grays, was also called the Richland Grays and the Columbia Greys.[87] It was organized on January 5 and accepted for state service on January 7, 1861.[88] Company C was one of the original companies in the 2nd Regiment. It mustered in state service on April 8 and in Confederate service for twelve months on May 23, 1861, near Richmond. Most of the men were from Richland District and had been part of the Upper Battalion of the 23rd Regiment, South Carolina Militia, though a few men came from the districts of Fairfield, Kershaw, Union, Horry, Darlington, Lexington, Greenville, Pickens and Clarendon. William W. Wallace, a general in the South Carolina Militia, raised the company and was elected captain on January 8, 1861. He enlisted in state service as captain on April 8, 1861. Wallace was slightly wounded in the cheek at First Manassas.[89] After the battle of Fredericksburg, Kershaw wrote of Wallace: "No braver man ever trod the field of battle."[90] He was promoted to major and First Lieutenant Solomon Lorick was promoted to captain on June 3, 1863. Lorick had been seriously wounded in the face at Sharpsburg on September 17, 1862. He was left permanently disfigured and with a facial paralysis that prevented him from closing his right eye, but he returned and fought with the regiment at Chancellorsville in May 1863. On May 23, a medical board of examiners recommended that Lorick be placed on light duty in response to his plea that "the warm weather was too much for me."[91] Only four days after he was promoted to captain, Lorick was sent from a Richmond hospital to Columbia. On September 20, he requested a transfer to the enrolling department and was assigned to enrolling duty in the conscription department in Columbia on September 24. After a month in the conscription department, Lorick accepted the rank of lieutenant and the assignment of drilling recruits at a camp of instruction.[92] Seeking retirement, Lorick applied for permission to appear before a medical board of examiners on June 11, 1864, but he was still serving in the conscription department as late as December. He did not return to Company C after the summer of 1863, and he retired to the Invalid Corps on February 2, 1865. He was assigned to duty at Columbia on February 6, 1865. Anderson Patterson Vinson was elected second lieutenant on October 8, 1863, and was promoted to first lieutenant on March 18, 1864. Vinson was wounded at Sharpsburg and again at Cedar Creek.[93] He was paroled as captain of Company C on May 2, 1865, at Greensboro.[94]

Company D, the Sumter Volunteers, was organized on January 7, 1861, in Sumter and mustered in state service on April 8. James D. Blanding raised the company which, ironically, did not remain with him in Charleston but went to Virginia with Kershaw.[95] Most of the men were from Sumter District, but a few came from Clarendon, Kershaw, Pickens and Darlington Districts.[96] John Smythe Richardson Jr. was the first captain; his commission was dated April 8, 1861. On May 9, he was elected major of the Western Battalion of Sumter's 20th Regiment, South Carolina Militia, an office that did not affect his position as captain of Company D.[97] Richardson was slightly wounded in the right arm at the battle of First Manassas on June 21. He was captured soon afterward but escaped.[98] The wound, and possibly an episode of jaundice in January 1862, left him disabled for further field service, and he resigned at the reorganization on May 13, 1862. Richardson subsequently served in the 23rd Regiment, SCV, as adjutant and assistant quartermaster, and he survived the war. On April 28, 1862, Sergeant Hugh R. Garden, a nephew of Captain Richardson and color bearer of the 2nd Regiment, recruited twenty-one of his fellow soldiers from the Sumter Volunteers to form the nucleus of a new independent artillery company called the Palmetto Light Battery.[99] Private Leonard White Bartlett was elected captain of Company D on May 13, 1862. He received wounds to the head and body at Savage's Station on June 29, and he died on July 1, 1862.[100] Major Gaillard wrote that Bartlett was "one of the most gallant and conscientious officers" in the 2nd Regiment.[101] First Lieutenant James Dupre Graham was promoted to captain, probably in late June or early July 1862. He was slightly wounded at Savage's Station and again at Gettysburg but remained with the company.[102] He received a flesh wound in the elbow at Chickamauga on September 20, 1863.[103] Graham was wounded again—a flesh wound in the left arm—while serving as acting lieutenant colonel at the battle of the Wilderness in May 1864.[104] He was admitted to the Officers' Hospital in Richmond on May 9, and he recovered.[105] Graham was promoted to lieutenant colonel of the Consolidated 2nd and 20th Regiment, SCV, on April 8, 1865. He was paroled at Greensboro on May 2.

Company E, the Camden Volunteers, was also called the Camden Light Infantry and the Kershaw Guards.[106] The company elected John Doby Kennedy captain as early as February 1860.[107] It was accepted by the governor on January 8, 1861, and was called into state service on April 9.[108] Most of the men were from Camden in Kershaw District, but a few came from Charleston, Anderson, Sumter and Newberry Districts. One of the original four companies to go to Virginia with Kershaw in May 1861, the Camden Volunteers mustered in Confederate service for twelve months near Richmond on May 23, 1861. John Doby Kennedy, commissioned the first captain on April 9, mustered in Confederate service as captain the same day. He was wounded at First Manassas and incapacitated by fever after Savage's Station. Kennedy was elected colonel on May 14, 1862. Wyckoff and Warner wrote that he was promoted to colonel in early 1862, raising the possibility that Kennedy may have been re-elected colonel in May. The *CSR* however, lists Kennedy as captain of Company E on the muster roll for April/May 1862, and a letter of recommendation in the *CSR* says he was promoted to colonel at the reorganization. First Lieutenant William Zachariah "Zack" Leitner was elected captain at the reorganization on May 13. While leading Company E at Gettysburg on July 2, 1863, canister shot wounded Leitner in the right leg. On hearing the news, his friend, brigade surgeon T.W. Salmond, left his post at the field hospital, rode to Leitner's aid and carried him off the field on his horse. The leg was amputated below the knee the next day.[109] Leitner was appointed enrolling officer for Kershaw District on October 31, and served in that capacity until at least September 16, 1864. He resigned effective August 13, 1864, on the grounds that he could no longer fill the position without serious injury to his health. Colonel John D. Kennedy recommended Leitner for a staff position on December 30, 1863. The last captain of Company E, Joseph J. Drakeford, was paroled at Greensboro on May 2, 1865.

Company F, the Secession Guards, was new to the 2nd Regiment in April 1861. It was also called Perryman's Company, the Abbeville Volunteers and the Abbeville Guards.[110] The Secession Guards had been organized on January 10, 1861, mostly with men from the towns of Greenwood, Ninety Six and New Market in the eastern part of Abbeville District, now Greenwood County; a few came from Richland and Laurens Districts.[111] The Secession Guards was originally Company A of the 7th Regiment, SCV, from January to April 28, 1861.[112] The company joined the 2nd Regiment on April 30 because the men wanted to serve in Virginia, and it became the right company of the 2nd Regiment.[113] The Secession Guards mustered in Confederate service in Richmond on May 23 for twelve months.[114] The company's original regiment, the 7th, was sent to Virginia in June. William Watson Perryman was elected captain on January 10 and mustered in state service on April 17. He was captain of the company in both the 7th and 2nd Regiments.[115] Re-elected on May 23, 1862, Perryman refused the office because he thought that allowing men to elect officers was subversive to good discipline. He left the regiment on June 1 but appears in the *CSR* as captain of Company F continuously on muster rolls through July and August 1863. By November 1862, Perryman was serving as enrolling officer in South Carolina's Second Congressional District. Colonel Jonathan J. Preston wrote that Perryman was "[t]he very best officer I have had on that duty. His intelligence, zeal, and industry, have been of the greatest benefit."[116] Incapacitated for further field service by typhoid fever on May 4, 1863, he was promoted to major in the Provisional Army of the Confederate States on June 5. One card in the *CSR* states he was promoted to colonel on September 10, 1864, and he was in command of the post and forces at Greenville, South Carolina, in January 1865. First Lieutenant George Marshall McDowell was promoted to captain on June 5, 1863. While under arrest for disobeying an order, he was mortally wounded at Gettysburg on July 2 and died the next day. McDowell was actually court-martialed posthumously. The court found him guilty and sentenced him to a private reprimand.[117] Alexander McNeil, lieutenant of Company F, wrote that McDowell was "[a] gallant soldier and in many respects a good officer."[118] Second Lieutenant William Calvin Vance was promoted to captain on July 3, replacing McDowell. Vance had been wounded during the Seven Days battles. He was also shot through the thigh at Bean's Station on December 14, 1863, and was wounded in the cheek at the Wilderness in May 1864.[119] Vance was paroled on May 2, 1865, at Greensboro.

Company G, the Flat Rock Guards, was organized on January 16, 1861, in Camden.[120] The men received orders to go to Virginia on April 24. They mustered in state service and left on the twenty-eighth, arriving in Richmond on April 30.[121] New to the 2nd Regiment, Company G was made up mostly of men from the Upper Battalion of Kershaw District's 22nd Regiment, South Carolina Militia, with a few from Lancaster District.[122] The company mustered in Confederate service for twelve months on May 22, 1861, near Richmond. Columbus Cureton Haile was commissioned captain on April 24. After receiving a head injury in a train accident, he was issued a twenty-one day sick furlough on December 19 and resigned at the reorganization on May 15, 1862. In 1862 and early 1863, Haile served as a captain in the 8th Regiment Reserves, and from July 1863 to February 1864, he served as captain of Company C of the 4th Regiment, South Carolina State Troops. Haile enlisted as a private in the 23rd Regiment, SCV, on February 1, 1864, and was elected lieutenant on March 7. He was captured on April 1, 1865, at Dinwiddie Court House, sent to Johnson's Island, Ohio, and released on June 18.[123] Dickert lists Thomas J. Clyburn as a captain of Company G. The *CSR* shows Clyburn as first lieutenant from April 24, 1861, but not as captain. He probably commanded the company in Haile's absence between December 1861 and May 1862, but there is no record that he ever actually held the rank of captain. Second Lieutenant Joseph P. Cunningham was elected to that post on May 13, 1862. He was mortally wounded in the knee at Gettysburg and died there on July 2, 1863. He was replaced by First Lieutenant Jesse Erasmus Truesdel on July 4, even though Truesdel himself had been seriously wounded in the neck two days earlier. When the 2nd and 20th Regiments were consolidated on April 8, 1865, Truesdel was not selected to command one of the new companies and was dropped from the rolls on April 21, 1865.

Company H, the Lancaster Invincibles, was organized on January 8, 1861, from the Lower Battalion of the 21st Regiment, South Carolina Militia.[124] Though most sources refer to the company as the Lancaster Invincibles, the company was known as the Lancaster Volunteers in early 1861; it was also called the Lancaster Guards.[125] Company H was made up of men from the town of Lancaster and the surrounding district. On April 28, 1861, the company entered state service and left its rendezvous site on foot for Camden, then traveled to Virginia by rail. The Lancaster Invincibles was new to the 2nd Regiment in late April 1861. The men mustered in for twelve months of Confederate service on May 22 near Richmond. Amos W. McManus, a veteran of the Mexican War, was elected captain on January 8; he enlisted in state service as captain on April 28.[126] Slightly wounded in the arm by a shell at First Manassas on July 21, McManus resigned on May 13, 1862, saying he was needed at home to fill the position of sheriff of Lancaster District. In July 1862, McManus attempted to raise a company of mounted men for the 1st Corps of Reserves, but whether or not this effort was successful is unclear.[127] The statue atop the Confederate monument in Lancaster was modeled after McManus. Lieutenant Benjamin R. Clyburn was elected captain on May 13, 1862.[128] He was wounded twice: slightly in the face at Sharpsburg and again, more seriously, at Gettysburg, where he sustained severe damage to the right leg and another slight facial wound on July 2, 1863.[129] Clyburn was promoted to major on August 10, 1864, with rank from May 6. James B. Horton was promoted to first lieutenant with rank from July 7, 1864, and to captain some time after that. He was slightly wounded at Sharpsburg and received a minor wound to the foot at Gettysburg.[130] Horton was paroled at Greensboro on May 2, 1865.

Company I, the Palmetto Guard, or Guards, was new to the 2nd Regiment in April 1861. A large prewar company in Charleston's 17th Regiment, South Carolina Militia, the Palmetto Guard was organized on June 28, 1851, and was ordered into state service on December 27, 1860. The men served in Charleston until January 9, 1861, when they were sent to Morris Island. The company was relieved there on February 12, 1861, but was sent back on March 11 to the Point Batteries under the command of Lieutenant Colonel W.G. DeSaussure of the 1st Regiment, South Carolina Artillery Militia. The Palmetto Guard participated in the bombardment of Fort Sumter on April 12 and April 13, and served on Morris Island and as garrison troops at Fort Sumter until May 1, when it was divided into two groups. About half the men, 130 in all, remained in Charleston under the command of Ensign George Lamb Buist to become the Palmetto Guard Artillery, also called the Buist Light Artillery, attached to the 18th Artillery Battalion.[131] The other half became known as the Palmetto Guard Volunteers.[132] This company volunteered for service in Virginia and left Charleston for Richmond on May 9.[133] It arrived in Richmond on May 11, where it was attached to the 2nd Regiment. The men mustered in Confederate service for twelve months near Richmond on May 22. They were mostly from Beaufort and Charleston, but the company included a few from Fairfield, Orangeburg, Richland, Greenville and Colleton Districts. George Barnwell Cuthbert was appointed captain on March 12, 1861.[134] He commanded the Iron Battery at Cummings Point during the bombardment of Fort Sumter in April.[135] Cuthbert enlisted as captain on May 9 and was mustered in Confederate service at that rank on the twenty-second. He was re-elected captain when the company signed up for the duration of the war in May 1862.[136] On June 18, 1862, Cuthbert received a severe flesh wound in the arm during a skirmish on the Nine Mile Road near Richmond. At Chancellorsville on May 3, 1863, he was struck in the breast by a ball that passed around his ribs and emerged just below his shoulder blade. He did well for a few days but died near Guiney's Station, Virginia, on May 10.[137] First Lieutenant Ralph Emmes Elliott, a physician from Pocotaligo and brother of Brigadier General Stephen Elliott, was promoted to captain in May, replacing Cuthbert.[138] Elliott had been slightly wounded in the thigh at Fredericksburg on December 13, 1862, and while he was leading the company at Cold Harbor on June 1, 1864, his men accidentally shot him in the right side of the head.[139] He died in a Richmond hospital on June 5 or June 6, 1864.[140] A memorial tablet inside St. Helena Episcopal Church in Beaufort, as well as the *Charleston Daily Courier*, the *Roll of the Dead* and Wyckoff give the date of death as June 6, but the *CSR* and Kirkland give it as the fifth.[141] Dickert described Elliott as "a brave soldier and a most estimable gentleman."[142] Robert Fishburne Jr., previously first lieutenant, was the last captain of the Palmetto Guard.[143] The *CSR* uses both Fishburne and Fishburn, but he signed official documents with the former. Fishburne was wounded in the head at Fredericksburg on December 13, 1862, before he became captain, and in the arm at Knoxville. He was promoted to captain on July 18, 1864, with rank from June 1 and was paroled on May 2, 1865, at Greensboro.

Company K, the Brooks Guard Volunteers, was new to the 2nd Regiment in April 1861. This company of Charlestonians originated as unit called the Brooks Guards or Brooks Home Guards, organized on January 9, 1861, with John E. Carew as captain.[144] The Brooks Home Guards was attached to the 17th Regiment, South Carolina Militia, and was stationed on Morris Island until after the bombardment of Fort Sumter in April. It never again saw active duty as a company. Most of its members were employed on the railroads during the war.[145] A volunteer detachment of the Brooks Guards elected Andrew Burnet Rhett captain on May 8 and called for additional volunteers to serve in Virginia.[146] The *CSR* spells Rhett's middle name Burnett, but his signature on official documents is Burnet. This volunteer detachment, augmented by recruits from Pickens District, became known as the Brooks Guard Volunteers.[147] It was organized in Charleston and entered state service on May 8. A.B. Rhett was commissioned captain on the twelfth, the same day the men left Charleston to join the 2nd Regiment in Virginia.[148] The Guard mustered in Confederate service near Richmond for twelve months on May 22 or May 23. The Confederate Congress passed an act in December giving a bounty and a furlough to men re-enlisting for two years. After serving only eight months of the initial enlistment, Rhett and sixty-one Company K men asked for and received special permission from the secretary of war to be furloughed and allowed to reorganize as an artillery corps.[149] On January 28, 1862, they re-enlisted for two years and three months and formed a new artillery company under Captain Rhett known as Rhett's Battery or the Brooks Light Artillery.[150] The battery was sent back to Charleston in early 1862 and was detached from the 2nd Regiment. Rhett was dropped as captain of Company K, 2nd Regiment, on May 13, 1862, but he retained command of the new artillery battery until about June 29, 1863.

Brevet Second Lieutenant Jacob F. Moorer was elected captain of a newly recruited Company K on May 13, 1862.[151] Moorer received a slight wound at Sharpsburg on September 17.[152] He received a mortal wound in the thigh at Gettysburg on July 2, 1863, and was left in the hands of the enemy.[153] Kirkland records the date of Moorer's death as July 5, and Wyckoff records it as July 27.[154] Neither the *CSR* nor the *Roll of the Dead* gives a date of death, but the *CSR* does state, in error, that Moorer died in a hospital in November 1862. First Lieutenant Jonathan "John" Webb Jr. was promoted to captain on April 30, 1864. The relatively late date of his promotion probably reflects uncertainty about what happened to Moorer after Gettysburg. Webb was shot through the heart and killed at Spotsylvania on May 12, 1864.[155] First Lieutenant James Elias Dutart, who had been wounded during the Seven Days campaign, was promoted to captain between May 12 and June 21.[156] He held the rank when he was mortally wounded at Petersburg on June 21, 1864, and died the next day.[157] Kirkland indicates that Dutart died on the twenty-first.[158] J.D. Kennedy wrote of Dutart: "He was a noble young man, and the best officer of his age I ever saw. He was cool and calm in the midst of danger, and yet at the same time active and energetic. He was brave to a fault, and his judgment was excellent. I had so much confidence in him that I placed him in command of two companies, and always felt that all was right when he was in command."[159] Samuel Jones Benton, previously first lieutenant of Company G, was elected lieutenant of Company K on September 29, 1864. He was slightly wounded in the arm at Gettysburg and in the chin at Cedar Creek on October 19, 1864. He was dropped from the rolls on April 24, 1865. He survived the war.

Brigade Affiliations

The 2nd Regiment, SCV, was part of C.H. Nelson's Brigade in Major General Milledge L. Bonham's Division while on Morris Island in April 1861.[160] For a brief period in May, the regiment was in Bonham's Palmetto Brigade along with Gregg's regiment.[161] It went to Virginia in May 1861, and it was brigaded from June 1861 to February 1862 with the 2nd, 3rd, 7th and 8th Regiments, SCV, as well as Kemper's Virginia Artillery, in Bonham's Brigade.[162] From February 1862 to December 1863, J.B. Kershaw commanded the same brigade, which added the 15th Regiment, SCV, and the 3rd Battalion, SCV, on November 26, 1862.[163] Kershaw's regiment was proudly known as the 1st Regiment, 1st Brigade, 1st Division, 1st Corps, Army of Northern Virginia. The brigade added the 20th Regiment, SCV, on May 28, 1864. James Conner commanded the brigade from August to October 1864, and John D. Kennedy commanded it from October until the war ended. On April 8, 1865, the regiments were consolidated, and the brigade comprised the "new" 2nd, 3rd and 7th Regiments. The 3rd Battalion, 8th, 15th and 20th Regiments ceased to exist on April 8, 1865.[164]

Major Movements and Engagements

The governor called the 2nd Regiment into state service on April 8, 1861, the same day Companies A, C and D arrived in Charleston. All the original companies, except for the Lancaster Grays, who arrived the next day, were in the field in Charleston by April 11.[165] Arriving on Morris Island just before the commencement of the bombardment of Fort Sumter, elements of the regiment were engaged in that action on April 12 and April 13.[166] Company D was stationed at the Trapier Battery, and Company I was at the Iron Battery and Pointe Battery. The regiment left Morris Island for Charleston on April 24.[167] Four companies—A, C, D and E—responded favorably to President Davis's appeal for volunteers to serve in Virginia, and all but Company D left Charleston at eleven o'clock on the night of April 25.[168] They arrived in Virginia between April 27 and May 4.[169] Company D left Charleston on May 17.[170] The remaining six companies—B, F, G, H, I and K—remained in Charleston under the command of Lieutenant Colonel J.D. Blanding. They served three days, from April 26 until April 29, as part of the garrison at Fort Sumter.[171] Three of these companies formed the nucleus of the 9th Regiment, SCV, and three served with other regiments. Six new companies went to Virginia in May to raise the 2nd Regiment to its full complement of ten. Company F was in Richmond by May 6.[172] Company I arrived on the ninth, and Company K arrived on May 13 to fill out Kershaw's regiment. Eight companies of the new 2nd Regiment were in camp near the Reservoir on May 22, and the ninth was expected to arrive that day.[173] Kershaw was considering several applications for the tenth company at that time.[174] The regiment mustered in Confederate service near Richmond on May 22, and it moved by rail two days later to Manassas Junction where it erected fortifications and breastworks until June.[175]

The 2nd Regiment marched to Fairfax Court House on the twenty-first and withdrew to Bull Run on July 16 and July 17. The brigade, consisting of the 2nd, 3rd, 7th and 8th Regiments, SCV, was shelled at Mitchell's Ford during the battle of Bull Run, or Blackburn's Ford, on July 18.[176]

The men of the 8th Regiment built earth works at Mitchell's Ford from July 18 to July 20. The 2nd and 8th Regiments were engaged in a charge at the Henry House Hill during the battle of First Manassas on July 21. The 3rd and 7th Regiments were on the field that day and endured heavy shellfire but were not actively engaged. The 3rd and 7th Regiments pursued Federal troops later that day.[177] The 3rd Regiment sustained no casualties on July 21. The brigade moved toward Washington and established a new camp at Flint Hill on August 14. The 2nd Regiment skirmished alone near Lewinsville and Georgetown on September 27.[178] The brigade was stationed at Flint Hill until mid-October when it moved to Centreville.[179] The men left Centreville on January 10, 1862, and moved into winter quarters near Blackburn's Bridge at Bull Run.[180] The brigade left camp on March 9 and marched toward the Rappahannock River, moving from there to Orange Court House on the nineteenth. Between March 28 and April 6, the brigade marched and countermarched before departing Orange Court House by rail for Richmond.[181] The men took the York River Railroad to West Point the next day and embarked on a schooner for Yorktown, arriving there late that night.[182] They spent the next few weeks marching, performing picket duty and constructing fieldworks. The brigade skirmished near Yorktown while covering Johnston's retreat on May 2. It withdrew on the third and marched through Williamsburg on the fourth, then it turned and marched back through the town. The 2nd and 8th Regiments were engaged there on the fourth, and the 3rd and 7th Regiments were shelled on the field but were not actively engaged.[183] The brigade then withdrew to a position eight miles from Richmond. The brigade was held in reserve at Seven Pines on May 31 and June 1.[184] The 2nd and 3rd Regiments, but not the 7th and 8th, were engaged on the Nine Mile Road below Richmond on June 18. Since it was south of the Chickahominy River, the brigade was not engaged at Mechanicsville on the twenty-sixth, at Gaines's Mill on the twenty-seventh or at Garnett's Farm on the twenty-eighth. The 3rd, 7th and 8th Regiments skirmished south of the Chickahominy on the twenty-seventh.[185] The brigade was heavily engaged at Savage's Station on June 29 and at Malvern Hill on July 1 but not at Frayser's Farm on June 30.[186] The brigade remained below Richmond for about seven weeks before moving north toward Manassas. Since Kershaw's Brigade did not arrive at the battlefield until September 2, it did not participate in the battle of Second Manassas.[187] The brigade arrived at Leesburg on September 3 and crossed the Potomac River into Maryland on the sixth. It marched to Frederick City, Maryland, on September 7 and remained there until the tenth, when it moved toward Maryland Heights. The brigade was lightly engaged at the north end of Maryland Heights near Harpers Ferry on September 12 and heavily engaged there the next day.[188]

The brigade came down from Maryland Heights early on September 15 and formed into a line of battle near Crampton's Gap, but Harpers Ferry surrendered that morning and Kershaw's Brigade was not engaged. Crossing the Potomac River into Virginia on the evening of the fifteenth, the brigade camped the next night about ten miles from Sharpsburg. The men recrossed the Potomac into Maryland at Boteler's Ford, near Shepherdstown, on the morning of September 17. The brigade was heavily engaged on the Confederate left near the Dunker Church at the battle of Sharpsburg on the seventeenth.[189] Recrossing the Potomac again late in the evening of September 18 and early in the morning of the nineteenth, the men marched to Martinsburg for a few days and then to Winchester, where they remained until October 28. They moved on to Culpeper, arriving on November 9, and left for Fredericksburg on the eighteenth, arriving two days later. The 3rd Battalion and the 15th Regiment, SCV, were reassigned to Kershaw's Brigade as it marched from Culpeper to Fredericksburg on November 26. Initially held in reserve, the brigade was fully engaged at Fredericksburg on December 13. The 2nd and 8th Regiments were engaged in the Sunken Road at Marye's Heights, and the 3rd and 7th Regiments were positioned on the plateau to the left of Marye's Mansion. The 3rd Regiment suffered particularly heavy casualties that day.[190] Company I, the Palmetto Guard of the 2nd Regiment, was detached and engaged to the right of Marye's Heights.[191] The 15th Regiment moved into the Sunken Road at Marye's Heights about 4:30 p.m. and was engaged there.[192] The 3rd Battalion took up a position in the railroad cut running from Fredericksburg to Marye's Heights, but since the men were somewhat protected by the bluff and railroad cut, they did not suffer as greatly as the rest of the brigade. Company A of the 3rd Battalion was engaged that day, but Company B was held in reserve and received shellfire only. Companies C, D and E endured shelling while in line of battle but were not engaged because their line was not attacked. Company F was placed at the Grist Mill on the west side of town to guard the railroad cut and suffered heavy shelling. The brigade remained in line of battle until December 16, when the 2nd, 7th and 15th Regiments moved into Fredericksburg, which the Federal troops had vacated.[193] The brigade set up winter camp nearby and performed picket duty in January and February 1863. The men left camp on April 29 and marched toward Chancellorsville. The brigade was engaged on May 1 near Chancellorsville and skirmished while in line of battle the next day. At that time, the 8th Regiment was temporarily assigned to Brigadier General Fitzhugh Lee's cavalry brigade to guard its wagon train. The 8th was engaged as skirmishers and flankers in that capacity without loss on May 1 and May 2 and rejoined the brigade the next day. The brigade saw action near the Chancellor House on May 3 before withdrawing toward Fredericksburg and engaging the enemy at Salem Church later the same day. On the fourth, the brigade skirmished between Salem Church and Fredericksburg.

The men left camp near Fredericksburg on June 3 and crossed the Potomac River into Maryland at Williamsport on the twenty-fifth. On July 1, during the first day of the battle of Gettysburg, the brigade was two miles away from the battlefield. Late in the afternoon of the second, however, the brigade was involved in Longstreet's attack, during which the 2nd Regiment suffered 52 percent casualties.[194] Though present on the battlefield on July 3, the brigade was not actively engaged. It remained on the field the next day but only the 8th Regiment saw light skirmishing. Withdrawing about midnight, the brigade marched toward Hagerstown on the fifth and sixth.[195] The men entrenched between Williamsport and Falling Waters on July 6 and July 7, and elements of the 3rd, 8th and 15th Regiments and 3rd Battalion skirmished at Antietam Creek near Hagerstown on the tenth and twelfth. The brigade remained in line of battle near Williamsport from July 11 to July 13 and finally crossed the Potomac into Virginia on July 14.[196] Only forty men of the 8th Regiment reported for duty after the Gettysburg campaign, and they skirmished near Front Royal on July 23.[197] The brigade arrived at Culpeper Court House on July 24 and moved on August 3 to the south side of the Rapidan River.

The brigade left its camp at Wallace's Tavern on September 8 and marched to Hanover Junction, where the men boarded a train for Richmond on the tenth. Transferred with Longstreet's corps to Tennessee, the brigade passed through Atlanta on the sixteenth, Dalton on the seventeenth and arrived at Catoosa Station, near Ringgold, Georgia, about two o'clock in the afternoon on the eighteenth.[198] The men camped at Tunnel Hill that night and marched to Ringgold the next morning. They deployed about three o'clock in the afternoon to guard a gap in the mountains nearby but were not engaged that day.[199] The brigade crossed the Chickamauga River after dark on the nineteenth and arrived on the battlefield about one o'clock in the morning on the twentieth. The brigade was heavily engaged later that day during the battle of Chickamauga.[200] It followed the retreating Federal army to Chattanooga on the twenty-second, but only the 8th Regiment saw action that day.[201] The brigade did not participate in the battle at Wauhatchie on the night of October 28 and left Chattanooga for Knoxville on November 4. The men arrived at Sweetwater on November 8 and crossed the Tennessee River on November 13. They pursued the enemy and skirmished on the fifteenth and at Campbell's Station on the sixteenth.[202] The 3rd Regiment and 3rd Battalion skirmished without the rest of the brigade along Kingston Road near Knoxville on November 17. The brigade marched in line of battle for five miles and drove Federal troops from Armstrong's Hill into Knoxville on the eighteenth.[203] The brigade invested Knoxville the next day and spent the next sixteen days in the rifle pits around the town. The brigade was present but not heavily engaged during the attack on Fort Loudon, also called Fort Sanders, near Knoxville, on November 29. Longstreet abandoned the siege and withdrew from Knoxville on December 4, arriving at Rogersville on the ninth. The brigade's last engagement in Tennessee was at Bean's Station on December 14.[204] The 3rd Regiment was on the field that day but was not actively engaged.[205] The brigade left Bean's Station on December 20 and two days later went into winter quarters on the east bank of the Tennessee River at Russellville, near Morristown. The 7th Regiment marched to Dandridge on December 28 but had returned to Russellville by the thirtieth. From January 4 to March 29, 1864, Companies H and M of the 7th Regiment were stationed at Broylesville, Tennessee, to guard the division shoe shop against bushwhackers. The brigade made a few brief excursions from Russellville that winter: to Dandridge from January 28 to February 1, to New Market on February 10 and to Greenville on February 21.

Leaving its winter quarters on February 22, the brigade ultimately arrived at Charlottesville, Virginia, on April 15 and at Gordonsville on the nineteenth, leaving that place on May 4. Though the brigade missed the first day of the battle of the Wilderness on May 5, it was heavily engaged there on the sixth. After burying their dead on the seventh, the men marched slowly to their right until evening, when they were force-marched to Spotsylvania Court House, arriving after midnight.[206] Racing the Federal vanguard to a crucial crossroads near Spotsylvania Court House, the brigade successfully delayed the Federal troops near there on the Brock Road on May 8. It saw skirmishing only during the heaviest fighting at Spotsylvania Court House on May 9, May 10 and May 12 and left the courthouse on the twenty-first. On May 23, the 8th and 15th Regiments were held in reserve when the rest of the brigade was heavily engaged near the Chesterfield Bridge on the North Anna River,[207] The 20th Regiment joined Kershaw's Brigade on the South Anna River on May 28. As the Overland campaign progressed, the brigade was engaged at Beulah Church near Cold Harbor on June 1 and skirmished near Gaines Farm on the second and the third.[208] The 20th Regiment suffered a few casualties on the fifth and twelfth.[209] The brigade left Cold Harbor on June 12 and marched to Malvern Hill by way of the old battlefield at Frayser's Farm. Leaving Malvern Hill on June 15, the men marched to Deep Bottom on the sixteenth and to Chaffin's Farm on the seventeenth. They crossed to the south side of the James River on the eighteenth and fought at Petersburg later that day.[210] The 2nd and 3rd Regiments were engaged there again on June 21, and the 20th Regiment suffered casualties from June 18 to June 24.[211] The brigade remained in the trenches until June 25, when it was transferred into the City of Petersburg and to the north side of the James River at Chaffin's Bluff on July 23. The men skirmished near Deep Bottom on the north side of the James on July 25 and July 26 and were engaged there on the twenty-seventh and twenty-eighth.[212] Transferred to the Shenandoah Valley on August 6, the brigade skirmished at Halltown on August 21 and August 26, near Berryville on September 3 and near Winchester on the thirteenth. The 8th Regiment was performing picket duty on September 13 on the Berryville and Winchester Pike near Winchester when all but two companies of the regiment were captured.[213] The remnants of the 8th were then temporarily consolidated with the 15th Regiment. The brigade left the valley on September 14, missing the battles at Winchester on September 19 and at Fisher's Hill on the twenty-second. The brigade arrived at Gordonsville on September 23 but returned to the valley on the twenty-fifth or twenty-sixth. Engaged at Strasburg on October 13, the brigade also participated in the debacle at Cedar Creek on the nineteenth, where most of the 3rd Battalion was captured.[214] It was transferred back to

Richmond about November 15, arriving there on the twentieth. The men went into winter quarters about seven miles below Richmond, north of the James River, and occupied the extreme left of the Confederate defenses.

Ordered to the Carolinas to help slow Sherman's advance, the brigade left Richmond by rail on January 4, 1865, arriving in Charleston on the seventh. After camping west of the Ashley River for about a week, the men moved to the railroad bridge over the Salkehatchie River. The 8th Regiment, and probably other units of the brigade, performed picket duty at the Salkehatchie River in late January and skirmished there on the thirty-first and on February 1st.[215] The men also guarded railroad bridges over the Edisto River. The brigade served as the rear guard during the evacuation of Charleston on February 18 and guarded the bridge over the Santee River from February 20 to February 23. The brigade was at Cheraw on February 25 and at Florence the next day.[216] It skirmished lightly at Thompson's Creek about five miles west of Cheraw on the twenty-eighth. Continuing its northward withdrawal on March 3, the brigade arrived at Fayetteville on the tenth. It was engaged at Averasboro on March 16 and at Bentonville on the nineteenth and twentieth. All the regiments in the brigade, with the exception of the 8th, suffered casualties on the nineteenth.[217] On April 9, the 2nd Regiment was consolidated with the 20th Regiment, along with parts of the 1st, 2nd, 6th and 7th Battalions of Albert G. Blanchard's South Carolina Reserves, at Smithfield. The consolidated regiment marched from there to Raleigh.[218] The regiment was paroled as the (New or Consolidated) 2nd Regiment, SCV. It surrendered with the Army of Tennessee near Greensboro on April 26, and the men were paroled on May 2 and May 3, 1865.

4.

THE 2ND REGIMENT, SOUTH CAROLINA VOLUNTEERS, CONSOLIDATED

The 2nd Regiment, SCV, Consolidated was created on April 9, 1865, by consolidating the 2nd Regiment, SCV; the 20th Regiment, SCV; and parts of the 1st, 2nd, 6th and 7th Battalions of Albert G. Blanchard's South Carolina Reserves.[1] The new Consolidated 2nd Regiment, SCV, was paroled as the 2nd Regiment, SCV, Infantry on April 26, 1865.

Colonel William W. Wallace wrote that about five hundred men were affected by the consolidation, and the new regiment retained the name and colors of the old 2nd Regiment.[2] Augustus Dickert wrote of the consolidation: "While in camp here there was a feeble attempt made to reorganize and consolidate the brigade by putting the smaller companies together and making one regiment out of two. As these changes took place so near the end, the soldiers never really realizing a change had been made, I will do no more than make a passing allusion to it, as part of this history. The only effect these changes had was the throwing out of some of our best and bravest officers (there not being places for all), but as a matter of fact this was to their advantage, as they escaped the humiliation of surrender, and returned home a few days earlier than the rest of the army."[3]

FIELD OFFICERS

William W. Wallace of Columbia was colonel of the Consolidated 2nd Regiment. Wallace was promoted to lieutenant colonel of the 2nd Regiment, SCV, on June 28, 1864, to date from May 6.[4] He was wounded in the right foot at Charlestown, Virginia, on September 13, 1864. At the suggestion of Brigadier General J.D. Kennedy, Wallace was named colonel of the Consolidated 2nd Regiment on April 8, 1865.[5] He was paroled on May 2. This Wallace should not be confused with Brigadier General William Henry Wallace of Union.

James Dupre Graham of Sumter was promoted from captain of Company D, 2nd Regiment, SCV, to lieutenant colonel of the 2nd Consolidated Regiment on April 8, 1865. Brigadier General J.D. Kennedy had suggested on April 5 that Graham be named major of the new Consolidated 2nd Regiment and that J.M. Partlow of the 20th Regiment become lieutenant colonel.

Godfrey Leaphart of Lexington District was promoted from captain of Company C, 20th Regiment, SCV, to major of the 2nd Consolidated Regiment on April 8, 1865. He was paroled on May 2, 1865, at Greensboro.

COMPANIES

Records of the companies of the 2nd and 20th Consolidated Regiment have not been well preserved. Many captains from the 2nd Regiment were paroled at Greensboro on May 2, 1865. These men probably commanded some of the companies of the Consolidated Regiment, but the letter designations of those companies are not known. Captains from the 2nd Regiment who were paroled with the Consolidated Regiment and their previous companies in the 2nd Regiment were: M.M. Maddrey (Company A), William Robert Powell (Company B), Lieutenant (paroled as captain) Jacob W. Cagle (Company B), Anderson P. Vinson (Company C), Joseph J. Drakeford (Company E), William C. Vance (Company F), James B. Horton (Company H) and Robert Fishburne Jr. (Company I). Captains from the 20th Regiment who were also captains in the Consolidated Regiment and their previous companies in the 20th Regiment were: G.T. Haltiwanger (Company C), James A. Cowan (Company E) and Soloman A. Haltiwanger (Company K).

Company C of the Consolidated Regiment was commanded by G.T. Haltiwanger. Haltiwanger had been first lieutenant in Company C of the 20th Regiment and was promoted to captain about April 8, 1865.[6] He was paroled as captain of Company C of the Consolidated 2nd and 20th Regiments on May 2 at Greensboro.

BRIGADE AFFILIATIONS

The Consolidated 2nd Regiment, SCV, was assigned to Kennedy's Brigade, Walthall's Division, 3rd Corps, Army of Tennessee, from April 9, 1865, until its surrender on April 26.[7]

Major Movements and Engagements

The Consolidated 2nd Regiment did not participate as such in any engagements during its brief existence. The men were paroled on May 2 at Greensboro.

5.

THE 6TH REGIMENT, SOUTH CAROLINA VOLUNTEERS

The 6th Regiment, SCV, was also called the 6th South Carolina Infantry; it was also known as both the "Old Sixth," a reference to the regiment before the reorganization in the spring of 1862, and the "New Sixth" afterward. This regiment was one of the ten authorized for twelve months' service by the act of December 17, 1860. The 6th was organized on February 8, 1861, and was received into state service by Governor Pickens on March 6. The regiment mustered in state service on April 10 or April 11 for one year.[1] The regiment, consisting of the usual ten companies, was transferred from Charleston to Summerville on June 3.[2] Later that month when it reorganized and mustered in Confederate service, however, three of the original companies—the Cedar Creek Rifle Company, the Fairfield Fencibles and the Little River Guard—elected not to enter Confederate service. Company A mustered in Confederate service on June 12, and Companies B through G mustered in on June 19. Three new companies—H, I and K—joined the regiment about June 21, increasing it to the full complement of ten.[3] By July 8, the regiment was at full strength, and by the tenth, all ten companies had mustered in Confederate service.[4] The 6th Regiment was severely affected by the reorganization in the spring of 1862. In February, anticipating the end of the initial twelve-month enlistment, many men of the 6th Regiment re-enlisted in the 5th and 17th Regiments, the 13th Battalion and a new regiment, the Palmetto Sharpshooters. The remaining men of the "Old Sixth" Regiment re-enlisted for two additional years or for the duration of the war and were reorganized into six companies. On March 27, one company of re-enlistees from Blanding's 9th Regiment joined the six at Orange Court House, Virginia, and on April 16 formed the 1st South Carolina Battalion of Re-enlisted Volunteers commanded by Lieutenant Colonel John Bratton. The battalion was increased to regiment size on April 22 by the addition of three more companies of re-enlisted men from Blanding's 9th Regiment, which, by then, had ceased to exist. Several re-enlistees from the old 5th Regiment and several new recruits were added to the companies of the "New Sixth" Regiment at that time. These ten companies formed the "New Sixth" Regiment, SCV, under the command of newly elected field officers. The effective date of enlistment for the "New Sixth" Regiment was April 10, 1862.[5] About January 20, 1864, the men voted unanimously to re-enlist for the duration of the war.[6]

FIELD OFFICERS

James Henry Rion of Winnsboro in Fairfield District was elected colonel of the regiment on February 19, 1861.[7] Rion was the first captain of the Fairfield Fencibles.[8] When the regiment mustered in Confederate service in June 1861, Colonel Rion allowed new elections of field officers. One veteran of the 6th Regiment wrote that Rion had learned of some opposition to his own election and ordered a new vote.[9] Rion lost the election by three or four votes and resigned on June 8.[10] Governor Pickens accepted his resignation.[11] Major Woodward wrote in 1883 that Rion's loss deprived the regiment of an efficient and astute head.[12] Rion later served in and eventually commanded the 7th Battalion, South Carolina Infantry.

Andrew Jackson Secrest of Chester was elected lieutenant colonel on February 19, 1861.[13] A distinguished officer in the Mexican War, Secrest was captain of the Calhoun Guards before the election.[14] Secrest refused promotion to colonel after Rion's resignation; the regiment had no colonel for several weeks.[15] Secrest was reappointed lieutenant colonel on June 20. The *Mercury* reported on July 11 that Secrest had replaced Rion as colonel; the replacement, however, was actually Charles S. Winder, whose commission was effective on July 8. Secrest relinquished command of the regiment to Winder on July 20 and remained lieutenant colonel until he lost re-election at the reorganization in the spring of 1862. Secrest applied for, but did not receive, command of a regiment or brigade in May. He later served as a private in the 13th (4th) Battalion and as colonel of the 6th Regiment, South Carolina Reserves, for ninety days in late 1862 and early 1863.[16] On September 11, 1863, Secrest was a private in Company B of the 4th Regiment, South Carolina Cavalry. At that time, he asked Governor Bonham for a commission, which he apparently never received. Secrest died in May 1865.

Thomas William Woodward of Fairfield District was elected major on February 19, 1861.[17] His commission as major in Confederate service dated from June 20. Woodward refused promotion to lieutenant colonel when Rion was defeated in June. He was severely wounded in the thigh at Dranesville on December 20, 1861.[18] Not re-elected at the reorganization, Woodward later re-enlisted as a private and eventually became quartermaster of the 20th Regiment, SCV, and assistant quartermaster of Kershaw's Brigade.[19]

Charles Sidney Winder of Maryland raised an artillery battery called Winder's Battery in Baltimore in early 1861. When he was appointed major of artillery in the Regular Confederate army with rank from March 16, 1861, he left the battery, and it eventually became Company C of the 15th Battalion, South Carolina Artillery, in November 1862. When the men of the 6th Regiment failed to re-elect Colonel Rion in June 1861, the remaining field officers and all line officers met and agreed to waive their own rights to promotion. They sent Major Woodward and Captain E.C. McLure to petition President Davis for a regular army officer, a stranger to the regiment, to fill the post of colonel.[20] After some discussion, Davis recommended Winder; the War Department appointed him colonel of the 6th Regiment on July 8, 1861.[21] Winder promptly joined the 6th Regiment and assumed command on July 20. He continued to lead the regiment until he was promoted to brigadier general in the Confederate States Provisional Army, effective March 1, 1862. He then commanded a brigade of Virginia regiments later known as the Stonewall Brigade. Winder was killed on August 9, 1862, at Cedar Mountain. Major James L. Coker wrote that Winder "was an officer of the old army, with the stern ideas of discipline and army etiquette incident to his training." Coker added that Winder left a "good mark" on the 6th Regiment.[22]

John Bratton, MD, of Winnsboro in Fairfield District was elected colonel at the reorganization, filling the post that had been vacant for two months. The men of the "New Sixth" Regiment, in fact, elected an entirely new slate of field officers at the reorganization.[23] Bratton had been captain of the Fairfield Fencibles when the 6th Regiment was in state service in early 1861. One of three companies declining Confederate service, the Fairfield Fencibles disbanded in June. Bratton re-enlisted as a private in Company C on June 13 and rose to the rank of second lieutenant. By April, he was universally respected in the "Old Sixth" Regiment and enjoyed a good reputation from his conduct at the battle of Dranesville.[24] He was elected lieutenant colonel of the 1st South Carolina Battalion of Re-enlisted Volunteers about April 16, 1862, and colonel of the 6th Regiment on the twenty-second. At the battle of Seven Pines on May 31, a ball struck Bratton in the left arm, penetrating the left side of his body; he was subsequently captured.[25] Bratton was sent to Hygeia United States Army General Hospital at Fort Monroe on June 4 and was transferred to Chesapeake United States Army General Hospital, also at Fort Monroe, on the eighth. By late July, his wounds were healing rapidly.[26] He was paroled at Fort Monroe, Virginia, on August 3, 1862, and was released for exchange on the thirty-first. The exchange took place at Aiken's Landing on the James River on September 1, and Bratton rejoined his regiment after the battle of Sharpsburg.[27] Promoted to brigadier general on May 6, 1864, Bratton was bruised in the side at the battle of Cold Harbor the next month. He was wounded in the left shoulder on the New Market Road on October 7 when a ball struck him in the chest and exited through the back.[28] The wound took two years to heal.[29] He was paroled at Appomattox Court House with the rank of brigadier general.[30] Coker wrote that Bratton "enforced obedience to army regulations as a part of the patriot soldiers' duty, while he accorded to the brave and intelligent men a kindly sympathy and consideration which won their confidence." Bratton, known to the men as "Old Reliable," evidently left an indelible impression on the regiment, one that it retained throughout the war.[31]

John Marcellus Steedman of Lexington was elected lieutenant colonel on April 22, 1862.[32] A graduate of the South Carolina Military Academy, he had previously served as major of Blanding's 9th Regiment, SCV.[33] Steedman was slightly wounded at Frayser's Farm on June 30, 1862, and also at Second Manassas. He was promoted to colonel replacing Bratton on July 20, 1864, with rank from May 6. Steedman was paroled with the regiment at Appomattox Court House on April 9, 1865.[34] He was considered "unsurpassed for courage, and endurance, and good judgment" and "a brave and sturdy officer."[35]

Edward Conrad McLure of Chester was elected major on either April 16 or April 22, 1862.[36] According to the *CSR*, McLure was major of the 1st South Carolina Battalion of Re-enlisted Volunteers before April 1862. He was also captain of Company F of the 6th Regiment before the reorganization. Afflicted with a bad heart, bad lungs, chronic diarrhea and dropsical attacks, McLure was frequently absent from the regiment. On June 4, 1863, he was appointed to the Enrolling Department with an effective date of June 30. He made a brief, unsuccessful attempt to return to the regiment on June 28 and transferred to the enrolling department in South Carolina's First Congressional District on July 1. McLure was discharged on a surgeon's certificate stating he had typhoid fever. Coker wrote that the regiment was fortunate to have elected Colonel Bratton and Lieutenant Colonel Steedman in April 1862, but he did not mention McLure.[37]

John M. White of Fort Mill in York District was promoted to major on July 4, 1863, replacing McLure. While serving as captain of Company B, White had been wounded at Seven Pines.[38] He was promoted to lieutenant colonel on July 20, 1864, with rank from May 6, to replace Steedman when Bratton was made brigadier general. Bratton wrote of White on July 31,

1864: "I am happy to add in this instance steady courage and merit as an officer generally are combined with rank as claims to promotion."[39] White was paroled at Appomattox Court House on April 9, 1865.[40]

James Lide Coker of Society Hill and Hartsville in Darlington District was promoted to major from captain of Company E on July 20, 1864, with rank from May 6, replacing White. The promotion, however, was not as simple as it seems: Coker's right thigh was fractured by a Minié ball during the night action at Lookout Creek, also called Wauhatchie, on October 28, 1863.[41] After the battle, Colonel Bratton, then in command of Jenkins's Brigade, wrote: "I have to regret the loss of the services of Captain J.L. Coker, 6th Regiment, SCV, acting assistant Adjutant General on my staff. He was seriously wounded while nobly performing his duty."[42] Carried off the battlefield by comrades, Coker was taken to the nearby home of the Hicks family and captured there when the house fell into Federal hands on November 25. Coker remained at the Hicks house for the next six months.[43] By April 30, 1864, he was a patient in a general field hospital near Chattanooga. Coker arrived at the military prison at Louisville, Kentucky, on May 9 and on the twentieth, he was sent to Fort McHenry, Maryland. On July 13, he was sent to Fort Monroe and exchanged three days later at City Point, Virginia. Coker's promotion to major came on July 20. He was still using crutches when he returned to the regiment in January or February 1865.[44] Remaining with the men for several weeks, though totally disabled for field service, Coker retired to the Invalid Corps on March 18, 1865. He was the brother of William Coker, captain of Company M, 8th Regiment, SCV. James L. Coker founded Coker College after the war.

COMPANIES

The companies below were originally attached to the 6th Regiment from its inception on February 8, 1861, until it mustered in Confederate service in June. These companies enlisted in state service on April 11 for twelve months. The *Mercury* listed them in the order given below but offered no documentation of alphabetic or numeric designations.[45] Edward J. McCrady, lieutenant colonel of the 1st Regiment, SCV, gave a speech on September 1, 1888, giving the same sequence of companies.[46] Major James L. Coker used a different sequence and assigned numeric designations to each company in an unpublished work.[47]

The Cedar Creek Rifle Company from Fairfield District was commanded by John B. Harrison. Coker called this Company #3.[48] This company existed as early as November 1860 under command of a Captain

Bookter.[49] It did not volunteer for Confederate service in June 1861. Its disposition is unknown, but it was probably disbanded. Company C of the 12th Regiment, SCV, organized in August 1861, was also called the Cedar Creek Rifles, but the connection between the two companies, if any, remains uncertain.

The Boyce Guards of Fairfield District was commanded by J.N. Shedd. It was called Company #2 in Coker's manuscript.[50] The Boyce Guards became Company D after June 19, 1861.

The Fairfield Fencibles of Fairfield District was originally commanded by Captain James Henry Rion, who was elected colonel of the regiment on February 19, 1861, and was succeeded by John Bratton, who was elected captain on the twenty-third.[51] Coker named this Company #1.[52] The Fairfield Fencibles remained with the 6th Regiment as it reorganized for Confederate service in June and July 1861. The company was still with the regiment as late as July 12, 1861, an indication that at least some of its men were willing to enter Confederate service.[53] In the end, however, the Fairfield Fencibles did not muster in Confederate service; the company was replaced in the 6th Regiment by the Limestone Springs Company and disbanded at that time. Bratton and twenty-three of his men mustered in Confederate service with the Buckhead Guards.[54]

The Chester Blues from Chester District was commanded by Edward C. McLure, captain of The Rifle Company of Chester, in early January 1861.[55] Not accepted as a rifle company, it disbanded and immediately reorganized as an infantry company on January 19. The new company was named the Chester Blues, and McLure was retained as captain.[56] The General Assembly incorporated the Chester Blues on January 28.[57] Coker's designation was Company #7.[58] The Chester Blues became Company F after June 19, 1861.

The Chester Guards from Chester District was commanded by Obadiah Harden, formerly colonel of the 26th Regiment, South Carolina Militia.[59] Company #6 to Coker, the Chester Guards became Company E after June 19, 1861.[60]

The Little River Guards of Fairfield District was commanded by James Michael "Mike" Brice, MD.[61] Coker called this Company #5.[62] The company failed to volunteer for Confederate service in June 1861 and was disbanded.[63] Brice served as captain of Company G of the 6th Regiment in 1864. Some men of the Little River Guards joined the Buckhead Guards and became Company C of the 6th Regiment in June 1861.[64]

The Buckhead Guards from Fairfield District was commanded by Edward J. Means. Company #4 to Coker, this company became Company C after June 19, 1861.[65]

The Catawba Guards from Richburg in Chester District was commanded by G.M.L. Strait, MD.[66] Coker termed this Company #8.[67] Its men began meeting as a volunteer company shortly after South Carolina seceded on December 20, 1860, and the company was raised from the 27th Regiment, South Carolina Militia.[68] It changed its name to the Catawba Light Infantry, probably on entering Confederate service, and became Company B after June 19, 1861.[69]

The Pickens Guards from the Hopewell Community in Chester District was commanded by J.M. "Mike" Moore.[70] Coker's Company #9, it was raised from the 27th Regiment, South Carolina Militia.[71] This company became Company G after June 19, 1861.

The Calhoun Guards from Chester in Chester District was a militia company that had been raised as a rifle company by Thomas S. Mills and Andrew J. Secrest.[72] Coker called it Company #10.[73] The Calhoun Guards, a volunteer company of light infantry, was incorporated by the South Carolina General Assembly on January 28, 1861, and was initially a company in the 26th Regiment, South Carolina Militia.[74] Its first captain, Secrest, was elected lieutenant colonel of the regiment on February 19, 1861. John T. Walker, who succeeded Secrest, mustered in state service with the company on April 11, 1861. According to the *CSR*, the company mustered in Confederate service on June 12, 1861, but Walker's commission was dated June 20. The Calhoun Guards became Company A after June 12, 1861.

The *History of Fairfield County* lists the Monticello Guards as a company in the 6th Regiment. The Monticello Guards was also called the Fairfield Volunteers and was commanded by John Bunyan Davis. It was Company I of Maxcy Gregg's 1st Regiment, SCV, during its six-month existence from early January to early July 1861, and it became Company E of the 15th Regiment, SCV, about August 30, 1861. It is possible that this company served briefly with the 6th Regiment between early July and late August 1861, though this possibility is not explored in sources like the *Compiled Service Records*, the *Memory Roll* or in Rion's Historical Sketch of the 6th Regiment.[75]

Following are the ten companies of the 6th Regiment after they mustered in Confederate service in June and July 1861. Company A mustered in on June 12 and six more, B through G, volunteered on the nineteenth. Three new companies, H, I and K, were added to the regiment about June 27 while it was in Summerville and mustered in Confederate service in early July.[76] All ten companies volunteered for twelve months' service to date from April 11, 1861.

Company A, the Calhoun Guard or Guards, was part of the 6th Regiment when it was in state service.[77] John T. Walker, who had commanded the company from February 19, mustered in Confederate service with the company on June 12. Walker died at the South Carolina Hospital at Warrenton Springs, Virginia, on January 23, 1862.[78] The *CSR* lists two causes of death: typhoid pneumonia and acute peritonitis. Private William Thad McFadden might have commanded the company during Walker's absence, but he never held the rank of captain.[79] Mortally wounded at Dranesville on December 20, 1861, McFadden died on January 13, 1862. First Lieutenant John L. Agurs was promoted to captain on January 24, by Special Order No. 6 from the headquarters of the 6th Regiment. He became assistant quartermaster of the 6th Regiment with the rank of captain on April 22.[80] At the reorganization, some men enlisted in Companies A, F and I of the 6th Regiment; others chose various companies of the reorganized 5th Regiment.

Company B, the Catawba Guards, was also known as the Catawba Light Infantry.[81] Its men were mostly from the town of Chester, but some came from Richburg, also in Chester District.[82] Company B was part of the 6th Regiment when it was in state service. Though it bore the same name, this was an entirely different unit from the first Company H of the 5th Regiment. The original captain, Gilbert M. Lafayette Strait, MD, commanded the company throughout its first year of enlistment, entering state service with the men on April 11 and entering Confederate service in June.[83] Most of the men followed Strait and enlisted in Company A of the 6th Regiment at the reorganization in the spring of 1862; though a few enlisted in Company B of the 5th Regiment, others chose Company F of the 6th Regiment, and still others joined the 17th Regiment.

Company C, the Buckhead Guards, was from the Buckhead area of Fairfield District.[84] Company C was part of the 6th Regiment when it was in state service, and about a quarter of its men came from the Fairfield Fencibles. Edward J. Means, the company's only captain, mustered in state service on April 11. The senior captain when Rion was not re-elected colonel in June 1861, Means was in line for but refused promotion to major. He was severely wounded in the arm at Dranesville on December 20, 1861.[85] Means did not run for re-election in the spring of 1862.[86] He applied for a commission as major in the P.A.C.S. on April 6 and received good recommendations from both Colonel Winder and Lieutenant Colonel Secrest. On May 5, Means was appointed to General R.H. Anderson's staff with the rank of captain. General Anderson also recommended Means in August for the rank of major of ordnance. On July 7, 1863, Means was appointed a lieutenant in the Confederate States Navy for the duration of the war. Though the *CSR* lists Means as captain of the second Company H of the 6th Regiment, the fact that W.B. Lyles was elected to that post on April 16, 1862, makes this entry unlikely. At the reorganization in the spring of 1862, some Company C men enlisted in Companies G and H of the 6th Regiment, and some men enlisted in other companies of the 6th and 17th Regiments.

Company D, the Boyce Guards from Fairfield District, was in the 6th Regiment when it was in state service. James Nelson Shedd, its only captain, enlisted in state service on April 11, 1861. Absent without leave from December 20, 1861, he relinquished his command from that date; he returned to the company on January 24, 1862, and commanded it until the expiration of its initial twelve-month enlistment. Not re-elected at the reorganization in the spring of 1862, Shedd served as lieutenant colonel of the 6th Regiment of South Carolina Reserves for ninety days in late 1862. In 1864, he was both lieutenant and captain in Company E of the 22nd Regiment, SCV. Lieutenant Colonel T.G. Burt of the 22nd Regiment recommended Shedd for the rank of major of his regiment on November 30, 1864; Shedd was promoted, effective December 2. Most of the men of Company D enlisted in Company G of the 6th Regiment at the reorganization in the spring of 1862.

Company E, the Chester Guards from western Chester District, was in the 6th Regiment when it was in state service.[87] Obadiah Harden, the original captain, mustered in state service on April 11. Mortally wounded in the shoulder at Dranesville, Virginia, on December 20, Harden died soon afterwards.[88] The *Memory Roll* states that he died the day after he was wounded, but the *Roll of the Dead* records the date of Harden's death as December 26. The *CSR* indicates that he died of tetanus on January 1, 1862. The last date seems the most plausible since Harden's successor, First Lieutenant Charles W. Sanders, was promoted to captain the same day. Sanders died of pneumonia on March 30, 1862, at the South Carolina Hospital at Post Jefferson in Charlottesville, Virginia. At the reorganization in the spring of 1862, some Company E men enlisted in Companies C and E of the 5th Regiment, and others in Companies F and I of the 6th Regiment.

Company F, the Chester Blues from Chester District, was in the 6th Regiment when it was in state service.[89] Edward Conrad McLure, the only captain of the company before the reorganization, enlisted in state service on April 11. He was elected major of the 6th Regiment at the reorganization in April 1862. Most of the men re-enlisted in Company I of the 6th Regiment for two years or for the duration of the war on March 29. Some chose Company F, also of the 6th Regiment.

Company G, the Pickens Guards from Chester District, mustered in state service with the 6th Regiment on April 11, 1861.[90] J.M. "Mike"

Moore, the only captain before the reorganization, was not re-elected but was elected first lieutenant of Company F of the reorganized 6th Regiment and was promoted to captain of that company. Moore was killed on June 27, 1862, at Gaines's Mill. In April 1862, some Company G men enlisted in Company B of the 5th Regiment, and others joined Companies F and I of the 6th Regiment.

Company H was called the York Volunteers, the York Guards and the York Guard.[91] Its men were from Fort Mill in York District. John M. White raised a company at Fort Mill in the fall of 1860. When it was refused by the governor on some unrecorded technicality, White offered his company to the governor of Alabama, who also refused it. White returned to Fort Mill and reorganized the company. This one evidently mustered in state service on April 11, 1861, but not, at first, with the 6th Regiment. White and his company left York District on June 22 with the intention of joining Blanding's 9th Regiment, SCV.[92] Though the company did not join that regiment, it did wind up in Confederate service. Shortly after June 27, White's Company, along with I and K, became new additions to the 6th Regiment, replacing those that refused to volunteer for Confederate service. Company H mustered in the 6th Regiment on July 2, 1861.[93] White was the only captain until the reorganization in the spring of 1862. At that time, some Company H men followed Captain White and enlisted in Company B of the 6th Regiment. Others enlisted in other companies of the reorganized 5th and 6th Regiments.

Company I, the Limestone Springs Infantry, was also called the Limestone Light Infantry and the Limestone Guards.[94] Most of its men were from Limestone Springs in Spartanburg District, though some came from Union District, and a few were possibly from York and Fairfield Districts. The company, which saw active service in the War of 1812, had as its motto "Victory or Death." The men offered their services to the governor as early as November 19, 1860. Company I, new to the regiment in the summer of 1861, mustered in Confederate service on July 10 and left Spartanburg by rail the same day to join the 6th Regiment already in Virginia.[95] William "Bill" Daniel Camp, who commanded the company in November 1860, was commissioned in Confederate service on July 10. He resigned on February 19, 1862, and was elected captain of Company I of the 5th Regiment at the reorganization later that spring. James F.V. Legg succeeded Camp as captain in February. Legg was not re-elected at the reorganization. In a letter dated June 5, 1863, Legg wrote that he had resigned on May 6, 1862, saying varicose veins in his left leg prevented him from performing his duties.[96] The *CSR* confirms Legg's claim that he resigned on May 6, and it also states that he held the ranks of both captain and first lieutenant at that time. On June

15, 1863, Legg was a private in Company K of the 6th Regiment and was physically infirm. He provided a substitute who was rejected. B.G. Rushing may have been temporarily attached to the company as its commander at some time before the reorganization, but whether or not he held the rank of captain is unclear. Some Company I men followed Camp and enlisted in Company I of the 5th Regiment at the reorganization. Others chose Company C of the 5th Regiment, and a few enlisted in the Palmetto Sharpshooters.

Company K, the Carolina Mountaineers from Greenville District, mustered in state service on April 11, 1861, but at that time, it was not associated with the 6th Regiment.[97] Shortly after June 27, Company K joined the 6th Regiment, and on July 2, it mustered in Confederate service. Spartan David Goodlett, the first captain, resigned on October 8, 1861, because of a "protracted and serious indisposition."[98] He became the first lieutenant colonel of the 22nd Regiment, SCV, on January 29, 1862. First Lieutenant Jasper N. Southern replaced Goodlett on October 10, 1861, and served until the reorganization in the spring of 1862.[99] At that time, most Company K men enlisted in various companies of the 13th (4th) Battalion, which was composed mostly of men from Greenville and Anderson Districts.

Following are the ten companies created at the reorganization in the spring of 1862 as the "New Sixth" Regiment.

Company A retained the name of Catawba Guards, or Catawba Light Infantry, since most of its men had previously served in Company B of the 6th Regiment. Its men were from Chester District. Some Chester District men were in Company A of the 6th Regiment, and some York District men were in Company H of the 5th Regiment before the reorganization. A few new recruits came from North Carolina. Gilbert M. Lafayette Strait, MD, captain of the Catawba Guards before the reorganization, was re-elected captain of Company A on April 16, 1862. His commission dated from March 29. Strait was severely wounded in the wrist at Second Manassas on August 30, 1862.[100] He resigned on February 19, 1863, to become assistant surgeon of the Palmetto Sharpshooters.[101] Strait died of dysentery at home in October 1863. The *Roll of the Dead* gives the date of his death as October 10, Kirkland gives it as October 15 and a sketch in *Recollections and Reminiscences* gives it as the eighteenth.[102] First Lieutenant William T.D. Cousar was promoted to captain on February 20, 1863, a date also recorded as February 4 and February 19. Cousar was wounded at Campbell's Station on November 16, 1863. According to a sketch in the *Confederate Military Series*, he was severely wounded in the shoulder at the Wilderness on May 6, 1864, and was absent from the company for many months.[103] The *CSR* states that Cousar was absent from November 16, 1863, to November or December

1864. This suggests that Cousar's debilitating wound was inflicted at Campbell's Station and not at the Wilderness. He was detailed as an enrolling officer in July and August 1864, and he returned to his company late in the year. Cousar was paroled with the company at Appomattox Court House on April 9, 1865.[104]

Company B, the Alston Riflemen, was composed of men who before the reorganization were in Company H of the 6th Regiment from York District, Company C of the 6th Regiment from Fairfield District and Company A of the 9th Regiment from Lancaster District. There were also a few men from other companies of the 5th Regiment as well as some new recruits. John M. White, captain of Company H before the reorganization, was re-elected captain in the spring of 1862. White was slightly wounded in the shoulder at the battle of Seven Pines on May 31, 1862.[105] He was promoted to major on July 4, probably effective on July 1, 1863. First Lieutenant Butler P. Alston replaced him as captain on July 1, a date also shown as June 30, 1863.[106] Alston had been slightly wounded in the hand at Dranesville, Virginia, on December 20, 1861, and suffered severe wounds at Frayser's Farm on June 30, 1862. He was wounded a third time at Fort Harrison on September 30, 1864. Alston was paroled with the regiment at Appomattox Court House on April 9, 1865.[107]

Company C was composed almost entirely of men from the 9th Regiment, SCV, before the reorganization. Some had been in Company E from Kershaw District, some in Company F from Sumter District and some in Company B from Richland District. There were also new recruits from Spartanburg, Colleton and Darlington Districts. Edward B. Cantey, who had been captain of Company E of the 9th Regiment before the reorganization, was elected captain of Company C on April 6, 1862. While commanding the regiment temporarily, Cantey was struck by four Minié balls at Sharpsburg on September 17, 1862. One passed through the lower third of the left femur and healed badly with contracture of the muscles. The second, which struck him in the back of the right thigh, was extracted from behind the knee. The third passed through his lower right leg splitting the smaller bone, the fibula, and injuring the calf. The fourth pierced Cantey's muscles at the front of his right thigh. These wounds left him unable to perform military duties. On August 13, 1863, Cantey was assigned a position as enrolling officer for Richland District; he was promoted to major on August 27.[108] First Lieutenant Richard M. "Dick" Cantey, who had been wounded at Second Manassas on August 30, 1862, was promoted to replace Edward Cantey. The *CSR* gives the date of his promotion as both August 13 and August 27, 1863. Dick Cantey was paroled with the regiment at Appomattox Court House on April 9, 1865.[109]

Company D was composed mostly of men from Company H of the 9th Regiment before the reorganization. These men were from Edgefield and Barnwell Districts, along with some from Colleton and Orangeburg Districts and a few new recruits. Jerome W. Walker, captain of Company H of the 9th Regiment before the reorganization, was elected captain of Company D on April 16, 1862. He was slightly wounded in the foot at Williamsburg on May 5.[110] About 4:30 p.m. on May 31, 1862, at the battle of Seven Pines, Walker was leading the company in a charge against a Federal battery when he was "shot dead." The *Roll of the Dead* records that he died the day after the battle. The fact that Walker's successor, First Lieutenant Robert G. Lanham, was promoted on May 31 tends to support this as the date of Walker's death.[111] Lanham received a flesh wound in the hand at New Market Hill on August 16, 1864. He was paroled with the company at Appomattox Court House on April 9, 1865.[112]

Company E was composed of men who had served previously in a Sumter District Company and a Darlington District Company. About twenty-five men from Bishopville and Lynchburg in Sumter District had served in the Sumter Grays, Company F of the 9th Regiment, before the reorganization.[113] Most of the rest had served in a Darlington District company called the Hartsville Light Infantry, Company G of the 9th Regiment, before the reorganization. A few others had served in other companies of the 9th Regiment. Company E was organized on April 22, 1862, and was mustered in for two years or for the duration of the war. The company joined the 6th Regiment at Yorktown. James Lide Coker, captain of Company G of the 9th Regiment before the reorganization, was elected captain of Company E on either March 27 or April 22, 1862. He was promoted to major on July 20, 1864, with rank from May 6. Coker was replaced as captain by First Lieutenant William J. McLeod who had commanded the company in Coker's absence after October 29, 1863; his commission, however, was dated May 6, 1864. McLeod received a flesh wound in the left arm from a shell fragment at the Wilderness on May 6, 1864. He was wounded in the right hip at Battery Harrison on September 30 the same year. McLeod was absent without leave, probably because of wounds, on January 27, 1865, but he had received a leave of absence by February. McLeod probably did not return to the company. He was not paroled with the regiment at Appomattox Court House on April 9, 1865.[114] Coker wrote that McLeod surrendered in 1865 but did not indicate where.[115] Melton lists E.W. Cannon as a captain of Company E, though his highest rank was probably first lieutenant.[116]

Company F, the Chester Blues, was composed mostly of men from Chester District who were in Companies A, B, E, F and G of the 6th

Regiment before the reorganization.[117] Rion wrote that most were from Companies F and G.[118] Some from Lancaster District had been in Company A of the 9th Regiment. A few others from the 5th Regiment came from York District, and a few hailed from North Carolina. The company retained the name of the prereorganization Company F. Joseph Lucius Gaston, a Chester lawyer and a private in Company F of the 6th Regiment before the reorganization, was unanimously elected captain of the second Company F on April 16, 1862.[119] He was killed at Seven Pines on May 31, 1862.[120] Though opposed to secession, Gaston was among the first to volunteer. He was "a man of the highest order and most scrupulous integrity."[121] He "performed his duties to the entire satisfaction of his company."[122] J.M. Moore, captain of Company G before the reorganization, was elected first lieutenant of Company F on April 16, 1862. He was promoted to captain on May 31 and was killed in action on June 27 at Gaines's Mill. First Lieutenant Robert A. Crawford replaced Moore on June 27. Crawford was severely wounded in the leg at Second Manassas on August 30, 1862.[123] He suffered an oblique fracture of the thigh just below the hip and, because proper extension was not maintained during convalescence, Crawford's wounded leg was left permanently shorter than the other leg. Unable to perform his military duties, Crawford tendered his resignation on October 19, 1863; acceptance came on January 8, 1864, a date also shown as the ninth. The *Confederate Military Series* states, probably incorrectly, that unspecified injuries, not the wound at Second Manassas, caused Crawford's resignation.[124] First Lieutenant Osmond A. Wylie was promoted to captain on January 8, 1864, replacing Crawford. Wylie was paroled with the company at Appomattox Court House on April 9, 1865.[125]

Company G retained the name of Boyce Guards because many of its men had served in Company D of the 6th Regiment before the reorganization. Those who had not came mostly from Company C of the 6th Regiment. Almost all Company G men were from Fairfield District. James Monroe Phinney of Fairfield District was first lieutenant in Company D before the reorganization. Phinney was elected captain on April 16, 1862, but his commission dated from March 29. He was killed at Seven Pines on May 31, 1862. The *Mercury* reported, incorrectly, that J.M. Hughs, captain of Company G, was killed at Seven Pines.[126] The *CSR* does not list J.M. Hughs as an officer in any South Carolina regiment. Phinney was replace by First Lieutenant James Douglas Cureton on May 30 or May 31. He left the company because of illness on June 9. Cureton was admitted to the Episcopal Church Hospital in Williamsburg, Virginia, with dysentery on June 25. He was released and then readmitted on July 8. Cureton might have returned, if only briefly, to the company but he left it again on September 9 at Frederick City, Maryland. He was captured, probably at Frederick City, in September or early October 1862 and was sent to Baltimore. Cureton was moved to Fort Monroe in Baltimore on October 11 and was exchanged at Aiken's Landing the next day along with twenty-seven other prisoners of war. He was present with the company from November 1862 to February 16, 1863, when he was admitted for three days to the Institute Hospital in Richmond. Two more attempts to return to the company failed, each time because of illness. Cureton was on sick furlough from June 3 and retired to the Invalid Corps on May 13, 1864. He was assigned to court martial duty on June 10 and to duty at Frog Level, now called Prosperity, in Newberry District on October 11, 1864. Re-examined on November 13, Cureton was found to be completely unfit for duty. James Michael Brice, MD, who had raised and commanded the Little River Guards of the 6th Regiment in early 1861, was promoted to captain replacing Cureton at the time of his retirement on May 13, 1864. Brice had been wounded in the thigh at Seven Pines on May 31, 1862. Suffering from diarrhea in early September 1862, he was unable to keep up with the regiment and was captured at Frederick, Maryland, on September 12.[127] Paroled at Fort Monroe on October 11, Brice was exchanged at Aiken's Landing two days later. Brice returned to the company; he was killed at Fort Harrison on September 30, 1864. William McCully, a second lieutenant, also commanded Company G. The *CSR* does not state that he held the rank of captain, but the *Appomattox Roster* shows him as captain of Company G when it was paroled at Appomattox Court House on April 9, 1865.[128]

Company H, the Buckhead Guards, was composed of Fairfield District men from Company C of the 6th Regiment and men from Richland District who were in Company B of the 9th Regiment before the reorganization. William Boykin Lyles of Fairfield District was elected captain on April 16, 1862; his commission dated from March 29. Lyles was killed at Seven Pines on May 31, 1862.[129] The *CSR* lists Edward J. Means as captain of the second Company H of the 6th Regiment, but the fact that W.B. Lyles was elected captain on April 16, 1862, makes this unlikely. Francis H. Weston was promoted to captain on May 31, 1862. Weston was severely wounded in the left leg at Second Manassas on August 30, 1862.[130] He sustained fatal wounds to the throat and shoulder during the night action at Lookout Creek on October 28, 1863, and he died on the thirtieth.[131] Henry W. Dixon was promoted to captain the same day. Dixon was wounded in the left shoulder on the Darbytown Road on October 4, 1864; his left arm was amputated just below the left shoulder. Still absent in February 1865, Dixon probably did not return to the company. He was not paroled at Appomattox.[132]

Company I, the Chester Guards, was composed of men from Chester District who enlisted on March 29, 1862, for two years or for the duration of the war. Many had served in Company F before the reorganization, and others had served in Companies A, E and G, all of the 6th Regiment. Dennis Colvin, second lieutenant in Company F before the reorganization, was elected captain of Company I on April 16, 1862. Colvin died of disease in Richmond only six days later. James M. Crosby, who was promoted to captain on April 27, was killed at Frayser's Farm on June 30, 1862. First Lieutenant William McAliley replaced Crosby as captain the same day.[133] While a sergeant in Company F, McAliley had been severely wounded in the hand at Dranesville, Virginia, on December 20, 1861. He was also wounded at Seven Pines on May 31, 1862, while still first lieutenant of Company I. Captain McAliley was wounded in the arm on September 20, 1864, and was paroled with the company at Appomattox Court House on April 9, 1865.[134]

Company K, the Dixie Guards, was composed of men from Spartanburg District who had served in Company C of the 9th Regiment before the reorganization.[135] In addition, there were a number of men from Sumter, Clarendon and Williamsburg Districts who had served in Companies D and F of the 9th Regiment. A few came from Chesterfield and Charleston Districts. William S. Brand, the company's only captain, was elected on April 22, 1862. He was wounded in the left hand by a Minié ball at Fort Harrison on September 30, 1864. Brand returned to duty on October 17 and was paroled with the company at Appomattox Court House on April 9, 1865.[136]

Brigade Affiliations

The 6th Regiment was attached to Nelson's Brigade in April 1861 and to the Charleston forces from April to July.[137] Part of Bonham's Brigade at First Manassas, the 6th was assigned to D.R. Jones's Brigade from July 28, 1861, to February 1862.[138] After the battle of First Manassas, Jones's Brigade comprised the 4th, 5th, 6th and 9th Regiments, SCV. R.H. Anderson assumed command of this brigade in February 1862. After the reorganization, Anderson's Brigade consisted of the 4th (13th) South Carolina Battalion, the 5th and 6th Regiments, the Palmetto Sharpshooters, the 2nd South Carolina Regiment of Rifles and the St. Paul (Louisiana) Battalion. Micah Jenkins assumed command in May 1862. The St. Paul Battalion was detached from the brigade after the battle of Seven Pines, and Hagood's 1st Regiment was added just before the battle of Second Manassas. In November 1862, the

13th (4th) Battalion merged with the Infantry Battalion, Hampton Legion, to form the Infantry Regiment, Hampton Legion, which remained with Jenkins's Brigade until March 1864. John Bratton commanded the brigade after Jenkins's death on May 6, 1864.

MAJOR MOVEMENTS AND ENGAGEMENTS

The 6th Regiment left home for state service on April 11, 1861, and arrived in Charleston that evening.[139] Five companies of the 6th Regiment were stationed on Morris Island during the bombardment of Fort Sumter on April 12 and April 13. The Fairfield Fencibles and the Buckhead Guards were sent to Battery Island on the twelfth. The Boyce Guards were sent to Cole's Island, and the Calhoun and Catawba Guards were sent to Sullivan's Island on the evening of April 12. W.A. Fudge, a veteran of Company A, wrote that his company, the Calhoun Guards, was sent to Mount Pleasant during the bombardment and the next day was sent to Sullivan's Island for about a week.[140] On April 30, the companies on Morris Island were transferred to Fort Pickens at Battery Island on the Stono River.[141] Companies of the regiment, some functioning as artillery, served in detachments on Sullivan's Island, Cole's Island, Battery Island and at Fort Johnson until June 3, when the regiment was ordered to Summerville.[142] It arrived at nearby Camp Woodward the next day. On June 21 while still in camp, the regiment reorganized to muster in Confederate service.[143] With seven of its original companies and three new additions, it mustered in between June 12 and July 10, 1861. The regiment was ordered to Virginia on the thirteenth.[144] The men left Summerville on July 16 and arrived in Richmond on the seventeenth and eighteenth.[145] Leaving Richmond on July 20, the regiment arrived at the Manassas battlefield on July 21, too late in the day to be engaged. The brigade left Camp Pettus on August 12 and moved to Germantown in Fairfax County, about seven miles nearer Washington.[146] The 6th Regiment skirmished with Federal pickets on September 13 near Manassas Hill, marched back to Bull Run in mid-October, and moved to Centreville in November.[147] The regiment's first battle in Virginia was at Dranesville on December 20. With some 330 men engaged that day, the 6th Regiment's casualties totaled 18 killed and 48 wounded.[148] After spending the fall and winter near Centreville in northern Virginia, the regiment left on March 10, 1862, and arrived at Richmond on April 14. Departing by steamer for Yorktown on the seventeenth, the men performed picket duty near the enemy. The regiment withdrew from Yorktown on May 3 and arrived at Williamsburg on the evening of the fourth. Engaged near

Williamsburg on May 5, the regiment evacuated the next day. It arrived at its camp within five miles of Richmond on May 17. The 6th Regiment was engaged at the battle of Seven Pines on May 31 when it and the Palmetto Sharpshooters made their famous charge. By the end of the day, the 6th Regiment had lost its colonel to wounds, had seen the deaths of four captains and had suffered about half its men killed, wounded and missing. After the battle of Seven Pines, the regiment set aside its Mississippi Rifles and "buck and ball" muskets, rearming itself with Enfield Rifles. The regiment crossed the Chickahominy River on June 26, but it was not engaged that day. It was engaged at Gaines's Mill on June 27; on June 30, Jenkins's Brigade opened the engagement at Frayser's Farm, where the 6th Regiment was heavily engaged.[149] Though not engaged during the remainder of the Seven Days battles, the brigade was shelled at Malvern Hill. The 6th Regiment returned to Richmond on July 8 and remained there until about August 13, when the men moved north with Longstreet's corps. About this time, Hagood's 1st Regiment, SCV, joined the 6th Regiment in Micah Jenkins's Brigade. Its further major movements and engagements are discussed in this volume under Hagood's 1st Regiment.

On April 9, 1865, the 6th Regiment surrendered with Bratton's Brigade at Appomattox Court House.[150] The men rested for the next two days and laid down their arms, accoutrements and colors on the twelfth. Between April 13 and April 15, the regiments started the long march home together, but the men soon broke up into smaller groups for the six-hundred-mile journey that lay before them.[151]

6.

The 7th Regiment, South Carolina Volunteers

The 7th Regiment, SCV, was also known affectionately as the "Old Seventh" Regiment.[1] It was one of ten regiments authorized by the South Carolina legislature's Act of December 17, 1860. All ten regiments consisted of men who volunteered for twelve months. The 7th Regiment enlisted in state service for one year on April 15, 1861. Company A transferred to the 2nd Regiment, SCV, in late April. The nine remaining companies, B through I and K, enlisted in Confederate service on June 4 at Camp Butler, near Johnson's Turnout (now Monmorenci).

The departure of Company A, the Secession Guards, created a deficit of one company in the 7th Regiment. On July 2, 1861, the Horry Volunteers joined as the tenth company and was designated Company L. Unlike many South Carolina infantry regiments raised early in 1861, the 7th suffered little when its men chose to enter Confederate service. During April, May and June 1861, South Carolina infantry regiments converting from state to Confederate service typically lost those few companies whose men refused to enter Confederate service. The 7th Regiment, on the other hand, lost Company A because its men wanted to enter Confederate service even before the rest of the regiment did so. In another unusual occurrence, the 7th Regiment lost no company through entering Confederate service.

After early July 1861, the 7th Regiment comprised ten companies, B through L, with J omitted, as was customary. According to the *CSR*, a redesignation in late June called for each company to be known by the letter preceding its former designation. Hence, Company B became Company A, Company C became Company B and so on. This state of affairs continued until May 1862, when the regiment was reorganized and increased from ten to twelve companies, lettered A through I and K through M. The regiment was kept in service for thirteen months from its initial enlistment until the reorganization in May 1862. During its retreat from Yorktown after the battle of Williamsburg, the regiment reorganized near New Kent Court House, Virginia; the men re-enlisted for two additional years on May 14. Like many other regiments, the men of the 7th voted that spring to completely replace the field officers and all but one company commander. Unlike a number of other regiments at the reorganization, the companies of the 7th remained relatively intact; no companies and few men left. Two years later, in March 1864, the regiment re-enlisted for the duration of the war. On April 9, 1865, the 7th Regiment was consolidated with the 15th Regiment, SCV, and parts of the 1st, 2nd, 6th and 7th Battalions of Blanchard's South Carolina Reserves to form the New, or Consolidated, 7th Regiment, SCV, which was paroled at Greensboro on May 2, 1865.[2]

Field Officers

Thomas Glascock Bacon of Edgefield was forty-eight years old when he was elected colonel of the regiment, probably on February 23, 1861.[3] Bacon's opponent was a gentleman named Moragne, probably W.C. Moragne, former colonel of the 19th Regiment, whom he defeated by a vote of 166 to 109.[4] Bacon had held the rank of major in the prewar South Carolina militia.[5] He was wounded in the left thigh when his navy revolver accidentally discharged sometime in March 1861.[6] By April 18, his recovery was progressing well.[7] Bacon enlisted as colonel in state service along with the regiment on April 15 and mustered in Confederate service, also with the regiment, on June 4, 1861. He resigned at the reorganization on May 14, 1862, declining to stand for re-election and citing poor health.[8] Bacon served as colonel of the 5th Regiment, South Carolina Reserves, a ninety-day regiment, in late 1862 and early 1863.[9] He was elected to the South Carolina Senate from Edgefield in 1863.[10] Dickert wrote: "Strong in his friendship and earnest in his affection, but with a peaceable and forgiving temperament, pure in his motives, charitable in all things, generous to the needy, affectionate to his friends and relatives, chivalric and honorable in every relation of life, brave in action, and with that fortitude in adverse circumstances that makes heroes of men, just and impartial to the officers and men under his command, pleasant and sociable towards his equals in rank, obedient and courteous to his superiors, few men lived or died with so much respect and admiration, genuine friendship, and love for all as Colonel Thomas G. Bacon."[11]

Robert Anderson Fair of Abbeville District was elected the first lieutenant colonel on February 23, 1861, with a vote of 270 to 6 each for opponents Bates and Perrin.[12] Originally captain of Company D, Fair enlisted in state service with the regiment as lieutenant colonel on April 15 and mustered in Confederate service on June 4, 1861.[13] He resigned on May 4, 1862, only ten days before the regiment was reorganized.[14] The *CSR* indicates that Fair was not re-elected and was dropped at the reorganization, but Major Seibels served as acting lieutenant colonel from May 4 to May 14, clearly indicating that Fair had resigned. The record indicates that "physical disability compelled him to quit the army. One year's service has told on him considerably."[15] Fair served in the South Carolina legislature for the remainder of the war.[16]

Emmet Seibels of Edgefield was elected the first major of the regiment, probably also on February 23, 1861, defeating D.W. Aiken and a gentleman identified only as Tompkins.[17] He enlisted as major in state service on April 15 and in Confederate service on June 4, 1861. Seibels and Elbert Bland, then captain of Company H, fought a duel with large-caliber pistols over a game of chess on November 26, 1861, at Mitchell's Ford on Bull Run.[18] Though Seibels fired at "one" and Bland at "three," Seibels was struck in the right side of the abdomen. The ball exited the left side but fortunately did not penetrate the abdominal cavity.[19] Seibels's recovery took several months.[20] He served ten days as acting lieutenant colonel after Fair's resignation but was probably not officially promoted to the position.[21] A pay voucher dated May 17, 1862, refers to Seibels as lieutenant colonel, though all other *CSR* references show him as major. Seibels wrote in a letter dated August 24, 1863, that he had been lieutenant colonel of the 7th Regiment. In another letter dated November 30, 1864, he said he was promoted to lieutenant colonel of the 7th Regiment on May 4, 1862, and was defeated in the election for colonel later that month. A letter from Matthew C. Butler contradicts these statements. In May 1864, Butler wrote that Seibels, an officer of great efficiency and ability, had served as major of the 7th Regiment.[22] Though Seibels ran for election to colonel of the 7th Regiment at the reorganization, he made himself unpopular by admonishing the men to remain in the service. D.W. Aiken, who had apparently gained popularity by urging the men to go home, defeated him.[23] Seibels was dropped from the rolls of the 7th Regiment on May 14, 1862. Milledge L. Bonham called him a faithful and efficient officer.[24] Seibels later served as a private in the 2nd Regiment, SCV. In May 1864, Matthew C. Butler helped him secure a position as quartermaster in Butler's command.[25] In November 1864, Seibels was acting aide-de-camp on General Butler's division staff.[26] The same month, he applied for command of the Foreign Battalion, but that post went to J.H. Brooks.

David Wyatt Aiken was originally from Winnsboro but moved to Abbeville before the war.[27] He was elected colonel of the 7th Regiment at the reorganization on May 14, 1862.[28] The thirty-two-year-old Aiken had lost to Emmett Seibels in a hotly contested election for major in February 1861. Though extremely upset by the outcome of that election, he volunteered to remain with the regiment as a private. Soon, however, Aiken was appointed adjutant of the 7th Regiment with the rank of captain, effective from March 9.[29] Aiken defeated Seibels in the election for colonel of the 7th Regiment in May 1862. At Sharpsburg on September 17, 1862, a rifle ball entered Aiken's left breast and exited his back along the edge of the shoulder blade.[30] Newspapers reported that he had been mortally wounded or killed in action.[31] In fact, he had survived and, though taken prisoner, was soon exchanged. The *Charleston Daily Courier* reported that Aiken was back home in Winnsboro by October 17.[32] According to the *CSR*, he was paroled and exchanged at Aiken's Landing on November 8. The exchange was probably made because Aiken's wound was thought "for a long time" to be fatal.[33] He returned to the regiment in June 1863, but he was wounded again the following month at Gettysburg. Aiken tendered his resignation on July 24, 1863. In early August however, before the letter left the adjutant's office, Aiken received orders to assume command of troops and defenses at the post at Macon, Georgia.[34] By August 26, he was personally in command at Macon.[35] Aiken resigned the position in Macon on July 14, 1864, based on a surgeon's statement that the Sharpsburg wound and his generally poor health left him unfit for duty. Dickert wrote: "Colonel Aiken was also one of nature's noblemen, bold, fearless, and incorruptible."[36] Not everyone agreed with this assessment. One private wrote in June 1863 when Aiken returned to the regiment: "Some hate to see him back. [Colonel] Bland is much better liked by the regiment than [Colonel] Aiken...the officers have no use for Aiken or at least the majority of them. For he makes them stand square up to the rack, fodder or no fodder. But he is not so overly strict with the privates."[37] Another source called him "firm and decisive when the occasion dictated, but...always generous and just and considerate."[38]

Elbert Bland, MD, of Edgefield District was elected lieutenant colonel on May 14, 1862.[39] Bland had been a surgeon in the Palmetto Regiment during the Mexican War and was a highly respected physician in Abbeville.[40] He had served as surgeon in Maxcy Gregg's 1st Regiment, SCV, between January and March 1861 and was captain of Company H of the 7th Regiment before the reorganization.[41] Bland was severely wounded in the arm at Savage's Station on June 29, 1862, and never completely recovered from the wound.[42] He was also slightly wounded at Fredericksburg on December 13, 1862, was wounded again at Chancellorsville in May 1863, and sustained still another wound, this time to the thigh, at Gettysburg.[43] The *Mercury* reported that Bland was promoted to colonel, replacing Aiken when the latter was transferred out of the regiment in August 1863.[44] Although Bland did command the regiment often between December 13, 1862, and September 20, 1863, and strongly desired the promotion, he never officially made colonel. He recommended himself for the promotion in 1863 based on Aiken's absence from the regiment, and Milledge L. Bonham added his recommendation in a letter to Secretary of War Seddon. Bland also tendered his resignation twice in 1863: on April 9 and on August 31. The second time, the men begged him to remain with the regiment, and he withdrew the resignation.[45] While leading the regiment at the battle of Chickamauga on September 20, 1863, Bland was shot down; he lived for about forty-five minutes.[46] The *Roll of the Dead* states, incorrectly, that he died of disease in Federal prison at Point Lookout, Maryland, in 1863. Dickert wrote: "Bland was the ideal soldier and a fighter 'par excellence'...His was a noble, generous soul, cool and brave almost to rashness. He was idolized by his troops and beloved as a comrade and commander."[47] In January 1864, J.B. Kershaw also wrote a letter praising Bland's personal characteristics. One sentence reads: "He possessed as an officer the military talent and disciplinary capacity of the highest order."[48]

William Capers White was elected major on May 14, 1862.[49] White was probably from Georgetown District, though one *Mercury* report gives Horry District as his home.[50] Dickert recorded, incorrectly, that he was from Edgefield.[51] White had been captain of Company L before the reorganization. On September 17, 1862, while acting lieutenant colonel at Sharpsburg, White had just ordered the 7th Regiment to retire when he was shot through the head by grapeshot and killed instantly.[52] White was buried at the Sharpsburg Cemetery.[53] The *Roll of the Dead* incorrectly states that he was killed at Maryland Heights on September 13, 1862. One of White's brothers was Richard Green White, first major of the 10th Regiment. Another was James Benjamin White, superintendent of The Citadel Academy and commanding officer of the Battalion of State Cadets.

John Stuart Hard of Graniteville in Edgefield District was promoted to major from captain of Company F on September 17, 1862, replacing Major White.[54] Hard was killed instantly while leading the regiment on the top of Pea Ridge during the battle of Chickamauga on September 20, 1863.[55] Krick gives Hard's middle name as Stewart, and contemporary newspapers spell it both Stuart and Stewart.[56] The *CSR* gives contradictory references: one states that Hard was "mustered in as major but was never actually promoted to major"; another says he was "promoted to major on September 17, 1862."[57] The fact that his successor as captain of Company F was promoted on September 17 strongly supports the notion that Hard was named major on that date as well. Dickert considered Hard "one of the finest officers in the brigade."[58] Kershaw wrote that he was "a gallant and accomplished officer, and has highly distinguished himself on every battlefield in which his regiment has been engaged."[59] His obituary reads in part: "During his brief but brilliant career, he won for himself not only the respect and esteem of his associates, but the confidence of his superiors."[60]

Elijah Jeremiah "Jerry" Goggans of Edgefield District was promoted to lieutenant colonel on January 12, 1865, retroactive to September 20, 1863. Goggans was captain of Company M, and his wartime biography is discussed there.

Thomas Allison Hudgens, MD, of Laurens District commanded the regiment after Goggans resigned, but his record is also unclear. Goggans commanded the regiment until he resigned in May 1864. That summer, though Captain Henry W. Addison claimed to be the senior captain in the regiment, Captain Hudgens of Company B was given command. Hudgens led the regiment as acting lieutenant colonel in October 1864 but still held the rank of captain at the time.[61] Hudgens was wounded several times, once at Fredericksburg.[62] The most severe wound was to the thigh at the Wilderness on May 6, 1864, while he was acting major.[63] Hudgens was promoted to lieutenant colonel on April 9, 1865, when the 7th Regiment was consolidated with other South Carolina units.[64] The fact that no other captain is listed for Company B supports the assumption that Hudgens was not promoted to lieutenant colonel in October 1864. Hudgens served until he was paroled on May 2, 1865, at Greensboro.

Robert Clayton Maffett, lieutenant colonel of the 3rd Regiment, SCV, was ordered to take command of the 7th Regiment on August 4, 1864; he assumed command the next day. Maffett's appointment was not altogether acceptable to the 7th Regiment, but as a "good officer and a perfect gentleman," he was expected to win the good will and confidence of his men.[65] Maffett commanded the regiment for only twenty-two days, until his capture near Halltown in the Shenandoah Valley on August 26, 1864.

COMPANIES

Following are the companies of the 7th Regiment from its enlistment in state service in April 1861 until the reorganization in May 1862:

Company A, the Secession Guards, was organized on January 10, 1861, at "Chalk Level," the muster ground of the local militia battalion.[66] The company was also called Perryman's Company, the Abbeville Volunteers and the Abbeville Guards.[67] Its men were from the towns of Greenwood, Ninety Six and New Market in the eastern part of Abbeville District, now

Greenwood County.[68] The Secession Guards was Company A of the 7th Regiment from January to April 28, 1861, when the men, unwilling to wait, left for Confederate service in Virginia.[69] Meanwhile, four companies of the 2nd Regiment also volunteered for service in Virginia in late April 1861; six companies of the 2nd chose to remain in South Carolina. The group of four in Virginia needed to add new companies to reach the regiment's complement; accordingly, on April 30 the Secession Guards opted for transfer to the 2nd Regiment, becoming Company F. William Watson Perryman was commissioned captain of the company on January 10, 1861, and he was commissioned again on April 17, when the regiment entered state service. He retained his commission when the company transferred to the 2nd Regiment.[70]

Company B, the Southern Guards, was also called the Cokesbury Minutemen.[71] Its men were from Abbeville District, where the company was organized at Drakes about January 18, 1861.[72] The company rendezvoused at Donalds about April 1, and the men mustered in Confederate service on June 4, 1861, at Camp Butler.[73] Gabriel M. Mattison commanded the company until poor health forced him to resign on May 31.[74] First Lieutenant W. Ludlow Hodges, a veteran of the Mexican War, succeeded Mattison as captain, with rank from May 15, a date also shown as May 20.[75] Not re-elected at the reorganization, Hodges resigned on May 13, 1862. He later served as lieutenant colonel of the 1st Regiment, South Carolina State Troops, in late 1863 and early 1864. This company was also called Company A from May 1861 to May 1862. At the reorganization in 1862, most of the men re-enlisted in Company B, but some chose Company A of the reorganized 7th Regiment.

Company C was composed of men from Abbeville District. One of two companies of minute men raised in Abbeville on October 15, 1859, in anticipation of armed conflict between the North and the South, Company C was officially organized at Bradley's about January 18, 1861.[76] Patrick H. Bradley was elected captain on January 21. He mustered in state service on April 15 and in Confederate service on June 4.[77] Bradley resigned on May 13, 1862. This company was also called Company B from May 1861 to May 1862. Most of its men re-enlisted in Company C at the reorganization.

Company D, Hester's Company, was also from Abbeville District. It was organized about January 18, 1861, at McCaw's.[78] The first captain, Robert Anderson Fair, was elected lieutenant colonel of the regiment on February 23, and First Lieutenant Samuel J. Hester took his place.[79] Hester was elected captain on March 9 and mustered in state and Confederate service with the company. Hester was not re-elected at the reorganization and was dropped from the rolls on May 13, 1862. This company was also called Company C from May 1861 to May 1862. At the reorganization in May 1862, most of its men re-enlisted in Company D.

Company E, the Mount Willing Guards, was composed of men previously in the Lower Battalion of the 10th Regiment, South Carolina Militia, from Edgefield District. David Denny, its only captain, was elected on February 7 and mustered in state and Confederate service with the company.[80] Denny resigned because of his age on May 13, 1862. This company was also called Company D from May 1861 to May 1862. Company E was deemed too large at the reorganization. Most of its men re-enlisted in Company E; many chose a new company designated M.

Company F was probably originally a company from Trenton in Edgefield District. W.L. Coleman commanded the company, which was raised from the Upper Battalion of the 7th Regiment, South Carolina Militia.[81] This was probably the same Wilson L. Coleman who was elected major of the Upper Battalion, 7th Regiment, South Carolina Militia, in February 1862.[82] Coleman's Company went into camp with the 7th Regiment at Montmorenci in early May 1861, an indication that it had probably mustered in state service with the regiment in April. Coleman was still captain on June 4, when the company failed to muster in Confederate service with the 7th Regiment.[83] Though its fate is unknown, the company was probably disbanded.[84] Some evidence suggests that Coleman served as a private in Company K after June 4, 1861. The *Edgefield Advertiser* reported on June 5 that a company, which it did not identify, refused service in Virginia—that is, it refused to muster in Confederate service—and was replaced by a new company from Graniteville under Captain Hard.[85] Hard's Company was raised from the Lower Battalion of the 7th Regiment, South Carolina Militia, and was from Graniteville in Edgefield District.[86] It existed as early as February 1861, but whether or not it was attached to a regiment before June is unclear.[87] The company, called the Davies Guard or Davies Guards, was named in honor of Major Thomas J. Davies, who saw to its welfare and was instrumental in its success.[88] The company name also appears, incorrectly, as the Davis Guard and Davis Guards.[89] The Graniteville Riflemen was another company from Graniteville in the part of Edgefield District now in Aiken County.[90] The Graniteville Riflemen was attached to the 7th Regiment as Company F. It is possible that Hard's Company was called the Graniteville Riflemen before it was known as the Davies Guards.[91] John Stuart Hard mustered in as captain of Company F on June 4, 1861. He was re-elected at the reorganization on May 13, 1862, a date also shown as April 16. From May 1861 to May 1862, this company was also called Company E. Most of its men re-enlisted with Captain Hard in Company F at the reorganization.

Company G, the Brooks Greys, was from Edgefield District.[92] Its men had served in the Upper Battalion of the 10th Regiment, South Carolina Militia, before the war.[93] John Hampden Brooks, who raised the company, was elected its captain on February 8, 1861.[94] Brooks mustered in state service on April 15 and in Confederate service on June 4, 1861. Captain Brooks named the company in honor of his brother, Preston S. Brooks, who had attacked Massachusetts Senator Charles Sumner with his cane in the United States Senate on May 22, 1856. Brooks's mother supplied the uniforms for the company.[95] Brooks served as Elbert Bland's second during the latter's duel with Major Seibels on November 26, 1861. From May 1861 to May 1862, this company was called Company F. On March 8, 1862, at Ninety Six, South Carolina, the men re-enlisted for three years or for the duration of the war—most of them in Company G and a few in the new company, M. Brooks was not re-elected at the reorganization. Dickert, historian of Kershaw's Brigade, wrote that Brooks did not seek re-election in the spring of 1862.[96] On July 14, 1862, Brooks was elected captain of a company of partisan rangers that eventually became Company H of the 7th Battalion, South Carolina Infantry.

Company H, the Ninety Six Rifles, was composed of men from Edgefield District.[97] A rifle company from the beginning, it had existed as early as January 30, 1861.[98] The men mustered in state service on April 15 and in Confederate service on June 4, 1861. Company H was the right company of the 7th Regiment.[99] Thomas G. Bacon and Elbert Bland raised the company. On March 16, 1861, Bacon was elected captain, Stewart Harrison was elected first lieutenant and Bland was elected second lieutenant.[100] When Bacon was elected colonel of the regiment in March, Bland became captain.[101] Bland was elected lieutenant colonel of the 7th Regiment on May 14, 1862, and may have been re-elected captain of the company the same day since the *CSR* names him as the first captain of Company A after the reorganization. From May 1861 to May 1862, this company was also called Company G. At the reorganization, most of the men re-enlisted in Company H, and some opted for Company A, which retained the company name.

Company I, the Red Hill Guard, was composed of men previously in the Lower Battalion of the 9th Regiment, South Carolina Militia.[102] It was organized at Red Hill in Edgefield District. William F. Prescott, elected captain on February 1, 1861, mustered in state service on April 15 and in Confederate service on June 4.[103] Prescott was in poor health in the spring of 1862 and was not re-elected captain. He was dropped from the rolls on May 13 and may have commanded Company C, 1st Regiment Junior Reserves, in 1864 and 1865.[104] From May 1861 to May 1862, this company was also called Company H. Most of its men re-enlisted in Company I at the reorganization.

Company K, the Ruffin Guards, was composed of men from Edgefield District.[105] Its men were from the Upper Battalion of the 9th Regiment, South Carolina Militia.[106] Bartley "Bart" M. Talbert, elected captain on February 19, 1861, mustered in state service on April 15 and in Confederate service on June 4.[107] Talbert was not re-elected and was dropped from the rolls on May 13, 1862. From May 1861 to May 1862, this company was also called Company I. Most of its men re-enlisted in Company K at the reorganization.

Company L, the Horry Volunteers from Horry District, was also called the Horry Guards, the All Saints Riflemen and the All Saints Rifles.[108] The *Horry Dispatch* referred to the company in April 1861 as the All Saints Rifles, and on May 9, the same newspaper called it the Horry Volunteers.[109] It is possible that the All Saints Rifles was a company in state service and that the Horry Volunteers was a group raised from the All Saints Rifles for Confederate service. William Capers White, elected captain by May 9, mustered at that rank on June 26, 1861.[110] He was elected major on May 14, 1862. The Horry Volunteers replaced Company A, which had left the 7th Regiment to join the 2nd Regiment in late April. The Horry Volunteers and the Waccamaw Light Artillery were stationed at Fort Randal on Little River in mid-April.[111] On June 7, Captain White was in Charleston to offer the services of his company to the governor.[112] The *Mercury* reported that the company left Conwayboro on June 22 to join the 7th Regiment in Virginia.[113] The *CSR* states that the company marched from Conwayboro on June 25 to Marion Court House, where it mustered in for twelve months' Confederate service the next day. The company arrived in Richmond on June 29, 1861. About July 2, the Horry Volunteers joined the 7th Regiment.[114] From May 1861 to May 1862, this company was also called Company K. Most of the men re-enlisted in Company L, and a few enlisted in Companies A, H and K at the reorganization.

Following are the companies of the 7th Regiment after the reorganization in May 1862:

Company A, the Ninety Six Riflemen, was composed of men who had been in Company B from Abbeville District and in Company H from Edgefield District. A few were previously in Company L from Horry District, and a few others were new recruits. The company was named for the village of Ninety Six, which was located on the extreme eastern edge of Abbeville District, now in Greenwood County. Formerly captain of Company H, Elbert Bland was elected lieutenant colonel of the 7th Regiment on May 14, 1862. Bland may have been re-elected captain of Company A the same day since the

CSR names him as the first captain of Company A after the reorganization. If this is correct, Bland served as captain for only a day. Stewart Harrison, formerly first lieutenant of Company H, was elected captain of Company A on May 14, 1862. Elected clerk of Court of Common Pleas and General Sessions for Edgefield District, Harrison resigned on March 18, 1864. On March 18, A.W. "Gus" Burt was promoted in absentia from first lieutenant to captain as Harrison's successor.[115] Burt had been wounded in the right knee, right shoulder and left ankle at Gettysburg on July 2, 1863. His foot was amputated, and he was left behind at Gettysburg, where he fell into the hands of the enemy. Burt was taken first to the School House Hospital in Chambersburg, Pennsylvania, on July 14 and from there to the United States Army General Hospital at the Cotton Factory in Harrisburg. He was sent to the West Walnut Street Hospital on November 5 before moving on to West's Buildings Hospital in Baltimore. On March 2, 1864, he was sent to Fort McHenry, Maryland, and on June 15, he was sent to Fort Delaware. Burt was moved to Hilton Head Island as part of the "Immortal Six Hundred" on August 20, but he was never placed with the six hundred Confederate officers on Morris Island. From the transport USS *Crescent* he was transferred to the United States General Hospital for Prisoners of War at Beaufort on August 28 and placed on parole. Burt was exchanged at Charleston Harbor on December 15, 1864. There is no evidence that anyone replaced him as captain of Company A.

Company B was composed of mostly Abbeville District men who had been in Company B. It is unclear whether the new Company B retained the name Southern Guards or the name Cokesbury Minutemen.[116] Some men came from Anderson and Union Districts. Thomas Allison Hudgens, MD, of Laurens District, previously third lieutenant in the first Company B, was elected captain on May 13, 1862. Hudgens was wounded several times, once slightly, at Fredericksburg in December 1862.[117] The most severe was a flesh wound to the right thigh sustained while he was acting major at the Wilderness on May 6, 1864.[118] The *CSR* shows Hudgens as captain in December 1864; he had functioned as acting lieutenant colonel since October.[119] Hudgens was promoted to lieutenant colonel on April 9, 1865, when the 7th Regiment was consolidated with other South Carolina units.[120] The fact that no other captain is shown for Company B suggests that Hudgens was not promoted to lieutenant colonel earlier. He served until he was paroled on May 2, 1865, at Greensboro.

Company C was composed primarily of men from Abbeville District who had been in Company C. Others came from Edgefield and Spartanburg Districts. Wade E. Cothran, a Citadel graduate and former first lieutenant of Company C, was elected captain on May 13, 1862.[121] Cothran was wounded and disabled at Maryland Heights on September 13 when a Minié ball passed through both thighs, leaving him with constant pain and a paralyzed right leg. Cothran probably never returned to the company; he resigned on a surgeon's certificate on August 25, 1863, a date also shown as August 20. Cothran was considered a brave and good officer.[122] N. Hodges Palmer was promoted from first lieutenant to captain on August 25. Palmer, who was hospitalized with gonorrhea in November 1861, was severely wounded at Fredericksburg on December 13, 1862, when he held the rank of second lieutenant. He was captured on July 2, 1863, at Gettysburg and was taken to Fort McHenry on the ninth. Later that month, he was sent to Fort Delaware, and on July 18, he was sent to Johnson's Island, near Sandusky, Ohio. On March 14, 1865, he was moved to Point Lookout, Maryland. Palmer was exchanged along with 305 other Confederate prisoners of war on March 22, 1865, at Cox's Wharf on the James River. First Lieutenant John Lyon commanded the company after Palmer was captured, but the *CSR* shows him as first lieutenant through December 17, 1864. Lyon was paroled with the rank of captain on May 2, 1865, at Greensboro, but the date of his promotion to captain is not recorded. It is possible that he was made captain when the 7th Regiment was consolidated with other units to create the "new" 7th Regiment on April 9, 1865. Lyon was wounded in the left knee at Hanover Junction on the North Anna River on May 26, 1864. He also sustained a wound to the shoulder at Cedar Creek, Virginia, and to the side at Bentonville, North Carolina. Lyon was captain of Company G, 7th Consolidated Regiment. He was considered a brave and efficient officer.[123]

Company D was composed of men from Abbeville District who had served in the previous Company D. A few new recruits also joined the company. Thomas Warren Allen, who had been first lieutenant of Company D, was elected captain on May 13, 1862.[124] Allen was slightly wounded at Chickamauga in September 1863.[125] He left the company in January or February 1864 and never returned. He applied for retirement on December 28, 1864, based on chronic rheumatism and disease of the aortic valve. The record does not show whether the application was approved, nor does it indicate that Allen was ever replaced as captain.

Company E was composed of Edgefield District men who came from the former Company E. Whether the company retained the name Mount Willing Guards is unclear. Some new men from Lexington, Williamsburg and Abbeville Districts joined Company E. James Mitchell, previously third lieutenant in Company E, was elected the company's only captain on May 13, 1862.[126] He was wounded at Sharpsburg on September 17 and severely wounded in the Shenandoah Valley on October 26, 1864.[127] Mitchell was probably furloughed and sent home. He was paroled at Augusta, Georgia, on May 19, 1865. The *Roll of the Dead* states that S.N. Hendrick, who died on December 20, 1864, was a captain in Company E. The *CSR* does not confirm this information. If the date of Hendrick's death is correct, his tenure as captain would have conflicted with Mitchell's. The *Roll of the Dead* probably confused S.N. Hendrick with George A. Hendricks, captain of Company E of the 2nd Regiment, South Carolina Rifles.

Company F was composed of men from Graniteville, in that part of Edgefield District that is now Aiken County. These men had also been in Company F, though we do not know if the names Davies Guards or Graniteville Riflemen were kept. A few new men came from Marion, Barnwell, Spartanburg, Abbeville and Anderson Districts. John S. Hard was re-elected captain on May 13, a date also shown as April 16, 1862. He was slightly wounded in the hand during the Seven Days battles.[128] Hard was promoted to major on September 17, 1862. First Lieutenant James E. Rearden, wounded at Sharpsburg on September 17, 1862, was promoted to captain the same day. Rearden was wounded so severely at Chickamauga on September 20, 1863, that he lost a leg and died six days later.[129] He is listed alphabetically in the *CSR* under the spelling Reardon; individual cards show his name as Rearden. Warren D. Brooks from Edgefield was promoted from first lieutenant to captain on September 26, 1863. Brooks was killed on May 6, 1864, at the Wilderness and was replaced by First Lieutenant Benjamin A. McKibben from Marion the same day. McKibben was badly wounded in the right arm at Cold Harbor on June 1, 1864.[130] He suffered a fracture to the upper end of the radius that produced inflammation of the elbow joint; the subsequent stiffening of the joint and contracture of the muscles limited the use of the right hand. McKibben was a brave officer, but his wounded arm prevented him from performing his duties efficiently.[131] He applied for retirement to the Invalid Corps on April 7, 1865. Though the application was forwarded, no documentation that it was finally approved exists, probably because the war ended before it could be acted upon. McKibben's wound caused him great suffering for many years after the war, essentially crippling him for the rest of his life.[132] His name is also shown as both McKibbon and McKibbin.[133] The *CSR* states that Company F was commanded by James Townsend, but this is probably Company F of the 7th and 15th Consolidated Regiment, not the 7th Regiment. Townsend was elected first lieutenant of Company B, 7th Regiment, on May 13, 1862. He was wounded in the left arm on September 13 at Maryland Heights. He was paroled as captain of Company F of the 7th Consolidated Regiment on May 2, 1865, at Greensboro. The *CSR* does not record the exact date of Townsend's promotion to captain, but it was probably April 9, 1865.

It is possible, though unlikely, that Townsend was promoted from first lieutenant of Company B to captain of Company F of the 7th Regiment after McKibben retired to the Invalid Corps. Townsend was a brave and efficient officer.[134]

Company G was composed of men from Edgefield District who had been in the first Company G. Whether or not the company retained the name Brooks Greys is unclear. The men of Company G re-enlisted for three years or for the duration of the war on March 8, 1862, at Ninety Six. William E. Clark, previously first lieutenant of Company G, was elected its captain on May 13. He was severely wounded in the left arm and side at Maryland Heights on September 12 or September 13.[135] The *CSR* states that Clark died in Charleston but gives two dates for his death: September 20 and September 22, 1862. The former is probably correct since his successor was promoted to captain that day. His tombstone in Saluda County, however, records the latter as the date of death.[136] A private in company G wrote: "There is no better man living than Captain Clark, for the men all complain of his being too easy. If a man goes to him for a favor if it is in his power to grant it he will do it."[137] John Wiley Kemp was promoted from first lieutenant to captain on September 20, 1862.[138] Kemp was leading Company G on May 6, 1864, at the Wilderness when he was struck in the chest by a volley and killed instantly.[139] He was "one of the best fellows that ever lived."[140] First Lieutenant James C. Williams was Company G's last captain. Williams had been slightly wounded at Fredericksburg. He was wounded again at the Wilderness on May 6, 1864. His promotion to captain was effective from the same day. Williams was a brave officer, but as a disciplinarian he was considered ordinary. Still absent from the company because of his wound in November, he returned before the end of the war. Williams was captain of Company D, 7th Consolidated Regiment, in April 1865.

Company H was composed mostly of men from Edgefield District who had been in the old Company H. It probably retained the name, Ninety Six Rifles. There were also a few Horry District men who had served in the previous Company L. Henry W. Addison, who had attended The Citadel, was first sergeant of the previous Company H and was elected captain on May 13, 1862.[141] He was wounded at Sharpsburg on September 17. On August 14, 1863, Addison applied for transfer to another post on the grounds that his company had been reduced by attrition to only fifteen men. Wounded in the left leg at Chickamauga on September 20, 1863, Addison lost the leg and was furloughed home.[142] In October 1863, he applied for an appointment as judge advocate. Addison was doing well at home in December, but he was missing most of one leg.[143] The *Edgefield Advertiser* reported in December that Addison, a "gallant and efficient young officer," would be made major of the 7th Regiment when he returned to duty.[144] He did return to the 7th Regiment for about two months in May and June 1864.[145] Claiming seniority over Captain Hudgens of Company B, Addison also made it clear that he wanted promotion to colonel of the 7th Regiment after Goggans resigned. Both men, Addison and Hudgens, had been elected captain on May 13, 1862. In a letter dated August 22, 1864, Addison claimed to have been the captain in command of Company H since the battle of Williamsburg, on May 5, 1862. He also stated that his commission was not sent forward at the time.[146] This seems unlikely since Elbert Bland was captain of Company H until he was elected lieutenant colonel of the regiment on May 14, 1862. Nevertheless, Hudgens received the promotion. Addison was absent without leave on November 28, 1864, and was deemed eligible for retirement, having been declared disabled by a proper medical authority. He returned to Edgefield and ran for the legislature. No steps were taken for his retirement throughout December, and there is no record of his being replaced as captain of Company H. He served as aide-de-camp to Governor Magrath in 1865.

Company I was composed of men from Edgefield District, most of whom were in the old Company I. It is unclear whether the company retained the name Red Hill Guard. Benjamin "Ben" Roper, a second lieutenant of the former Company I, was elected captain on May 13, 1862.[147] He was severely wounded in the hip at Fredericksburg on December 13 and slightly wounded at Chickamauga.[148] Roper was elected to a four-year term as tax collector of Edgefield District on October 11, 1864, and resigned his commission as captain on December 19. Roper was not replaced as captain of Company I.

Company K was composed mostly of men from Edgefield District who had served in the old Company K. It is unclear if the company retained the name Ruffin Guards. John F. Burress, first lieutenant of the old Company K, was elected captain on May 13, 1862.[149] Slightly wounded in the tibia, he was captured at Sharpsburg on September 17, 1862. By October 14, Burress had been taken to Fort McHenry, Maryland. He was paroled and exchanged at Aiken's Landing, Virginia, on November 8. Burress was furloughed and resigned on September 11, 1863, as a result of the Sharpsburg wound. The *CSR* gives his name as Bowers on one card. Jiles Mastin Berry was promoted from first lieutenant to captain on October 8, with rank from September 11, 1863. Berry had commanded the company as first lieutenant for almost a year after Burress was wounded.[150] Berry was wounded several times. He sustained a severe wound to the arm at Savage's Station and was wounded again at Sharpsburg.[151] He also suffered a slight wound to the left thigh at the Wilderness on May 6, 1864.[152] Berry retired to the Invalid Corps on September 7, probably because of his wounds but possibly also because of the chronic dysentery he had endured in July and August. First Lieutenant James Wesley Cheatham was promoted to captain as Berry's replacement on September 7.[153] Cheatham had been wounded in the thigh at Chickamauga on September 20, 1863. He also sustained a severe wound to the right leg at Cedar Creek on October 19, 1864.[154] Cheatham died on January 7, 1865, at Staunton, Virginia.[155] Kirkland gives the date of death as January 8. Cheatham was not replaced as captain of Company K.

Company L was composed of former Company L men from Horry District. The company probably retained the name Horry Volunteers. John L. Litchfield, a graduate of The Citadel and second lieutenant of the old Company L, was elected captain on May 13, 1862.[156] While leading his company in an attack on Federal breastworks at Maryland Heights on September 13, 1862, Litchfield was mortally wounded by a gunshot wound to the neck. He died at the Pleasant Valley Hospital in Washington County, Maryland, on the 16th.[157] The *CSR* gives the date of his death as both September 15 and 16, and the *Charleston Daily Courier* the sixteenth.[158] The *Roll of the Dead* states, incorrectly, that he died on October 15, while Kirkland states he was killed in action on September 13, 1862.[159] Litchfield's brother, First Lieutenant George T. Litchfield, was promoted to captain on September 13, a date also shown as the seventeenth and eighteenth. George was captured at Strasburg, Virginia, on October 19, 1864, and was taken soon afterward to Harpers Ferry. On October 25, Litchfield was moved to Fort Delaware. He was released there on May 28, 1865. George Litchfield was called "a very good officer."[160]

Company M, the Saluda Riflemen, was created in the spring of 1862.[161] It was composed of men from Edgefield District. Most Company M men had been in the old Company E, and a few had been in Company G. Considered too large, the original Company E was split into two companies, E and M, in the spring of 1862. Elijah Jeremiah "Jerry" Goggans, a second lieutenant in the old Company E, was elected captain of Company M on May 9, 1862.[162] Goggans was wounded in the face at Savage's Station on June 29, 1862.[163] The *Memory Roll* shows that he was promoted to major at Sharpsburg in September 1862 and to lieutenant colonel at Chickamauga in September 1863. The promotion to major was probably made unofficially in the field, and the promotion to lieutenant colonel was made in 1865, retroactive to September 1863. The *Mercury* reported correctly that Goggans was still captain of Company M in October 1863.[164] At the time, the regiment had no field officers; Colonel Aiken had resigned in August 1863, and both Lieutenant Colonel Bland

and Major Hard had been killed at Chickamauga in September. Goggans commanded the regiment as its senior captain from the Knoxville campaign in late 1863 until the battle of the Wilderness on May 6, 1864.[165] While leading the regiment at the Wilderness on May 6, he was severely wounded in the right forearm; the arm was resected, a procedure involving removal of the injured part in an effort to avoid amputation.[166] Goggans resigned later in May.[167] His record after May 1864 is unclear, but he appears to have remained in the service in some capacity. He arrived at home in Edgefield on September 7, having come directly from Kershaw's Division in the Shenandoah Valley only ten days earlier.[168] His arm was considerably twisted, and the wound was still open. He was hospitalized with syphilis on November 22. Though no longer with the regiment, Goggans was promoted to lieutenant colonel on January 12, 1865, retroactive to September 20, 1863. Wyckoff spelled his name Goggin.[169] First Lieutenant Andrew P. Bouknight replaced Goggans as captain, but the date is uncertain. Bouknight was slightly wounded at Fredericksburg on December 13, 1862, and was slightly wounded again in the left leg at Cedar Creek on October 19, 1864.[170] He was promoted to captain of Company C of the 7th Consolidated Regiment on April 9, 1865, and was paroled at Greensboro on May 2, 1865.

BRIGADE AFFILIATIONS

The 7th and 8th Regiments, SCV, constituted A.C. Garlington's 3rd Brigade from April to early June 1861.[171] While in Virginia, the 7th Regiment was in M.L. Bonham's Brigade from July 1, 1861, to February 1862, along with the 2nd, 3rd and 8th Regiments, SCV, as well as Kemper's Virginia Artillery.[172] From February 1862 to December 1863, J.B. Kershaw commanded the brigade, which added the 15th Regiment, SCV, and the 3rd Battalion, South Carolina Infantry, on November 26, 1862. The brigade added the 20th Regiment, SCV, on May 28, 1864. James Conner commanded the brigade from August to October 1864; John D. Kennedy was in command from then until the end of the war. About April 9, 1865, the regiments of the brigade were consolidated so that the brigade comprised the "New" or Consolidated 2nd Regiment, "New" or Consolidated 3rd Regiment and "New" or Consolidated 7th Regiment. The 3rd Battalion and the 8th, 15th and 20th Regiments all ceased to exist at that time.[173]

MAJOR MOVEMENTS AND ENGAGEMENTS

The companies of the 7th Regiment were ordered to Charleston on April 13, 1861. Company H left Edgefield Court House, and Company I left Hamburg in Edgefield District by rail for Charleston on April 15.[174] Companies A and B left Abbeville on the seventeenth and arrived in Charleston the same day.[175] Companies C and D left Abbeville on the eighteenth.[176] Company G was in Charleston by the next day.[177] In April 1861, the companies of the 7th Regiment came together at the German Schutzenplatz (Shooting Place) near Rikersville in Charleston.[178] Held in reserve in Charleston, the regiment was not engaged during the bombardment of Fort Sumter on April 12 and April 13. It was encamped at Charleston's Race Course on May 1 but was transferred the same day to Camp Butler by order of Governor Pickens.[179] The regiment had arrived at Camp Butler near Pole Cat Ponds, now Montmorenci, by the fifth.[180] The regiment went home on May 27 for a week's furlough.[181] The 7th mustered in Confederate service on June 4, 1861, and departed by rail for Richmond the same day, arriving there on the seventh.[182] The regiment was at Camp Pickens at Howard's Grove near Richmond for a few days before moving to Bull Run by the fourteenth.[183] Company L joined the 7th Regiment on July 2 at Fairfax Court House. From there, the men performed picket duty along the road to Washington, D.C.[184] The regiment withdrew to Bull Run on July 17.

From this time until the end of the war, the 7th Regiment was in a brigade commanded successively by Bonham, Kershaw, Conner and Kennedy. The major movements and engagements of the regiment are discussed in this volume under the 2nd Regiment. On April 9, 1865, the 7th Regiment was consolidated with the 15th Regiment and parts of the 1st, 2nd, 6th and 7th Battalions of Blanchard's South Carolina Reserves to form the "New" or Consolidated 7th Regiment, SCV.[185] It was this regiment that surrendered with the Army of Tennessee near Greensboro on April 26. The men were paroled on May 2 and May 3.

7.

The 7th Regiment, South Carolina Volunteers, Consolidated

The 7th Regiment, SCV, Consolidated was also called the (New) 7th Regiment, SCV. It was among those formed at Smithfield, North Carolina on April 9, 1865, when some battalions of Blanchard's South Carolina Reserves were consolidated with several first-line units—3rd Battalion, 2nd, 3rd, 7th, 8th, 15th and 20th Regiments, SCV,— to form the (New) or Consolidated 2nd, 3rd and 7th Regiments, SCV. The 7th Consolidated Regiment was formed by uniting the 7th Regiment, the 15th Regiment and elements of the 1st, 2nd, 6th and 7th Battalions of Blanchard's Reserves. Dickert takes a balanced view: "While in camp here there was a feeble attempt made to reorganize and consolidate the brigade by putting the smaller companies together and making one regiment out of two. As these changes took place so near the end, the soldiers never really realizing a change had been made, I will do no more than make a passing allusion to it, as part of this history. The only effect these changes had was the throwing out of some of our best and bravest officers (there not being places for all), but as a matter of fact this was to their advantage, as they escaped the humiliation of surrender, and returned home a few days earlier than the rest of the army."[1]

Field Officers

John Bunyan Davis of Fairfield District became colonel of the Consolidated 7th Regiment on April 9, 1865. Previously colonel of the 15th Regiment, he was paroled at Greensboro on May 2, 1865.

Thomas Allison Hudgens, MD, of Laurens District was promoted from senior captain in the old 7th Regiment to lieutenant colonel when the 7th Consolidated Regiment was created on April 9. Hudgens served as acting lieutenant colonel in command of the 7th Regiment in October 1864, but he was not promoted to the position at that time.[2] He was paroled on May 2 at Greensboro.

James W. McCutcheon of Kingstree became major of the Consolidated 7th Regiment on April 9, 1865. Previously captain of Company G of the 15th Regiment, McCutcheon, too, was paroled on May 2, 1865.

Companies

Company A was commanded by Captain Holloway I. Bird, previously captain of Company K, 15th Regiment.[3] The men of Company A had served previously in Company K of the 15th Regiment.[4]

Company B was commanded by Captain Cornelius Benton Burns, previously captain of Company D, 15th Regiment.[5] The men of Company B had served previously in Companies A, B and D of the 15th Regiment.[6]

Company C was commanded by Captain Andrew P. Bouknight, previously captain of Company M, 7th Regiment.

Company D was commanded by Captain James C. Williams, previously captain of Company G, 7th Regiment.

Company E was commanded by Captain Francis Marion Farr, previously captain of Company H, 15th Regiment. The men of Company E had served previously in Companies E, H and I of the 15th Regiment.[7]

Company F was commanded by Captain James A. Townsend, previously first lieutenant of Company B, 7th Regiment.

Company G was commanded by Captain John Lyon, previously first lieutenant of Company C, 7th Regiment.

Company H was commanded by Captain David J. Griffith, previously captain of Company C, 15th Regiment. The men of Company H had served previously in Company C of the 15th Regiment.[8]

Company I was commanded by Captain William W. Kirkland, previously first lieutenant of Company E, 15th Regiment. The men of Company I had served previously in Companies F and G of the 15th Regiment.[9]

Company K was commanded by Captain Edmund H. Covar, previously first lieutenant in Company A, 7th Regiment.[10]

Brigade Affiliations

The 7th Regiment (Consolidated), SCV, was attached to Kennedy's Brigade, Walthall's Division, 3rd Corps, Army of Tennessee.

MAJOR MOVEMENTS AND ENGAGEMENTS

The 7th Regiment (Consolidated) participated in no major engagements during its brief existence.

8.

The 7th Battalion, South Carolina Infantry

The 7th Battalion, South Carolina Infantry was also called the Enfield Rifles, the Enfield Battalion and Nelson's Battalion.[1] In August 1861, Major General P.H. Nelson of the South Carolina militia proposed raising a regiment consisting of two rifle companies and eight infantry companies for the duration of the war.[2] Nelson and militia Colonels Rion, Blair, Jones, Sligh and Boykin began concentrating on this particular battalion in January and February 1862. It was raised specifically for Confederate service under the call for 2,500 men who would volunteer for the duration. All companies were armed with Enfield rifles. The battalion mustered in Confederate service on February 22, 1862, with five companies—A, B, C, D and E—all of which had mustered in service in late 1861 and early 1862. Companies F and G were formed on May 22, 1862, with transfers from the original five. Company H was organized on July 14 as an independent company of Partisan Rangers and assigned to the battalion on October 14. This large battalion, only two companies shy of full regimental strength, maintained its integrity and fought as a battalion until March 1865, when its companies were consolidated with remnants of the 11th, 21st, 25th and 27th Regiments, SCV. This new unit of twelve companies was called Rion's Regiment.

Field Officers

Patrick Henry Nelson, a major general in the South Carolina militia before the war, was appointed brigadier general of South Carolina volunteer forces as a result of the act of December 17, 1860. A planter from Kershaw District, he was born in Clarendon District. Nelson was appointed major of the 7th Battalion on February 24, 1862, and was promoted to lieutenant colonel on July 10. Nelson was in charge of the

11th, 21st and 27th Regiments positioned north of the City Point Road in late June 1864. He was killed on June 24 near Petersburg while leading the skirmish line of Hagood's Brigade against the extreme right of the Union works.[3] Nelson's name appeared on the list of those missing in action but when the record was updated nearly four months later, on October 19, 1864, he was declared killed in action and dropped from the rolls. Johnson Hagood wrote that Nelson was "a gentleman of high culture and fine presence, and an excellent office…a devoted patriot, a gallant soldier, and a courteous gentleman."[4]

Lovick William Rochelle Blair of Kershaw District was captain of Company K of the Holcombe Legion from November 14, 1861, to February 22, 1862. Company A of the 7th Battalion was Company K of the Holcombe Legion from December 11, 1861, until February 22, 1862, when, through transfer, it became Company A of the 7th Battalion. Blair was appointed major of the battalion on August 16 with rank from July 10, 1862. Suffering from remittent typhus and the sequelae of typhoid fever, which had necessitated a four-month absence, Blair failed in an effort to return to the regiment and resigned on February 24, 1863, effective on April 1.[5] When Blair resigned, the officers of the 7th Battalion unanimously approved a statement in which they expressed their "great loss to ourselves, the battalion, and to the public service."[6]

James Henry Rion, a prominent lawyer from Winnsboro in Fairfield District, was colonel of the 6th Regiment, SCV, from February 19 to June 8, 1861. He then served as captain of Company B, 7th Battalion from November 1861 until he was promoted to major with rank from March 5, 1863, as Blair's replacement. Rion received a bayonet wound at Morris Island on July 14, 1863.[7] From September 1863 to February 1864, he temporarily commanded the 22nd Regiment, SCV. He was twice offered and twice refused permanent command of the 22nd.[8] Rion was slightly wounded at Drewry's Bluff on May 16, 1864, but remained on the field until nightfall.[9] He was promoted to lieutenant colonel effective June 24, 1864, when Nelson was killed. Wounded in the arm at Petersburg on June 18, 1864, Rion again remained on the field until after dark. In March 1865, Hagood's Brigade was consolidated into one regiment of twelve companies under Rion's command; it was called Rion's Regiment. Rion was paroled at Greensboro on May 2, 1865. Johnson Hagood wrote that, largely because of Rion's zeal and ability, the 7th Battalion came nearer to regulars in discipline and uniform efficiency at all times and under all circumstances than any volunteer troops he met during the war.[10]

COMPANIES

Company A, the Lucas Guards, was originally Company K of the Holcombe Legion.[11] The index to the *Southern Historical Society Papers* refers to the company erroneously as the Washington Mounted Artillery, which was, in fact, Company A of the Artillery Battalion of the Hampton Legion. The Holcombe Legion mustered in service on November 21, 1861, though this company was not among the legion's original eight. The Lucas Guards probably mustered in service on November 14 and was in camp at the old Cornwallis Headquarters in Camden the next day.[12] The company joined the Holcombe Legion as Company K on December 11. When the 7th Battalion was organized on February 22, 1862, Company K transferred to the 7th Battalion, where it became Company A. The men were from Camden in Kershaw District.[13] Lovick William Rochelle Blair was elected captain on November 14, 1861, and remained captain after the transfer. He was appointed major on August 16, effective July 10, 1862. Benjamin S. Lucas Jr. was promoted from first lieutenant to captain as Blair's replacement on July 10. Lucas was severely wounded in the left arm on June 3, 1864, in a skirmish near Gaines's Mill. The *Mercury* reported, incorrectly, that he was wounded on June 7 or June 8 but was doing well in Jackson Hospital in Richmond.[14] Lucas's wound resulted in the amputation of his arm, leaving him an invalid. He tendered his resignation on January 10, 1865, but the records fail to indicate whether or not the resignation was officially accepted. He was never replaced as captain of Company A.

Company B, the Lyles Rifles, was composed of men from Fairfield District. The company mustered in Confederate service for the duration of the war on December 9, 1861, at Columbia. At first, Company B did not belong to a regiment because the one for which it was intended, possibly the 17th, had not yet been organized.[15] Company B was attached to the Holcombe Legion, temporarily, from its inception until about January 23, 1862.[16] The company was not assigned a letter designation while part of the legion. It was detached for picket duty at Walter's Battery on the Toogoodoo River until February 2, when it was sent to Pineburg. The company moved on to Adams Run on February 22 to join the other four companies of the 7th Battalion. Some original members of Company B transferred to the newly created Company G on May 27.

James Henry Rion, who was elected captain of Company B on November 13, 1861, had been elected colonel of the 6th Regiment, SCV, on February 19, 1861, but had not been re-elected when the regiment mustered in Confederate service on June 8. Brigadier General N.G. Evans arrested Rion and three lieutenants of Company B on February 15, 1862, on charges of disobeying orders.[17] General Lee ordered a court-martial, but the affair's conclusion is unknown. Rion was promoted to major of the 7th Battalion on April 29, 1863, with rank from March 5, and First Lieutenant John R. Harrison became captain on April 1, effective March 5. Harrison had suffered for twenty years from rheumatism, especially in the spine and hips, and was unfit for active duty. He resigned on October 24 and was replaced by First Lieutenant John L. Kennedy the same day. Kennedy died of typhoid fever at the South Carolina Hospital near Petersburg on August 8, 1864.[18] The *Roll of the Dead* states that he died of dysentery on August 10, 1864, at Petersburg. Kirkland also gives the date of Kennedy's death as the tenth, but the date of August 8 seems more plausible since Kennedy's successor, Lieutenant Swanson Wade Douglass, became captain on August 9.[19] Douglass's promotion might not have been confirmed. He received a flesh wound in the left thigh during the famous charge of Hagood's Brigade on the Weldon Railroad near Petersburg on August 21, 1864, and was admitted to Jackson Hospital in Richmond at the rank of lieutenant. The wound subsequently became infected, and Douglass died. The death certificate in the *CSR* gives the date of death as September 26, 1864, but the *CSR* also shows both September 9 and September 27, 1864.[20] John L. Tidwell was elected first lieutenant on September 7, 1864. He commanded the company with the rank of lieutenant but was never officially promoted to captain. Hagood states that Tidwell was promoted to captain on December 18, 1864.[21]

Company C, the McCullough Rifles, was composed of men from Richland District.[22] Elections for company officers were held at Brown's Mill on October 19, 1861, and the company mustered in Confederate service for the duration of the war on December 28 at Camp Hampton near Columbia.[23] On January 4, 1862, the men were sent to Magnolia in Charleston and on the nineteenth to Adams Run, where, on February 22, the company joined the four other original companies of the 7th Battalion. Some members of Company C transferred to the newly created Company G on May 27, 1862. William H. Sligh was elected captain on December 28, 1861. He commanded the 7th Battalion at the battle of Pocotaligo on October 22, 1862.[24] Sligh wrote on May 5, 1863, that he had requested assignment "about 7 weeks ago" to some duty other than field service.[25] His preference was either a camp of instruction, discharge on medical grounds or permission to resign. An accompanying surgeon's letter stated that Sligh was unfit for duty because of violent asthma attacks brought on by exposure. Sligh resigned, but the exact date is unclear. The *CSR* gives two dates, May 18 and June 29, 1863. It is possible that Sligh's resignation was accepted on June 29, but the effective date was May 18. Andrew Wallace

Pearson was promoted from first lieutenant to captain on June 29. Pearson was wounded at Battery Wagner on July 11 or July 12, 1863.[26] He and an enlisted man became intoxicated on the night of September 20, 1864. They left camp without permission, attempted to break into the home of a widow and actually threatened rape. Pearson was charged with disobeying orders, being absent from camp without permission, intoxication and conduct unbecoming an officer. In the face of such serious charges, he tendered his resignation, which became effective on October 25, 1864. First Lieutenant Joel R. Mankin was promoted to captain the same day. He received a flesh wound in the left calf at Petersburg on August 12, 1864. Mankin was still absent in December but was present when Rion's Regiment was paroled at Greensboro on May 1, 1865.

Company D, the Kershaw Grays, or Greys, was composed of men from Kershaw District.[27] It was organized at Camden on November 11, 1861, and was still recruiting new members as it prepared to go into camp on the twenty-ninth.[28] By December 20, the men were in camp and preparing to be mustered in service, and on the thirtieth they left Camden for Camp Hampton near Columbia.[29] At the camp on January 2, 1862, the company mustered in Confederate service for the duration of the war. Twelve days later, the company was sent to Magnolia in Charleston, and on the twentieth, it was sent to Adams Run to join the other four original companies of the 7th Battalion. On May 27, 1862, some Company D men transferred to the newly created Company G.

John L. Jones from Liberty Hill, a major in the South Carolina militia, was elected captain on December 7, 1861.[30] He mustered in Confederate service with his men on January 2, 1862.[31] Jones sustained a slight head wound in early June 1864.[32] He was wounded again at Petersburg and captured while in command of the battalion during the charge of Hagood's Brigade on the Weldon Railroad on August 21, 1864. He was taken to the Old Capitol Prison in Washington, D.C., on the twenty-third and to Fort Delaware six days later. The *Mercury* reported in late September that Jones was in prison and doing well at Fort Delaware.[33] Never replaced as captain, Jones was released from Fort Delaware on June 30, 1865.

Company E was composed mostly of men from Kershaw, Sumter and Colleton Districts, along with a few from Richland, Clarendon, Barnwell, Fairfield, Lexington and Orangeburg Districts.[34] It mustered in Confederate service at Camp Hampton, probably on January 14, 1862. Burwell E. Boykin was elected captain the same day. Boykin suffered from complications of secondary syphilis, a condition that left him unfit for duty. He resigned on May 25, 1863, and was replaced by First Lieutenant Phillip Porcher Gaillard the same day. In October 1864, Gaillard was detailed to command a company of one hundred picked men serving as sharpshooters in Hagood's Brigade. The record is unclear as to whether the men were Company E or another company.[35] Gaillard was paroled on May 1, 1865, at Greensboro.

Company F, the Lucas Rifles, was organized on May 27, 1862, primarily with former Company A men from Kershaw District.[36] The *Memory Roll*, however, states that the men of Company F were from Chesterfield and Lancaster Districts, not from Kershaw District. Dove Segars, also shown in the *CSR* as Seagars, served as second lieutenant in Company A until he was elected captain of Company F on May 27. The *Mercury* refers to Segars as both Don and David.[37] He was severely wounded in the left side by a Minié ball during the charge of Hagood's Brigade on the Weldon Railroad near Petersburg on August 21, 1864.[38] Segars recovered and commanded the company until the end of the war. He was paroled at Greensboro on May 1, 1865.

Company G, the Moffatt Rifles, was organized on May 27, 1862, with transfers from other companies of the 7th Battalion.[39] Most of the men were from Company B (Fairfield District), Company C (Richland District) and Company D (Kershaw District), but a few came from Chesterfield and Lancaster Districts. The company was named for "the gallant Moffatt, our mutual friend," a soldier in the Mexican War who contracted a disease, came home and soon died.[40] William Clyburn of Camden, who had been first lieutenant in Company D, organized Company G and was elected its captain on May 27. On March 13, 1863, Clyburn requested a leave of absence because he held the office of clerk of Court of Common Pleas in Kershaw District, and his designee there had died. Whether or not Clyburn was granted leave is unknown, but the act that would have exempted him from active duty because he held public office at home had not yet been passed. When the color bearer of the 7th Battalion was shot down on July 10, 1863, at Morris Island, Clyburn stopped to help him. At that instant, an exploding shell stunned him momentarily. Alone and surrounded by Federal troops, Clyburn was taken prisoner.[41] He was sent to Hilton Head Island on July 14, and on October 6, he was sent to Fort Columbus in New York Harbor. Clyburn was moved to Johnson's Island near Sandusky, Ohio, on October 9.[42] He was taken to Baltimore, Maryland, on February 9, 1864, and was exchanged at Point Lookout on March 3.[43] By June 1864, Clyburn had returned to the command of Company G.[44] He was wounded on August 21, 1864, and was in command of the company when it was paroled on May 1, 1865.

Company H, the Joe Johnston Rifles, was also called the Johnston Rifles, the Partisan Rangers and the Brooks Infantry Partisan Rifles.[45] An advertisement appeared in the *Daily Southern Guardian* on June 27, 1862, announcing that the secretary of war had authorized John Hampden Brooks, on the recommendation of Joe Johnston, to raise a company for partisan service. According to the advertisement, the company would probably be assigned to Kershaw's Brigade as an independent sharpshooter company. Brooks was given thirty days to raise the company.[46] The men mustered in Confederate service at Columbia on July 14, 1862, for the duration of the war. The secretary of war appointed Brooks captain of the company the same day. Three South Carolina organizations were raised as partisan rangers: Brooks's Company, M.J. Kirk's Cavalry Company and H.K. Aiken's Cavalry Battalion.[47] Brooks's mother supplied the uniforms for the men of the Johnston Rifles.[48] Previously captain of Company G of the 7th Regiment, Brooks was not re-elected at the reorganization in the spring of 1862. He raised this independent company of partisan rangers shortly afterward.[49] The men were from Edgefield, Fairfield, Richland, Abbeville and Chester Districts. On October 14, 1862, the company was assigned to the 7th Battalion as Company H, the color company of the battalion.[50] Brooks applied for promotion to lieutenant colonel of the 22nd Regiment, SCV, on May 9, 1864, but the application was rejected. He was wounded three times, in both arms and a leg, at Drewry's Bluff on May 16, 1864; he left the field only on General Hagood's orders.[51] More than 90 percent of Brooks's men were killed or wounded in that battle, and he was left without a command.[52] General Hagood cited Brooks for conspicuous gallantry at Drewry's Bluff. Thanks in part to that citation, he was selected to command the 2nd Foreign Battalion. In October 1864, he was promoted to lieutenant colonel of the 2nd Foreign Battalion and commanded it until it was dissolved in late December 1864. Brooks returned to command Company H, 7th Battalion. He applied, unsuccessfully, for promotion on January 10, 1865.

BRIGADE AFFILIATIONS

The 7th Battalion served in the Department of South Carolina, Georgia and Florida until early 1864. It was part of States Rights Gist's Brigade from about March to about August 1863. In August and September, the battalion was part of the Clingman's Second Subdivision of the 1st South Carolina Military District, under command of Roswell Ripley. On September 20, 1863, General P.G.T. Beauregard issued a special order creating a new brigade from the 7th Battalion, the Charleston Battalion and the 11th, 21st and 25th, SCV, Regiments.[53] The Charleston Battalion became the 27th Regiment on September 30 and remained with the brigade. Johnson Hagood was its commander. In early March 1865, the 7th Battalion was consolidated with the remnants of the 11th, 21st, 25th and 27th Regiments to form a new twelve-company regiment under command of Lieutenant Colonel James H. Rion. This consolidated regiment of about five hundred men was placed in a new brigade commanded by Johnson Hagood. Other major components of Hagood's new Brigade were Hedricks's 40th North Carolina Regiment and Taylor's Consolidated 36th North Carolina, along with the 1st North Carolina Battalion of Heavy Artillery. On March 31, 1865, the North Carolina troops were reassigned to other brigades; Rion took command of Hagood's Brigade, which reverted back to its original composition.

MAJOR MOVEMENTS AND ENGAGEMENTS

After its creation on February 22, 1862, the 7th Battalion served along the South Carolina coast, mostly in the Charleston area. The 7th and 5th Battalions, the Holcombe Legion and the Washington Artillery were engaged on Little Edisto Island on March 29.[54] On May 15, Company B was detached from the battalion and sent from Adams Run to Church Flats, where it served as heavy artillery for more than a year until August 1863. From July 3, 1862, to January 11, 1863, the rest of the battalion was stationed at Camp Cantey near Adams Run on the Charleston and Savannah Railroad.[55] Nelson's Battalion, the Holcombe Legion, the 17th Regiment and Jenkins's Rebel Troop participated in an expedition to Jehossee Island on July 7, 1862, but none saw action there.[56] The battalion was engaged at the battle of Pocotaligo on October 22, 1862; the *Mercury* reported that the 7th Battalion "saved the day."[57] It soon returned to Adams Run.[58] On December 15, the battalion left Adams Run and went to Wilmington, North Carolina, arriving there two days later.[59] The 7th Battalion was accompanied by the 16th, 24th and 25th Regiments, as well as the 46th Georgia Regiment and Preston's, Waties's and Culpeper's Batteries.[60] The battalion returned to Adams Run on January 3, 1863, but was sent back to Wilmington on January 11. It returned to Adams Run on February 9. Three months later, most, if not all, of its companies were sent to John's Island. From there, they were soon detached to various places along the South Carolina coast. Companies A, E and H were sent to Toogoodoo Creek on May 16 and to Kings Creek on June 8. Company F was detached on May 14 and sent to Yonges Island, where it performed picket duty along the Stono River. Companies C, D and G were detached on the fifteenth and sent to Church Flats, where some of the men served as heavy artillery. Company B had sole charge of the batteries at Church Flats from July 21, 1862, to August 1863.[61] All 7th Battalion companies, except Company B, were sent to Charleston on July 9, 1863. Seven were transferred to Battery Wagner on Morris Island on the tenth to meet the Union assault on that position. Company B remained behind at Church Flats. Companies A, E and G supported the artillery at the south end of Morris Island during the Federal assault there on the tenth, but the men arrived at the scene too late to be of material assistance.[62] All seven companies became part of the garrison at Battery Wagner on the afternoon of July 10 and saw action there the next morning.[63] A 150-man force, from the 7th Battalion, the 20th Regiment, the 51st North Carolina Regiment and the 12th and 18th Georgia Battalions, joined in an effort to drive Federal pickets from their rifle pits near Battery Wagner in the early morning hours of July 15.[64] The seven companies of the 7th Battalion were transferred to Battery Gregg on Morris Island on July 15 and were sent by steamer to Sullivan's Island the same day.[65] They were based at the Moultrie House until July 19 or July 20, when they were sent to Battery Marshall on Sullivan's Island. Throughout July, August and September, Company B was at Adams Run; the rest of the battalion was at Sullivan's Island.[66] When Hagood's Brigade was created in September 1863, the 7th Battalion was assigned to it. The battalion remained on detached service at Sullivan's Island, however, during November and December 1863 and January 1864.[67] The men stayed at Battery Marshall until February 9, 1864, when they were sent to Fort Johnson on James Island.[68] The battalion remained there until about April 28.

Hagood's Brigade was ordered to Virginia by way of Wilmington on April 28, 1864. The 11th Regiment actually left Sullivan's Island on May 1 and arrived in Wilmington on the fourth.[69] Most of the 21st Regiment left James Island by rail for Wilmington on April 28 and arrived there the next day.[70] Company G of the 21st had been on garrison duty at Fort Sumter, and it left Charleston on May 2. Company A of the 21st left Charleston on May 29.[71] The 27th Regiment, leaving Company G behind, departed James Island for Wilmington on April 29.[72] The 25th Regiment left Charleston on May 3 and arrived at Wilmington the next day.[73] The 7th Battalion also moved to Wilmington about that time.

Seven companies of the 21st Regiment, along with three of the 25th—G, H and I—left Wilmington by rail on May 5 and arrived at Drewry's Bluff about five o'clock the next morning. They marched to Walthall Junction, arriving there after dark on the sixth.[74] The remainder of the 21st Regiment arrived by train at Walthall Junction about the same time. The 21st Regiment and Companies G, H and I of the 25th skirmished that evening near Walthall Junction, also called Mrs. Howlett's farm.[75] The rest of the brigade—the 11th and 27th Regiments, seven companies of the 25th Regiment and the 7th Battalion—arrived at Drewry's Bluff by train on the sixth and marched to Walthall Junction, arriving after dark and missing the day's action.[76] Three regiments—the 21st, 25th and 27th—were also engaged at Walthall Junction on May 7.[77] The 7th Battalion and 11th Regiment arrived after the action on the seventh. That day, the 21st Regiment broke and ran under a flank attack, during which Colonel Graham was wounded and Lieutenant Colonel Dargan was killed. Companies B and K of the 21st were used as skirmishers on the right of the regiment and were not engaged on the seventh.[78]

Eight companies of the 11th Regiment, eight or nine of the 21st and three—A, H and K—of the 25th were engaged in a reconnaissance action at Swift Creek on May 9.[79] The brigade left for Drewry's Bluff on the tenth and arrived there the next day. It skirmished from May 12 to May 15 in front of the Drewry's Bluff fortifications and was engaged there again on May 16.[80] The brigade moved to Bermuda Hundreds on the seventeenth and eighteenth, skirmishing heavily there from May 18 to May 31 in a series of maneuvers, during which Beauregard bottled up Butler at the Bermuda Hundreds Neck.[81] Hagood's Brigade was ordered from the trenches at six in the morning on May 31 and moved by foot and rail through Richmond to Cold Harbor, arriving there about one in the morning on June 1. The brigade was engaged at Cold Harbor from June 1 to 3 and from June 5 to June 6, 1864.[82] Company E of the 11th Regiment and Company G of the 27th finally arrived on June 4, having missed all the action in Virginia up to that time.

Leaving Cold Harbor at eight o'clock in the morning on June 13, the men crossed the Chickahominy River and moved to Malvern Hill. The brigade moved to the pontoon bridge over the James River near Drewry's Bluff on the fourteenth, and crossed to the south side of the river the next day. It arrived at Petersburg after dark on the fifteenth and occupied the lines later the same night. The brigade saw action at Petersburg on June 16, skirmished under shellfire on June 17 and was engaged at Hare's Hill on the eighteenth. Three regiments—the 11th, 21st and 27th—attacked the extreme right of the Union trenches on the south bank of the Appomattox River near Petersburg on June 24. Lieutenant Colonel Nelson of the 7th Battalion was temporarily in command of the skirmish line that day, but his battalion was not engaged. He was killed, and the 27th Regiment was "cut to pieces" during the attack.[83] Hagood's Brigade remained under constant fire and suffered many casualties as it occupied the Petersburg trenches from June 18 to August 20.[84] The brigade withdrew on August 20 and made its famous charge against Warren's Federal army corps, which was numerically superior and well entrenched, along the Weldon Railroad on the twenty-first. Hagood took 740 men into the action and returned with only 292 unscathed. The 27th Regiment again suffered heavy casualties, counting only about 40 men remaining after the engagement.[85] The men of the brigade considered this charge their most desperate encounter.[86]

From August 31 to September 2, the 7th Battalion was stationed at the Iron Bridge in Petersburg. The brigade was sent to Dunlop's Park near Swift Creek north of Petersburg for rest and recuperation from September 2 to September 15. The 7th Battalion was stationed along the Boydton Plank Road from September 16 to September 18. The brigade returned to the Petersburg trenches on September 28 and was sent the next day to the north side of the James River, where the men built and occupied a new line of works between the New Market and Darbytown Roads. The brigade, except for Companies D, E and G of the 21st Regiment, was held in reserve during the assault on Fort Harrison on September 30, but suffered casualties while in the trenches at Chaffins Farm on October 2.[87] The 25th Regiment was actively engaged that day. Leaving Chaffins Farm for the Darbytown Road on October 6, the brigade was held in reserve there the next day but suffered casualties nevertheless because of shellfire.[88] The brigade skirmished, again on the Darbytown Road, on October 13 and October 27. It occupied the lines around Richmond in October and November and was engaged below the capital on October 27.[89]

The brigade conducted an armed reconnaissance involving some skirmishing around the Federal right flank on December 10 and marched on the twenty-first to Richmond, where the men boarded trains for Danville. Between the twenty-second and the twenty-sixth, the brigade was transported by rail to Greensboro, North Carolina. Most of the brigade arrived at Wilmington on the twenty-sixth, left by steamer for Fort Fisher the same day, and returned to Wilmington on the thirty-first.

In early January 1865, Hagood's Brigade moved to Fort Anderson, about fifteen miles south of Wilmington on the Cape Fear River. The 21st Regiment skirmished on January 13 and January 14. The 21st and 25th Regiments moved by steamer on January 14 and January 15 from Gander Hall Landing on the Cape Fear River down to Battery Buchanan and back up the peninsula to Fort Fisher. Unable to move into the fort because of Federal naval shellfire, the 7th Battalion and 11th Regiment were sent across the river to Smithville. While the 27th was still at Fort Anderson, and the 7th Battalion and most of the 11th Regiment at Smithville, most of the 21st and 25th Regiments were captured during an engagement at Fort Fisher on January 15.[90] The few men of the 21st and 25th Regiments who were not captured remained with the brigade. A few men of the 11th Regiment were captured at Fort Fisher.[91] The remainder of the brigade skirmished below Fort Anderson from February 17 until they abandoned the fort and withdrew to Town Creek two days later. The brigade was engaged at Town Creek, about nine miles below Wilmington on the opposite side of the Cape Fear River, on the twentieth, and most of the remnant of the 25th Regiment was captured there. The 7th Battalion was held in reserve during that action.

Hagood's Brigade evacuated Wilmington on February 22 and marched on the twenty-third to Rockfish Creek, where it remained until March 5. The brigade arrived at Kinston, North Carolina, by rail on March 8 and was soon consolidated into a twelve-company regiment, named for its commander, Lieutenant Colonel Rion. Rion's Regiment comprised the 7th Battalion and remnants of the 11th, 21st, 25th and 27th Regiments, an aggregate of about five hundred men. Rion's Regiment skirmished near Kinston from March 8 to March 10 and remained in the lines for two or three more days. It was not engaged at Averasboro on the sixteenth, but it saw action at Bentonville from March 19 to March 21.

Rion's Regiment withdrew to Black Creek on the twenty-second and marched through Smithfield on April 10. Two days later, the men marched through Raleigh. From April 13 to April 17, the regiment marched to Chapel Hill, Greensboro and finally to Salisbury. Men began leaving in significant numbers as rumors of surrender circulated in mid-April. On April 26, Generals Johnston and Sherman agreed to articles of a military convention, in effect surrendering Johnston's army. The surrender was announced the next day, and officers signed for and received paroles for the men on May 1 and May 2. Rion's Regiment surrendered 40 officers and 510 men. The men broke camp on the third and left on foot for Lancaster Court House in South Carolina, where they were given their paroles. Hagood's Brigade (Rion's Regiment) was disbanded there on May 7, 1865.

9.

The 9th Regiment, South Carolina Volunteers

The 9th Regiment, SCV, was also called the 9th Regiment, South Carolina Infantry. It was not among the regiments raised in response to the legislative act of December 17, 1860, calling for ten regiments of twelve-month volunteers. The history of the 9th Regiment is based on the organization of the 2nd Regiment, which was authorized by the act. According to the *Mercury*, the 2nd Regiment was complete on March 12, 1861.[1] It was received into state service on April 9.[2] Four of its companies volunteered to go to Virginia and mustered in Confederate service on May 22 and May 23.[3] Six companies, totaling about 540 men, chose to remain at Morris Island under the command of Lieutenant Colonel Blanding, thus permanently dividing the 2nd Regiment. Three of the six—A, B and D—became the nucleus of a new regiment called Blanding's Regiment. The final three companies were dispersed as follows: one went into Gregg's regiment, another went into the Hampton Legion and the third joined the 12th Regiment, SCV. New elections were held on May 23 to replace Blanding, but he was re-elected.[4] His battalion was relieved of duty at Morris Island on May 30 and sent to Camp Quitman in Ridgeville, located in a part of Colleton District now in Dorchester County.[5] At that time, the press clearly still associated Blanding's Battalion with Kershaw's Regiment by referring to it as the 2nd Regiment, the 2nd Battalion of Kershaw's Regiment, and the detachment of the 2nd Regiment under Lieutenant Colonel Blanding.[6] Governor Pickens urged the men to serve out the remaining ten months of their state enlistment by mustering in Confederate service; by late June, Blanding and his men had settled their differences with the governor and agreed to Confederate service in Virginia.[7] The ranks of Blanding's companies increased so rapidly that full regimental strength was achieved by July 10.[8] Companies A, B, C and D mustered in Confederate service on June 27 at Ridgeville for twelve months, effective from April 8 and elected field officers on July

5.[9] On July 10, Companies E, F, G, H, I and K also mustered in Confederate service for twelve months with the same effective date. Because there were now six new companies in the regiment, Blanding called for a new election of field officers on July 10.[10] Elections were actually held on the twelfth, and by that day, the regiment of ten companies was organized for twelve months' Confederate service to date from April 8, 1861. The regiment left for Virginia on July 18.[11] During this time and as late as July 24, the public press continued to refer to Blanding's as the 2nd Regiment.[12] The press called Blanding's the 9th Regiment for the first time in early August.[13] It failed to reorganize in the spring of 1862 and was disbanded on April 28.[14] The War Department authorized Colonel Blanding to raise a new regiment and gave him until May 16 to accomplish the task; Blanding tried but was unsuccessful. At the reorganization, the men of the 9th Regiment mustered in the 5th and 6th Regiments, SCV, and in a new South Carolina infantry regiment, the Palmetto Sharpshooters.

FIELD OFFICERS

James Douglass Blanding, a lawyer from Sumter, raised Company D, the Sumter Volunteers.[15] Blanding had served in the Mexican War as a lieutenant in Company A of the Palmetto Regiment; he was later promoted to captain and given a staff position. He was also colonel of the 22nd Regiment, South Carolina Militia, in the 1840s.[16] Blanding was elected lieutenant colonel at the organization of the 2nd Regiment in early February 1861.[17] His commission actually dated, however, from April 8, when the regiment entered state service. Elected colonel of the 9th Regiment on July 5, 1861, Blanding was re-elected on July 12.[18] The 9th Regiment ceased to exist on April 28, 1862, and Blanding was relieved from duty. During late April and early May, he attempted, unsuccessfully, to raise a new regiment. Blanding advertised between May and August, attempting to raise a company of mounted partisan rangers for attachment to a battalion of similar companies as called for by the Executive Council.[19] Blanding probably had some success in this endeavor, but the commanding general refused to accept the partisan rangers, and Blanding's efforts again came to naught.[20] In July 1862, Blanding was the enrolling officer in Sumter District.[21] He later became inspector general of seacoast batteries and reserve regiments from Charleston to the North Carolina line. He also served in the Ordnance Department.[22] In late 1863 and early 1864, he is shown in the record as first sergeant of Company I, 4th Regiment, South Carolina State Troops. He also commanded a small company of mounted men during Potter's Raid in

April 1865.[23] Blanding had some health problems during the war; he was considered "disabled but anxious to continue service."[24] Coker wrote that Blanding was "very popular with the men, and would certainly have led them bravely in battle if the opportunity had been presented."[25]

Dixon Barnes of Lancaster District was elected lieutenant colonel of the 9th Regiment on July 5, 1861.[26] When new elections for field officers were held on the twelfth, Companies A, B and D—those originally attached to the 2nd Regiment—voted nearly unanimously for Barnes as colonel, but the seven new companies swung the vote to Blanding.[27] Barnes had been major of the 2nd Regiment earlier in 1861, but he remained in South Carolina when four companies of the 2nd went to Virginia in May. Later that summer, he raised Company I of the 12th Regiment and was elected its captain on August 28.[28]

Duncan William Ray, MD, of Richland District was captain of the States Rights Guards in the 2nd Regiment. This company became Company B, the Fork Troop, of the 9th Regiment. Ray was elected lieutenant colonel of the 9th at the election held on July 12, 1861.[29] Coker wrote that Ray was "a civilian of fine position and influence at home."[30]

John Marcellus Steedman of Lexington had attended the South Carolina Military Academy and was captain of Company K until July 5, 1861, when he was elected major of the 9th Regiment.[31] He was re-elected on July 12. When the 9th Regiment was disbanded in April 1862, Steedman was elected lieutenant colonel of the 6th Regiment.[32] He was wounded at Frayser's Farm on June 30, 1862, and at Second Manassas. He was promoted to colonel of the 6th Regiment, replacing John Bratton, on May 6, 1864. Steedman was called "plain, unassuming, and brave."[33]

COMPANIES

Company A, the Lancaster Greys, was composed of men from that district. It was one of the three 2nd Regiment companies that refused to serve in Virginia in April 1861.[34] Company A remained in Charleston and helped form the nucleus of the 9th Regiment.[35] Company A mustered in Confederate service on June 27 for twelve months, effective April 8. At that time, Companies A and G were the only two in the 9th Regiment armed with Mississippi Rifles. John Dunovant Wylie, who had attended The Citadel, raised the company and was its only captain. Wylie was appointed brigade engineer on November 3, 1861, but was relieved from that duty on December 22 when he was appointed provost marshal. When the 9th Regiment was disbanded in April 1862, Wylie, like most of the other men, enlisted in Company A of the 5th Regiment and was elected its captain.[36] A few men chose other companies of the 5th Regiment, and some enlisted in Companies B and F of the 6th Regiment.

Company B, the States Right Guards, was also called the Fork Troop.[37] Originally part of the 2nd Regiment, Company B was one of the three that refused to go to Virginia in April 1861. It remained in Charleston and became part of the nucleus of the 9th Regiment.[38] Company B men were from the lower part of Richland District.[39] While at Ridgeville on June 27, Company B mustered in Confederate service for twelve months from April 8, 1861. Duncan William Ray, who mustered in state service as captain on April 8, was elected lieutenant colonel of the 9th Regiment on July 12. Robert Adams was promoted from first lieutenant to captain on July 12. When the 9th Regiment was disbanded in April 1862, some of its men enlisted in Companies C and H of the 6th Regiment, and two enlisted in Company A of the 5th Regiment.

Company C, the Clarendon Blues, was composed of men from that district.[40] It left Sumter for Ridgeville on June 4, 1861, to join Blanding's regiment.[41] While at Ridgeville on June 27, Company C mustered in Confederate service, effective from its original enlistment date of June 4 to April 8, 1862. John Shaw Whitworth mustered in state service as captain on June 4 and in Confederate service with the regiment on the twenty-seventh. Whitworth was Company C's only captain. "No man is loved better by his men than Captain John S. Whitworth."[42] The *Memory Roll* calls Company C the Cowpens Guards. The *CSR* and the *Mercury* both state, however, that the Cowpens Guards was a company in the 9th Regiment at this time, but it was most likely Company I. Some men of Company C enlisted in Company K of the 6th Regiment at the reorganization.

Company D, the Chicora Guards, was also called the Salem Company.[43] It mustered in Confederate service on June 27 at Ridgeville for twelve months effective from April 8. James D. Blanding raised this company in Sumter District, but some of its men came from Williamsburg and Clarendon Districts.[44] Company D, one of the three companies originally in the 2nd Regiment that refused to go to Virginia in April 1861, remained in Charleston and, along with Companies A and B, formed the nucleus of the 9th Regiment.[45] S.D.M. Lacoste commanded Company D, probably from the time Blanding was elected lieutenant colonel of the 2nd Regiment in February 1861 to June 26. Lacoste was later a sergeant in Company K, 23rd Regiment, SCV. Second Lieutenant Alexander "Aleck" Colclough, who had attended The Citadel, was promoted to captain on June 26, 1861.[46] In April 1862, some Company D men enlisted in Company E of the Palmetto Sharpshooters, and some enlisted in Company K of the 6th

Regiment. Colclough was elected captain of Company E of the Palmetto Sharpshooters at that time.

Company E, the Kershaw Troop, was composed of men from that district.[47] It was a cavalry company before the war and converted to infantry when the war came.[48] The company's captain, Edward B. Cantey, offered its services to Governor Gist on November 12, 1860. Cantey was re-elected on June 25, 1861. At Ridgeville on July 10, Cantey and his men mustered in Confederate service for a term to expire on April 8, 1862. In April 1862, some Company E men enlisted in Company A of the 5th Regiment. Others chose Company C of the 6th Regiment and elected Cantey captain on April 6.

Company F, the Sumter Grays, was composed mostly of men from that district.[49] A few men were from Chester, Chesterfield, Charleston and Williamsburg Districts. Organized on June 8, 1861, it was the fourth company raised in Sumter District.[50] It mustered in Confederate service at Ridgeville on July 10 for a term to expire on April 8, 1862. Dwight W. Harrington, the only captain, enlisted on July 4 and mustered in service with the men on the tenth.[51] Harrington, then in the Palmetto Sharpshooters, was killed on June 30, 1862, at Frayser's Farm. At the reorganization in April 1862, some Company F men enlisted in Company E of the Palmetto Sharpshooters. A few chose Companies C and K of the 6th Regiment, and about twenty-five men from Bishopville and Lynchburg enlisted in Company E of the 6th Regiment.[52]

Company G, the Hartsville Light Infantry, was composed of men from Darlington District. Coker wrote that the company was formed in 1859 under a charter from the South Carolina legislature.[53] On January 28, 1861, the General Assembly authorized a "new" company, called the Hartsville Light Infantry, to be received into the Upper Battalion of the 29th Regiment, South Carolina Militia.[54] Whatever its origins, the Hartsville Light Infantry offered its services to the governor in the early months of the war but was not accepted. The men applied to the 8th Regiment, SCV, in early 1861, but were turned down again.[55] The company probably enlisted in state service on June 29, 1861. While at Ridgeville on July 10, Company G mustered in Confederate service as part of the 9th Regiment. At that time, Companies A and G were the only two in the 9th Regiment armed with the Mississippi Rifle. The company's term of service was from the original date of enlistment, June 29, to April 8, 1862. James Lide Coker raised Company G and enlisted with the men on June 29, 1861, though his commission as captain dated from July 10. Coker was the only captain of Company G.[56] Company G had planned to re-enlist as an artillery company when its initial term expired, but "the exigencies of service forbade any changes."[57]

Most of the men followed Coker and re-enlisted in Company E of the 6th Regiment in April 1862. Elected captain of that company as well, Coker was severely wounded and captured at Wauhatchie on October 28, 1863. He was promoted to major of the 6th Regiment on July 20, 1864, while still in prison.

Company H, the Blanding Blues, was composed mostly of men from Edgefield and Barnwell Districts along with a few from Colleton and Orangeburg Districts.[58] At Ridgeville on July 10, 1861, Company H mustered in Confederate service for a period from its initial date of enlistment, July 4, 1861, to April 8, 1862. Company H's only captain, Jerome W. Walker, enlisted with the men on July 4, though his commission dated from the tenth. In April 1862, most of the men followed Walker into Company D of the 6th Regiment.

Company I, the Cowpens Guards or Guard, was composed of men from Spartanburg District.[59] While at Ridgeville on July 10, 1861, Company I mustered in Confederate service for a term from its original date of enlistment, June 29, 1861, to April 8, 1862. William Moultrie Foster, the only captain of Company I, enlisted on June 28 and was commissioned captain on July 10. Foster had been captain of a company called the Cowpens Cavalry in May 1861, and he was attempting to have the company attached to the Hampton Legion.[60] It is probable that the Cowpens Cavalry converted to infantry and joined the 9th Regiment instead. In April 1862, Foster was elected major of the 5th Regiment. Some men followed him into Companies I and K of the 5th, but most enlisted in Company H of the Palmetto Sharpshooters.

Company K, the Pickens Sentinels, was composed of men from Lexington District.[61] From late May to late June 1861, it was probably associated with Johnson Hagood's 1st Regiment, SCV. On July 10, 1861, Company K mustered in Confederate service at Ridgeville. Its term of service was from the original date of enlistment, July 8, 1861, to April 8, 1862. John Marcellus Steedman, who enlisted as captain of Company K on July 8, 1861, was elected major of the 9th Regiment on July 12. Joseph E. Lee was promoted from first lieutenant to captain on July 12 with rank from the fourteenth.[62] Most of the men followed Captain Lee and enlisted in Company F of the Palmetto Sharpshooters in April 1862.

A company called the Clarendon Volunteers, or Clarendon Riflemen, was attached to Blanding's regiment in late April 1861.[63] The Clarendon Volunteers, commanded by Captain W. Elliott Keels at the time, may have been attached previously to the 2nd Regiment.[64] The Clarendon Rifles was discharged from service on June 20, 1861. Many of the men wanted to enter Confederate service and reorganized themselves under Captain James

McCauley, MD. There is no evidence that McCauley's Company was ever accepted into a South Carolina regiment, and it was probably disbanded again.[65]

Brigade Affiliations

The 9th Regiment was in D.R. Jones's Brigade from July 25 to December 22, 1861, when R.H. Anderson took command of the brigade.[66] The 4th, 5th and 6th Regiments, SCV, were also part of this brigade.

Major Movements and Engagements

The 9th Regiment was organized at Ridgeville and ordered to Virginia on July 13, 1861.[67] It left for Virginia on the eighteenth and arrived at Richmond on July 20.[68] The regiment camped briefly in Richmond before moving by rail to Manassas, but it arrived there on the evening of July 21, too late to participate in that day's battle. The regiment moved to Centreville on July 28 and set up Camp Pettus, named for the governor of Mississippi.[69] On August 12, the regiment, along with its brigade, left Camp Pettus and moved to Germantown in Fairfax County, which was about seven miles closer to Washington.[70] The regiment was camped at Germantown on September 14, its men suffering from various diseases. From September 14 to September 20, the regiment performed picket duty and participated in light picket firing. Around the twenty-fifth, the regiment was on picket duty for three days near Lewinsville and was on picket duty again from October 5 to October 9 at Wells Cross Roads. The regiment left Germantown for McLean's Ford on October 16 and was engaged in picket firing the next day near the Makeley house, where it mistakenly fired on a Georgia regiment. The 9th took one or two prisoners only to discover they were Georgians. On October 29, the 9th Regiment performed picket duty, again at the Makeley house, for three days. The regiment was stationed at Centreville, Virginia, from November 1861 to February 5, 1862. During March 1862, the 9th Regiment was temporarily attached to J.E.B. Stuart's command, acting as its rear guard near Warrenton while most of the Confederate forces concentrated on Richmond and Yorktown. The 9th Regiment then withdrew to join the brigade at the Rapidan River. It participated in no major engagements during its nine-month existence. The 9th Regiment was disbanded at Yorktown on April 28, 1862.[71]

10.

The 14th Regiment, South Carolina Volunteers

The 14th Regiment, SCV, was also called the 14th Regiment, South Carolina Infantry. It was one of four created in response to President Davis's call for three thousand additional volunteers from South Carolina in late June 1861. The *Mercury* announced in late July that the regiment was to be raised.[1] As the summer wore on, companies that would soon become the 12th, 13th, 14th and 15th Regiments gathered at both Lightwood Knot Springs, about seven miles north of Columbia, and at Camp Butler at Pole Cat (now Montmorenci) in Barnwell District. According to the *Mercury*, the 14th Regiment was complete and fully organized by August 3.[2] The ten-company 14th Regiment mustered in Confederate service at Camp Butler on September 10, 1861. Because the men enlisted for the duration of the war, the 14th was not affected by the reorganization in the spring of 1862.

Field Officers

James Jones of Columbia and Edgefield was unanimously elected colonel of the 14th Regiment on September 9, 1861.[3] Jones had served before the war as both a general in the militia and adjutant general of South Carolina. He served less than a year with the 14th Regiment. When States Rights Gist, then adjutant general of South Carolina, was appointed brigadier general in the Provisional Army of the Confederate States on March 20, 1862, Jones felt slighted because he thought he, not Gist—who was his junior in rank—should have received the appointment instead. Although he deeply regretted leaving the regiment he had formed, Jones felt bound by military etiquette and resigned on April 11.[4] Colonel Dunovant of the 12th Regiment resigned for the same reason. Maxcy Gregg appealed, without success, to the secretary of war to reject Jones's resignation, writing that he was "an excellent officer…[whose] loss will be felt by the regiment."[5] Jones served as quartermaster general for South Carolina after he resigned.

Samuel McGowan of Abbeville, who was appointed brigadier general in the South Carolina Army on December 17, 1860, commanded a brigade of South Carolina troops at Fort Sumter in April 1861 and served as a volunteer aide to General M.L. Bonham at First Manassas. He was elected lieutenant colonel of the 14th Regiment on September 9, 1861, defeating Thomas G. Lamar, later commander of the 2nd Artillery Regiment, by a vote of 451 to 372.[6] Lamar moved on to become captain of Company D, 2nd Battalion, South Carolina Artillery by October; he soon rose to command both the 2nd Battalion and its successor, the 2nd Regiment. McGowan was promoted to colonel about April 11, 1862. He was severely bruised by grapeshot across the abdomen at Gaines's Mill on June 27.[7] He also received a flesh wound in the thigh at Second Manassas on August 29.[8] Rhea states this wound was to the forearm.[9] McGowan was promoted to brigadier general on January 17, 1863, replacing Maxcy Gregg, who was killed at Fredericksburg. McGowan was wounded again at Chancellorsville on May 3, 1863, this time shot in the ankle as he stood atop the fieldworks. He was still walking painfully, and only with the aid of crutches, four months later.[10] McGowan returned to the brigade on February 4, 1864, only to be wounded on May 12 at Spotsylvania Court House by a bullet that, fortunately, passed between the two bones of his forearm.[11] He returned during the summer but took still another wound at Reams Station on August 25. McGowan was paroled with the regiment at Appomattox Court House on April 9, 1865.[12] Caldwell, writing while McGowan was still alive, said: "As a military man he was very successful. Although not so rigid and minute in his discipline and management as many others, he excelled most officers of equal rank in efficiency. He was an excellent drillmaster, a constant maintainer of good order and regularity, and (which is his great merit) has always succeeded in inspiring confidence in himself and in imparting to others the magnetism of his own enthusiasm. Enough has been already written to satisfy us of his courage."[13]

William Dunlap Simpson of Laurens was elected major of the regiment on September 9, 1861, defeating R.B. Watson by a vote of 553 to 261.[14] Simpson had served as a delegate to the first Provisional Congress held in Montgomery, Alabama, in 1861. He was promoted to lieutenant colonel on May 31, 1862, retroactive to April 11. Simpson was wounded at Gaines's Mill on June 27 and again, but only slightly, at Germantown.[15] Milledge L. Bonham's election as governor in late 1862 left his seat in the Confederate Congress vacant; when Simpson was elected to represent the 4th Congressional District in early 1863, he resigned as lieutenant colonel on February 4 to serve in Bonham's place.[16] That service continued until the end of the war.[17] Simpson built a long career in South Carolina politics. In 1876 and 1878, he was elected lieutenant governor, and he became governor when the General Assembly sent Wade Hampton to the United States Senate in 1879. Simpson did not serve out his term. Elected chief justice of the South Carolina Supreme Court, he resigned the governorship on September 1, 1880.

William Ingram Carter of Darlington District was promoted to major from captain of Company A on May 31, 1862, with rank from April 11. Carter was wounded at Gaines's Mill. He was dropped from the rolls on January 16, 1863, an action revoked on the thirtieth. Suffering from chronic nephritis, Carter resigned on February 20. He volunteered as a private in Company E of the Palmetto Battalion Light Artillery in August 1863 and remained in the field until his health failed again in January 1864. On December 15, 1864, Carter applied as a bonded agent in the Quartermaster Department of the Confederate States Army and served in that capacity until the end of the war.

Abner Monroe Perrin of Edgefield was promoted to major from captain of Company D on January 17, 1863, and to lieutenant colonel when Simpson resigned on February 4. He was promoted to colonel of the 14th Regiment on April 2, 1863, retroactive to February 20. Perrin was wounded at Chancellorsville while in command of the 14th Regiment. He was promoted to brigadier general on September 17, 1863, with rank from September 10, for gallantry at Gettysburg. Perrin commanded McGowan's Brigade from some point in 1863 until McGowan, who had recovered from a wound sustained at Chancellorsville, returned to duty in February 1864. Next, Perrin was assigned to command Wilcox's Alabama brigade. He was killed at Spotsylvania Court House on May 12, 1864.[18] Caldwell wrote that Perrin was "an officer of remarkable gallantry as [*sic*] remarkable discipline, and, perhaps, more distinguished than for these qualities by his devotion to, and concentration upon, the military life. He was always and entirely a soldier, and appeared to by far the greatest advantage amidst the greatest danger and tumult."[19] Captain H.P. Griffith held a different view: "Captain Perrin was a man of great ambition and seemed to have no regard for the feelings of any man who crossed his purposes, or in any respect stood in his way. He was of nervous temperament, overbearing and tyrannical at times, but brave to recklessness."[20] Colonel J.N. Brown wrote: "He was a martinet in discipline and every inch a soldier."[21] A.C. Haskell wrote in October 1863: "I confess I give up Perrin with much regret. He is a soldier every inch of him."[22]

Joseph Newton Brown, a lawyer from Laurens and Anderson Districts, was promoted from captain of Company E to major on February 4, 1863, and to lieutenant colonel on the twentieth. He was promoted to colonel on October 7, with rank from September 10, when Perrin became brigadier general. Brown's left shoulder was fractured on July 3, 1863, at Gettysburg. He commanded McGowan's Brigade at Spotsylvania after McGowan and Colonel Brockman of the 13th Regiment were wounded.[23] The *Mercury* initially reported that Brown, who was commanding the brigade, was killed at Jericho Ford on the North Anna River on May 23, 1864.[24] Though not killed, Brown was captured there and sent to the Old Capitol Prison in Washington on the twenty-ninth. He was moved to Fort Delaware on June 17 and sent aboard the *Dragoon* to Hilton Head Island on the twenty-fifth. Brown was among the fifty Confederate officers exchanged in Charleston Harbor on August 3, 1864.[25] He was recommended for promotion to brigadier general on March 20, 1865, but was never confirmed because the War Department failed to act.[26] Brown was captured again on April 2, 1865, during the battle at Sutherland's Station on the South Side Railroad. He was confined for a week at the Old Capitol Prison and was sent on to Johnson's Island, Ohio, where he was released on July 25, 1865. James Armstrong wrote that Colonel Brown "is as bold in battle as he is generous and good."[27]

Edward Croft, born and raised in Greenville District but residing in Edgefield District, was promoted to major from captain of Company H on April 2, 1863, retroactive to February 20. Croft, a graduate of the South Carolina Military Academy, was shot through the chest and right hand at Gettysburg.[28] According to the *CSR*, he was wounded in July 2, 1863, but Brown makes that date July 3.[29] Croft was able to accompany the army as it withdrew into Virginia. A note in the *CSR* states that he received a gunshot wound that fractured his right wrist on July 25, 1863. It is unclear whether this was the Gettysburg wound and only a misprint or was a separate wound entirely. Captured about July 30 at Winchester, Virginia, Croft was held for a time at the United States Army Hospital there. He was exchanged shortly thereafter and sent home to recover.[30] Croft was promoted to lieutenant colonel on October 7, 1863, with rank from September 10. He was wounded again on December 23, 1864, and though shot in the foot at Hatcher's Run on March 30 or March 31, 1865, Croft remained on the field. He was paroled with the regiment at Appomattox Court House on April 9, 1865.[31]

Henry Holcombe Harper of Abbeville was promoted from captain of Company I to major on October 7, 1863, with rank from September 10, a date also shown as both the seventeenth and the nineteenth. Harper was slightly wounded in the thigh at the Wilderness on May 5, 1864.[32] According to Krick, Harper was wounded four times.[33] He was also captured, at Deep

Bottom on July 28, 1864, and sent to the Old Capitol Prison in Washington on August 3.[34] He was moved to Fort Delaware on August 11 and was released on July 21, 1865.[35] Harper is listed out of alphabetical order under the "Hamptons" in the *CSR*.

COMPANIES

Company A, the Lynch Creek Guards, was composed mostly of men from Darlington District, though Edgefield, Sumter and Chesterfield Districts each contributed one man. William Ingram Carter, who was elected captain on August 10, mustered in with the company at Camp Butler on September 10. He was promoted to major on April 11, 1862, and First Lieutenant Charles M. Stuckey replaced him as captain.[36] Stuckey's date of promotion does not appear in the *CSR*; presumably the date was April 11 also. A pay voucher dated July 2 lists him as captain. Stuckey was wounded in the hand on June 30, 1862, at Frayser's Farm.[37] He also sustained a severe wound—a shot through the lungs that disabled him—at Second Manassas in August 1862.[38] The *Memory Roll* records, oddly and erroneously, that he was killed at Chancellorsville in May 1863 and that he resigned on September 20, while Thomas believed Stuckey was disabled at Chancellorsville.[39] Actually, he resigned on August 19, 1863. First Lieutenant Thomas W. Carwile was promoted to captain on August 1, 1864, for conspicuous gallantry he displayed at Frayser's Farm.[40] Carwile was paroled with the regiment at Appomattox Court House on April 9, 1865.[41]

Company B, the Dearing Guards, was composed of men from Edgefield District and named in honor of Colonel Alfred Dearing, who contributed $1,000 to outfit the company.[42] Pinckney West, who had enlisted as captain on August 12, mustered in Confederate service with the company at Camp Butler on September 10. He was wounded at Ox Hill, also called Chantilly, on September 1, 1862, when a ball entered near the right elbow and lodged between the two bones of the forearm, causing stiffening of the elbow joint and partial paralysis of the right arm. Disabled, West resigned on January 31, 1863.[43] He ran for sheriff of Edgefield District in March 1863. An advertisement in the *Edgefield Advertiser* sponsored by the men of the 14th Regiment reads: "His integrity and energy of character, his business qualities, and his bearing as a soldier and gentleman, as known to us by a long acquaintance through the most trying scenes of the service, render him particularly fit for the office."[44] James Boatwright was promoted from first lieutenant to captain on January 31, 1863.[45] Boatwright, who had received a contusion from a shell at Port Royal on

January 1, 1862, was paroled with the regiment at Appomattox Court House on April 9, 1865.[46]

Company C, called Company Raiborn, was composed of men from the Rabon Creek section of Laurens District.[47] There are many variations of the spelling of Rabon Creek, including Rabun, but Raiborn appears most often when referring to Company C.[48] The men had served in the Upper Battalion of the 40th Regiment, South Carolina Militia, a Laurens District battalion.[49] Company Raiborn was one of the twelve original companies of the 3rd Regiment, SCV, when it was in state service in early 1861.[50] When the 3rd Regiment entered Confederate service on June 6, 1861, only seventy-two Company Raiborn men were willing to volunteer. Company Raiborn was not one of the ten companies accepted into the 3rd Regiment for Confederate service, and it was disbanded on June 10.[51] About seventeen of the men transferred to other companies in the 3rd Regiment, and the rest left for home.[52] Nearly seventy of the original members met to reorganize the company and elect new officers in early July.[53] Company Raiborn was reorganized on July 27 by William L. Wood, a third lieutenant in the original company, and it went into camp at Lightwood Knot Springs on August 12.[54] The company mustered in the Provisional Army of the Confederate States at Camp Butler on September 10 as Company C of the 14th Regiment.[55] Wood, who had enlisted as captain on August 12, mustered in with the company on September 10. The forty-seven-year-old Wood tendered his resignation on July 16, 1862, citing poor health and advanced age; the resignation was accepted on October 1.[56] George Washington Culbertson was promoted from first lieutenant to captain in March or April 1863.[57] Culbertson was wounded in the left leg at Gettysburg in July 1863. He was injured again on May 19, 1864, near Spotsylvania Court House when an exploding shell burned his face, both his hands and his arms.[58] Captured on April 3, 1865, at the Appomattox River near Petersburg, he was taken to the Old Capitol Prison in Washington on the fourteenth and to Johnson's Island, Ohio, on the seventeenth. He was released on June 18, 1865.

Company D, the Edgefield Rifles, was composed of men from Edgefield district.[59] The company might also have been known as the Confederate Light Guards.[60] More than twenty of its men had served in Company C, the Edgefield Riflemen, of Maxcy Gregg's six month Regiment in early 1861.[61] Abner Monroe Perrin, who had been an officer in the Mexican War, enlisted as captain on August 10 and mustered in with the company on September 10 at Camp Butler.[62] He was promoted to major on January 17, 1863, and was replaced by First Lieutenant Erasmus H. Youngblood whose promotion date is unclear. Youngblood had sustained a wound to the thigh at Ox Hill on September 1, 1862. Though it healed, he was left with a contracture of the leg. Still recuperating in January and February 1863, Youngblood was probably promoted in absentia. On August 10, 1863, he applied for permanent transfer to the conscript service. Three days later, Youngblood was detached from Company D and appointed enrolling officer in the conscription department for South Carolina. He was replaced by First Lieutenant Erasmus "Ras" S. Mims, who had been wounded at Malvern Hill while serving as the lieutenant in command of the company.[63] Mims suffered a severe wound to the right knee at Deep Bottom on July 28, 1864.[64] He applied for retirement on November 20, but the records do not show whether or not the application was accepted. Mims had not returned to duty as late as February 28, 1865.

Company E, the Enoree Mosquitoes, or Mosquitos, was composed of men from the Upper Battalion of the 41st Regiment, South Carolina Militia, from Laurens District.[65] It might also have been called the Enoree Rifles.[66] The company was raised by early August 1861, but it was organized officially at Riddle's Old Field near Laurens on August 14 and arrived in Columbia two days later.[67] After a week or two at Lightwood Knot Springs, the company moved on to Camp Butler at Montmorenci. Joseph Newton Brown, previously a private in Company D of Gregg's 1st Regiment, SCV, was elected captain on August 16 and mustered in with the company on September 10. He was slightly wounded in the arm at Gaines's Mill on June 27, 1862.[68] He was slightly injured again when a ball grazed his neck, another hit a knuckle and a piece of shell bruised his left hand at Second Manassas.[69] Brown sustained still another wound, this time to the shoulder, at Shepherdstown Ford on September 20, 1862.[70] Brown was promoted to major on February 4, 1863, and was replaced by First Lieutenant Harrison Patillo Griffith, whose promotion came on the twentieth.[71] Griffith was hit in the leg while charging near the Lutheran Seminary at Gettysburg on July 1, 1863. He was also severely wounded in both ankles and disabled at the Wilderness on May 5, 1864.[72] Retiring to the Invalid Corps on January 17, 1865, Griffith was assigned to the Reserve Forces of South Carolina on the twentieth. He had not fully recovered from his wounds as late as 1900.[73] Brown found Griffith "genial and gallant."[74] First Lieutenant Samuel L. Dorroh, who was promoted to captain on January 17, 1865, had been wounded at Gaines's Mill on June 27, 1862, and at Chancellorsville on May 3, 1863. Dorroh was paroled with the regiment at Appomattox Court House on April 9, 1865.[75]

Company F, the Carolina Bees, was also called the South Carolina Bees.[76] The company was probably named for Barnard E. Bee, who was killed at First Manassas. Composed of men from Laurens District, the Bees went into camp at Lightwood Knot Springs on August 19, 1861, and moved to Camp Butler soon afterward.[77] Robert Spencer Owens, who raised the company, was elected its captain on August 18 and mustered in with the men on September 10.[78] He was mortally wounded at Frayser's Farm on June 30, 1862.[79] According to the *Memory Roll*, he died on the day he was wounded, but both the *CSR* and a sketch in *Recollections and Reminiscences* say he died in Richmond on July 11.[80] Kirkland believed Owens died on the fourteenth.[81] James H. Dunlap was promoted from first lieutenant to captain on June 30, a date also shown as July 11. Dunlap was killed at Shepherdstown, or Boteler's Ford, on September 20, 1862. He was replaced by First Lieutenant James M. McCarley on the twentieth.[82] McCarley had been wounded the previous June 27 at Gaines's Mill and was slightly injured in the thigh at the Wilderness on May 5, 1864. He also sustained serious injury to the right arm at Spotsylvania Court House on May 12.[83] Disabled, McCarley retired to the Invalid Corps on December 30, 1864. He was assigned to the superintendent of the bureau of conscripts at Laurens Court House on January 3, 1865. The record shows James P. Sloan as an officer in Company F, but whether or not he ever made captain is unclear. Sloan was promoted to second lieutenant on January 29, 1863. He was wounded at Chancellorsville on May 3 and again at Gettysburg on July 1, this time in the left leg. Left behind at Gettysburg, Sloan was captured on July 4 and was sent to Johnson's Island, Ohio, on August 31. He was paroled there and moved to Point Lookout, Maryland, on March 14, 1865, for exchange. Only one card in the *CSR*, dated September 1, 1864, lists Sloan as captain; all those before and after that date show him as second lieutenant. In addition, his parole was at the rank of second lieutenant. It is likely that he neither returned to the company nor ever commanded it as captain. Sloan's name does not appear with the other officers of the 14th Regiment paroled at Appomattox Court House on April 9, 1865.[84]

Company G, the McGowan Greys, was also known as Captain Jay's Company.[85] It was composed mostly of men from Abbeville District, though at least eight came from Edgefield District. Its captain, William Jay, who had enlisted on August 17, was injured on September 10, the day the company mustered in service; he resigned on September 22.[86] First Lieutenant Moses C. Taggart, "a practicing physician of high respectability," was promoted to captain the next day.[87] The *Mercury* gives the captain's name, erroneously, as Faggarts.[88] Taggart suffered a wound through the muscles of the thigh at Gaines's Mill on June 27, 1862, and was sent home on furlough. He was still absent as late as February 1863. He attempted to return to duty in early March but discovered that he could not perform active duty in the field. Since Taggart was still capable of duty in the medical department, he resigned on March 20 and was replaced by First Lieutenant Edmund

Cowan the same day.[89] Cowan was slightly wounded in the heel by a shell fragment at Spotsylvania Court House on May 12, 1864. Only three months later, on August 16, both his left tibia and fibula were fractured at Fussell's Mill.[90] Listed as absent on February 28, 1865, his name does not appear with the other officers of the 14th Regiment paroled at Appomattox Court House on April 9, 1865.[91] Most likely, Cowan neither returned to the company nor resigned his commission.

Company H, Ryan's Guards or the Ryan Guard, was composed of men from those sections of Edgefield and Barnwell Districts in present-day Aiken County.[92] Edward Croft, who was elected captain on August 16, mustered in with the company on September 10.[93] Croft took a flesh wound to the shoulder at Gaines's Mill on June 27, 1862.[94] He was promoted to major on February 24, 1863; William N. Jordan was moved up to captain about that time.[95] Jordan was wounded in the left thigh at Gettysburg on July 1, 1863. The *CSR* states, probably erroneously, that he was captured there, but a muster roll for July and August 1863, also in the *CSR*, lists him as wounded and on leave. Since nothing else in the *CSR* refers to details of imprisonment, exchange or release, Jordan probably was never captured. He was wounded again—however, this time a flesh wound in the right leg at Fussell's Mill on August 16, 1864. Since he was still recuperating on January 27, 1865, he probably never returned to the company.[96] His name does not appear on the list of officers of the 14th Regiment paroled at Appomattox Court House on April 9, 1865.[97]

Company I, the McCalla Rifles, was composed of men from Lowndesville in Abbeville District. It was named in honor of George R. McCalla of Lowndesville. He had outfitted and equipped the company, and his wife presented it with a banner.[98] The company was organized, and Henry H. Harper was elected its captain on August 21, 1861.[99] Harper, who had enlisted on September 3, mustered in with the company on the tenth.[100] Wounded at Frayser's Farm on June 30, 1862, he was promoted to major on September 17, 1863.[101] William R. White, who had been wounded in the right arm at Gettysburg, was promoted from first lieutenant to captain two days later. White was captured at the South Side Railroad on April 2, 1865, and was sent to the Old Capitol Prison in Washington on the sixth. He was moved three days later to the prison at Johnson's Island, Ohio, and was released on June 20, 1865.

Company K, the Meeting Street Saludas, was composed of men from Edgefield District. It was organized in the community of Meeting Street in August 1861.[102] Dewitt Clinton "Clint" Tompkins, MD, who had enlisted as captain on August 26, mustered in with the company on September 10.[103] Tompkins was wounded at Gaines's Mill in June 1862 and at Ox

Hill the following September 1.[104] Incapacitated by chronic rheumatism in the heels and ankles, he tendered his resignation on September 5, 1862; it was accepted on October 1. Tompkins went home to serve in the medical department. He died from paralysis at Meeting Street on September 11, 1895. Tompkins's replacement was First Lieutenant Orsamus W. Allen, MD, who was promoted on October 1. He had been slightly wounded in the leg at Gaines's Mill on June 27, 1862.[105] His promotion to captain might never have been confirmed. Suffering from chronic kidney problems and general debility, he wrote a formal letter of resignation on November 1 and signed it as first lieutenant. He was paroled as lieutenant, Company K, on May 25, 1865, at Augusta, Georgia. A sketch written by Tompkins's children in *Recollections and Reminiscences* fills the gaps. It seems that Company K's section of Edgefield District was left without a physician when both Tompkins and Allen left for active duty. Concerned about the home front, the citizens took their case to General Jackson, who determined that both should be allowed to resign and do their duty at home. The sketch adds that the men of Company K regretted the departure of Captain Tompkins in early October 1862. Orsamus Allen, who was ill with typhoid fever at the time, resigned in early November. His departure, too, was considered a great loss, according to the sketch.[106] O.W. Allen died from apoplexy in 1877.

First Lieutenant William L. Stevens, Allen's brother-in-law, was promoted to captain on November 1, 1862. Stevens had been wounded at Port Royal Ferry on January 1, 1862, and again at Gaines's Mill on June 27, this time in the neck. He was wounded a third time, a slight leg injury, at Chancellorsville on May 2 or May 3, 1863.[107] Stevens resigned on September 18, 1863, for medical reasons. He wrote that a year of suffering from frequent and profuse hemorrhages caused by hemorrhoidal tumors had left him nearly prostrate. According to a sketch in *Recollections and Reminiscence*, Stevens resigned because of malarial fever.[108] W.L. Stevens died from heart disease at Meeting Street in 1896.

First Lieutenant James Hamilton Allen, Orsamus's brother, moved up to captain on September 18, 1863. Seriously wounded at Second Manassas, Allen was injured again, though only slightly, some time between May 5 and May 15, 1864.[109] A subsequent wound would leave him disabled. He was hit in the right thigh by a ball from a sharpshooter's rifle while conversing with the 7th Cavalry Regiment's Colonel, Alexander C. Haskell, near Riddell's Shop on June 13, 1864.[110] The sketch in *Recollections and Reminiscences* calls him a "gallant officer" who was "universally loved by his men" and adds that he resigned sometime in 1864.[111] We know that Allen was absent from June 13, 1864, until at least January 27, 1865, but there is no evidence that he resigned, retired to the Invalid Corps, or returned to the company after that date. We also know that he suffered from the wound's effects for the rest of his life, and that he died at Meeting Street in 1896 of pneumonia.

Still another brother, Walter Scott Allen, was the last commander of Company K, though he was never actually promoted to captain.[112] He had been wounded in the arm and shoulder at Gaines's Mill and in the breast at Chancellorsville.[113] Also, at Spotsylvania Court House on May 12, 1864, the then fifth Sergeant Allen was severely injured by a Minié ball that entered one cheek and exited the other. Allen was advanced to second lieutenant by direct appointment from the secretary of war on January 6, 1865, effective the preceding December 23. The appointment was made pursuant to an April 16, 1862, act of the Confederate Congress that allowed promotion for extraordinary valor and skill displayed on the field.[114] The expectation was that Allen would request reassignment to the Trans-Mississippi Department when he recovered from the facial wound, but he acquiesced when men of Company K begged him to accept command of the company.[115] *Recollections and Reminiscences* states, incorrectly, that W.S. Allen was promoted to captain of Company K to replace his brother, James.[116] Actually, James Allen never resigned his commission as captain, and strong evidence suggests that W.S. Allen was never officially promoted to that rank.[117] John P. Thomas said W.S. Allen "may have never been promoted to captain."[118] D.A. Tompkins, too, said W.S. Allen was brevetted captain, an indication that promotion was not confirmed.[119] Even so, W.S. Allen commanded Company K until the end of the war and was paroled with the regiment at Appomattox Court House on April 9, 1865, as second lieutenant.[120]

BRIGADE AFFILIATIONS

The 14th Regiment, along with the 12th and 13th, made up Maxcy Gregg's Brigade in the fall of 1861. Gregg's old regiment, the 1st SCV, and Orr's regiment of rifles were added about June 20, 1862, creating a five-regiment brigade known as Maxcy Gregg's 2nd Brigade. Samuel McGowan, Abner Perrin and James Conner later commanded this brigade. In Virginia, it was part of A.P. Hill's Light Division of the Army of Northern Virginia.

MAJOR MOVEMENT AND ENGAGEMENTS

On September 10, 1861, the 14th Regiment mustered in Confederate service for the duration of the war at Camp Butler near Montmorenci in Barnwell District. It remained at Camp Butler until October 1 when it was ordered to the coast. The regiment was transferred to the Schutzenplatz in Charleston for a few days in early November before being sent to Port Royal Ferry in anticipation of a Federal assault there.[121] By November 31, the regiment was stationed at Gardner's Corner, below Pocotaligo.[122] Company B was engaged with a Federal gunboat at Port Royal Ferry on December 18.[123] The regiment remained at Tomotley near Pocotaligo from December 1861 until at least February 28, 1862, and possibly until late April.[124] The 14th Regiment was the only full regiment to see action at Port Royal Ferry on January 1, 1862.[125] On April 22, the 14th Regiment was sent to Fredericksburg, Virginia, passing through Richmond on May 1.[126] In April and May, the 14th Regiment was in the Army of the Rappahannock; it became part of the Army of Northern Virginia in June.[127] On May 24, the brigade marched back to Richmond, where the men encamped along the Nine Mile Road, just south of the capital. It was here that the 1st Regiment and Orr's Rifle Regiment joined the other regiments of Gregg's Brigade.

From this time to the end of the war, the 14th Regiment shared the major movements and engagements of Gregg's Brigade, which are discussed in this volume under the 1st (Gregg's) Regiment. On April 9, 1865, the 14th Regiment surrendered with the brigade at Appomattox Court House. The men surrendered their arms and marched for home on April 12.

11.

THE 15TH REGIMENT, SOUTH CAROLINA VOLUNTEERS

The 15th Regiment, SCV, was also called the 15th Regiment, South Carolina Infantry, and DeSaussure's regiment, SCV. Another of the four regiments created in response to President Davis's call in late June 1861 for three thousand South Carolinians to volunteer for the duration of the war, the 15th gathered that fall for training at Lightwood Knot Springs near Columbia to prepare for Confederate service. The regiment did not hold all new recruits; many men who had served in Maxcy Gregg's recently disbanded six-month Regiment re-enlisted in the 15th. Though six of its companies mustered in before September 10, and the field officers' commissions were dated either the ninth or tenth, a letter from Governor Pickens dated September 28 indicates, albeit indirectly, that the 15th had not yet mustered in service.[1] The process was evidently completed on October 1 or October 2 when Companies I and K mustered in service. Because its men enlisted for the duration of the war, the regiment was not affected by the reorganization in the spring of 1862. Shortly before the war ended, however, it was consolidated with the 7th Regiment, SCV, and parts of the 1st, 2nd, 6th and 7th Battalions of Blanchard's South Carolina Reserves to form a (New) 7th Regiment, South Carolina Infantry.[2] The 15th Regiment ceased to exist on April 9, 1865.

FIELD OFFICERS

William Davie DeSaussure of Columbia, had served both in the Mexican War as captain of the Palmetto Regiment's Company H and as a captain in the dragoons in the United States Army on the western plains. He was commissioned colonel of the 15th Regiment on September 9, 1861.[3] On January 28, 1861, he was appointed to the rank of major in the South

Carolina Regular Army where he commanded DeSaussure's Squadron Cavalry, Regulars. Though he resigned in early June 1861, he retained the Regular Army commission even after he was elected colonel of the 15th Regiment.[4] DeSaussure was forty-one years old when he was appointed captain in the P.A.C.S. on July 19, 1861, retroactive to March 16. According to an article in the September 11 issue of the *Mercury*, he had recently been voted in as colonel of the 15th Regiment in an election that probably took place on September 9.[5] The *Memory Roll* states, incorrectly, that he was appointed, not elected, colonel. In December 1862, Joseph B. Kershaw recommended DeSaussure for promotion to brigadier general, and on May 9, 1863, his fellow officers presented him with the gift of a horse as "a token of their esteem and appreciation of [his] ability and efficiency as an officer, and of their personal regard for [him] as a gentleman."[6] DeSaussure, still holding the rank of colonel, was shot in the chest and instantly killed near Stony Hill at Gettysburg on July 2, 1863.[7] In a singular tribute, Dickert wrote: "Colonel DeSaussure was one of the most gallant and efficient officers that South Carolina ever produced. His attainments were such as fitted him for much higher position in the service."[8] Kershaw's opinion was similar: "His loss to his regiment is irreparable."[9] The *Charleston Daily Courier* tempered its enthusiasm somewhat; its reporter noted that DeSaussure was "not a student and very far from being a book-worm. He possessed a quick mind, ready apprehension, a tenacious memory, and a judgment which, though rapid, was sound and generally correct" and "He possessed many of the qualities to make him an eminent commander."[10]

Richard F. Anderson was elected lieutenant colonel on September 10, 1861.[11] He had held the rank of captain in the South Carolina Richland Rangers from January to May 1861.[12] On October 18, while still in camp at Lightwood Knot Springs, Anderson's servant rushed in when he heard his master fall inside his tent. Though he continued to breathe for a couple of hours, Anderson died without regaining consciousness; his death was attributed to apoplexy, or stroke.[13] A tribute published in the *Daily Southern Guardian* called Anderson an "able and accomplished officer."[14]

Joseph Fincher Gist of Union District was elected major on September 10, 1861.[15] The oldest brother of Brigadier General States Rights Gist, he was promoted to lieutenant colonel on October 22, retroactive to the nineteenth, replacing Anderson. The *Mercury* reported, probably in error, that Gist was severely wounded in the hip at Boonsboro on September 14, 1862.[16] He was unpopular among the men. John Jeffries, who served later as captain of Company F, wrote that the men would protest if Gist was promoted to colonel and that he (Jeffries) would even leave the regiment.[17] Gist was promoted to colonel on July 2, 1863, as DeSaussure's replacement. He was wounded again, at Chickamauga on September 20, 1863. After suffering for at least two years from poor health, including an anal fistula, hemorrhoids and rheumatism, Gist submitted his letter of resignation on October 22, 1863, pronouncing himself physically unable to perform military duties. There is no reference to an incapacitating wound in his resignation papers. The resignation was accepted on January 5, 1864.

William Moreno Gist of Union District was promoted from captain of Company B to major, effective October 19, 1861.[18] The *Memory Roll* supports this date, as do most cards in the *CSR*, though one states that his promotion came on December 14, 1861. This apparent discrepancy has a simple explanation: Thomas W. Radcliffe, captain of Company A, was senior to Gist when the vacancy created by Anderson's death arose in October. He was routinely promoted on October 22, retroactive to the nineteenth. But Radcliffe fell ill, left the regiment and resigned about December 14.[19] He declined the promotion in either October or December, though the record is unclear which, and the next senior captain, who happened to be Gist, was promoted in his stead.[20] W.M. Gist was also rather unpopular. Some of the men were not pleased to see him return after an absence in January 1863, and the same John Jeffries who had reviled J.F. Gist said W.M. had behaved badly under fire at Boonsboro in September and again at Fredericksburg in December 1862.[21] Gist was shot through the head and killed instantly while leading the regiment at Fort Loudon near Knoxville on November 18, 1863.[22] Gist had evidently foreseen his own death; he is reported to have said the day before: "I will be killed if the fight comes tomorrow."[23] Slated for promotion to lieutenant colonel following DeSaussure's death on July 2, 1863, Gist was killed before the commission could reach him; the record shows no such promotion. Krick spells Gist's middle name as Murena.[24] Dickert, who by his own admission was very rarely critical of any South Carolina officer, offered a favorable assessment of this one: "Major [W.M.] Gist was a young man of rare qualities–open, frank, generous, brave. He commanded the respect and esteem of all." and "He was beloved by his men, and they appreciated his worth."[25]

Frederick Sims Lewie, MD, of Lexington District was promoted to major from captain of Company C on July 5, 1864, with rank from November 18, 1863, as William Gist's replacement.[26] He advanced to lieutenant colonel on December 8, 1864, retroactive to January 5, the date of Joseph Gist's resignation. Lewie was severely wounded in the left side by shrapnel in late July 1864.[27] He was elected to the South Carolina Senate in 1864 and could have used that as a legal reason to leave the regiment, but he chose to remain with the men. Lewie was placed in temporary command of the 20th Regiment in late 1864. Granted a furlough home in the early spring of

1865, he was on the way when he was captured and released by Sherman's troops in South Carolina about April 5.[28] General Kershaw recommended Lewie as colonel of the Consolidated 3rd Regiment, SCV, on April 5, 1865.[29] Lewie was paroled at Augusta, Georgia, on May 27, 1865.

John Bunyan Davis, MD, of Fairfield District was promoted to colonel from captain of Company E on February 5, 1864, with rank from January 19, following Joseph Gist's resignation. His was another promotion that was awarded for extraordinary valor and skill under the terms of an act passed by the Confederate Congress on April 16, 1862. Clearly, he also enjoyed the confidence of the men.[30] Davis became colonel of the (New) 7th Regiment when the 15th and 7th Regiments were consolidated with parts of the 1st, 2nd, 6th and 7th South Carolina Reserve Battalions on April 9, 1865. He was paroled at Greensboro on May 2, 1865. Dickert wrote that Davis was a "good disciplinarian, brave, resolute, and an all round good officer…one of the best tacticians in the command."[31]

James M. McCutcheon of Kingstree was promoted from captain of Company G to major when the 15th and 7th Regiments were consolidated on April 9, 1865. McCutcheon was paroled with the regiment at Greensboro on May 2, 1865.

COMPANIES

Company A, the Columbia Rifles, was composed primarily of men from Columbia in Richland District.[32] It was organized on August 13, 1861.[33] From early January to early July, some of its men were in the Richland Volunteers, also called the Richland Rifles, which was Company A of Maxcy Gregg's 1st Regiment, SCV. Others had been members of Company H of the 4th Regiment, SCV, from Pickens District. The Columbia Rifles mustered in Confederate service at Lightwood Knot Springs on September 5. Thomas W. Radcliffe enlisted as captain on August 15 and mustered in with the company. He soon fell ill however, as documented earlier, and after declining promotion to major and resigning his captain's commission about December 14, became drillmaster at the camp of instruction in Columbia.[34] He was promoted to captain on November 26, 1862, and served as quartermaster; on August 20, 1863, he was promoted to major. First Lieutenant Henry Beard succeeded Radcliffe as captain of Company A on October 19, 1861, "with satisfaction to us all."[35] Beard, who suffered from chronic dyspepsia and a severely impaired constitution, resigned on April 23, 1862, and was replaced by First Lieutenant Presly Brown the same day.[36] Brown signed documents as Presley, but the *CSR* gives his first name as both Presly and Pressley. Slightly wounded in the heel at Gettysburg, Brown was injured again, this time in the fingers, at Spotsylvania on May 12, 1864.[37] Hospitalized for a time in Columbia, he returned to Virginia; he was captured at Halltown on August 26, 1864, and was held at Harpers Ferry. He was moved to Washington and then sent on to Fort Delaware on August 30.[38] Brown was released from Fort Delaware on June 17, 1865.

Company B, the Gist Guards, was composed mostly of men from Union District with some from Spartanburg and Laurens Districts.[39] A notice in the August 13, 1861, issue of the *Mercury* announced that the company was soon to be organized.[40] It mustered in Confederate service on September 5, 1861. William "Bill" Moreno Gist, who was elected captain on August 22, mustered in with the company. The son of former Governor W.H. Gist, he had served as a member of Governor Pickens's staff. Gist was promoted to major on either October 19 or December 14, 1861, and First Lieutenant Stephen H. Sheldon advanced to captain on one of those two days.[41] Sheldon was struck in the thigh by a rifle ball at Chancellorsville on May 3, 1863; the ball was extracted.[42] On May 24, he was sent to a hospital in Columbia to recuperate. Sheldon returned to the company by July or August and was wounded again at Bean's Station, probably on December 14, 1863. He was sent once again to a hospital in Columbia and did not return to Company B.[43] Instead, Sheldon was placed in temporary command of the Confederate States military prison at Charleston on September 5, 1864. He died of yellow fever on October 4 at the First Louisiana Hospital in Charleston while supervising Federal prisoners there.[44] *Recollections and Reminiscences* reprints a story from the *Union Times* of 1914 naming Sheldon one of the "Immortal Six Hundred" Confederate officers who, as prisoners of war, were intentionally exposed to Confederate cannon fire on Morris Island. According to the article, Sheldon contracted scarlet fever while on Morris Island and died on August 4, 1864.[45] Both the date of his death and the claim that Sheldon was one of the "Immortal Six Hundred" were incorrect.[46]

Company C was called the Lexington Rifles and the Lexington Guards.[47] Its men were from the Dutch Fork section of Lexington District.[48] The company mustered in Confederate service at Lightwood Knot Springs on September 10, 1861. Frederick Sims Lewie, who raised the company, was elected captain on August 16. He was promoted to major on July 5, 1864, retroactive to November 18, 1863. James Henry Lewie was promoted from first lieutenant to captain some time between July 5 and August 30, 1864. Lewie, who had been wounded in the right hand at Spotsylvania on May 8, 1864, was captured at Halltown, Virginia, on August 26, 1864. Taken first to Harpers Ferry, Lewie was sent to Fort Delaware on the thirtieth and was held there until his release on June 17, 1865.[49] Lieutenant David Jefferson Griffith was promoted to captain sometime after December 20, 1864. Since J.H. Lewie was in prison until the end of the war, it is most likely that Griffith's promotion came on April 9, 1865, when the 15th Regiment was consolidated into the (New) 7th Regiment. He was wounded twice—once at the North Anna River and again at Charlestown, Virginia.[50] Appointed captain of Company H, 7th (Consolidated) Regiment, Griffith was paroled with the rank of captain on May 2, 1865, at Greensboro.

Company D, the Kershaw Guards, was composed of men from Kershaw District.[51] A few had served previously in the DeKalb Guards, one of the original companies of the 2nd Regiment, SCV. The Dekalb Guards left the 2nd Regiment and became Company N of Maxcy Gregg's 1st Regiment, SCV, about May 1, 1861, two months before the expiration of its six-month enlistment. The company mustered in Confederate service at Lightwood Knot Springs on September 6, 1861. Thomas "Tom" J. Warren, former editor of the *Camden Journal*, organized the company.[52] Elected captain on August 16, he mustered in Confederate service with the company. The thirty-nine-year-old Warren was killed at Gettysburg on July 2, 1863, while acting as major of the regiment.[53] Cornelius Benton Burns was promoted from first lieutenant to captain on October 5, 1863, retroactive to July 2. In December 1864, Burns was in the hospital, and he may have been a prisoner of war at one time. Appointed captain of Company B of the 7th (Consolidated) Regiment, he was paroled on May 17, 1865, at Charlotte.

Company E, the Monticello Guards, was composed of men from Fairfield District and was organized on August 30, 1861. Some of its men had served in Company I of Maxcy Gregg's 1st Regiment, SCV, from January to early July 1861. The company mustered in Confederate service at Lightwood Knot Springs on September 6. John Bunyan Davis, formerly captain of Gregg's Company I, raised the Monticello Guards, was elected captain at organization and mustered in with the company. Davis was promoted to colonel on January 19, 1864, for valor and skill. He was replaced by First Lieutenant William J. Dawkins on March 26 with rank from January 19, 1864. Dawkins was captured at Deep Bottom on July 27, 1864, and was sent to the Old Capitol Prison in Washington on August 3. Transferred to Fort Delaware on August 11, he was released on June 17, 1865.[54] William W. Kirkland commanded the company with the rank of first lieutenant after Dawkins's capture. Kirkland was promoted to captain of Company I when the 15th Regiment was consolidated into the (New) 7th Regiment on April 9, 1865. He was paroled on May 2, 1865.

Company F, the Thicketty Rifles, was composed mostly of men from Union and Spartanburg Districts, though a few came from Laurens,

Darlington, Fairfield, Clarendon and Marlboro Districts.[55] The company mustered in Confederate service at Lightwood Knot Springs on September 7, 1861. Charles "Charley" Wesley Boyd, who was elected captain on August 29, mustered in with the company.[56] Boyd was highly thought of by the men.[57] He was shot in the head and killed at Chancellorsville on May 2, 1863, a date also shown as the third.[58] First Lieutenant John Randolph Jeffries was promoted to captain on May 3.[59] He was severely wounded in the upper arm at Gettysburg on July 2, 1863. The *Mercury* reported, incorrectly, that Jeffries was killed at the Wilderness in May 1864.[60] Diagnosed with a tumor in the right eye in November 1864, Jeffries was admitted to Jackson Hospital in Richmond on the twenty-second. He returned to duty on January 12, 1865, but was readmitted to the same hospital the next day. He was sent to Columbia on January 15, but nothing further appears in the record. Moses Wood was in command of the company at the surrender. He was paroled on May 2, 1865, at the rank of first lieutenant.

Company G, the Williamsburg Riflemen, was composed of men from Williamsburg District along with a few from Georgetown.[61] The company was organized on August 17, 1861, at Indiantown in Williamsburg District and mustered in Confederate service at Lightwood Knot Springs on September 16.[62] Joseph Benson Chandler, who mustered in as captain that day, resigned on December 1.[63] James M. McCutcheon was promoted from first lieutenant to captain on the fifth. McCutcheon was slightly wounded at Fredericksburg on December 13, 1862.[64] When all but two companies of the 8th Regiment were captured while on picket duty near Winchester, Virginia, on September 13, 1863, the 8th and 15th Regiments were temporarily field-consolidated. McCutcheon commanded this unit near Strasburg on October 13, 1864.[65] He was promoted to major of the consolidated 7th and 15th Regiments on April 9, 1865, and was paroled at Greensboro on May 2.

Company H, the Mount Tabor Company, was also called the Pinckney Guards.[66] Its men were from Union District. The company mustered in Confederate service at Lightwood Knot Springs on September 16, 1861. William Henry Simms, who enlisted as captain on September 11, mustered in with the company.[67] Suffering from chronic enlargement of the prostate gland and chronic catarrh of the bladder, he resigned on July 8, 1862, and was replaced by First Lieutenant William P. Farr. Farr was killed at Fox's Gap near South Mountain on September 14, 1862. His replacement was Second Lieutenant William Riley Briggs, whose promotion came no later than October 17 and probably as early as September 14.[68] Briggs, who suffered for twelve months with chronic dysentery complicated by ascites, was absent from the company from

January to November 1863. He resigned on November 12, a date also shown as the seventh, and was replaced by First Lieutenant John L. Bailey, who was promoted on July 28, 1864. Bailey, who suffered from diarrhea and chronic debility, waived his right to promotion in favor of Second Lieutenant Francis Marion Farr. Accordingly, Farr was promoted to captain on August 15, 1864. Farr was a private in Company F when he was wounded in the right shoulder and captured at Gettysburg on July 2, 1863. He was taken to Decamp General Hospital at Davids Island in New York Harbor on the twenty-first and was paroled there on September 27. He was transferred to City Point, Virginia, for exchange.[69] Farr was elected brevet lieutenant of Company H on March 1, 1864, with rank from July 3, 1863. Wounded in the right shoulder at the Wilderness, Farr was appointed captain of Company E, 7th (Consolidated) Regiment and paroled at Greensboro on May 2, 1865.[70]

Company I, the Dutch Fork Guards, was composed mostly of men from Lexington District, along with a few from Fairfield and Newberry Districts. The company mustered in Confederate service at Lightwood Knot Springs, on October 1, 1861. John Henry Koon had been commissioned captain one month earlier on August 30.[71] Though sick and absent from the company from August 23, 1862, until he resigned on March 2, 1863, Koon did not cite health reasons in his letter of resignation; he wrote instead that he had been elected tax collector for Lexington District. First Lieutenant Robert William Frick commanded the company in September 1862. He sustained a wound through the thigh at Fox's Gap on September 14, 1862.[72] Furloughed home, Frick attempted to return to the regiment in January or February, but he soon left again and was ultimately disabled by the wound. Though promoted to captain no later than May 2, 1863, and probably as early as March 2, Frick resigned on July 28, 1863, because of disability and poor general health caused by the 1862 wound. He was replaced by First Lieutenant Joshua A. Derrick. Derrick had commanded the company as a lieutenant in Frick's absence. Injured slightly at Fredericksburg on December 13, 1862, Derrick was wounded again and captured at Gettysburg on July 2, 1863.[73] Taken to Fort McHenry on July 9, he was moved to Fort Delaware on the twelfth and to Johnson's Island, Ohio, on July 20. Paroled there, he was moved to City Point, Virginia, and exchanged on February 24, 1865. Derrick was promoted to captain of Company I on April 5, 1864, retroactive to July 28, 1863.

Company K, the Dorn Volunteers, was also called the Dorn Invincibles and might have been known as the Independent Guards as well.[74] Composed of men from Edgefield and Abbeville Districts, the company was organized at Dorn's Gold Mine in present-day McCormick County on September 4, 1861.[75] It was named in honor of W.B. Dorn, who not only furnished uniforms and equipment but also helped members' families who might otherwise have been destitute. The company mustered in Confederate service at Lightwood Knot Springs on October 2, 1861. Holloway Ivanhoe Bird, who raised the company, was elected its captain on September 4 and mustered in with the company on October 2.[76] His Christian name is also shown as Hobson and nickname as Hob. Multiple listings in the *Abbeville Press* show his middle initial as J; many others in the *Edgefield Advertiser* use I.[77] The *Mercury* lists him as H.L. Bird.[78] Bird tendered his resignation on April 14, 1864, but apparently it was not accepted. In May 1864, he was wounded in the left arm and heel while acting as major of the regiment.[79] Bird was captured at Halltown, Virginia, on August 26, was moved to Harpers Ferry on September 1, and was sent on to Fort Delaware and paroled on October 11, 1864.[80] He was probably exchanged at Cox's Wharf on the James River on October 15, one of more than three hundred prisoners of war. Bird was absent on parole for the rest of the year. A note in the *CSR* dated December 28, 1864, reads: "No measures have been taken to have him retired as we were not notified of his parole."[81] Bird returned to the company in 1865 and was appointed captain of Company A, 7th (Consolidated) Regiment. He was paroled at Greensboro on May 2.

Brigade Affiliations

In 1862, the 15th Regiment was attached to Thomas F. Drayton's Brigade along with the 3rd Battalion, South Carolina Infantry, the 50th and 51st Georgia Regiments and the Phillips Legion from Georgia.[82] After the battle of Sharpsburg, Drayton was reassigned and his brigade was broken up.[83] On November 26, 1862, the 15th Regiment and the 3rd Battalion were attached to J.B. Kershaw's Brigade, which already consisted of the 2nd, 3rd, 7th and 8th Regiments, SCV. Kershaw was in command until December 1863. The brigade added the 20th Regiment, SCV, on May 28, 1864. James Conner commanded the brigade from August to October 1864, and John D. Kennedy served as brigade commander from October 1864 to the end of the war. When its regiments were consolidated on April 9, 1865, the brigade consisted of the "new" 2nd, 3rd and 7th Regiments, SCV.[84] At that time, the 15th Regiment was consolidated with the 7th and part of Blanchard's Reserve Battalion to form the "new" 7th Regiment. The 3rd Battalion and the 8th, 15th and 20th Regiments ceased to exist at this time.[85]

MAJOR MOVEMENTS AND ENGAGEMENTS

Following its organization at Lightwood Knot Springs in September 1861, the 15th Regiment left for the South Carolina coast in early November in anticipation of a Federal assault there. It passed through Summerville on the fourth and moved via Charleston to Hilton Head Island, arriving on November 6.[86] The 15th provided infantry support for the garrison at Fort Walker and was shelled during the battle of Port Royal on November 7.[87] It evacuated the island that evening, marching over a four-day period, first to Bluffton and then to Hardeeville. The men moved on to the New River Bridge on November 18; by December 5, the regiment was back in Hardeeville.[88] Nearly two weeks later, on the seventeenth, the regiment left again, this time for Jonesville; it moved to Camp DeSaussure at Major Pritchard's plantation on December 29. Some companies left Major Pritchard's plantation for Camp Elliott on February 4; two months later, they were joined by Companies E, G, H and I.

The 15th Regiment moved to James Island in early June 1862 but was not engaged at the battle of Secessionville on June 16. Drayton's Brigade went to Virginia in July. The 15th Regiment left on the eighteenth of the month.[89] The entire brigade lay in camp below Richmond until August 13. It skirmished at Thoroughfare Gap on August 28 and was held in reserve on the extreme right of the Confederate lines at Second Manassas on August 29.[90] Drayton's Brigade did see action late in the day on August 30. After crossing the Potomac River into Maryland on September 6, the men rested at Frederick City for a few days. The brigade was engaged at Fox's Gap on South Mountain on September 14 and at Sharpsburg on the seventeenth before recrossing the Potomac on the eighteenth.[91] Because of its small size, Drayton's Brigade was dissolved in mid-November.[92] On November 26, during the march from Culpeper to Fredericksburg, the 3rd Battalion and the 15th Regiment were reassigned to Kershaw's Brigade. From this time until the end of the war, the 15th Regiment was in Kershaw/Conner/Kennedy's Brigade. The major movements and engagements of the regiment are discussed in this volume under the 2nd Regiment. On April 9, 1865, the 15th was consolidated with the 7th Regiment and parts of the 1st, 2nd, 6th and 7th Battalions of Blanchard's South Carolina Reserves to create the (New) or Consolidated 7th Regiment, South Carolina Infantry. Though the 15th Regiment ceased to exist as a separate entity at that time, the Consolidated 7th Regiment, of which it was a part, surrendered with the Army of Tennessee near Greensboro on April 26, and its men were paroled on May 2 and 3.

12.

THE 17TH REGIMENT, SOUTH CAROLINA VOLUNTEERS

The 17th Regiment, SCV, was raised in November and December 1861 and early 1862. The South Carolina legislature, then in special session, passed resolutions in November and on December 7, 1861, authorizing Governor Pickens to call for volunteers to enlist for twelve months' service in the state. Governor Pickens called for twelve thousand volunteers on December 9 primarily because of the threat to Charleston after the Federal invasion of Port Royal in early November 1861.[1] Companies that would eventually make up the 17th Regiment had assembled at Camp Hampton, near Columbia, as early as November 18. For the first few days, the 17th Regiment was a battalion, with J.H. Means as lieutenant colonel and F.W. McMaster as major.[2] On December 18, less than ten days after the governor's call, enlistment in state service came, and field officers were elected. The regiment was reorganized and the men enlisted in Confederate service at John's Island on May 1, 1862; Edwards gives the date of re-enlistment as May 22.[3] Re-enlistment for the duration of the war came on February 16, 1864.[4]

FIELD OFFICERS

John Hugh Means of Fairfield District was elected colonel of the 17th Regiment on December 18, 1861, and was re-elected without opposition at the reorganization on May 1, 1862.[5] Means had been governor of South Carolina from 1850 to1852, and he could have avoided field service because of his age.[6] Struck in the chest by a shell fragment at Second Manassas on August 30, 1862, he died about two in the afternoon on September 1 at Gainesville, Virginia.[7] Means was originally buried near Haymarket, Virginia; the next winter, however, his body was moved home to Buckhead and placed in an unmarked grave. A battery near the Wappoo Cut in Charleston was named in his memory.[8] The only field officer of the 17th Regiment to be killed in the war, Means was a "noble man," one who was "beloved by the whole brigade."[9] He was popular, and when he died, the men of the regiment felt as if they had lost a father.[10]

Fitz William McMaster was a lawyer from Winnsboro in Fairfield District. He also practiced law in Richland District. He was elected lieutenant colonel on December 18, 1861, and was also re-elected at the reorganization on May 1, 1862, without opposition.[11] McMaster was promoted to colonel on June 22, 1864, retroactive to the date of Means's death on September 1, 1862. McMaster, too, was wounded at Second Manassas in August 1862 and at Sharpsburg in September. At the battle of Clay's farm on May 20, 1864, he was bruised in the chest and shoulder by a spent ball. Shortly after the battle of Kinston in December 1862, most of the officers of Evans's Brigade signed a petition to the secretary of war requesting reassignment to another brigade on the grounds of a "want of confidence" in General Evans.[12] Evans promptly arrested McMaster as the instigator and charged him with misconduct before the enemy, cowardice and disrespect. Colonel Goodlett of the 22nd Regiment retaliated with charges against Evans, among them drunkenness, conduct unbecoming an officer, incompetence and cowardice. Evans was acquitted of the drunkenness charge, and the other charges were dropped. McMaster's court-martial took place in March 1863. He was acquitted of everything except conduct prejudicial to military discipline. The court determined that the finding itself was sufficient punishment and ordered McMaster to resume his command by May 4.[13] A copy of McMaster's court-martial proceedings appears in the *CSR*.[14] Bitterness between McMaster and Evans continued for the rest of the war. Upon assuming command of the brigade in July 1864, Brigadier General Stephen Elliott wrote: "McMaster is just about what you might expect—a man who has been writing pamphlets against his superior officers to be—but I have had no trouble with him and do not expect to have."[15] Only a few days later Elliott wrote that McMaster "is a hypocrite and I strongly, yea powerfully, suspect that his regard for his hide is paramount."[16] McMaster was wounded again at the battle of the Crater on July 30, 1864.[17] Captured on March 25, 1865, at Fort Stedman, he was moved on the twenty-seventh to the Old Capitol Prison in Washington and to Fort Delaware on March 30. He was released on July 24.[18] A.H. Edwards, captain of Company A of the 17th Regiment, wrote in 1908 that many officers of Evans's Brigade felt that Colonel McMaster should have been promoted to brigadier general on September 20, 1864, instead of Colonel Wallace of the 18th Regiment.[19] The men called McMaster "our beloved colonel."[20] Lieutenant Logan of

Company F wrote: "Our Colonel is a man respected and loved by every man in the regiment."[21]

Julius Mills of Chester, previously a private in Company A, was elected major on December 19, 1861. Though he ran for re-election at the reorganization, Mills lost to Robert S. Means by a margin of sixty-two votes.[22] W.L. Edwards, captain of Company A, wrote that he lost "because Mills was a strict disciplinarian and a fine drill officer, and the men did not like to be under him as a drill officer, and they were afraid he would become colonel of the regiment, and they knew he would require them to chalk the line."[23] Dropped from the rolls of the 17th Regiment on April 29, 1862, he later served as second lieutenant in Company F, 23rd Regiment, SCV; he was promoted to captain of that company on September 29, 1864.

Robert Stark Means of Fairfield District, son of its first colonel, was elected major at the reorganization on May 1, 1862, with rank from April 28. He was promoted to lieutenant colonel on April 25, 1864, retroactive to September 1, 1862, when his father was killed. Means was severely wounded in both knees, was disabled and was captured at Boonsboro on September 14, 1862.[24] The *Mercury* reported two weeks later that his wounds were not dangerous.[25] Means was exchanged at Aiken's Landing, Virginia, on October 24. Though Means's left knee was not severely damaged and healed well, the injury to the right knee was more severe. The popliteal nerve was damaged and stiffening of the knee joint followed. A shortened right leg and constant pain in the foot resulted in permanent disability. Means retired to the Invalid Corps on August 29, 1864; he was placed in command of the military prisons at Charleston on September 27. There is evidence that he later became an enrolling officer at Columbia, where he commanded the post guard and the provost guard.

John Ripley Culp of Chester District was promoted to major from captain of Company A on August 25, 1864, with rank from September 1, 1862. Culp had been wounded at Second Manassas. He was promoted to lieutenant colonel on September 26, 1864, retroactive to the date of Means's retirement, August 29. Culp was wounded in the head and captured on April 1, 1865, at Five Forks near Dinwiddie Court House, Virginia.[26] He was taken to the Old Capitol Prison in Washington four days later and was moved to Johnson's Island, Ohio, on April 9. Culp was released on July 25, 1865.

John William Avery of York District was promoted to major from captain of Company F on September 26, 1864, with rank from August 29, when Means retired. Avery was slightly wounded on March 25, 1865, near Petersburg.[27] He was severely wounded in the left foot at Appomattox on April 9 while in command of the remaining fragment of the regiment. He was sent to the Field (Flying) Hospital of the 24th Army Corps, Army of the James. Probably Avery was still hospitalized at the surrender since his name does not appear on the roster of officers paroled at Appomattox Court House.[28]

COMPANIES

Company A, the right color company, was composed of men from Richburg in Chester District. Organized in the summer of 1861, it elected John Ripley Culp its captain and mustered in state service on November 18. Culp's commission was dated November 26. According to Krick, however, Culp was commissioned on March 26, a full eight months before the company entered service.[29] Culp was re-elected at the reorganization about April 16, 1862, and mustered in Confederate service with the regiment on May 1. Culp received a flesh wound in the arm at Second Manassas. He was promoted to major on August 25, 1864, retroactive to September 1, 1862.[30] First Lieutenant William Henry Edwards, who became known as "Captain Bill," followed Culp in that rank effective September 1. He was severely wounded when a shell exploded in the Petersburg lines on June 17, 1864, and was injured again in the left side at Fort Stedman on March 25, 1865. Taken to Jackson Hospital in Richmond on the twenty-seventh, Edwards was moved to the Confederate States General Hospital at Farmville on April 7 and was captured there. His name does not appear on the roster of officers paroled at Appomattox Court House because he was lying wounded at Farmville at the time.[31] Edwards was paroled some time between April 11 and April 21, 1865. His wound took eighteen months to heal.[32]

Company B, formerly called Company G, was composed of men from Fairfield District.[33] It mustered in state service on December 14, 1861, and in Confederate service on May 1, 1862. Its captain, William Preston Coleman, mustered in with the company on December 14 and was re-elected at the reorganization on May 1, 1862. He lost a leg to amputation on the battlefield at Second Manassas in August 1862.[34] He was furloughed home to Fairfield District and died there on January 31, 1863. We do not know the cause of his death, though Kirkland believed that he died from the effects of his wound, probably at Warrenton, Virginia.[35] Noah A. Burley was promoted from first lieutenant to captain on January 31, 1863, a date also shown as February 1. His name also appears in the *CSR* as Bailey, Berlin and Barley. Burley was wounded at the battle of Second Manassas. Captured on March 25, 1865, at Fort Stedman, he was taken to the Old Capitol Prison in Washington on March 27 and to Fort Delaware on March 30. Burley was released on June 17, 1865, and was still alive in 1908.[36]

Company C, the Defenders of Right, was formerly designated Company H.[37] The company might also have been known as the Broad River Light Infantry.[38] Its men were from York District. Organized on December 19, 1861, the company was accepted by the South Carolina adjutant and inspector general the next day. The men went to Camp Hampton in Columbia on the twenty-seventh and mustered in Confederate service on January 3, 1862, for twelve months of special state defense duty. John Alfred Witherspoon was elected captain on December 27, 1861.[39] He had attended the theological seminary in Columbia before the war and entered the army as a chaplain. A great favorite among the men, it was he who raised Company C of the 17th Regiment.[40] Witherspoon was re-elected captain at the reorganization on May 1, 1862. He suffered a wound to the thigh, described only as "frightful," at Second Manassas.[41] He lingered in great pain for seven weeks before he died of its effects on October 19, 1862, at Warrenton. Witherspoon was remembered for his "spirit of self-denial, uncalculating patriotism, spotless virtue, and devoted piety."[42]

In early December 1862, the men of Company C unanimously requested that first Lieutenant D.J. Logan of Company F be transferred to the command of Company C, but the request was not honored.[43] The company's second lieutenant, William H. Moore, was wounded at both Second Manassas and South Mountain and died on October 1, 1862. The muster roll for November and December shows Moore as captain even though he was already dead. The fact that Moore died eighteen days before Witherspoon, coupled with the fact that the effective date of the next captain's promotion coincided with Witherspoon's death, makes it unlikely that Moore was ever actually promoted to the rank of captain. A note in the *CSR* states that the listing was probably an error. First Lieutenant John W. Mitchell was promoted to captain as Witherspoon's replacement on October 19. Mitchell was slightly wounded at Second Manassas. He was also frequently absent from the company and was inefficient when on duty.[44] A sufferer from chronic rheumatism, Mitchell resigned on February 11, 1864, effective from the fourth. William Dunovant, who served as first sergeant of Company F until April 1864, was promoted to captain of Company C on April 30 for valor and skill displayed at the battle of Second Manassas. Severely wounded in the right arm at Second Manassas, Dunovant lost his left arm at the Crater on July 30, 1864.[45] He retired to the Invalid Corps on January 4, 1865. The nephew of both R.G.M. Dunovant, colonel of the 12th Regiment, and Brigadier General John Dunovant, William survived the war and settled in Texas; he was killed there in 1902.[46]

Company D, the Palmetto Rifles, was also called The Palmettoes.[47] Originally called Company K, its men were from Chester and Fairfield Districts. The company mustered in state service on December 18, 1861. According to the *CSR*, the men enlisted for three years or for the duration of the war. This information is probably incorrect since the company's first captain was re-elected in May 1862, an event that would not have occurred if the men had originally enlisted for three years. James C. Beaty was elected captain on January 14, 1862, and re-elected at the reorganization on either April 16 or May 1, 1862. He was slightly wounded in the head and shoulder at Second Manassas.[48] Beaty also served as both acting major and lieutenant colonel in late 1863 and early 1864. He transferred out of the company when he was appointed assistant quartermaster of the 17th Regiment on February 19, 1864.[49] William Grafton Stevenson, who was promoted to captain on July 23, 1864, had been wounded by his own men near Legareville on John's Island on June 8, 1862, when the 17th Regiment mistakenly fired on Confederate cavalrymen.[50] He was also wounded at Petersburg about August 4, 1864, and again at Farmville, Virginia, in April 1865, this time in the right leg. Admitted to the Field (Flying) Hospital of the 24th Army Corps, Army of the James, on April 11, 1865, Stevenson was not present at Appomattox.[51] There is no record of his parole in the *CSR*.

Company E, the Indian Land Tigers, was formerly called Company B.[52] According to the *Mercury*, the company was known as the Indian Land Rifles, but the *Southern Historical Society Papers Index* records the company name as the York Rangers.[53] Made up of men from York District, the company was the left flank guide of the 17th Regiment. Organized in November 1861, it mustered in state service on December 18.[54] The *CSR* states that the men initially enlisted for three years or for the duration of the war. This information is probably incorrect, since the first captain was dropped from the rolls at the reorganization in May 1862, an event that would not have occurred if the enlistment had been for three years. Thomas Boyd Meacham, MD, who was elected captain on November 26, 1861, was not re-elected at the reorganization and was dropped from the rolls on April 28, 1862.[55] Edwards implies that Meacham did not run for re-election.[56] First Lieutenant John C. Holley was elected captain on May 1, 1862. He died of a heart attack a month later at John's Island. W.L. Edwards, captain of Company A, wrote that Holley suddenly "fell dead, of heart failure" as the regiment stood in line after a march. First Lieutenant D.J. Logan of Company F wrote that he "dropped dead without a struggle or a moment's reflection."[57] Edwards called Holley "a fine officer and an educated Christian gentleman."[58] The *Memory Roll* states that he died from a heart attack at John's Island on June 8, 1862, but according to the *Roll of*

1. Johnson Hagood was colonel of the 1st Regiment, SCV, and was later promoted to brigadier general. Chairman of the Board of Visitors at The Citadel and governor of South Carolina after the war, he also wrote *Memoirs of the War of Secession*. *Courtesy The Citadel Archives & Museum*

2. Edward E. McCrady Jr. of Charleston, previously captain of Company K, 1st Regiment, was promoted to major in December 1861 and lieutenant colonel in June 1862. He was badly injured by a falling tree while in camp near Fredericksburg in January 1863 and resigned in March 1864. McCrady served as an enrolling officer and as commander of a camp of instruction in Madison, Florida, where he was paroled in May 1865. *From* Cyclopedia of Eminent and Representative Men of the Carolinas.

3. William T. Haskell, brother of A.C. Haskell, was captain of Company H, 1st (Gregg's) Regiment. As commander of the brigade's battalion of sharpshooters, he was killed at Gettysburg. *Courtesy of South Caroliniana Library, University of South Carolina, Columbia.*

4. James Armstrong Jr. was promoted to captain of the Irish Volunteers, Company K, 1st (Gregg's) Regiment, in November 1864. Wounded at Sharpsburg, Fredericksburg, Gettysburg and Spotsylvania, his right tibia was shattered and he was captured at Sutherland's Station in April 1865. A popular public speaker after the war, he spoke at more dedication ceremonies of Confederate monuments in South Carolina than any other veteran. *Courtesy Hibernian Society of Charleston.*

5. Joseph Brevard Kershaw of Camden was elected colonel of the 2nd Regiment in February 1861. He was promoted to brigadier general a year later and to major general in May 1864. Kershaw played a distinguished role in the Army of Northern Virginia until his capture in April 1865. He was very popular among the troops. *Courtesy of South Caroliniana Library, University of South Carolina, Columbia.*

6. William Zachariah Leitner was captain of the Camden Volunteers, Company E, 2nd Regiment. When he was wounded in the right leg at Gettysburg, his friend, brigade surgeon T.W. Salmond, left his post at the field hospital, rode to Leitner's aid and personally carried him off the field. The leg was amputated the next day. He resigned in August 1864 and served as an enrolling officer in Kershaw District. *Courtesy Old Darlington District Chapter SCGS and the War Between the States Museum.*

7. Thomas William Woodward of Fairfield District was elected major of the 6th Regiment in February 1861. Severely wounded in the thigh at Dranesville in December 1861, he was not reelected at the reorganization in 1862 and eventually became quartermaster of the 20th Regiment and assistant quartermaster of Kershaw's Brigade. *From* Cyclopedia of Eminent and Representative Men of the Carolinas.

8. John Bratton, MD, colonel of the 6th Regiment and known to the men as "Old Reliable," held several ranks—from private to brigadier general. Wounded and captured at the battle of Seven Pines, he was soon released, only to be wounded again in 1864. He was paroled at Appomattox Court House with the rank of brigadier general. *Courtesy the South Carolina Room, Greenville Public Library.*

9. James Lide Coker, captain of Company E, 6th Regiment, was severely wounded at Lookout Creek in October 1863 and captured soon afterward. Exchanged the following July, he was also promoted to major of the 6th Regiment that month. Totally disabled for field service, Coker retired to the Invalid Corps in March 1865. He founded Coker College after the war. *Courtesy of South Caroliniana Library, University of South Carolina, Columbia.*

10. David Wyatt Aiken was elected colonel of the 7th Regiment in May 1862. Severely wounded and captured at Sharpsburg, he was soon exchanged only to be wounded again at Gettysburg. Aiken resigned in July 1863 and commanded the post at Macon, Georgia, for the next year. *Courtesy of South Caroliniana Library, University of South Carolina, Columbia.*

11. Wade E. Cothran was a Citadel graduate and captain of Company C, 7th Regiment. SCV. Wounded and disabled at Maryland Heights in September 1862, he resigned in August 1863. *Courtesy The Citadel Archives & Museum.*

12. James Douglass Blanding, a veteran of the Mexican War and a lawyer from Sumter, was lieutenant colonel of the 2nd Regiment in early 1861 and was elected colonel of the 9th Regiment in July. The 9th Regiment ceased to exist in April 1862, and Blanding was relieved from duty, serving later as an enrolling officer in Sumter District, an inspector general of seacoast batteries and reserve regiments and in the Ordnance Department. *Courtesy of South Caroliniana Library, University of South Carolina, Columbia.*

13. James Henry Rion of Winnsboro was colonel of the 6th Regiment in early 1861. He then served as captain, major and lieutenant colonel in the 7th Battalion and temporarily commanded the 22nd Regiment. Finally, he commanded a consolidated unit called Rion's Regiment at the end of the war. He was paroled at Greensboro in 1865. *Courtesy of South Caroliniana Library, University of South Carolina, Columbia.*

14. John Stuart Hard was promoted to major from captain of Company F, 7th Regiment, in September 1862. He was killed instantly while leading the regiment at the top of Pea Ridge during the battle of Chickamauga in September 1863. *Courtesy J.S. Taylor and the South Carolina Confederate Relic Room and Museum, Columbia.*

15. *Above left*: William Dunlap Simpson of Laurens, a delegate to the first Provisional Congress in Montgomery, Alabama, in 1861, resigned as lieutenant colonel of the 14th Regiment when he was elected to the Confederate Congress in early 1863. Simpson built a long career in South Carolina politics after the war, serving as lieutenant governor, governor and chief justice of the South Carolina Supreme Court. *Courtesy of South Caroliniana Library, University of South Carolina, Columbia.*

16. *Above right*: Fitz William McMaster, a lawyer from Winnsboro, was elected lieutenant colonel of the 17th Regiment in December 1861 and promoted to colonel in June 1864. Wounded several times, he was captured at Fort Stedman in March 1865 and released in July. Loved by his men, McMaster had difficulties with his superiors. *Courtesy of South Caroliniana Library, University of South Carolina, Columbia.*

17. Edward Croft was a graduate of The Citadel and lieutenant colonel of the 14th Regiment. Wounded three times and captured once, he was paroled with his regiment at Appomattox. *Courtesy The Citadel Archives & Museum.*

18. Charles W. Boyd was captain of the Wickety Rifles, Company F, 15th Regiment. Highly thought of by his men, he was shot in the head and killed at Chancellorsville in May 1863. *Courtesy Old Darlington District Chapter SCGS and the War Between the States Museum.*

19. Robert William Frick was captain of the Dutch Fork Guards, Company I, 15th Regiment. Disabled by a wound in September 1862, he resigned in July 1863. *Courtesy Old Darlington District Chapter SCGS and the War Between the States Museum.*

20. Samuel McGowan of Abbeville, colonel of the 14th Regiment, was promoted to brigadier general in January 1863. Wounded five times, McGowan was paroled with his regiment at Appomattox Court House. He enjoyed a successful political career after the war. *From* Cyclopedia of Eminent and Representative Men of the Carolinas.

21. William Blackburn Wilson was elected captain of Company F, 17th Regiment, in November 1861, but he was overage and retired from the service in April 1862. He later served as colonel of the 7th Regiment, South Carolina Reserves. *From* Cyclopedia of Eminent and Representative Men of the Carolinas.

22. Laurence Massillon Keitt, a lawyer from St. Matthews Parish in Orangeburg District, raised the 20th Regiment and was commissioned its colonel in January 1862. He had been a member of the United States Congress and the Secession Convention, and a delegate to the First Provisional Confederate Congress in 1861. Keitt was mortally wounded during his first battle in Virginia as he led his men in a charge near Cold Harbor on June 1, 1864. *Courtesy of South Caroliniana Library, University of South Carolina, Columbia.*

23. Joseph Newton Brown, a lawyer from Laurens and Anderson Districts, served as captain, major, lieutenant colonel and colonel in the 14th Regiment. He was captured at Jericho Ford in May 1864 but exchanged in August. Captured again in April 1865 during the battle at Sutherland's Station, he was sent to Johnson's Island, Ohio, where he was released in July. *Courtesy* The State *Printing Company.*

24. Augustus Marshall Smith of Abbeville served as major and lieutenant colonel in the 1st (Gregg's) Regiment. Fighting while sick, he was mortally wounded at the battle of Gaines's Mill in June 1862. *Courtesy of South Caroliniana Library, University of South Carolina, Columbia.*

25. Thomas Jefferson Lipscomb commanded an independent company bearing his name before becoming major of the 2nd Regiment, South Carolina Cavalry, in October 1862. Promoted to lieutenant colonel in July 1863 and to colonel in October, he was captured near Goldsboro, North Carolina, in March 1865. *Courtesy of South Caroliniana Library, University of South Carolina, Columbia.*

26. Frank Hampton, brother of Wade Hampton, was lieutenant colonel of the 2nd Regiment, South Carolina Cavalry. Shot through the body while fighting hand-to-hand with a sabre during the First Battle of Brandy Station in June 1863, he died a few hours later. *From* Hampton and His Cavalry in '64.

27. Thomas Gresham Lamar of Edgefield District commanded the 2nd Battalion, South Carolina Artillery, and its successor, the 2nd Regiment. He was wounded while directing the defense of the Tower Battery during the battle of Secessionville in June 1862 and died from the effects of malaria that October. Not long after Lamar's death, General Pemberton ordered the Tower Battery works at Secessionville to be renamed Fort Lamar. *From MSS 80, Benjamin Ryan Tillman Papers, Special Collections, Clemson University Libraries, Clemson, SC.*

28. Thomas Jamison Glover of Orangeburg was lieutenant colonel and colonel of the 1st (Hagood's) Regiment. Mortally wounded at Second Manassas, he died the next day. A battery on the north side of James Island near the Ashley River was named in Glover's memory. *Courtesy* The State *Printing Company.*

29. David J. Griffith was appointed captain of Company H, 7th (Consolidated) Regiment, in April 1865. Wounded twice, he was paroled in May 1865 at Greensboro. *From* Men of the Times.

30. Matthew Calbraith Butler of Edgefield District was major in command of the Cavalry Battalion, Hampton Legion, in 1862. Elected colonel of the 2nd Regiment, South Carolina Cavalry, in August 1862, he was promoted to brigadier general in September 1863 and to major general a year later. After the war, Butler was a U.S. senator and major general in the U.S. Army. *Courtesy* The State *Printing Company.*

the Dead, he died at James Island on June 9 from an unspecified illness. The *Mercury* published an obituary dated June 11 in its June 16 issue.[59] The date in the *CSR*'s account, June 18, is incorrect.

Edwin Ruthwin Mills was promoted to captain on June 18, 1862.[60] His middle name is also given as Ruthven.[61] While stationed in Brandon, Mississippi, in 1863, Mills suffered a sunstroke followed by worsening vision.[62] He retired to the Invalid Corps on January 21, 1865, because of amaurosis, a loss of sight. On January 27, he was assigned to Major General J.M. Withers in Alabama. Mills's replacement on January 21 was First Lieutenant Elijah Hyatt Cherry, who had been wounded twice before. The first injury came at Boonsboro while he was a sergeant, and he also suffered a contusion to the left thigh from a shell fragment on July 30, 1864, at the Crater. Cherry was paroled at Appomattox Court House on April 9, 1865.[63]

Company F, the Carolina Rifles, the color company of the 17th Regiment, was composed of men from York District.[64] It left York for Columbia on November 26, 1861, and mustered in state service at the College Green on December 18.[65] The *CSR* notes, incorrectly, that the initial enlistment was for three years or for the duration of the war. In fact, the company reorganized and re-enlisted for the duration of the war on April 28, 1862.[66] The first captain, William Blackburn Wilson, was elected on November 29, 1861.[67] He had served for nine months in the Beaufort Volunteer Artillery. Wilson was overage and retired from the service at the reorganization; he was dropped from the rolls on April 28, 1862. Wilson later served as colonel of the 7th Regiment, South Carolina Reserves.[68] First Lieutenant John William Avery was elected captain on either April 28 or May 1, 1862.[69] He was slightly wounded in the knee by a shell fragment at Second Manassas and slightly injured again during the Maryland campaign.[70] The *CSR* records that Avery was wounded on a Tuesday in September 1862 and did not see action on Wednesday, an indication that he was injured on September 16. Avery served as acting major in early June 1864, and on July 8, he was in the hospital recovering from a wound. He was promoted to major on September 26, 1864, retroactive to August 29. First Lieutenant David J. Logan, who corresponded with the *Yorkville Enquirer* using the sobriquet L, commanded the company from time to time when Avery was absent but was never actually promoted to captain.[71] Logan was wounded in the chest at Second Manassas. In early December 1862, the men of Company C unanimously requested that Logan be transferred to their command, but the transfer never came.[72] Near Petersburg on June 18, 1864, Logan was shot in the forehead by a sharpshooter and died instantly.[73] First Lieutenant William "Bill" Shakespeare Moore was promoted in absentia to captain to succeed

Avery effective from August 29.[74] Moore had sustained a flesh wound to the leg at Second Manassas and was wounded again at Boonsboro.[75] On May 20, 1864, he was wounded and disabled at Clay's farm. He was absent until at least February 1865, and he probably never returned to the company. Moore's name does not appear on the list of officers of the 17th Regiment paroled at Appomattox on April 9, 1865, nor is there a parole card for him in the *CSR*.[76] Moore was still alive in 1908.[77]

Company G, formerly called Company I, was composed of men from Barnwell District. It mustered in for twelve months of special service and home defense about January 9, 1862. According to one source, the company's first captain in November 1861 was James Sanders, a Baptist preacher at least forty-five years old, though "of sterling integrity and great force of character."[78] Since the *CSR* does not show a Captain James Sanders for this or any other company in the 17th Regiment, Sanders probably commanded the company before its enlistment. Henry J. Kearse was elected captain on January 9, 1862. Kearse, who was older than thirty-five, was not re-elected at the reorganization and was dropped from the rolls on April 28, 1862. First Lieutenant William J. "Joe" Dickinson was elected instead on either April 28 or May 1. He was severely wounded at Second Manassas on August 30, 1862; a Minié ball struck him in the left side of the abdomen, traveled downward near the superior spinous process of the ilium and lodged near the symphysis pubis. Dickinson retired to the Invalid Corps on August 3, 1864, and was paroled at Augusta, Georgia, on May 19, 1865. First Lieutenant George H. Kearse, who had been slightly wounded at Boonsboro, was promoted to captain on August 3, 1864. He was furloughed home after a shell fragment struck his left buttock on October 11, 1864, at Petersburg. Kearse was still absent as late as January 26, 1865, on the authority of a board of medical examiners. He had not returned by February 27, though this time he was listed as absent without leave. Kearse probably never came back. His name is not on the list of officers of the 17th Regiment paroled at Appomattox Court House on April 9, 1865, and no parole card appears in the *CSR*.[79]

Company H, formerly called Company F, was composed of men from Barnwell District. William Thomas Sanders was elected its captain on December 9, 1861. Sanders died while stationed at John's Island in March 1862, probably from typhoid pneumonia.[80] Kirkland gives the date of his death as March 15.[81] The *CSR* shows him dropped from the rolls on April 28, 1862, and lists him among other deceased officers in September 1864. First Lieutenant David H. Rice commanded the company from March to April 28, 1862, when he was dropped from the rolls. Rice was never promoted to captain. He later commanded the 2nd Regiment, Junior

Reserves, in 1864 and 1865. Second Lieutenant Hughie M. Ray was elected captain on May 1, 1862, with rank from April 28. Ray was severely wounded and disabled at Second Manassas on August 30, 1862. The wound caused partial paralysis on the left side; he resigned on February 9, 1863, and was replaced the same day by Second Lieutenant Henry Martin Ulmer, also wounded at Second Manassas. Ulmer was captured at Petersburg on March 25, 1865, and was moved two days later to the Old Capitol Prison in Washington. He was transferred to Fort Delaware on March 30 and was released on June 17, 1865.

Company I, the Lancaster Tigers, was formerly designated Company D.[82] Composed of men from Lancaster District, the company was organized for twelve months' service on November 21, 1861.[83] James Dixon Caskey was elected captain on December 9, and the company left Lancaster for Columbia the next day.[84] Caskey's commission is dated December 14, which is probably the date the company mustered in service. Caskey, who was not re-elected and was dropped from the rolls on April 28, 1862, served as captain of Company I, 3rd Regiment, South Carolina State Troops, in 1863 and as captain of Company I, 3rd Regiment, Junior Reserves, in late 1864 and 1865. First Lieutenant James F. Steele was elected captain on May 1, 1862, with rank from April 28.[85] Steele was severely wounded in the shoulder at Second Manassas and in the right leg at Appomattox on April 9, 1865.[86] He was admitted to the Field (Flying) Hospital of the 24th Corps, Army of the James, on April 11; the *CSR* shows no parole card for Steele.

Company K, the Lacy Guards, was formerly designated Company E.[87] Composed of men from York District, it mustered in service at the College Green in Columbia in late November 1861.[88] Lucian P. Sadler was elected captain on December 14, 1861. Not re-elected, he was dropped from the rolls on April 28, 1862. Sadler served as major of the 5th Regiment, South Carolina State Troops, in 1863. Third Lieutenant Edward Alexander Crawford was elected captain on May 1, 1862, with rank from April 28.[89] Wounded at Second Manassas, Crawford was also slightly wounded in the head at the Crater.[90] He was paroled with the company at Appomattox Court House on April 9, 1865.[91]

Brigade Affiliations

The 17th Regiment was assigned to Nathan George "Shanks" Evans's command in the Department of South Carolina, Georgia and Florida on December 20, 1861, along with the 16th Regiment and the 3rd Battalion.[92] A new independent brigade under the command of Evans was created about June 20, 1862, and the 17th Regiment was attached to it in July. At the beginning, the 18th, 22nd and 23rd Regiments, SCV, as well as the Holcombe Legion, were also part of the brigade. The 26th Regiment was added in May 1863, and the Macbeth Artillery was attached until the end of that year. Evans's Brigade acquired the name "Tramp Brigade," a reference to its ubiquity east of the Mississippi River. The brigade had four commanders: N.G. Evans served the longest, from July 7, 1862, to April 16, 1864. His successor was William S. "Live Oak" Walker whose term was the shortest; he assumed command the same day he was wounded and captured at Clay's farm on May 20, 1864. Next came Stephen Elliott Jr., who served for two months—from May 24 until he too was seriously wounded at the Crater on July 30. The tenure of William H. Wallace, the last commander, lasted from July 30, 1864, to the surrender on April 9, 1865. The Tramp Brigade served at various times in the following commands: the Department of South Carolina, Georgia and Florida; the Army of Northern Virginia; the Department of North Carolina and Southern Virginia; the Department of the West; and the Department of Mississippi and East Louisiana.[93]

Major Movements and Engagements

The companies of the 17th Regiment were stationed at Camp Hampton near Columbia from mid-November to December 19, 1861. Several, including Companies D, E, F and K, camped at the College Green before moving to Camp Hampton in early December.[94] Seven companies left the camp on December 19 and arrived in Charleston later the same day.[95] The men set up their tents at Camp Lee, which was across the Ashley River about three miles from Charleston near the mouth of the Wappoo Cut.[96] Company C arrived in Charleston on January 4, 1862; all except Company B were there by January 15.[97] The 17th was poorly armed and ill equipped then.[98] Only two companies, A and E, had Enfield rifles; the other eight were armed with smoothbore muskets, which had been converted from flintlock to percussion.[99]

The regiment, based near Charleston from December 1861 until July 21, 1862, remained at Camp Lee from December 19 to January 30, 1862, when it marched across John's Island to Wadmalaw Island. Arriving on February 1, the men set up Camp Craft near Rockville.[100] The regiment soon pulled back to Camp Pillow on John's Island about six miles from the ferry.[101] The men drilled and performed picket duty from this base for three months, and by April, the regiment was well equipped and thoroughly drilled.[102] Leaving John's Island on May 19, the men spent a few days at Camp Simons near

Rantowles Station before moving to Church Flats on the Stono River on the twenty-third. The 17th Regiment boarded a train for Pocotaligo on May 29 but arrived after the battle and merely followed Federal troops as they withdrew toward Port Royal Ferry.[103] On the morning of May 30, Companies A and F supported the Beaufort Volunteer Artillery as it fired into the Federal rear guard. About June 1, after a few more days at Camp Simons, the regiment moved to a camp near Ravenel, also called Camp Simons, on the Charleston and Savannah Railroad.[104] It was soon ordered back to John's Island to meet an anticipated Federal advance. On June 8, one company of the 17th Regiment accidentally fired into friendly forces—pickets of the 1st Regiment, South Carolina Cavalry—killing four and wounding four.[105] Several men of the 17th were wounded in the crossfire.[106] The 17th Regiment did not participate in the battle of Secessionville on June 16, but the next day, it moved to the mainland and returned to Camp Simons on the railroad. On July 7, the regiment marched to Adams Run to participate in an expedition to Jehossee Island.[107]

N.G. Evans's Brigade, comprising the 17th, 18th, 22nd and 23rd Regiments and the Holcombe Legion, was created about June 20. The 17th, 18th and 23rd Regiments, the Holcombe Legion and the Macbeth Light Artillery were ordered to Virginia on July 17. They left by rail between July 18 and July 21. The 18th left on July 18 and arrived in Richmond on the twenty-fourth.[108] The 23rd left on July 19 and arrived in Richmond on the twenty-seventh.[109] The 17th Regiment left for Virginia by rail on July 21 and arrived in Richmond on the twenty-fifth. The rest of the brigade, except for the 22nd Regiment, left for Virginia about July 21 and arrived in Richmond on the twenty-fourth. The 22nd Regiment was not included in this order and remained in South Carolina for a few more weeks.[110]

On July 30, the men marched about seven miles down the Darbytown Road to Camp Mary, named for Lieutenant Colonel McMaster's wife.[111] The brigade skirmished while on an armed reconnaissance near Malvern Hill on August 6.[112] Leaving camp on August 11, the men marched towards Richmond; they left the capital by rail for Gordonsville on the thirteenth and crossed the Rapidan River at Raccoon Ford on August 21.[113] The 22nd Regiment joined the brigade about then.[114] The brigade lost about ninety men while acting as infantry support in a largely artillery battle at Rappahannock Station on August 23.[115] The brigade was not present on the first day of the battle of Second Manassas, August 28. It crossed through Thoroughfare Gap on the morning of the twenty-ninth and was under constant fire and lightly engaged during reconnaissance that day. It was heavily engaged late in the afternoon of the thirtieth.[116] The Tramp Brigade provided the Holcombe Legion and three other regiments—the 17th, 18th and 23rd—to the fighting on August 30; the 22nd Regiment was not engaged because it was on detached service.[117] Nearly 70 percent of men in the 17th were killed or wounded that day.[118] The *Mercury* printed a lengthy list of casualties from the 23rd Regiment from the fighting on August 30.[119] The Holcombe Legion suffered casualties in the fighting on both the twenty-ninth and thirtieth and mustered only about one hundred men for duty after the battle.[120]

A much-weakened brigade crossed the Potomac River into Maryland at White's Ford on September 5 and arrived at Frederick City on the seventh. The brigade marched through Boonsboro to Hagerstown on September 14 and arrived about four in the afternoon at South Mountain (Boonsboro Gap), where it was heavily engaged until dark. Because of the heavy losses at Second Manassas, Company F of the 23rd Regiment took only one man into the battle at South Mountain on the fourteenth. The brigade was present, and most of its regiments were engaged at Sharpsburg on September 17. The 18th Regiment was heavily engaged there; about sixty men of the 17th were on the battlefield but detached from Evans's Brigade and only partially engaged along the advance line of Longstreet's Division.[121] The men remained on the battlefield on September 18 and crossed the Potomac into Virginia that night. The brigade was in camp at Winchester from September 20 to October 30; it participated in the Grand Review in October. Leaving Winchester for Culpeper by foot on October 30, the men boarded trains bound for North Carolina on November 7 and arrived at Weldon the next day. The brigade passed through Halifax Court House and Tarboro before reaching Kinston on November 13.[122] The 18th Regiment was detached from the brigade and ordered to Greenville, North Carolina, on December 3 to perform picket duty on the Tar River. One company of the 22nd Regiment was captured while on picket duty about two miles from Kinston on the night of December 12.[123] The 17th, 22nd, 23rd, the Holcombe Legion and the Macbeth Artillery saw action at Kinston on December 13 and December 14.[124] The 18th Regiment was not engaged at Kinston and rejoined the brigade there on December 22.

The brigade moved on December 17 by rail to Goldsboro, where it was engaged at the Neuse River Bridge that evening.[125] Ordered back to Kinston on the twenty-fourth, the brigade participated in the defense of the Kinston Railroad until early February 1863. It left Kinston by rail on the evening of the seventh and arrived at Wilmington the next day.[126] The men were sent to Topsail Island for picket duty on February 10, and on the twenty-fifth, they marched to Mansonboro Sound about four miles from Wilmington. The Holcombe Legion returned to Charleston about April 18 in advance of the brigade and was based at the Four Mile House.[127] The legion was "in fine health and under excellent discipline" at that time.[128] The rest of the brigade left by rail for Charleston on April 25 and arrived there on the twenty-sixth. The men camped between the Four Mile House and the Cooper River for two days before moving to the south side of the Ashley River. The brigade was sent to Secessionville on May 4, and though ordered to John's Island on the ninth, it was not engaged and returned to Secessionville on the evening of the eleventh.[129] Companies F and I of the 23rd Regiment were detached from the regiment in early May. Company I served as heavy artillery at Battery Palmer near the John's Island Ferry for about two weeks.[130]

The 26th Regiment was added to the brigade on May 16, and Evans's entire command was sent by rail to Jackson, Mississippi, the same day. Arriving at the railroad terminus on the twenty-third, the men marched from there to Jackson.[131] The brigade remained in camp along the Pearl River near Jackson until June 22. It was stationed about sixteen miles north of Jackson until the surrender at Vicksburg on July 4. The brigade was within three miles of the Big Black River that day and did not hear about the capitulation until the fifth. It marched back to Jackson two days later,[132] entered the town on the morning of the ninth and participated in the siege that lasted until the evening of July 16. Engaged on the sixteenth, the brigade evacuated Jackson that night, withdrawing eastward through Brandon to Forest Station. By July 19, the brigade was described as "almost worn out physically and badly depressed mentally."[133] Still, within a few days, the brigade had moved into a new camp, Camp Sprawls, about thirteen miles from Forest along Caney Creek in Scott County.[134] On August 4, the men boarded a train at Forest Station for Meridian; from there they proceeded by rail and steamboat to Demopolis, Alabama, arriving on the fifth.[135] Another train trip to Selma, followed by a riverboat ride to Montgomery, occupied another day; August 7 found the men en route by train to Columbus, Georgia. The brigade continued to move, still by rail, through Macon and on to Savannah on the eighth and ninth. Though bareheaded, barefoot and in rags by this time, the men marched the next day ten miles down the Skidaway Shell Road to Camp Johnson at the Wormsloe plantation along the Skidaway River on the Isle of Hope.[136] A much-needed two-week rest and recuperation followed.

On August 26, the brigade, except for the 22nd Regiment, was sent by rail to Sullivan's Island near Charleston, arriving the next morning. The men went into camp at Mount Pleasant on the twenty-eighth and were occupied with building breastworks all the way from the south tip of Long Island (Isle of Palms) to the Cooper River. By the end of August five regiments—the 17th, 18th, 23rd, and 26th and the Holcombe Legion—had been put to work clearing timber for one and a half miles in front of the works, guarding the land approach to Charleston from the north, and providing emergency infantry support for Sullivan's Island.[137] The men also performed guard duty on Sullivan's Island every fifth night. The 22nd Regiment remained near Savannah in late August and rejoined the brigade about September 20.[138]

On September 30, the brigade moved to a position seven miles northeast of Mount Pleasant near the breastworks. Company A of the 23rd Regiment reported no men for duty on October 17, Companies B and C reported one and Company D reported two.[139] The 23rd was stationed at Hamlin's Farm on the road to Georgetown until early November when it was ordered to Battery Marshall on Sullivan's Island. It remained there until April 1864.[140] Company F of the 23rd was detached and based at Long Island (Isle of Palms) from November 1863 to February 1864. The 18th Regiment was stationed at Bonneau's Landing during September and early October 1863. On October 10, October 17 and October 18, the regiments were ordered to James Island. Arriving at Secessionville on October 12, they performed picket duty in front of Fort Lamar, near the spot they had evacuated just before leaving for Mississippi the previous summer.[141] Brigade headquarters remained at Mount Pleasant.[142] The 26th Regiment moved from Sullivan's Island to Charleston on October 24 but was ordered back to Mount Pleasant about November 29.[143] The 18th Regiment was ordered back to Mount Pleasant on October 24 and probably arrived there two days later.[144]

Though many of the men of the 17th Regiment were still shoeless and in rags during October and November 1863, they somehow managed to stay physically healthy.[145] Lieutenant Colonel Alfred Roman, assistant inspector general, wrote on November 6: "The general condition of Evans's Brigade, as regards discipline, military appearance, and efficiency in drill, is far from being satisfactory…The *materiel* of which the brigade is composed is as good as can be found in any part of the Confederacy. The men are willing to do their duty, to fight for their rights, and to be disciplined to that effect." Roman added that though the field officers were doing a good job, the men were neglected by their company commanders, who showed great want of efficiency, energy and firmness. He also wrote that the 22nd was far behind the other regiments as regards discipline, soldierly bearing and drill, and the Holcombe Legion showed a lack of discipline, practice and attention to drill, as well as considerable deficiencies in arms and ammunition.[146] At that time, the 26th Regiment suffered from defective discipline and ammunition, a dirty camp and an imperfectly kept adjutant's office.[147]

The 17th Regiment endured frequent shelling while at James Island.[148] On November 9, about a hundred men from Companies B, E, G and K of the 17th were sent to perform garrison duty at Fort Sumter. They repulsed a Federal barge attack on the fort that day.[149] The four companies suffered a continual barrage of shot and shell at Fort Sumter until November 22, when they returned to James Island. The regiment was ordered back to Mount Pleasant on the twenty-eighth. The 17th Regiment left James Island on the evening of the thirtieth and arrived at Mount Pleasant at two in the morning on December 1. Several companies of the 26th were detached from the regiment about this time. Company C of the 26th was sent to Venning's Landing from September 1863 to February 1864.[150] Company I of the 26th was sent from Mount Pleasant to Accommodation Wharf in Charleston on October 25 and remained there until April 15, 1864; Company H was also sent to Accommodation Wharf on October 28. Company E of the 26th was detached to serve guard duty at the Charleston Arsenal on January 24, 1864. Between November 1863 and January 1864, the Holcombe Legion was based in the vicinity of Mount Pleasant, Christ Church and Sullivan's Island.[151] The brigade resumed picket duty on the beaches in front of the batteries and rifles pits in the center of Sullivan's Island in December 1863 and January 1864.[152] Company B of the 18th Regiment was sent to Fort Sumter on February 12, and another company of the 18th went to Fort Sumter on February 20.[153] Both companies left the fort on February 21.[154] The rest of the brigade was sent to James Island on February 12, was sent back to Sullivan's Island on the thirteenth and was ordered to Green Pond on February 14, arriving the next day.[155]

The brigade re-enlisted for the duration of the war on February 16; the 17th Regiment's vote was unanimous. From February to April, the regiments served in various locations. The 17th Regiment performed picket duty, built a battery on the Combahee River, worked on a battery at Stock's Causeway and built roads and breastworks until April 13. One company of the 22nd Regiment was sent to Fort Sumter on February 20.[156] Other detachments from the 22nd were at Fort Sumter throughout March and April.[157] The 22nd Regiment was sent to James Island on April 7, and Company C was detached for duty at Fort Sumter the same day. The last detachment of the 22nd left Fort Sumter on April 23.[158] Company C eventually rejoined the regiment at Kinston, North Carolina, on May 3. On February 25, a detachment of the 23rd Regiment was sent to Fort Sumter.[159] About half the men of the 23rd Regiment were sent to Fort Sumter for thirty days on March 1.[160] Another fifty-man detachment of the 23rd was sent to Fort Sumter on March 4 and was relieved on the twelfth.[161] Company G of the 23rd was at Fort Sumter on March 12 and was probably relieved on April 7.[162] The last detachment of the 23rd Regiment left Fort Sumter on April 22.[163]

The 18th Regiment was detached from the Tramp Brigade on February 20 and was sent to Baldwin, Florida, near Lake City.[164] While in Florida, the 18th Regiment was attached to Colonel George P. Harrison's Brigade, along with the 11th Regiment, SCV, the 32nd Georgia Regiment and the 59th Virginia Regiment.[165] The 18th Regiment was not engaged during the battle of Ocean Pond on February 20, but it participated in the pursuit of Federal troops toward Jacksonville and was engaged nearby at Cedar Creek. The 18th Regiment left Camp Milton, Florida, on April 16 or April 17, arriving at Savannah on April 20 and Charleston on the twenty-first or twenty-second.[166] The 18th Regiment was ordered to Sullivan's Island, but Brigadier General Roswell Ripley, commander of that military district, objected on the grounds that he lacked confidence in the experience of any regiment in Evans's Brigade.[167] He succeeded in having the 11th Regiment ordered to Sullivan's Island and the 18th to Charleston.[168] The 18th Regiment left Charleston on April 29 and arrived at Wilmington on May 1, leaving on the fifteenth and arriving at Weldon the next day.

The Holcombe Legion was also detached from the Tramp Brigade, left Charleston for Savannah on February 22, 1864, and arrived in Savannah on February 24.[169] From this time until October 17, the legion was detached from the brigade. The legion was soon sent to Oatland Island, Georgia, leaving on April 15 for Savannah.[170] It left Savannah by rail on April 16 for Weldon, North Carolina, and arrived there on the twenty-first. It got to Tarboro the next day. The legion went to Kinston on May 5 and two days later was back at Weldon to guard the Petersburg and Weldon Railroad. Companies I and K were captured on May 7 while defending the railroad at Stony Creek Station, Virginia, and the rest of the legion was engaged with Federal cavalry at Jarratt's Station, near Chester, Virginia, on May 8.[171] On May 10, the legion arrived at the Nottoway Bridge in Sussex County, Virginia, where it continued to guard the same railroad. Two companies guarded the bridge over the Nottoway River eighteen miles south of Petersburg, four were posted at the bridge over Stony Creek two miles farther south and four were posted at the Nottoway River Bridge five more miles south.[172] The legion stayed in that vicinity throughout the summer. It was engaged with Wilson's Raiders at Sappony Church under the command of Wade Hampton on June 28 and June 29, and it may have been engaged at the Ware House on July 1. The Holcombe Legion was not present with the brigade on July 30 during the battle of the Crater. Leaving Stony Creek on October 15, the Holcombe Legion rejoined the Tramp Brigade in the Petersburg trenches on the seventeenth.

The 17th, 22nd, 23rd and 26th Regiments were sent to Wilmington by rail on April 15, 1864, arriving there the next day.[173] The four regiments left Wilmington on the twenty-second and moved the next day to Tarboro with orders to guard Federal prisoners there. The 17th Regiment arrived just as the Holcombe Legion was preparing an offensive strike.[174] Companies

A and F of the 17th Regiment left Tarboro on the twenty-sixth, escorting Federal prisoners captured by General Hoke at Plymouth, North Carolina; it reached Charleston on April 28. The two companies left Charleston the next day, rejoined the rest of the regiment at Wilmington on April 30 or May 1, and were assigned to provost duty in Wilmington for the next two weeks. On April 23, the 26th Regiment left Weldon, arrived at Kinston the next day, and left again by May 3. The 22nd and 26th Regiments arrived at New Bern on May 6 and drove in the enemy pickets there the same day.

The brigade left Wilmington by rail on May 16 and arrived at Petersburg before daylight three days later. Ordered immediately into the rifle pits south of the Appomattox River near Petersburg, the brigade returned to the city after dark the same day.[175] The brigade remained in that theater until the surrender at Appomattox; it was under fire daily for nearly a year, from May 20, 1864, until April 9, 1865. The Tramp Brigade left Petersburg on the evening of May 19 and arrived at Chester Station near Clay's Farm about two in the morning on the twentieth. The 17th, 18th, 22nd and 26th Regiments fought together that day at Hewlett's house; the 23rd Regiment was engaged at Clay's Farm, also called Ware Bottom Church.[176]

The brigade was engaged in the lines at Bermuda Hundreds from May 21 to June 15. It moved by forced march to Petersburg on June 16, built breastworks all night and was lightly engaged there on the seventeenth and eighteenth.[177] The 22nd Regiment was detached from the brigade but was heavily engaged those two days, and five companies of the 23rd Regiment were also independently engaged on the seventeenth.[178] Lieutenant Colonel Joshua Hilary Hudson of the 26th Regiment wrote in 1903 that "it was an unbroken fight from June 17, 1864, until April 2, 1865 [the day after he was wounded]."[179] From June 18 to June 23, the brigade was in the Petersburg trenches alternating periods of hard fighting with hard work. The brigade left the lines about June 23 but returned to the trenches on July 4.

On July 30, Federal forces blew up a mine filled with eight thousand pounds of gunpowder directly under the Tramp Brigade's position. During the ensuing battle of the Crater, the regiments of the Tramp Brigade were dispersed as follows: from left to right were the 26th, 17th, 18th, 22nd and 23rd, with Pegram's Battery between the 18th and 22nd Regiments.[180] The Holcombe Legion, detached at the time, did not rejoin the brigade until October 17. The 18th and 22nd Regiments were directly over the mine. Five companies of the 18th were blown up when the mine exploded; 83 men of that regiment were killed or wounded in the explosion and 119 were killed in retaking the crater. Companies E and H of the 22nd Regiment were blown up, and nearly all the men in Companies B, C, G and H were captured.[181] The 22nd listed only 48 men for duty the next day.[182] On the right edge of the crater, three companies of the 23rd Regiment were overwhelmed, and the regiment lost 49 men killed or wounded. To the left of the crater, Company A, the right company of the 17th Regiment, was completely overwhelmed. The 17th and 23rd Regiments managed to hold the gap in the thin Confederate line for four critical hours until Mahone's Division arrived.

With the exception of only a few days, the brigade was in the trenches flanking either side of the Crater from September 1, 1864, to March 13, 1865. During that time, the men endured almost constant sharpshooting and desultory shelling. The 22nd and 23rd Regiments and the Holcombe Legion were engaged in a picket battle to recapture rifle pits in front of the Crater on October 27.[183] The Holcombe Legion was engaged again south of the Crater on November 5. Company D of the 17th Regiment was detached from the regiment in early November and worked every other night on the construction of Battery Harrison. It returned to the trenches on November 9.

The entire brigade left its position on March 13, 1865, and marched about twelve miles to a new position near Five Forks on the right of the Confederate lines.[184] It saw action at Hatcher's Run that day; on the twenty-fourth, the men marched twelve miles back to Petersburg. The next day, they launched an attack on Fort Stedman on Hare's Hill. The brigade was also engaged on March 29 near the sawdust pile on the Boydton Plank Road; it remained in the lines at Burgess Mill on the thirtieth and was held in support during the engagement at Dinwiddie Court House on March 31. The brigade was engaged at Five Forks on April 1; only a remnant avoided capture. The remainder was involved in continuous skirmishing from April 1 to April 9 on the retreat to Appomattox Court House. Major Avery and about 119 men of the 17th Regiment surrendered with the brigade there on April 9, 1865.

13.

THE 19TH REGIMENT, SOUTH CAROLINA VOLUNTEERS

The 19th Regiment, SCV—originally called the 19th Regiment, South Carolina State Troops—was organized on January 3, 1862, in Columbia.[1] The South Carolina legislature, then in special session, had passed resolutions in November and on December 7, 1861, authorizing Governor Pickens to call for volunteers to enlist for twelve months of service in defense of the state. Primarily because of the Federal invasion of Port Royal in early November and the subsequent threat to Charleston, Governor Pickens had called for twelve thousand volunteers on December 9.[2] The ten companies of the 19th Regiment, A through K, had been raised for a twelve-month enlistment in November and December 1861. They mustered in state service in early December and in Confederate service between December 28, 1861, and January 3, 1862. The regiment was reorganized in May 1862. The 19th Regiment re-enlisted for the duration of the war on February 13, 1864.[3] It was consolidated with the 10th Regiment from February 1863 until April 1864.[4] In February 1863, twelve companies of the 10th Regiment were consolidated into six, numbered 1 through 6; the companies of the 19th Regiment were consolidated into four, numbered 7 through 10.[5] The two regiments were then consolidated into one until April 1864.[6] In early February 1864, the "gallant remnants" of the 19th Regiment re-enlisted for the duration of the war.[7] The 10th and 19th Regiments were deconsolidated in April 1864 but were consolidated again on April 9, 1865, to form Walker's Battalion, South Carolina Infantry. Walker's Battalion, probably also designated the 10th South Carolina Battalion, consisted of Companies A through F. Companies C, D, E and F were made up men from the former 19th Regiment; they were paroled on May 1, 1865.

FIELD OFFICERS

William Cain Moragne, a lawyer from Edgefield, was elected colonel of the regiment on January 3, 1862.[8] Moragne had been an officer in a company called the Ninety Six Boys in the Palmetto Regiment during the Mexican War; he had also served on M.L. Bonham's staff at the battle of First Manassas on July 21, 1861. Moragne and Colonel Abney of the 22nd Regiment, who had attempted to raise a regiment together in December 1861, competed for the office of colonel of the 19th Regiment, and Moragne won.[9] A victim of "the seeds of disease [that] rapidly developed by exposure in camp," the new colonel suffered for several months from an illness that ravaged both body and mind. Finally, too feeble to perform his military duties, Moragne reluctantly resigned his post on March 14, 1862.[10] He died at home on October 5, less than seven months later.[11] Moragne was "a high-souled man and a citizen of remarkable worth and usefulness."[12]

Augustus Jackson Lythgoe of Abbeville District had served as first lieutenant of Company G since December 19, 1861, and was elected lieutenant colonel on January 3, 1862.[13] He was promoted to colonel upon Moragne's resignation the following March.[14] Though the promotion date was not recorded in the *CSR*, his commission probably ranked from March 14. Lythgoe was almost unanimously re-elected colonel at the reorganization in May 1862; that commission dated from May 19.[15] During the first of three charges at the battle of Murfreesboro on December 31, a Minié ball shattered Lythgoe's left thigh. The leg was amputated, and he died "the same day about 12 p.m. from the effects of the amputation."[16] Lythgoe's name was engraved on one of the four cannon captured by the 10th and 19th Regiments at Murfreesboro.[17] Other cannon carried the names of Captain Nettles, Company H of the 10th Regiment; Captain Palmer, Company K of the 10th Regiment; and Second Lieutenant John T. Norris, Company A of the 19th Regiment. General A.M. Manigault cited Lythgoe for his courage and coolness under fire at Murfreesboro.[18] "All loved and respected this generous and kind-hearted officer."[19] Another notation reads: "Colonel Lythgoe is ever kind and lenient in the discharge of the duties of his office, and he has won for himself the good will and respect of every man he commands."[20]

Abraham Jones of Edgefield was elected major on January 3, 1862.[21] The *Mercury* gives his first name as Abraham, while the *Charleston Daily Courier* spelled it Abram.[22] Jones had previously served as captain of Company K from about December 21, 1861. He was promoted to lieutenant colonel at some point between Colonel Moragne's resignation in March and April 1862.[23] His promotion date was not recorded in the *CSR*, but his commission probably ranked from March 14 as well. Jones was not re-elected lieutenant colonel at the reorganization and was dropped from the rolls on May 16, 1862.

Tilman Watson was promoted to major from captain of Company A in March 1862 when Moragne resigned. His promotion date was not recorded in the *CSR*, but his commission probably dated from March 14. Only two weeks later, on March 28, the sixty-year-old Watson tendered his resignation, citing age and general physical disability. His resignation was accepted on April 16. The *Edgefield Advertiser* records his name as Tillman.[24]

Thomas Pickens Shaw of Edgefield, previously captain of Company B, was elected lieutenant colonel at the reorganization on May 19, 1862. Though Colonel Lythgoe was killed at Murfreesboro on December 31, 1862, Lieutenant Colonel Shaw, absent on sick leave at the time, was not immediately promoted to fill the vacancy. Neither was he included as a field officer when the 19th and 10th Regiments were consolidated in February 1863. Shaw was required to submit to the inquiry of an examining board convened for the purpose of relieving the army of disabled and disqualified officers before he was allowed to take command of the regiment. He appeared before the board on March 4, 1863, and by April, certain investigations into his conduct, probably those of the examining board, had not yet been acted upon by President Davis.[25] Shaw was listed by order of army headquarters as "under arrest" on the muster rolls for July and August as well as September and October 1863. On August 31, he was suspended from duty pending a decision from the secretary of war, but the War Department still had not acted on the board's recommendations by November 20. It is unclear whether the secretary of war rejected the board's recommendations or simply ignored them, but the record shows that on June 1, 1864, Shaw was promoted to colonel of the 19th Regiment, such rank to date from December 31, 1862. Shaw was seriously wounded in the upper lobe of the left lung at Franklin, Tennessee, on November 30, 1864.[26] The *Edgefield Advertiser* reported that he had been mortally wounded, and the *Mercury* reported, erroneously, that he had died of the wound in December.[27] Because his condition was such that he could not be moved, Shaw was left at Franklin when the Confederate army retreated after the debacle at Nashville; he was captured there by Federal forces.[28] On December 17, 1864, Shaw was moved to Nashville, and on March 7, 1865, he was moved to the military prison at Louisville, Kentucky. After three days, Shaw was moved to Camp Chase, Ohio, where he was paroled and transferred to Point Lookout, Maryland, on March 18, 1865. By March 27, Shaw was a patient at the Stuart Hospital in Richmond. He was viewed as a "universally popular and beloved officer."[29]

John A. Crowder of Edgefield was elected major on May 25, 1862. He served in Company H of Gregg's six-month Regiment and later as first lieutenant in Company D of the 19th Regiment before the reorganization.[30] Crowder was severely wounded in the leg at Murfreesboro on December 31, 1862. The *CSR* states that he left the regiment on January 30, 1863, to recruit, but probably he left the regiment because of his wound. He went home to Edgefield, where he died on February 12, 1863, in the home of a Mr. Curry after a long and severe illness, probably precipitated by the wound.[31] The *CSR* and *Memory Roll* give his date of death as February 14. General A.M. Manigault cited Crowder for his courage and coolness at the battle of Murfreesboro, and Crowder was awarded the Medal of Honor for bravery under fire.[32] He was "ardently devoted to the cause of his country" and was "devotedly attached to this regiment."[33]

James Leonard White of Abbeville District was promoted to major from captain of Company H on August 12, 1863, the rank to date from February 14.[34] The *Abbeville Press* reported that the men were "extremely well pleased at having him commissioned major."[35] White served as major of the Consolidated 10th and 19th Regiment from August 1863 until April 1864.[36] White received a severe chest wound at the battle of Atlanta on July 22, 1864. The *Edgefield Advertiser* initially reported that he was mortally wounded.[37] Much to the sorrow and regret of his devoted comrades, White never recovered sufficiently to return to the regiment.[38] Though he managed to survive the war, the *CSR* does not show a parole card in White's name.

James Fowler Pressley, colonel of the 10th Regiment, commanded the Consolidated 10th and 19th Regiments from February 1863 until April 1864.[39] He ranked as lieutenant colonel in command of the Consolidated 10th and 19th Regiments from February 1863 until his promotion to colonel on July 30, after which he commanded the Consolidated Regiment until April 1864.

COMPANIES

Company A, initially designated Company G, was composed of men from Edgefield District.[40] Company A mustered in state service on November 27, 1861, and in Confederate service a month later on December 28. Tilman Watson was commissioned captain then and was promoted to major about March 14, 1862. Sixty-year-old Ezekiel Watson Perry, first lieutenant of Company A, was promoted to captain on March 14, 1862.[41] Perry was not re-elected at the reorganization and was dropped from the rolls on May 8. Elijah W. Horne was elected captain at the reorganization on May 21,

1862. Horne had served as chaplain of the 19th Regiment from January 13, 1861, until he was elected lieutenant of Company A on March 27, 1862. Considered an efficient officer, Horne was wounded at Atlanta in 1864 and also slightly wounded in the leg at Chickamauga.[42] In February 1863, Horne was appointed captain of Company Number 8, which was formed by the consolidation of Companies A and B of the 19th Regiment.[43] By October 1863, this company had been redesignated Company Number 10, with Horne still in command.[44] Horne was consistently present until about September 18, 1864, when he was listed as absent because of illness. In 1865, Horne requested permission to either resign or to be reassigned to the Invalid Corps. His request for resignation was granted.[45] First Lieutenant Ezekiel Randall was promoted to captain in 1865. He appeared as captain of Company C in Walker's Battalion in April and May 1865, and he is also listed as captain of Company A of the 19th on May 2, 1865, after the regiment had ceased to exist. The record is unclear as to whether Randall was captain of Company A, 19th Regiment, or if his promotion to captain took place when Walker's Battalion was created. Randall was paroled at Augusta, Georgia, on May 18, 1865. Second Lieutenant John Thomas Norris was never in command of the company, but because of unusual bravery, his name was engraved on one of the four cannon captured at Murfreesboro.[46] He received a flesh wound in the leg at Murfreesboro and died from its complications on January 9 at Chattanooga.[47]

Company B, the Lamar Guards, initially designated Company F, was composed of men from Edgefield District.[48] Company B, organized in late November 1861, mustered in state service on December 1 and in Confederate service on December 28, 1861.[49] Its first captain, Thomas Pickens Shaw, was elected captain in late November 1861. He retained his rank until the reorganization on May 19, 1862, when he was elected lieutenant colonel.[50] Third Lieutenant Thomas Washington Getzen was elected captain at the reorganization.[51] He was placed on detached service with the conscript and enrolling department from January 26, 1863, until March 13, 1864. Getzen was wounded at Chickamauga on September 20, 1863, and at Atlanta on July 28, 1864. He also lost a leg at Bentonville, North Carolina.[52] Getzen was paroled at Greensboro on May 1, 1865, while he was a patient at General Hospital #3 at High Point. Company B was consolidated with Company A to form Company Number 8 in February 1863, but the company was redesignated Company Number 10 in October.[53]

Company C, the Dorn Guards, was composed mostly of men from Edgefield District, though a few men came from Laurens District.[54] Company C mustered in state service on December 5, 1861, and in Confederate service on December 28. John Quattlebaum was commissioned captain on December 28 but was not re-elected at the reorganization and was dropped from the rolls on May 8, 1862. H. Rufus Dean was elected captain on May 21. Dean had previously served as captain of Company C of Maxcy Gregg's six-month Regiment from January until July 1861. He enlisted in Company C of the 19th Regiment as a private in late 1861 or early 1862 and was elected captain at the reorganization. Considered an efficient officer, Dean was captain of the consolidated Companies C, F and K, which formed the 9th Consolidated Company.[55] On April 1, 1864, Dean was placed on extra duty as inspector general for Manigault's Brigade; he served as assistant adjutant general for the brigade from April 13. He was sick in the hospital on July 22, 1864, and, for that reason, was not present during the battle of Atlanta that day.[56] Dean was promoted to assistant adjutant general and inspector general on Manigault's staff on August 8. He was severely wounded at Franklin, Tennessee, and was captured there on December 17, 1864.[57] Dean was initially taken to Camp Chase, Ohio, and was moved on March 18, 1865, to Point Lookout for exchange. On March 27, Dean was admitted to Stuart Hospital in Richmond with a diagnosis of debilitas from the wound. A sketch in *Recollections and Reminiscences* states that Dean was with the army when it surrendered, but the *CSR* did not record a parole card for him.[58]

Company D was composed of men from Edgefield District and a few from Newberry, Chester, Sumter, Union and Fairfield Districts. Company D mustered in state service on December 5 and in Confederate service on December 28, 1861, at which time Ira Cromley was commissioned captain. Because he was overage, Cromley probably did not offer himself for re-election at the time of the reorganization. He was dropped from the rolls on May 8, 1862.[59] Cromley shows up later as captain of Company D, 6th Battalion, South Carolina Reserves.[60] Private William Spencer "Bass" Peterson was elected captain on May 20, 1862.[61] When the 10th and 19th Regiments were consolidated, Peterson was placed on enrolling and recruiting service from February 28, 1863, until about May 23, 1864. Peterson was shot through the head and killed instantly at Atlanta on July 28, 1864.[62] First Lieutenant John William Denny was promoted to captain in September 1864, the promotion to date from July 28. Denny was regarded as a satisfactory officer.[63] He was paroled at Augusta, Georgia, on May 22, 1865. Companies D and G were merged to form the Consolidated Company Number 7 in February 1863.[64]

Company E, made up of men from Sumter District, mustered in state service on December 17, 1861, went into camp on December 25, and mustered in Confederate service on December 28, 1861.[65] William M. Green was commissioned captain on that date but was not re-elected at the reorganization. He was dropped from the rolls on May 8, 1862. Probably elected captain at the reorganization, First Lieutenant B. Rufus Richbourg was on sick leave from June 4, 1862, to about December 1862. Richbourg was not given a command when the 10th and 19th Regiments were consolidated on January 31, 1863; instead, he was ordered to the camp of instruction at Chattanooga from February 23, 1863, until April 1, 1864. He rejoined Company E on May 26, 1864, but was placed on detached service under General Pillow on August 31. Chronic dysentery forced Richbourg to resign on October 13; at that time, he asked to join the cavalry service. General Manigault agreed that Richbourg's resignation was beneficial to Company E. First Lieutenant Robert Young McLeod commanded the company from the reorganization until he was shot through the upper third of his right thigh at Jonesboro on August 31, 1864; the wound disabled him. Though McLeod was considered a satisfactory officer, he was never promoted to captain.[66] Company E was consolidated with Companies H and I to form the 10th Consolidated Company in February 1863.[67] It was redesignated Company Number 8 in October.[68]

Company F, initially designated Company H, was composed of men from the area around Bethel Church in Edgefield District.[69] Company F mustered in state service on December 18 and in Confederate service on December 30, 1861. Wade Holstein was commissioned captain at that time, but resigned on February 15, 1862. First Lieutenant William H. Norris was promoted to captain upon Holstein's resignation. Norris was not re-elected at the reorganization and was dropped from the rolls on May 8, 1862. After an illness of several weeks, Norris died from an unnamed disease at Crawfordville, Mississippi, on May 28, 1862.[70] He was a "beloved and efficient officer."[71] Kirkland records, incorrectly, that Norris was killed in action on May 28, 1862, at Atlanta.[72] Brevet Second Lieutenant John W. Turner was elected captain, probably on May 8, 1862. Sick and left behind at Thompkinsville, Turner was taken prisoner and paroled in November or December 1862. He was not given a command when the 19th and 10th Regiments were consolidated on January 31, 1863. He was placed on duty under General Bragg at Atlanta about February 23. Turner commanded the guard at the Medical College in Atlanta until April 1, 1864. Shortly after, he returned to command Company F and was in the field with the regiment on August 18, 1864. Turner was captured at Macon, Georgia, on April 20 or April 21, 1865. Company F was consolidated with Companies C and K to form the 9th Consolidated Company in February 1863.[73]

Company G, initially designated Company B and composed of men from Abbeville District, mustered in state service on December 19, 1861, and in Confederate service on January 3, 1862, with Joseph "Joe" H. Cunningham as captain.[74] Cunningham was not re-elected at the reorganization and was dropped from the rolls on May 8. He died of disease on June 9, 1862, at Meridian, Mississippi. Both the *Confederate Military History Series* and the *Confederate Veteran* record, incorrectly, that A.J. Lythgoe became captain after Cunningham resigned and before Lythgoe was elected lieutenant colonel on January 3, a temporal impossibility because Cunningham's resignation came in May.[75] First Lieutenant Lythgoe of Company G was elected lieutenant colonel of the 19th Regiment on January 3, 1862.

Edward Noble had been first lieutenant of Company G from January 11, 1862, and he might have been elected captain on May 21; on the other hand, he might have been promoted to captain that day if Cunningham's resignation occurred before the reorganization. The *CSR* was unclear about Noble's status throughout this period. It did not state clearly that he was ever elected captain at the reorganization, but it did refer to Noble as "Ex-Captain Noble." The *CSR* also records that Noble was not re-elected captain, implying that he had held that rank before the reorganization and merely failed to be re-elected. Noble resigned on May 24, 1862, and was dropped from the rolls two days later. At most, Noble was captain of Company G for only a few days.

Robert N. Chatham was elected first lieutenant in May 1862; he was promoted to captain on June 19.[76] Several sources give his name as Cheatham.[77] Chatham was severely wounded in the shoulder at Chickamauga.[78] He served as captain of the 7th Consolidated Company formed by Companies D and G in February 1863.[79] Company G's picket line was overrun by a Federal line of battle at New Hope Church on the night of May 29, 1864. Lying with the other men in the supporting line of battle, Chatham was accidentally shot in the abdomen by one of his own men, the only casualty Company G suffered in that night's action.[80] He died the next day at the division hospital and was buried there.[81] Chatham's death was considered a great loss to the regiment because he was an efficient officer, a splendid gentleman and "an amiable and good man, a brave and good officer, and loved by all his men."[82] Kirkland records that Chatham died on May 25, 1864.[83] Described as a satisfactory officer, Second Lieutenant John M. McDonald was promoted to captain on May 29, 1864. He had been slightly wounded at Murfreesboro when a bullet, deflected by a button on his coat, struck him in the shoulder.[84] He died of wounds received at Nashville on December 15, 1864.

Company H, initially designated Company A, was composed of men from Abbeville District.[85] It mustered in state service on December 19, 1861, and in Confederate service on January 3, 1862, when Robert W. Lites was commissioned captain. Lites was not re-elected at the reorganization and was dropped from the rolls on May 8. First Lieutenant James Leonard White was elected captain on May 20.[86] He was promoted to major on August 12, 1863, the rank to date from February 14. First Lieutenant Robert F. McCaslan was promoted to captain on February 14, 1864, the rank to date from March 14, 1863.[87] The *Mercury* gives his name as R.H. McCastin, and one card in the *CSR* spells the name McCaslin.[88] McCaslan, a satisfactory officer, commanded the regiment for nine months in 1864.[89] He was stunned by a shell on December 31, 1862, at Murfreesboro and wounded again at Nashville in December 1864.[90] McCaslan was paroled on May 2, 1865, as captain of Company F, 10th South Carolina Battalion. Companies E, H and I formed Consolidated Company Number 10 in February 1863.[91] The company was redesignated Company Number 8 in October 1863.[92]

Company I, initially designated Company D and composed of men from Abbeville District, was organized on December 17 and mustered in state service on December 19, 1861.[93] The men marched into Camp Hampton, near Columbia, on December 27 and mustered in Confederate service on December 30, 1861. Hugh Robinson was commissioned captain on January 3, 1862. Past middle age at the time, Robinson resigned when the company re-enlisted at the reorganization in May 1862.[94] Some confusion exists in the record; though the effective date of resignation was May 8, Robinson did not actually resign until June 16. The *Due West Times* of June 20, 1862, reported that Robinson became ill and died before leaving "the west."[95] A week later, the same paper reported that Robinson was not only not dead but was on his way home.[96] Robinson was "an excellent man, highly esteemed by his neighbors and well liked by his company."[97] First Lieutenant Addison Clinkscales was elected captain at the reorganization in May 1862, but his commission was dated June 16, further evidence of the "confusion." Clinkscales was regarded as an efficient officer.[98] He was captain of Consolidated Company Number 10, formed from Companies E, H and I.[99] In October 1863, the company was redesignated Company Number 8.[100] Clinkscales was paroled at Greensboro on May 1, 1865. He had served as captain of Company E of Walker's Battalion in April 1865.

Company K was composed of men from Graniteville in that part of Edgefield District now located in Aiken County.[101] A few men were from Abbeville and Lexington Districts. The company was organized at Old Wells on December 21, 1861, and Abraham Jones was elected captain, probably that day.[102] His first name also appears as Abram. Jones was elected major at the organization of the regiment on January 3, 1862, and First Lieutenant William Gregg Jr. was promoted to captain.[103] Gregg was not re-elected at the reorganization and was dropped from the rolls on May 8, 1862. He was replaced by First Lieutenant Washington Hodges Timmerman MD. Poor health forced Timmerman's resignation on July 5, 1862.[104] In late 1864 and 1865, Timmerman served as a captain in the 2nd Regiment, South Carolina Junior Reserves. First Lieutenant Jordan B. Courtney, MD, was promoted to captain of Company K in January 1863.[105] He was not given a command when the 10th and 19th Regiments were consolidated in late January; instead, on January 28, 1863, Courtney was placed on detached duty as a recruiting officer. He returned to the company in August 1864. He was injured in an accident on the Mobile and Ohio Railroad near Enterprise, Mississippi, on April 24, 1862; he was also slightly wounded in the thigh at Nashville on December 15, 1864.[106] Company K, along with Companies C and F, made up the Consolidated Company Number 9.[107]

Brigade Affiliations

The 19th Regiment was attached to the Department of South Carolina, Georgia and Florida from February to April 1862.[108] For a day or two that spring, the regiment became part of David S. Donelson's Brigade along with the 10th Regiment, SCV, and the 8th and 16th Tennessee Regiments. On April 28, 1862, the 10th and 19th Regiments, with the 28th Alabama Regiment, the 44th Mississippi Regiment and Waters's Alabama Battery were formed into James H. Trapier's 4th Brigade in the Army of the Mississippi. Trapier was soon sent back east, and Arthur Manigault took over command of the brigade. In June 1862, the 44th Mississippi was replaced with the 34th Alabama Regiment. On November 15, the 24th Alabama Regiment was added to the brigade. Thus, Manigault's Brigade comprised the 10th and 19th South Carolina Regiments and the 24th, 28th and 34th Alabama Regiments.[109] Manigault's Brigade was transferred to the Army of Tennessee about November 1862. In late March 1865, it comprised the 10th and 19th South Carolina Regiments and the 24th and 34th Alabama Regiments.[110] On April 9, 1865, the 10th and 19th Regiments were consolidated into Walker's Battalion, and Manigault's Brigade was consolidated with Brigadier General Jacob H. Sharp's Brigade under Sharp's command.[111]

Major Movements and Engagements

Most of the men of the 19th Regiment enlisted at Camp Hampton near Columbia.[112] On January 4, 1862, the 19th Regiment left Camp Hampton for Charleston, arriving at Camp Wappoo, a camp of instruction across the Ashley River from Charleston, on January 6. It remained there until April 11. Between January and April, P.G.T. Beauregard refused almost all requests for furloughs from men of the 19th Regiment.[113] In the early morning hours of April 12, one week after the battle of Shiloh, the regiment left Charleston by rail for Corinth, Mississippi.[114] A controversy arose as the train passed near Edgefield District, which was home to many of the men in the regiment. Nearly all the officers and privates felt that they had enlisted for local defense within the borders of South Carolina and were not liable to be sent out of state. Against orders, about 150 of the men, many from Company C, left the train to say goodbye to their families. Though they had no intention of deserting, a good number were left behind when the train pulled out. The men's actions were condemned by some, but Lieutenant Colonel Jones defended his men.[115] Captain Quattlebaum of Company C agreed; he wrote that the men were young and uneducated and believed their enlistment was for service only in South Carolina. Because he was absent on recruiting duty when the train passed near Edgefield District, his men refused to go on to Georgia without him. When Quattlebaum returned, the men agreed to follow him anywhere; he passed off the incident as simply "poor judgment."[116]

On April 13 or April 14, the regiment was in Augusta, Georgia, heading west toward Atlanta. On April 23, it was at Mobile, Alabama.[117] Five men from Companies C, H and K were killed, thirteen seriously wounded and fifteen to twenty slightly injured in a Mobile and Ohio Railroad accident that occurred six miles north of Enterprise, Mississippi, about ten at night on April 25.[118] The 19th Regiment arrived at Corinth, Mississippi, on April 27. From this time until the end of the war, the 19th Regiment served with the 10th Regiment.

Both regiments were engaged in a skirmish at Farmington on May 17, 1862.[119] The two regiments evacuated Corinth on May 29 and arrived at Tupelo, Mississippi, on June 7. They left Tupelo about July 6 and marched fourteen miles north to Saltillo.[120] Leaving Saltillo by rail on July 30 or July 31, the regiments arrived at Tyner's Station, near Chattanooga, in early August. On August 28, the regiments crossed the Tennessee River, and on the thirtieth, they participated in the opening of Braxton Bragg's Kentucky campaign. The 10th and 19th Regiments were part of Bragg's march through Tennessee and Kentucky from August 30 to late October 1862. The men passed into Kentucky on September 10. On September 17, both regiments were engaged at Munfordville, where the 10th Regiment, being in advance of the brigade, drove in the Federal pickets. The regiments also participated in the attack on Lawrenceburg and took part in several smaller skirmishes in the Kentucky campaign, but they were not engaged at Perryville on October 8, 1862.

The regiments returned to Tennessee via Cumberland Gap on October 20 and marched to Knoxville on the twenty-fourth. Next, on November 1, they moved by rail to Bridgeport, Alabama, and then they marched to Tullahoma, Tennessee, arriving there on November 24. The *CSR*'s caption of events for the 19th Regiment shows that it left Tullahoma on November 24 and arrived at Murfreesboro on the twenty-sixth. The 10th Regiment left Tullahoma and marched to Murfreesboro about the same time. Manigault's Brigade formed a line of battle there on December 28, 1862.[121] Company A of the 10th Regiment was engaged as brigade skirmishers near Murfreesboro on December 29.[122] Company I of the 19th Regiment skirmished at Murfreesboro on December 30. The two regiments were engaged in their first major action at Murfreesboro on December 30 and December 31. The 10th and the 19th Regiments captured a Federal Battery—Company C, 1st Illinois Light Artillery—that day, which General Bragg presented to General Beauregard, then commanding the Department of South Carolina, Georgia and Florida. The four captured guns were three-inch rifled, steel cannon, two Wiards and two Parrotts, though another source records them as Napoleons.[123] The cannon were engraved with the names of two men from the 10th and two from the 19th Regiment who had shown outstanding bravery during the battle.[124] Those men from the 10th Regiment were Captains John R. Nettles of Company H and John S. Palmer of Company K. Men from the 19th Regiment were Colonel A.J. Lythgoe and Second Lieutenant John T. Norris of Company A. In late February, the four cannon were shipped to Charleston for use there.[125] The Santee Light Artillery received two of the Murfreesboro cannon in March.

The men remained in line of battle on from January 1 to January 3, 1863, and on January 24, the regiments withdrew from Murfreesboro with the Army of Tennessee, marching south twenty-five miles in one day to Shelbyville, where they set up winter quarters.[126] In February 1863, the 10th and 19th Regiments were consolidated into one; the 10th Regiment furnished six companies, and the 19th supplied four.[127] Those commissioned officers who no longer had a company to command were allowed to retain their commissions and ordered to report to General Polk for duty.[128] The Consolidated Regiment remained in winter quarters near Shelbyville, performing picket and scout duty around that area and the Duck River until late June 1863.[129] On June 27, the regiments arrived back at Tullahoma, Tennessee, and on July 1, they retreated from there with Bragg's army.[130] The army crossed the Tennessee River on July 4 and marched ninety miles to McFarland's Springs at the foot of Lookout Mountain near Chattanooga, arriving July 8.[131] The regiment left Chattanooga on August 30, arrived at Tyner's Station, near Chickamauga, the same day, then moved back to McFarland's Springs and left again on September 8. From September 8 to September 12, the men marched and countermarched. On September 11 at McLemore's Cove and on September 12 at Lafayette, the consolidated regiment participated in unsuccessful maneuvers designed to entrap Major General George H. Thomas's Federal troops.[132] The regiment left Lafayette, Georgia, on September 17 and went into line of battle the next day during a skirmish on the south side of the Chickamauga River near Lee and Gordon's Mill. The regiment also lay in line of battle near Chickamauga during most of September 19; at dusk it crossed the river and engaged in still another light skirmish. The lull ended on the twentieth when the Consolidated 10th and 19th Regiment found itself heavily engaged at the battle of Chickamauga. On September 21, the men pursued the enemy to Chattanooga and advanced the next day to the Chattanooga Valley. Here, the regiment was deployed at the foot of Missionary Ridge as a heavy picket line on September 23, and it participated in the siege of Chattanooga.[133] Engaged at the foot of Missionary Ridge on November 25, the regiment withdrew to its crest that afternoon, retreated from the Ridge later in the day, and crossed Chickamauga Creek that night. It moved through Ringgold, Georgia, on November 26 but was not engaged there. Arriving at Dalton, Georgia, about November 27, it went into winter quarters.

The men were placed in line of battle again on February 23 and February 28, but no engagements ensued. The 10th and 19th Consolidated Regiment was de-consolidated that spring. The 10th Regiment remained at Dalton until April 11, when the men left camp to repair the public road running between Dalton and Resaca. On April 23, the 19th Regiment left Dalton to build fortifications near the front at Ault's Mill.

The 10th Regiment left Dalton on May 7, opening the Georgia campaign. The regiments skirmished every day and were frequently engaged between May 7 and June 25.[134] The 19th and 10th were in line of battle at Rocky Face near Mill Creek Gap but were not engaged there on May 8. They suffered heavy shelling while in line of battle on the fourteenth at Resaca and were engaged during the Second Battle of Resaca, or Oostanaula, on May 15.[135] The regiments crossed the Oostanaula River that night and withdrew with the army in the direction of Atlanta. They marched to Adairsville on May 17, skirmished there the same day, and marched to Cassville the next. The men skirmished near Cassville on May 19 and were engaged there on the twentieth as well. The two regiments withdrew from the lines near Cassville after dark on May 20 and crossed the Etowah River. They arrived at New Hope Church on May 25, were engaged that day and skirmished on May

26 and May 27. Both regiments remained in line of battle, skirmishing daily near New Hope Church, until June 4, when they withdrew to Lost Mountain. By June 19, the men of the 10th and 19th Regiments were within two miles of Marietta. They were engaged again at Zion Church near Marietta on June 22 and remained in position until July 2.

Manigault's Brigade was not actively engaged during the battle of Kennesaw Mountain on June 27. On the night of July 2, the army evacuated Marietta; on July 3, it withdrew to Smyrna Church; and on the fifth, it withdrew to the Chattahoochee River, where it was engaged. It crossed the river on July 9 and marched to within three miles of Atlanta where, from July 10 to July 17, the men experienced a week of relative calm. The 10th and 19th Regiments were not engaged at the battle of Peachtree Creek on July 20, they skirmished on July 21 and they fell back to the works surrounding Atlanta that night. On July 22, at the battle of Atlanta, the 10th and 19th Regiments were heavily engaged in attacking, capturing and then abandoning the same works they had evacuated the preceding night. The men rested in their trenches for the next five days. On July 27, the regiments moved through Atlanta to a point about two miles southwest of the city. There on July 28, they were engaged at the battle of Ezra Church, also called the battle of the Poor House and the battle of Lick Skillet Road. Every captain of the 19th Regiment was either killed or wounded in this battle, and Adjutant James O. Ferrell was forced to take command.[136] Company A of the 10th Regiment had only eight men present for duty on the morning of July 29. The regiments skirmished almost continuously for the next thirty days from their heavily fortified position about three to four miles southwest of Atlanta between the Lick Skillett Road and the Sandtown Road.[137] The regiments evacuated their trenches on August 30, marched south of Atlanta toward Jonesboro, and were engaged there on the thirty-first. The 10th and 19th Regiments marched northward toward Atlanta in the early morning hours of September 1, but turned south and marched to Lovejoy's Station on the Macon and Atlanta Railroad as Hood's army evacuated Atlanta on September 2. The Federal army occupied Atlanta on the night of September 7, thus ending Atlanta campaign. A.M. Manigault wrote that he had been under fire for the entire four-month period except for twelve days.[138]

Following a ten-day truce, on September 18, the regiments marched northwest toward Palmetto Station on the Atlanta and West Point Railroad. The troops left by train from Palmetto Station on the twenty-ninth, crossed the Chattahoochee River and moved north. The army then moved through Dalton, Georgia, to Gadsden and Florence, Alabama. On November 20, Hood's army started for Tennessee, arriving at Spring Hill on the twenty-ninth. The field-consolidated 10th and 19th Regiments were engaged during the debacle at Franklin on November 30. Before the battle of Franklin, the companies of the 10th Regiment had not been uniformly armed. Company A carried the English-made Enfield rifle, Company B carried the Mississippi rifle and Company E carried the Harpers Ferry rifle. The other nine companies were originally armed with smoothbore muskets, and it wasn't until after the battle of Murfreesboro that those had been replaced with the Austrian rifle. After the battle of Franklin, the entire regiment was armed with Enfield rifles. After Franklin, the men moved to Nashville and were engaged there on December 15 and December 16. Manigault's Brigade managed to withdraw in an orderly manner during the chaotic retreat of Hood's army from Nashville on December 16. The regiments crossed over the Tennessee River on December 27 and arrived at Tupelo, Mississippi, on January 7, 1865. Hood's winter campaign took a severe toll on the men. The battered regiments left Tupelo by rail for South Carolina on January 19, passed through Augusta, Georgia and Branchville, South Carolina, and arrived at the defensive lines along the Edisto River, where they were placed in position near Holman's Bridge and soon moved to Jones's Bridge. Next, the regiments moved to a defensive line on Mill Creek, near Columbia, and crossed the Congaree River into the capital on February 16. The next day, the regiments moved to Granby to support the artillery at the ferry there. On the evening of February 17, the 10th and 19th Regiments moved to the Broad River Bridge, where its pickets were driven in the next morning. The regiments soon withdrew toward Winnsboro.

On February 18, 1865, about 150 men of the 10th Regiment took an unprecedented and unauthorized five-day leave of absence, leaving only about 83 men in the regiment. Many men from the 19th also took voluntary leave. Those from the 10th Regiment were unable to return because they were cut off by Sherman's troops, but some did gather under Pressley's command at Marion Court House, thus avoiding the penalty for desertion.[139] Most of the men who left the 19th Regiment were able to return during its march through Winnsboro and on to Charlotte, North Carolina. In early March, the regiments moved to Smithfield, North Carolina; they were engaged at Kinston on March 8 and March 9 and at Bentonville on the fifteenth. On April 10, the regiments retraced their steps to Smithfield.

On April 9, the 10th and 19th Regiments were consolidated into Cornelius I. Walker's Battalion, and the two regiments ceased to exist. There were only enough men left in the 10th Regiment to make up two companies in Walker's Battalion, but enough remained in the 19th to make up four companies.

The men of the 10th Regiment composed Companies A and B of Walker's Consolidated Battalion, and those from the 19th became Companies C, D, E and F. Walker's Battalion surrendered near High Point, North Carolina, on April 26; the troops were paroled on May 1 at Greensboro.[140] A discussion of Walker's Battalion follows.

14.

Walker's Battalion, South Carolina Infantry

Walker's Battalion, South Carolina Infantry, was also popularly known as the 10th Battalion, South Carolina Infantry. The 10th and 19th Regiments, SCV, were consolidated on April 9, 1865, to form Walker's South Carolina Battalion Infantry.[1] Sifakis records that the two consolidated regiments were called the (new) 19th Regiment. Walker's Battalion comprised six companies designated A to F. The men of the former 10th Regiment constituted Companies A and B, and the men of the former 19th made up Companies C, D, E and F. Many men from both regiments had taken unauthorized leaves of absence about February 18, 1865. Technically, this action was desertion, but as Walker wrote: "If ever desertion was excusable, this was. The majority had not been home since they left South Carolina in 1862."[2] Most of the men of the 19th Regiment returned to their command, but those in the 10th were unable to get back because the position of Sherman's army at the time made it impossible. Walker's Battalion was assigned to Brigadier General Jacob H. Sharp's Brigade, to which the 10th and 19th Regiments had originally belonged.[3] Sharp's Brigade was part of D.H. Hill's Division, 2nd Corps, Army of Tennessee.[4] Walker's Battalion accompanied the army to Greensboro and was encamped near High Point when the surrender took place on April 26, 1865. The men were paroled at Greensboro on May 1, 1865.

Field Officers

Cornelius Irvine Walker, the lieutenant colonel in command of the battalion, had served previously as lieutenant colonel of the 10th Regiment, SCV. He was paroled with his battalion at Greensboro on May 1, 1865.[5]

James O. Ferrell was promoted to major of Walker's Battalion on April 10, 1865.[6] He had been appointed sergeant major of the 19th Regiment on January 21, 1862, and had been promoted to adjutant of the regiment with the rank of first lieutenant on December 4, 1862. Ferrell, considered a very efficient officer, was paroled on May 1 at Greensboro.[7]

COMPANIES

Company A, composed of men from Companies A, C, D, G, H and I of the 10th Regiment, was commanded by Captain Robert Z. Harllee, previously captain of Company D, 10th Regiment. Harllee was paroled at Greensboro on May 2, 1865.

Company B, composed of men from Companies B, E, F, K, L and M of the 10th Regiment, was commanded by Captain G.P. Anderson, previously captain of Company E of the 10th Regiment.

Company C was commanded by Ezekiel Randall, who was probably an officer in Company A, 19th Regiment. Randall was promoted from first lieutenant to captain in 1865. He served as captain of Company C in Walker's Battalion in April and early May and was also listed as captain of Company A of the 19th Regiment on May 2, after the regiment had ceased to exist. It is unclear whether Randall was captain of Company A of the 19th Regiment or if his promotion to captain took place when Walker's Battalion was created. He was paroled at Augusta, Georgia, on May 18, 1865.

Company D was commanded by Henry Earlyburry Vansant. He enlisted as a private in Company D of the 19th Regiment on December 5, 1861, and had advanced to the rank of first lieutenant by September 10, 1864. He was promoted to captain of Company D when the regiments were consolidated. Vansant was paroled on May 1, 1865, at Greensboro. He was known as a satisfactory officer.[8]

Company E was commanded by Addison Clinkscales, who had previously served as captain of Company I, 19th Regiment. Clinkscales was paroled at Greensboro on May 1, 1865.

Company F was composed of men who were previously in the 19th Regiment; its commander is unknown.

15.

The 20th Regiment, South Carolina Volunteers

The 20th Regiment, SCV, was also called Keitt's regiment. Because it was so large when it went to Virginia in May 1864, men of the other regiments in Kershaw's Brigade referred to it mockingly as the 20th Army Corps. As early as May 1863, men of the 20th Regiment, recognizing their relatively easy service to that point, were calling themselves the "Pound Cake Regiment," a name that stuck until the end of the war.[1]

The 20th Regiment was raised in response to the governor's call on December 9, 1861, for twelve thousand volunteers to enlist for twelve months of service in defense of the state. Governor Pickens's authorization had come from resolutions passed by the legislature in special session in November and December. The immediate concern was the threat to Charleston posed by the Federal invasion of Port Royal in early November.[2] Companies of the regiment were organized in the fall of 1861; they gathered in Orangeburg in December and early January 1862. On January 11, 1862, after returning to Columbia, the regiment itself was organized with ten companies, A through I and K.[3] Company L, an infantry company, was added as the eleventh in April 1862; it was converted to a cavalry company and detached from the regiment in April 1863. The 20th was reorganized on April 29, 1862. Three additional cavalry companies were added in 1863: Company M on July 17, Company N on August 1 and Company O on September 25. A light artillery battery was also added on September 9, 1863. The four additional companies, however, were soon either disbanded or transferred, leaving a regiment of ten infantry companies. On April 9, 1865, the 20th was consolidated with the 2nd Regiment, SCV, and parts of the 1st, 2nd, 6th and 7th Battalions of Blanchard's South Carolina Reserves to create the (New) 2nd Regiment, SCV.[4] The 20th Regiment did not exist after that.

FIELD OFFICERS

Laurence Massillon Keitt, a lawyer from St. Matthews Parish in Orangeburg District, raised the 20th Regiment and was commissioned its colonel on January 11, 1862.[5] Keitt had been a member of the United States Congress, a member of the Secession Convention and a delegate to the First Provisional Confederate Congress in Montgomery, Alabama, in 1861. He was thirty-seven years old when he was re-elected colonel of the 20th Regiment at the reorganization.[6] Keitt was placed on detached duty as commander of Sullivan's Island from October 1862 until at least April 1863. Roswell Ripley, and others, recommended him for promotion to brigadier general in early 1863. Keitt commanded the Confederate forces on Morris Island in August and early September that year, and he supervised the evacuation of Morris Island on September 6 and September 7. On June 1, 1864, Keitt was mortally wounded during his first battle in Virginia as he led his men in a charge at Beulah Church near Cold Harbor.[7] Shot through either the lung or the liver, or both, he died the next day in Richmond.[8] Several incorrect accounts of his death appear in the records. The *CSR* states that Keitt was wounded and died on June 2. Krick says he was mortally wounded at Cold Harbor on June 2 and died in Richmond on the fourth.[9] A sketch in *Recollections and Reminiscences* claims that Keitt was wounded on June 3 and died on June 4.[10] Dickert gives the most details, writing that Keitt was commanding the brigade on June 1 as the senior colonel present and led the regiment into battle while on horseback, an action Dickert had never before witnessed in Kershaw's Brigade. Dickert believed Keitt's lack of experience in open-field battle led directly to his death.[11] The *Mercury* spells Keitt's first name as Lawrence.[12] Brigadier General Johnson Hagood wrote of Keitt: "He was a gentleman of honor and fine intellect, but his previous training and the bent of his mind qualified him for the political arena rather than a soldier's career."[13]

Olin Miller Dantzler of St. Matthews Parish in Orangeburg District was commissioned lieutenant colonel of the 20th Regiment on January 11, 1862, and was re-elected at the reorganization in the spring.[14] Before service in the 20th Regiment, Dantzler had served as a lieutenant in the St. Matthews Rifles, Company D of Hagood's 1st Regiment, SCV.[15] Though unharmed, Dantzler was shot through the breast of his coat while leading his men in driving back Federal pickets outside Battery Wagner on August 21, 1863.[16] He was appointed colonel of the 22nd Regiment on April 29, 1864.[17] Dickert wrote: "He was a fine officer, a good tactician, and a thorough disciplinarian" and "he was greatly loved by officers and men, and it was with feelings of universal regret that the regiment was forced to give him up [to the 22nd Regiment]."[18]

Alfred Mims of Lexington District was commissioned major of the regiment on January 11, 1862.[19] He refused to stand for re-election, probably because of impaired health following a severe case of measles.[20] Mims resigned as major on March 27, 1862.[21] He later served on ordnance duty at Augusta and Macon, Georgia.[22]

Stephen Madison Boykin of Kershaw and Sumter Districts was promoted to major from captain of Company A—which became Company G after the reorganization—on April 1, a date also shown as April 4, 1862; he was re-elected at the reorganization.[23] Boykin was promoted to colonel on July 6, with rank from June 2, 1864, after Keitt was killed.[24] He was slightly wounded in the head and captured at Cedar Creek, also called Belle Grove, near Strasburg, Virginia, on October 19, 1864.[25] He was taken first to Harpers Ferry and then, on October 25, to Fort Delaware, where he was released on July 24, 1865. Boykin was "a very dignified and intelligent middle aged gentleman."[26] He died in 1897.[27]

Paul Agabus McMichael of Orangeburg District was promoted to lieutenant colonel from captain of Company B on August 15, 1864, effective June 2. He was also captured on October 19, 1864, at Cedar Creek, near Strasburg. His imprisonment, in fact, was identical to Boykin's: he was taken first to Harpers Ferry, then to Fort Delaware and was then released on July 24, 1865.[28] McMichael's middle name is given variously as Agabus, Agalus and Agbarus.

John M. Partlow of Pickens District was promoted to major from captain of Company A on August 15, 1864, effective June 2. Partlow was shot through the right shoulder by a ball that fractured the spine of his shoulder blade at New Market Heights, near Deep Bottom, on July 28, 1864.[29] Nothing in the *CSR* suggests that Partlow ever returned to duty, but Dickert says he rejoined the regiment near the end of the war.[30] On April 5, 1865, Brigadier General John D. Kennedy recommended Partlow as lieutenant colonel of the Consolidated 2nd Regiment, SCV, a statement that strongly indicates he was present and fit for duty.[31] Kennedy's recommendation was not accepted, and Partlow was left out of the Consolidated 2nd Regiment.

Godfrey Leaphart of Lexington District was promoted to major of the (New) or Consolidated 2nd Regiment from captain of Company C on April 8, 1865. He was paroled at that rank on May 2, 1865.

Frederick Sims Lewie of Lexington District was promoted to lieutenant colonel of the 15th Regiment on January 5, 1864. He was placed in temporary command of the 20th Regiment late in 1864 after both Colonel Boykin and Lieutenant Colonel McMichael were captured. It is unclear from the *CSR* how long Lewie was in command, but Dickert wrote that he was furloughed home in the early spring of 1865 only to be captured before he got there.[32] Lewie was paroled at Augusta, Georgia, on May 7, 1865.

COMPANIES

Company A, which had been Company K before the reorganization, was composed of men from Anderson and Pickens Districts. At least one source calls it Company C.[33] John M. Partlow was elected captain on December 17, 1861, mustered in service on January 2, 1862, and was re-elected at the reorganization.[34] Partlow was promoted to major on August 15, 1864, with rank from June 2. His replacement was First Lieutenant Charles H.A. Woodin, whose promotion was also effective on June 2. Woodin was killed in action at Cedar Creek on October 19, 1864.[35] The *Mercury* incorrectly spelled his name as Wooden.[36] Considered "a good citizen soldier and officer," Woodin was also remembered as one who "won his way to captaincy by his fine business and social qualities, his skill and gallantry."[37] John Lee was promoted from first lieutenant to captain as Woodin's replacement on October 19. Lee had suffered a contusion to the right shoulder at Cold Harbor the previous June 3; he was wounded again at Cedar Creek the same day he was promoted. Lee's record after October 19, 1864, is non-existent. He might have been incapacitated by the wound, or he might never have returned to the company.

Company B, designated Company E before the reorganization, was composed of men from Orangeburg District. One source refers to it as Company D.[38] Paul Agabus McMichael raised the company, was elected its captain on December 30, 1861, was re-elected at the reorganization and was promoted to lieutenant colonel on August 15, 1864, retroactive to June 2.[39] McMichael was replaced as captain by First Lieutenant Benjamin H. Barton, whose promotion was effective as of June 2, 1864. Wounded in the right shoulder at Cold Harbor the same day, Barton's record ends there.[40]

Company C, the Evans Guards, was either Company C or H before the reorganization.[41] It was composed of men from the Dutch Fork section of Lexington District, along with a few from Edgefield, Newberry and Orangeburg Districts. Another source refers to this as Company E.[42] It was organized about December 14, 1861.[43] Godfrey Leaphart was commissioned captain on January 8, 1862; he was re-elected at the reorganization.[44] Leaphart took slight wounds to the head and leg at Battery Wagner on either August 21 or August 23, 1863.[45] He was promoted to major on April 8, 1865, when the 20th and 2nd Regiments were consolidated. First Lieutenant

George T. Haltiwanger, who had been wounded at Cedar Creek in October 1864, was promoted to captain about April 8.[46] He was paroled as captain of Company C of the Consolidated 2nd and 20th Regiments on May 2, 1865, at Greensboro.

Company D, the Bull Swamp Guards, was also designated Company F before the reorganization.[47] Most of its men were from the communities of North and Neeses near Bull Swamp in Orangeburg District, but a few came from Lexington District. Richard "Dick" V. Dannelly was commissioned captain on January 10, 1862, and was re-elected at the reorganization.[48] Dannelly tendered his resignation on January 22, 1865, citing chronic bronchitis and chronic diarrhea over the preceding eight months. His resignation was accepted on February 7, 1865. His name was spelled Dannerley in a sketch in *Recollections and Reminiscences*, and J.P. Thomas spelled it as Danelly.[49]

Company E, designated Company D before the reorganization, was composed mostly of men from Anderson District, along with a few from Abbeville District. Another source calls it Company I.[50] The only captain of the company, James Addison Cowan, was elected on December 28, 1861, and mustered in service on January 9, 1862. Re-elected at the reorganization, Cowan surrendered with the company at the war's end.[51]

Company F, the Kinard Phalanx, was designated Company G before the reorganization and was composed primarily of men from Newberry District and a few from Laurens District.[52] John P. Kinard, who was elected captain on December 24, 1861, transferred to the Quartermaster Department on January 15, 1862. His nephew, First Lieutenant John Martin Kinard, was promoted to captain the same day, a date also shown as both the eleventh and the seventeenth. He was re-elected at the reorganization.[53] Kinard was killed in action at Strasburg, Virginia, on October 13, 1864.[54] According to Dickert, a bullet actually pierced his heart.[55] Dickert viewed Kinard as "one of the finest line officers in the command—a good disciplinarian and tactician, and a noble-hearted, kind-hearted gentleman of the 'Old School.'"[56] Still another Kinard, First Lieutenant William M., was promoted to captain effective October 13, 1864.

Company G, the Spring Hill Volunteers, was designated Company A before the reorganization.[57] One source calls it Company B.[58] It was composed of men from Sumter District. Stephen M. Boykin, who was elected captain on December 24, 1861, was promoted to major on April 1, 1862. His replacement, First Lieutenant Robert LaRoche Heriot, was promoted to captain sometime in April and was re-elected at the reorganization.[59] Heriot tendered his resignation on December 15, 1862, citing poor health arising from "ascites and its accompaniment."[60] His resignation was accepted on

January 8, 1863. The *CSR* spells his name Herriott, but his signature on official documents is Heriot.[61] First Lieutenant Alexander Moseley was promoted to captain on January 8, 1863.[62] The last records for Moseley in the *CSR* were a thirty-day furlough for diarrhea on August 4 and a pay voucher on December 7, both in 1864.

Company H, designated either C or H before the reorganization, was composed of men from Lexington District, though some probably came from Orangeburg District as well. It was organized at Platt Springs in Lexington District on December 26, 1861.[63] Company H was the left center company in the 20th Regiment. Edward Kinsler, who was commissioned captain on January 10, 1862, lost the election for major of the regiment that spring. He refused to stand for re-election to captain and was dropped from the rolls in May.[64] Kinsler served as captain of Company A, 2nd Regiment, South Carolina State Troops, in late 1863 and early 1864.[65] Samuel "Sam" M. Roof was unanimously elected captain on May 3, 1862.[66] One source calls him Ruff. Roof, wounded in the right arm and side, was also captured at Cedar Creek on October 19, 1864.[67] Having sustained a comminuted fracture of the lower third of the right humerus, his arm had to be amputated above the elbow in a field hospital. Roof was taken to the United States Army Field Hospital in Winchester, Virginia, the next day, transferred to another hospital on November 19 and moved to the United States Army General Hospital at West's Buildings in Baltimore on November 30. Presumably recovered, Roof was sent to Fort McHenry, Maryland, on December 9 and to Fort Delaware later that month. He was released from Fort Delaware on June 14, 1865.[68] The *Memory Roll* states that Roof was promoted to major the day he was wounded. No other evidence supports this statement.

Company I, the Edisto Guards, was designated Company B before the reorganization. It was composed of men from Lexington and Orangeburg Districts.[69] A few men came from Edgefield District. Originally intended for the 22nd Regiment, the company was exchanged with the one that became Company E of the 22nd Regiment.[70] A company called the Edisto Guards, commanded by R. Allen Willis, was organized on July 20, 1861, at Maple Cane.[71] It is unclear whether this was the same as Company I of the 20th Regiment. J. Mat Jones, who was elected captain on December 28, 1861, did not stand for re-election at the reorganization and was dropped from the rolls. First Lieutenant Elbert Gunter was elected captain instead.[72] Two undated cards in the *CSR*, most likely in error, indicate that Gunter was captain of Company K. A sketch in *Recollections and Reminiscences*, however, notes that Gunter and Captain Harman of Company K "changed places" after the reorganization.[73] This reference probably means simply that the companies changed their letter designations after the reorganization, thereby changing their positions in the regimental line of battle. It would have been extremely unusual for any duly elected captain of one company to "change places" and assume command of another. Gunter was paroled at Augusta, Georgia, on May 18, 1865.

Company K, the Lexington Volunteer Rifle Company, was also called the Lexington Riflemen.[74] Made up of men from Lexington District, it was designated Company I before the reorganization.[75] William D.M. Harman, was commissioned captain on January 10, 1862, and was re-elected at the reorganization.[76] His name also appears as Harmon in the record.[77] Harman was absent from the company for almost five months in 1864, suffering from syphilis and nephritis. He was discharged on April 10, 1865, an indication that he was not given command of one of the companies in the consolidated regiment. J.P. Thomas names Soloman A. Haltawanger as captain of this company, but Haltawanger's highest rank after the reorganization was second lieutenant.[78] Possibly he was named captain of one the consolidated companies in April 1865, but the *CSR* does not address this issue.

Company L, the Ripley Rangers, was composed of men from Lexington, Marion and Marlboro Districts.[79] There were also a few from Sumter, Chesterfield, Darlington Anderson and Union Districts. This company, organized as an infantry company on April 3, 1862, was converted to a cavalry troop sometime between that date and April 1863. It was attached to the 20th Regiment soon after it was organized but was detached on April 30, 1863. According to the *Memory Roll*, the company was discharged at Mount Pleasant in 1863, and its men were dispersed to other commands. The *CSR* notes that the men detached from the regiment became known officially as Captain A.D. Sparks's Company, South Carolina Cavalry, and became Company E, 19th Battalion, South Carolina Cavalry, on December 20, 1864. Alexander D. Sparks, commissioned captain on April 3, 1862, was re-elected at the reorganization.[80] It was he who commanded the company after it was detached from the 20th Regiment; Sparks resigned on January 7, 1865.

Company M, designated Captain Keitt's Company Mounted Riflemen and, simply, the Mounted Riflemen, was composed mostly of men from Newberry, Richland, Anderson and Marlboro Districts. Some came from Orangeburg, Charleston, Fairfield, Edgefield, Abbeville, Lexington and Spartanburg Districts. Organized on June 10, 1863, it was made up of men who had transferred from other companies of the 20th Regiment. The company was received into service on July 17 and was attached to the 20th Regiment as Company M about that time. Before the organization of the 20th Regiment, the Emmett Guards, a company in the Volunteer Battalion from Columbia, organized in November 1860, was commanded by Ellison Summerfield Keitt.[81] Men of the Emmett Guards were all Irishmen.[82] Still captain of the Emmett Guards in early 1861, Keitt contracted typhoid fever; it was complicated by neuralgic rheumatism that spring, and Keitt resigned in late April.[83] The Emmett Guards was still in existence in late July 1861, but it disbanded shortly afterward, and its men joined various other commands.[84] Keitt apparently regained his health, mustered in service as a private in Company B of the 20th Regiment, raised what would become Company M and was commissioned its captain on June 10, 1863.[85] The new *Official Records Index* states that Company M was the Emmett Guards. The *Southern Historical Society Papers Index* says the company name was the Emmett Guards-Keitt's Mounted Riflemen. These two publications probably confused Keitt's two companies, though quite possibly some men from the original Emmett Guards enlisted in the 20th Regiment and later in Keitt's Company when it was organized in 1863. It is also possible that Keitt resurrected the name Emmett Guards in 1863. In any event, Company M was detached from the 20th Regiment and designated Keitt's Company Mounted Riflemen, SCV, on April 30, 1864. On December 20, 1864, it became Company B, 19th Battalion, South Carolina Cavalry.

Company N was probably called the Peterkin Rangers. Some of its men were from Marlboro District. A cavalry company organized on August 1, 1863, it joined the 20th Regiment about that time.[86] James A. Peterkin, previously a lieutenant in Company L, was appointed captain on August 1.[87] The company performed picket duty at Mount Pleasant, Sullivan's Island and Christ Church Parish for its entire existence.[88] The adjutant and inspector general's office determined that the company had been organized without proper authority and disbanded it on April 1, 1864, ordering the men to report to the commandant at the camp of instruction in Columbia. Some of the men later served in various companies, including C and H of the Hampton Legion.

Company O, Venning's Company, a cavalry troop organized on September 25, 1863, joined the 20th Regiment about that time.[89] Elias Venning was commissioned captain at the organization. This company performed picket duty near Mount Pleasant, and possibly at Sullivan's Island and Christ Church Parish, for its entire existence.[90] The adjutant and inspector general's office, determining that the company had been organized without proper authority, disbanded it on April 1, 1864, and ordered the men to report to the commandant at the camp of instruction in Columbia. Some men later served in the Hampton Legion and other cavalry companies.

Buist's Company Light Artillery was attached to the 20th Regiment for about eight months in 1863 and 1864. The secretary of war authorized the raising of an artillery company to be incorporated into the 20th Regiment about August 26, 1863. Henry Buist, captain of Company G of the 27th Regiment, was appointed captain of the new company at a request from Colonel L.M. Keitt made on October 2. Buist's Light Artillery was to have been composed of men transferring from other companies of the 20th Regiment, as well as officers and some men from Company G of the 27th Regiment. The rolls of Company G, in fact, show a large number of men joining Buist's Company under Special Order No. 323 on September 9, 1863. The company served at Mount Pleasant for its seven-month existence. The creation of the company was later determined to be illegal, and Buist's Artillery Company was never officially organized. Its men, including those from the 27th Regiment, returned to their former commands on April 11, 1864. Those from Company G of the 27th Regiment left Charleston on May 29 to rejoin the 27th in Virginia.[91] The men were mostly from Charleston, Spartanburg, Orangeburg, Laurens and Union Districts, with a few from Newberry, Marion, Barnwell and Lexington Districts.

Brigade Affiliations

The 20th Regiment was attached to the Department of South Carolina, Georgia and Florida from January 1862 to May 1864.[92] It was assigned to Kershaw's Brigade in Virginia on May 28, 1864. At that time the brigade consisted of the 2nd, 3rd, 7th, 8th and 15th Regiments and the 3rd Battalion, South Carolina Infantry. James Conner was in command of the brigade from August to October 1864, followed by John D. Kennedy who led the brigade to the end of the war. About April 9, 1865, when its regiments were consolidated, the brigade consisted of the (New) 2nd, 3rd and 7th Regiments, SCV. The 20th Regiment was consolidated with the 2nd and parts of the 1st, 2nd, 6th and 7th Battalions of Blanchard's South Carolina Reserves to form the (New) 2nd Regiment, SCV. The 3rd Battalion and the 8th, 15th and 20th Regiments ceased to exist at that time.

Major Movements and Engagements

Captain Kinsler's Company H was ordered to Camp Hampton near the present-day State Fair Grounds in Columbia on January 1, 1862, where it mustered in service on the eleventh. Company K, and probably other companies of the 20th Regiment, also gathered there in early January.[93] The 20th Regiment was scheduled to leave for the South Carolina coast on

January 14 but did not depart until March 4.[94] Company H, and probably the rest of the regiment as well, was based at the Charleston Race Course in March.

The 20th Regiment served near Charleston and along the South Carolina coast in the Department of South Carolina, Georgia and Florida from March 1862 to May 1864. It was transferred to Sullivan's Island on April 20, 1862.[95] Shortly after the battle of Secessionville on June 16, the 20th was ordered to James Island for a few months but had returned to Moultrieville on Sullivan's Island by September or October.[96] Company A was stationed at the Breech Inlet in September and October 1862, and at Battery Marshall from January to April 1863. Company K was detached to garrison the Palmetto Battery at Dewee's Inlet on Long Island for several months, including June 1862.[97] On January 4, 1863, three companies, which had been on detached service in Charleston, returned to the regiment at Sullivan's Island.[98] Companies H and I participated as sharpshooters in the capture of the USS *Isaac P. Smith* on the Stono River on January 30, 1863.[99] Stationed on James Island in February 1863, the regiment was transferred back to Sullivan's Island and Christ Church Parish on March 13.[100] Company G was based at the Palmetto Battery in Christ Church Parish from January to April 1863. Colonel Keitt was present at Battery Bee during the engagement on April 7; some companies of the 20th Regiment provided infantry support to the Upper Batteries, but were not engaged.[101] The 20th, ordered to Rantowles on May 9, conducted an armed reconnaissance with some of the regiments of N.G. Evans's Brigade to John's Island from May 9 to May 11.[102]

The three new cavalry companies, M, N and O, as well as Buist's Artillery, served as detached forces. Company L was based at Christ Church Parish in June and July 1863 and may also have been detached from the regiment.[103] Company M was stationed at McClellanville from June 10, 1863, to November 1863, when it was detached from the regiment and sent to Battery White near Georgetown.[104] Company N was based at Mount Pleasant in late 1863 and early 1864, and Company O was based at Camp Anderson in September and October 1863 and at Camp Allston in Christ Church Parish after November. Seven companies of the regiment were at Secessionville, three were at Sullivan's Island and a detachment of Company G was at the Palmetto Battery in Christ Church Parish in late June.[105] Buist's Artillery was stationed in Charleston in November and at Mount Pleasant in December 1863.

The 20th Regiment was sent to Morris Island in early July 1863 and suffered battle casualties there on the fourteenth.[106] Also, during the early morning hours of July 15, some men from the 20th participated in a night sortie from Battery Wagner, along with some men from the 7th South Carolina Battalion, the 51st North Carolina Regiment and the 12th and 18th Georgia Battalions.[107] Three companies were relieved on July 15, and Company E was relieved on the seventeenth.[108] The rest of the 20th Regiment probably rotated to Sullivan's Island but returned to Morris Island on July 19.[109] The 20th suffered more casualties on Morris Island between July 20 and July 24 and was probably sent back to Sullivan's Island on the twenty-fourth.[110] It returned to Morris Island on the night of July 30 and took more casualties between July 31 and August 7.[111] The regiment was engaged on the picket line on August 1.[112]

Six companies left Morris Island on August 3, leaving four behind.[113] These four were relieved on the fifth.[114] The 20th Regiment rotated back to Morris Island on August 15 and was engaged at Battery Wagner that day.[115] It was relieved on August 21 but returned on the twenty-fifth.[116] The regiment was relieved again only to return at daylight on August 27.[117] The 20th Regiment, the 23rd Georgia Regiment and the 61st North Carolina Regiment were being evacuated from Morris Island by the steamer *Sumter* when it was sunk by friendly fire from Fort Sumter and Fort Moultrie on the night of August 30, 1863.[118] After spending the thirty-first at Fort Sumter, the men were transported to Sullivan's Island the next day. Lieutenant Colonel Dantzler was in command of transportation during the evacuation of Morris Island on September 6, but the regiment was already at Sullivan's Island by that time. It was stationed at Mount Pleasant from September 1863 to February 1864.[119]

The regiment left Mount Pleasant on February 10, 1864, and arrived the same day at Battery Marshall on Sullivan's Island, where it remained until May 19, 1864; during that time, detachments were periodically sent to Fort Sumter. On April 16, four companies were at Battery Marshall, two were at the Palmetto Battery, two were serving in the 4th Military District and the rest were at Branchville.[120] Companies H and I were based at Kinloch's Landing in Christ Church Parish from September 1863 to May 1864. Detachments were sent to Fort Sumter on April 22, April 23 and May 15.[121] The four companies on Sullivan's Island were ordered on May 20 to join the rest of the regiment at Mount Pleasant in preparation for the move to Virginia.[122] The regiment was transferred to Richmond on May 24, 1864.[123] It joined Kershaw's Brigade on the South Anna River on the twenty-eighth. The *Mercury* reported that the regiment reached Lee's army on May 31.[124] From this time to the end of the war, the 20th Regiment was in Kershaw/Conner/Kennedy's Brigade. The major movements and engagements of the regiment are discussed in this volume under the 2nd Regiment. On April 9, 1865, the 20th Regiment was consolidated with the 2nd and parts of the

1st, 2nd, 6th and 7th Battalions of Blanchard's South Carolina Reserves to create the (New) 2nd Regiment, SCV. The 20th ceased to exist as a separate unit then. The (New) 2nd Regiment surrendered with the Army of Tennessee near Greensboro on April 26; the men were paroled on May 2.

16.

Independent Infantry Organizations

The South Carolina College Cadets

The company known as the South Carolina College Cadets, also called the College Cadets, underwent a series of transformations in 1861. Three attempts to go to war as a body failed that year, largely because the college's faculty and trustees wanted to keep it functioning in spite of the war. Ironically, by the spring of 1862, the college had closed, and most of its students were scattered among various regiments. The company was organized by South Carolina College students on January 16, 1861.[1] Sixty-three had signed on by January 19, and one hundred were on the roll by the twenty-first.[2] The students elected John Hilary Gary of Abbeville as captain and E. Dawkins Rogers of Union as first lieutenant the same day.[3] Gary, later captain of Company A, 15th Battalion, South Carolina Artillery, was mortally wounded at Battery Wagner on August 12, 1863.

Governor Pickens gave the Cadets permission to go to Charleston on April 11, 1861, and seventy of its members left Columbia by train the next day.[4] They observed the bombardment of Fort Sumter from the city but did not participate.[5] Assigned to duty at the Moultrie house on Sullivan's Island later that month, the students were relieved on April 30.[6] They returned to Charleston the next day. Though the governor and General Beauregard praised their service, both also urged the cadets to go back to school but to maintain their company structure.[7] The Cadets left for Columbia later that day and were careful to retain their integrity as a company.[8] In May or June, the Cadets offered their services to President Davis, who accepted the company for a three-month term of service to coincide with the school's summer vacation which began on July 1.[9] The president's position was contingent upon the governor's approval;

accordingly, two lieutenants visited Governor Pickens on June 21 seeking his approval.[10] Though reluctant to do so, Pickens accepted the cadets into state service because he believed his refusal would result in a mass exodus from the college. He did, however, insist on several conditions: all cadets had to agree to return to school on October 1, each had to obtain permission from his parent or guardian and a majority of the faculty had to endorse the plan.[11] The faculty, however, declined to go along, and the other conditions might also have been unmet. Many of the students enlisted in other military units immediately after final examinations in June.[12] Those remaining reorganized the College Cadets on June 24, electing their mathematics professor, Charles S. Venable, as the new captain. His careful planning in disarray, Governor Pickens refused to accept the company for service.[13] The College Cadets disbanded on June 25, 1861.[14]

When the college reopened in October, many returning students reorganized the College Cadets and elected their former first lieutenant, E. Dawkins Rogers, as the new captain.[15] William T. Gary was elected first lieutenant, and the company itself was called the 3rd Cadet Company.[16] By November, the sixty-man company was drilling and otherwise preparing itself for field service.[17] Port Royal fell to a Federal fleet on November 7; the next day, the College Cadets voted unanimously to offer their services to Governor Pickens. The faculty, vehemently against the cadets' proposal, tried unsuccessfully to dissuade the governor from accepting the company; the students left Columbia bound for Port Royal via Charleston on November 8. Governor Pickens detained the cadets in Charleston, ostensibly as his bodyguard, and placed them in camp at the Washington Race Course. At the time, the company was attached to the 17th Regiment, South Carolina Militia. Even as the cadets practiced their drills in Charleston, their professors back in Columbia worked to ensure the reopening of the college in January 1862.[18] The company was mustered out of service on December 10, and the students were ordered to return to college on January 1, 1862. Most joined other commands; few returned to school. Many cadets probably joined a new company raised by Rogers and Gary in late 1861 or early 1862. Named the Stevens Light Infantry, it was ordered to report to Adams Run to muster into the Holcombe Legion on January 4, 1862. The company was not accepted into the legion and was probably disbanded then.[19]

Though the college was open in January and February, results were unsatisfactory. On March 8, 1862, the Executive Council decreed that all white males eighteen or older would be subject to the draft. This order was communicated to the students at breakfast, and before dinner most had enlisted. Not until then was the college "virtually broken up."[20] Seventy students were enrolled and attending classes on April 30, but only nine by May 3.[21] The trustees, scheduled to meet on the seventh, were expected to suspend college activities.[22]

Captain Hamilton's Company-Provost Guard

Captain Hamilton's Company-Provost Guard, SCV, Columbia, South Carolina, was also called the State Provost Guard Company and the Provost Guard of Columbia. Captain D.H. Hamilton Jr. commanded the company. It was organized on December 18, 1863, at Columbia and was intended for local defense only under the authority of the War Department. Lieutenant Colonel Robert Stark Means, previously lieutenant colonel of the 17th Regiment, SCV, commanded both this company and the Post Guard under Captain R.D. Senn. The company was stationed at the capital from December 1863 to February 1865.[23] The Provost Guard was paroled at Chester on May 5, 1865.

Conscripts in the Camp of Instruction at Columbia, South Carolina

Major Thomas W. Radcliffe Jr. commanded the conscripts in the camp of instruction at Columbia, South Carolina.[24] The only muster roll for this unit is dated November 16, 1862. In the summer of 1861, Radcliffe had commanded another company called the Chicora Greys or Chicora Rifles. The Greys was made up of fourteen- to eighteen-year-old boys from the City of Columbia.[25] Armed with rifles supplied by the city, they camped at Barhamville.[26] Radcliffe enlisted as captain of Company A, 15th Regiment, SCV, in August 1861 and resigned that December. He then served as drillmaster in Columbia and was promoted to major in August 1863. Radcliffe also served as lieutenant colonel of the First Regiment of Detailed Men in the spring of 1864.

The Post Guard, South Carolina

The Post Guard, South Carolina, was also called the Post Guard of Columbia, South Carolina, and Captain Senn's Company. Commanded by Rufus D. Senn, the company was organized at Columbia from conscripts about February 9, 1863.[27] Senn's Company was stationed at Columbia under Lieutenant Colonel Robert Stark Means, who also commanded Captain Hamilton's Company-Provost Guard, SCV. Means was previously lieutenant colonel of the 17th Regiment, SCV. The Post Guard lasted for two years, from February 1863 to February 1865.[28] It probably remained in Columbia until the city was evacuated in February. Records indicate that the Provost Guard was paroled at Chester on May 5, 1865, but the ultimate fate of Senn's Company, the Post Guard, is not recorded.

Shiver's Company-Local Defense Troops, South Carolina

Shiver's Company-Local Defense Troops, South Carolina, also called the Rebel Guards, was commanded by Captain William Shiver. It was organized under an act of the Confederate Congress dated August 21, 1861, and was called into service on November 6. The men, who enlisted to guard prisoners and to defend Columbia, mustered in Confederate service on November 6, 1861, and mustered out on March 6, 1862.

The (Columbia) Volunteer Battalion

The Volunteer Battalion existed in Columbia in late 1860; the *Mercury* reported its organization in November.[29] Artemas Darby Goodwyn of Gadsden in Richland District was named colonel in command of the battalion. He was elected major of the 2nd Regiment, SCV, on May 21, 1861, replacing Dixon Barnes in that post.[30] Since no listing of this organization appears in the *CSR* (an indication that the battalion was never in Confederate service) and because most of its companies were included in other organizations by early 1861, the Volunteer Battalion appears to have been a short-lived unit. It consisted of five companies, all from Columbia.

Companies

The Richland Volunteer Rifle Company was commanded by Captain Daniel B. Miller. It became Company A of Maxcy Gregg's six-month Regiment on January 3, 1861.

The Cedar Creek Riflemen was commanded by a Captain Bookter, probably Edwin Faust Bookter, later captain of the Richland Guards, one of six original companies of the 2nd Regiment, SCV, that refused to go to Virginia in April 1861. The Guards later became Company D of the

12th Regiment, SCV. Another company called the Cedar Creek Rifles, commanded by Captain J.R. Harrison, was part of the 6th Regiment, but it dropped out when that regiment entered Confederate service in June 1861. These were probably two different companies; the confusion over the similarity of their names might have arisen from the fact that one Cedar Creek runs through southern Richland District and another through southern Fairfield and northern Richland Districts.

The Governor's Guards was commanded by Captain William H. Casson. This company, which became Company A of the 2nd Regiment, SCV, was received into state service on March 6, 1861.

The Emmett Guards was commanded by Captain Ellison Summerfield Keitt.[31] Composed of Irishmen, it was still in existence in July 1861 when another company of Irishmen from Charleston was expecting the Emmett Guards to join.[32] When Keitt was about to take his men to Virginia, he contracted typhoid fever complicated by neuralgic rheumatism and was compelled to resign.[33] Shortly after July 1861, the company was disbanded, and its men scattered to other commands. On February 5, 1863, Keitt mustered in as a private in Company B, 20th Regiment, SCV. Later that year, on June 10, he raised a cavalry company called the Emmett Guards-Keitt's Mounted Riflemen, which became Company M of the 20th Regiment. On April 30, 1864, the Emmett Guards was detached from the 20th Regiment as an independent cavalry company. It became Company B of the 19th Battalion, South Carolina Cavalry, on December 20, 1864.

The Columbia Artillery was commanded by Captain Allen Jones Green Jr. of Gadsden in Richland District. This battery, organized about the time the Mexican War ended, left Columbia on January 2, 1861, arriving in Charleston later the same day.[34] The battery crossed the harbor to Morris Island on January 2, returned to Charleston on the third and went to Sullivan's Island on January 4, the men taking quarters on board the steamer *Excelsior*. After three days, the battery moved to Fort Moultrie. There the men helped the Washington Artillery and a detachment of the Marion Artillery unspike and remount the guns that Major Anderson's men had left behind when they evacuated the fort on December 26, 1860. The Columbia Artillery remained at Fort Moultrie until at least mid-February.[35] Next, the battery manned a five-gun installation on Sullivan's Island. Because of his long service record, Green, given his choice of location, chose a site he felt most likely to see action. His command soon moved to its new location on Morris Island at the Star of the West Battery, which overlooked the channel entrance to Charleston Harbor.[36] Actually, Green's choice resulted in his battery not being actively engaged during the bombardment of Fort Sumter on April 12 and April 13, in spite of his request to General James Simons to be allowed to open fire.[37] The Columbia Artillery was relieved from duty on April 25, and it returned to Columbia, where it was disbanded.[38]

The battery was reorganized on May 25, 1861, to serve in Virginia; the men unanimously re-elected Green captain.[39] The Columbia Artillery had reorganized earlier in May, hoping to join the Hampton Legion, but the Washington Artillery of Charleston was chosen instead. A sketch in *Recollections and Reminiscences* states, incorrectly, that the men elected John Waties captain in April 1861, but according to the *CSR*, Waties was elected on September 20.[40] Serving as a volunteer in the summer of 1861, Captain Green saw action at the battle of First Manassas.[41]

The Columbia Artillery mustered in service for the duration of the war on September 20, 1861, and became Company B of the 3rd Battalion, South Carolina Light Artillery, at the same time. Green, no longer associated with the Columbia Artillery, became the first lieutenant colonel of the 23rd Regiment, SCV, on November 11, 1861, but he was not re-elected at the reorganization and was dropped from the rolls the following May. In January 1864, he raised six volunteer companies of mounted men for South Carolina service, arresting deserters and repelling raiders.[42] On April 14, 1864, he held the rank of major in the conscript service in South Carolina.[43]

First Regiment of Detailed Men

The 1st Regiment of Detailed Men, also called the City Regiment of Reserves, was raised for the defense and protection of Columbia in May 1864.[44] Its colonel, John Baylis Earle Sloan, was elected on or about May 30, 1864.[45] Sloan, who had been colonel of the 4th Regiment, SCV, in 1861 and early 1862, had also served as colonel of the 4th Regiment Reserves. Thomas W. Radcliffe won the election for lieutenant colonel, and T.B. Sharp was elected major. New elections for field officers were held on August 15.[46] The men chose John Peyre Thomas, superintendent of The Arsenal Academy in Columbia, as colonel of the Regiment of Detailed Men.[47] They also elected Benjamin F. Evans, a Charleston printer associated with Evans and Cogswell, lieutenant colonel, and they elected John Alexander major.[48] The regiment comprised ten companies totaling about a thousand men.[49] On February 15, 1865, the Board of Visitors of the South Carolina Military Academy determined that Thomas's position as colonel was incompatible with his duties at The Arsenal Academy.[50] Bowing to the decision, Thomas turned command over to Evans and resumed leadership of the Battalion of Arsenal Cadets. Thus, Thomas commanded three different organizations during the war: the Battalion of Arsenal Cadets throughout the war, Thomas's Battalion in 1863, and the Regiment of Detailed Men in 1864 and 1865. When Sherman reached Columbia in February 1865, the regiment was disbanded so the men could perform their various duties in saving or destroying government stores in the area.[51]

Companies

Company #1, made up of Arsenal employees, was commanded by Captain C.C. McPhail.

Company #2, commanded by Captain B.F. Evans, consisted of employees of Evans and Cogswell and Stebbins, Bayne, and Company.

Company #3, employees of John Judge and Company and Kraft, Goldsmith, and Kraft, was commanded by Captain John Judge.

Company #4, commanded by Captain J.J. Chisolm, was made up of employees of the Quartermaster Department, the Commissary, the Medical Department, the Central Bureau and C.F. Jackson's Company.

Company #5 was commanded by Captain S.G. Jamison. It consisted of personnel connected with S.G. Jamison, William Giese and Gray and Valory.

Company #6, commanded by Captain L.F. Robertson, was made up of workers in several areas, among them banks, the Depository, the post office, the Naval Powder Mills and the deputy marshal's office, as well as businesses run by W.Y. Leitch and Henry Hunt.

Company #7 was manned by employees of the South Carolina Railroad Company and its workshops. It was commanded by Captain W.B. Smith.

Company #8, another railroad company, was commanded by Captain Thomas R. Sharp. Its men worked for the Charlotte and South Carolina Railroad Company.

Company #9, the Ball Guard, was commanded by Captain Edward A. Keatinge.[52] Employees at Keatinge and Ball and John Alexander made up the company.

Company #10 was commanded by Captain J.B. LaSalle. Employees of the South Carolina Railroad Company probably made up the company.

Thomas's Battalion

Thomas's Battalion was organized in 1863 in response to a call from General P.G.T. Beauregard for volunteers to help defend Charleston. On February 17, Beauregard published an order saying movements of the

Federal fleet indicated an imminent attack by land and sea.[53] He requested that all able-bodied men from Georgia and South Carolina rush to arms to "share with us our dangers, our brilliant victory, or our glorious death."[54] John Peyre Thomas, superintendent of The Arsenal Academy in Columbia, immediately began to raise a company there for the defense of Charleston in case of attack; by February 27, he was raising a battalion.[55] The men enlisted specifically "for and during the attack on Charleston."[56] One Columbia company was composed of "boys, lexagenerians, and valetudinarians."[57] Major Thomas soon became commander of the battalion, which consisted of about a hundred men in mid-March 1863. By the seventeenth, Beauregard had accepted the unit into service; he ordered Thomas to have his men ready to move to the coast "as soon as the enemy's movements indicate an immediate attack upon the city."[58] On April 7, Companies A and B were ordered to rendezvous at The Citadel in Charleston as soon as they could get there.[59] Stationed at the Wappoo Cut near Charleston, the men were organized into several companies and thoroughly drilled. The battalion suffered no casualties during its brief deployment in the field.[60] Thomas's Battalion was disbanded on April 15 "when the emergency passed—with the praise of Beauregard," and the men returned to Columbia two days later.[61] During the war, J.P. Thomas commanded three different organizations—the Battalion of Arsenal Cadets throughout, Thomas's Battalion in 1863 and the Regiment of Detailed Men in 1864 and 1865.

17.

THE 1ST BATTALION/1ST REGIMENT, SOUTH CAROLINA CAVALRY

The 1st Battalion, South Carolina Cavalry, the precursor of the 1st Regiment, South Carolina Cavalry, was organized on October 31, 1861, with five companies designated A through E, all of which had enlisted for the duration of the war between August 23 and October 26.[1] Its commander, Lieutenant Colonel John L. Black, accepted the challenge of turning the battalion into a regiment, which became known as Black's Regiment.[2] The *Confederate Veteran*, probably referring to the regiment, records, incorrectly, that the battalion was authorized on December 31.[3] Initially, Governor Pickens called up Companies A, B, C and D, which had been raised in the summer of 1861, to serve for the duration of the war.[4] Of particular note is the fact that, during the ten-month interval between secession and the creation of the 1st Battalion, the only cavalry units of battalion or regimental strength raised in the state were militia units and the sole squadron of regular cavalry. Both the *Mercury* and the *Edgefield Advertiser* announced in January 1862 that the battalion had been authorized to grow to regimental strength.[5] By late 1861, and certainly no later than late January 1862, Company F was part of the battalion. In addition, Companies G and H had been raised, had been mustered in service and had joined the battalion by late January.[6] Company I was added about April 16.[7] The tenth, Company K, was formed by transfers from Companies C, D and F, along with unattached recruits about June 25, 1862. All ten companies had enlisted for the duration of the war. The ten companies were redesignated the 1st Regiment, South Carolina Cavalry, on June 25. At the same time, Lieutenant Colonel J.L. Black was promoted to colonel, and Major J.D. Twiggs was promoted to lieutenant colonel. Captain M.T. Owen declined promotion to major, and Captain W.A. Walker accepted it nearly a year later.

FIELD OFFICERS

John Logan Black, born in York District and living in Fairfield District before the war, was commissioned lieutenant colonel of the 1st Battalion at its organization on October 31, 1861. He commanded the battalion throughout its eight-month existence.[8] He had attended West Point but resigned before graduation.[9] Black had served as captain of Company E, 1st Regiment, South Carolina Infantry Regulars. He resigned that post between August 31 and October 23, 1861. He was promoted to colonel of the 1st Cavalry Regiment on July 28, 1862, with rank from June 25, and commanded the regiment until the war ended. Black suffered a head wound from a shell fragment on June 21, 1863, at Upperville, and for that reason was separated from the regiment until early July. On reaching Gettysburg, he accepted Lee's assignment to a special command comprising Hart's Battery and some unattached cavalrymen—a small force charged on July 2 and July 3 with guarding the extreme right of the line. Black reported to Longstreet's corps headquarters on July 2 and to Hood's Division headquarters the next day. Ordered to the left of the line on July 4, he was finally able to take command of his own regiment as the retreat began. At the Second Battle of Brandy Station on August 1, 1863, he received a painful wound when a Minié ball struck his right hand.[10] He was furloughed for sixty days and unable to use his hand for six months. Black commanded the east lines on James Island while on detached service from May to December 1864, but he commanded the regiment for the rest of the war. Black was wounded nine times during the war.[11]

John David Twiggs, MD, of Hamburg in Edgefield District was promoted from captain of Company C to major of the 1st Battalion on May 26, 1862. Promotion to lieutenant colonel of the 1st Regiment came on July 28, effective from its organization on June 25, 1862. Twiggs was temporarily disabled when his horse was struck and fell during the skirmish at Stevensburg on November 8, 1863. Black described Twiggs as a "home man and always sick at heart to get home."[12] Twiggs was granted a seventeen-day leave of absence on September 2, 1864, specifically to handle some trouble between his family and a neighbor. On the evening of the fifteenth, Twiggs encountered the troublesome neighbor, Robert J. Butler Sr., at the intersection of Martintown and Five Notch Roads about a mile from Hamburg.[13] Though Twiggs missed when he fired at Butler, the bullet struck Butler's seventeen-year-old son, a namesake, who was waiting for his father in a nearby buggy, whereupon Butler shot and killed Twiggs. Mortally wounded, the son died within a few hours. The *Edgefield Advertiser* reported that Twiggs died while defending his home from violence and his wife, little children, aged father-in-law and mother-in-law from insult.[14] In a tribute of respect, the men of the 1st Regiment wrote that Twiggs "always manifested the deepest interest in the cause of our country."[15] His obituary stated that Twiggs was "a man of deeds, not words. Not an advocate of secession, he rushed to arms when the vandal foe dared to invade his beloved South."[16] Twiggs was also called "a gentleman and a soldier of the highest and most irreproachable character."[17]

Moses Taggart Owen of Abbeville, captain of Company A of the 1st Battalion, South Carolina Cavalry, was elected major at the organization of the regiment on June 25, 1862. He declined the promotion but retained command of Company A, leaving the regiment without a major from June 1862 to April 1863.[18]

William Alexander "Alex" Walker of Chester, captain of Company D in the 1st Battalion, was promoted to major on April 2, 1863. He was wounded in the left calf at Gettysburg on July 3 by the same projectile that killed his horse. Walker was promoted to lieutenant colonel on November 22, 1864, with rank from September 15 when Twiggs was killed. Walker may have commanded the 18th Battalion, South Carolina Artillery, in the withdrawal into North Carolina from February to April 1865.

Niles Nesbitt of Spartanburg District was promoted to major from captain of Company B with rank from September 15, 1864, replacing Walker. Black found him "a man of no stamina," writing that he (Black) would have forgiven a trooper who deserted to the enemy if only he had taken Nesbitt with him.[19]

COMPANIES

The companies' letter designations were identical in both the 1st Battalion and its successor, the 1st Regiment.

Company A, the Abbeville Troop, was composed of men from that district.[20] The *CSR* erroneously lists it as Company B and calls it the Ferguson Rangers. It was one of the original five companies in the battalion.[21] W. James Lomax raised the company in the summer of 1861. When it was organized on July 20, Moses Taggart Owen was elected captain, and Lomax was elected first lieutenant.[22] The company was based at Lightwood Knot Springs, north of Columbia, when it mustered in Confederate service on August 23, 1861. Owen was senior captain in the 1st Battalion and was elected major when the 1st Regiment was created in June 1862, but he declined the promotion and retained command of Company A throughout the war. Owen was struck in the left foot by a pistol ball as he led the regiment near Boonsboro on July 9, 1863.[23] He was hospitalized in Richmond until the twenty-second. Though he managed to get home, Owen died from tetanus on August 4.[24] Black called him "a gallant man."[25] A Columbia newspaper described him as a "brave and efficient officer."[26] Kirkland believed Owen suffered his death wound at Williamsport.[27] S. Henry Jones succeeded him as captain.

Company B, the Ferguson Rangers, was composed of men from two districts.[28] The fact that it was also called the Spartanburg and Laurens Rangers indicates that its men were from those areas, though the *Edgefield Advertiser* reported that the company may have been from Laurens and Newberry Districts instead.[29] It may also have been called the Enoree Rangers. The *CSR* erroneously identified it as Company A, the Albemarle South Carolina Cavalry. Company B, one of the battalion's original five companies, mustered in Confederate service while based at Lightwood Knot Springs north of Columbia on August 25, 1861.[30] Niles Nesbitt was elected captain on August 22, 1861, and retained command in the 1st Regiment. He was promoted to major on December 5, 1864, retroactive to September 15. First Lieutenant W.J. Leak succeeded Nesbitt as captain, effective September 15, 1864.[31]

Company C, the Edgefield and Barnwell Rangers, was also called the Edgefield Rangers.[32] Another of the original five, its men came from those districts.[33] The company mustered in Confederate service on September 18 while based at Camp Johnson near Lightwood Knot Springs. Elected captain on August 27, 1861, John David Twiggs had commanded the company in the 1st Battalion. He was promoted to major of the battalion on May 26, 1862, and later to lieutenant colonel of the regiment. Thomas W. Whatley replaced Twiggs as captain on May 26 while the company was still in the 1st Battalion, and he commanded it until the war ended. He was paroled at Augusta, Georgia, on May 20, 1865.

Company D, the Chester Troop, was one of the original five companies in the 1st Battalion and was composed of men from that district.[34] Its men arrived at Camp Johnson near Lightwood Knot Springs on September 10, 1861. The men mustered in Confederate service on October 2. William Alexander Walker was elected captain the same day and commanded the company in the 1st Battalion. He was promoted to major on April 2, 1863, but the effective date was probably much earlier. His successor, First Lieutenant John S. Wilson, commanded the company from April 1863 until the end of the war. He was wounded at Brandy Station on June 9, 1863.

Company E, the Fort Motte Rangers, was composed of men from Orangeburg District and was the last of the 1st Battalion's original five companies.[35] Its men mustered in Confederate service on October 26,

1861, at Fort Motte. James Davis Trezevant, who enlisted the same day, was probably elected captain at about that time. Trezevant commanded the company in both the 1st Battalion and 1st Regiment.[36]

Company F, the Allen Hussars, was composed of men from Pickens District. It was named in honor of the Honorable J.D. Allen.[37] A newcomer to the battalion, Company F mustered in Confederate service for the duration on December 4, 1861, at Pickens Court House.[38] Forty-year-old Elam Sharpe, who enlisted the same day, was probably elected captain about the same time. The company moved through Charleston on December 26 en route to join the battalion at Adams Run.[39] Sharpe commanded the company in both the battalion and regiment. He was frequently absent because of illness, and his poor health forced his resignation on November 2, 1863.[40] His replacement, First Lieutenant Alfred "Alf" T. Clayton, was promoted on November 1.[41] Colonel Black regarded Sharpe as one of his "very best officers."[42]

Company G, L.J. Johnson's Cavalry, was composed of men from Abbeville District. Johnson, known as "Old Hickory," was elected captain on January 8, 1862, probably the date of the company's organization.[43] Johnson commanded the company in both the battalion and regiment. He was wounded at Williamsport on September 18, 1862, and again when he was struck in the shin by a spent ball at Second Brandy Station on August 1, 1863.[44] Black wrote that Johnson was "ever to be relied on."[45]

Company H, Robin Jones's Cavalry, was composed of men from Rock Hill in York District.[46] It was probably organized shortly before leaving Rock Hill on February 12, 1862.[47] Robin ap Cadwallader "Bob" Jones raised the company and commanded it in both battalion and regiment.[48] One source gives a middle name of Catesby. Jones was killed in a charge at Brandy Station on June 9, 1863. Several versions of his death were recorded: one from the *Yorkville Enquirer* states that Jones, who had captured several Federal troopers in a charge, was collecting their weapons when one of them shot him.[49] Another version, this one from his obituary, has him disabling and capturing a trooper who then shot him in the chest, killing him instantly.[50] Still another, which appeared later, records that Jones, who rode ahead of his men during the charge, attacked a dismounted trooper and cut off his thumb, but the wounded man managed to get off the fatal shot from his revolver as Jones rode past.[51] Black called Jones "one of my most gallant officers" and among the "very best captains."[52] M.C. Butler, colonel of the 2nd Regiment, described him as "the very highest type of gentleman and soldier."[53] Both Jones's father and older brother were officers in the 12th Regiment, SCV, Infantry.[54] James H. "Jim" Barry, who succeeded Jones as captain in September or October 1863, was wounded in the right foot about August 7, 1863; part of the foot next to the great toe was amputated.[55] He remained in command of Company H until his resignation on January 27, 1865. Barry resigned for several reasons: age (he was forty-seven), his three-year enlistment had expired on January 9 and he had enrolled in the reserves.

Company I, the Round O Troop, was composed of men from Colleton District. The company had probably served in the 11th Regiment as the Round O Guards under Captain Hugo Sheridan but had refused to enter Confederate service in late 1861 and was disbanded. It is unclear when the men reorganized, and it is also unclear if Sheridan commanded the company between late 1861 and April 1862. The company was added to the 1st Battalion about April 16, 1862.[56] John R.P. Fox, who was elected captain on April 3, 1862, commanded the company in both battalion and regiment. Wounded in the arm, Fox was captured at Brandy Station on June 9, 1863.[57] He was in a federal hospital at Alexandria, Virginia, until about July 11, when he was sent to the Old Capitol Prison in Washington. Ordered to Fort McHenry on September 24, he arrived on the twenty-ninth only to be transferred shortly afterwards to Johnson's Island, near Sandusky, Ohio.[58] On April 22, 1864, Fox was moved to the Hammond General Hospital at Point Lookout, Maryland, and was paroled on May 3. He was exchanged at Aiken's Landing, Virginia, on May 8, along with 401 other Confederate prisoners, including 50 officers. He arrived at Richmond the next day.[59] Fox retired to the Invalid Corps on January 16, 1865, and on the twentieth, he was assigned to the South Carolina Reserve Forces. He may have commanded Company I of the 1st Regiment, Junior Reserves, in 1865. He had been wounded on James Island earlier, probably before the regiment went to Virginia in the fall of 1862, but the date is unclear. Black called Fox one of his "very best captains."[60] Fred Horsey commanded the company after Fox's capture, but his highest rank was first lieutenant. Even so, Black credited Horsey with the rank of captain and called him a very reliable officer.[61]

Company K was composed of men from York, Chester, Barnwell, Edgefield and Pickens Districts.[62] Authorized by special permission from the War Department, it was created with transfers from companies C, D and F and unattached recruits on June 2, 1862, a date also shown as the twenty-fifth; the men enlisted for the duration of the war. Angus P. Brown was its only captain—his commission was dated June 26, 1862. Brown was wounded in the head and leg while holding a crucial bridge at the battle of Upperville on June 21, 1863. He appeared initially to be mortally wounded and unable to be moved. Two Federal troopers tried to trample Brown as they crossed the bridge, but their horses balked.[63] Taken prisoner and held at Old Capitol

Prison in Washington, Brown was moved on August 8 to Johnson's Island, Ohio.[64] He was sent to Baltimore on February 9, 1864, and was exchanged at Point Lookout, Maryland, on March 10, returning to duty afterward.[65] Brown survived the war. Black called him a man of "stubborn coolness."[66]

BRIGADE AFFILIATIONS

The 1st Battalion was attached to the Department of South Carolina, later the Department of South Carolina, Georgia and Florida, for its eight-month existence, and the 1st Regiment was assigned to the same Department from June until September 1862. It served next in Wade Hampton's Brigade of the Army of Northern Virginia, along with the 2nd Regiment, South Carolina Cavalry; the 1st Regiment, North Carolina Cavalry; the Jefferson Davis Legion (Georgia); the Cobb Legion (Georgia); the Phillips Legion (Georgia); and Hart's South Carolina Battery from October 1862 until March 1864. The 10th Virginia Cavalry Regiment was attached to the brigade briefly in 1862 until the 1st Regiment was added. Successive brigade commanders were Wade Hampton, M.C. Butler, W.H.F. Lee and P.M.B. Young. In the spring of 1864, the 1st and 2nd Regiments, South Carolina Cavalry, were sent back to the Department of South Carolina, Georgia and Florida. By November 20, nine companies of the 1st Regiment were in Taliaferro's Brigade, Company K was in Roswell Ripley's Brigade, and Company D was under the command of Colonel George P. Harrison Jr. at the Post of Florence, South Carolina.[67] By January 31, 1865, Company K was in Mercer's Brigade, Company E was not brigaded and the remainder of the 1st Regiment was in Stephen Elliott's Brigade, along with three companies of the 1st Regiment, South Carolina Artillery, two companies of the 2nd Regiment, South Carolina Artillery, the Battalion of State Cadets, Company D of the South Carolina Siege Train and some Georgia units.[68] By February 10, the regiment was attached to Harrison's Brigade with the 5th, 32nd and 47th Georgia Regiments.[69] The 1st, 2nd and 3rd Regiments, South Carolina Cavalry, were placed in a new brigade under Brigadier General M.L. Bonham on March 29.[70] During March and April, the 1st Regiment was part of Logan's Brigade, Butler's Division, Hampton's Cavalry.[71]

MAJOR MOVEMENTS AND ENGAGEMENTS

The 1st Battalion operated in the Charleston area and along the South Carolina coast during late 1861 and the first six months of 1862. Company

A left Abbeville for Lightwood Knot Springs on August 20, 1861, and moved to Sullivan's Island on September 22.[72] The 1st Platoon of Company B left Lightwood Knot Springs for Edisto Island on October 17, while the Second Platoon departed for Edisto Island on November 1. Company E left Fort Motte and arrived in Charleston on October 30, and Company C left Lightwood Knot Springs for Charleston the next day. Company D arrived at Mars Bluff in Marion District on November 2. It moved to Florence on the fourth and to Camp Marion on November 7.

Company E left Charleston and arrived at Coosawhatchie on the sixth and moved to Bee's Creek on the nineteenth. Company C left Charleston for Adams Run on November 14, and Company A marched to Adams Run some time during this period. Company D arrived at Cat Island near Georgetown on November 19 and was ordered to nearby South Island on December 3.

Company B left Edisto Island for Adams Run on November 24. Leaving South Island on the twenty-sixth, Company D arrived at Adams Run three days later.[73] Companies A, D and F were based at Adams Run until January 2, when they moved to Camp Ripley. Company A moved to Church Flats on the tenth and to Wadmalaw Island on the thirteenth.

The battalion skirmished on John's Island on April 19, 1862.[74] Two companies were engaged at Pocotaligo on May 29, and two others were held in reserve that day.[75] The men of the 1st Battalion were on picket duty when they skirmished with Federal troops on John's Island on June 7.[76] On June 25, 1862, the ten companies were designated the 1st Regiment, South Carolina Cavalry.

Company A, and probably several other companies as well, was stationed at Adams Run in July and August; four were based at McPhersonville on September 25.[77] Companies B and E participated in an expedition to Edisto Island from August 29 to August 31. The regiment moved to Summerville in late August or early September and left for Staunton, Virginia, in late September and early October.[78] Company G left on September 23, the horses and handlers started on foot on the twenty-eighth and the rest departed by train on October 1.[79] Company G arrived in Virginia on October 7, and the others at various times between October 17 and October 24. The regiment joined Wade Hampton's Brigade about that time.

The 1st and 2nd South Carolina Cavalry Regiments saw action at Barber's Cross Roads on November 5 and also skirmished at Broad Run near Warrenton on the seventeenth. The 1st participated in the Hartwood Church Raid on November 27. Three raids took place around Fredericksburg in December. The 2nd Regiment was involved in the Dumfries Raid from December 10 to October 14, and the 1st was engaged at Ellis's Ferry. The

1st Regiment participated in the second raid, called the Occoquan Raid, from December 17 to December 20. The third, or Dumfries/Occoquan Raid, used ten men from each company of the 1st and 2nd Regiments. Leaving camp with the rest of the cavalry on December 25, they crossed the Rappahannock River the next day. The 1st and 2nd Regiments attacked Occoquan on the twenty-seventh and returned to their camp near Culpeper Court House four days later. Winter quarters were set up at Stevensburg.

Wade Hampton's Brigade, sent to southern Virginia in late February 1863, missed the battles at Kelly's Ford on March 17 and Chancellorsville in early May. The brigade returned to northern Virginia later in May; the 1st Regiment was engaged at Culpeper that month. The regiment also participated in General Lee's grand review held on June 8 on the plain between Culpeper and Brandy Station. The 1st Regiment saw action at the First Battle of Brandy Station on June 9 and helped the Cobb Legion prevent the capture of Hart's Battery.[80] Soon afterward, the cavalry marched in support of Lee's second invasion of the north.

The 1st and 2nd Regiments were engaged at Rectors Crossroads near Middleburg on June 19. Left behind to guard the wagon train on June 21, the 1st saw action later that day at Upperville.[81] It also skirmished at Warrenton on June 23 and crossed the Potomac River on the twenty-sixth. The 1st was engaged at Rockville, Maryland, on the twenty-seventh and at Hanover, Pennsylvania, on June 30. It and probably saw action at Hunterstown, Pennsylvania, on July 2 as well. The 1st, though not the 2nd, was engaged near Emmitsburg on July 3 and skirmished at Gettysburg the same day. A detached command comprising one company from the 1st Regiment, one from the 2nd, Hart's Battery and other displaced men protected the extreme right of the Confederate lines at Gettysburg on July 2 and July 3.[82] The entire brigade moved to the left of the army on the third.[83] The regiment withdrew from Gettysburg after dark on July 4 and arrived at Williamsport on the evening of July 6. Elements of the 1st Regiment were also engaged during the "wagoners' fight" at Williamsport on the sixth. The 1st Regiment skirmished near Antietam Mountain on July 7 and July 8 and at Benviola at the foot of South Mountain on the ninth. The regiment was engaged at Funkstown, Maryland, on July 10 and crossed the Potomac River into Virginia on the thirteenth or fourteenth. Frequent skirmishes occupied the men during the withdrawal into Virginia from July 17 to July 20. Late in July, the regiment marched to Culpeper Court House and camped near Stevensburg.

The 1st Regiment was engaged at the Second Battle of Brandy Station on August 1, 1863. It skirmished at Funkstown on August 4 and at Upperville on the eleventh.[84] The regiment saw action and sustained losses at Piney

Mountain on September 13 and near Raccoon Ford on the Rapidan River the next day.[85] The 1st Regiment skirmished near Madison's Mill on September 20, and both the 1st and 2nd were engaged at Jack's Shop on the twenty-second. The 1st Regiment saw action at Bristoe Station on October 9, and its men skirmished with Federal infantry from the Rapidan River to James City on the tenth; there was also skirmishing on October 12 near Culpeper Court House. After crossing the Rappahannock River on October 13, the men faced the enemy again on the seventeenth. The 1st Regiment was engaged at the Buckland Races on October 19, skirmished at Stevensburg on November 8 and participated in a series of small fights on the south side of the Rapidan River beginning on the sixteenth. The regiment was engaged in the Mine Run campaign from November 26 to December 2 before moving to its winter camp at Hamilton Crossroads and to picket duty along the Rappahannock River below Fredericksburg.

The 1st and 2nd Regiments were ordered back to South Carolina on February 15, 1864, to recruit and obtain fresh mounts. The order first appeared in the *Official Records* on March 17.[86] The two battle-weary regiments marched to Hanover Junction in early March. The 2nd left on March 20, and the 1st Regiment between the twenty-third and the twenty-sixth. The 4th, 5th and 6th South Carolina Cavalry Regiments replaced them in Virginia.

The men of the 1st traveled by rail, and their horses went overland. Part of the 1st Regiment arrived in Columbia during the last two days of March.[87] Black wrote that the regiment remained in the capital for about two weeks before moving in mid-April to James Island via Charleston.[88] According to the *Official Records*, however, part or all the regiment was ordered from Columbia to Charleston more than a month later, on May 17.[89]

Company A, and probably other companies as well, was sent to Green Pond from April 16 to April 26. On the twenty-eighth, Colonel Black, accompanied by an escort of one officer and four men, was sent on a personal reconnaissance of the mountain passes between Walhalla and Greenville, concentrating on the Jones Gap area of Greenville District.[90] By May 20, the entire regiment was stationed on the east lines of James Island, with Black in command.[91] The regiment camped in the rear center of the east lines and functioned as a mobile force of mounted rifles and pickets. On May 26, detachments of Companies I and F were engaged as sharpshooters at the battle of Chapman's Fort on the Ashepoo River when Earle's Battery sank the transport USS *Boston*.[92] The 1st Regiment was engaged with black troops on James Island during this time, and Company B skirmished along the western lines on James Island on July 1 and July 2.

Companies of the regiment were scattered along the coast of South Carolina throughout 1864. Company K was stationed at White Point in Charleston from March 1864 to February 1865 but spent some time at Sullivan's Island and Christ Church Parish in October 1864.[93] By July 31, 1864, one company was stationed north of Charleston, while the other nine were based on James Island.[94] On October 31, five companies were stationed at James Island, and a detachment was at Florence.[95] The dismounted men of the 1st Regiment were sent to Coosawhatchie in November or December. A detachment of the 1st Regiment, including Company E, was present on the Confederate left flank during the engagements at the Tullifinny River on December 7 and December 9. In late December, Company E remained near the Tullifinny River, while another detachment of the regiment was at Grahamville.[96] Company E was at Broxton's Bridge and Dubois Landing on the Salkehatchie River probably as early as January 17 and no later than January 28, 1865.[97] Company E was detached and served as dismounted troops in Colonel Harrison's Brigade in late January and February 1865.[98] About thirty men of the 1st Regiment were engaged in the infantry skirmish at Grimball's Causeway near the Stono River on February 10.[99] The regiment guarded the bridge over the Santee River at Holly Hill on the twelfth.[100]

During the Carolinas campaign, a few men from the regiment skirmished at Florence on March 5. The regiment withdrew from Florence and marched through Darlington, Society Hill, Chesterfield Court House, Wadesboro and Ashboro on the way to Raleigh. It also marched to Smithfield and saw action at Moccasin Hill (or Moccasin Creek) near Goldsboro on March 28.[101] The regiment was engaged at Averasboro and skirmished at Hillsboro, North Carolina. The 1st Regiment was included in the surrender at Greensboro on April 26, 1865, but it was probably not present. Colonel Black wrote in the *Memory Roll* that the 1st Regiment was fully armed and equipped when Johnson surrendered, and it marched out of camp and was disbanded by companies in York District.[102]

18.

The 2nd Regiment, South Carolina Cavalry

The 2nd Regiment, South Carolina Cavalry, also called Lipscomb's regiment, was formed by merging the Cavalry Battalion of the Hampton Legion, comprising four companies; Easley's Squadron—the 4th (or 3rd) Battalion, South Carolina Cavalry—also four companies; and two independent companies under A.H. Boykin and T.J. Lipscomb. It was created on August 22, 1862. Scarcely a week later, all except Troop A were with the regiment in Virginia. When Troop A reported to Colonel M.C. Butler on September 9 at Urbana, Maryland, the completed regiment was in the field facing the enemy.

Field Officers

Matthew Calbraith Butler of Edgefield, who had served as major-in-command of the Cavalry Battalion, Hampton Legion, since July 21, 1861, was elected colonel of the newly created 2nd Regiment on August 22, 1862. Nearly a year later, on June 9, 1863, at the battle of Brandy Station, Butler was struck by a cannon ball just above the right ankle.[1] Dr. Benjamin W. Taylor amputated the remainder of the stump on the field soon afterward. Butler was promoted to brigadier general on September 1, 1863, returned to duty in May 1864, and was elevated to major general on September 19. Wade Hampton found Butler "the coolest man in danger and the grandest man in a fight I ever saw."[2]

Frank Hampton of Richland District, brother of Wade Hampton, became the first lieutenant colonel of the regiment on October 7, with rank from August 22, 1862. He had served as captain of Company B of the 4th (3rd) Battalion, South Carolina Cavalry, which became Company C of the 2nd Regiment. Hampton was mortally wounded during the first battle of Brandy Station on June 9, 1863, and died a few hours later. Butler recorded that he suffered a pistol shot to the abdomen and died later that afternoon.[3] Henderson also recorded that Hampton died from a gunshot wound, and E.L. Wells added the detail that he was shot through the body while fighting hand-to-hand with the saber.[4] U.R. Brooks wrote that while Hampton was engaging one Federal cavalryman with his saber another shot him through the body, and he died about eight in the evening in a house near Stevensburg.[5] According to Wellman, Hampton suffered a terrible saber wound to the face but died the night of the battle from a gunshot wound to the abdomen.[6] The *CSR* records that he died on June 10, indicating the time of death as after midnight. Krick's account is that Hampton was wounded by a saber cut across the face and head near Stevensburg and died that night.[7] Colonel Butler described Hampton as "the very highest type of gentleman and soldier."[8]

Thomas Jefferson Lipscomb, who was raised in Edgefield District but was living in Newberry District in 1861, was a physician and captain of an independent company bearing his name before the regiment was created.[9] That company became Company G of the 2nd Regiment, and Lipscomb became the regiment's first major on October 7, 1862, retroactive to August 22. He was promoted to lieutenant colonel on July 23, 1863, with rank from June 10, replacing Frank Hampton. Lipscomb was wounded at the second battle of Brandy Station on August 1, 1863. He was promoted to colonel on October 24, effective from September 1, 1863, when Butler was made brigadier general. Wade Hampton, recommending Lipscomb for promotion to brigadier general, wrote: "His gallantry and dash has [*sic*] been conspicuous wherever he has been engaged and his judgment and his management of troops of a superiority [*sic*] character."[10] Lipscomb was captured on the Goldsboro Road near Goldsboro, North Carolina, on March 25, 1865.

Thomas Edward Screven of Beaufort District was promoted from captain of Company B to major, effective June 10, 1863, as Lipscomb's replacement. He was promoted again, this time to lieutenant colonel, on September 22, 1864, with rank from September 1, 1863, when Butler became brigadier general.

COMPANIES

Company A, the Boykin Rangers, was composed mostly of men from Kershaw District, along with a few from Richland, Darlington, Charleston, Barnwell, Chester, Lexington, Spartanburg and Laurens Districts. It may also have been called the Hampton Scouts.[11] Before joining the regiment in September 1862, the company was called Boykin's Independent Company, South Carolina Cavalry and also the Mounted Rangers or the Independent Mounted Rangers. Alexander Hamilton "Ham" Boykin, a member of the South Carolina Senate from Kershaw District, personally raised and equipped the company at a cost of more than $10,000.[12] The Boykin Rangers was sent to Virginia in April 1861 and was based at Camp Pickens near Richmond in the brigade commanded by General Milledge L. Bonham. It was accepted into Confederate service on June 26, 1861, for the duration of the war. Boykin's commission as captain dated from July 1, though he had commanded the company since its inception several months earlier. The company served in Bonham's Brigade in Virginia as scouts, couriers and pickets.[13] Along with two other cavalry companies, it was ordered on July 8 to march to Ashland, Virginia, about twenty miles north of Richmond, under the command of Lieutenant Colonel C.W. Field.[14] Moving farther north, the Boykin Rangers performed picket duty near Leesburg on the Potomac River. On the sixteenth, the company was sent to Manassas.

Under Bonham's command, the company was engaged while on picket duty on July 21 at the battle of First Manassas. It remained at Camp Gregg near Vienna in northern Virginia from August to October 1861, skirmishing on August 16 with Federal cavalry at Falls Church near the Potomac River.[15] It was also attached for a short time to Radford's Virginia Cavalry Regiment. On October 15, the troop moved to Flint Hill. Leaving Bull Run for Yorktown, it was in camp near Williamsburg by March 8, 1862.

Men of the Boykin Rangers re-enlisted on March 17 for the duration of the war, an unusual move since most troops who originally mustered in service for the duration in 1861 did not need to re-enlist during the reorganization of the Confederate army in the spring of 1862. Engaged at Williamsburg on May 5, the company, throughout the Peninsula campaign, was attached to the Jeff Davis Legion as Company G. A few of its men were with J.E.B. Stuart on his ride around McClellan from June 12 to June 15.[16]

The Boykin Rangers became Company A, 2nd Regiment, South Carolina Cavalry, in September 1862. Bonham recommended Boykin for promotion to lieutenant colonel when the regiment was organized. The post should have gone to Major Easley of the 3rd (4th) Battalion, but when he resigned it was given to Frank Hampton instead. Protracted dyspepsia and a nervous irritation forced Boykin to resign. His resignation was effective on October 1, 1862. He was known as a meritorious and efficient officer.[17] He was appointed judge advocate but declined the appointment.[18] Boykin may have served with another cavalry unit in 1865.[19] His replacement, First

Lieutenant John Chesnut, commanded the company until at least March 10, 1865.[20] He was considered "brave enough, [but] strongly inclined to dandyism and luxury."[21]

Company B, the Beaufort District Troop or Beaufort Dragoons, was a group of volunteers who had served in a prewar Home Guard company of the same name. Most of the men were from Grahamville in Beaufort District, though some represented Charleston and Colleton Districts as well, and seven Marion Men of Combahee joined the troop as it was organizing in June 1861.[22] The company rendezvoused at Gillisonville and left Green Pond on the nineteenth to muster in service at Charleston. Two days later, the Beaufort District Troop left Charleston to join the Hampton Legion Cavalry Battalion in Columbia, where it was designated Company C. Thomas Edward Screven was elected captain on June 22, 1861, and he retained command when the troop became Company B of the 2nd Regiment in late August 1862. Screven was promoted to major, effective June 10, 1863, and Lieutenant Abram Miles Ruth was moved up to captain on November 2 as his replacement.[23] Ruth had been wounded in the left shoulder at the second battle of Brandy Station on August 1. The wound was nearly fatal, and the shoulder joint had to be resected by surgeons at Hospital #10 in Richmond.[24] Ruth retired to the Invalid Corps on September 26, 1864, and was assigned to Andersonville Military Prison on October 14. He surrendered at Augusta, Georgia, on May 29, 1865.

Company C, the Congaree Rangers from Richland District, was previously Company B of the 3rd (4th) Battalion. Frank Hampton was captain when it was in the 3rd Battalion. He was promoted to lieutenant colonel of the 2nd Regiment when it was created in August 1862, and Ireland native John F. Meighan was commissioned captain of Company C as his replacement on the twentieth.[25] Despite his frequent hospitalizations for dyspepsia and rheumatism, Meighan was the company's only captain in the 2nd Regiment. T.G. Barker, adjutant general of Hampton's Division of Cavalry, wrote that Meighan served "four years of gallant, patriotic, and devoted as well as efficient service."[26] U.R. Brooks called him "the very soul of honor."[27]

Company D, the Wassamassaw Cavalry or Wassa Massaw Rangers, was composed mostly of men from Goose Creek in Charleston District, along with a few from Orangeburg and Colleton Districts. It had also been Company D in the 3rd (4th) Battalion, and Captain J.C. McKewn retained command when the company became part of the 2nd Regiment. In failing health since September 1862, McKewn resigned on May 22, 1863, probably for that reason. Andrew J. Hydrick replaced him as captain on the twenty-third.[28]

Company E, Dean's Company from Spartanburg, Greenville and Laurens Districts, had been Company C of the 3rd (4th) Battalion. Alvin H. Dean, its captain, retained command when the 2nd Regiment was formed. He resigned the commission, however, on February 23, 1863, on the grounds that his wife was in poor health, and he had two small children. Dean returned to the company in September or October 1864, and he served as brevet second lieutenant until the close of the war. First Lieutenant George Bobo Dean, who replaced his brother as captain on February 23, was wounded at the second battle of Brandy Station on August 1, 1863.

Company F was composed primarily of men from Pickens District, though some came from Greenville and Anderson and a few came from Lancaster and Spartanburg Districts.[29] It was previously Company A of the 3rd (4th) Battalion. John Westfield, who commanded the company in the battalion, was also its only captain in the 2nd Regiment.

Company G, the Bonham Light Dragoons, was also called Lipscomb's Troop.[30] From April 10 until August 22, 1862, it was known as Lipscomb's Independent Company, South Carolina Cavalry. Thomas Jefferson Lipscomb, MD, raised the company in December 1861 from Company B of the 3rd Regiment, South Carolina Infantry. He was Company B's second lieutenant and was promptly elected captain of the new company. While serving in Virginia, the company mustered in service on April 10, 1862, for the duration of the war and on June 20, it became a mounted company. Most of the men were from Newberry, Abbeville and Laurens Districts, but a few came from Richland, Charleston and Edgefield Districts. The *Edgefield Advertiser* claimed the company for Edgefield District.[31] Lipscomb remained its commander from April 10 until the regiment became a reality, and he became its major on August 22, 1862. Jesse Wistar Gary replaced him as captain of Company G the same day.[32]

Company H, the Congaree Troop, had been Company D in the Hampton Legion, Cavalry Battalion. It was known by several names: the *Mercury* reported on July 8, 1861, that the Congaree Mounted Riflemen, or Rifles, had changed its name to the Congaree Troop, the name most commonly used.[33] The *Memory Roll*, however, referred to the company as the Congaree Mounted Infantry, and the *Confederate Veteran* referred to it as the Richland Light Dragoons.[34] Though its men were from both Fairfield and Richland Districts, it was considered a Richland District company.[35] Thomas "Tom" Taylor, the first captain, was not re-elected at the reorganization. He served later as an aide to Wade Hampton.[36] James "Jim" P. Macfie was elected captain on April 28, 1862, and retained command when the company became part of the 2nd Regiment.[37]

Company I, the Edgefield Hussars, was previously Company A of the Hampton Legion, Cavalry Battalion. It was also called the Edgefield Dragoons.[38] Though most of the men were from Edgefield District, a number of them came from Abbeville District, and a few, who came from Richland, Fairfield and Orangeburg District, might have joined the company at the reorganization in April 1862.[39] Matthew Calbraith Butler became the first captain of the Edgefield Hussars on June 12, 1861, and was promoted to major in command of the Cavalry Battalion about July 21. Jeremiah J. Bunch, Butler's successor, resigned at the reorganization in April 1862, and Tillman H. Clark was elected captain with rank from April 28.[40] Clark, who retained command in the 2nd Regiment, was wounded near Stevensburg on September 13 or September 14, 1863.[41] The *Memory Roll* spells his name Clarke.

Company K, the Brooks Troop from Greenville District, was also called the Brooks Guards and the Brooks Dragoons.[42] It was previously Company B of the Hampton Legion, Cavalry Battalion. Its first captain, Furman professor John F. Lanneau, was not re-elected at the reorganization but served afterward as chief engineer with the rank of first lieutenant in General W.H.C. Whiting's Division.[43] Leonard Williams, who was elected captain from May 1, retained command of the company in the 2nd Regiment. He received a flesh wound in the lower neck and upper shoulder from a pistol shot in hand-to-hand fighting on August 1, 1863, at the second battle at Brandy Station but managed to wound his assailant with a saber during the fight.[44] Williams continued to serve as captain until the close of the war. The Brooks Troop re-enlisted as a body for the duration of the war when its initial term of enlistment expired, probably in the spring of 1862.

Brigade Affiliations

The 2nd Regiment, South Carolina Cavalry, was attached to Wade Hampton's Cavalry Brigade in the Army of Northern Virginia. Also in Hampton's Brigade were the 1st Regiment, South Carolina Cavalry, the 1st Regiment, North Carolina Cavalry, the Jeff Davis Legion (Georgia), the Cobb Legion (Georgia), the Phillips Legion (Georgia) and Hart's South Carolina Battery from August 1862 to March 1864. Successive commanders of the brigade were Wade Hampton, M.C. Butler, W.H.F. Lee and P.M.B. Young.

The 1st and 2nd South Carolina Regiments were sent back to the Department of South Carolina, Georgia and Florida in March 1864 and served afterward mainly in Robertson's Brigade. By January 1865, the 2nd was attached to the Department of North Carolina, and on March 29, the

1st, 2nd and 3rd Regiments, South Carolina Cavalry, were placed in a new brigade under Brigadier General M.L. Bonham.[45] The 2nd Regiment is not listed with other South Carolina Cavalry Regiments attached to Logan's Brigade, Butler's Division, Hampton's Cavalry Command of the Army of Tennessee in April 1865.[46]

MAJOR MOVEMENTS AND ENGAGEMENTS

The 2nd Regiment, South Carolina Cavalry, reached its final configuration on September 9, 1862, in the field near Urbana, Maryland. Companies of the 3rd (4th) Battalion were based in South Carolina until August, and those of the Cavalry Battalion of the Hampton Legion served on the Peninsula below Richmond, as had the two independent companies. The Cavalry Battalion of the Hampton Legion was based near White Oak Swamp below Richmond on August 19, but by the twenty-sixth, it was in camp on the North Anna River, thirty-five miles above the capital.

Company A joined the regiment in September 1862. The other nine companies, B through I and K, were together but not engaged at either Cedar Mountain or Second Manassas in August, though all participated in pursuing the Federal army after Second Manassas. Hampton's Brigade crossed the Potomac River on September 5 at White's Ford and skirmished at Poulsville, Maryland, and probably at Rockville also. The 2nd Regiment performed picket duty along the Potomac River and skirmished almost daily during September—at Urbana on the tenth, at Frederick and Burkittsville on the twelfth and near Middletown on the thirteenth. On September 14, the brigade was engaged at Cotoctin Ridge, and it was present, though primarily held in support on the flanks, during the battle of Sharpsburg on the seventeenth. The brigade skirmished daily from the fifth to the nineteenth, and the 2nd Regiment was engaged during the delaying action at Williamsport on September 19 and September 20. In addition, 175 of its men took part in the Chambersburg Raid from October 9 to October 12.[47] The men bivouacked on the night of the ninth at Hedgesville, Virginia, crossed the Potomac River at dawn on October 10 and captured Chambersburg, Pennsylvania, about eight that night. Returning, the column passed through Cashtown near Gettysburg on October 11, recrossed the Potomac at White's Ford on the twelfth and arrived safely at Leesburg, Virginia.

The 1st and 2nd Regiments were engaged at Barber's Cross Roads on November 5 and skirmished at Broad Run near Warrenton on the seventeenth. The 2nd also skirmished at Berryville, Flint Hill and Little

Washington at about the same time.[48] A detachment of the 2nd Regiment crossed the Rapidan River and skirmished during the Hartwood Church Raid on November 27 and November 28. In early December, the regiment, stationed first at Fredericksburg and afterward at Hamilton's Crossing, performed picket duty along the Rappahannock and Rapidan Rivers.[49] Three raids were launched around Fredericksburg in December 1862. First came the Dumfries Raid, from December 10 to December 13, when Hampton attacked a large sutler's train bound for Fredericksburg on the twelfth. The 2nd Regiment was part of that operation, and the 1st was engaged at Ellis's Ferry. Though the 2nd was not engaged at Fredericksburg on December 13, it did support Pelham's horse artillery during the battle. The 2nd was part of the second Dumfries Raid, also called the Occoquan Raid, on December 17; its men had returned to camp by the twentieth.[50] The third and last raid, the Dumfries/Occoquan, used ten men from each company of the 1st and 2nd Regiments. Leaving camp with the rest of the cavalry on Christmas Day, the raiders crossed the Rappahannock River on the twenty-sixth and attacked Occoquan on the twenty-seventh, returning to their camp near Culpeper Court House on the thirty-first.

The 2nd Regiment spent the winter near Fredericksburg. It was based at Kelly's Ford and Raccoon Ford in January 1863 and at Stevensburg in Culpeper County in February. The brigade was in Nelson County in March and was soon sent to southern Virginia, missing the battles at Kelly's Ford on March 17. The 2nd Regiment performed picket and outpost duty during the battle of Chancellorsville in early May.[51] It was also engaged at Culpeper that month and scouted in Prince William County in the vicinity of Brenstville, Greenwood Church and Occoquan Village. The 2nd Regiment was part of General Lee's grand review on the plain between Culpeper and Brandy Station on June 8. The regiment helped repel a Federal reconnaissance force at the first battle at Brandy Station the next day, actually engaging the enemy at Dagget's farm near Stevensburg during the battle.[52] On June 17, the regiment crossed the Rappahannock River in support of Lee's second invasion of the north, marched to Warrenton and saw action there. The 1st and 2nd Regiments were engaged at Rectors Crossroads near Middleburg on June 19 and at Upperville on the twenty-first.

The 2nd Regiment was engaged for fifty-two consecutive days during the Gettysburg campaign. It skirmished at Warrenton, Virginia, on the twenty-third and at Thoroughfare Gap four days later, and it crossed the Potomac River into Maryland on June 27 or June 28.[53] The 2nd saw action at Rockville on the twenty-seventh, and at Hanover, Pennsylvania, on the thirtieth. It was engaged on July 2 at Hunterstown, about five miles north of Gettysburg.[54] The 1st Regiment, though not the 2nd, saw action near Emmitsburg,

Pennsylvania, on July 3 and skirmished at Gettysburg the same day, while the 2nd arrived at Gettysburg, probably on the second, and fought there on July 3. A detached command comprising one company of the 1st Regiment, one from the 2nd, Hart's Battery and other displaced men protected the extreme right of the Confederate lines on July 2 and 3.[55] The entire brigade moved to the left of the army on the third.[56]

The 2nd Regiment arrived at Williamsport on the evening of July 6 and was engaged there during the "wagoners' fight" that night. The 1st and 2nd Regiments skirmished at Benviola near Boonsboro at the foot of South Mountain on July 9. The 2nd, involved in a number of skirmishes for several days, crossed the Potomac into Virginia on July 14. It was engaged again at the second battle of Brandy Station, or Beverly's Ford, on August 1, skirmished at Funkstown, Maryland, on the fourth and skirmished again at Upperville on August 11.[57] The 2nd suffered losses during action near Stevensburg on September 13 and September 14.[58] The 2nd Regiment fell back across the Rapidan River on the thirteenth.

The 1st and 2nd Regiments were engaged at Jack's Shop on September 22, while the 2nd Regiment saw action at Bristoe Station on October 9 and at the Buckland Races about six miles from Warrenton on the nineteenth. Occupied with picket duty at the fords on the Rappahannock River, the regiment was engaged on November 8 and again in the Mine Run campaign from November 26 to December 2. It made camp for the winter at Hamilton Crossroads near Fredericksburg and performed picket duty along the nearby Rappahannock before participating in an engagement at Todd's Tavern. The 2nd Regiment took part in the attack on General Kilpatrick during his Richmond raid on February 29, 1864.

An order dated February 15 remanded the 1st and 2nd Regiments to South Carolina to recruit and remount, though it first appeared in the *Official Records* on March 17.[59] So it was that the two battle-weary regiments marched to Hanover Junction in early March and were replaced in Virginia by the 4th, 5th and 6th Regiments, South Carolina Cavalry. The 2nd left its camp on March 20 bound for Columbia, the men by rail and the horses traveling overland. It arrived in Columbia about April 2 and was sent to James Island via Charleston in mid-April.[60] The *Official Records* notes that the regiment was ordered to Charleston on May 17.[61] The regiment remained on James Island only a day or two before it was ordered elsewhere.[62] Its companies were separated and sent to various locations along the coast. Company G went to Pawleys Island, where it endured shelling from Federal naval vessels for three hours on June 23. The company was ordered to Battery White near Georgetown in August, and it remained until October 1864. Elements of the 2nd Regiment were engaged on John's Island in June

1864, though most of its companies were stationed at Adams Run from May to October.[63] Company K was sent to Georgetown in May and was based at Camp Jefferson about nine miles below town. It left Georgetown for Mount Pleasant at some point between July 3 and July 13 and marched to Chisolmville near Green Pond on the eighteenth, arriving on or about July 20. Parts of the 2nd Regiment were stationed first at Pocotaligo, then at Green Pond and Chisholmville, where the men performed picket duty along the Combahee River during July while other elements returned to John's Island. A forty-man detachment from Companies A, B, F, I and possibly E, was engaged on July 7 as dismounted troops at Gervais Field near Waterloo Place on Johns Island.[64] Another part of the 2nd Regiment was engaged at Burden's Causeway on John's Island on July 9. On August 20, 1864, a detachment of Company I and an independent company known as the Stono Scouts participated in burning Legareville on John's Island.[65] Company G was still at Georgetown, and the rest of the regiment was at Adams Run on October 31.

On November 4, the 2nd Regiment was sent to Summerville en route to Wilmington, North Carolina. Arriving on the twenty-eighth, the men performed picket duty in the vicinity of Mansonboro Sound and Topsail Island. The regiment was engaged at Fort Fisher in late December and at Fort Anderson on February 2, 1865. The men skirmished for three days, from February 17 to February 19, in the vicinity of Fort Anderson below Wilmington, and withdrew to Town Creek on the nineteenth. Though the 2nd Regiment covered the Confederate right flank at the Upper Town Creek Bridge, it was otherwise not engaged on February 20.[66] Evacuating Wilmington with Hagood's Brigade on February 22, the 2nd moved to the North East River on February 23. At Goldsboro, North Carolina, on March 10, it was ordered to march to Raleigh that day.[67] March 11 brought another order to stop the march at Smithfield.[68] On the twelfth, the regiment was occupied with picket duty on the South River, also called the Black River, between Goldsboro and Fayetteville.[69] The men marched to Goldsboro on the seventeenth, and on April 1, 1865, the 2nd Regiment drew picket duty again, this time along the Cape Fear River twenty miles below Fayetteville.[70] Ordered to march to Charlotte and from there to Chester, South Carolina, the 2nd Regiment was furloughed at Chester Court House before the end of the month.[71]

19.

THE 10TH BATTALION, SOUTH CAROLINA CAVALRY

The 10th Battalion, South Carolina Cavalry, created for special service and local defense, was organized about January 19, 1862, at Camp Hampton near Columbia with four companies that were designated A through D. The initial enlistment period was twelve months.[1] The battalion mustered in service originally as the 2nd Battalion, also known as Adams's Battalion, South Carolina Cavalry.[2] Though popularly called the 2nd Battalion, it was officially designated the 3rd Battalion, South Carolina Cavalry, for its first nine months.[3] Reorganized with new elections on May 6, 1862, as required by the April 21 act of the Confederate Congress, its company designations were changed at the same time.[4] The official designation of the 3rd Battalion was changed to the 10th in September 1862. The 10th Battalion merged on December 16, 1862, with Major Emanuel's 12th Battalion and two independent companies commanded by Captains B.H. Rutledge and Thomas Pinckney to form the 4th Regiment, South Carolina Cavalry.

FIELD OFFICERS

James Pickett Adams of Kershaw and Richland Districts was the battalion's first major.[5] Colonel of the 5th Regiment, South Carolina Cavalry Militia, before the war, he was elected major of the newly created battalion on January 21, 1862, defeating A.G. Salley of Orangeburg.[6] William Stokes wrote that the men "do not think so well of Adams, as he cannot do everything they want done." As the time for new elections neared, Adams became more polite than usual and granted "almost every request," but the men "laughed at him about it."[7] Adams was not re-elected at the reorganization on May 6, 1862. Stokes wrote further that Adams's men were "down on him" to the point they "forced him out" at the election.[8]

William Stokes of Branchville in Orangeburg District and Colleton District, captain of the Evans Light Dragoons, was elected major at the reorganization on May 6, 1862.[9] He was promoted to lieutenant colonel of the 4th Regiment when it was created on December 16, 1862.

COMPANIES

Company A, the Palmetto Rangers, was known as both Captain Barber's Company and Company C before the reorganization and Company A afterward.[10] According to Stokes, it was the original Company A.[11] Two-thirds of its men were from Chester and the rest were from Fairfield District.[12] Osborne Barber, who enlisted on January 20, 1862, was the only captain in the 3rd/10th Battalion. He retained command when the company entered the 4th Regiment as Company B in December 1862.[13]

Company B, the Calhoun Troop, also called Captain Cary's Company, was designated Company B before the reorganization and Company B of the 3rd Battalion thereafter. Stokes cites this company as the original Company D.[14] Its men were from Pendleton in Anderson District and from sections of Pickens District now in Oconee and Pickens Counties, especially the Fort Hill area. John W.L. Cary enlisted as the first captain on January 19, 1862, but he may have been commissioned as early as December 20, 1861.[15] He was defeated at the reorganization by John Caldwell Calhoun, who received the unanimous vote of the men. Calhoun retained command when the company became Company C of the 4th Regiment in December 1862.[16]

Company C, the Evans Light Dragoons, or Captain Stokes's Company, enlisted originally with only fifty-five men.[17] Some had served in the Hammond Hussars of the 4th Regiment, South Carolina Cavalry Militia.[18] Stokes had served as captain of the Hussars from 1855. Designated Company D before the reorganization, the Evans Light Dragoons, according to Stokes, was the original Company B.[19] The Dragoons, originally an independent cavalry company in state service, had been ordered to Bluffton in November 1861, just after the battle of Port Royal. After about a month, the men went home to reorganize for Confederate service; early in 1862, the company traveled to Columbia to muster in the 3rd Battalion.[20] Most of the men re-enlisted for the duration of the war at the reorganization that spring when the company became Company C of the 3rd Battalion.[21] Its men were from Colleton and Orangeburg Districts.[22] William Stokes enlisted as captain on January 17, 1862, a date also shown as both the fourth and the sixth. Stokes was elected major of the 3rd Battalion at the reorganization on May 6, and

W.P. Appleby was elected captain of the Evans Light Dragoons. Appleby retained command when the Evans Light Dragoons became Company G of the 4th Regiment in December 1862.

Company D, the Catawba Rangers, was known as both Captain McIlwain's Company and Company A before the reorganization. It was known as Company D, 3rd Battalion afterward.[23] Stokes cites the Rangers as the original Company C.[24] Organized on November 21, 1861, it was first called both the Lancaster Troop and the Lancaster Cavalry.[25] The *Daily Southern Guardian* referred to it at the time as the Catawba Guards.[26] Its men were from Lancaster District.[27] The Catawba Rangers was slated for attachment to Colonel Martin's 1st Regiment, South Carolina Militia, which was stationed at Pocotaligo in late December 1861.[28] But the plan never materialized, and the company passed through Camden on January 9, 1862, on its way to Camp Hampton below Columbia, where the men soon mustered in service.[29] James D. McIlwain enlisted as captain on January 9, 1862, a date also shown as December 30, 1861.[30] At his request, McIlwain did not stand for re-election at the reorganization and was dropped from the rolls on May 6, 1862.[31] He also commanded a Lancaster District militia company called the Hew Hope Mounted Men at some point during the war.[32] Another McIlwain, this one W.J., was elected captain on May 6 but resigned on August 1 for health reasons—he suffered from a chronically enlarged prostate gland that rendered him incapable of discharging his duties.[33] John C. Foster was promoted to captain on December 28, 1862, and commanded the company until the surrender. The Catawba Rangers became Company H of the 4th Regiment in December 1862.

BRIGADE AFFILIATIONS

The 2nd/3rd/10th Battalion was assigned to the Department of South Carolina, Georgia and Florida for its eleven-month existence.

MAJOR MOVEMENTS AND ENGAGEMENTS

All four companies of the 2nd/3rd Battalion were at Camp Hampton, near Columbia, until January 23, 1862, when they moved to the Broad River near Grahamville in Beaufort District.[34] The Palmetto Rangers drew picket duty at nearby Honey Hill from early February to late April, and one ranger was killed while on picket duty at Fripp's plantation in St. Luke's Parish in Beaufort District on February 5. About March 12, Companies B and C left

Camp Gregg and marched seventeen miles to Camp McIlwain about seven miles from the Coosawhatchie River and three miles from the Broad River.[35] The two companies were assigned picket duty at Boyd's Landing and other sites along the Broad River until about May 1, when the battalion returned to Grahamville for nearly three months.[36] Though sent to Pocotaligo on May 29, the battalion arrived late and missed the battle earlier that day.[37] The battalion left Grahamville on July 25, and its companies were dispatched to other lowcountry sites: the Palmetto Rangers and the Evans Light Dragoons went to Camp Jackson near Bluffton on the May River, while the Calhoun Troop and Catawba Rangers were based at Camp Pritchard near Hardeeville and were joined there by the others for September and October.[38] Company C skirmished with a Federal gunboat on the May River on October 18.[39] The Palmetto Rangers, and possibly other companies, were also engaged at Old Pocotaligo near the Coosawhatchie Bridge on October 22. The 10th Battalion, South Carolina Cavalry, merged into the 4th Regiment, South Carolina Cavalry, on December 19, 1862.

20.

THE 14TH BATTALION, SOUTH CAROLINA CAVALRY

The 14th Battalion, South Carolina Cavalry, was also called the 1st Battalion, the 1st Squadron, the 2nd Battalion and Felder's Squadron.[1] It was organized in late December 1861 and early January 1862 with four companies, A through D. Though officially designated by the adjutant and inspector general as the 2nd Battalion, South Carolina Cavalry, it mustered in service in the field as the 1st Battalion (or 1st Squadron), South Carolina Cavalry. When the battalion was disbanded and reorganized in May 1862, the resulting battalion was officially designated the 14th. Eight months later, on January 18, 1863, the 14th Battalion was consolidated with the 17th Battalion and two independent cavalry companies to form the 5th Regiment, South Carolina Cavalry.

FIELD OFFICERS

Paul Stroman Felder, the first major in command of the 1st/2nd Battalion, was commissioned major on January 8, 1862.[2] He may have served also for a time as lieutenant colonel. Felder was not re-elected at the reorganization in May 1862.

Joseph Hargrove Morgan, MD, of Orangeburg District was elected major of the battalion on May 3, 1862.[3] Morgan had previously served as colonel of the 3rd Cavalry Regiment, South Carolina Militia, in 1860 and also as a private in S.D. Lee's Battery in 1861 and early 1862.[4] He suffered a severe wound to the right ankle at Pocotaligo on October 22, 1862.[5] Morgan became the first major of the 5th Regiment on January 18, 1863.[6]

COMPANIES

Company A, the Santee Guerillas or Santee Rangers, had been Company B in the 1st/2nd Battalion before the reorganization. Also called Captain William Nettles's Company, it mustered in service at Camp Hampton below Columbia on January 2, 1862. Though most of its men were from Sumter District, some came from Clarendon District and one was from Williamsburg District. William Nettles, who enlisted on January 2, 1862, was the first captain; his commission may have dated from as early as December 17, 1861.[7] Nettles was absent for a prolonged period in 1862, probably because of poor health, and he was dropped by order of the War Department on November 14. There is evidence that he served as commissary agent in Sumter District in 1863 and 1864. Richard M. Skinner, who succeeded Nettles as captain, had been wounded at both the first and second battles of Pocotaligo on May 29 and October 22, 1862. He retained command when the company became Company H of the 5th Regiment on January 18, 1863.

Company B was probably the St. Matthews Troop.[8] It existed as early as July 1860, and it was known as Captain J.C. Edwards's Company, SCV, probably before it joined the 1st/2nd Battalion in early 1862. The company, which mustered in service at Camp Hampton below Columbia on January 7, carried the designation of Company D until it became Company B of the 14th Battalion in May 1862.[9] The men were from St. Matthews Parish in Orangeburg District.[10] John Cubbage Edwards, who was commissioned captain on December 24, 1861, probably commanded the company even before then. The only captain in the 2nd/14th Battalion, he retained command when the company became Company A in the 5th Cavalry Regiment on January 18, 1863.

Company C, the Light Dragoons, had been designated Company C in the 1st/2nd Battalion before the reorganization.[11] It was also called Captain W.F. Caughman's Company, SCV. The company, made up of men from Lexington District, mustered in service at Camp Hampton on December 28, 1861. Thirty-seven-year-old Wesley F. Caughman enlisted as captain the same day, though his commission may have dated from the nineteenth.[12] Caughman was not re-elected at the reorganization having "declined to run for office, not being able to stand the service."[13] Another Caughman, Augustus Henry, was elected instead on May 13 and retained command when the company became Company F of the 5th Cavalry Regiment on January 21, 1863. One of the Caughmans, probably the latter, was wounded at Fayetteville, North Carolina.

Company D mustered in on January 6 or January 7, 1862, for twelve months of service in local defense. Called Captain James W. Reed's Company, it was Company A of the 1st/2nd Battalion between January and May 1862. Most of its men were from Orangeburg and Barnwell Districts, along with a few from Lexington and Edgefield Districts. James W. Reed was the first captain in the 1st/2nd Battalion, with a commission that may have dated from as early as December 28, 1861.[14] Reed was not re-elected at the reorganization, perhaps because he was recovering from an illness at home, or possibly because he had unknowingly lost the confidence of the officers and men. In any event, Peter Andrew Raysor was elected captain on May 13, 1862, and Reed soon requested a commission as captain of conscripts. Raysor tendered his resignation on August 9; it was accepted on the twenty-sixth. Brigadier General W.S. Walker provided an explanation of Raysor's resignation: "He has lost the confidence of the men and officers of his command." First Lieutenant Thomas W. Tyler commanded the company from August 26, 1862, until it became Company I in the 5th Regiment on January 18, 1863.

Brigade Affiliations

The 2nd/14th Battalion was in the Department of South Carolina, Georgia and Florida for its entire twelve-month existence.

Major Movements and Engagements

The four companies of the 2nd Battalion mustered in service at Camp Hampton in late December 1861 and early January 1862.[15] By late January, Companies B and C were performing picket duty at Page's Point, Cunningham's Bluff and Mackay's Point.[16] Company C, and probably the other three as well, were based at McPhersonville in Beaufort District by May. The 14th Battalion saw action at Old Pocotaligo on May 29, and a detachment was engaged at Pinckney Island on August 21.[17] The battalion retained its base at McPhersonville until at least October; all four companies fought at Old Pocotaligo and Coosawhatchie on October 22.[18] Company B was based at Tullifinny, and Companies C and D were based at Pocotaligo during November and December. The 14th Battalion merged into the 5th Regiment, South Carolina Cavalry on January 18, 1863.

21.

The 16th Battalion, South Carolina Cavalry

The 16th Battalion, South Carolina Cavalry, was also called the 16th Battalion, South Carolina Partisan Rangers and the 6th Battalion, South Carolina Cavalry. Hugh K. Aiken received permission in May 1862 to raise a unit called the Regiment of Partizan Rangers under an act passed on April 21, 1862.[1] He had received seven companies into his new organization by June 12.[2] The 16th Battalion was organized on July 21, 1862, at Camp Preston near Columbia. Six of the seven original companies, designated A through F, mustered in service from July 10 to July 23. A report in the *Mercury* noted that the "Partisan Rangers" mustered in the 6th Battalion, South Carolina Cavalry, on July 27, indicating that the Rangers had existed as a separate organization before the creation of the battalion.[3] Additional evidence supporting the existence of an organization before July 21 is the fact that the captains of Companies B, C, E and F enlisted in service in May or June. The seventh company, designated Company G, existed as early as June but was officially added to the battalion on August 6, 1862, and all seven volunteered for the duration of the war at their initial enlistment in July and August.[4] An eighth company joined Aiken's organization in late July, but whether or not it was the one eventually designated Company H in the 6th Regiment is unclear.[5] Possibly it was, since at the time Aiken was trying to add two more to complete a regiment of ten companies.[6] E.B. Turnipseed was authorized in late August to raise the tenth company, but his efforts probably failed.[7] So it was that in September and October 1862, Aiken and eight companies were camped in Columbia with expectations of two more companies soon joining them.[8]

Apparently Aiken ran into a good deal of bureaucratic red tape in establishing his regiment.[9] He may, in fact, have lost one of his eight companies, possibly Turnipseed's, since three were finally added to his seven-company battalion to make it a full regiment in November 1862. A letter from Major General John C. Pemberton to Adjutant and Inspector General Samuel

Cooper dated September 10 sheds light on the creation of Aiken's Partisan Battalion.[10] Cooper had issued an order to disband all those partisan corps in South Carolina and Georgia that had been organized without proper authority. Pemberton noted that the secretary of war had said partisan groups could not include men between the ages of eighteen and thirty-five. He also revealed that he had learned on September 6 that South Carolina authorities believed the age restrictions had been annulled, and some six hundred men from that age group had already joined these "comparatively useless organizations." Most of these men were the seven companies of Aiken's Partisan Rangers.[11] Pemberton emphasized his conviction that these groups had not been raised under the proper authority and should be disbanded, pending a ruling by the secretary of war.[12] He was probably technically correct and, in fact, was supported by Governor Bonham who wrote in February 1864 that Aiken's Battalion had been improperly organized since it consisted primarily of conscripts who legally should have been placed in existing regiments.[13] But the issue was never pursued in late 1862 and apparently the matter was dropped.

Not only was Aiken's Battalion allowed to remain in existence, but it was augmented to regimental size. About November 1, 1862, the addition of three companies increased the size of the battalion, and by January 19, 1863, the new ten-company regiment was designated the 6th Regiment, South Carolina Cavalry. Two other South Carolina organizations were raised as partisan rangers: Brooks's Company H, 7th Battalion (Infantry) and M.J. Kirk's Cavalry Company.[14]

Field Officer

Hugh Kerr Aiken of Charleston commanded the 16th Battalion with the rank of lieutenant colonel. He was commissioned on September 11, 1862, with rank from July 21. Aiken was attacked in Columbia on September 23, 1862, by a man wielding a policeman's club, but his injuries were not severe.[15] The only field officer of the 16th Battalion, Aiken was promoted to colonel of the 6th Regiment, South Carolina Cavalry, when it was created in November 1862. He was the brother of David Wyatt Aiken, colonel of the 7th Regiment, South Carolina Infantry.

Companies

Company A, the Carolina Guerrillas, was also called Captain M.A. Sullivan's Company. It was composed of men from Laurens, Greenville, Pickens,

Abbeville and Anderson Districts, along with a few from Spartanburg District. The company was in the process of organization in May 1862; its members mustered in service in Columbia on July 10 for the duration of the war.[16] Milton A. Sullivan, commissioned captain on July 10, commanded the company in the 16th Battalion and retained command when it became Company A in the 6th Regiment.

Company B, the Edgefield Rangers, was also called the Edgefield Partisan Rangers and Captain Lewis Jones's Company.[17] It was composed mostly of men from Edgefield District, though a few came from Richland, Abbeville, Lexington, Marlboro and Colleton Districts. Captain Lewis Jones, who enlisted on June 30, raised, equipped and mounted the company in June and July 1862. The men left Edgefield for Columbia on June 30.[18] The company mustered in service in Columbia on July 14, 1862, for the duration of the war.[19] Jones commanded the company in the 16th Battalion and retained command when it became Company B in the 6th Regiment.

Company C, also called Captain P.W. Goodwyn's Company, consisted mostly of men from Abbeville and Fairfield Districts, along with a few from Spartanburg, Anderson, Orangeburg and Laurens Districts. Its men mustered in service in Columbia on July 18, 1862, for the duration of the war. Peter W. Goodwyn, who enlisted on June 15, was commissioned captain on July 18. He commanded the company in the 16th Battalion and retained command when it became Company C in the 6th Regiment.

Company D was also called Captain W.M. Hale's Company. The record does not reveal where its men were from, only that they mustered in service in Columbia on July 19, 1862, for the duration of the war. William M. Hale retained command, briefly, after the company became Company D in the 6th Regiment.

Company E, the Laurens Partizans, was also called Captain J.P. Knight's Company.[20] It was composed of men from Laurens and Spartanburg Districts. Though scheduled to appear at Laurens Court House to prepare for muster on July 1, 1862, the men actually mustered in service for the duration of the war at Camp Preston in Columbia on July 21.[21] The *CSR* records that the company was stationed at Adams Run on June 1, 1862, an indication that it existed before its Confederate service muster date. James P. Knight, who had enlisted on May 1 and was commissioned captain on July 21, commanded the company in the 16th Battalion and retained command when it became Company E of the 6th Regiment.

Company F was called the Cadet Company, the Cadet Troop, the Cadet Rangers and Captain M.B. Humphrey's Company.[22] It was formed with thirty-six Citadel cadets who marched out en masse, formed a company and mustered in state service on June 9, 1862. The company's membership represented the entire state. Aiken's original request to enlist the Cadet Company in his battalion was refused by the Executive Council on the grounds that the students' suspension from The Citadel did not terminate their connection with the institution.[23] While stationed in Columbia on July 23, Captain Moses Benbow Humphrey and his men mustered in Confederate service for the duration of the war as Company F of the 16th Battalion. Though suspended by the superintendent and expelled by the Board of Visitors, the men of Company F were accepted as members in good standing by the Association of Graduates after the war.[24] Humphrey commanded the company in the 16th Battalion and retained command when it became Company F in the 6th Regiment.

Company G was called Captain John R. Miot's Company. Miot's Company probably existed as an independent company as early as June 12, 1862. The men were from Richland, Abbeville and Edgefield Districts. They mustered in service in Columbia on August 6, 1862, for the duration of the war. John R. Miot commanded the company in the 16th Battalion and retained command of the company when it became Company G in the 6th Regiment.

Brigade Affiliations

The 16th Battalion spent its entire three-month existence along the South Carolina coast in the Department of South Carolina, Georgia and Florida.

Major Movements and Engagements

The seven original companies of the 16th Battalion mustered in service at Camp Preston in July and early August 1862. The camp was located near the Saluda Factory on the Lexington side of the Congaree River near Columbia.[25] The battalion, eight companies strong, was ordered to Charleston on September 10.[26] By the twenty-fifth, it was at Green Pond, and within the next month it had moved to Adams Run.[27] Company B performed picket duty at Bennett's Point on Bear Island on the Ashepoo River.[28] The *Mercury* reported that the Partisan Rangers, probably a reference to the 16th Battalion, saw action at Pocotaligo on October 22.[29] The battalion was stationed at Adams Run when it merged into the 6th Cavalry Regiment on or about November 1, 1862.

22.

Independent Cavalry Organizations

Captain E.M. Boykin's Squadron

Captain E.M. Boykin's Squadron was also called Boykin's Squadron, Mounted Rifles. It was created about November 5, 1862, when Boykin's original company was expanded to create a new two-company squadron. Boykin's Company became Company A, and W.N.G. Rodgers's new company was designated Company B. Both enlisted as state troops. Some time between October 1863 and January 1864, Governor Bonham allowed Boykin's Squadron to leave state service and muster in Confederate service.[1] Though the squadron transferred about January 28, 1864, the men actually mustered in service on March 11, 1864. Meantime, on February 3, Company A, the Wateree Mounted Rifles, was assigned to the 7th Cavalry Regiment as Company K; with that, the squadron was effectively disbanded. Rodgers's Company served independently in South Carolina until it was attached to the 19th Battalion, South Carolina Cavalry, in December 1864.

Field Officer

Edward Mortimer Boykin, MD, commanded the squadron at the rank of captain.

Companies

Company A, known as Boykin's Company Mounted Rifles, was also called the Wateree Mounted Rifles and Boykin's Rangers.[2] Though this one was raised by E.M. Boykin in the summer of 1862, another company called the Boykin Rangers existed as early as September 1861.[3] H.H. Boykin was its commander in November 1861, but the connection between the two companies, if any, is unclear.[4] The *Camden Confederate* reported on July 4, 1862, that the governor and Executive Council had passed a resolution calling for a "Battalion of Mounted Men, volunteers for the 1st Corps of Reserves."[5] At that time, E.M. Boykin was a first lieutenant in the Kirkwood Rangers of the Holcombe Legion. He placed an ad in the same paper in which he described himself as "relieved from duty" and asked for middle-aged men currently exempt from service to serve in "defending our state and homes."[6] On August 8, Boykin was still raising the company.[7] The *Mercury* reported that month that the company was adding ten to fifteen men in its attempt to raise a "battalion of mounted riflemen" to serve in the defense of the coast north of Georgetown.[8] The company was finally organized and Boykin was elected its captain on August 27, 1862.[9] Boykin's commission as captain of the Mounted Squadron of Rifles, made up of men from Camden in Kershaw District, was dated September 5. Company A was assigned to the 7th Cavalry Regiment as Company K on February 3, 1864, even though the regiment was not officially created until March 18.

Company B was organized on November 5, 1862, as an independent company in state service known as Captain W.N.G. Rodgers's Company, Cavalry (State Troops) South Carolina. Made up of men from Georgetown and Williamsburg Districts, it became Company B of Boykin's Squadron soon after it was organized. It mustered in Confederate service on March 11, 1864. Two nearly simultaneous events complicated matters at this point: first, Company B men received permission to reorganize and elect a new captain who turned out to be J.J. Steele, and, second, Company A joined the 7th Cavalry Regiment, effectively disbanding Boykin's Squadron and leaving Company B independent. Known as Captain J.J. Steele's Company, South Carolina Cavalry, it became Company D of the 19th Battalion, South Carolina Cavalry, on December 20, 1864. Rodgers commanded a company, probably one of home guards, in April 1865 during Potter's Raid along the Black River.[10]

Major Movements and Engagements

Boykin's Company went into camp at the Race Course near Camden on October 22, 1862.[11] It left for the coast about the middle of November, and by the twenty-eighth, it was stationed in Horry District.[12] Thereafter, Boykin's Company—Boykin's Squadron after November 5—operated along the coast around Murrell's Inlet. Nearly a year later, in late August 1863, Governor Bonham ordered Company A to the mountainous regions of Spartanburg, Greenville and Pickens Districts to clear out a large number of deserters and draft dodgers hiding there.[13] The company arrived in Camden on its way to the mountains on September 4.[14] Its mission was changed by late October, and it was ordered to remain in the upcountry and western North Carolina to repel an expected Federal raid near Asheville.[15] The governor also probably ordered Company B to join Company A in late October 1863.[16]

Company A and a unit of North Carolina Mounted Infantry saw action at Parrottsville in east Tennessee in early December 1863.[17] By early 1864, the squadron had returned to Greenville, where it continued to arrest deserters and conscripts from early February until sometime in March.[18] Company A was ordered to Virginia on March 17 and left the squadron to join the 7th Cavalry Regiment.[19] Company B, which remained in South Carolina, was stationed at Clam Bank from March 11 to April 30, 1864. Its base was at Murrell's Inlet near the line separating Horry and Georgetown Districts from late April to October.[20] Company B was placed in Trapier's Brigade in late November 1864.[21] Based at Battery White near Georgetown in November and December, Company B became Company D of the 19th Battalion, South Carolina Cavalry, in December 1864.

KEITT'S MOUNTED RIFLEMEN

Keitt's Mounted Riflemen was commanded by Ellison Summerfield Keitt.[22] He also commanded a company called the Emmett Guards, organized in Columbia in November 1860 and attached to the city's Volunteer Battalion.[23] Ordered by S.R. Gist to prepare the Emmett Guards for service in Virginia in the spring of 1861, Keitt contracted typhoid fever complicated by neuralgic rheumatism and resigned as captain of the guards in April. When the company disbanded that summer, its men joined other commands. Keitt was ill for almost two years.[24] On February 5, 1863, he enlisted as a private in Company B of the 20th Regiment, South Carolina Infantry. Keitt recruited men from the 20th Regiment to form a new cavalry company, which was organized on June 10, 1863. Keitt and the men mustered in service on July 17 as the Mounted Riflemen Company; their official designation was Company M, 20th Regiment, SCV. Most of Keitt's men were from Richland, Newberry, Anderson and Marlboro Districts, though a few came from Orangeburg, Charleston, Fairfield, Edgefield, Abbeville, Lexington and Spartanburg Districts. Detached from the 20th Regiment on April 30, 1864, the company assumed independent status and a new name: Keitt's Company Mounted Riflemen, SCV. It became Company B of the 19th Cavalry Battalion on December 20, 1864. John Peyre Thomas shows

Keitt's Company as Company C of Kirk's Squadron, but no other sources confirm the listing.[25]

Major Movements and Engagements

From the time it became independent until December 1864, Keitt's Company served between Charleston and Georgetown, specifically at McClellanville, Andersonville, Buck Hall, Mount Pleasant and Sullivan's Island.[26] During April and May 1864, it was stationed on the western side of Winyah Bay near Georgetown.[27] Ordered to Andersonville, twenty miles above Mount Pleasant, on May 23, the company was sent to Mount Pleasant on July 9 and to Sullivan's Island for picket duty on August 7. Ordered back to Andersonville on the twenty-ninth, the men marched to Mount Pleasant on September 19 to observe a twenty-five-mile segment of Charleston's left flank. Though still in the vicinity on October 31, Keitt's Company was back at Andersonville in November.[28] It remained there until December 20, when it became Company B of the 19th Battalion and part of Roswell Ripley's Brigade.[29] At the end of the war, Keitt brought his men home and disbanded them in York District.

Captain W.F. Percival's Company

Captain William F. Percival commanded two different companies during the war.[30] The first was the Pickens Rangers, and the second was the Aiken Mounted Infantry.[31] The Rangers, which enlisted under local state law on November 15, 1861, was from Aiken in Barnwell District and was attached to the 1st Regiment, South Carolina Mounted Militia.[32] Its men furnished their own horses and arms. Breaking camp at "Wasteaway" near Montmorenci on November 25, the men marched to the coast, spending successive nights near Barnwell Courthouse, Allendale and Pocotaligo, until all seventy-one had arrived at nearby Camp Martin by December 4.[33] This movement, the only significant action taken by Percival's first company, was apparently in response to the Federal capture of Hilton Head Island on November 7, though it may also have been present during the engagement at Port Royal Ferry on January 1, 1862.[34] The Rangers was disbanded in late February 1862 when its regiment ceased to exist. After offering their services to Colonel Martin, who was attempting to raise a new cavalry regiment at the time, the men either went home or enlisted in other organizations.

In May 1862, the *Mercury* ran an advertisement announcing that Percival was attempting to raise a company of Partizan Rangers consisting of men between eighteen and thirty-five.[35] Whether this effort succeeded is unclear, but by September 1864, Percival had formed a company of men exempt from Confederate service, including a number of former Pickens Rangers, called the Aiken Mounted Infantry and Percival's Independent Mounted Infantry.[36] Pension records indicate that the company was attached to the 3rd Regiment, South Carolina State Troops, and Colcock's Independent Regiment. Neither connection can be confirmed by other sources; it is possible that this is a reference to the fact that C.J. Colcock, colonel of the 3rd Cavalry Regiment, commanded the entire 3rd Military District in 1864 and 1865. Percival's Company was probably raised under authority of an act passed by the General Assembly on September 30, 1863, entitled "An Act to Provide for Volunteer Companies of Mounted Infantry."[37] This act might have resulted from a special order from the secretary of war, who ordered the Bureau of Conscription in September 1863 to authorize South Carolina to raise a six-company battalion of mounted men not otherwise liable for the draft to arrest deserters, assist with conscription and provide local defense. These men would be expected to serve for one year.[38] Another provision of the act empowered the governor to accept an unlimited number of mounted infantry companies to suppress insurrection and repel actual or threatened raids on the state.[39] Further, the governor was authorized to enroll all white males between eighteen and forty-five in companies, battalions and regiments of infantry for the same purpose and to raise one or more companies of artillery. Finally, the act permitted the governor to retain the men in service solely at his discretion. Accordingly, Governor Bonham called for all those exempt from Confederate service to form new companies during the summer of 1864. Men from Barnwell, Edgefield and Lexington Districts enlisted in a new company of mounted infantry under Percival's command for state defense.[40] Percival's goal was to recruit up to a hundred men; by late January 1865, he had signed up about sixty.[41] They were armed with Morse's patent breech-loading carbines.

Even as Sherman marched from Atlanta to Savannah, Percival's new company was occupied with picket duty at the ferries and crossings on the Savannah River between Hamburg and Whistler's Ferry. Part of the Aiken Mounted Infantry was engaged in the successful defense of Aiken on February 12, 1865. The company was probably disbanded at Aiken in April, and it was paroled at Augusta, Georgia, on May 23, 1865.

23.

The 2nd Battalion/2nd Regiment, South Carolina Artillery

The 2nd Battalion, South Carolina Artillery was also called Lamar's Artillery Battalion and the Lamar Artillery.[1] It was formed in October 1861 with four companies, all of which mustered in service for the duration of the war.[2] According to an article in the *Southern Historical Society Papers*, the battalion was raised following a call from the Executive Council for ten regiments whose field officers would be appointed by the governor and Executive Council.[3] A fifth company, commanded by Captain Frederick Warley, joined the battalion in March 1862. The 2nd Regiment, South Carolina Artillery, was created on April 12, 1862, as the result of a call from the secretary of war on February 2 for more South Carolina troops. Five new artillery companies, raised over the two-month period from February to April 1862 were consolidated with the 2nd Battalion to form the new ten-company 2nd Regiment, South Carolina Artillery. In addition to its official designation, it was also called the 2nd Heavy Artillery Regiment, Lamar's regiment and Frederick's regiment. For several weeks, the 2nd was also called the 1st Regiment, South Carolina Artillery Volunteers.[4] The name was soon changed to avoid confusion with the 1st Regiment, South Carolina Artillery Regulars, created only a few weeks earlier on March 25. With the exception of Company B, the companies' letter designations did not change then. The regiment was organized in Charleston and all ten companies enlisted for the duration of the war. Though the men wanted to elect their own field officers, the Executive Council chose to appoint them instead.[5]

Field Officers

Thomas Gresham Lamar of Beech Island in Edgefield District initially commanded the 2nd Battalion as its major. He held the rank of lieutenant colonel when the Executive Council appointed him colonel of the 2nd Regiment on April 16, 1862.[6] The only field officer of the 2nd Battalion, he was originally captain of Company D. As he directed the defense of the Tower Battery during the battle of Secessionville on June 16, 1862, Lamar was struck by a Minié ball that passed through his ear and out the back of his neck.[7] He was at home in Edgefield and had nearly recovered from the wound by July 23.[8] Having returned to Charleston some time between late July and mid-October, Lamar died in a hotel from the effects of malaria at 5:00 a.m. on October 17, 1862.[9] His obituary was glowing: "As an artillery officer, Colonel Lamar had few rivals or equals, and no superiors among volunteers now in our service. Faithful and vigorous in enforcing all the essential conditions of military discipline, he was as far as possible removed from a Martinet."[10] Not long after Lamar's death, General Pemberton ordered the Tower Battery works at Secessionville to be renamed Fort Lamar.[11]

Andrew David Frederick, MD, of Orangeburg was appointed lieutenant colonel of the regiment on May 7, 1862.[12] He had served as captain of Company A in the 2nd Battalion, and possibly as captain of Company I of the 2nd Regiment, though only for a short time. Serving as acting colonel, Frederick was probably elected to that post in January 1863, when a new vote was held for the field officers, who had originally been appointed.[13] Frederick was officially promoted to colonel on April 23, 1863, retroactive to the date of Lamar's death. He commanded both the east and west lines on James Island in 1863 and 1864, and he was present with the regiment there as late as January 25, 1865.[14]

James Welsman Brown of Charleston was appointed major of the regiment on May 7, 1862.[15] Brown had served as captain of Company C of the 2nd Battalion and possibly for a brief time as captain of Company K of the 2nd Regiment. Serving as acting lieutenant colonel, he was probably elected to the post in January 1863, when a new vote was held for the field officers, who had originally been appointed. He was probably officially appointed in April 1863, retroactive to October 17, 1862.[16] Some evidence, though inconclusive, suggests Brown may have been wounded and briefly captured on September 4, 1863, at Battery Wagner. He was detached for service on a board of inquiry in September and October 1863. Brown surrendered at Goldsboro, North Carolina, in April 1865 as commander of Elliott's Brigade. One observer called him "one of the most brilliant ornaments that formerly graced the halls of the Citadel."[17]

Frederick Fraser Warley of Darlington, previously captain of the Inglis Light Artillery, was promoted to major on April 29, 1863, with rank from October 17, 1862. He suffered severe wounds to the left leg and ankle from a shell splinter on September 4, 1863, at Battery Wagner, while acting as chief of artillery.[18] That evening, Warley was placed on a small boat belonging to Brigadier General Roswell Ripley for the short trip across the harbor to Charleston. Unfortunately, a Federal picket boat captured Warley and the crew about nine in the evening between Battery Wagner and Battery Gregg.[19] L.T. Izlar, a member of Company G, 25th Infantry Regiment, wrote that Warley was captured during the evacuation of Battery Wagner on September 6.[20] Izlar had personally participated in that operation, but he probably simply got the date of the capture wrong. On the sixth, Warley was taken to the steamer *Cosmopolitan*, where he was held for about two weeks. Then he was hospitalized in Beaufort until December 4. Still a prisoner, Warley arrived at Fort Columbus on Governor's Island in New York Harbor in early December; on the eleventh, he was transferred to Fort McHenry, Maryland. Warley was moved again, first to Fort Delaware on June 16, 1864, and then to Hilton Head Island on June 25. Warley was among the fifty Confederate officers exchanged in Charleston Harbor on August 3, 1864.[21] He briefly commanded the prison stockade at Florence that fall and returned to the 2nd Regiment no later than April 9, 1865.[22] He was paroled at Greensboro on April 28, 1865. Warley was considered "a most able and gallant officer."[23]

COMPANIES

Company A was composed of men from Barnwell District.[24] Previously Company B of the 2nd Battalion, it was probably given the same designation when the regiment was called the 1st Artillery Regiment, SCV. Though Arthur Buist raised the company, he resigned shortly after. J.T. Youngblood, who was promoted to captain of Company B in the 2nd Battalion on December 28, 1861, retained command for about a year in the 2nd Regiment.[25] Youngblood was dismissed following a court-martial on December 6, 1862, and ten days later William M. Hunter was promoted to captain. Hunter, a member of the South Carolina legislature then, resigned his commission on April 2, 1865. Though Lieutenant Robert S. Millar Jr. also commanded the company, he was never promoted to captain.

Company B, Thomas G. Lamar's Company of Heavy Artillery, was originally composed of men half of whom were from Barnwell District and half of whom were from Edgefield District.[26] It had many names and was successively designated: Captain Tom Lamar's Company, South Carolina Artillery; Captain Tom Lamar's Company, 2nd Battalion, South Carolina Artillery; Company D, 2nd Battalion, South Carolina Artillery; Company

D, 1st Regiment, South Carolina Artillery; Company B, 1st Regiment, South Carolina Artillery; and, finally, Company B, 2nd Regiment, South Carolina Artillery. The men mustered in service for the duration of the war on October 1, 1861, while stationed at Camp Butler near Montmorenci.[27] Thomas Gresham Lamar, elected captain on October 10, 1861, was promoted soon after to major of the battalion. Samuel J. Reed was promoted to captain on January 20, 1862, and retained command in the 2nd Regiment.[28] Reed was killed at Secessionville on June 16, 1862; soon after, the Clark House Battery near Secessionville was renamed Battery Reed.[29] J. Wyatt Lancaster, was promoted to captain as Reed's replacement on June 16 and was paroled at Greensboro.

Company C, the Edisto Artillery, was composed of men from Orangeburg District.[30] According to an unpublished sketch of the company, its men were from Colleton District.[31] Not part of the 2nd Battalion, the company was designated C when the regiment was called the 1st Artillery Regiment, SCV. The men mustered in service for the duration of the war on March 19, 1862. Chronic hepatitis forced the first captain, F.H.W. Briggmann, to resign on September 10, 1862.[32] First Lieutenant Medicus Rickenbacker was promoted to captain the same day. His widow spelled his first name Medicor on her pension application.

Company D, the Inglis Light Artillery, was also called Charles's Independent Light Battery. It was named in honor of a father and son: John A. Inglis was a lawyer from Cheraw and chairman of the committee that drafted the Ordinance of Secession. His oldest son, Captain John Cowper Inglis, adjutant of the 8th Regiment, SCV, died of typhoid fever at Richmond on October 18, 1861.[33] The men mustered in Confederate service for the duration of the war on March 20, 1862, at Darlington Court House. Originally an independent light battery, the company had been raised by special order of the secretary of war and had been given permission to go immediately to Virginia or to the western army.[34] But with no light artillery pieces immediately available, the battery was equipped as heavy artillery and ordered to Fort Johnson on James Island, where it was attached as an unlettered company to Lamar's Battalion for two to three weeks before it became a regiment.[35] This happened in March and early April 1862. The company was briefly designated Company D when the regiment was called the 1st Artillery Regiment, SCV.

The company was considered a Darlington District unit since it was composed mostly of men from Darlington, Williamsburg and Charleston Districts, along with a few from Chesterfield, Georgetown, Sumter, Marlboro and Marion Districts. Frederick Fraser Warley, elected captain on March 20, 1862, had been captain of the Darlington Guards for two years—from June

1859 to June 1861. From January to June 1861, the Darlington Guards was Company B of Maxcy Gregg's 1st Regiment (six-months), SCV. Warley and many of the Darlington Guards refused to follow Gregg to Virginia in April 1861, and Warley led this segment of the company home to Darlington in May.[36] These men formed a new company and re-elected Warley captain on June 24, 1861.[37] Whether this company was related to the Inglis Light Artillery is unclear, but F.F. Warley and W.E. Charles appear on both company rolls. Warley was promoted to major of the 2nd Regiment on April 29, 1863, with rank from October 17, 1862. His replacement, First Lieutenant William E. Charles, was promoted to captain, effective October 17, 1862. He was paroled at Greensboro on May 1, 1865.

Company E was composed mostly of men from Aiken in Barnwell District, along with some from Lexington and Edgefield Districts.[38] Though not part of the 2nd Battalion, it was briefly designated Company E when the regiment was called the 1st Artillery Regiment, SCV. The men mustered in service for the duration of the war about March 19, 1862, while stationed at Fort Johnson. Many, if not most, had served in the Allen Guards, Company E in Johnson Hagood's regiment, in early 1861. In the summer of 1861, the Allen Guards volunteered for Confederate service and was attached as Company E to the 25th Mississippi Regiment, also called the 1st Mississippi Valley Regiment, which was organized on August 10, 1861. The 25th Mississippi Regiment was redesignated the 2nd Confederate Regiment on January 31, 1862, but it was officially disbanded about May 8, 1862. Its remaining companies scattered among other regiments. Reorganized for the duration of the war on March 19, 1862, the Allen Guards left its Mississippi regiment soon afterward and was attached to the 2nd Regiment, South Carolina Artillery, known at the time as the 1st. B.E. Dickson, previously a second lieutenant in Company E of the 25th Mississippi Regiment, was elected captain of Company E of the 2nd Regiment on March 22, 1862.[39] He was paroled at Greensboro on April 28, 1865.

Company F, the Carolina Artillery, was composed of men from Orangeburg and Branchville in Orangeburg District.[40] Before the reorganization in the spring of 1862, most of its members were in the Glover Guards, Company C, of Johnson Hagood's 1st Volunteer Regiment, though a few were members of other companies in Hagood's regiment. The men were based at Cole's Island when they re-enlisted in the 2nd Artillery Regiment on April 12, 1862, for the duration of the war. According to the *Mercury*, the men re-enlisted again for the duration of the war in February 1864, though this probably represented a reaffirmation of their original commitment.[41] One source states that this company was briefly Company F in Lamar's 2nd Battalion, an unlikely stint since Lamar's Battalion was converted into a regiment on the same day the Carolina Artillery mustered in service. It was designated Company F when the regiment was called the 1st Artillery Regiment, SCV. Thomas K. Legare, its only captain, was elected on March 23, 1862.[42]

Company G, the Silverton Artillery, was composed mostly of men from Barnwell District.[43] Silverton was an earlier name for Jackson, a town in the district. Both the *Mercury* and the *Edgefield Advertiser* recorded, incorrectly, that Company G men were from Darlington District.[44] Until March 1862, most had served in Company G and other companies of Johnson Hagood's 1st Regiment, SCV. One source records that the company was designated Company G in Lamar's 2nd Battalion in March and early April 1862, an unlikely supposition. It was designated Company G when the regiment was called the 1st Artillery Regiment, SCV. Frederick J. Sanders, who had organized the company while he was first lieutenant of Company G in Hagood's regiment, was court-martialed for conduct unbecoming an officer and a gentleman while still in Hagood's regiment. Though under arrest and awaiting sentence when the reorganization took place, he was nevertheless elected captain of the company he had raised.[45] Hagood wrote: "The sentence of the court was promulgated shortly after he [Sanders] reported to Lamar and he was dismissed from the service. He went home and in a few weeks afterwards was licensed as a Baptist preacher."[46] Sanders was popular with the men, and they thought him competent.[47] The *CSR* lists Robert M. Willis as captain of Company G, but he was more likely captain of Company H.[48] George W. Stallings enlisted as captain of Company G for two years or for the duration of the war on April 9, 1862, though his commission was dated the seventeenth. Hagood wrote that he commanded the company well for the remainder of the war. Stallings was a patient at Hospital #2 in Greensboro when he was paroled on May 2, 1865.[49]

Company H, composed of men from Barnwell District, was also designated H when the regiment was called the 1st Volunteers.[50] Robert M. Willis was probably its first captain.[51] Though the *CSR* and the minutes of the Executive Council list him as being captain of Company G, his dates of service appear more compatible with the record of Company H.[52] Willis resigned on June 2, 1862. The *CSR* records that William H. Kennady was promoted to captain on June 2, but it also lists Kennady as captain on the muster roll for March 20 to April 30, 1862. Wounded in the right arm on March 26, 1865, at Bentonville, Kennady was furloughed on April 12 from Hospital #11 at Charlotte, North Carolina.

Company I, the Orangeburg Artillery, was composed mostly of men from Orangeburg District, though a few came from Barnwell and Laurens Districts.[53] Previously Company A in the 2nd Battalion, it was briefly designated Company I of the 1st Artillery Regiment, SCV. The Orangeburg

Artillery mustered in the Confederate States Provisional Army for the duration of the war on November 11, 1861, a date also shown as the nineteenth. According to the *CSR*, the men mustered in while stationed at Orangeburg in November 1861, but it also records the site as Fort Johnson and the date sometime between October 4 and December 28. Andrew David Frederick, MD, raised the company and enlisted on November 11, 1861. The only captain in the 2nd Battalion, he may have commanded the company briefly in the 2nd Regiment before he was elected lieutenant colonel on May 7, 1862.[54] George D. Keitt, who was promoted to captain on May 7, 1862, resigned on September 9 to fulfill his responsibilities as state senator at the next meeting of the legislature.[55] First Lieutenant Joseph B. Humbert was promoted to captain as Keitt's replacement on September 9, and he commanded the company until the end of the war.[56]

Company K, known as Captain J. W. Brown's Company in the 2nd Battalion, was composed mostly of men from Edgefield District, along with a few from Abbeville, Lexington, Charleston, Laurens and Newberry Districts.[57] It was previously Company C of the 2nd Battalion.[58] James Welsman Brown, elected captain on January 1, 1862, was the only company commander in the 2nd Battalion and was promoted to major of the 2nd Regiment on May 7, 1862. H.C. Culbreath replaced him as captain of the company in the 2nd Regiment the same day. Culbreath's first name appears, variously, as Harry, Hay and Henry.[59] The fifty-one-year-old captain resigned on November 23, 1864, because of an unspecified physical disability of twenty-five years' duration. Philemon B. Waters succeeded Culbreath and served until the end of the war.[60] Waters was paroled at Greensboro. Company K was large; its roster numbered 180 men in December 1863.[61]

BRIGADE AFFILIATIONS

The 2nd Battalion, South Carolina Artillery served in several military districts of the Department of South Carolina, Georgia and Florida during its six-month existence.[62] From its creation in April 1862 to early 1865, the 2nd Regiment was also attached to various subdivisions and military districts of the Department of South Carolina, Georgia and Florida.[63] By November 20, 1864, two of the regiment's companies, probably C and D, had been attached to Brigadier General Beverly H. Robertson's Brigade and the other eight had been attached to Brigadier General William B. Taliaferro's Brigade.[64] The regiment also served briefly as part of A.M. Rhett's Brigade, which was formed on December 28, 1864, with the 1st Regiment, South Carolina Artillery (Regulars), the 2nd Regiment, South Carolina Artillery and the 1st Regiment, South Carolina Infantry (Regulars).[65] By January 31, 1865, six companies of the 2nd Artillery Regiment were unbrigaded, while the others were widely scattered: Company D was attached to Brigadier General John K. Jackson's Brigade; Company C was in Mercer's Brigade; and two companies were attached to Stephen Elliott's Brigade along with the Battalion of State Cadets, eight companies from the 1st Cavalry Regiment, three from the 1st South Carolina Artillery, Company D of the South Carolina Siege Train and some Georgia units.[66] On April 9, 1865, the 2nd Regiment was attached to Elliott's Brigade with several Georgia artillery organizations.[67]

Major Movements and Engagements

Companies C and D of the 2nd Battalion were originally based at Camp Butler near Montmorenci in Barnwell District. Company D was the first company in the battalion to arrive at Fort Johnson on James Island in early October 1861; Company B was there by the fourth. The others arrived in Charleston in late October and prepared to serve as part of the garrison of Fort Johnson.[68] Company D was transferred to Sullivan's Island on the twenty-sixth.[69] Companies B and D were engaged at Fort Walker during the battle of Port Royal on November 7. The battalion had returned to Fort Johnson by November 19.[70] The 2nd Battalion merged into the 1st Regiment, South Carolina Artillery Volunteers, shortly after redesignated the 2nd Regiment, on April 12, 1862.

The 2nd Regiment served primarily in the Charleston area from April 1862 until the evacuation of Charleston in February 1865. Some of its companies served often in a detached capacity. The 2nd Regiment erected the permanent batteries known as the "west lines" on James Island; some of its companies manned those works from mid-June 1862 to February 1865. The 2nd Regiment also provided its quota of companies for service at Battery Wagner until its evacuation in early September 1863.

Company A was stationed at Fort Johnson and Battery Cheves on James Island from July 1862 to December 1864. Company B's base was at the western end of James Island in June 1862. Company C was stationed in the east lines and at Battery Means on James Island from March 19, 1862, to April 1863. Company D was at James Island in the summer of 1862, while Company E was stationed on Morris Island from March 19, 1862, to April 30, 1862, when it was sent to James Island. Company F was probably at James Island in the summer of 1862, while Company G was definitely there then. Company H served in the "west lines," at Fort Lamar, in the "east lines" and at Battery #5 on James Island from March 1862 to December 1864. Company I was stationed at Fort Johnson, in the "west lines," at Fort Lamar, and in the "new lines" from November 1861 to December 1864. Company K was based at Fort Lamar from July 1862 to December 1864.

Company B saw action at the western end of the James Island lines on June 2, 1862. Companies B and I were engaged at the Tower Battery during the battle of Secessionville on June 16, 1862. Company D, though present during the battle of Secessionville, was not engaged because the terrain kept the men from firing for fear of endangering their own troops. Company B remained at Fort Lamar (formerly the Tower Battery) and in the "west lines" of James Island from June 16, 1862, until the evacuation in February 1865. In November 1862, Company D was sent to Battery White on Winyah Bay near Georgetown. There it was engaged with Federal gunboats on two occasions as both heavy and light artillery. One fight took place on November 11.[71] The company remained at Battery White until May 1863, when it was sent across the bay to the Waccamaw Neck. Company D, which moved to Mount Pleasant in July 1863, was at Sullivan's Island on August 31 and returned to James Island in September.[72] Company G was stationed at Battery Glover, in the "west lines," and in the "new lines" on James Island from July 1862 to December 1864.

Most of the regiment was stationed on James Island in October 1862. The *Mercury* reported that it was serving as infantry then.[73] Detachments from Companies B and K participated in the capture of the USS *Isaac P. Smith* on the Stono River on January 30, 1863.[74] On March 13, 1863, the regiment was stationed at James Island and at St. Andrews Parish.[75] Company I was at Fort Johnson on April 7 and was engaged during the ironclad attack on Fort Sumter.[76]

In April 1863, Company C was sent to Batteries Palmer and Haig in St. Andrews Parish. It remained there until April 30, 1864. Companies B and K were at Fort Lamar in June 1863, Company I was at Fort Johnson, Company G was at Battery Glover, Company C was at Batteries Haig and Palmer, and four were at the east lines on James Island.[77] Company D was stationed near Georgetown then.[78]

In the spring and summer of 1863, the 2nd Regiment was based at James Island, but a number of its companies participated in the defense of Morris Island and Battery Wagner. During the siege of Battery Wagner, the regiment rotated its companies.[79] Company E served on Morris Island in March and April 1863 before returning to James Island. Company A arrived at Battery Wagner on July 19 and was relieved after several days.[80] Company A returned to the battery from Charleston on July 31 and was relieved on August 6.[81] Company G, sent to Morris Island on July 31, remained there until about August 15.[82] On August 5, Company C was at Battery Gregg on Morris Island.[83] Company H arrived at Wagner on August 20 and remained until the end of the month.[84] A detachment of Company F was at the battery from August 27 to September 1.[85] Company B was sent to Wagner on August 31, and Company A returned on September 1 to relieve Company F.[86] Company A participated in the evacuation of Battery Wagner on September 6.[87]

James Island continued as the regiment's base after Morris Island was evacuated on September 6.[88] By November 1, eight companies were stationed at the eastern division of James Island as heavy artillery, Company C was at Battery Palmer in St. Andrews Parish, and Company D was at the eastern division of James Island as light artillery.[89] Later in November, Company D moved to Adams Run. Company D was engaged with the USS *Marblehead* near Legareville on the Stono River on December 25, 1863.[90]

From the autumn of 1863 until November 1864, the same eight companies remained in the batteries and forts on James Island, while Companies C and D were at Adams Run and St. Andrews Parish.[91] Company D was engaged at the Haulover Cut on John's Island on February 10 and February 11, 1864.[92] Company C moved from St. Andrews Parish to Godfrey's on April 30 and remained there until October. Companies F, G, H and I occupied Batteries 1, 2, 3, 4 and 5 of the new lines on James Island in April. Company F was based at the "new lines" when some of its pickets were captured at Legare's house on James Island on May 13, 1864. Companies H and I, along with a detachment of Company F, skirmished at the same spot on the twenty-second. Detachments from Companies A and E saw action during the Federal boat assault on Fort Johnson and Battery Simkins on July 3, 1864.[93] One howitzer from Company D skirmished at Huntscum's Corner on John's Island on July 5 and again the next day at Grimball's Waterloo Place on John's Island.[94] Two howitzers of Company D were engaged at Gervais's Field on John's Island on the seventh.[95] Company D fought again on July 9 at Burden's Causeway on John's Island.[96] Company D saw action at Legareville, probably on August 20. Company E left James Island in October. Company C moved to Kirkland in November and remained there for about a month. Company D was sent to Grahamville to demonstrate during the battle of Honey Hill in late November.[97] It remained based at Honey Hill until the end of December and sent detachments to the Bee Creek works on the Coosawhatchie River, to Grahamville and to Sister's Ferry on the Savannah River.[98] A detachment of Company B was ordered to Pocotaligo from December 14 to December 17 and to Green Pond on December 25.

Company C was stationed at Battery Burnett on the Combahee River when it destroyed the Federal gunboat *Dai-ching* at Tar Bluff on January 26,

1865.[99] About a hundred men of the 2nd Regiment were part of the infantry skirmish at Grimball's Causeway near the Stono River on February 10.[100] Company H skirmished at Secessionville the same day. When Confederate forces evacuated Charleston in February, the 2nd Regiment was converted to infantry. According to one source, Company D withdrew from Sisters Ferry through Robertville, Honey Hill, Branchville and St. Stephen's Depot as part of Delaware Kemper's Artillery Regiment.[101] Another source records that Company D evacuated Charleston on the night of February 17 before marching via Moncks Corner to St. Stephens Depot.[102] From that point they traveled by rail to Kingstree, Florence, Darlington and Cheraw and marched to Rockingham and Fayetteville. The 2nd Regiment also fought as infantry at Averasboro on March 16 and withdrew from the battlefield that evening.[103] The regiment was also heavily engaged at Bentonville on March 19. The next day, it performed picket duty near Bentonville, and on March 21 the regiment was engaged again.[104] After Averasboro and Bentonville, the regiment retreated to Smithfield and marched on to Raleigh. By April 10, it was at Hillsboro.[105] Some men of the Inglis Light Artillery left for home on the twenty-first. Still on the move, the regiment marched to Burlington and Greensboro where it surrendered with the Army of Tennessee on April 26, 1865.

24.

Independent Artillery Organizations

Captain Garden's Company-the Palmetto Light Battery-South Carolina Light Artillery

Captain Garden's Company-the Palmetto Light Battery-South Carolina Light Artillery, was also called the Palmetto Light Artillery; the Palmetto Light Battery; and Garden's Battery, SCV, Confederate States Provisional Army. It was raised in March and April 1862 in Charleston and was accepted by the secretary of war on March 25.[1] On April 8, Sergeant Hugh Richardson Garden of Company D, 2nd Regiment, SCV, recruited twenty-one men from his infantry company to establish the nucleus of the Palmetto Light Artillery.[2] Some from the 8th and 9th Regiments also enlisted in Garden's new unit.[3] Garden's men were from Sumter District.[4] Others came from Chesterfield, Greenville and Laurens Districts, and a few represented Clarendon, Kershaw, Lancaster, Williamsburg and Charleston Districts. The men elected Garden captain of the new artillery battery. Sumter's Baptist, Methodist, Presbyterian and Episcopal Churches donated their bells to be made into cannons for the Palmetto Light Battery.[5] By April 1863, those donated by the Baptist Church had been returned, though the reason remains unclear.[6] Garden was wounded at Cold Harbor and paroled at Appomattox on April 9, 1865.

Brigade Affiliations

The Palmetto Light Battery served with the Army of Northern Virginia and in the Department of North Carolina and Southern Virginia.[7] It was part of B.W. Frobel's Battalion along with Bachman's German Artillery in the summer of 1862. It was also attached to Kemper's Artillery Battalion and later to M.W. Henry and J.C. Haskell's Battalions of Reserve Artillery in the Army of Northern Virginia. Both Henry and Haskell's Battalions were composed of batteries that were from various states and that subsequently served as independent commands.

Major Movements and Engagements

The Palmetto Light Artillery left Sumter for Camp Hampton in Columbia on April 27, 1862.[8] For about two months, from late April to late June, it spent time on guard duty at Branchville.[9] Sometime after June 25, the battery was ordered to Virginia. Present but not engaged at the battle of Second Manassas on August 29, the battery did see action there on the thirtieth. It crossed the Potomac into Maryland with the Army of Northern Virginia on September 4. The battery skirmished on September 15, and Garden wrote that his men were "desperately engaged" at Sharpsburg on the seventeenth.[10] Two of the battery's guns were disabled, but neither was lost. The battery recrossed the river into Virginia on the night of September 18, and by the twenty-third, it was at Martinsburg. It moved from there to Culpeper. By November 23, the men were at Fredericksburg but did not participate in the fighting on December 13. The Palmetto Light Artillery left Fredericksburg in late February 1863 and moved with Longstreet's corps to southern Virginia a month or so later. About April 11, the battery was ordered to Suffolk; the men skirmished with the enemy at nearby Hill's Point throughout late April.[11] On May 3, the battery saw action while serving as the rear guard near Suffolk; later the same day, it moved out to rejoin the Army of Northern Virginia.[12] The Palmetto Light Artillery was not present for the battles around Chancellorsville in May 1863. Moving north, the battery crossed the Potomac at Williamsport on June 26.

During the battle of Gettysburg, the Palmetto Light Artillery was engaged on July 2 on the Confederate right wing and moved with the infantry of Hood's Division as it charged up Round Top.[13] The next day, the battery fought at the center of the Confederate line; one of its guns was part of Pickett's Charge.[14] It remained on the field until about six in the evening on July 4. Withdrawing from the area, the men recrossed the Potomac on the evening of July 13 and had reached Culpeper Court House by the twenty-first. The battery spent the rest of July and August at Culpeper; it did not go with Longstreet's corps to Tennessee in September. It was present but not engaged during the Bristoe campaign from October 9 to October 22 and during the Mine Run campaign in November and December.[15] The Palmetto Light Artillery spent that winter at Green Spring Valley near Charlottesville and Gordonsville.[16] Though not engaged at the Wilderness in early May 1864, it did fight at Spotsylvania Court House on May 8, May 9, May 11 and May 18. During the Overland campaign, the battery saw action at the North Anna River on May 23 and at Cold Harbor from June 1 to June 3. It marched to the south bank of the Chickahominy River on June 7 and crossed the James on the sixteenth at Drewry's Bluff, arriving at Petersburg two days later.[17] The Palmetto Light Artillery was in the Petersburg lines but was not engaged on June 18. The battery was engaged at Port Walthall on June 19; the next day it was posted some six hundred yards behind Elliott's Salient, where it fought in the battle of the Crater on July 30. Crossing to the north side of the James on September 30, it engaged the enemy again at Fort Harrison that day and the next. Following another encounter along the Darbytown Road on October 7, the battery was engaged again on the thirteenth on the Williamsburg Road and along the Nine Mile Road on October 27.

The Palmetto Light Artillery was stationed north of the James River in January, February and March 1865.[18] Leaving the lines after dark on April 2, the battery passed through Richmond later that night.[19] The men marched toward Amelia Court House on April 4 and arrived there at mid-morning on the fifth. The battery continued its march that day and the next and arrived at Farmville on April 7.[20] Acting as the rear guard, the battery met the enemy one last time at the Appomattox River near Farmville on the seventh. The march continued later that day and the next, and the Palmetto Light Artillery abandoned its guns on the eighth.[21] Following the surrender at Appomattox on April 9, the men left on the twelfth to make their way home.[22]

Appendix 1.

Infantry Companies with Unknown Regimental or Battalion Affiliations

1. The Southern Guards was a company of Wofford College students organized on February 22, 1860. According to one source, the captain was Talliaferro Simpson; another source names T.B. Anderson.[1] Anderson is not listed in the CSR, probably because the company was never in Confederate service.
2. The Charleston Guard, commanded by Captain Myer Jacobs, was composed of alarm men and those otherwise exempted from service.[2] Myer is not listed in the CSR, probably because the company was never in Confederate service.
3. The Snow Hill Guards was a company from Newberry District.[3]
4. The Magrath Guard, a company of Irishmen probably from Charleston, was commanded by a Captain Farrelly.[4] Henry S. Farley was captain of Companies D and H of the 1st Regiment, South Carolina Artillery Regulars, but no Captain Farrelly appears in the CSR.
5. The Hudson Street Guard, a company of "armed juveniles," probably took its name from Hudson Street in Charleston.[5]
6. The Gasper Guards was a company of boys, probably of school age, commanded by Master Algernon Alston.[6] Alston is not listed in the CSR.
7. The Southern Boys was a company commanded by Captain Sam Thomas.[7] Thomas is not listed in the CSR.
8. The University Riflemen, from Greenville, was made up of Furman University students. It existed in January 1861, and it may have become the Brooks Troop, Company B of the Hampton Legion.[8]
9. The Marion Men was commanded by Captain G.B. Lartigue.[9] In July 1861, the *Mercury* announced that Lartigue was unable to complete the organization of the company.[10] He is not listed as a captain in the CSR.
10. The Sumter Cadets was a company of "juveniles."[11]

11. The Hope Guard, a Charleston company, was probably raised from the Hope Fire Engine Company.[12] Company H of the 13th Regiment, SCV, was a Lexington District company also known as the Hope Guards.
12. The Confederate Guards was a home guard company from Williston in Barnwell District.[13]
13. The Citizen Guards was a Chesterfield District company commanded by a Captain Tawh.[14] Tawh is not listed as a captain in the CSR.
14. The Home Guard of Union District was commanded by Captain F. Scaife.[15] This was probably Ferdinand D. Scaife who, in November 1861, became captain of Company A of the 18th Regiment, SCV, and later became its lieutenant colonel.
15. The Carolina Greys was a Charleston company commanded by Captain F. Marion Ronan.[16] Ronan was a lieutenant in the 16th Regiment, South Carolina Militia, but the record is unclear on whether or not the Carolina Greys was a company in that regiment.
16. Captain William Greene was attempting to raise the Manigault Guards in Georgetown in late December 1861.[17] The result of that effort is unknown.
17. Captains O'Connell, Stewart and Pulliam were from Pickens District.[18]
18. The Keitt Guard was commanded by Captain H. Smith Bass.[19] Bass is not listed in the CSR.
19. John W. Carr, a private in the St. George's Volunteers, served later in the 18th Regiment, SCV.[20] Carr was disabled in December 1861. He is not listed in the CSR.
20. Captain Samuel Y. Tupper commanded a "force" of exempt men and others who provided auxiliary services to the army in the defense of Charleston in June 1864.[21] Tupper had been captain of the Vigilant Rifles, part of the 4th Brigade, South Carolina Militia, in 1861. Later that year, he served in the 1st Regiment, S.C. Artillery Militia. Tupper enlisted on July 11, 1863, as captain of Company H of the 1st Regiment, Charleston Guard, South Carolina. An order dated May 29, 1864, authorized him to raise a company of volunteers from those citizens exempt from immediate military duty for service at batteries in Charleston. Another order, this one dated September 23, detached Tupper for duty as an agent of the state commissioners assisting in the removal of noncombatants from Charleston.
21. Captain James K. Mackett of the 1st Battalion was exchanged on October 15, 1864. He was not listed in the CSR.
22. The Foreign Legion was organized on January 18, 1865, to maintain good order in Charleston. It was commanded by Captain Nicholas

Scherhammer, previously captain of Beat #1 of the 16th Regiment, South Carolina Militia.[22]

23. Captain W.R. Holmes commanded the Burke Sharpshooters.[23] Holmes is not listed in the CSR.
24. A company of boys called the Davis Guards was raised at the military school in Anderson. The boys were taught by Major B.F. Sloan and Captain Joseph Adams, who probably commanded the company.[24]
25. James Long was captain of Company A of Perryman's Battalion. Either the company or battalion was from Pickens District and was named the Mountain Rangers, but the battalion cannot be definitely identified. The Mountain Rangers served from July 1864 to May 1865 and was disbanded at Greenville. Another captain in this company was George A. Rankin. Pension records show that Long's Company was designated D of the 1st or 8th Reserves in May 1864, or possibly A or B of the 1st Regiment, South Carolina State Troops. Possibly the same James Long was captain of both Company D, 4th Regiment, SCV, and Company A, 13th Battalion, SCV, in 1862 and was colonel of the 42nd Regiment, Militia.
26. Two companies of "Old Men's Home Guards" from the Oconee section of Pickens District were commanded by Captains C.F. Seeba and E.P. Verner.[25]
27. Gregg Light Infantry, probably a militia company in Columbia in 1863, was commanded by William J. Taylor.[26]
28. The Mountain Guards, men exempt from military service, was raised on January 5, 1861, to protect homes and families and quell insurrection.[27] It was commanded by Captain J.J. Quinn. Another company, G of the 18th Regiment, SCV, may have had the same name.
29. The Bethel Guards, a company of exempt men, was organized about January 17, 1861, to protect homes and families in an emergency.[28] Its captain was J.J. Wilson. Thomas and Silverman wrote that the Bethel Guards was Company B of the 5th Regiment, SCV.[29]
30. The Walhalla Riflemen was a Pickens District company in January 1861. Captain __ Hershel may have commanded the company at first, but Jonathan M. Hencken was captain in June 1861.[30] Although the men desired to muster in Orr's Rifles that month, there is no record of the company either there or in Moore's (2nd) Rifles.
31. A company of exempt men was organized in January 1861 in the northwest part of York District; it was commanded by Captain John B. Mintz.[31]
32. A company of exempt men was organized in January 1861 in the Kings Mountain part of York District; its commander was Captain M.R. Bird.[32]

33. The Bull Swamp Guards, organized in Orangeburg District in January 1861, was commanded by Captain L.W. Dash.[33]
34. The Broad River Light Infantry was organized in February 1861 and was commanded by Captain John S. Crosby.[34]
35. The Rich Hill Guards existed in February 1861.[35]
36. The Home Guards of Yorkville, organized in April 1861, was commanded by Captain Asbury Coward.[36]
37. In May 1861, Captain John B. Jackson organized a new company in York.[37]
38. The Carolina Home Guards was raised in February 1861 by W.T. Field and R.C. Clayton. It was probably from Pickens District.[38]
39. The Mountain Creek Home Guards, organized on May 4, 1861, at Kirksey's Cross Roads in Edgefield District, was commanded by W.H. Holloway.[39] Holloway raised another company in the summer of 1861, which became part of Company G, Gregg's 1st Regiment, SCV.
40. A company of Home Guards, organized in Edgefield District on June 1, 1861, was commanded by G.D. Huiet.[40]
41. The Pleasant Lane Home Guards, organized in Edgefield District in June 1861, was commanded by Luke Culbreath.[41]
42. The Greenville Riflemen was organized in June 1861 from an artillery company unable to procure a battery of field artillery.[42] Whether or not this company was related to Company M of Maxcy Gregg's regiment is unknown.
43. A cavalry company of the Home Guards of Edgefield District was organized in June 1861; its captain was Lewis Jones.[43]
44. A company called the Confederate Stars was organized in Columbia in July 1861. Its members were boys who were five to thirteen years old.[44]
45. The Lanham Guards, organized in August 1861, was commanded by T.W. Lanham.[45]
46. The Dean Guards was a mounted infantry company organized in the Pine Grove section of Edgefield District in July 1863 for domestic defense. Theodore Dean was its captain.[46]
47. The Chichester Guards, organized in July 1864 for local defense in Edgefield District, was commanded by E.J. Dawson. It consisted of about fifty managers and operatives at Bath Paper Mills and Southern Porcelain Company and was named in honor of the owner of the Bath Paper Mills.[47]
48. A Home Defense Company, organized on March 16, 1865, in Edgefield, was commanded by E.H. Youngblood. It was made up of about seventy men, most of them either exempt from service or in the 2nd Class militia.[48]

49. The Golden's Creek Company, organized on June 1, 1861, for home defense, was commanded by William Hunter.[49] This company was probably from the Golden's Creek area northeast of Columbia.
50. The Pendleton Home Guard, organized in June 1861, was commanded by F.A. Hoke.[50]
51. The Anderson's Mills Home Guard, commanded by A.G. Field, was organized in July 1861.[51]
52. The Village Creek Home Guard, organized in July 1861, was commanded by Patterson Orr. Members were required to be older than twelve.[52]
53. The Mile Creek Home Guard, commanded by Levi N. Robins, was organized in July 1861.[53]
54. The Claremont Vigilance and Military Volunteer Committee elected Major John C. Miller as president in July 1861.[54]
55. The Snow Creek Vigilant Committee elected J.A. Elrod as president in July 1861.[55]
56. The Pumpkin Town Home Guard was organized in July 1861; G.W. Keith was its captain. It was also called the Mountain Rangers.[56]
57. The Battleground Home Guard, organized at Gill's Creek in May 1861, was commanded by Dr. D.A. Belk.[57]
58. The Independent Blair Guards, a home guard company organized in the lower part of Lancaster District in May 1862, was commanded by T.R. Clyburn.[58]
59. A Home Guard company commanded by John D. Andrews was organized in Lancaster District in May 1862.[59]
60. The Pleasant Hill Guard, organized in May 1861, was commanded by J.E. Rutledge.[60]
61. The Wild Cat Vigilant Company, commanded by J. Funderburk, was organized in May 1861.[61]
62. A Home Guard Company was organized in Lancaster District in May 1861; W.W. Baskin was its captain.[62]
63. The Lynches Creek Home Guards was organized in September 1861 in the lower part of Lancaster District; its commander was the Reverend N. Faile.[63]
64. The Greenville Home Guard was organized in January 1861. C.J. Elford was its captain.[64]
65. A Home Guard Company of Mounted Riflemen, also called the Greenville Home Guards–State Troops, was organized on July 1, 1863, in Greenville District. T.S. Arthur was its captain.[65] In its sole engagement, it forced General I.N. Palmer's Federal raiding column, which was in pursuit of President Davis, from its direct route.

66. A Home Guard Company of Infantry, organized in Greenville District on July 1, 1863, was commanded by G.E. Elford.[66]
67. The Hanging Rock Home Guards was organized in April 1862 in Lancaster District.[67]
68. The Brooks Boys, named for Preston Brooks, was organized in February 1861 from the Upper Battalion of the 2nd Regiment, South Carolina Militia, from Pickens District. Warren R. Marshall was its captain.[68]
69. The Anderson Home Guard, organized in February 1861, was commanded by a Captain Cox.[69]
70. W.P. McKellar was captain of a Greenwood company in September 1861.[70]
71. Captain Alfred J. Frederick commanded a company of South Carolina Militia in January 1865.[71]
72. The Home Guard of Charleston was commanded by Captain G.S. Hacker in May 1861.[72]
73. The City Guard of Charleston was a three-company battalion commanded by Captain H.S. Bass in May 1861.[73]
74. The Palmetto Reserve Guards #6 elected T.W. Holwell as captain on August 25, 1861. This company was composed of harbor pilots, shipmasters and others exempt from military duty.[74]
75. The Yeadon Blues was raised by G.E. Steedman in the summer of 1862 and named in honor of Richard Yeadon, senior editor of the *Charleston Daily Courier*. It was also called the "boys from Aiken."[75] G.E. Steedman's name does not appear in the CSR as captain or lieutenant of any company.
76. The Georgetown Reserves was commanded by Captain David Henry Smith.[76]
77. Willis Wilkinson Shackelford was captain of the Georgetown Home Guard.[77]
78. Captain J.H. Simons's Company, South Carolina Infantry, was commanded by J. Hume Simons. It enlisted in Confederate service for the duration of the war on May 14, 1862, at Charleston; Simons was elected at about the same time. The term of service dated from April 15. It might have been called the Miles Grenadiers.[78]
79. The Chesterfield Eagles, commanded by Neill F. Graham, was probably raised in Chesterfield for special state defense. Graham was captain of Company E of the 9th Battalion, but whether or not the two companies were the same is unclear.
80. The St. Paul's Home Guards was stationed at Adams Run and was charged with local defense. The St. Paul's Rifles, probably the same company, took over garrison duty from the Calhoun Artillery when

it was disbanded in June 1861. A Captain Smith commanded the St. Paul's Rifles.[79]

81. Captain Dougherty's Reserve Corps was commanded by Captain John Dougherty.
82. The Edgefield Reserves, commanded by Captain Joseph Abney, volunteered for twelve months of state service. Upon its organization, the company, in early December 1861, requested service with other Edgefield Companies; whether that request was honored is unknown. A company called the Edgefield Riflemen, however, commanded by Joseph Abney, became Company A of the 22nd Regiment at its organization in May 1862.
83. The Walhalla State Guards from Pickens District was commanded by Captain James O'Connell. See Company D, 22nd Regiment, SCV.
84. The Signal Corps was commanded by Captain Joseph Manigault and Captain C.G. Memminger.
85. The Port Royal Guards was commanded by Lieutenant Randolph Peyton.[80]
86. The Independent Men of Waxhaws, a militia company from Lancaster, was commanded by R.M. Sims.[81]
87. William Shivers commanded the Rebel Guards, a local defense company.[82]
88. Captain H.A. Shaw commanded an Edgefield District company that existed as early as April 1864. It served as a ferry guard at Vienna, South Carolina, before moving to Waynesboro, Georgia, to observe Sherman's troops. It was sent next to Beaufort and then served along the courier line between Augusta and Columbia until February 1865. The company was discharged at Trenton, South Carolina, in April 1865.
89. E.J. Dennis commanded a company of scouts in Charleston District in 1865.
90. Peter Sudduth, or Suddeth, was captain of a company of home guards, also described as a company of reserves, raised in 1864 from Spartanburg and Greenville Districts. The men performed bridge duty and were discharged at Columbia in April 1865.
91. The "Boy Cavalry" was in the 2nd Reserves and was commanded by B.B. McCoy.
92. In late 1864 and 1865, a Captain McMurphy commanded a home guard company of sixteen-year-olds from the part of Beaufort District that is now Hampton County.
93. John Lovell, or Lowell, commanded a home guard company of sixteen-year-olds from Horry District in late 1864 and 1865.

94. E.H. Peeples commanded a company of "old men" in one of the reserve organizations in late 1864 and 1865.
95. George Camp commanded an independent company organized at New Prospect. It performed patrol duty for three to four months.

Appendix 2

Cavalry Organizations with Unknown Regimental or Battalion Affiliations

1. The Horry Hussars from northern Horry District are not mentioned in the CSR.
2. Patterson's Rangers is mentioned in *Saddle Soldiers* as one of the few active cavalry organizations left to guard the South Carolina coast in March 1864, when most of the other organizations were transferred to Virginia. The possibility exists, however, that it was neither a South Carolina unit nor part of a militia or reserve force.[1] No Captain Patterson appears in either the CSR for South Carolina cavalry units or the *Official Records* for March 1864.
3. The Spartan Rangers, commanded by Captain Thomas Hall, was in the process of organizing in January 1861.[2] It may have failed to organize completely, or, instead, it could have been a militia unit since Hall's name does not appear in the CSR. Alternatively, the company may have been the predecessor of Company L, 3rd Regiment, South Carolina Cavalry. A company called the Seneca Rangers, commanded by Captain Thomas Hall, existed in early 1861.[3] It volunteered for service in the 4th Militia Regiment on January 3, 1861.[4] Whether or not the Spartan Rangers and the Seneca Rangers were the same company remains unclear.
4. A Home Guard of Cavalry in St. Paul's Parish at Adams Run existed in January 1861.[5] Since Hawkins S. King, its captain, is not listed in the CSR, the company was probably a militia unit.
5. The Newberry Chargers from Newberry District existed in February 1861.[6] No further information on this company appears in the record.
6. The Columbia Mounted Rifles was on duty in Charleston in April 1861.[7]
7. In June 1861, a Captain Lucas commanded a company of juveniles called the Lone Star Dragoons; it was probably a militia unit.[8]

8. The Ashepoo Guerillas, probably a militia company, was commanded by Charles Witsell, MD, in October 1861.[9]
9. The Black River Troop, commanded by W.J.N. Hammett, is listed in the index to the *Southern Historical Society Papers*, and Hammett's name appears as a sergeant in the Hampton Legion in the CSR. Hammett commanded the Black River Troop in the fall of 1860.[10]
10. The cavalry of the Western Battalion of the Sumter District South Carolina Militia, organized on July 25, 1863, elected South Carolina Senator F. J. Moses Jr. as its captain.[11] The Claremont Troop, probably the same unit, was a Sumter District militia company also called the Sumter Cavalry, South Carolina Militia. It was organized for home defense in November 1863 and was also commanded by Moses.[12] It is unlikely that this company and the Claremont Cavalry, Company A of the Holcombe Legion Cavalry Battalion, later Company I of the 7th Cavalry Regiment, were the same.
11. Captain Edward Avery commanded a company of boys under the age of eighteen in July 1863.[13] The company mustered in state service that month. When Avery's requests for active field service were denied, the company disbanded on January 1, 1864.[14] Avery is not listed in the CSR.
12. The Spartan Troop of Spartan Village was created by the General Assembly on January 28, 1861, and was attached to the Upper Battalion of the 9th Regiment, 5th Brigade, South Carolina Cavalry Militia.[15]
13. The South Carolina Executive Council authorized the creation of a company called the Combahee Rangers and accepted it for police duty and state service on May 26, 1862. Its captain was T.J. Allen.[16]
14. The Richland Rangers, which existed before the war, was commanded by Colonel R. Anderson, probably Richard Anderson who was elected lieutenant colonel of the 15th Infantry Regiment in September 1861. Its men tendered their services to the governor in January 1861, and they also offered themselves to the Confederacy. Although the company existed in April 1861 and was in Columbia the following October, any further activity is unknown.[17] It probably disbanded in the fall of 1861.
15. The Anderson Troop, commanded by Captain John W. Guyton, volunteered for service in the 4th Militia Regiment on January 3, 1861.[18]
16. The Mountain Cavalry, commanded by Captain Miles M. Norton, was in the 1st Regiment (probably the 1st Regiment, South Carolina Militia) in January 1861. Norton was later captain of Company E, Orr's Rifles.[19]

17. The Saluda Rangers, also called the Saluda Sentinels, existed in January 1861. Its captain was A.D. Bates.[20]
18. The Jefferson Nullifiers, which existed in February 1861, was commanded by Captain John F. Talbert.[21] The company, probably from Edgefield District, was disbanded at some point before September 4.[22] Governor Pickens ordered the company to return its arms by September 30. In 1862 and 1863, Talbert commanded Company F, 5th Regiment Reserves.
19. The Little River Rangers, commanded by Captain James L. Boyd, existed as a Home Defense Company in June 1861.[23]
20. The Salem Mounted Men, a Home Guard Company in Sumter District, commanded by Captain William Harris, existed in August and September 1863.[24]
21. Farmer's Rangers was commanded by Claus Volmer, who was elected captain on January 16, 1865.[25] Volmer served as first sergeant in the German Hussars when it was part of the South Carolina Militia earlier in the war.
22. Companies existing in Abbeville in April 1861 were: the Abbeville Light Infantry under Captain James C. Calhoun, the Mounted Minute Men under Captain J. Wardlaw Perrin, the Abbeville Squadron and the Southern Rights Dragoons.[26]

Appendix 3

Artillery Organizations with Unknown Regimental or Battalion Affiliations

1. Wood's Battery was based on the Black River. Whether it was a militia battery, a South Carolina battery called by an unrecognized name or, possibly, not a South Carolina battery at all, remains unclear.
2. There may have been a Captain Daniell or Daniell's Battery.
3. The McDuffie Artillery was probably a prewar militia organization from Newberry.
4. Moore's Battery was at Coosawhatchie in November 1861. We do not know if it was a militia battery, a South Carolina battery called by an unrecognized name or if it was not a South Carolina battery at all.
5. Thomas's Battery was engaged briefly at Columbia on February 15, 1865. It is described as "a small two-gun battery armed with obsolescent six pounders, which guarded the Congaree River Bridge at the foot of Gervais Street."[1] It was almost certainly manned by The Arsenal Cadets under the command of John Peyre Thomas.[2]
6. Nelson's Battery was engaged at Pocotaligo on October 22, 1862.[3] A Lieutenant Massie commanded the Nelson Light Artillery in January 1864.[4] It was probably a battery from Virginia.
7. Crenshaw's Battery was probably not a South Carolina battery.
8. The Camden Artillery Company was commanded by Captain A.W. Thames in June 1861.[5] Once again, it may have been a militia battery, a South Carolina battery called by an unrecognized name or one that was never accepted into service and was disbanded.
9. The Fairfield Artillery was commanded by Captain S.M. Smart, who was elected captain on September 14, 1861.[6] Whether this battery was a militia battery, a South Carolina battery called by an unrecognized name or a company that was never accepted into service and was disbanded is unclear.

10. From the fall of 1861 to December 1861, the Star Battery existed as a forty-man detachment of the 5th Regiment, South Carolina Infantry. It had two cannon detached from the Calhoun Artillery, probably indicating that it was Company A, Calhoun's Company, of the 1st Battalion, South Carolina Artillery (Regulars). The Star Battery was commanded by Lieutenant F.G. Latham of Company G.[7]
11. The Georgetown Artillery, also called Henning's Battery and the Georgetown Artillery Company, was commanded by Captain James G. Henning. This was a militia battery composed of older men of the community, many of whom had sons in Company A—the Georgetown Rifle Guards of the 10th Regiment, SCV. The General Assembly incorporated the battery on January 28, 1861.[8] That summer it participated in a brief expedition up the Waccamaw River with Company A of the 10th Regiment.[9] Although available for service, the battery had not been called up by late 1861 and early 1862.[10]

Appendix 4

Company Nicknames

1st Regiment, Infantry (Regulars) after May 1861

Company D, the Calhoun Light Infantry, Company K, Rivers's Battery

The 1st Regiment, South Carolina Volunteers (Hagood's)

Following are the companies that mustered in Confederate service on August 22, 1861:

Company A, the Edisto Rifles
Company B, the Jamison Guards
Company C, the Glover Guards
Company D, the St. Matthews Rifles or the Keitt Guards
Company E, the Allen Guards, later the Wee Nee Volunteers
Company G, the Johnson Guards
Company I, the Republican Blues, later the Pickens Sentinels and the Buford's Bridge Guards
Company K, the Bamberg Guards

Following are the companies of Hagood's regiment created at the reorganization on April 12, 1862:

Company A, the Bamberg Guards
Company C, the Buford's Bridge Guards
Company D, the Waxhaw Guards
Company F, the Dixie Guards
Company H, the Winsmuth Guards

The 1st Regiment, South Carolina Volunteers (Six Months) and the 1st Regiment, South Carolina Infantry, Provisional Army (Gregg's)

Gregg's 1st (six-month) Regiment was made up of the following companies:

Company A, the Richland Rifles, the Richland Volunteer Rifle Company, the Richland Volunteer Rifles, the Richland Riflemen
Company B, the Darlington Guards
Company C, the Edgefield Rifles, the Edgefield Riflemen
Company D, the Abbeville Volunteers, the Abbeville Minute Men
Company E, the Union Volunteers, the Union District Volunteers
Company F, the Wee Nee Volunteers
Company G, the Hamburg Volunteers, the Hamburg Company, the Hamburg Minute Men
Company H, the Cherokee Pond Volunteers, the Cherokee Pond Guards, the Meriwether Guards
Company I, the Monticello Guards, the Fairfield Volunteers, the Monticello Volunteers
Company K, the Marion Volunteers
Company L, the Rhett Guards
Company M, the Richardson Guard
Company N, the DeKalb Rifle Guards, the DeKalb Rifles, the DeKalb Guards, the Camden Rifle Guards
Company O, the Saluda Guard

Gregg's regiment, after the reorganization in the summer of 1861, was made up of the following companies:

Company A, the Gregg Guards
Company B, the Rhett Guards
Company C, the Richland Rifles, the Richland Volunteer Rifle Company
Company D, the Pee Dee Rifles
Company E, the Marion Rifles, the Marion Volunteers
Company F, the Horry Rebels, Horry Rifles
Company G, the Butler Sentinels, the Edgefield Company
Company H, Haskell's Rifle Corps, the Models
Company I, the Richardson Guards
Company K, the Irish Volunteers, the Irish Volunteers For The War
Company L, the Carolina Light Infantry Volunteers, the Carolina Light Infantry for the War, the Boy Company
Company M, the Furman Guards

THE 1ST REGIMENT, SOUTH CAROLINA RIFLES (ORR'S)

Company A, the Keowee Riflemen, the Keowee Rifles, the Keowee Volunteers, the Keowee Volunteer Company
Company B, the McDuffie Rifles, the McDuffie Guards
Company C, the Mountain Boys, the Pickens Boys
Company D, Orr's Rifles
Company E, the Oconee Riflemen, Oconee Rifles, the Mountain Cavalry, the Pickens Mountain Cavalry
Company F, the Blue Ridge Riflemen, the Blue Ridge Volunteers
Company G, the Marshall Riflemen, the Marshall Rifles, the Abbeville Riflemen
Company H, the PeeDee Guards
Company K, the Marshall Guards
Company L, the Calhoun Guards

THE 1ST REGIMENT, CHARLESTON (SOUTH CAROLINA) GUARDS

Company H, the Vigilant Rifles

THE 1ST (CHARLESTON) BATTALION, INFANTRY

Company A, the Charleston Riflemen
Company B, the Charleston Light Infantry
Company C, the Irish Volunteers
Company D, the Sumter Guards, the Sumter Guard Volunteers, the Gamecocks
Company E, the Calhoun Guards or Guard
Company F, the Union Light Infantry Volunteers, the Union Light Infantry Volunteers and German Fusiliers
Company G, the Charleston Light Infantry

THE 1ST BATTALION, SOUTH CAROLINA SHARPSHOOTERS

Company A, the Union Light Infantry and German Fusiliers
Company B, the Sumter Guards
Company C, the Charleston Sharpshooters, the Palmetto Guards

The 2nd Regiment, South Carolina Volunteers

Following are the six companies that refused to go to Virginia in May 1861:
The Claremont Rifles
The DeKalb Rifle Guards, the DeKalb Rifles, the DeKalb Guards
The Lancaster Grays, the Lancaster Greys
The Richland Guards
The Salem Company, the Chicora Guards
The States Rights Guards, the Fork Troop

The following ten companies made up the 2nd Regiment after it entered Confederate service in April 1861:
Company A, the Governor's Guards
Company B, the Butler Guards
Company C, the Columbia Grays, the Richland Grays, the Columbia Greys
Company D, the Sumter Volunteers
Company E, the Camden Volunteers, the Camden Light Infantry, the Kershaw Guards
Company F, the Secession Guards, Perryman's Company, the Abbeville Volunteers, the Abbeville Guards
Company G, the Flat Rock Guards
Company H, the Lancaster Invincibles, the Lancaster Volunteers, the Lancaster Guards
Company I, the Palmetto Guard or Guards
Company K, the Brooks Guard Volunteers, the Brooks Guards, Brooks Home Guards

The 3rd Regiment, South Carolina Volunteers

Company A, the State Guards, the State Guards Rifle Company, the Laurens Guards, the Garlington Rifles
Company B, the Williams Guard
Company C, the Pickens Guards, the Yahoo
Company D, the Cross Anchor Volunteers, the Cross Anchors
Company E, the Quitman Rifles, the Quitman Guard, the Quitman Riflemen, the Quitmans
Company F, the Wadsworth Guards, the Wadsworth Volunteers
Company G, the Briers, the Briars, the Laurens Briers, the Liars Briers

Company H, the Brooks Guards, the Brooks Palmetto Guards, the Dutch, the Dutch Fork Boys
Company I, the Musgrove Volunteers, the Musgrove Guards, the Clinton Company, the Clinton Divers
Company K, the Blackstock Volunteers, the Blackstock Company
No letter designation, the Helena Guard
No letter designation, Company Raiborn, Company Rabun

THE 3RD BATTALION, SOUTH CAROLINA INFANTRY

Company B, the Williams Company
Company E, the Hunter Guards
Company F, the Harper Rifles
Company G, the Aiken Guards

THE 4TH REGIMENT, SOUTH CAROLINA VOLUNTEERS

Company A, the Butler Guards, Hoke's Rifle Company
Company B, the Palmetto Riflemen, the Palmetto Rifles, Whitner's Rifle Company
Company C, Dean's Infantry Company
Company D, the Piercetown Guards, Long's Infantry Company
Company E, the Calhoun Mountaineers, the Calhoun Guards, Kilpatrick's Infantry Company
Company F, the Tyger Volunteers, Poole's Infantry Company
Company G, the Saluda Volunteers, Hawthorne's Infantry Company
Company H, the Twelve Mile Volunteers
Company I, the Pickens Guards, Hollingsworth's Infantry Company
Company J, the Confederate Guards, Ashmore's Infantry Company
Company K, the Fort Hill Guards, Shanklin's Company

THE 5TH REGIMENT, SOUTH CAROLINA VOLUNTEERS

The following companies of the 5th Regiment existed from early March 1861 until the regiment was reorganized and mustered in Confederate service on June 4, 1861:
Company A, the Johnson Rifles, Johnson Riflemen
Company B, the Pea Ridge Volunteers
Company C, the Batesville Volunteers

Company D, the Pacolet Guards
Company E, the Jasper Light Infantry
Company F, the Lawson's Fork Volunteers
Company G, the Kings Mountain Guard
Company H, the Catawba Light Infantry
Company I, the Morgan Light Infantry, the Morgan Rifles
Company J, the Whyte Guards, the "Wild Geese"
Company K, the Tyger Volunteers, Tyger River Volunteers, the Goshen Hill Volunteers
Company L, the Spartan Rifles

Following are the companies of the 5th Regiment existing from June 4, 1861, to April 13, 1862:
Company A, the Johnson Rifles or Riflemen
Company B, the Kings Mountain Guards
Company C, the Lawson's Fork Volunteers
Company D, the Tyger River Volunteers, Tyger Volunteers, the Goshen Hill Volunteers
Company E, the Pea Ridge Volunteers
Company F, the Morgan Light Infantry, Morgan Rifles
Company G, the Pacolet Guards, the Limestone Spring Company
Company H, the Catawba Light Infantry
Company I, the Jasper Light Infantry
Company K, the Spartan Rifles
The Star Battery

Following are those companies of the 5th Regiment existing from April 23, 1862, to the end of the war:
Company A, the Lancaster Greys, the Lancaster Grays
Company B, the Catawba Light Infantry
Company C, the Limestone Southern Rights Guards
Company D, the Tyger River Volunteers, Tyger Volunteers, the Goshen Hill Volunteers
Company E, the Turkey Creek Grays
Company F, the Kings Mountain Guards
Company H, the Pea Ridge Volunteers
Company K, the Lawson's Fork Volunteers

THE 6TH REGIMENT, SOUTH CAROLINA VOLUNTEERS

The following companies were originally attached to the 6th Regiment from its inception on February 8, 1861, until it mustered in Confederate service in June:
The Boyce Guards
The Buckhead Guards
The Calhoun Guards
The Catawba Guards
The Cedar Creek Rifle Company, the Cedar Creek Rifles
The Chester Blues
The Chester Guards
The Fairfield Fencibles
The Little River Guards
The Monticello Guards, the Fairfield Volunteers
The Pickens Guards

Following are the ten companies of the 6th Regiment after they mustered in Confederate service in June and July 1861:
Company A, the Calhoun Guard or Guards
Company B, the Catawba Guards, the Catawba Light Infantry
Company C, the Buckhead Guards
Company D, the Boyce Guards
Company E, the Chester Guards
Company F, the Chester Blues
Company G, the Pickens Guards
Company H, the York Volunteers, the York Guards, the York Guard
Company I, the Limestone Springs Infantry, the Limestone Light Infantry, the Limestone Guards
Company K, the Carolina Mountaineers

Following are the companies created at the reorganization in the spring of 1862:
Company A, the Catawba Guards, Catawba Light Infantry
Company B, the Alston Riflemen
Company F, the Chester Blues
Company G, the Boyce Guards
Company H, the Buckhead Guards
Company I, the Chester Guards
Company K, the Dixie Guards

Manigault's Battalion South Carolina Volunteers

Company A, the St. James Santee Mounted Riflemen, the Mounted Rifles Company, Captain Thomas Pinckney's Company, Thomas Pinckney's Independent Mounted Riflemen
Company B, the Santee Light Artillery, Gaillard's Company of Light Artillery
Company C, the Trenholm Rifles, the Infantry Company–Trenholm Rifles, the Palmer Rifles
Company D, the Infantry Company–Chesnut Guards
Company E, the Kickapoo Riflemen

The 6th Battalion South Carolina Infantry

Company B, the Chesnut Guards
Company C, the Kickapoo Riflemen
Santee Light Artillery
St. James Santee Mounted Riflemen

The 7th Regiment, South Carolina Volunteers

Following are the companies of the 7th Regiment from its enlistment in state service in April 1861 until the reorganization in May 1862:
Company A, the Secession Guards, Perryman's Company, the Abbeville Volunteers, the Abbeville Guards
Company B, the Southern Guards, the Cokesbury Minutemen
Company D, Hester's Company
Company E, the Mount Willing Guards
Company F, the Davies Guard, Davies Guards, the Graniteville Riflemen
Company G, the Brooks Greys
Company H, the Ninety Six Rifles
Company I, the Red Hill Guard
Company K, the Ruffin Guards
Company L, the Horry Volunteers, the Horry Guards, the All Saints Riflemen, the All Saints Rifles

Following are the companies of the 7th Regiment after the reorganization in May 1862:
Company A, the Ninety Six Riflemen
Company B, the Southern Guards, Cokesbury Minutemen
Company E, the Mount Willing Guards
Company F, the Davies Guards
Company G, the Brooks Greys
Company H, the Ninety Six Rifles
Company I, the Red Hill Guard
Company K, the Ruffin Guards
Company L, the Horry Volunteers
Company M, the Saluda Riflemen

THE 7TH BATTALION, SOUTH CAROLINA INFANTRY

Company A, the Lucas Guards
Company B, the Lyles Rifles
Company C, the McCullough Rifles
Company D, the Kershaw Grays or Greys
Company F, the Lucas Rifles
Company G, the Moffatt Rifles
Company H, the Joe Johnston Rifles, the Johnston Rifles, the Partisan Rangers, the Brooks Infantry Partisan Rifles

THE 8TH REGIMENT, SOUTH CAROLINA VOLUNTEERS

Company A, the Darlington Rifleman
Company B, the Chesterfield Rifles
Company C, the Chesterfield Guards
Company D, the Jackson Guards
Company E, the Timmonsville Minute Men
Company F, the Darlington Grays
Company G, the Marlboro Guards, the Marlborough Guards
Company H, the Jeffries Creek Company, the Jeffries Volunteers
Company I, the Marion Guards
Company K, the McQueen Guards
Company L, the Spartan Band

THE 9TH REGIMENT, SOUTH CAROLINA VOLUNTEERS

Company A, the Lancaster Greys
Company B, the States Right Guards, the Fork Troop
Company C, the Clarendon Blues
Company D, the Chicora Guards, the Salem Company
Company E, the Kershaw Troop
Company F, the Sumter Grays
Company G, the Hartsville Light Infantry
Company H, the Blanding Blues
Company I, the Cowpens Guards or Guard, the Cowpens Cavalry
Company K, the Pickens Sentinels
Unlettered, the Clarendon Volunteers, Clarendon Riflemen, Clarendon Rifles

THE 9TH BATTALION, SOUTH CAROLINA INFANTRY

Company A, the Bull Creek Guerillas, the Bull Creek Rangers
Company C, the Irby Rifles
Company D, the Watchesaw Rifles, the Wachitaw Rifles
Company E, the Chesterfield Eagles
Company G, the Eutaw Rifles, the Floyd Guerillas

THE 10TH REGIMENT, SOUTH CAROLINA VOLUNTEERS

Companies attached to the 10th Regiment in early 1861:
Original Company D, the Wee Nee Volunteers, the Williamsburg Company
Original Company G, the Coast Guards
Original Company I, the Carver's Bay Palmetto Rifle Guards, the Carver's Bay Sharpshooters
Joshua Ward's Artillery Company, Mayham Ward's Company, South Carolina Light Artillery
The North Santee Mounted Rifles
The Sampit Rangers

Following are the twelve companies of the 10th Regiment after it mustered in Confederate service in August 1861:
Company A, the Georgetown Rifle Guards
Company B, the Brooks Guards, Brooks Rifle Guards

Company C, the Lake Swamp Volunteers
Company D, the Marion Volunteers
Company E, the Black Mingo Rifle Guards, Black Mingo Riflemen
Company F, the Pee Dee Rangers
Company G, the Horry Rough and Readys
Company H, the Liberty Volunteers
Company I, the Swamp Fox Guards
Company K, the Eutaw Volunteers
Company L, the Liberty Guards
Company M, the Horry Dixie Boys, the Horry Volunteers

The 11th Regiment, South Carolina Volunteers

Company A, the Beaufort Volunteer Artillery
Company B, the Calhoun Artillery, the St. Paul's Rifles
Company C, the Summerville Guards
Company D, the Whippy Swamp Guard
Company E, the Hamilton Guards or Guard
Company F, the Republican Blues, the Yemassee Volunteers
Company G, the Butler Guards, Butler Rifles
Company H, the St. George Volunteers, St. George's Volunteers
Company I, the Colleton Rifles
Company K, the Eutaw Volunteers
Bellinger's Company–the Colleton Guard, Colleton Rifles
Sheridan's Company–the Round O Guards

The 11th Battalion, South Carolina Infantry

The Beauregard Light Infantry
The Edisto Rifles
The Marion Light Infantry
The Ripley Guards, Gordon's Company
The St. Matthews Rifles, or Riflemen
The Washington Light Infantry, Company A
The Washington Light Infantry, Company B
The Wee Nee Volunteers, the Williamsburg Company
The Yeadon Light Infantry

THE 12TH REGIMENT, SOUTH CAROLINA VOLUNTEERS

Company A, the Palmer Guards
Company B, the Campbell Rifles, the Sevier Rifles, the Rock Hill Campbell Riflemen
Company C, the Cedar Creek Rifles
Company D, the Richland Guards
Company E, the Blair Guards
Company F, the Means Light Infantry, the Long Run Company, the Monticello Guards
Company G, the Bonham Rifles Volunteers, the Bonham Rifles, the Confederate Guards
Company H, the Indian Land Guards
Company I, the Lancaster Hornets
Company K, the Grisham Rifles
Unlettered, the Lancaster Guards

THE 13TH REGIMENT, SOUTH CAROLINA VOLUNTEERS

Company A, the Martin Guards
Company B, the Brockman Guards
Company C, the Forest Rifles, the Forest Guards
Company D, the Newberry Riflemen
Company E, the Cherokee Guards
Company F, the Pacolet Volunteers, Pacolet Guards
Company G, the DeKalb Guards
Company H, the Hope Guards
Company I, the Iron District Volunteers
Company K, the Johnson Rifles, Johnson Riflemen

THE 14TH REGIMENT, SOUTH CAROLINA VOLUNTEERS

Company A, the Lynch Creek Guards
Company B, the Dearing Guards
Company C, Company Raiborn
Company D, the Edgefield Rifles, the Confederate Light Guards
Company E, the Enoree Mosquitoes, the Enoree Rifles
Company F, the Carolina Bees, the South Carolina Bees
Company G, the McGowan Greys, Captain Jay's Company

Company H, Ryan's Guards, the Ryan Guard
Company I, the McCalla Rifles
Company K, the Meeting Street Saludas

The 15th Regiment, South Carolina Volunteers

Company A, the Columbia Rifles
Company B, the Gist Guards
Company C, the Lexington Rifles, the Lexington Guards
Company D, the Kershaw Guards
Company E, the Monticello Guards
Company F, the Thicketty Rifles
Company G, the Williamsburg Riflemen
Company H, the Mount Tabor Company, the Pinckney Guards
Company I, the Dutch Fork Guards
Company K, the Dorn Volunteers, the Dorn Invincibles, the Independent Guards

The 16th Regiment, South Carolina Volunteers

Company A, the Mountain Rebels, the Reedy Rifles
Company C, the Croft Mountain Rangers
Company D, the Elford Guards
Company E, the McCullough Lions
Company K, the Goodlett Guard, the Buttermilk Rangers, the Greenville Guard

The 17th Regiment, South Carolina Volunteers

Company C, the Defenders of Right, the Broad River Light Infantry
Company D, the Palmetto Rifles, the Palmettoes
Company E, the Indian Land Tigers, the Indian Land Rifles, the York Rangers
Company F, the Carolina Rifles
Company I, the Lancaster Tigers
Company K, the Lacy Guards

THE 18TH REGIMENT, SOUTH CAROLINA VOLUNTEERS

Company A, the Unionville Rifles
Company B, the Union District Volunteers, the York Rangers
Company C, the Cross Keys Company
Company G, the Mountain Guards
Company H, the Bethel Rifles
Company I, the Darlington Rifles
Company K, the Broad River Guards

THE 19TH REGIMENT, SOUTH CAROLINA VOLUNTEERS

Company B, the Lamar Guards
Company C, the Dorn Guards

THE 20TH REGIMENT, SOUTH CAROLINA VOLUNTEERS

Company C, the Evans Guards
Company D, the Bull Swamp Guards
Company F, the Kinard Phalanx
Company G, the Spring Hill Volunteers
Company I, the Edisto Guards
Company K, the Lexington Volunteer Rifle Company, the Lexington Riflemen Company L, the Ripley Rangers
Company M, Keitt's Company Mounted Riflemen, the Mounted Riflemen
Company N, the Peterkin Rangers
Company O, Venning's Company
Buist's Company Light Artillery

THE 21ST REGIMENT, SOUTH CAROLINA VOLUNTEERS

Company B, The Wilds Rifles
Company C, the Clarendon Guards
Company D, the Cheraw Guards
Company F, the Thomas Guards
Company G, the Williams Guards
Company K, the Timmonsville Minutemen

THE 22ND REGIMENT, SOUTH CAROLINA VOLUNTEERS

Company A, the Edgefield Riflemen, the Edgefield Reserves, the Edgefield Blues, the Confederate Light Guards
Company B, the Cedar Hill Guards
Company C, the Chapel Guards
Company D, the Hopewell Guards
Company E, the Lancaster Guards
Company F, the Hagood Guards

THE 23RD REGIMENT, SOUTH CAROLINA VOLUNTEERS

Company A, the Bee Rifles
Company B, the Chicora Rifles
Company C, the Johnson Rifles or Riflemen
Company D, the Duryea Guards, Duryea Coast Guard
Company E, the Marion Blues, the Marion Rifles
Company F, the Chester Grays
Company G, the Douglass Rifles
Company H, the Roberts Guards
Company I, the Sprott Guards
Company K, the Lee Guard

THE 24TH REGIMENT, SOUTH CAROLINA VOLUNTEERS

Company A, the Marion Rifles
Company B, the Pee Dee Rifles
Company C, M.T. Appleby's Company
Company D, the Evans Guard
Company E, the Colleton Guard
Company F, Hill's Company
Company G, Pearson's Company
Company H, Thomas's Company
Company I, the Edgefield Light Infantry, the Edgefield Guard
Company K, Tompkins's Company

THE 25TH REGIMENT, SOUTH CAROLINA VOLUNTEERS

Company A, the Washington Light Infantry, Company A
Company B, the Washington Light Infantry, Company B
Company C, the Wee Nee Volunteers
Company D, the Marion Light Infantry
Company E, the Beauregard Light Infantry
Company F, the St. Matthews Rifles or Riflemen
Company G, the Edisto Rifles
Company H, the Yeadon Light Infantry
Company I, the Clarendon Guards
Company K, the Ripley Guards

THE 26TH REGIMENT, SOUTH CAROLINA VOLUNTEERS

Company A, the Bull Creek Guerillas
Company D, the Irby Rifles
Company E, the Watchesaw Rifles
Company F, the Chesterfield Eagles
Company H, the Chesnut Guards
Company I, the Kickapoo Riflemen
Company K, the Eutaw Rifles, the Floyd Guerillas

THE 27TH REGIMENT, SOUTH CAROLINA VOLUNTEERS

Company A, the Calhoun Guards or Guard
Company B, the Charleston Light Infantry
Company C, the Union Light Infantry Volunteers
Company D, the Sumter Guards, the Sumter Guard Volunteers, the Gamecocks
Company E, the Union Light Infantry and German Fusiliers
Company F, the Sumter Guards
Company G, the Charleston Sharpshooters, the Palmetto Guard
Company H, the Irish Volunteers
Company I, the Charleston Riflemen
Company K, the Charleston Light Infantry

THE HAMPTON LEGION

Infantry Battalion

Company A, the Washington Light Infantry, the Washington Light Infantry Volunteers
Company B, the Watson Guards
Company C, the Manning Guards or Guard
Company D, the Gist Rifles, the Gist Guards, the Gist Riflemen
Company E, the Bozeman Guards
Company F, the Davis Guards
Company G, the Claremont Rifles
Company H, the German Artillery Volunteers, the South Carolina Zouaves

Cavalry Battalion

Company A, the Edgefield Hussars, the Edgefield Huzzars, the Edgefield Dragoons
Company B, the Brooks Troop, the Brooks Guards, the Brooks Dragoons, the University Riflemen
Company C, the Beaufort District Troop, the Beaufort Dragoons
Company D, the Congaree Troop, the Congaree Mounted Riflemen, Congaree Mounted Rifles, the Congaree Mounted Infantry, the Richland Light Dragoons

Artillery Battalion

Battery A, the Washington Artillery Volunteers, the Washington Mounted Artillery, the Washington Artillery for Confederate service, Lee's Battery, Hampton Horse Artillery
Company B, the German Artillery, the German Light Artillery, the German Flying Artillery, the German Volunteers, Hampton Legion, Bachman's Battery

THE HOLCOMBE LEGION

Infantry Battalion

Company A, Smith's Riflemen, the Palmetto Riflemen
Company B, the Batesville Volunteers
Company C, the Morgan Rifles
Company D, the Stevens Guards

Company E, the Spartan Guards
Company F, the Ripley Rifles
Company H, the Frog Level Scouts
Company I, the Fort Prince Guards
Company K, the Lucas Guards
Unlettered, the Stevens Light Infantry

Cavalry Battalion

Company A, the Claremont Cavalry
Company B, the Congaree Mounted Guard, the Congaree Mounted Riflemen, the Congaree Cavaliers
Company C, the Newberry Rangers, the Palmetto Light Dragoons
Company D, the McKissick Rangers, McKissick's Rangers
Company E, the Kirkwood Rangers, the Kirkwood Cavalry, the Kirkwood South Carolina Cavalry, The Kirkwoods, the Camden Rangers

The Palmetto Sharpshooters

Company A, the Johnson Rifles
Company B, the Calhoun Mountaineers
Company C, the Palmetto Riflemen
Company D, the Morgan Light Infantry
Company E, the Darlington Sentinels
Company F, the Pickens Sentinels
Company G, the Jasper Light Infantry
Company H, the Cowpens Guards
Company I, the Pickens Guards
Company K, the Spartan Rifles
Company L, the Confederate Guards
Company M, the Pacolet Guards

The Battalion of South Carolina State Cadets, Local Defense Troops

Company A, The Citadel Cadets
Company B, The Arsenal Cadets

THE SOUTH CAROLINA COLLEGE CADETS

The South Carolina College Cadets, the College Cadets, the Third Cadet Company, the Stevens Light Infantry

CAPTAIN RHETT'S COMPANY, SOUTH CAROLINA

Captain Rhett's Company, the Brooks Home Guards, the Brooks Guards

CAPTAIN JOHN SYMONS'S COMPANY, NAVAL BRIGADE, SOUTH CAROLINA VOLUNTEERS

The Sea Fencibles

HARLEE'S LEGION, SOUTH CAROLINA MILITIA

The Black River Rangers
The Williamsburg Light Dragoons

CAPTAIN L.H. CHARBONNIER'S COMPANY, SOUTH CAROLINA MILITIA

The Pickens Rifles, the Pickens Guard, the Pickens Cadets

SHIVER'S COMPANY–LOCAL DEFENSE TROOPS, SOUTH CAROLINA

The Rebel Guards

THE FIRE COMPANIES OF CHARLESTON

The Aetna Fire Company, the Aetna Rifles, the Aetna Guard
The Phoenix Fire Company, the Phoenix Rifles
The Vigilant Fire Engine Company, the Vigilant Rifles, Vigilant Light Infantry

THE (COLUMBIA) VOLUNTEER BATTALION

The Cedar Creek Riflemen
The Columbia Artillery
The Emmett Guards
The Governor's Guards
The Richland Volunteer Rifle Company

1ST REGIMENT CHARLESTON RESERVES, SOUTH CAROLINA MILITIA

Company A, the Hibernian Guard
Company B, the Charleston Home Guard
Company C, the Pickens Rifles

THE 7TH REGIMENT RESERVES (90 DAYS 1862–1863)

Company B, the Rocky Creek Troop

THE 9TH REGIMENT RESERVES (90 DAYS 1862–1863)

Company K, the Yemassee Volunteers

THE 2ND BATTALION SOUTH CAROLINA RESERVES

Company C, the Spartan Rangers, the Spartanburg Rangers, the Spartan Rangers Independent Cavalry-Reserves
Company H, Captain Kay's Detachment, South Carolina Mounted Reserves the Palmetto Mounted Infantry

THE 8TH BATTALION SOUTH CAROLINA RESERVES

Company B, the Confederate Reserve Corps of Colleton District

2nd Regiment, Junior Reserves, South Carolina State Troops

Company B, the Saluda Company

3rd Regiment, Junior Reserves, South Carolina State Troops

Company K, the Bonham Guards

4th Regiment, Junior Reserves, South Carolina State Troops

Company B, the Union Laddies

South Carolina Militia Units-Cavalry

The 1st Regiment, South Carolina Mounted Militia
The Allendale Mounted Guard
The Beaufort District Guerillas, the Coosawhatchie Guerillas
The Beech Hill Rangers
The Bluffton Troop, the May River Troop
The Calhoun Minute Men
The Charleston Mounted Guard
The Colleton Rangers
The Dorchester Guerillas
The Etiwan Rangers
The Grey Riders of St. Bartholomew Parish, the Colleton Grey Riders, the Walterboro Home Guard
The Hardeeville Guerillas
The Marion Men of Combahee
The Marion Troop, the Marion Rangers, the Marion Scouts
The May River Troop, the Bluffton Troop
The Palmetto Hussars
The Palmetto Rangers
The Parish Mounted Rangers, the Parish Rangers
The Pickens Rangers
The Red Oak Rangers

The Salkehatchie Guerillas, the Saltketcher Guerillas
The Savannah River Guards
The South Carolina Rangers
The St. Helena Mounted Rifles, St. Helena Volunteer Mounted Riflemen
The St. Paul Home Guard, St. Paul Mounted Men
The St. Paul Rangers
The St. Peter's Guards

The 4th Regiment, South Carolina Militia

The Beaufort District Troop, Beaufort Troop
The Charleston Light Dragoons
The Combahee Troop, the Combahee Rangers
The German Hussars
The Hammond Huzzars, or Hussars, the Evans Light Dragoons
The Marion Troop
The McDonald Troop
The Palmetto Troop
The Wassamassaw Troop

The 1st Regiment Artillery, South Carolina Militia

Company A of the German Artillery Battalion
Company B of the German Artillery, the German Flying Artillery
The Lafayette Artillery
The Marion Artillery
The Rutledge Mounted Riflemen
The Vigilant Fire Engine Company, the Vigilant Rifles, Vigilant Light Infantry
The Washington Artillery of Charleston

The 1st Regiment Rifles, South Carolina Militia

The Beauregard Light Infantry
The Carolina Light Infantry
The Chichester Zouaves, the Charleston Zouave Cadets, the Zouave Cadets

The German Riflemen
The Jamison (or Jamieson) Riflemen
The Meagher Guards, the Emerald Light Infantry
The Moultrie Guard or Guards
The Palmetto Riflemen
The Pickens Rifles
The Sarsfield Light Infantry
The Washington Light Infantry, the Washingtons

The 1st Regiment, South Carolina Militia

Piney Mountain Company
The Saluda Battalion
The Tyger Battalion

The 5th Regiment, South Carolina Militia

The Pickensville Silver Greys

The 7th Regiment, South Carolina Militia

The Edgefield Riflemen

The 13th Regiment, South Carolina Militia

The Colleton Rifle Corps, the Colleton Rifle Company
The Palmetto Volunteers
The St. Paul's Rifles

The 15th Regiment, South Carolina Militia

The Lexington Rifle Company

THE 16TH REGIMENT, SOUTH CAROLINA MILITIA

The Jackson Guard
The Marion Rifles
The Pickens Rifles, Pickens Guards

THE 17TH REGIMENT, SOUTH CAROLINA MILITIA

The Brooks Guards or Brooks Home Guards
The Cadet Rifles or Riflemen
The Calhoun Guards or Guard
The Charleston Riflemen
The Emmet Volunteers
The German Fusiliers
The Highland Guards
The Irish Volunteers
The Jasper Greens
The Montgomery Guard or Guards
The Palmetto Guard
The Phoenix Rifles or Riflemen
The Richardson Guard
The South Carolina College Cadets
The Sumter Guards, the Gamecocks
The Union Light Infantry

THE 18TH REGIMENT, SOUTH CAROLINA MILITIA

Company E, the Dorchester Company
The Goose Creek Company

THE 26TH REGIMENT, SOUTH CAROLINA MILITIA

The Calhoun Guards
The Chester Rifles

The 33rd Regiment, South Carolina Militia

The All Saints Riflemen, All Saints Rifles
Blantons Cross Roads Volunteers
Bull Creek Rangers
The Carolina Greys
Conwayboro Palmetto Guards
Cool Springs Home Guard
Dog Bluff Home Guards
Floyd Guerillas
Waccamaw Guerillas
The Waccamaw Light Artillery
Wachitaw Rifles
The Watchesaw Riflemen

The 36th Regiment, South Carolina Militia

The Johnson Volunteers
Lawson's Fork Volunteers
The Morgan Rifles
Pacolet Volunteers
The Spartanburg Light Infantry

The 1st Battalion/1st Regiment, South Carolina Cavalry

Company A, the Abbeville Troop
Company B, the Ferguson Rangers, the Spartanburg and Laurens Rangers, the Enoree Rangers
Company C, the Edgefield and Barnwell Rangers, the Edgefield Rangers
Company D, the Chester Troop
Company E, the Fort Motte Rangers
Company F, the Allen Hussars
Company G, L.J. Johnson's Cavalry
Company H, Robin Jones's Cavalry
Company I, the Round O Troop

THE 2ND REGIMENT, SOUTH CAROLINA CAVALRY

Company A, the Boykin Rangers, the Hampton Scouts, Boykin's Independent Company, South Carolina Cavalry, the Mounted Rangers, the Independent Mounted Rangers
Company B, the Beaufort District Troop, Beaufort Dragoons
Company C, the Congaree Rangers
Company D, the Wassamassaw Cavalry, Wassa Massaw Rangers
Company E, Dean's Company
Company G, the Bonham Light Dragoons, Lipscomb's Troop
Company H, the Congaree Troop, the Congaree Mounted Riflemen or Rifles, the Congaree Mounted Infantry, the Richland Light Dragoons
Company I, the Edgefield Hussars, the Edgefield Dragoons
Company K, the Brooks Troop, the Brooks Guards, the Brooks Dragoons

THE 2ND BATTALION CAVALRY, SOUTH CAROLINA RESERVES

Company B, the Marion Men of Combahee
Company F, the Savannah River Guard or Guards
The Ashley Dragoons or Ashley Rangers
The Barnwell Dragoons
The Beaufort District Troop
The Calhoun Minute Men, Calhoun Mounted Men
The Colleton Rangers
The Spartan Rangers

THE 3RD REGIMENT, SOUTH CAROLINA CAVALRY

Company A, the Marion Men of Combahee
Company B, the Colleton Rangers
Company C, the Beaufort District Troop
Company C, Captain John H. Howard's Company
Company D, the Barnwell Dragoons
Company E, the Calhoun Minute, Calhoun Mounted Men
Company F, the St. Peter's Guards
Company G, the German Hussars
Company H, the Ashley Dragoons, Ashley Rangers

Company I, the Rebel Troop
Company K, the Savannah River Guards or Guard
Johnson's Section of Horse Artillery, Johnson's Mounted Artillery, Colcock's Light Artillery, Colcock's Section Light Artillery

THE 3RD BATTALION, SOUTH CAROLINA CAVALRY

Company B, the Congaree Rangers
Company D, the Wassamassaw Cavalry, Wassa Massaw Rangers

THE 4TH REGIMENT, SOUTH CAROLINA CAVALRY

Company A, the Chesterfield Light Dragoons
Company B, the Palmetto Rangers
Company C, the Calhoun Troop
Company D, St. James Mounted Riflemen, Company A
Company E, previously Company C of the 12th Battalion, South Carolina Cavalry
Company F, the E.M. Dragoons
Company G, the Evans Light Dragoons
Company H, the Catawba Rangers
Company I, the Williamsburg Light Dragoons
Company K, the Charleston Light Dragoons

THE 5TH REGIMENT, SOUTH CAROLINA CAVALRY

Company A, the St. Matthews Troop
Company B, the Dixie Rangers
Company C, the Beech Hill Rangers
Company D, the South Carolina Rangers, Carolina Rangers
Company E, the St. James Mounted Riflemen, Company B
Company F, the Lexington Light Dragoons
Company G, the Willington Rangers
Company H, the Santee Guerillas, Santee Rangers
Company K, the Mountain Rangers

THE 6TH REGIMENT, SOUTH CAROLINA CAVALRY

Company A, the Carolina Guerrillas
Company B, the Edgefield Rangers, the Edgefield Partisan Rangers
Company E, the Laurens Partizans
Company F, the Cadet Company, the Cadet Troop, the Cadet Rangers, The Citadel Troop
Company H, the Yeadon Rangers

THE 7TH REGIMENT, SOUTH CAROLINA CAVALRY

Company A, the Marion Men of Winyah, Company A
Company B, the Rutledge Mounted Riflemen
Company C, the McKissick Rangers, McKissick's Rangers
Company D, the Congaree Mounted Guard, the Congaree Mounted Riflemen, the Congaree Cavaliers
Company E, the Newberry Rangers, the Palmetto Light Dragoons
Company F, the Marion Men of Winyah, Company B
Company G, the Rutledge Mounted Riflemen
Company H, the Kirkwood Rangers, the Kirkwood Cavalry, the Kirkwood South Carolina Cavalry, the Kirkwoods, the Camden Rangers
Company I, the Claremont Cavalry
Company K, the Wateree Mounted Rifles, Boykin's Company Mounted Rifles, the Boykin Rangers

THE 10TH BATTALION, SOUTH CAROLINA CAVALRY

Company A, the Palmetto Rangers
Company B, the Calhoun Troop
Company C, the Evans Light Dragoons
Company D, the Catawba Rangers, the Lancaster Troop, the Lancaster Cavalry, the Catawba Guards

THE 12TH BATTALION, SOUTH CAROLINA CAVALRY

Company A, the Chesterfield Light Dragoons
Company B, the Williamsburg Light Dragoons
Company D, the E.M. Dragoons
The Waccamaw Light Artillery

THE 14TH BATTALION, SOUTH CAROLINA CAVALRY

Company A, the Santee Guerillas, Santee Rangers
Company B, the St. Matthews Troop
Company C, the Light Dragoons

THE 16TH BATTALION, SOUTH CAROLINA CAVALRY

Company A, the Carolina Guerrillas
Company B, the Edgefield Rangers, the Edgefield Partisan Rangers
Company E, the Laurens Partizans
Company F, the Cadet Company, the Cadet Troop, the Cadet Rangers

THE 17TH BATTALION, SOUTH CAROLINA CAVALRY

Company A, the South Carolina Rangers, Carolina Rangers
Company B, the Willington Rangers
Company C, the Dixie Rangers
Company D, the Beech Hill Rangers

THE 19TH BATTALION, SOUTH CAROLINA CAVALRY

Company A, Kirk's Company, South Carolina Partisan Rangers, the May River Troop
Company B, Captain E.S. Keitt's Company Mounted Riflemen, South Carolina Volunteers
Company C, Kirk's Squadron of Partisan Rangers, Company B
Company D, Captain J.J. Steele's Company
Company E, the Ripley Rangers

INDEPENDENT CAVALRY ORGANIZATIONS

Captain Manning J. Kirk's Company, South Carolina Partisan Rangers, Kirk's Partisan Rangers, the May River Troop
The Etiwan Rangers
The German Hussars
Keitt's Mounted Riflemen

The North Santee Mounted Rifles
The Pickens Rangers, the Aiken Mounted Infantry
The Ripley Rangers
The Stono Scouts, Stono Rangers

The 1st Battalion/1st Regiment, South Carolina Artillery Regulars

Company A, the Sumter Battery, the Calhoun Battery, the Calhoun Artillery, the Calhoun Flying Artillery, the Light Battery
Company B, the Brooks Flying Artillery

The 2nd Battalion/2nd Regiment, South Carolina Artillery

Company C, the Edisto Artillery
Company D, the Inglis Light Artillery
Company E, the Allen Guards
Company F, the Carolina Artillery
Company G, the Silverton Artillery
Company I, the Orangeburg Artillery

The 3rd Battalion, South Carolina Light Artillery

Company A, the Furman Artillery, Earle's Battery Light Artillery
Company B, the Columbia Flying Artillery, the Columbia Artillery, the Blake Artillery
Company C, the Wilson Light Artillery, Culpeper's Light Battery
Company D, the Wagner Light Artillery, Kanapaux's Light Artillery
Company E, the Yeadon Light Artillery
Company F, the Chesnut Light Artillery
Company G, the DeSaussure Light Artillery, the DePass Light Battery
Company I, Bowden's Battery Light Artillery
Company K, Richardson's Company

The 18th Battalion, South Carolina Artillery

The Beauregard Louisiana Artillery
The German Artillery, Company B
The Gist Guard, Gilchrist's Independent Company, South Carolina

Heavy Artillery
The Horry Light Artillery, the Alston Light Artillery
Mathewes's Artillery
The McQueen Light Artillery, Gregg's Battery
The Palmetto Guard Artillery, the Palmetto Guards, the Buist Light Artillery
The Pee Dee Artillery, McIntosh's Battery

INDEPENDENT ARTILLERY BATTERIES

The Beaufort Volunteer Artillery
Beauregard's Battery–South Carolina Artillery, T.B. Ferguson's Company, Light Artillery
Brooks Guard Battery Artillery, Captain Fickling's Company, South Carolina Artillery, Fickling's Battery–Brooks Light Artillery, South Carolina; Rhett's Company, Rhett–Fickling's Battery
The Calhoun Artillery
The Chesterfield Light Artillery
The German Artillery Battalion, SCV
The German Light Artillery, the German Flying Artillery, the Charleston German Artillery, Captain Bachman's Company, South Carolina Artillery–German Light Artillery, Captain William K. Bachman's Battery
The Gist Guard Light Artillery, Captain Gilchrist's Company–the Gist Guard-South Carolina Heavy Artillery, Robert C. Gilchrist's Company, South Carolina Heavy Artillery
The Lafayette Artillery, Kanapaux's Battery—Lafayette Light Artillery—South Carolina, the Lafayette Light Artillery
The Macbeth Light Artillery, Captain Jeter's Company, South Carolina Light Artillery, Robert Boyce's Company, South Carolina Light Artillery
The Marion Artillery, the Marion Light Artillery, SCV
The Mathewes Artillery, Captain Mathewes's Company, South Carolina Heavy Artillery, Mathewes's Battery, Mathewes's Independent Company, F.N. Bonneau's Company Artillery, SCV, Confederate States Provisional Army
The McQueen Light Artillery
The Palmetto Light Artillery, Captain Garden's Company—the Palmetto Light Battery—South Carolina Light Artillery, the Palmetto Light Battery; Garden's Battery, SCV, Confederate States Provisional Army
The Pee Dee Light Artillery, Captain Zimmerman's Company, the Pee Dee Artillery, South Carolina Artillery, Captain McIntosh's Battery, Captain McIntosh's Company Light Artillery, Captain Brunson's Company, South Carolina Light Artillery

The Santee Light Artillery, Captain Christopher Gaillard's Company, Light Artillery, SCV, Gaillard's Light Artillery
Stephen D. Lee's Battery–South Carolina Artillery
The Waccamaw Light Artillery, Captain Mayham Ward's Battery, Captain Joshua Ward's Company, South Carolina Light Artillery
The Washington Artillery, Captain George H. Walter's Company, South Carolina Light Artillery, Walter's Battery–the Washington Artillery, Walter's Company–the Washington Artillery, Walter's Light Battery
The Washington Artillery, Captain Hart's Company of Horse Artillery, Hart's Battery, the Washington Light Artillery, Lee's Battery of Hampton's Horse Artillery, Halsey's Battery

Infantry Companies with Unknown Regimental or Battalion Affiliations

The Anderson Home Guard
The Anderson's Mills Home Guard
The Battleground Home Guard
The Bethel Guards
The Boy Cavalry
The Broad River Light Infantry
The Brooks Boys
The Bull Swamp Guards
The Burke Sharpshooters
The Carolina Greys
The Carolina Home Guards
The Charleston Guard
The Chesterfield Eagles
The Chichester Guards
The Citizen Guards
The City Guard of Charleston
The Claremont Vigilance and Military Volunteer Committee
The Confederate Guards
The Confederate Stars
The Davis Guards
The Dean Guards
The Edgefield Reserves
The Gasper Guards
The Georgetown Home Guard
The Georgetown Reserves
The Golden's Creek Company

The Greenville Home Guard
The Greenville Home Guards–State Troops
The Greenville Riflemen
Gregg Light Infantry
The Hanging Rock Home Guards
The Home Guard
The Home Guard of Charleston
The Home Guards of Edgefield District
The Home Guards of Yorkville
The Hope Guard
The Hudson Street Guard
The Independent Blair Guards
The Independent Men of Waxhaws
The Keitt Guard
The Lanham Guards
The Lynches Creek Home Guards
The Magrath Guard
The Manigault Guards
The Marion Men
The Mile Creek Home Guard
The Miles Grenadiers
The Mountain Creek Home Guards
The Mountain Guards
The Mountain Rangers
Old Men's Home Guards
The Palmetto Reserve Guards #6
The Pendleton Home Guard
The Pleasant Hill Guard
The Pleasant Lane Home Guards
The Port Royal Guards
The Pumpkin Town Home Guard, the Mountain Rangers
The Rebel Guard
The Rich Hill Guards
The Snow Creek Vigilant Committee
The Snow Hill Guards
The Southern Boys
The Southern Guards
The St. George's Volunteers
The St. Paul's Home Guards
The Sumter Cadets
The University Riflemen

The Village Creek Home Guard
The Walhalla Riflemen
The Walhalla State Guards
The Wild Cat Vigilant Company
The Yeadon Blues

Cavalry Organizations with Unknown Regimental or Battalion Affiliations

The Abbeville Squadron
The Anderson Troop
The Ashepoo Guerillas
The Black River Troop
The Claremont Troop, the Sumter Cavalry
The Columbia Mounted Rifles
The Combahee Rangers
Farmer's Rangers
Home Guard of Cavalry in St. Paul's Parish
The Horry Hussars
The Jefferson Nullifiers
The Little River Rangers
The Lone Star Dragoons
The Mountain Cavalry
The Mounted Minute Men
The Newberry Chargers
Patterson's Rangers
The Richland Rangers
The Salem Mounted Men
The Saluda Rangers, the Saluda Sentinels
The Southern Rights Dragoons
The Spartan Rangers, the Seneca Rangers
The Spartan Troop

Artillery Organizations with Unknown Regimental or Battalion Affiliations

The Camden Artillery
The Fairfield Artillery
The Georgetown Artillery
The McDuffie Artillery

Notes

Introduction

1. William J. Rivers, "Annual Report of the State Historian of Confederate Records For The Year 1899." Microcopy 13, Roll 29, South Carolina Department of Archives and History.

Overview

1. Charles E. Cauthen, *South Carolina Goes to War, 1860–1865*, 113. (Hereafter cited as Cauthen, *South Carolina Goes to War.*); Alexander S. Salley, comp., *South Carolina Troops in Confederate Service,* 1: 429. (Hereafter cited as Salley, *SC Troops.*)
2. *Acts of the General Assembly of the State of South Carolina, passed in November and December 1860 and January 1861,* 848. (Hereafter cited as *Acts.*)
3. *Acts,* 849.
4. Cauthen, *South Carolina Goes to War,* 114.
5. Confederate Historian, "Annual Report For The Year 1899, " 9, South Carolina Department of Archives and History. (Hereafter cited as Confederate Historian, "Annual Report.")
6. The county system of subdivision was not adopted until 1868.
7. Lockwood Tower, ed., *A Carolinian Goes To War, The Civil Narrative of Arthur Middleton Manigault, Brigadier General, C.S.A., R.*, 5. (Hereafter cited as Tower, *A Carolinian Goes To War.*)
8. Johnson Hagood, *Memoirs of the War of Secession, From the Original Manuscripts of Johnson Hagood,* 27. (Hereafter cited as Hagood, *Memoirs.*)
9. Charles E. Cauthen, ed., *Journals of the South Carolina Executive Councils 1861 and 1862,* 4. (Hereafter cited as Cauthen, ed., *Journals.*)
10. Cauthen, *South Carolina Goes to War,* 114.
11. Ibid.; Douglas Southall Freeman, *Lee's Lieutenants*, 1, 518. (Hereafter cited as Freeman, *Lee's Lieutenants.*)
12. Cauthen, ed., *Journals,* 17, 18; Salley, *SC Troops,* 1:1; United States War Department, *The War of the Rebellion: A Compilation of the Official Records of the Union and Confederate Armies*, series 4, volume 1, page 913. (Hereafter cited as *OR*. It should be noted that some volumes in this series are broken into parts, while some are not. Entries for volumes with parts are listed with a series, a volume, a part and a page number or numbers; entries for volumes without parts are listed only with a series, a volume and a page number or numbers.)
13. *Acts,* 854; *OR*, 4, 1, 914.
14. Confederate Historian, "Annual Report," 11.
15. *OR,* 4, 1, 914.
16. Ibid.
17. *Charleston Mercury*, 12-30-1861. (Hereafter cited as *CM.*)
18. *OR,* 1, 1, 265
19. Southern Historical Society Papers, 14, 51. (Hereafter cited as SHSP.)
20. Salley, *SC Troops,* 3:284; Cauthen, ed., *Journals,* 67, 68; Cauthen, *South Carolina Goes to War,* 135.
21. Confederate Historian, "Annual Report," 24.

22. Cauthen, ed., *Journals*, 77–79.
23. United Daughters of the Confederacy, South Carolina Division, *Recollections and Reminiscences, 1861–1865 through World War 1*. 9, 242. (Hereafter cited as *RR*.)
24. Confederate Historian, "Annual Report," 26.
25. Cauthen, *South Carolina Goes to War*, 116; *OR*, 4, 1, 412.
26. Confederate Historian, "Annual Report," 30.
27. *Lancaster Ledger*, 9-4-61. (Hereafter cited as *LL*.)
28. Cauthen, *South Carolina Goes to War*, 136.
29. *Camden Confederate*, 11-15-1861. (Hereafter cited as *TCC*.)
30. Cauthen, *South Carolina Goes to War*, 137.
31. *OR*, 4, 1, 779; *TCC*, 12-20-61.
32. Cauthen, *South Carolina Goes to War*, 138.
33. Confederate Historian, "Annual Report," 44.
34. *CM*, 12-18-61.
35. Confederate Historian, "Annual Report," 46.
36. Ibid.
37. *CM*, 2-19-62.
38. Ibid.
39. Cauthen, ed., *Journals*, 102
40. *CM*, 5-1-62; *Edgefield Advertiser*, 5-7-62. (Hereafter cited as *EA*.)
41. *OR*, 4, 1, 973; Cauthen, *South Carolina Goes to War*, 144; *CM*, 5-1-62.
42. *OR*, 4, 1, 963.
43. Cauthen, *South Carolina Goes to War*, 144.
44. *EA*, 3-19-62.
45. *CM*, 5-1-62; Cauthen, ed., *Journals*, 305.
46. *OR*, 4, 1, 975.
47. *CM*, 3-13-62; Cauthen, ed., *Journals*, 107.
48. *CM*, 3-13-62.
49. Cauthen, ed., *Journals*, 103; *OR*, 4, 1, 973–975; *EA*, 3-19-62.
50. *CM*, 5-1-62.
51. Cauthen, ed., *Journals*, 127.
52. *CM*, 4-21-62; Cauthen, ed., *Journals*, 154.
53. Ibid.
54. *OR*, 4, 1, 1062.
55. Confederate Historian, "Annual Report," 47, 57, 58; *CM*, 5-1-62.
56. *Yorkville Enquirer*, 9-17-62. (Hereafter cited as *YE*); *EA*, 9-1-62.
57. D. Augustus Dickert, *History of Kershaw's Brigade*, 105. (Hereafter cited as Dickert, *Kershaw's Brigade*.)
58. *CM*, 4-21-62; *LL*, 10-8-62.
59. Dickert, *Kershaw's Brigade*, 332.
60. *Charleston Daily Courier*, 2-9-64. (Hereafter cited as *CDC*.)
61. *OR*, 1, 35, 1, 518, 577.
62. J.F.J Caldwell, *The History of a Brigade of South Carolinians*, 170.
63. *Daily Southern Carolinian*, 2-22-64. (Hereafter cited as *DSC*.)
64. *CM*, 7-12-62.
65. Confederate Historian, "Annual Report," 58
66. Ibid., 25.
67. Ibid., 57–58.
68. Cauthen, *South Carolina Goes to War*, 110.
69. Confederate Historian, "Annual Report," 25, 53.
70. *LL*, 10-8-62.
71. Cauthen, ed., *Journals*, 154.
72. Ibid.
73. *LL*, 7-30-62.
74. *CM*, 5-16-62; Cauthen, ed., *Journals*, 154–156; *TCC*, 5-2-62.

75. *YE*, 8-13-62.
76. Cauthen, ed., *Journals*, 154.
77. *CM*, 5-16-62; Cauthen, ed., *Journals*, 154; *YE*, 6-24-63.
78. Cauthen, ed., *Journals*, 228.
79. Ibid., 172.
80. Ibid., 173.
81. *CM*, 11-6-62.
82. Cauthen, ed., *Journals*, 154; *TCC*, 8-22-62.
83. *OR*, 4, 2, 155–56.
84. Ibid., 4, 2, 176.
85. *YE*, 11-12-62.
86. Cauthen, ed., *Journals*, 293; *TCC*, 11-14-62.
87. Cauthen, *South Carolina Goes to War*, 161.
88. *OR*, 1, 53, 281; Judith N. McArthur and Orville Vernon Burton, *A Gentleman and An Officer—A Military and Social History of James B. Griffin's Civil War*, 262. (Hereafter cited as McArthur, *Griffin*.)
89. McArthur, *Griffin*, 266.
90. *YE*, 2-11-63.
91. *OR*, 1, 14, 784–785.
92. Ibid., 1, 14, 816.
93. Cauthen, ed., *Journals*, 228.
94. *TCC*, 7-25-62.
95. Cauthen, *South Carolina Goes to War*, 146.
96. *TCC*, 11-14-62.
97. Cauthen, ed., *Journals*, 292.
98. *OR*, 4, 2, 580–582; *TCC*, 7-31-63; *Triweekly Watchman*, 7-18-63.
99. *OR*, 1, 28, 2, 145.
100. Ibid., 4, 2, 580.
101. Ibid., 1, 28, 2, 145.
102. *Greenville Southern Enterprise*, 7-30-63; Cauthen, *South Carolina Goes to War*, 192; *LL*, 6-24-63; *OR*, 1, 28, 2, 144.
103. *OR*, 1, 28, 2, 145; *YE*, 6-24-63.
104. *OR*, 1, 28, 2, 145.
105. *LL*, 7-15-63; *OR*, 4, 3, 38–39.
106. *OR*, 3, 38–39; 4, 2, 665; *YE*, 6-24-63; 7-29-63; *Carolina Spartan*, 8-27-63. (Hereafter cited as *CS*.)
107. *CM*, 8-14-63.
108. *OR*, 1, 28, 2, 339; 4, 2, 1058.
109. Ibid., 1, 28, 2, 339.
110. Ibid., 1, 35, 1, 562; 4, 2, 1058; *CM*, 2-15-64.
111. Lloyd Halliburton, *Saddle Soldiers, The Civil War Correspondence of General William Stokes 4th South Carolina Cavalry*, 125 (Hereafter cited as Halliburton, *Saddle Soldiers*.); *Sumter Watchman*, 1-18-63.
112. *OR*, 1, 35, 2, 456.
113. *DSC*, 3-15-64.
114. *LL*, 3-2-64; *EA*, 2-24-64.
115. *YE*, 3-2-64.
116. Cauthen, *South Carolina Goes to War*, 194.
117. *EA*, 2-24-64.
118. *YE*, 3-23-64.
119. *DSC*, 4-8-64.
120. *YE*, 6-15-64.
121. Ibid., 6-22-64.
122. Ibid., 7-13-64
123. Ibid., 7-20-64.
124. *EA*, 8-17-64; *LL*, 12-18-64.

125. *EA*, 1-4-65; *Compiled Service Records of Confederate Soldiers Who Served in Organizations from the State of South Carolina*, National Archives and Records Administration, M267, 391. (Hereafter cited as *CSR*.)
126. *RR*, 7, 27.
127. *CM*, 9-6-64.
128. *YE*, 3-29-65.
129. *EA*, 4-19-65
130. Ibid.
131. Ibid., 4-5-65.
132. Confederate Historian, "Annual Report," 84.
133. Ibid., 80.
134. Randolph W. Kirkland Jr, *Broken Fortunes—South Carolina Soldiers, Sailors & Citizens Who Died in the Service of Their Country and State in the War for Southern Independence, 1861–1865*, xiv. (Hereafter cited as Kirkland, *Broken Fortunes*.)
135. Confederate Historian, "Annual Report," 84.
136. *CM*, 4-21-62.
137. *Confederate Veteran*, 34, 221. (Hereafter cited as *CV*.)
138. *Due West Telescope*, 5-2-62. (Hereafter cited as *DWT*.)

Chapter 1

1. CM, 4-27-61; CSR M267, roll 119.
2. Walter Brian Cisco, *States Right Gist, A South Carolina General of the Civil War*, 50.
3. Hagood, *Memoirs*, 28.
4. *CM*, 3-12-61.
5. Hagood, *Memoirs*, 29.
6. James R. Hagood, "Memoirs of the First South Carolina Regiment of Volunteer Infantry in the Confederate War for Independence from April 12, 1861, to April 10, 1865," 14 (hereafter cited as Hagood, "Memoirs of the First Regiment.").
7. Hagood, "Memoirs of the First Regiment," 14.
8. Ibid., 14.
9. *OR*, 4, 1, 413.
10. Hagood, "Memoirs of the First Regiment," 14.
11. Ibid., 15.
12. Salley, *SC Troops*, 1: 430.
13. Hagood, "Memoirs of the First Regiment," 17.
14. Ibid., 16, 17.
15. Salley, *SC Troops*, 1: 430; Hagood, *Memoirs*, 40.
16. Salley, *SC Troops*, 1: 430
17. Hagood, "Memoirs of the First Regiment," 22.
18. Ibid., 23.
19. Ibid., 25.
20. Ibid., 29.
21. *CM*, 8-3-61.
22. Salley, *SC Troops*, 1: 431.
23. *CM*, 8-27-61.
24. Hagood, "Memoirs of the First Regiment," 30.
25. Ibid., 30.
26. *CM*, 5-20-62.
27. Hagood, "Memoirs of the First Regiment," 48; Cauthen, ed., *Journals*, 136.
28. Cauthen, ed., *Journals*, 138.
29. *CM*, 2-7-61.
30. Salley, *SC Troops*, 1: 433.
31. Hagood, "Memoirs of the First Regiment," 26.
32. *CM*, 5-20-62.
33. *OR*, 1, 12, 568.

34. Salley, *SC Troops*, 1: 433.
35. *CM,* 8-12-62.
36. William Valmore Izlar, *A Sketch of the War Record of the Edisto Rifles, 1861–1865,* 96-9. (hereafter cited as Izlar, *Sketch*).
37. *CM,* 2-7-61.
38. Salley, *SC Troops*, 1: 433.
39. *CM,* 5-20-62.
40. Ibid., 8-30-62.
41. James J. Baldwin, *The Struck Eagle—A Biography of Brigadier General Micah Jenkins, and a History of the Fifth South Carolina Volunteers and the Palmetto Sharpshooters*, 156 (hereafter cited as Baldwin, *The Struck Eagle*); *CM,* 9-16-62; *Confederate Military History Extended Edition, Volume 6, South Carolina*, 601 (hereafter cited as *CMH*); Hagood, "Memoirs of the First Regiment," 72.
42. Salley, *SC Troops*, 1: 433.
43. *RR,* 5, 325.
44. *CM,* 9-27-62.
45. Hagood, "Memoirs of the First Regiment," 72.
46. SHSP, 14, 92.
47. *LL,* 11-26-62.
48. *CDC,* 9-6-62.
49. *CM,* 2-7-61.
50. Hagood, "Memoirs of the First Regiment," 49.
51. Robert K. Krick, *Lee's Colonels, A Biographical Register of the Field Officers of the Army of Northern Virginia*, 125 (hereafter cited as Krick, *Lee's Colonels*).
52. Hagood, "Memoirs of the First Regiment," 100; Frank M. Mixson, *Reminiscences Of A Private*, 36 (hereafter cited as Mixson, *Reminiscences).*
53. Hagood, "Memoirs of the First Regiment," 101.
54. Baldwin, *The Struck Eagle,* 188; Krick, *Lee's Colonels*, 125.
55. Hagood, *Memoirs,* 68.
56. Krick, *Lee's Colonels*, 240.
57. Hagood, "Memoirs of the First Regiment," 85; Mixson, *Reminiscences,* 30.
58. Hagood, "Memoirs of the First Regiment," 101.
59. Ibid., 134.
60. Ibid.
61. Krick, *Lee's Colonels*, 240.
62. Hagood, *Memoirs,* 68.
63. Krick, *Lee's Colonels,* 223.
64. Hagood, *Memoirs,* 68.
65. South Carolina Department of Archives and History, *Roll of the Dead, South Carolina Troops Confederate States Service* (hereafter cited as SCDAH, *Roll of the Dead*); *CM,* 11-11-63; Hagood, "Memoirs of the First Regiment," 221; Mixson, *Reminiscences*, 46.
66. *CV,* 18, 473; James Lide Coker, *History of Company G, Ninth S.C. Regiment, Infantry, South Carolina Army and of Company E, Sixth S.C. Regiment, Infantry, South Carolina Army*, 133 (hereafter cited as Coker, *History);* Baldwin, *The Struck Eagle,* 236.
67. *CMH*, 616; *CM,* 3-7-64.
68. *CM,* 3-7-64; Mixson, *Reminiscences,* 122.
69. Hagood, "Memoirs of the First Regiment," 220.
70. Ibid., 217-220.
71. R.A. Brock and Philip Van Doren Stern, *The Appomattox Roster*, 121 (hereafter cited as Brock, *The Appomattox Roster*).
72. *CM,* 11-11-63.
73. Hagood, "Memoirs of the First Regiment," 132-133.
74. SCDAH, *Roll of the Dead*; *CSR* M267, roll 121.
75. Krick, *Lee's Colonels,* 224.
76. Brock, *The Appomattox Roster*, 121.
77. Mixson, *Reminiscences,* 54-55.

78. *CM,* 2-3-63.
79. *CV,* 32, 420-21.
80. Izlar, *Sketch,* 18.
81. *CV,* 32, 420.
82. Izlar, *Sketch,* 33.
83. *CV,* 21, 350.
84. Ibid., 32, 420.
85. Izlar, *Sketch,* 33.
86. *CM,* 4-13-61.
87. Ibid.
88. Hagood, *Memoirs,* 391; Kirkland, *Broken Fortunes,* 70.
89. *CM,* 6-5-61; 8-8-61.
90. *CDC,* 1-9-61.
91. *EA,* 8-221-61; Confederate Historian, "Annual Report," 14.
92. Joseph H. Crute, Jr, *Units of the Confederate Army*, 181 (hereafter cited as Crute, *Units*).
93. *CDC,* 9-16-61.
94. Ibid; *CM,* 9-16-61; 2-20-64.
95. *CV,* 35, 103.
96. SHSP, 16, 116.
97. *Acts,* 934.
98. *CM,* 9-19-61; 10-24-61.
99. Ibid., 11-2-61.
100. SHSP, Index; *CV,* 35, 103.
101. *CDC,* 2-20-64.
102. SHSP, 16, 133.
103. Ibid.
104. *CM,* 2-20-64.
105. Hagood, *Memoirs,* 28; *RR,* 8, 348; Confederate Historian, "Annual Report," 14.
106. Hagood, "Memoirs of the First Regiment," 4.
107. Confederate Historian, "Annual Report," 14; Hagood, "Memoirs of the First Regiment," 5.
108. *CM,* 9-23-61; Mixson, *Reminiscences,* 23.
109. *Barnwell Sentinel*, 8-31-61.
110. *CM,* 9-23-61.
111. Ibid.
112. Confederate Historian, "Annual Report," 14; Hagood, *Memoirs,* 29; Hagood, "Memoirs of the First Regiment," 5.
113. Izlar, *Sketch,* 19.
114. *CDC,* 9-28-61.
115. Ibid.
116. SHSP, Index.
117. *CM,* 11-14-60.
118. Ibid. 1-14-61.
119. Hagood, *Memoirs,* 40.
120. *CM,* 5-3-61.
121. Ibid., 5-20-62; 9-11-62; *CDC,* 5-21-62.
122. Hagood, "Memoirs of the First Regiment," 45.
123. *RR,* 3, 524, 527.
124. *CM,* 5-20-62.
125. Salley, *SC Troops*, 1: 475.
126. Hagood, "Memoirs of the First Regiment," 99.
127. *CM,* 5-20-62.
128. Hagood, "Memoirs of the First Regiment," 198.
129. Brock, *The Appomattox Roster*, 121.
130. *CDC,* 9-28-61.
131. Hagood, "Memoirs of the First Regiment," 229.

132. Brock, *The Appomattox Roster*, 121.
133. Hagood, "Memoirs of the First Regiment," 136.
134. *CV,* 23, 162.
135. *LL,* 5-21-62.
136. Mixson, *Reminiscences,* 23.
137. *LL,* 11-26-62.
138. Ibid., 4-2-6.
139. *CM,* 5-20-62.
140. Salley, *SC Troops*, 1: 544.
141. Hagood, "Memoirs of the First Regiment," 233.
142. *LL,* 9-17-62; 11-26-62.
143. Ibid., 4-29-63; SCDAH, *Roll of the Dead*; Baldwin, *The Struck Eagle,* 196; Coker, *History*, 122.
144. Hagood, "Memoirs of the First Regiment," 236.
145. Ibid., 108; *LL,* 4-29-63.
146. The author holds the typewritten list.
147. *CM,* 11-11-63; Hagood, "Memoirs of the First Regiment," 235; Salley, *SC Troops*, 1: 544.
148. *CM,* 10-12-64.
149. Hagood, "Memoirs of the First Regiment," 268.
150. *LL,* 10-25-64.
151. *RR,* 12, 319.
152. Mixson, *Reminiscences,* 23.
153. *LL,* 11-26-62.
154. Ibid; SCDAH, *Roll of the Dead*; *CM,* 10-13-62; Hagood, "Memoirs of the First Regiment," 238.
155. Hagood, "Memoirs of the First Regiment," 71.
156. *LL,* 11-26-62.
157. Hagood, "Memoirs of the First Regiment," 71.
158. Mixson, *Reminiscences,* 105-106.
159. *CM,* 10-12-64, Mixson, *Reminiscences,* 105.
160. Hagood, "Memoirs of the First Regiment," 74.
161. *Daily Southern Guardian*, 7-17-62 (hereafter cited as *DSG*); *Greenville Southern Enterprise,* 3-26-63.
162. Cauthen, ed., *Journals,* 182; *CM,* 5-20-62.
163. Hagood, "Memoirs of the First Regiment," 94.
164. *Greenville Southern Enterprise*, 3-26-63.
165. Brock, *The Appomattox Roster*, 121.
166. *CM,* 5-20-62.
167. Hagood, "Memoirs of the First Regiment," 246.
168. Ibid., 46.
169. Ibid., 89.
170. SCDAH, *Roll of the Dead*; Hagood, "Memoirs of the First Regiment," 248.
171. Hagood, "Memoirs of the First Regiment," 120.
172. SCDAH, *Roll of the Dead*; *CM,* 10-12-64.
173. Hagood, "Memoirs of the First Regiment," 268.
174. Ibid., 134.
175. Brock, *The Appomattox Roster*, 121.
176. Mixson, *Reminiscences,* 24.
177. *CM,* 5-20-62; 10-12-64.
178. Hagood, "Memoirs of the First Regiment," 54, 200.
179. Ibid., 135.
180. Ibid., 253.
181. *CMH*, 761.
182. Brock, *The Appomattox Roster*, 121.
183. *CM,* 5-20-62.
184. Hagood, "Memoirs of the First Regiment," 89.
185. Ibid., 198.
186. Ibid., 55.

187. *CM,* 10-12-64.
188. Hagood, "Memoirs of the First Regiment," 135.
189. Ibid., 200.
190. *CM,* 5-20-62.
191. Hagood, "Memoirs of the First Regiment," 89.
192. Ibid., 89, 104.
193. *CMH,* 617; *CDC,* 11-9-63.
194. Hagood, "Memoirs of the First Regiment," 101.
195. *CM,* 10-12-64; Brock, *The Appomattox Roster*, 121.
196. Stewart Sifakis, *Compendium of the Confederate Armies—South Carolina and Georgia*, 52 (hereafter cited as Sifakis, *Compendium*).
197. Hagood, "Memoirs of the First Regiment," 8.
198. *CM,* 4-12-61; 4-13-61; *CV,* 32, 420; Hagood, "Memoirs of the First Regiment," 8.
199. Hagood, *Memoirs,* 30.
200. *OR,* 1, 53, 158.
201. Ibid., 1, 53, 174.
202. *CM,* 5-24-61; *CV,* 32, 420; Izlar, *Sketch*, 21.
203. *CV,* 32, 420.
204. *CM,* 8-31-61.
205. *CDC,* 4-15-62; *CM,* 4-13-62.
206. Hagood, "Memoirs of the First Regiment," 57; *CM,* 6-11-62
207. Hagood, "Memoirs of the First Regiment," 61.
208. Ibid., 238.
209. *CDC,* 9-27-62.
210. Linda Sparks Starr, *W.R.Rankin, Manassas to Appomattox*, 2. (hereafter cited as Starr, *W.R. Rankin*).
211. *CM,* 9-9-62.
212. Starr, *W.R. Rankin,* 23.
213. Hagood, "Memoirs of the First Regiment," 74.
214. *CM,* 10-3-62.
215. *CDC,* 10-1-62.
216. Starr, *W.R. Rankin,* 36.
217. Hagood, "Memoirs of the First Regiment," 92.
218. *CM,* 12-20-62.
219. Baldwin, *The Struck Eagle,* 187.
220. *CM,* 10-30-63.
221. Baldwin, *The Struck Eagle,* 192; *CM,* 10-30-63; *CDC,* 10-29-63.
222. Baldwin, *The Struck Eagle,* 194; Asbury Coward, N.J. Bond and O.L. Coward, eds., *The South Carolinians*, 76. (hereafter cited as Coward, *The South Carolinians*).
223. Baldwin, *The Struck Eagle,* 195; *CM,* 10-30-63; *CDC,* 10-29-63.
224. Baldwin, *The Struck Eagle,* 195.
225. Ibid., 200.
226. *CM,* 10-30-63; *RR,* 2, 89.
227. Starr, *W.R. Rankin,* 46.
228. Mixson, *Reminiscences,* 45; *CM,* 9-29-63.
229. *CM,* 10-30-63.
230. Hagood, "Memoirs of the First Regiment," 235; Richard Lewis, *Camp Life of a Confederate Boy*, 58 (hereafter cited as Lewis, *Camp Life*); Starr, *W.R. Rankin,* 47; Baldwin, *The Struck Eagle,* 223; *CM,* 10-30-63.
231. *CM,* 11-11-63; *CDC,* 11-5-63.
232. Mixson, *Reminiscences,* 50.
233. *CDC,* 11-5-63.
234. Baldwin, *The Struck Eagle,* 243.
235. Mixson, *Reminiscences,* 52.
236. Baldwin, *The Struck Eagle,* 371.
237. Hagood, "Memoirs of the First Regiment," 232; *CM,* 12-16-63; Baldwin, *The Struck Eagle,* 246.

238. J. Luke Austin, *General John Bratton: Sumter to Appomattox In Letters to His Wife*, 174 (hereafter cited as Austin, *Letters*).
239. Baldwin, *The Struck Eagle*, 252.
240. *CM,* 3-1-64; 4-29-64; *DSG,* 1-30-64; *CDC,* 2-1-64.
241. *CM,* 3-1-64.
242. Coward, *The South Carolinians*, 132.
243. Freeman, *Lee's Lieutenants,* 3, 384; *CM,* 5-24-64.
244. Baldwin, *The Struck Eagle,* 371; SHSP, 8, 550.
245. Baldwin, *The Struck Eagle,* 371.
246. Ibid.
247. Hagood, "Memoirs of the First Regiment," 265; *CM,* 8-25-64; *CDC,* 8-29-64.
248. Baldwin, *The Struck Eagle,* 319.
249. *CM,* 10-12-64.
250. Confederate Historian, "Annual Report," 20.
251. *CM,* 2-3-65.
252. *CMH*, 517.
253. Baldwin, *The Struck Eagle,* 356.
254. Ibid., 360; Coward, *The South Carolinians*, 180.

Chapter 2

1. *CV,* 7, 198; *CM,* 1-19-61.
2. *EA,* 5-15-61.
3. Freeman, *Lee's Lieutenants,* 1, 518.
4. Louise Haskell Daly, Alexander Cheves Haskell, *The Portrait of a Man*, 51 (hereafter cited as Daly, *Portrait*).
5. *LL,* 5-29-61.
6. *EA,* 5-15-61.
7. *OR,* 1, 53, 141; Cauthen, ed., *Journals,* 79.
8. SHSP, 13, 495; Hagood, "Memoirs of the First Regiment," 13.
9. *EA,* 5-8-61.
10. *OR,* 4, 1, 468.
11. Cauthen, ed., *Journals,* 79; *OR,* 4, 1, 468.
12. Freeman, *Lee's Lieutenants,* 1, 518.
13. *EA,* 7-26-61.
14. *OR,* 1, 6, 268.
15. Ibid., 1, 6, 275.
16. Ibid., 4, 1, 42.
17. Susan Williams Benson, ed., *Berry Benson's Civil War Book, Memoirs of a Confederate Scout and Sharpshooter*, 55 (hereafter cited as Benson, *Berry Benson*).
18. *CM,* 10-4-62.
19. *CV,* 8, 428; *CM,* 12-15-62; 12-24-62; Freeman, *Lee's Lieutenants,* 2, 375, 518.
20. Caldwell, *History,* 98.
21. Daly, *Portrait*, 49.
22. *EA,* 5-15-61.
23. *CDC,* 4-15-62.
24. Ibid.
25. *CM,* 2-19-61; *CDC,* 1-18-61.
26. *CM,* 4-8-62; 4-15-62; Caldwell, *History,* 30; *CDC,* 4-15-62.
27. *CM,* 2-19-61; 3-2-61; 4-23-61.
28. Ibid., 12-28-61.
29. Daly, *Portrait*, 112.
30. Freeman, *Lee's Lieutenants*, 3, 237; *CM,* 1-16-64.
31. Caldwell, *History,* 158
32. *Abbeville Press*, 7-12-61 (hereafter cited as *AP*).
33. *CM,* 3-2-61; 4-23-61.

34. *EA,* 7-23-62.
35. Ibid., 7-23-62; SCDAH, *Roll of the Dead*; *CM,* 7-1-62.
36. Caldwell, *History,* 46.
37. Confederate Historian, "Annual Report," 11.
38. *CMH*, 722.
39. Krick, *Lee's Colonels*, 248; *CMH*, 722; *CM,* 10-31-62.
40. *CM,* 9-15-62; *CDC,* 9-6-62.
41. *CDC,* 2-10-63.
42. Caldwell, *History,* 86.
43. Krick, *Lee's Colonels*, 249; *CM,* 9-3-61; 10-31-62.
44. Krick, *Lee's Colonels*, 248.
45. *CDC,* 5-7-64; Krick, *Lee's Colonels*, 249.
46. *CDC,* 7-18-64; *CM,* 7-19-64; *DSC,* 6-8-64.
47. Caldwell, *History,* 275; Krick, *Lee's Colonels*, 249; *CV,* 3, 281.
48. Caldwell, *History,* 276.
49. *CV,* 31, 53.
50. *CDC,* 5-7-64; Krick, *Lee's Colonels*, 343.
51. *CM,* 7-19-64; *CV,* 3, 281; Caldwell, *History,* 197; *CDC,* 7-18-64.
52. Caldwell, *History,* 195.
53. Ibid., 198.
54. Varina D. Brown, *A Colonel at Gettysburg and Spotsylvania*, 103 (hereafter cited as Brown, *A Colonel*).
55. *CDC,* 5-7-64; Krick, *Lee's Colonels*, 33.
56. *CM,* 6-6-64.
57. *CV,* 13, 156; *CM,* 5-24-64; 7-1-64.
58. *CV,* 13, 156; *CM,* 6-6-64.
59. *CM,* 6-19-64; 7-19-64; *CDC,* 7-18-64.
60. *DSC,* 6-30-64.
61. Krick, *Lee's Colonels*, 33.
62. *CM,* 7-1-64; SCDAH, *Roll of the Dead.*
63. *DSC,* 8-25-64; *CDC,* 8-23-64.
64. Brock, *The Appomattox Roster,* 367.
65. *CM,* 5-25-64; 8-17-63.
66. Brock, *The Appomattox Roster,* 367.
67. *CV,* 18, 233; *CM,* 3-2-61.
68. *DSG,* 8-2-61.
69. *CM,* 1-4-61; 4-23-61; 5-6-61; *DSG,* 1-4-61.
70. *CM,* 11-20-60; 3-2-61.
71. *DSG,* 1-4-61.
72. Confederate Historian, "Annual Report," 11.
73. *CM,* 1-8-61.
74. Ibid., 4-23-61; 5-10-61.
75. *DSG,* 7-25-61.
76. *CMH*, 725; *Acts,* 934.
77. *RR,* 9, 482.
78. *CM,* 1-4-61; 3-2-61; 4-23-61.
79. Confederate Historian, "Annual Report," 11; *RR,* 9, 483.
80. *RR,* 9, 485.
81. *CMH*, 725.
82. *CM,* 5-2-61; 5-14-61.
83. Ibid., 6-29-61; *YE,* 7-4-61.
84. *CM,* 5-10-61.
85. *EA,* 1-9-61; *RR,* 11, 388.
86. *CM,* 1-8-61; 3-2-61; 7-8-62; *EA,* 1-9-61.
87. *Acts,* 869.
88. *CM,* 4-23-61; *YE,* 5-2-61.

89. *EA*, 10-9-61.
90. Ibid., 1-9-61; 5-10-61.
91. *CM*, 1-11-61; 3-2-61; *CMH*, 559; SHSP, Index.
92. *RR*, 6, 396.
93. *AP*, 1-4-61.
94. *Ibid.*, 1-4-61; 1-18-61.
95. *Ibid.*, 1-18-61; *CM*, 1-26-61.
96. *AP*, 1-11-61; *CM*, 1-11-61.
97. *LL*, 5-29-61; Daly, *Portrait*, 51; *CM*, 5-10-61.
98. *AP*, 5-3-61; *RR*, 6, 399; 9, 176.
99. *YE*, 5-2-61; *CM*, 3-2-61; 4-23-61.
100. *LL*, 5-29-61; *CM*, 5-10-61.
101. DeWitt Boyd Stone, Jr., *Wandering to Glory*, 22 (hereafter cited as Stone, *Wandering*).
102. *CV*, 18, 233.
103. Ibid., 35, 103.
104. *CM*, 11-5-60.
105. Ibid., 1-5-61.
106. SHSP, 13, 481.
107. *CM*, 1-5-61; 2-7-61; 3-2-61; 4-23-61; 4-29-61; 5-10-61; *CDC*, 2-20-64; *CV*, 18, 233.
108. *CDC*, 2-14-61.
109. *LL*, 5-29-61; *CM*, 5-10-61.
110. SHSP, 13, 495.
111. *Horry Dispatch*, 5-23-61; *RR*, 5, 598; Walker, *Rolls and Historical Sketch of the Tenth Regiment, So. Ca. Volunteers in the Army of the Confederate States*, 70-72 (hereafter cited as Walker, *Rolls*).
112. *EA*, 1-16-61; *CM*, 3-2-61; 4-23-61; *RR*, 1, 615; Benson, *Berry Benson*, 4.
113. *CM*, 3-21-61; *EA*, 1-16-61.
114. *LL*, 5-29-61; *CM*, 5-10-61.
115. *CM*, 3-2-61; *RR*, 1, 615; *EA*, 1-30-61; Benson, *Berry Benson*, 1.
116. *EA*, 1-16-61.
117. Ibid., 7-20-64.
118. *CM*, 5-10-61; *LL*, 5-29-61.
119. *CM*, 1-11-61; 3-2-61; 4-23-61; 5-10-61; *AP*, 1-11-61.
120. *CM*, 5-10-61; *LL*, 5-29-61.
121. *DSG*, 7-24-61.
122. SHSP, 16, 15.
123. *GPM* 3-7-61; *AP*, 3-8-61; *CM*, 3-2-61; 4-23-61; Confederate Historian, "Annual Report," 10.
124. *LL*, 5-29-61.
125. *CM*, 5-10-61.
126. *RR*, 9, 400.
127. *CM*, 1-14-61; *CV*, 14, 360.
128. *CM*, 1-14-61; *CV*, 22, 198.
129. *CM*, 3-2-61.
130. Ibid., 5-10-61.
131. *LL*, 5-29-61; *CM*, 4-23-61; 5-10-61.
132. *CM*, 1-11-61.
133. Ibid., 4-23-61; 7-11-62.
134. Ibid., 1-1-61; 7-11-62.
135. Ibid., 1-11-61.
136. Ibid., 3-2-61.
137. Ibid., 4-23-61.
138. Ibid; Daly, *Portrait*, 55.
139. *CM*, 5-10-61; 7-11-61; *LL*, 5-29-61.
140. *CM*, 5-1-61.
141. Ibid., 5-10-61; *EA*, 5-8-61.
142. *CM*, 6-28-60; *LL*, 5-8-61.

143. Woodward, C. Vann and Elisabeth Muhlenfeld, *The Private Mary Chesnut, The Unpublished Civil War Diaries*, 62 (hereafter cited as Woodward, *Mary Chesnut*).
144. *LL*, 5-29-61.
145. Ibid., 5-8-61.
146. *CM*, 1-8-61; 4-29-61.
147. *RR*, 9, 576.
148. *CM*, 1-8-61.
149. Ibid., 12-3-64.
150. Ibid., 5-10-61; *LL*, 5-28-61.
151. *DSG*, 7-15-61.
152. *CM*, 8-19-61.
153. Ibid., 9-23-61.
154. Ibid., 8-30-64.
155. Krick, *Lees Colonels*, 249; *CM*, 9-3-61.
156. *CM*, 5-16-63; 7-19-64.
157. Ibid., 8-4-64; *CDC*, 8-9-64.
158. *CM*, 9-29-64.
159. *CV*, 14, 360.
160. Salley, *SC Troops*, 1: 235.
161. Krick, *Lee's Colonels*, 489; *CV*, 3, 281.
162. Salley, *SC Troops*, 1: 235.
163. Ibid., 236.
164. Ibid.
165. *RR*, 5, 93.
166. Caldwell, *History*, 67.
167. SCDAH, *Roll of the Dead*.
168. *RR*, 9, 149.
169. *CM*, 5-16-63; 7-18-63; 7-19-63.
170. *CDC*, 7-18-64; *CM*, 7-19-64; *Memory Roll: Rolls of South Carolina Volunteers in the Confederate States Provisional Army*, South Carolina Department of Archives and History, Microcopy No. 16 (hereafter cited as *Memory Roll*).
171. *DSG*, 5-31-64; *CM*, 7-31-61.
172. *DSG*, 8-6-61; *CDC*, 8-7-61.
173. *CM*, 7-31-61.
174. *CV*, 3, 281.
175. *CM*, 5-16-63; 7-18-63; 7-19-64.
176. Brock, *The Appomattox Roster*, 367.
177. Salley, *SC Troops*, 1: 252.
178. *CMH*, 725.
179. *CV*, 32, 207; *CM*, 8-23-64; William W. Sellers, *A History of Marion County, South Carolina, from its earliest times to present*—1910, 585; *EA*, 9-4-61.
180. Krick, *Lee's Colonels*, 343.
181. Ibid.
182. Caldwell, *History*, 119.
183. Brock, *The Appomattox Roster*, 368.
184. SHSP, Index.
185. *DSG*, 12-25-62.
186. *CDC*, 7-18-64.
187. *EA*, 11-6-61; *CM*, 8-20-61.
188. *EA*, 9-4-61.
189. *RR*, 3, 57.
190. *EA*, 8-21-61.
191. Ibid., 8-7-61.
192. Ibid., 5-22-61.
193. Ibid., 8-10-64; *CDC*, 8-9-64.

194. Brock, *The Appomattox Roster,* 368.
195. *CM,* 7-24-61.
196. Benson, *Berry Benson,* 7.
197. Salley, *SC Troops*, 1: 327.
198. *AP,* 7-19-61; Daly, *Portrait*, 106.
199. Benson, *Berry Benson,* 47; *CM,* 9-15-62; 7-18-63; 8-17-63.
200. Caldwell, *History,* 146.
201. Daly, *Portrait*, 107.
202. Benson, *Berry Benson,* 6-7.
203. Ibid., 24.
204. *CDC,* 5-26-64; 7-18-64.
205. *CM,* 8-17-63; 7-19-64; 8-8-64; *CDC,* 8-9-64.
206. Benson, *Berry Benson,* 75.
207. Brock, *The Appomattox Roster,* 368.
208. Benson, *Berry Benson,* 49.
209. *CM,* 8-23-63.
210. *CM,* 5-25-64; *CV,* 33, 420.
211. *CM,* 7-26-61.
212. Ibid., 7-26-61.
213. Ibid., 8-1-61; 8-3-61; 8-5-61; Daly, *Portrait*, 235.
214. *DSG,* 8-6-61.
215. Daly, *Portrait*, 55.
216. *CM,* 1-1-61.
217. Salley, *SC Troops*, 1: 347.
218. *CM,* 7-2-62; 7-11-62; 8-18-62.
219. *CDC,* 7-9-62.
220. Krick, *Lee's Colonels*, 66.
221. *CDC,* 5-25-64; 7-18-64; Benson, *Berry Benson,* 75.
222. Krick, *Lee's Colonels*, 66.
223. *CMH*, 434, *Memory Roll.*
224. *CM,* 6-8-61.
225. Ibid., 3-19-61.
226. *CMH*, 721.
227. *CM,* 5-7-61.
228. Ibid., 5-28-61.
229. Ibid., 1-29-62.
230. Ibid., 6-24-61.
231. Ibid., 6-8-61.
232. Confederate Historian, "Annual Report," 30; Salley, *SC Troops*, 1: 370.
233. *CM,* 7-2-61; *CDC,* 7-2-61.
234. *DSG,* 7-24-61; *CDC,* 7-22-61.
235. *DSG,* 7-24-61.
236. *CDC,* 7-2-61; 7-24-61.
237. Confederate Historian, "Annual Report," 30.
238. Ibid., 25.
239. *CM,* 1-24-62; *Memory Roll.*
240. *CDC,* 9-30-62; *CM,* 9-15-62.
241. *CMH*, 433.
242. *CDC,* 5-26-64; *CMH*, 434; *CM,* 7-18-63; *CV,* 38, 415.
243. *CV,* 38, 415.
244. *CDC,* 7-18-64; *CV,* 3, 281.
245. *CV,* 3, 281.
246. Ibid., 38, 415.
247. *CM,* 8-6-61; James Armstrong, *The Carolina Light infantry's Record in the Great War*, 1.
248. *CM,* 8-15-61; 8-27-61.

249. *CDC,* 9-26-62; *CM,* 8-6-61; 9-25-62; *CMH*, 447.
250. *CM,* 9-15-62; *CDC,* 9-6-62.
251. SCDAH, *Roll of the Dead*; *CDC,* 9-26-62.
252. *Memory Roll*; *CM,* 7-18-63; 7-25-63.
253. *CV,* 31, 51.
254. Ibid.
255. *Memory Roll.*
256. *CM,* 8-23-63.
257. *CDC,* 5-26-64; 7-18-64.
258. *CM,* 5-25-64.
259. Brock, *The Appomattox Roster,* 368.
260. *CM,* 8-14-61.
261. SHSP, 26, 238.
262. *Greenville Southern Enterprise*, 10-10-61.
263. SHSP, 26, 238.
264. *CMH*, 497.
265. *CM,* 4-16-61; 5-27-61.
266. *Keowee Courier (Walhalla),* 6-1-61.
267. Freeman, *Lee's Lieutenants*, 2, 418.
268. *CV,* 18, 233.
269. *CM,* 1-4-61; 1-7-61; 1-8-61.
270. Ibid., 1-11-61.
271. Ibid., 1-14-61; *CDC,* 2-5-61.
272. *RR,* 9, 483.
273. *CM,* 1-8-61; 1-14-61.
274. *EA,* 1-16-61.
275. *CM,* 1-26-61.
276. Ibid., 2-14-61; 3-2-61.
277. *EA,* 5-15-61.
278. *RR,* 9, 484.
279. *EA,* 5-15-61.
280. *CM,* 4-23-61; Daly, *Portrait,* 52.
281. *CM,* 4-23-63; *YE,* 5-2-61.
282. *CM,* 4-23-61.
283. Ibid., 4-22-61; 4-23-61.
284. *EA,* 5-8-61.
285. *CM,* 4-29-61; 5-4-61; *EA,* 5-8-61.
286. *CDC,* 4-30-61.
287. *CV,* 22, 198.
288. *CM,* 5-25-61.
289. Ibid., 6-19-61; 2-9-63.
290. Guy R. Everson and Edward H. Simpson, Jr. eds., *Far Far from Home—The Wartime Letters of Dick and Tally Simpson, 3rd South Carolina Volunteers*, 21 (hereafter cited as Everson, *Far from Home*); *CM,* 7-8-61; *TriWeekly Watchman,* 7-8-61.
291. *CM,* 7-6-61; 7-11-61.
292. Ibid., 7-17-61.
293. Ibid., 7-26-61.
294. Benson, *Berry Benson,* 6.
295. *CM,* 8-27-61; 10-12-61.
296. *EA,* 9-4-61.
297. *CDC,* 9-28-61.
298. *CM,* 3-26-62.
299. Ibid., 2-9-63.
300. Ibid.
301. Ibid.

302. Ibid.
303. Ibid.
304. Ibid.
305. Ibid.
306. Ibid., 9-17-62; 2-9-63; Benson, *Berry Benson,* 25.
307. *CM,* 2-9-63.
308. Brown, *A Colonel*, 70.
309. Benson, *Berry Benson,* 30; *CM,* 10-2-63.
310. Caldwell, *History,* 87.
311. Spencer G. Welch, A Confederate Surgeon's Letters to his Wife, 36 (hereafter cited as Welch, *A Confederate Surgeon's Letters*).
312. Caldwell, *History,* 93.
313. *CM,* 12-24-62.
314. Ibid., 5-8-63.
315. Ibid.
316. *RR,* 9, 236.
317. Brown, *A Colonel*, 86.
318. *CV,* 31, 51.
319. *CM,* 8-4-63.
320. Ibid. 7-19-64; SHSP, 6, 149.
321. *CM,* 7-19-64.
322. *CDC,* 8-4-64
323. *CM,* 8-4-64; 8-23-64.
324. Freeman, *Lee's Lieutenants,* 3, 589.

Chapter 3

1. *CM,* 3-12-62.
2. Mac Wyckoff, *A History of the 2nd South Carolina Infantry, 1861–1865*, viii (hereafter cited as Wyckoff, *2nd South Carolina Infantry*); *CSR* M267, 153.
3. Wyckoff, *2nd South Carolina Infantry*, x.
4. *CM,* 6-4-61.
5. *OR,* 1, 47, 3, 757, 773.
6. *CM,* 2-5-61; Ezra J. Warner, *Generals in Blue, Lives of the Union Commanders*, 171 (hereafter cited as Warner, *Generals in Blue*).
7. Wyckoff, *2nd South Carolina Infantry*, x.
8. J.C. Garlington, *Men of the Time, Sketches of Living Notables, A Biographical Encyclopedia of Contemporaneous South Carolina Leaders*, 33 (hereafter cited as Garlington, *Men of the Time*).
9. *CM,* 4-10-61; *LL,* 1-30-61.
10. *CM,* 7-10-61; 7-13-61.
11. Ibid., 4-10-61; *LL,* 1-30-61.
12. *LL,* 1-30-61.
13. Ibid., 7-17-61.
14. Krick, *Lee's Colonels*, 46.
15. *CSR* M267, 156; *CM,* 5-23-61; *LL,* 5-2-61; 5-29-61.
16. *LL,* 5-29-61.
17. *CDC,* 5-23-61; Wyckoff, *2nd South Carolina Infantry*, 201; Krick, *Lee's Colonels*, 213.
18. *LL,* 5-29-61; Wyckoff, *2nd South Carolina Infantry*, 201; Salley, *SC Troops*, 2: 5
19. *CSR* M267, 156.
20. Krick, *Lee's Colonels*, 213; Warner, *Generals in Blue,* 170.
21. *CM,* 11-20-60.
22. *CMH*, 603; *CM,* 5-23-61.
23. *CSR* M267, 153; *LL,* 5-22-61.
24. *LL,* 5-29-61.
25. Woodward, *Mary Chesnut*, 43.
26. Wyckoff, *2nd South Carolina Infantry*, 187.

27. *CSR* M267, 154.
28. Wyckoff, *2nd South Carolina Infantry*, 168.
29. Ibid., 234.
30. Salley, *SC Troops*, 2: 6
31. *CMH*, 505.
32. Wyckoff, *2nd South Carolina Infantry*, 168.
33. *CMH*, 505.
34. Wyckoff, *2nd South Carolina Infantry*, 203.
35. Warner, *Generals in Blue,* 170.
36. *CM,* 7-21-63; 5-17-64; 5-27-64.
37. Dickert, *Kershaw's Brigade,* 475.
38. *CM,* 5-22-62.
39. Salley, *SC Troops*, 2: 6
40. *Greenville Southern Enterprise*, 1-15-63; *CM,* 12-20-62.
41. *DSC,* 5-18-64; 5-9-64; *CM,* 5-18-64; 5-21-64.
42. Dickert, *Kershaw's Brigade,* 355.
43. *CM,* 7-21-63.
44. Dickert, *Kershaw's Brigade,* 479.
45. *LL,* 11-8-64.
46. Ibid.
47. SHSP, 11, 523.
48. *CM,* 4-11-61.
49. Ibid., 5-1-61.
50. Ibid., 5-10-61; *EA,* 5-8-61.
51. *CM,* 6-28-60; *LL,* 5-8-61.
52. *CM,* 5-1-61.
53. *LL,* 5-1-61; 5-8-61.
54. *CM,* 5-1-61.
55. *LL,* 1-30-61.
56. *CM,* 4-16-61.
57. *CV,* 7, 398.
58. *LL,* 11-1-64; *CM,* 4-11-61.
59. *CM,* 7-24-61.
60. *RR,* 7, 177.
61. Ibid.
62. *CM,* 7-24-61.
63. Ibid., 4-11-61.
64. *RR,* 3, 281.
65. *CV,* 32, 64.
66. *CM,* 7-29-61.
67. *RR,* 5, 97; *CMH*, 506.
68. *CM,* 11-20-60.
69. *CDC,* 4-30-61.
70. See Casson's record under Field Officers.
71. Wyckoff, *2nd South Carolina Infantry*, 234.
72. *CM,* 6-5-62.
73. Ibid., 7-21-63.
74. *CDC,* 11-30-64.
75. *CM,* 11-30-63.
76. *CV,* 21, 342.
77. *CM,* 5-8-61.
78. Ibid., 6-24-61; Wyckoff, *2nd South Carolina Infantry*, x; *CMH*, 494.
79. *CDC,* 11-9-63; *CMH*, 644.
80. *CM,* 7-31-61; 8-8-61; *CMH*, 645.
81. *CM,* 7-21-63; 8-28-63; SCDAH, *Roll of the Dead.*

82. *Greenville Southern Enterprise*, 7-23-63; 8-6-63.
83. *CDC*, 11-9-63.
84. *Greenville Southern Enterprise*, 7-23-63.
85. *CMH*, 494; Dickert, *Kershaw's Brigade,* 108; Wyckoff, *2nd South Carolina Infantry*, 166.
86. *Greenville Southern Enterprise*, 7-23-63.
87. *CM,* 1-9-61; 4-24-61; 8-22-64; Wyckoff, *2nd South Carolina Infantry*, x.
88. *DSG,* 1-8-61.
89. *CM,* 7-31-61.
90. Wyckoff, *2nd South Carolina Infantry*, 62.
91. Ibid., 207.
92. Ibid.
93. Ibid., 2, 242.
94. Dickert, *Kershaw's Brigade*, 547.
95. Garlington, *Men of the Time*, 33; *CV,* 15, 38.
96. *Memory Roll.*
97. *CM,* 5-17-61.
98. Ibid., 7-31-61; 8-8-61.
99. Woodward, *Mary Chesnut*, 107; Glenn Dedmondt, *Southern Bronze, Captain Garden's (SC) Artillery Company During the War Between the States*, 2 (hereafter cited as Dedmondt, *Southern Bronze*); *TriWeekly Watchman,* 4-29-61.
100. SCDAH, *Roll of the Dead*; Wyckoff, *2nd South Carolina Infantry*, 158.
101. Wyckoff, *2nd South Carolina Infantry*, 31.
102. *TriWeekly Watchman*, 7-20-63.
103. Ibid., 9-28-63.
104. *CM,* 5-16-64; *TriWeekly Watchman*, 5-25-64; *CDC,* 5-16-64.
105. *DSC,* 5-14-64.
106. *CM,* 3-1-60.
107. Ibid.
108. Ibid., 4-24-61; Wyckoff, *2nd South Carolina Infantry*, xii.
109. Dickert, *Kershaw's Brigade,* 253.
110. *DSG,* 5-6-61; *AP,* 5-10-61.
111. Ulysses Robert Brooks, ed., *Stories of the Confederacy,* 47 (hereafter cited as Brooks, *Stories*); Wyckoff, *2nd South Carolina Infantry*, xii-xiii; *CMH*, 724.
112. *CM,* 4-18-61.
113. *LL,* 5-27-61.
114. Ibid.
115. *CM,* 6-5-62.
116. Wyckoff, *2nd South Carolina Infantry*, 224.
117. Ibid., 209.
118. Ibid.
119. *DSG,* 1-1-64; *CM,* 5-17-64.
120. *CM,* 5-2-61.
121. Ibid., 5-3-61.
122. Ibid., 2-28-61.
123. *Cyclopedia of Eminent and Representative Men of the Carolinas of the Nineteenth Century,* 448 (hereafter cited as *Cyclopedia*.)
124. *LL,* 5-1-61; 5-29-61; 1-8-61; 6-3-61.
125. *YE,* 829-61; *LL,* 1-8-61.
126. Wyckoff, *2nd South Carolina Infantry*, 211.
127. *LL,* 7-9-62.
128. *CM,* 6-5-62.
129. Ibid., 7-21-63.
130. Wyckoff, *2nd South Carolina Infantry*, 196.
131. *CM,* 5-10-61.
132. Ibid., 5-1-61.

133. Ibid., 5-9-61; *CDC,* 5-27-61.
134. *CM,* 3-13-61; 5-22-63.
135. Ibid., 5-16-63.
136. *CDC,* 5-23-62; *CM,* 5-23-62.
137. *CM,* 5-16-63; 5-22-63; *CDC,* 5-14-63.
138. *CM,* 7-28-64.
139. Ibid.,7-28-64; *CDC,* 7-29-64.
140. *CM,* 7-28-64.
141. Wyckoff, *2nd South Carolina Infantry*, 180; *CDC,* 7-29-64; Kirkland, *Broken Fortunes,* 104.
142. Dickert, *Kershaw's Brigade,* 371.
143. *CMH*, 573.
144. *CM,* 1-11-61.
145. Ibid., 4-7-63; *Memory Roll.*
146. *CDC,* 5-9-61; *CM,* 5-1-61; 5-9-61; Confederate Historian, "Annual Report," 64.
147. *CM,* 5-13-61.
148. *CDC,* 5-13-61.
149. *CMH*, 595.
150. Wyckoff, *2nd South Carolina Infantry*, 18; *CM,* 2-12-62.
151. *CM,* 6-5-62.
152. *DSC,* 9-27-62.
153. *CSR* M267, 158; *CM,* 7-21-63.
154. Kirkland, *Broken Fortunes,* 235; Wyckoff, *2nd South Carolina Infantry*, 217.
155. *CM,* 6-6-64; SCDAH, *Roll of the Dead.*
156. Wyckoff, *2nd South Carolina Infantry*, 179.
157. *CDC,* 11-29-64; *CSR* M267, 155; SCDAH, *Roll of the Dead.*
158. Kirkland, *Broken Fortunes,* 100.
159. Wyckoff, *2nd South Carolina Infantry*, 179; *CDC,* 11-29-64.
160. *CM,* 4-16-61.
161. Ibid., 5-27-61; *Keowee Courier (Walhalla),* 6-1-61.
162. *CM,* 7-22-61.
163. Wyckoff, *2nd South Carolina Infantry*, 53.
164. *CV,* 4, 6.
165. *CM,* 4-11-61; 4-13-61; 4-16-61.
166. Ibid., 4-11-61.
167. Ibid., 4-25-61.
168. *CDC,* 4-26-61.
169. *Keowee Courier (Walhalla),* 5-4-61; *CM,* 5-4-61; *CMH*, 603; Wyckoff, *2nd South Carolina Infantry*, x.
170. *Keowee Courier (Walhalla),* 5-11-61.
171. *TriWeekly Watchman*, 4-29-61.
172. *DSG,* 5-6-61.
173. *LL,* 5-22-61.
174. Ibid.
175. *CM,* 5-25-61; 5-26-61.
176. Everson, *Far from Home,* 33.
177. *CM,* 2-27-62.
178. *CMH*, 464.
179. Everson, *Far from Home,* 106.
180. Ibid., 109.
181. Ibid., 113.
182. Ibid.
183. Ibid., 125; *CM,* 6-13-62.
184. *CM,* 6-3-62.
185. Ibid., 6-27-62; Everson, *Far from Home,* 132.
186. *CM,* 7-23-62; 7-24-62.
187. Ibid., 9-10-62; *CDC,* 9-10-62.

188. *CM,* 10-2-62; 1-1-63; *EA,* 10-8-62.
189. *CM,* 10-2-62.
190. *CDC,* 12-22-62.
191. Wyckoff, *2nd South Carolina Infantry*, 58.
192. *CM,* 12-29-62.
193. Wyckoff, *2nd South Carolina Infantry*, 61.
194. Ibid., 84.
195. SHSP, 4, 183.
196. Ibid., 13, 210.
197. *CM,* 7-20-63.
198. *LL,* 11-4-63; SHSP, 16, 377.
199. Freeman, *Lee's Lieutenants*, 3, 229; Mac Wyckoff, *A History of the 3rd South Carolina Infantry 1861–1865*, 135 (hereafter cited as Wyckoff, *3rd South Carolina Infantry*).
200. *CDC,* 10-24-63; Everson, *Far from Home,* 283; *CM,* 9-26-63.
201. *CM,* 10-2-63.
202. SHSP, 16, 387.
203. *CM,* 12-22-63.
204. *CDC,* 12-29-63.
205. SHSP, 16, 390.
206. Ibid., 7, 129.
207. *CM,* 5-31-64.
208. Freeman, *Lee's Lieutenants*, 3, 506; *CM,* 6-13-64; 6-20-64.
209. *CDC,* 7-19-64.
210. Freeman, *Lee's Lieutenants*, 3, 506.
211. *CDC,* 7-19-64.
212. *CM,* 8-3-64; 8-8-64; *CDC,* 8-9-64.
213. *CDC,* 9-24-64.
214. *CM,* 10-24-64.
215. *OR,* 1, 47, 2, 1074.
216. Ibid., 1, 47, 2, 1282; 1, 47, 2, 262.
217. Ibid., 1, 47, 1, 1111.
218. SHSP, 7, 131.

Chapter 4

1. *CV,* 3, 281.
2. SHSP, 7, 130.
3. Dickert, *Kershaw's Brigade,* 526-527
4. *CM,* 7-21-63.
5. *Cyclopedia,* 97.
6. *CM,* 10-31-64; 11-2-64.
7. Sifakis, *Compendium,* 60.

Chapter 5

1. J.H. Rion, "History of the 6th Regiment, South Carolina Infantry," Miscellaneous Sketches, 1868–1898, South Carolina Department of Archives and History, S108121 (hereafter cited as "History of the 6th Regiment," SCDAH, S108121).
2. *CM,* 6-27-61.
3. "History of the 6th Regiment," SCDAH, S108121; *CM,* 6-27-61; *OR,* 4, 1, 413.
4. *CM,* 7-8-61; *YE,* 7-11-61.
5. History of the 6th Regiment," SCDAH, S108121.
6. *YE,* 4-13-64.
7. *CM,* 2-22-61.
8. *YE,* 1-31-61.
9. *RR,* 6, 343.
10. *LL,* 6-19-61; T. W. Woodward, "History of the 6th Regiment, S.C. Volunteers," 9 (hereafter cited as Woodward, "History").

11. *CM,* 6-13-61; 6-27-61.
12. Woodward, "History," 9.
13. *CM,* 2-22-61.
14. SHSP, 16, 16.
15. *CM,* 6-27-61.
16. Krick, *Lee's Colonels*, 338.
17. *CM,* 2-22-61.
18. Ibid., 12-20-61.
19. *Cyclopedia,* 433.
20. Woodward, "History," 11; Confederate Historian, "Annual Report," 19.
21. Warner, *Generals in Blue,* 340; Woodward, "History," 14.
22. "History of the 6th Regiment," SCDAH, S108121.
23. *CM,* 5-6-62; Baldwin, *The Struck Eagle,* 87.
24. Coker, *History*, 51.
25. *YE,* 7-31-62; *CV,* 8, 407.
26. *CDC,* 7-29-62.
27. *CM,* 9-4-62.
28. Ibid., 10-8-64.
29. Austin, *Letters*, 241.
30. SHSP, 15, 122.
31. "History of the 6th Regiment," SCDAH, S108121; Austin, *Letters*, 245.
32. *CM,* 5-6-62.
33. *CDC,* 11-9-63.
34. Brock, *The Appomattox Roster,* 122.
35. Coker, *History,* 51; "History of the 6th Regiment," SCDAH, S108121.
36. *CM,* 5-6-62.
37. Coker, *History,* 51.
38. *CV,* 7, 209.
39. *CSR* M267, 212.
40. Brock, *The Appomattox Roster,* 122.
41. *CM,* 11-11-63.
42. Coker, *History,* 134.
43. Ibid., 135.
44. Ibid., 170.
45. *CM,* 6-11-61.
46. SHSP, 16, 15.
47. "History of the 6th Regiment," SCDAH, S108121.
48. Ibid.
49. *CM,* 11-20-60.
50. "History of the 6th Regiment," SCDAH, S108121.
51. *YE,* 1-31-61; Austin, *Letters*, 6.
52. "History of the 6th Regiment," SCDAH, S108121.
53. *YE,* 7-11-61; *Laurensville Herald*, 7-12-61 (hereafter cited as *LH*).
54. Austin, *Letters*, 21.
55. *CM,* 1-21-61.
56. *YE,* 1-24-61.
57. *Acts,* 934.
58. "History of the 6th Regiment," SCDAH, S108121.
59. *YE,* 1-31-61.
60. "History of the 6th Regiment," SCDAH, S108121.
61. *CMH*, 477; *RR,* 8, 6.
62. "History of the 6th Regiment," SCDAH, S108121.
63. *CMH*, 477.
64. *RR,* 3, 281.
65. "History of the 6th Regiment," SCDAH, S108121.

66. *CM,* 6-11-61.
67. "History of the 6th Regiment," SCDAH, S108121.
68. *RR,* 6, 454; *YE,* 1-24-61.
69. *CM,* 7-25-61.
70. *RR,* 6, 410.
71. "History of the 6th Regiment," SCDAH, S108121; *YE,* 1-24-61.
72. *YE,* 1-31-61; *CM,* 1-22-61; *CMH*, 521.
73. "History of the 6th Regiment," SCDAH, S10812.
74. *Acts,* 865.
75. "History of the 6th Regiment," SCDAH, S108121.
76. *CM,* 6-27-61.
77. Ibid., 12-27-61.
78. *RR,* 6, 1; *CSR* M267, 212.
79. Robert J. Stevens, *Captain Bill, The Records and Writings of Captain William Henry Edwards, Seventeenth Regiment (and others) Company A, 17th Regiment South Carolina Volunteers, Confederate States of America*, 1, 80 (hereafter cited as Stevens, *Captain Bill*).
80. *CSR* M267, 203.
81. *YE,* 7-11-61; *LH,* 7-12-61; *CM,* 6-11-61; 7-25-61.
82. *RR,* 6, 454.
83. *CM,* 6-11-61.
84. Ibid., 12-27-61; *RR,* 4, 516.
85. *CM,* 12-23-61; 12-27-61.
86. *RR,* 12, 454.
87. *CM,* 12-27-61.
88. Ibid., 12-23-61.
89. Ibid., 12-27-61.
90. Ibid.
91. *YE,* 7-11-61; 1.1.62; *LH,* 7-12-61; *CM,* 7-8-61; 12-27-61.
92. *CM,* 6-29-61.
93. *YE,* 7-11-61.
94. Ibid., 1-2-61; *Carolina Spartan,* 7-11-61; *CM,* 12-27-61; SHSP, Index; *CSR* M267, 204; *CDC,* 2-8-62.
95. *Carolina Spartan,* 7-11-61.
96. *CSR* M267, 208.
97. *CM,* 7-8-61; 12-27-61.
98. *Greenville Southern Enterprise*, 10-17-61.
99. *RR,* 2, 558.
100. *CM,* 9-12-62; *RR,* 6, 455.
101. Baldwin, *The Struck Eagle,* 176.
102. Kirkland, *Broken Fortunes,* 335; *RR,* 9, 514.
103. *CMH*, 517.
104. Brock, *The Appomattox Roster,* 123.
105. *LL,* 6-1-62.
106. *RR,* 1, 443.
107. Brock, *The Appomattox Roster,* 123.
108. *CM,* 9-12-63.
109. Brock, *The Appomattox Roster,* 123.
110. *EA,* 7-2-62; *CM,* 5-10-62.
111. *CM,* 9-12-62.
112. Brock, *The Appomattox Roster,* 123; *CV,* 21, 177.
113. *TriWeekly Watchman*, 6-27-62.
114. Coker, *History,* 191; SHSP, 15, 123.
115. Coker, *History,* 44.
116. E. Frank Melton, *War Between the States*, 65 (hereafter cited as Melton, *War*).
117. SHSP, 15, 17.

118. History of the 6th Regiment," SCDAH, S108121.
119. *DWT,* 7-4-62.
120. SCDAH, *Roll of the Dead.*
121. SHSP, 16, 17.
122. *DWT,* 7-4-62.
123. *CM,* 9-12-62.
124. *CMH,* 521.
125. Brock, *The Appomattox Roster,* 123.
126. *CM,* 6-5-62.
127. *RR,* 12, 456.
128. Brock, *The Appomattox Roster,* 123; SHSP, 15, 123.
129. *CM,* 6-7-62.
130. Ibid., 9-10-62.
131. SCDAH, *Roll of the Dead*; *CM,* 11-11-63.
132. SHSP, 15, 123.
133. *CM,* 9-12-62.
134. Brock, *The Appomattox Roster,* 123.
135. *TriWeekly Watchman,* 5-18-63.
136. Brock, *The Appomattox Roster,* 123.
137. Sifakis, *Compendium,* 72.
138. Baldwin, *The Struck Eagle,* 65.
139. *CM,* 4-12-61; *RR,* 11, 425.
140. *RR,* 6, 454.
141. *OR,* 1, 53, 159; *CM,* 5-1-61; *RR,* 6, 342.
142. *OR,* 1, 53, 167, 170.
143. *YE,* 7-18-61; *CM,* 6-4-61; *RR,* 6, 343.
144. *OR,* 1, 53, 178.
145. *CM,* 7-17-61.
146. Jesse E. Reid, *History of the Fourth Regiment, S.C. Volunteers, from the Commencement of the War until Lee's Surrender,* 35 (hereafter cited as Reid, *History*).
147. Austin, *Letters,* 45.
148. *CMH,* 560; *CM,* 1-4-62.
149. *CM,* 7-14-62.
150. Baldwin, *The Struck Eagle,* 356.
151. Ibid., 360; Coward, *The South Carolinians,* 180.

Chapter 6

1. *EA,* 12-9-63.
2. *OR,* 1, 47, 3, 773.
3. *CM,* 3-9-61.
4. *EA,* 3-6-61.
5. *CM,* 7-12-60.
6. *EA,* 3-20-61; *CM,* 3-16-61; 3-22-61.
7. *CDC,* 4-18-61.
8. *CM,* 6-6-62.
9. Ibid., 10-8-62.
10. Ibid., 8-23-63.
11. Dickert, *Kershaw's Brigade,* 102.
12. *CM,* 3-9-61; *EA,* 3-6-61.
13. *AP,* 1-18-61.
14. *CM,* 7-29-63.
15. *DWT,* 6-13-62.
16. Krick, *Lee's Colonels,* 133.
17. *EA,* 3-6-61; *CM,* 3-9-61; McArthur, *Griffin,* 205.
18. Krick, *Lee's Colonels,* 338; *CM,* 12-17-61.

19. *TCC,* 12-20-61.
20. *CM,* 12-17-61.
21. Ibid., 7-29-63.
22. *CSR* M267, 221.
23. Ibid.
24. Ibid.
25. Krick, *Lee's Colonels*, 338.
26. C.M. Calhoun, "Liberty Dethroned," 15 (hereafter cited as Calhoun, "Liberty").
27. *CDC,* 9-30-62.
28. *CM,* 6-6-62.
29. L.E. Estilow, ed. "A Historical Sketch of the Georgetown Rifle Guards," 2 (hereafter cited as Estilow, "Sketch").
30. *CDC,* 10-17-62; *CM,* 9-25-62.
31. *EA,* 10-1-62; *CDC,* 9-30-62.
32. *CDC,* 10-17-62.
33. Dickert, *Kershaw's Brigade,* 164.
34. *CM,* 8-13-63.
35. *OR,* 1, 28, 2, 307.
36. Dickert, *Kershaw's Brigade,* 165.
37. *RR,* 10, 396.
38. *CDC,* 9-30-62.
39. *CM,* 6-6-62.
40. *EA,* 9-30-63.
41. Ibid.
42. Ibid; *CM,* 7-4-62; 8-2-62.
43. *CM,* 1-5-63; 7-21-63; Dickert, *Kershaw's Brigade,* 283.
44. *CM,* 8-13-63.
45. *EA,* 9-30-63.
46. Ibid; *RR,* 9, 407.
47. Dickert, *Kershaw's Brigade,* 282.
48. *EA,* 1-6-64.
49. *CM,* 6-6-62.
50. Ibid., 2-3-62; 6-6-62.
51. Dickert, *Kershaw's Brigade,* 111.
52. *EA,* 10-15-62; *For Love of a Rebel*, Arthur Manigault Chapter of the U.D.C., 119 (hereafter cited as *For Love of a Rebel*).
53. *CM,* 12-3-62.
54. Ibid., 10-2-63.
55. *EA,* 11-4-63.
56. Ibid., 10-7-63; 11-4-63; Krick, *Lee's Colonels*, 178.
57. *CSR* M267, 218.
58. Dickert, *Kershaw's Brigade,* 281.
59. SHSP, 13, 392.
60. *EA,* 11-4-63.
61. Ibid., 11-2-64; *CM,* 5-27-64; *CMH*, 657.
62. *CM,* 1-5-63.
63. Ibid., 5-27-64.
64. Krick, *Lee's Colonels*, 200.
65. *EA,* 8-24-64.
66. Calhoun, "Liberty Dethroned," 95, 100; *AP,* 1-18-61.
67. *DSG,* 5-6-61; *AP,* 5-10-61.
68. Brooks, *Stories*, 47; Wyckoff, *2nd South Carolina Infantry*, xii-xiii; *CMH*, 724.
69. *CM,* 4-18-61.
70. Ibid., 6-5-62.
71. *AP,* 5-31-61; *DWT,* 3-7-62; *CM,* 4-18-61.

72. *AP,* 1-18-61.
73. *RR,* 11, 32.
74. *AP,* 5-31-61.
75. Ibid.
76. *RR,* 6, 396; *AP,* 1-18-61.
77. *CM,* 6-3-61.
78. *AP,* 1-18-61.
79. Ibid; *CM,* 6-3-61.
80. *CM,* 6-3-61.
81. *EA,* 2-6-61.
82. Ibid., 2-19-62.
83. *CM,* 6-3-61.
84. Dickert, *Kershaw's Brigade,* 38.
85. *EA,* 6-5-61.
86. Ibid., 2-6-61.
87. Ibid.
88. Ibid., 9-18-61.
89. Ibid., 9-11-61, *AP,* 10-25-61.
90. *CV,* 31, 186; *CMH,* 441.
91. *EA,* 6-5-61.
92. *CM,* 4-19-61; 4-23-61.
93. *RR,* 3, 552.
94. *CM,* 6-3-61.
95. *RR,* 4, 318.
96. Dickert, *Kershaw's Brigade,* 481.
97. *RR,* 9, 407.
98. *EA,* 1-20-61.
99. Ibid., 9-30-63.
100. Ibid., 3-20-61.
101. *CM,* 6-3-61.
102. *EA,* 2-6-61.
103. *CM,* 6-3-61.
104. *Cyclopedia,* 474.
105. *EA,* 9-11-61.
106. Ibid., 2-6-61.
107. *CM,* 6-3-61; Dickert, *Kershaw's Brigade,* 37.
108. *Horry Dispatch,* 4-11-61; *CM,* 10-21-63; SHSP, Index.
109. *Horry Dispatch,* 4-11-61; 5-9-61.
110. Ibid., 5-9-61.
111. Ibid., 4-11-61.
112. *CDC,* 6-7-61.
113. *CM,* 6-26-61.
114. *EA,* 7-24-61.
115. Dickert, *Kershaw's Brigade,* 113.
116. *AP,* 5-31-61; *DWT,* 3-7-62; *CM,* 4-18-61.
117. *CM,* 1-5-63.
118. Ibid., 5-27-64; *CDC,* 5-16-64.
119. *CM,* 5-27-64; *CMH,* 657.
120. Krick, *Lee's Colonels,* 200.
121. *CDC,* 11-9-63.
122. *CSR* M267, 216.
123. Ibid., M267, 219.
124. *CM,* 7-24-62.
125. Ibid., 10-2-63.
126. Ibid., 7-24-62.

127. *DSC,* 9-23-64; *EA,* 9-21-64.
128. *EA,* 7-16-62.
129. Ibid., 10-7-63; 11-25-63; *CM,* 10-2-63.
130. Gasper Loren Toole, *Ninety Years in Aiken County* (hereafter cited as Toole, *Ninety Years*), 12.
131. *CSR* M267, 219.
132. *CMH*, 441.
133. *Memory Roll*; *RR,* 3, 157.
134. *CSR* M267, 222.
135. *EA,* 10-8-62; *RR,* 10, 384.
136. *RR,* 12, 95
137. Ibid., 10, 384.
138. *CMH*, 694.
139. *EA,* 6-15-64; *CM,* 5-27-64; *RR,* 3, 257; 10, 403.
140. *EA,* 5-25-64; 6-15-64.
141. *CM,* 7-24-62; *CDC,* 11-9-63.
142. *CM,* 10-2-63.
143. *EA,* 12-9-63.
144. Ibid.
145. Ibid., 7-6-64.
146. *CSR* M267, 214.
147. *CM,* 7-24-62.
148. Ibid., 1-5-63; 10-2-63.
149. Ibid., 7-2-462.
150. Ibid., 7-21-63; 10-2-63.
151. *EA,* 7-23-62.
152. Ibid., 6-1-64; *CV,* 20, 286; *CM,* 5-27-64.
153. *EA,* 2-14-65.
154. Ibid., 11-2-64.
155. Ibid., 2-14-65.
156. *CDC,* 11-9-63; *CM,* 7-24-62.
157. *EA,* 11-26-62.
158. *CDC,* 10-20-62.
159. Kirkland, *Broken Fortunes,* 211.
160. *CSR* M267, 219.
161. *EA,* 6-11-62.
162. *CM,* 7-24-62.
163. Ibid., 8-2-62.
164. Ibid., 10-2-62.
165. CM 5-27-64.
166. *CDC,* 5-16-64.
167. *CM,* 5-27-64.
168. *EA,* 9-7-64.
169. Wyckoff, *2nd South Carolina Infantry*, 138.
170. *EA,* 11-2-64.
171. *CM,* 6-3-61.
172. Ibid., 7-22-61.
173. *OR,* 1, 47, 3, 773.
174. *EA,* 4-17-61.
175. *AP,* 4-19-61; *CM,* 4-18-61.
176. *AP,* 4-19-61.
177. *CM,* 4-19-61.
178. *CDC,* 4-18-61.
179. *CM,* 5-2-61.
180. *EA,* 5-8-61; 5-22-61; *CM,* 5-10-61.
181. *AP,* 5-31-61.

182. *CM,* 6-4-61; 6-6-61.
183. Ibid., 6-15-61.
184. Estilow, "Sketch," 6.
185. *OR,* 1, 47, 3, 773.

Chapter 7

1. Dickert, *Kershaw's Brigade,* 526-527
2. *CM,* 5-27-64; *CMH,* 657.
3. *EA,* 4-26-65.
4. James B. Clary, *A History of the 15th South Carolina Infantry 1861–1865,* 285. (Hereafter cited as Clary, *15th SC Regiment.*)
5. *EA,* 4-26-65
6. Clary, *15th SC Regiment,* 285.
7. Ibid.
8. Ibid.
9. Ibid.
10. *EA,* 4-26-65.

Chapter 8

1. *OR,* 1, 6, 114.
2. *TriWeekly Watchman,* 8-12-61.
3. SCDAH, *Roll of the Dead*; Bruce S. Allardice, *More Generals in Gray*, 174 (hereafter cited as Allardice, *Generals*).
4. Hagood, *Memoirs,* 209, 278.
5. *CM,* 4-13-63; Krick, *Lee's Colonels*, 55.
6. *TCC,* 4-10-63.
7. SHSP, 16, 27.
8. Ibid., 16, 26.
9. *CM,* 5-24-64.
10. Hagood, *Memoirs,* 209.
11. *TCC,* 11-16-61; Woodward, *Mary Chesnut*, 201.
12. *TCC,* 11-15-61.
13. Woodward, *Mary Chesnut*, 201.
14. *CM,* 6-15-64; 6-24-64.
15. Samuel N. Thomas, Jr. and Jason H. Silverman, eds., *A Rising Star of Promise: The Civil War Odyssey of David Jackson Logan, 17th South Carolina Volunteers, 1861–1864*, 213 (hereafter cited as Thomas, *Rising Star*).
16. *Carolina Spartan,* 1-23-62.
17. *OR,* 1, 6, 383-386.
18. *CSR* M267, 226.
19. Kirkland, *Broken Fortunes,* 194.
20. SCDAH, *Roll of the Dead*; Kirkland, *Broken Fortunes,* 96.
21. Hagood, *Memoirs,* 375.
22. SHSP, Index.
23. *DSG,* 10-22-61.
24. Ulysses Robert Brooks, ed., *Butler and His Cavalry in the War of Secession, 1861–1865*, 66 (hereafter cited as Brooks, *Butler*).
25. *CSR* M267, 228.
26. *CM,* 7-13-63.
27. *TCC,* 1-3-62; SHSP, Index.
28. *TCC,* 11-29-61.
29. Ibid., 1-3-62.
30. Ibid., 12-13-61.
31. *RR,* 11, 11.
32. *DSG,* 6-6-64.

33. *CM,* 9-29-64.
34. *CMH*, 585.
35. Ibid., 586.
36. *TCC,* 11-14-62.
37. *CM,* 5-24-64; 8-29-64.
38. Ibid., 8-29-64.
39. *Cyclopedia,* 396.
40. *TCC,* 7-11-62.
41. Ibid., 8-28-63.
42. *CDC,* 11-30-63; *CM,* 11-30-63.
43. *CDC,* 3-14-64.
44. *CM,* 3-14-64; 6-24-64.
45. *EA,* 10-22-62; SHSP, Index.
46. *DSG,* 6-27-62.
47. *OR,* 4, 2, 82-83.
48. *RR,* 4, 318.
49. Dickert, *Kershaw's Brigade,* 481.
50. *RR,* 12, 538.
51. Hagood, *Memoirs,* 248.
52. *CM,* 5-24-64; Brooks, *Stories*, 310.
53. *OR,* 1, 28, 2, 368.
54. *OR,* 1, 6, 113-123; *CM,* 4-1-62; *CDC,* 4-15-62.
55. *OR,* 1, 53, 255.
56. Thomas, *Rising Star*, 33.
57. *CM,* 10-27-62.
58. *OR,* 1, 14, 711.
59. Ibid., 1, 14, 742.
60. Ibid.
61. Ibid., 1, 28, 2, 169.
62. Ibid., 1, 28, 1, 73.
63. *CM,* 7-11-63; 7-13-63; 7-17-63.
64. *OR,* 1, 28, 1, 75; *CM,* 7-16-63.
65. *OR,* 1, 28, 1, 372.
66. Ibid., 1, 28, 2, 245, 246, 269, 325, 367.
67. Ibid., 1, 28, 2, 467, 601; 1, 35, 1, 557.
68. Ibid., 1, 35, 1, 377.
69. Ibid., 1, 35, 2, 454.
70. Ibid.
71. Ibid., 1, 35, 2, 518.
72. Ibid.
73. SHSP, 16, 179.
74. *CV,* 25, 458.
75. *CM,* 5-13-64; *CV,* 23, 458.
76. *CM,* 5-24-64; 6-2-64.
77. Ibid., 5-16-64; *CM,* 6-2-64.
78. *CDC,* 5-23-64.
79. *CM,* 5-23-63; SHSP, 16, 190.
80. *CM,* 5-23-64; 5-24-64; 5-26-64; 6-2-64.
81. Ibid., 6-2-64; *CM,* 6-13-64.
82. *CDC,* 8-13-64.
83. *DSG,* 7-14-64.
84. *CM,* 7-29-64; *CDC,* 7-29-64; 8-13-64; Confederate Historian, "Annual Report," 72.
85. *CM,* 8-26-64.
86. Hagood, *Memoirs,* 473.
87. *CM,* 10-18-64.

88. Ibid.
89. Ibid., 1-8-64.
90. *CDC,* 1-25-65; *CM,* 1-23-65.
91. *CM,* 1-30-65.

Chapter 9

1. *CM,* 3-12-62.
2. Wyckoff, *2nd South Carolina Infantry*, viii.
3. Ibid., x.
4. *CM,* 5-23-61.
5. *LL,* 6-5-61; *CM,* 5-31-61; *CDC,* 5-31-61.
6. *CM,* 5-31-61; 6-4-61; *LL,* 7-10-61.
7. *CM,* 6-27-61.
8. Ibid., 6-29-61; 7-8-61; 7-10-61.
9. *YE,* 7-5-61; *DSG,* 7-15-61.
10. *CM,* 7-10-61.
11. Ibid., 7-17-61.
12. Ibid., 7-24-61; *TriWeekly Watchman*, 7-26-61.
13. *LL,* 8-7-61; *TriWeekly Watchman*, 8-12-61; *CM,* 8-28-61.
14. Baldwin, *The Struck Eagle,* 86.
15. Garlington, *Men of the Time*, 33.
16. *CV,* 15, 38.
17. *CM,* 4-10-61.
18. Ibid., 7-10-61; 7-13-61.
19. *TriWeekly Watchman*, 5-30-62; *CDC,* 8-12-62.
20. *TriWeekly Watchman*, 9-8-62.
21. Ibid., 7-14-62.
22. *CV,* 15, 38.
23. Allan D. Thigpen, *Recollections of Potter's Raid*, 289 (hereafter cited as Thigpen, *Potter's Raid*).
24. *CV,* 15, 28.
25. Coker, *History,* 17.
26. *YE,* 7-18-61.
27. *LL,* 7-17-61.
28. Krick, *Lee's Colonels*, 46.
29. *CM,* 7-17-61.
30. Coker, *History,* 17.
31. *YE,* 7-18-61; *CM,* 7-13-61.
32. *CM,* 5-6-62.
33. Coker, *History,* 17.
34. *CDC,* 4-30-61.
35. *CM,* 7-24-61.
36. *LL,* 5-7-62.
37. *TriWeekly Watchman*, 7-26-61; *CM,* 7-24-61.
38. *CDC,* 4-30-61; *CM,* 7-24-61.
39. *RR,* 3, 281.
40. *TriWeekly Watchman*, 6-5-61; *CM,* 7-24-61.
41. *TriWeekly Watchman*, 6-4-61.
42. Ibid., 6-12-61.
43. Ibid., 7-26-61; *CM,* 7-24-61.
44. *LL,* 9-4-61, *CV,* 15, 38.
45. *CM,* 7-24-61.
46. Thigpen, *Potter's Raid*, 226.
47. *CM,* 7-24-61; SHSP, Index.
48. *LL,* 7-10-61.
49. *CM,* 7-24-61; *CMH* 555.

50. *TriWeekly Watchman*, 6-10-61; *RR*, 7, 177.
51. *TriWeekly Watchman*, 6-10-61; 6-19-61.
52. Ibid., 6-27-62.
53. Coker, *History*, 14; *CM*, 7-24-61.
54. *Acts*, 868.
55. Coker, *History*, 16.
56. *CMH*, 509.
57. Coker, *History*, 38.
58. *EA*, 8-7-61; *CM*, 7-24-61.
59. *CM*, 7-8-61; 7-24-61.
60. *Carolina Spartan*, 5-16-61.
61. *LL*, 9-4-61; *CM*, 7-24-61; *Lexington Dispatch*, 6-9-86.
62. *CM*, 7-24-61.
63. *CDC*, 4-30-61.
64. Ibid.
65. Ibid., 7-1-61; *CM*, 6-20-61.
66. *TriWeekly Watchman*, 8-12-61.
67. *OR*, 1, 53, 178.
68. *TriWeekly Watchman*, 7-26-61; *CM*, 7-17-61; *OR*, 4, 1, 487.
69. *TriWeekly Watchman*, 8-12-61; Coker, *History*, 32.
70. Reid, *History*, 35.
71. Coker, *History*, 43.

Chapter 10

1. *CM*, 7-29-61.
2. Ibid., 8-3-61.
3. *EA*, 9-18-61; *CM*, 9-11-61.
4. *EA*, 4-3-62.
5. *CSR* M267, 273.
6. *CM*, 9-11-61; *EA*, 9-18-61.
7. *CM*, 7-1-62; 8-27-62.
8. Ibid., 9-11-62.
9. Gordon C. Rhea, *Carrying the Flag*, 90 (hereafter cited as Rhea, *Carrying the Flag*).
10. *CM*, 9-21-63; *OR* 25, 1, 803, 889.
11. *CV*, 33, 420; *CM*, 2-24-64; 5-23-64.
12. Brock, *The Appomattox Roster*, 367.
13. Caldwell, *History*, 104.
14. *EA*, 9-18-61; *CM*, 9-11-61.
15. *Cyclopedia*, 102.
16. *CV*, 35, 18.
17. *Cyclopedia*, 103.
18. *EA*, 5-25-64.
19. Caldwell, *History*, 169.
20. Brown, *A Colonel*, 53-54.
21. Ibid., 88.
22. Daly, *Portrait*, 113.
23. *CV*, 33, 376; Brown, *A Colonel*, 72, 89.
24. *CM*, 5-31-64; *LL*, 6-7-64.
25. *CM*, 8-4-64.
26. Brown, *A Colonel*, 141.
27. Ibid., 121.
28. *Greenville Southern Enterprise*, 3-5-63.
29. Brown, *A Colonel*, 72, 87.
30. *RR*, 3, 63.
31. Brock, *The Appomattox Roster*, 368; *CMH*, 524.

32. *EA,* 5-25-64; *CM,* 5-18-64.
33. Krick, *Lee's Colonels*, 182.
34. *CM,* 8-3-64.
35. Ibid., 8-30-64; 9-29-64
36. Ibid., 7-4-62.
37. *DSG,* 7-15-62; *CM,* 7-14-62.
38. *CM,* 9-11-62.
39. Confederate Historian, "Annual Report," 33.
40. *CV,* 17, 91.
41. Brock, *The Appomattox Roster,* 368.
42. *EA,* 9-4-61.
43. Ibid., 3-18-63; *CM,* 1-9-62; 7-4-62.
44. *EA,* 3-18-63.
45. *CM,* 5-16-63.
46. Brock, *The Appomattox Roster,* 368; *CV,* 8, 88.
47. *LH,* 3-15-61.
48. Ibid., 8-16-61; *DSG,* 8-29-61.
49. *LH,* 1-18-61; 6-14-61.
50. Ibid., 2-1-61.
51. Ibid., 6-14-61;
52. Ibid., *RR,* 1, 18.
53. *LH,* 7-5-61.
54. Ibid., 3-15-61; 8-16-61.
55. Ibid., 8-2-61.
56. *CM,* 1-6-62; 7-1-62.
57. Ibid., 5-16-63.
58. *DSG,* 5-31-64.
59. *EA,* 8-7-61.
60. Ibid., 5-15-61.
61. Ibid., 8-7-61.
62. *CM,* 7-1-62; 9-11-62.
63. Ibid., 5-16-63; *EA,* 9-7-64.
64. *CM,* 8-3-64.
65. *LH,* 8-9-61; 8-23-61.
66. ac Wyckoff, Website on South Carolina in the Civil War, <http://www.members.ripod.com/mwyckoff/ (hereafter cited as Wyckoff, Website).
67. *LH,* 8-9-61; 8-17-61; *CV,* 35, 105; *RR,* 3, 476; Brown, *A Colonel*, 38.
68. *CM,* 7-4-62.
69. Ibid., 9-11-62; Brown, *A Colonel*, 44.
70. *CM,* 10-2-62; Brown, *A Colonel*, 44.
71. *CM,* 5-16-63; *CV,* 27, 347.
72. *EA,* 5-25-64; *CM,* 5-18-64; Brown, *A Colonel*, 102.
73. Brown, *A Colonel*, 8.
74. Joseph N. Brown, "Account of the Battle of Gettysburg," 103 (hereafter cited as Brown, "Account").
75. Brock, *The Appomattox Roster,* 368.
76. *LH,* 8-16-61.
77. Ibid; *The State*, 9-29-1910.
78. *CM,* 7-4-62; *RR,* 10, 227.
79. *CM,* 7-14-62.
80. *CSR* M267, 275; *RR,* 10, 227.
81. Kirkland, *Broken Fortunes,* 266.
82. *CM,* 5-16-63.
83. *EA,* 5-25-64; *CM,* 5-18-64; 5-24-64.
84. Brock, *The Appomattox Roster,* 368.

85. *DWT,* 5-2-62.
86. Confederate Historian, "Annual Report," 33.
87. *CSR* M267, 276.
88. *CM,* 7-4-62.
89. Ibid., 1-9-62; 5-16-63.
90. Ibid., 8-23-64.
91. Brock, *The Appomattox Roster,* 368.
92. Toole, *Ninety Years*, 13; *CMH*, 325.
93. *CM,* 1-9-62; 7-4-62.
94. Ibid., 7-4-62.
95. Ibid., 5-16-63.
96. Ibid., 8-23-64.
97. Brock, *The Appomattox Roster,* 368.
98. *AP,* 9-6-61; 9-13-61.
99. Ibid., 8-23-61.
100. *CM,* 7-4-62.
101. Ibid., 7-14-62; 5-16-63.
102. *RR,* 6, 421.
103. *CM,* 1-9-62; 7-14-62; 9-11-62; *RR,* 7, 215.
104. *RR,* 6, 422, 429.
105. *DSG,* 7-8-62.
106. *RR,* 6, 423.
107. *DSG,* 7-8-62; *EA,* 5-27-63; *CM,* 5-16-63; *RR,* 1, 505.
108. *RR,* 1, 505.
109. *EA,* 6-1-64.
110. Ibid., 9-7-64; *RR,* 6, 425.
111. *RR,* 6, 423.
112. Ibid., 9, 379.
113. Ibid., 5, 553.
114. Ibid., 6, 422.
115. Ibid., 6, 425.
116. Ibid., 1, 505.
117. *CSR* M267, 270.
118. Confederate Historian, "Annual Report," 34.
119. D.A. Tompkins, *Company K, 14th S.C.V.*, 11 (hereafter cited as Tompkins, *Company K*).
120. *RR,* 6, 156; Brock, *The Appomattox Roster,* 368.
121. *CDC,* 11-8-61; *RR,* 6, 422.
122. *YE,* 12-5-61; *CM,* 12-3-61.
123. *CM,* 12-20-61.
124. *RR,* 6, 422.
125. *CM,* 1-1-62; 2-9-63.
126. Toole, *Ninety Years,* 18.
127. *CM,* 5-19-62.

Chapter 11

1. *OR,* 4, 1, 624.
2. Ibid., 1, 47, 3, 773.
3. *CM,* 7-18-63.
4. Ibid., 1-29-61; 4-8-62.
5. Ibid., 9-11-61.
6. *TCC,* 5-29-63.
7. *CM,* 4-8-62; 7-20-63; Clary, *15th SC Regiment,* 121.
8. Dickert, *Kershaw's Brigade,* 251.
9. SHSP, 4, 183.
10. *CDC,* 9-18-63.

11. *CM,* 9-11-61.
12. *DSG,* 5-4-61.
13. *EA,* 10-23-61; SCDAH, *Roll of the Dead*; *CM,* 10-22-61.
14. *DSG,* 10-23-61 or 10-24-61.
15. *CM,* 9-11-61.
16. Ibid., 9-26-62.
17. *RR,* 2, 252.
18. *CM,* 9-26-62.
19. *DSG,* 3-5-62.
20. Ibid., 1-4-64.
21. *RR,* 2, 252.
22. *DSG,* 1-4-64.
23. Ibid.
24. Krick, *Lee's Colonels*, 158.
25. Dickert, *Kershaw's Brigade,* 175, 312.
26. *CDC,* 7-18-64.
27. *DSG,* 8-7-64.
28. *OR,* 1, 47, 3, 758; Dickert, *Kershaw's Brigade,* 335.
29. *OR,* 1, 47, 3, 757.
30. *RR,* 2, 252.
31. Dickert, *Kershaw's Brigade,* 333, 334.
32. *CM,* 8-15-61; 12-15-62.
33. *DSG,* 8-14-61; *CM,* 8-15-61.
34. *DSG,* 3-5-62; 1-4-64.
35. Ibid., 3-5-62.
36. *CM,* 7-21-63.
37. Ibid.
38. Ibid., 9-29-64.
39. Ibid., 8-9-61; 8-15-61.
40. Ibid., 8-13-61.
41. *RR,* 2, 606.
42. *CDC,* 5-14-63; *CM,* 5-12-63.
43. Clary, *15th SC Regiment,* 481.
44. *CM,* 10-29-64; *CDC,* 10-28-64.
45. *RR,* 5, 440.
46. J. Ogden Murray, 124–125; *The Immortal 600,*
47. *CM,* 12-15-62; *CDC,* 12-9-61.
48. *CDC,* 12-9-61.
49. *CM,* 9-29-64.
50. Calhoun, "Liberty Dethroned," 367.
51. *CM,* 8-17-61; 112-15-62; Woodward, *Mary Chesnut*, 62.
52. Woodward, *Mary Chesnut*, 62.
53. *CM,* 7-21-63.
54. Ibid., 9-29-64.
55. Ibid., 12-15-62.
56. Everson, *Far from Home,* 225.
57. *RR,* 2, 252.
58. *CDC,* 5-14-63; *CM,* 5-12-63; 5-19-63.
59. Clary, *15th SC Regiment,* xvi.
60. *CM,* 7-21-63; 5-27-64.
61. Ibid., 12-15-62.
62. Ibid., 9-17-61.
63. Clary, *15th SC Regiment,* xvi.
64. *CDC,* 12-27-62.
65. *CM,* 10-24-64.

66. Ibid., 12-15-62.
67. Clary, *15th. SC Regiment,* 483.
68. Ibid., 9-26-62; 10-2-62.
69. *RR,* 3, 101.
70. *CM,* 5-18-64
71. Clary, *15th. SC Regiment,* 2.
72. Ibid., 10-2-62.
73. Ibid., 7-21-63.
74. *EA,* 9-25-61; 11-20-61; *AP,* 10-11-61.
75. *CM,* 12-15-62.
76. *DSG,* 9-22-63; *AP,* 9-13-61.
77. *EA,* 9-30-63; 6-24-64.
78. *CM,* 9-29-64.
79. *DSG,* 5-29-64.
80. *CM,* 9-29-64; 10-22-64; *CDC,* 10-22-64; Clary, *15th. SC Regiment,* 2.
81. *CSR* M267, 278.
82. SHSP, 1, 418.
83. Freeman, *Lee's Lieutenants,* 2, 326.
84. *OR,* 1, 47, 3, 773.
85. *CV,* 4, 6.
86. *RR,* 8, 25.
87. *TCC,* 11-15-61.
88. *CM,* 12-3-61; *YE,* 12-5-61.
89. *OR,* 1, 14, 587.
90. Clary, *15th. SC Regiment,* 38.
91. *CM,* 10-2-62.
92. SHSP, 1, 418.

Chapter 12

1. *CM,* 12-18-61.
2. W.H. Edwards, *A Condensed History of the Seventeenth Regiment, S.C.V. C.S.P.A.*, 3 (hereafter cited as Edwards, *Seventeenth Regiment*).
3. Edwards, *Seventeenth Regiment*, 5.
4. *CM,* 2-20-64.
5. Thomas, *Rising Star*, 6.
6. *CMH,* 744.
7. *CM,* 9-9-62; 10-4-62; 11-8-62; Edwards, *Seventeenth Regiment*, 18; *CDC,* 9-6-62.
8. *RR,* 5, 325; Stone, *Wandering*, 54.
9. SHSP, 16, 23.
10. Ibid; Thomas, *Rising Star*, 11
11. Thomas, *Rising Star*, 6
12. James L. Conrad, "The Sad History of 'Shanks' Evans," 36 (hereafter cited as Conrad, "Shanks Evan.").
13. *CDC,* 5-4-63; 7-16-63; Conrad, "Shanks Evans," 33–38; Stone, *Wandering*, 274.
14. *CSR* M267, 294; *YE,* 7-22-63.
15. Stone, *Wandering*, 180.
16. Ibid., 181.
17. *YE,* 6-1-64; *DSG,* 5-27-64.
18. *CV,* 9, 79.
19. Edwards, *Seventeenth Regiment*, 48.
20. *RR,* 9, 208.
21. *YE,* 1-7-63.
22. Thomas, *Rising Star*, 6; *RR,* 12, 461.
23. Edwards, *Seventeenth Regiment*, 6.
24. *CM,* 9-27-62.

25. Ibid., 10-3-62.
26. *CMH*, 527.
27. *YE*, 4-5-65.
28. Brock, *The Appomattox Roster*, 402.
29. Krick, *Lee's Colonels*, 107.
30. *CDC*, 9-10-62.
31. Brock, *The Appomattox Roster*, 402; Stevens, *Captain Bill*, 1, 30.
32. Stevens, *Captain Bill*, 1, v.
33. *CM*, 4-26-65.
34. *RR*, 3, 248.
35. Kirkland, *Broken Fortunes*, 70.
36. Edwards, *Seventeenth Regiment*, 54.
37. *DSG*, 12-31-61.
38. Thomas, *Rising Star*, 184.
39. *YE*, 10-29-62; Thomas, *Rising Star*, 208.
40. *CDC*, 10-23-62.
41. *YE*, 10-22-62; 10-29-62; *CM*, 9-8-62.
42. *CDC*, 10-23-62.
43. Thomas, *Rising Star*, 55.
44. *CSR* M267, 294.
45. *YE*, 8-10-64; *CV*, 10, 422.
46. *CV*, 10, 422.
47. *CDC*, 1-24-62.
48. Ibid., 9-10-62.
49. *CM*, 9-10-62.
50. Stone, *Wandering*, 138.
51. SHSP, 15, 402.
52. *YE*, 1-2-62.
53. *CM*, 6-16-62; SHSP, Index.
54. *YE*, 1-2-62.
55. Thomas, *Rising Star*, 199.
56. Edwards, *Seventeenth Regiment*, 6.
57. Thomas, *Rising Star*, 26.
58. Edwards, *Seventeenth Regiment*, 8.
59. *CM*, 5-16-62; 6-16-62.
60. *RR*, 8, 101.
61. Ibid., 11, 217.
62. Ibid., 11, 216.
63. Brock, *The Appomattox Roster*, 402.
64. *YE*, 11-21-61; 4-3-62; *Cyclopedia*, 228.
65. *YE*, 11-28-61.
66. Ibid., 5-1-62; 7-10-62.
67. *CM*, 4-16-62.
68. *Cyclopedia*, 228.
69. Thomas, *Rising Star*, 6.
70. *YE*, 10-1-62; 10-22-62.
71. *RR*, 8, 299.
72. Thomas, *Rising Star*, 55.
73. *YE*, 6-29-64.
74. Thomas, *Rising Star*, 201.
75. *YE*, 9-10-62.
76. Brock, *The Appomattox Roster*, 402; SHSP, 15, 402.
77. Edwards, *Seventeenth Regiment*, 54.
78. Ibid., 4-9.
79. Brock, *The Appomattox Roster*, 402; SHSP, 15, 402.

80. *RR,* 6, 441.
81. Kirkland, *Broken Fortunes,* 308.
82. *LL,* 12-25-61; *CM,* 4-16-62.
83. *LL,* 11-27-61.
84. Ibid.
85. Ibid., 5-14-62.
86. Ibid., 9-17-62; SHSP, 16, 25.
87. *YE,* 1-16-62.
88. Thomas, *Rising Star,* 4.
89. Ibid., 182.
90. *YE,* 9-24-62; 8-10-64.
91. Brock, *The Appomattox Roster,* 402; *CMH* 520.
92. *OR,* 1, 6, 348.
93. Sifakis, *Compendium,* 92.
94. *RR,* 11, 100; Thomas, *Rising Star,* 4.
95. *YE,* 1-16-62.
96. *OR,* 1, 6, 362; *YE,* 1-2-62; *CM,* 12-20-61; *RR,* 11, 100; Thomas, *Rising Star,* 5.
97. *RR,* 9, 202.
98. *OR,* 1, 6, 362.
99. *RR,* 9, 202; Edwards, *Seventeenth Regiment,* 4.
100. Thomas, *Rising Star,* 4.
101. Ibid., 5.
102. *RR,* 11, 110; *YE,* 4-24-62.
103. *CM,* 6-3-62; *OR,* 1, 14, 25.
104. Thomas, *Rising Star,* 7, 20.
105. *OR,* 1, 14, 34.
106. Thomas, *Rising Star,* 26.
107. Ibid, 33.
108. *OR,* 1, 14, 587.
109. Ibid., 1, 14, 587; Sketches of the 23rd. Regiment, SCV, Miscellaneous Sketches, 1868–1898, South Carolina Department of Archives and History, S108121 (hereafter cited as Sketches of the 23rd Regiment, SCDAH, S108121).
110. *OR,* 1, 14, 587.
111. Thomas, *Rising Star,* 40.
112. *RR,* 8, 410.
113. Ibid., 11, 12; Edwards, *Seventeenth Regiment,* 15.
114. Stone, *Wandering,* 28, 36.
115. *CM,* 9-8-62; *CDC,* 8-30-62; 9-27-62.
116. Sketches of the 23rd Regiment, SCV, Miscellaneous Sketches, 1868–1898, South Carolina Department of Archives and History, S108121.
117. *LL,* 9-17-62; *CM,* 9-9-62; 9-10-62; 9-20-64; 9-27-64.
118. Stevens, *Captain Bill,* 1, 27.
119. *CM,* 9-9-62.
120. Ibid., 9-13-62; 9-25-62; Stone, *Wandering,* 56.
121. *YE,* 1-28-63; *RR,* 11, 14.
122. Everson, *Far from Home,* 159; Thomas, *Rising Star,* 54.
123. Thomas, *Rising Star,* 56.
124. *TriWeekly Watchman,* 1-5-63; *CM,* 12-23-62.
125. *TriWeekly Watchman,* 1-5-63.
126. *YE,* 2-18-63.
127. *DSG,* 4-18-63.
128. *YE,* 4-22-63.
129. *CM,* 5-9-63.
130. *RR,* 8, 421; A.A. James, "Brief History of the 18th South Carolina Volunteers," Miscellaneous Sketches, 1868–1898, South Carolina Department of Archives and History, S108121 (hereafter cited as James, "18th SCV," SCDAH, S108121).

131. *LL,* 7-1-63.
132. *YE,* 8-5-63.
133. Ibid.
134. Ibid., 8-12-63.
135. Ibid., 9-9-63; *OR,* 1, 28, 2, 255.
136. *YE,* 8-26-63; 9-9-63; 9-16-63; *CM,* 8-18-63.
137. *OR,* 1, 28, 2, 309, 325.
138. Ibid., 1, 28, 2, 327, 345, 367; *RR,* 2, 215.
139. Ibid., 1, 28, 2, 590.
140. *RR,* 8, 433.
141. *YE,* 10-11-63; 10-28-63.
142. Ibid., 10-25-63.
143. *OR,* 1, 28, 2, 444, 468, 587, 529.
144. Ibid., 1, 28, 2, 444, 467, 587.
145. *YE,* 11-11-63.
146. *OR,* 1, 28, 2, 587-589.
147. Ibid., 1, 28, 2, 590.
148. *YE,* 11-11-63; *OR,* 1, 28, 2, 468, 587.
149. *OR,* 1, 28, 1, 160, 637.
150. Ibid., 1, 35, 1, 557-559.
151. Ibid., 1, 28, 2, 467, 587, 601; 1, 35, 1, 558.
152. Ibid., 1, 28, 2, 467, 529, 587, 601; 1, 35, 1, 557.
153. Ibid., 1, 35, 1, 189-191.
154. Ibid., 1, 35, 1, 191.
155. Ibid., 1, 35, 1, 604.
156. Ibid., 1, 35, 1, 191.
157. Ibid., 1, 35, 1, 194–203.
158. Ibid., 1, 35, 1, 204.
159. Ibid., 1, 35, 1, 192.
160. James, "18th SCV," SCDAH, S108121.
161. *OR* 1, 35, 1, 194, 196.
162. Ibid., 1, 35, 1, 196, 200.
163. Ibid., 1, 35, 1, 204.
164. Ibid., 1, 35, 1, 621.
165. *CM,* 2-24-64.
166. *OR* 1, 35, 1, 372; 1, 35, 2, 422, 427, 430.
167. Ibid., 1, 35, 2, 435.
168. Ibid., 1, 35, 2, 436.
169. Ibid., 1, 35, 1, 193, 633.
170. Ibid., 1, 35, 2, 426.
171. *CMH,* 740; *CM,* 5161-64; 5-21-64.
172. *RR,* 1, 89.
173. *YE,* 5-11-64; *OR,* 1, 35, 2, 425.
174. *YE,* 5-11-64.
175. Ibid., 5-19-64, 6-8-64.
176. Ibid., 6-1-64; 6-8-64 *DSG,* 5-31-64; *CDC,* 6-4-64; *CM,* 5-28-64.
177. *CM,* 6-24-64.
178. *EA,* 6-29-64; *CDC,* 7-20-64
179. Joshua Hilary Hudson, *Sketches and Reminiscences*, 41 (hereafter cited as Hudson, *Sketches*).
180. *YE,* 8-17-64.
181. *LL,* 8-9-64.
182. *EA,* 8-10-64.
183. *CM,* 11-9-64.
184. Stevens, *Captain Bill*, 1, 62.

Chapter 13

1. *LL*, 4-23-62; *EA*, 1-8-62; *CM*, 1-9-62.
2. *CM*, 12-18-61.
3. Ibid., 2-18-64.
4. Ibid., 2-24-63.
5. Ibid., 2-24-63; 10-5-63.
6. Ibid., 10-5-63; 12-8-63.
7. *CDC*, 2-18-64.
8. *CM*, 1-9-62; 1-4-63.
9. *EA*, 2-5-62.
10. Ibid.
11. Ibid., 10-8-62; SCDAH, *Roll of the Dead*; *CM*, 10-9-62.
12. *EA*, 10-8-62.
13. *CM*, 1-9-62.
14. *CV*, 8, 87.
15. *CMH*, 716.
16. *AP*, 1-30-63; *CM*, 1-14-63.
17. Gary R. Baker, *Cadets in Gray*, 67 (hereafter cited as Baker, *Cadets*); *CMH*, 717.
18. Tower, *A Carolinian Goes To War*, 60.
19. *AP*, 2-27-63.
20. *EA*, 12-10-62.
21. Ibid., 4-30-62; *CM*, 1-9-62.
22. *CM*, 1-9-62; *CDC*, 5-2-62.
23. *EA*, 4-30-62.
24. Ibid., 2-19-62.
25. *CSR* M267, 306.
26. *CM*, 1-4-65; *Memory Roll*; *CDC*, 1-7-65.
27. *EA*, 12-28-64; *CM*, 12-30-64.
28. *EA*, 2-8-65.
29. Ibid.
30. Ibid., 4-15-63.
31. Ibid; *CM*, 1-14-63.
32. Tower, *A Carolinian Goes To War*, 60.
33. *EA*, 4-15-63.
34. *RR*, 6, 48.
35. *AP*, 7-17-63.
36. Tower, *A Carolinian Goes To War*, 103; *RR*, 12, 359.
37. *EA*, 8-3-64.
38. *RR*, 5, 358; 6, 48.
39. *CM*, 2-24-63; 12-8-63.
40. *EA*, 2-19-62.
41. *RR*, 3, 529.
42. Ibid., 3, 530; *EA*, 10-7-63.
43. *CM*, 2-24-63.
44. Ibid., 10-5-63; *CDC*, 10-5-63.
45. *RR*, 3, 530.
46. Baker, *Cadets*, 67.
47. *DSG*, 1-12-63.
48. *EA*, 2-12-62; 2-19-62.
49. Ibid., 11-27-61.
50. Ibid.
51. *CM*, 1-14-63.
52. *CV*, 30, 266.
53. *CM*, 2-24-63; 10-5-63; *CDC*, 10-5-63.
54. *EA*, 2-12-62.

55. *CM,* 2-24-63; 10-5-63; *CSR* M267, 305; *CDC,* 10-5-63.
56. *EA,* 8-3-64.
57. *CM,* 12-30-64; *RR,* 3, 537.
58. *RR,* 3, 537.
59. Ibid., 9, 380.
60. Ibid., 2, 533.
61. CM, 1-14-63.
62. *EA,* 9-21-64.
63. *CSR* M267, 305.
64. *CM,* 2-24-63; 10-5-63; *CDC,* 10-5-63.
65. *CM,* 1-9-62; *CMH*, 729.
66. *CMH*, 729; *CM,* 1-14-63; *CSR* M267, 307.
67. *CM,* 2-24-63.
68. Ibid., 10-5-63; *CDC,* 10-5-63.
69. *EA,* 2-19-62; *RR,* 8, 29.
70. *EA,* 7-30-62.
71. Ibid.
72. Kirkland, *Broken Fortunes,* 261.
73. *CM,* 2-24-63; 10-5-63; *CDC,* 10-5-63.
74. *EA,* 2-19-62.
75. *CMH*, 716; *CV,* 8, 87.
76. *CM,* 1-14-63; *DWT,* 8-29-62.
77. *RR,* 1, 336; *CSR* M267, 304; Kirkland, *Broken Fortunes,* 64.
78. *CDC,* 10-5-63; *CM,* 10-5-63.
79. *CM,* 2-24-63; 10-5-63; *CDC,* 10-5-63.
80. *DSC,* 6-16-64; *RR,* 1, 336.
81. *RR,* 1, 336.
82. Ibid., 1, 336; 8, 31; *CSR* M267, 304.
83. Kirkland, *Broken Fortunes,* 64.
84. *AP,* 1-30-63; *CSR* M267, 307.
85. *EA,* 2-19-62.
86. *RR,* 6, 47.
87. *AP,* 1-30-63.
88. *CM,* 1-14-63.
89. *CMH*, 717; *CSR* M267, 307.
90. *EA,* 1-14-63.
91. *CM,* 2-24-63.
92. Ibid., 10-5-63; *CDC,* 10-5-63.
93. *EA,* 2-19-62.
94. *DWT,* 6-20-62.
95. Ibid.
96. *Ibid.,* 6-27-62.
97. *Ibid.,*6-20-62.
98. *CSR* M267, 304.
99. *CM,* 2-24-63; *CDC,* 10-5-63.
100. *CM,* 10-5-63.
101. Ibid., 4-15-62.
102. *EA,* 4-30-62; *CM,* 1-9-62.
103. *CM,* 1-9-62.
104. *Cyclopedia,* 310; *RR,* 11, 211.
105. *RR,* 12, 97.
106. *EA,* 2-1-65.
107. *CM,* 2-24-63; 10-5-63; *CDC,* 10-5-63.
108. Sifakis, *Compendium,* 94.
109. Tower, *A Carolinian Goes To War*, xiii.

110. *OR,* 1, 47, 3, 734.
111. Ibid., 1, 47, 1, 1064.
112. *RR,* 5, 257.
113. *CDC,* 5-2-62.
114. *CM,* 4-13-62.
115. *EA,* 4-30-62; *CDC,* 5-2-62.
116. *CDC,* 4-22-62.
117. *CM,* 4-15-62.
118. *EA,* 4-30-62; 5-7-62; *DWT,* 5-9-62; *CM,* 4-29-62; 5-8-62; *RR,* 5, 258.
119. *DWT,* 7-4-62; *CM,* 5-20-62; *RR,* 8, 453.
120. *CDC,* 7-29-62.
121. Tower, *A Carolinian Goes To War*, 55, 61.
122. *CM,* 3-30-63.
123. *CDC,* 2-18-63; 3-7-63; *CM,* 3-21-63.
124. *CV,* 15, 263; 28, 128.
125. *CDC,* 3-7-63; *RR,* 9, 168.
126. *CM,* 1-14-63; *CDC,* 2-18-63.
127. *CM,* 2-24-63.
128. *AP,* 2-20-63.
129. Ibid., 5-15-63; 6-5-63; 6-19-63; 6-26-63; 7-3-63.
130. Ibid., 7-10-63; 7-17-63.
131. Walker, *Rolls,* 98.
132. *CDC,* 10-17-63.
133. *CM,* 10-1-63.
134. Ibid., 5-30-64.
135. Ibid.
136. *RR,* 5, 358; Tower, *A Carolinian Goes To War*, 265.
137. Tower, *A Carolinian Goes To War*, 219.
138. Ibid., 251.
139. Walker, *Rolls,* 132.
140. S. Emanuel, "A Historical Sketch of the Georgetown Rifle Guards."

Chapter 14

1. *OR,* 1, 47, 1, 1064.
2. Walker, *Rolls,* 132.
3. *OR,* 1, 47, 1, 1064.
4. Sifakis, *Compendium,* 95.
5. *CV,* 6, 335.
6. Sifakis, *Compendium*, 95.
7. *CSR* M267, 305.
8. *CSR* M267, 308

Chapter 15

1. Edwards, *Seventeenth Regiment*, 29.
2. *CM,* 12-18-61.
3. *DSG,* 1-13-62; *CM,* 1-13-62.
4. *OR,* 1, 47, 3, 773.
5. *CDC,* 6-6-64; Krick, *Lee's Colonels*, 220.
6. *CM,* 1-13-62; 6-2-62.
7. *EA,* 6-15-64; *DSC,* 6-8-64.
8. Freeman, *Lee's Lieutenants,* 3, 506; *CM,* 6-13-63; 6-6-64; 6-20-64; Dickert, *Kershaw's Brigade,* 375; *RR,* 6, 202.
9. *CV,* 35, 18; Krick, *Lee's Colonels,* 220.
10. *RR,* 9, 155.
11. Dickert, *Kershaw's Brigade,* 370.

12. *CM,* 6-20-64.
13. Hagood, *Memoirs,* 257.
14. *CM,* 10-26-61; 1-13-62.
15. Krick, *Lee's Colonels*, 110.
16. *OR,* 1, 28, 1, 440.
17. *CM,* 6-2-62; 4-29-64.
18. Dickert, *Kershaw's Brigade,* 366.
19. *CM,* 1-13-62.
20. *RR,* 11, 347.
21. Ibid., 5, 568.
22. Ibid., 11, 347; Krick, *Lee's Colonels*, 272.
23. *CM,* 6-2-62.
24. *CDC,* 7-18-64.
25. *CM,* 11-2-64.
26. SHSP, 3, 184.
27. Melton, *War,* 47.
28. *CM,* 11-2-64.
29. Ibid., 8-8-64; *CDC,* 8-9-64.
30. Dickert, *Kershaw's Brigade,* 368.
31. *OR,* 1, 47, 3, 757.
32. Dickert, *Kershaw's Brigade,* 335.
33. Roster of Officers, Confederate Historian, South Carolina Department of Archives and History, S108079 (hereafter cited as Roster of Officers, SCDAH, S108079).
34. *CM,* 6-2-62; 8-11-63.
35. *CDC,* 10-26-64; *CM,* 11-2-64.
36. *CM,* 6-2-62; 10-31-64.
37. *CDC,* 11-19-64.
38. Roster of Officers, SCDAH, S108079.
39. *CM,* 6-2-62.
40. Ibid., 10-31-64; *RR,* 168.
41. *DSG,* 12-31-61.
42. Roster of Officers, SCDAH, S108079.
43. *DSG,* 12-31-61.
44. *CM,* 6-2-62.
45. Ibid., 8-27-63.
46. Ibid., 10-31-64; 11-2-64.
47. Ibid., 2-18-62.
48. Ibid., 6-2-62; *RR,* 5, 123.
49. *RR,* 7, 357; Confederate Historian, "Annual Report," 49.
50. Roster of Officers, SCDAH, S108079.
51. *CM,* 6-2-62; 8-11-63.
52. *RR,* 12, 296.
53. *CDC,* 10-26-64; *CM,* 6-2-62; 8-11-63.
54. *CMH*, 695; SCDAH, *Roll of the Dead*; *Memory Roll*; *CM,* 10-31-64.
55. Dickert, *Kershaw's Brigade,* 442.
56. Ibid., 441.
57. *SW,* 2-17-64.
58. Roster of Officers, SCDAH, S108079.
59. *CM,* 6-2-62; 1-17-63.
60. *CSR* M267, 312.
61. Ibid.
62. *CM,* 8-11-63; 10-31-64.
63. *RR,* 5, 564.
64. *CM,* 6-2-62.
65. *RR,* 5, 565.

66. *CM,* 6-2-62; 11-2-64; *RR,* 5, 563.
67. *CM,* 10-31-64; 11-2-64.
68. *RR,* 5, 556.
69. *CDC,* 12-9-61; 3-31-62.
70. *LL,* 2-19-62.
71. *CM,* 8-8-61.
72. Ibid., 6-2-62; 8-11-63.
73. *RR,* 5, 568.
74. *DSG,* 3-3-62.
75. *RR,* 2, 304.
76. *CM,* 6-2-62; 8-11-63.
77. *RR,* 5, 568.
78. Confederate Historian, "Annual Report," 49.
79. *CM,* 1-14-63.
80. Ibid., 6-2-62.
81. Ibid., 11-20-60; 7-23-61.
82. *RR,* 5, 519.
83. Ibid.
84. *CM,* 7-23-61.
85. *RR,* 5, 519.
86. *CM,* 6-2-62.
87. *OR,* 1, 35, 1, 558.
88. Ibid., 1, 28, 2, 367, 467, 601; 1, 35, 1, 548, 558.
89. *CM,* 6-2-62.
90. *OR,* 1, 28, 2, 467, 601; 1, 35, 1, 548, 558.
91. Ibid., 1, 35, 2, 518.
92. Sifakis, *Compendium*, 96.
93. *RR,* 5, 567.
94. *CM,* 1-13-62; 3-5-62.
95. *CDC,* 4-22-62; *CM,* 4-22-62; 11-12-62.
96. *RR,* 5, 569; *CM,* 4-22-62.
97. *RR,* 5, 570.
98. *OR,* 1, 14, 925.
99. *CM,* 2-2-63; *CDC,* 2-3-63.
100. *OR,* 1, 14, 823.
101. Ibid., 1, 14, 272.
102. Ibid., 1, 14, 932; Edwards, *Seventeenth Regiment*, 30.
103. *OR,* 1, 28, 2, 162, 245.
104. Ibid., 1, 28, 2, 468, 602.
105. Ibid., 1, 28, 2, 162.
106. *CM,* 7-21-63; 8-11-63; *CDC,* 8-11-63.
107. *CM,* 7-16-63.
108. *OR,* 1, 28, 1, 372.
109. Ibid.
110. *CM,* 8-11-63; *OR,* 1, 28, 2, 219, 223.
111. *OR,* 1, 28, 1, 375; 1, 28, 2, 245; *CM,* 8-11-63.
112. *RR,* 8, 40.
113. *OR,* 1, 28, 1, 384, 458.
114. Ibid., 1, 28, 1, 383, 385.
115. *CM,* 8-27-63; *OR,* 1, 28, 1, 387, 466.
116. *OR,* 1, 28, 1, 393, 396; *CDC,* 8-27-63.
117. *OR,* 1, 28, 1, 500.
118. *CM,* 9-1-63; *OR,* 1, 28, 1, 398.
119. *OR* 1, 28, 2, 367, 467, 601; 1, 35, 1, 557.
120. Ibid., 1, 35, 2, 435.

121. Ibid., 1, 35, 1, 203, 204, 212, 214; 1, 35, 2, 485.
122. Ibid., 1, 35, 2, 495.
123. Ibid., 1, 35, 1, 119; 1, 35, 2, 505.
124. *CM,* 6-6-64.

Chapter 16

1. *AP,* 1-25-61; *CM,* 1-23-61; 1-25-61.
2. *CDC,* 1-23-61.
3. Ibid; *AP,* 1-25-61.
4. *DSG,* 4-13-61.
5. *CMH*, 688; *Cyclopedia,* 176.
6. *CM,* 4-18-61; 5-2-61.
7. *OR,* 1, 53, 159; *CDC,* 5-2-61.
8. *CDC,* 5-2-61; *CM,* 6-4-61.
9. *CM,* 6-18-61.
10. *EA,* 6-26-61; *CDC,* 6-27-61.
11. *EA,* 6-26-61.
12. SHSP, 30, 138-141.
13. *CM,* 7-3-61.
14. Ibid., 6-29-61; 7-3-61.
15. *AP,* 1-25-62; *DSG,* 2-24-62.
16. SHSP, 30, 138-141.
17. *OR,* 1, 6, 326.
18. SHSP, 30, 138-141.
19. *DSG,* 2-24-62.
20. *CDC,* 5-3-62.
21. Ibid., 4-30-62.
22. Ibid., 5-3-62.
23. *OR,* 1, 35, 2, 646; 1, 44, 876; 1, 47, 2, 1073.
24. *CSR* M267, 361.
25. Brooks, *Stories*, 23.
26. *EA,* 7-10-61.
27. *CSR* M267, 391, 445.
28. *OR,* 1, 35, 2, 646; 1, 44, 876; 1, 47, 2, 1073.
29. *CM,* 11-20-60.
30. *CMH*, 603; *CM,* 5-23-61.
31. *RR,* 5, 519.
32. *CM,* 7-23-61; *DSG,* 7-24-61.
33. *RR,* 5, 519.
34. *YE,* 1-10-61; *DSG,* 1-4-61.
35. *CM,* 2-11-61.
36. *OR,* 1, 1, 46; *RR,* 5, 562; Confederate Historian, "Annual Report," 39.
37. *OR,* 1, 1, 38.
38. *CDC,* 4-26-61.
39. Ibid., 5-25-61.
40. *CMH*, 626.
41. *DSG,* 8-3-61.
42. *YE,* 1-27-64; *CM,* 1-26-64.
43. Krick, *Lee's Colonels*, 167.
44. *DSC,* 6-29-64; 8-17-64; *DSG,* 5-29-64.
45. *CDC,* 5-20-64.
46. *DSC,* 8-13-64.
47. Ibid., 8-17-64.
48. Walker, *Rolls,* introduction, 2.
49. *DSG,* 5-30-64.

50. Baker, *Cadets*, 156.
51. *RR*, 5, 557.
52. *DSC*, 6-11-64.
53. *CDC*, 2-18-63.
54. Ibid.
55. *DSG*, 2-17-63; 2-27-63; *CM*, 3-17-63.
56. *YE*, 4-22-63.
57. Ibid.
58. *CDC*, 3-17-63.
59. *DSG*, 4-7-63.
60. *YE*, 4-22-63.
61. *DSG*, 4-18-63; Confederate Historian, "Annual Report," 82.

Chapter 17

1. *OR*, 1, 53, 182; *YE*, 11-14-61.
2. *CDC*, 11-9-61.
3. *CV*, 35, 214.
4. Eleanor D. McSwain, ed., Crumbling Defenses or Memoirs and Reminiscences of John Logan Black, 17 (hereafter cited as McSwain, *Crumbling Defenses*).
5. *CM*, 1-27-62; *EA*, 1-15-62.
6. *CM*, 1-27-62.
7. *CDC*, 4-16-62.
8. Ibid., 11-7-61.
9. Ibid., 9-22-62.
10. *CM*, 8-6-63.
11. *CV*, 35, 214; McSwain, *Crumbling Defenses*, 59.
12. McSwain, *Crumbling Defenses*, 72.
13. *EA*, 9-21-64, 11-16-64.
14. *EA*, 10-5-64; *CM*, 10-11-64; McSwain, *Crumbling Defenses*, 85.
15. *EA*, 10-12-64.
16. Ibid., 10-5-64.
17. Ibid., 9-21-64.
18. Ibid., 3-11-63.
19. McSwain, *Crumbling Defenses*, 75.
20. *CM*, 4-21-62; 8-12-61; 9-26-63.
21. *OR*, 1, 53, 183.
22. *AP*, 7-26-61.
23. *CM*, 7-27-63.
24. *AP*, 8-7-63.
25. McSwain, *Crumbling Defenses*, 48.
26. *DSG*, 9-12-63.
27. Kirkland, *Broken Fortunes*, 265.
28. *CDC*, 2-8-62; Confederate Historian, "Annual Report," 45; *LH*, 9-27-61; *EA*, 1-15-62; *Carolina Spartan*, 1-30-62; 2-6-62; *CM*, 4-21-62; 9-26-63.
29. *EA*, 3-11-63.
30. *OR*, 1, 53, 183.
31. *LH*, 9-27-61.
32. *CM*, 4-21-62; *EA*, 11-26-62; *CDC*, 11-24-62.
33. *OR*, 1, 53, 183.
34. Ibid.
35. Ibid., .
36. *CM*, 6-20-63; 7-27-63.
37. *CDC*, 12-27-61.
38. *OR*, 1, 53, 183.
39. *CDC*, 12-27-61.

40. *CM,* 6-20-63; 7-27-63.
41. *CMH,* 460.
42. McSwain, *Crumbling Defenses,* 100.
43. *OR,* 1, 53, 183.
44. McSwain, *Crumbling Defenses,* 58.
45. Ibid., 116.
46. *OR,* 1, 53, 183.
47. *YE,* 2-13-62.
48. *CM,* 6-12-62; 6-20-63; *RR,* 6, 456; 8, 279; Brooks, *Butler*, 160.
49. *YE,* 6-24-63.
50. Ibid., 7-8-63.
51. Brooks, *Stories*, 308.
52. McSwain, *Crumbling Defenses,* 20.
53. Brooks, *Butler*, 137.
54. *YE,* 6-17-63.
55. *CM,* 7-27-63; *RR,* 8, 279.
56. *CDC,* 4-16-62; *OR,* 1, 53, 183.
57. *CM,* 6-20-63.
58. Ibid., 2-5-64; 5-23-64.
59. *DSC,* 5-14-64.
60. McSwain, *Crumbling Defenses,* 20.
61. Ibid., 38-39.
62. *OR,* 1, 53, 183.
63. Brooks, *Butler*, 178.
64. *CDC,* 11-30-63.
65. *CM,* 11-30-63.
66. McSwain, *Crumbling Defenses,* 25.
67. *OR,* 1, 44, 875.
68. Ibid., 1, 47, 2, 1070.
69. Ibid., 1, 47.2.1145.
70. Ibid., 1, 47, 3, 712.
71. Ibid., 1, 47, 1, 1065.
72. *AP,* 8-23-61.
73. *OR,* 1, 6, 360.
74. *CM,* 4-21-62.
75. *OR,* 1, 14, 25.
76. Ibid., 1, 14, 32.
77. Ibid., 1, 14, 624.
78. *CDC,* 10-1-62.
79. *CM,* 10-1-62.
80. McSwain, *Crumbling Defenses,* 19.
81. Brooks, *Butler*, 178.
82. McSwain, *Crumbling Defenses,* 32.
83. SHSP, 16, 225.
84. *CM,* 8-3-63.
85. Ibid., 9-26-63.
86. *OR,* 1, 35, 2, 362.
87. *CM,* 4-2-64.
88. McSwain, *Crumbling Defenses,* 75.
89. *OR,* 1, 35, 2, 487.
90. *CV,* 35, 214; McSwain, *Crumbling Defenses,* 78; *OR,* 1, 35, 2, 455; 1, 53, 331.
91. *CV,* 35, 214.
92. Warren Ripley, *The Battle of Chapman's Fort, May 26, 1864*, 166 (hereafter cited as Ripley, *Chapman's Fort*); *OR,* 1, 35, 1, 400.
93. *OR,* 1, 35, 2, 644.

94. Ibid., 1, 35, 2, 598-599.
95. Ibid., 1, 35, 2, 644, 646.
96. Ibid., 1, 44, 992, 999.
97. Ibid., 1, 47, 2, 199, 1053.
98. Ibid., 1, 47, 2, 1069, 1205.
99. Ripley, *Chapman's Fort,* 244.
100. *CV,* 35, 214; *OR,* 1, 47, 2, 1169.
101. *CV,* 35, 214.
102. McSwain, *Crumbling Defenses,* 119.

Chapter 18

1. Brooks, *Stories*, 148; Freeman, *Lee's Lieutenants,* 3, 14.
2. Brooks, *Butler*, 552.
3. Ibid., 153.
4. E. Prioleau Henderson, Autobiography of Arab, E. Prioleau Henderson, 112 (hereafter cited as Henderson, *Autobiography*); Edward L. Wells, *Hampton and His Cavalry in '64*, 71 (hereafter cited as Wells, *Hampton*).
5. Brooks, *Butler*, 167, 171.
6. Manly Wade Wellman, *Giant in Gray, A Biography of Wade Hampton of South Carolina*, 109 (hereafter cited as Wellman, *Giant in Gray*).
7. Krick, *Lee's Colonels*, 177.
8. Brooks, *Butler*, 137.
9. *EA,* 2-11-63.
10. Wyckoff, *3rd South Carolina Infantry,* 274.
11. SHSP, Index.
12. Richard Manning Boykin, *Captain Alexander Hamilton Boykin, One of South Carolina's Distinguished Citizens*, 122 (hereafter cited as Boykin, *Alexander Hamilton Boykin*).
13. *CMH*, 456.
14. Boykin, *Alexander Hamilton Boykin,* 124.
15. *Ibid.,* 135.
16. *RR,* 7, 700; Freeman, *Lee's Lieutenants,* 1, 279.
17. Boykin, *Alexander Hamilton Boykin,* 162.
18. Ibid., 170.
19. Ibid., 183.
20. Ripley, *Chapman's Fort,* 297.
21. Wellman, *Giant in Gray,* 131.
22. Henderson, *Autobiography,* 10.
23. *RR,* 11, 210.
24. Ibid., 11, 211.
25. *EA,* 2-11-63.
26. Brooks, *Butler*, 63.
27. Ibid., 65.
28. *OR,* 1, 35, 2, 645.
29. *CM,* 1-29-62; *Memory Roll.*
30. *CDC,* 6-20-63.
31. *EA,* 2-11-63; *Greenville Southern Enterprise*, 1-22-63.
32. *CV,* 23, 420; *EA,* 2-11-63.
33. *CM,* 7-8-61.
34. *CV,* 12, 240.
35. *Greenville Southern Enterprise*, 1-22-63.
36. *CV,* 12, 240.
37. *CM,* 5-22-62.
38. Ibid., 7-10-61; SHSP, Index.
39. *CM,* 6-21-61.
40. Ibid., 5-27-62.

41. *EA,* 9-30-63.
42. *CM,* 7-1-61; SHSP, Index.
43. *DSG,* 6-19-62.
44. *EA,* 8-13-63.
45. *OR,* 1, 47, 3, 712.
46. Ibid., 1, 47, 1, 1065.
47. Raymond P. Boylston, *Butler's Brigade, That Fighting Civil War Cavalry Brigade from South Carolina*, 91 (hereafter cited as Boylston, *Butler's Brigade*).
48. Henderson, *Autobiography,* 52.
49. Ibid., 54.
50. Boylston, *Butler's Brigade,* 100-102.
51. Henderson, *Autobiography,* 57.
52. Freeman, *Lee's Lieutenants,* 3, 14; Brooks, *Stories*, 148.
53. Boylston, *Butler's Brigade,* 128.
54. SHSP, 7, 245; Freeman, *Lee's Lieutenants,* 3, 139.
55. McSwain, *Crumbling Defenses,* 32.
56. SHSP, 16, 225.
57. *CM,* 8-3-63.
58. *EA,* 9-30-63; *CM,* 9-26-63.
59. *OR,* 1, 35, 2, 362.
60. *CM,* 4-2-64.
61. *OR,* 1, 35, 2, 487.
62. McSwain, *Crumbling Defenses,* 79.
63. *OR,* 1, 35, 2, 598.
64. Ibid., 1, 35, 1, 263.
65. Ripley, *Chapman's Fort,* 229.
66. Hagood, *Memoirs,* 344-346.
67. *OR,* 1, 47, 2, 370.
68. Ibid., 1, 47, 2, 1378.
69. Ibid., 1, 47, 2, 1381.
70. Ibid., 1, 47, 2, 1045; 1, 47, 3, 741.
71. *RR,* 11, 231.

Chapter 19

1. Halliburton, *Saddle Soldiers,* 13; William Stokes, "Sketch of Co G, 4th South Carolina Cavalry," Miscellaneous Sketches, 1868–1898, South Carolina Department of Archives and History, S108121 (hereafter cited as "Sketch of Co. G, SCDAH, S108121).
2. Confederate Historian, "Annual Report," 57.
3. Halliburton, *Saddle Soldiers,* 239.
4. *CM,* 5-19-62.
5. Ibid., 4-5-60.
6. Halliburton, *Saddle Soldiers,* 14.
7. Ibid., 25.
8. Ibid., 19, 24.
9. *CM,* 5-19-62; 12-27-62.
10. *CDC,* 1-24-62.
11. "Sketch of Co.G, SCDAH," S108121.
12. *CDC,* 1-24-62; *CM,* 1-6-64.
13. *CM,* 5-6-62.
14. "Sketch of Co.G, SCDAH," S108121.
15. Roster of Officers, SCDAH, S108079.
16. *CM,* 12-27-62; Brooks, *Butler*, 189.
17. *CDC,* 1-30-62; Halliburton, *Saddle Soldiers,* 13.
18. Halliburton, *Saddle Soldiers,* 239.
19. "Sketch of Co. G, SCDAH," S108121.

20. Ibid.
21. Halliburton, *Saddle Soldiers,* 20.
22. *CM,* 1-6-64; *Memory Roll.*
23. *LL,* 1-15-62; 1-22-62; 2-5-62; 3-26-62.
24. Sketch of Co. G, SCDAH," S108121.
25. *LL,* 11-27-61, *TCC,* 12-20-61.
26. *DSG,* 1-9-62.
27. *CM,* 1-6-64.
28. *TCC,* 12-20-61.
29. Ibid., 1-10-62; *RR,* 1, 459.
30. Roster of Officers, SCDAH, S1008079.
31. *LL,* 5-14-62.
32. Wyckoff, Website.
33. *LL,* 5-14-62.
34. Ibid., 2-5-62.
35. Ibid., 3-26-62.
36. Ibid., 5-14-62.
37. *CM,* 6-3-62.
38. *OR,* 1, 14, 624.
39. *CM,* 10-21-62.

Chapter 20

1. Confederate Historian, "Annual Report," 57.
2. Roster of Officers, SCDAH, S1008079.
3. *CM,* 6-3-62.
4. *RR,* 12, 43.
5. *CM,* 10-25-62; 10-28-62; Halliburton, *Saddle Soldiers,* 167; *RR,* 12, 43.
6. *CM,* 1-27-63.
7. Roster of Officers, SCDAH, S1008079.
8. *CM,* 7-23-60.
9. Roster of Officers, SCDAH, S1008079.
10. *CM,* 2-7-61.
11. *YE,* 1-31-61.
12. Roster of Officers, SCDAH, S1008079.
13. *CSR* M267.
14. Roster of Officers, SCDAH, S1008079.
15. *RR,* 7, 207.
16. Ibid.
17. *CM,* 5-30-62; *OR,* 1, 14, 25; Sifakis, *Compendium,* 47.
18. *CM,* 10-27-62; *CDC,* 10-25-62.

Chapter 21

1. *CDC,* 5-21-62; 6-16-62.
2. Ibid., 6-12-62.
3. *CM,* 8-1-62.
4. Ibid., 2-18-64.
5. *CDC,* 7-31-62.
6. Ibid.
7. Ibid., 8-27-62.
8. *CDC* 9-9-62; 10-7-62.
9. Ibid., 9-9-62.
10. *OR,* 1, 14, 603.
11. Ibid., 1, 53, 257.
12. Ibid., 1, 14, 603.
13. Ibid., 4, 3, 166.

14. Ibid., 4, 2, 82-83.
15. *CDC,* 9-25-62.
16. *DSG,* 5-19-62.
17. *EA,* 7-9-62.
18. Ibid., 7-30-62.
19. Ibid., 6-18-62.
20. *DSG,* 6-27-62.
21. Ibid.
22. *CM,* 6-23-64.
23. Cauthen, ed., *Journals,* 204.
24. *CMH*, 648.
25. *EA,* 9-24-62.
26. Ibid.
27. *OR,* 1, 14, 624; 1, 53, 257.
28. Hagood, *Memoirs,* 104.
29. *CM,* 1-6-64.

Chapter 22

1. *YE,* 11-28-64; *OR,* 1, 28, 2, 458.
2. Woodward, *Mary Chesnut*, 240; Confederate Historian, "Annual Report," 80.
3. Daly, *Portrait*, 240.
4. *TCC,* 11-1-61.
5. CC, 7-4-62.
6. *TCC,* 7-4-62.
7. Ibid., 8-8-62.
8. *CM,* 8-29-62.
9. *TCC,* 8-29-62.
10. Thigpen, *Potter's Raid*, 26.
11. *TCC,* 10-24-62.
12. Ibid., 11-7-62; 11-28-62.
13. *OR,* 4, 2, 741.
14. *TCC,* 9-4-63.
15. *OR,* 1, 28, 2, 457.
16. Ibid., 1, 28, 2, 463.
17. *TCC,* 12-11-63.
18. *OR,* 1, 35, 2, 377.
19. Ibid., 1, 35, 2, 362.
20. Ibid., 1, 35, 2, 457, 598, 644.
21. Ibid., 1, 44, 875.
22. *RR,* 5, 519.
23. *CM,* 11-20-60; 7-23-61.
24. *RR,* 5, 519.
25. Confederate Historian, "Annual Report," 81.
26. *RR,* 5, 519.
27. *OR,* 1, 35, 2, 598.
28. Ibid., 1, 35, 2, 644.
29. Ibid., 1, 44, 875.
30. *Memory Roll.*
31. *EA,* 1-25-65.
32. *CDC,* 12-4-61; *CM,* 11-30-61.
33. *CDC,* 12-4-61.
34. *CM,* 1-7-62; *OR,* 1, 6, 68.
35. *CM,* 5-26-62.
36. *EA,* 1-25-65.
37. *LL,* 10-14-63.

38. *OR,* 4, 2, 796.
39. *TCC,* 9-11-63; 10-9-63.
40. *EA,* 1-25-65.
41. Ibid.

Chapter 23

1. *CDC,* 11-26-61; *EA,* 2-5-62.
2. *CM,* 10-28-61.
3. SHSP, 14.51.
4. *CM,* 6-19-62; *EA,* 6-18-62; *OR,* 1, 14, 575.
5. *CDC,* 6-21-62.
6. Cauthen, ed., *Journals,* 149; *CDC,* 6-21-62; *CM,* 5-29-62; 1-8-63.
7. *CM,* 6-17-62; *CDC,* 6-19-62.
8. *EA,* 7-23-62.
9. *CM,* 10-17-62; 10-18-62; *EA,* 10-22-62; *CDC,* 10-18-62.
10. *EA,* 10-22-62.
11. *CDC,* 8-15-62.
12. *CM,* 1-8-63; 5-29-64; *CDC,* 6-21-62.
13. *CM,* 1-8-63.
14. Ripley, *Chapman's Fort,* 292.
15. *CM,* 5-29-62; *CDC,* 6-21-62.
16. *CM,* 1-8-63.
17. *CDC,* 8-1-64.
18. *OR,* 1, 28, 1, 400; *CM,* 9-7-63; 9-10-63.
19. SHSP, 16, 159.
20. *RR,* 7, 76.
21. *CM,* 8-4-64.
22. *OR,* 1, 47, 1, 1063.
23. *CDC,* 8-1-64.
24. *CM,* 5-29-62.
25. Ibid.
26. Ibid., 5-29-62; 10-18-62; *RR,* 1, 100.
27. *CDC,* 6-21-62.
28. *CM,* 5-29-62.
29. Ibid., 6-17-62.
30. Ibid., 5-29-62.
31. Sketch of the 2nd Artillery Regiment, Miscellaneous Sketches, 1866–1898, South Carolina Department of Archives and History, S108121 (hereafter cited as Sketch of the 2nd Artillery, SCDAH, S108121).
32. *CM,* 5-29-62.
33. *CDC,* 4-22-62, SCDAH, *Roll of the Dead.*
34. *RR,* 5, 560.
35. Ibid; Confederate Historian, "Annual Report," 62.
36. *CM,* 5-21-61.
37. Ibid., 6-24-61.
38. Ibid., 5-29-62.
39. Ibid;
40. Ibid; *RR,* 7, 358; Confederate Historian, "Annual Report," 54.
41. *CM,* 2-20-64.
42. Ibid., 5-29-62.
43. *CDC,* 4-22-62.
44. *CM,* 5-29-62; *EA,* 6-18-62.
45. Hagood, *Memoirs,* 65; *CDC,* 4-22-62.
46. Hagood, *Memoirs,* 65; *CM,* 5-29-62; *RR,* 6, 439.
47. *RR,* 6, 439.

48. Sketch of the 2nd Artillery, SCDAH, S108121.
49. Hagood, *Memoirs*, 65.
50. *CM*, 5-29-62.
51. Ibid.
52. Cauthen, ed., *Journals*, 195.
53. *CM*, 3-4-62.
54. *RR*, 5, 117.
55. *CM*, 5-29-62.
56. *CMH*, 659.
57. *EA*, 2-26-62; *CM*, 5-29-62.
58. *CM*, 5-8-62.
59. Ibid., 5-29-62; *RR*, 2, 228; *EA*, 2-26-62.
60. *RR*, 3, 550; 11, 348.
61. *EA*, 12-23-63.
62. Sifakis, *Compendium*, 7.
63. Ibid., 6.
64. *OR*, 1, 44, 875.
65. Ibid., 1, 44, 997.
66. Ibid., 1, 47, 2, 1070, 1073.
67. Ibid., 1, 47, 1, 1063; 1, 47, 3, 1732.
68. *CM*, 10-28-61.
69. *CDC*, 10-28-61.
70. *OR*, 1, 6, 326.
71. *CDC*, 11-13-62.
72. *OR*, 1, 28, 2, 325.
73. *CM*, 10-11-62.
74. *CM*, 2-2-63; *OR*, 1, 14, 202.
75. *OR*, 1, 14, 282.
76. Ibid., 1, 14, 277.
77. Ibid., 1, 28, 2, 162.
78. Ibid., 1, 28, 1, 159; 1, 28, 2, 246.
79. Ibid., 1, 28, 2, 245, 325.
80. Ibid., 1, 28, 1, 383, 390.
81. Ibid., 1, 28, 1, 454.
82. Ibid., 1, 28, 1, 467, 494; 1, 28, 2, 249.
83. Ibid., 1, 28, 1, 461.
84. Ibid., 1, 28, 1, 439, 476, 499; *CDC*, 8-31-63.
85. *OR*, 1, 28, 1, 448, 500; 1, 28, 2, 325.
86. Ibid., 1, 28, 1, 479.
87. Ibid., 1, 28, 1, 541; 1, 28, 2, 249; *CDC*, 9-9-63.
88. *OR*, 1, 28, 2, 367.
89. Ibid., 1, 28, 2, 469.
90. *CM*, 12-24-63; *OR*, 1, 28, 2, 562; 1, 53, 16.
91. *OR*, 1, 28, 2, 603; 1, 35, 1, 538; 1, 35, 2, 458, 598, 644.
92. *CM*, 2-15-64.
93. *OR*, 1, 35, 1, 167.
94. Ibid., 1, 35, 1, 266.
95. Ibid.
96. *CM*, 7-18-64.
97. *RR*, 5, 561.
98. *OR*, 1, 44, 993, 1000.
99. *CM*, 1-26-65; 2-10-65.
100. Ripley, *Chapman's Fort*, 244.
101. *RR*, 5, 561.
102. *CV*, 33, 255.

103. Ibid., 34, 215.
104. Ibid., 37, 460.
105. *OR,* 1, 47, 3, 782.

Chapter 24

1. *CM,* 3-18-62; Dedmondt, *Southern Bronze,* 20.
2. Woodward, *Mary Chesnut*, 107.
3. Dedmondt, *Southern Bronze,* 16.
4. *CM,* 3-28-62.
5. *DSG,* 3-28-62.
6. Ibid., 4-29-63
7. Sifakis, *Compendium*, 32.
8. Dedmondt, *Southern Bronze,* 17.
9. Cauthen, ed., *Journals,* 214.
10. *TriWeekly Watchman*, 10-1-62; *RR,* 12, 465.
11. Dedmondt, *Southern Bronze,* 72.
12. *CDC,* 5-21-63.
13. Brooks, *Stories*, 283.
14. Dedmondt, *Southern Bronze,* 97.
15. Ibid., 109, 117.
16. Ibid., 118.
17. Ibid., 143.
18. *CDC,* 1-31-65.
19. Dedmondt, *Southern Bronze,* 171.
20. Ibid., 173.
21. Ibid., 175.
22. Ibid., 177.

Appendix 1

1. *CS,* 2-28-61; *CM,* 2-25-60.
2. *CM,* 1-11-61.
3. Ibid., 2-22-61.
4. Ibid., 3-1-61.
5. Ibid., 3-14-61.
6. Ibid., 3-27-61; *YE,* 4-4-61.
7. *CM,* 6-5-61.
8. *YE,* 1-24-61.
9. *CM,* 6-13-61.
10. Ibid., 7-13-61.
11. Ibid., 7-2-61.
12. Ibid., 8-16-61; *CDC,* 4-13-63.
13. *CM,* 8-19-61.
14. Ibid., 9-19-61.
15. Ibid., 9-23-61.
16. Ibid., 10-4-61.
17. Ibid., 12-25-61.
18. Ibid., 1-29-62.
19. Ibid., 4-14-62.
20. Ibid., 5-12-63.
21. Ibid., 6-3-64.
22. Ibid., 1-19-65.
23. SHSP, Index.
24. UDC, *RR,* 7, 23.
25. Ibid., 10, 337.
26. *DSG,* 9-4-63.

27. *YE,* 1-10-61.
28. Ibid., 1-17-61.
29. Thomas, *Rising Star*, 177.
30. *YE,* 1-24-61; *Keowee Courier (Walhalla),* 1-12-61; 6-29-61.
31. *YE,* 1-24-61.
32. Ibid.
33. Ibid., 1-31-61.
34. Ibid., 2-21-61.
35. Ibid., 2-28-61.
36. Ibid., 4-25-61; *CM,* 5-6-61.
37. *YE,* 5-30-61.
38. *Keowee Courier (Walhalla),* 2-2-61.
39. *EA*, 5-22-61.
40. Ibid., 6-12-61; 7-3-61.
41. Ibid., 6-19-61.
42. Ibid., 6-26-61.
43. Ibid., 7-3-61.
44. Ibid., 7-10-61.
45. Ibid., 8-7-61.
46. Ibid., 7-8-63.
47. Ibid., 7-21-64; *CDC,* 9-15-64.
48. *EA*, 3-22-65.
49. *Keowee Courier (Walhalla),* 6-29-61.
50. Ibid., 6-29-61.
51. Ibid., 7-6-61.
52. Ibid., 7-13-61.
53. Ibid.
54. Ibid., 7-20-61.
55. Ibid.
56. Ibid.
57. *LL,* 5-1-61.
58. Ibid., 5-22-62.
59. Ibid.
60. Ibid., 5-29-61.
61. Ibid., 5-12-61.
62. Ibid.
63. Ibid., 9-18-61.
64. PM1-3-61.
65. *Greenville Southern Enterprise*, 7-2-63.
66. Ibid.
67. *LL,* 4-30-62.
68. *Anderson Intelligencer,* 2-7-61.
69. Ibid., 2-21-61.
70. *AP,* 9-20-61.
71. *OR,* 1, 47, 2, 1073.
72. *CDC,* 5-2-61.
73. Ibid., 5-31-61.
74. Ibid., 8-26-61.
75. Ibid., 8-30-62.
76. *For Love of a Rebel*, 50.
77. Ibid, 103.
78. Wyckoff, Website.
79. Brooks, *Stories*, 293.
80. Wyckoff, Website
81. Ibid.
82. Ibid.

Appendix 2

1. Halliburton, *Saddle Soldiers*, 130.
2. *CM,* 1-12-61.
3. *Anderson Intelligencer,* 1-3-61, 1-10-61.
4. *Keowee Courier (Walhalla),* 1-19-61.
5. *CM,* 1-31-61.
6. Ibid., 2-22-61.
7. Ibid., 4-19-61.
8. Ibid., 6-1-61.
9. Ibid., 10-9-61.
10. UDC, *RR,* 7, 343.
11. *Triweekly Watchman,* 7-27-63.
12. *CM,* 11-14-63.
13. *CMH,* 687.
14. Ibid.
15. *Acts,* 878.
16. Cauthen, ed., *Journals,* 190.
17. *YE,* 1-10-61; *DSG,* 1-8-61; 5-4-61.
18. *Anderson Intelligencer,* 1-10-61; *Keowee Courier (Walhalla),* 1-19-61.
19. *Keowee Courier (Walhalla),* 1-12-61.
20. *EA*, 1-30-61.
21. Ibid., 2-27-61.
22. Ibid., 9-4-61.
23. *Keowee Courier (Walhalla),* 6-15-61.
24. *Triweekly Watchman,* 8-14-63; 9-18-63.
25. *CDC,* 1-17-65.
26. *AP,* 1-4-61.

Appendix 3

1. Baker, *Cadets in Gray*, 155.
2. *CMH,* 437.
3. *CM,* 10-29-62.
4. Ibid., 1-6-64.
5. Ibid., 6-27-61.
6. Ibid., 9-19-61.
7. James J. Baldwin, *The Struck Eagle—A Biography of Brigadier General Micah Jenkins, and A History of the Fifth South Carolina Volunteers and the Palmetto Sharpshooters*, 75.
8. *Acts,* 934.
9. *For Love of a Rebel*, 17.
10. Tower, *A Carolinian Goes To War*, 12.

BIBLIOGRAPHY

Abbeville Banner

Abbeville Press

Acts of the General Assembly of the State of South Carolina, passed in November and December 1860 and January 1861. Columbia, South Carolina: Charles P. Pelham, 1861.

Allardice, Bruce S. *More Generals in Gray*. Baton Rouge: Louisiana State University Press, 1995.

Anderson Intelligencer

Andrews, Robert W. *The Life and Adventures of Captain Robert W. Andrews of Sumter, South Carolina*. Boston, Massachusetts: E.P. Whitcomb, 1887.

Andrews, Welburn J. *Sketch of Company K, 23rd SCV in the Civil War from 1862–1865*. Richmond, Virginia: Whittet and Shepperson, n.d. Repr. South Carolina Division, United Daughters of the Confederacy. *Recollections and Reminiscences 1861–1865 through World War I*.

Armstrong, James. *The Carolina Light Infantry's Record in the Great War*. Charleston, South Carolina: Walker, Evans, and Cogswell, 1912.

Austin, J. Luke. *General John Bratton: Sumter to Appomattox In Letters to His Wife*. Sewanee, Tennessee: Proctor's Hall Press, 2003.

Baker, Gary R. *Cadets in Gray*. Columbia, South Carolina: Palmetto Bookworks, 1989.

Baldwin James J. *The Struck Eagle—A Biography of Brigadier General Micah Jenkins, and A History of the Fifth South Carolina Volunteers and the Palmetto Sharpshooters*. Shippensburg, Pennsylvania: Burd Street Press, 1996.

Barnwell Sentinel

Batson, Steve. Website on the 16th Regiment, SCV. http://www.geocities.com/BourbonStreet/Square/3873/franklina.html.

Baxley, Neil. *No Prouder Fate: The Story of the 11th South Carolina Volunteer Infantry*. Bloomington, Indiana: AuthorHouse, 2005.

Bell, L.M., ed. *Rebels In Grey, Soldiers from Pickens District 1861–1865*. Clemson, South Carolina: Joyce's Print Shop, 1984.

Benson, Susan Williams, ed. *Berry Benson's Civil War Book, Memoirs of a Confederate Scout and Sharpshooter*. Athens: The University of Georgia Press, 1992.

Boykin, Edward Mortimer. *The Falling Flag*. New York: E.J. Hale and Son, 1874.

Boykin, Richard Manning. *Captain Alexander Hamilton Boykin, One of South Carolina's Distinguished Citizens*. Repr. Camden, South Carolina: J.J. Fox, 1991.

Boyles, J.R., Lt. *Reminiscences of the Civil War, Company C, 12th Regiment, SCV.* Columbia, South Carolina: R. L. Bryan Co., 1890.

Boylston, Raymond P. *Butler's Brigade, That Fighting Civil War Cavalry Brigade from South Carolina*. Raleigh, North Carolina: Jarrett Press and Publications, 2000.

Bradshaw, Timothy E., Jr. *Battery Wagner, The Siege, The Men Who Fought and The Casualties*. Columbia, South Carolina: Palmetto Historical Works, 1993.

Brasington, Bill. Website "South Carolina State Troops Seed Corn Units, 1864–1865." Website deals with reserves and state troops. www://geocities.com/sc_seedcorn.

Brennan, Patrick. *Secessionville, Assault on Charleston*. Campbell, California: Savas Publishing Company, 1996.

Brock, R.A., and Philip Van Doren Stern. *The Appomattox Roster.* New York: Antiquarian Press, Ltd. 1962.

Brooks, Ulysses Robert, ed. *Butler and His Cavalry in the War of Secession 1861–1865, 1909*. Repr. Camden, South Carolina: J.J. Fox, 1991.

———. *Stories of the Confederacy.* Columbia, South Carolina: The State Company, 1912.

Brown, Joseph N., Col. "Account of the Battle of Gettysburg." Speech given in Anderson, South Carolina. March 23, 1901. (Available from the Greenville County Public Library. Microfiche SC 973.7457, Fiche 109.)

———. An Address Delivered on the Battle of the "Bloody Angle" at the November 1900 Meeting of the Robert E. Lee Chapter of the Daughters of Confederacy May 12, 1864. Anderson, South Carolina: The Association Publishing Company, 1900.

Brown, Varina D. *A Colonel at Gettysburg and Spotsylvania*. Columbia, South Carolina: The State Company, 1931.

Brunson, Joseph Woods, Sgt. *Pee Dee Light Artillery of Maxcy Gregg's (Later Samuel McGowan's) Brigade First South Carolina Volunteers (Infantry) C.S.A. A Historical Sketch and Roster*. University of Alabama: Confederate Publishing Company, 1983.

Buzhardt, Beaufort Simpson. "Diary of Beaufort Simpson Buzhardt." (Available from the Greenville County Public Library. Microfiche 973.7457, fiche 89.)

Caldwell, J.F.J. *The History of a Brigade of South Carolinians*. Philadelphia: King and Baird Printers, 1866. Repr. Dayton, Ohio: Morningside Press, 1984.

Calhoun, C.M. *Liberty Dethroned*. N.p., n.d. (Available from author.)

Camden Confederate

Carolina Spartan

Cauthen, Charles E. *South Carolina Goes to War, 1860–1865.* Chapel Hill: University of North Carolina Press, 1950.

———, ed. *Journals of the South Carolina Executive Councils 1861 and 1862*. Columbia: South Carolina Archives Department, 1956.

Charleston Daily Courier

Charleston Mercury

Chisolm, Robert. Papers. N.p., n.d. (Available from the Greenville County Public Library. Microfiche SC 973.7457, fiche 123.)

Cisco, Walter Brian. *States Rights Gist, A South Carolina General of the Civil War*. Shippensburg, Pennsylvania: White Mane Publishing Company, 1991.

The Civil War in Southwestern South Carolina December 1864–January 1865. Montmorenci, South Carolina: Western Carolina Historical Research, 1997.

Clary, James B. *A History of the 15th South Carolina Infantry 1861–1865*. Cary, NC: James B. Clary in cooperation with the South Carolina Department of Archives and History, 2007.

Coker, James Lide. *History of Company G, Ninth S.C. Regiment, Infantry, South Carolina Army and of Company E, Sixth S.C. Regiment, Infantry, South Carolina Army.* Greenwood, South Carolina: The Attic Press, Repr. 1979.

Confederate Military History Extended Edition, Volume 6, South Carolina. Wilmington, North Carolina. Broadfoot Publishing, 1987.

Confederate Veteran, Nashville, Tennessee. 40 vols.

Conrad, James L. The Sad History of 'Shanks' Evans." *The Civil War Times Illustrated*, Vol. 22 (Sept. 1983): 32–38.

Coward, Asbury, N.J. Bond, and O.L. Coward, eds. *The South Carolinians.* New York: Vantage Press, 1968.

Crute, Joseph H., Jr. *Units of the Confederate Army*. Midlothian, Virginia: Derwent Books, 1987.

Cyclopedia of Eminent and Representative Men of the Carolinas of the Nineteenth Century. Vol. 1. Madison, Wisconsin: Brant and Fuller, 1892.

Daily South Carolinian

Daily Southern Guardian

Daly, Louise Haskell. *Alexander Cheves Haskell, The Portrait of a Man*. Wilmington, North Carolina: Broadfoot Publishing Company, 1989.

Darlington Southerner

Davis, Nora M., comp. *Military and Naval Operations in South Carolina 1860–1865: A Chronological List, With References to Sources of Further Information*: South Carolina Archives, 1959.

Davis, Sam. Conversation with author.

Dedmondt, Glenn. *Southern Bronze, Captain Garden's (S.C.) Artillery Company During the War Between the States*. Columbia, South Carolina: Palmetto Bookworks, 1993.

Dickert, D. Augustus. *History of Kershaw's Brigade*. Dayton, Ohio: Morningside House, 1988.

Douglas, David G. *A Boot Full of Memories: Captain Leonard Williams, 2nd South Carolina Cavalry.* Camden, South Carolina: Gray Fox Publishing, 2003.

DuBose, Henry Kershaw. *The History of Company B, 21st Regiment (Infantry) SCV C.S.P.A*. Columbia, South Carolina: The R.L. Bryan Company, 1909.

Due West Telescope

Dunlop, W.S. *Lee's Sharpshooters or, The Forefront of Battle*. W.S. Dayton, Ohio: Morning House Inc, 1988.

Edgefield Advertiser

Edwards, W.H., Capt. *A Condensed History of the Seventeenth Regiment, SCV, C.S.A.* Columbia, South Carolina: The R.L. Bryan Company, 1908.

Elliott, Charles P., Maj. "Elliott's Brigade and how it held the Crater at the Battle of Petersburg. Speech given 5 December 1895. The Fitz William McMaster Collection. (Available from the Greenville County Public Library. Microfiche SC 973.7457, Fiche 113.)

Emanuel, S. "A Historical Sketch of the Georgetown Rifle Guards." Speech delivered on 17 November, 1909. (Available from the Greenville County Public Library. Microfiche 973.7457, fiche 100.)

Estilow, L.E., ed. "Doing My Duty—The Wartime Experiences of John S. Hard 1861–1863." Unpublished. (Available from author.)

Evans, Clement, ed. *Confederate Military History Extended Edition*, Vol. 6, *South Carolina*. Atlanta: Confederate Publishing Company, 1899. Repr. Wilmington, North Carolina: Broadfoot Publishing Company, 1987.

Everson, Guy R., and Edward H. Simpson Jr., eds. *Far, Far from Home—The Wartime Letters of Dick and Tally Simpson, 3rd South Carolina Volunteers*. New York: Oxford University Press, 1994.

Ewell, S.P.H. *Recollections of War Times*. Bamberg, South Carolina: The Bamberg Herald Printers, 1895.

For Love of a Rebel. Georgetown, South Carolina: The Arthur Manigault Chapter of the U.D.C., 1964.

Ford, A.P., and M.J. Ford. *Life in the Confederate Army*. New York: The Neale Publishing Company, 1905.

Freeman, Douglas Southall. *Lee's Lieutenants*. 3 vols. New York: Charles Scribner's Sons, 1944.

Garlington, J.C. *Men of the Time, Sketches of Living Notables, A Biographical Encyclopedia of Contemporaneous South Carolina Leaders.* Spartanburg, South Carolina: Garlington Press, 1902.

Gibson, John Mendinghall. *Those 163 Days; A Southern Account of Sherman's March from Atlanta to Raleigh.* New York: Bramhall House, 1961.

Greenville Mountaineer

Greenville Patriot and Mountaineer

Greenville Southern Enterprise

Hagood, James R. "Memoirs of the First South Carolina Regiment of Volunteer Infantry in the Confederate War for Independence from April 12, 1861 to April 10, 1865." Unpublished MS. Columbia: South Caroliniana Library.

Hagood, Johnson. *Memoirs of the War of Secession, From the Original Manuscripts of Johnson Hagood.* Columbia, South Carolina: The State Company, 1910.

Halliburton, Lloyd. *Saddle Soldiers, The Civil War Correspondence of General William Stokes 4th South Carolina Cavalry.* Orangeburg, South Carolina: Sandlapper Publishing Company, 1993.

Heller, J. Roderick, and Carolynn Ayres Heller, eds. *The Confederacy Is on Her Way Up the Spout, Letters to South Carolina 1861–1864.* Columbia: University of South Carolina Press, 1998.

Henderson, E. Prioleau. *Autobiography of Arab, E. Prioleau Henderson.* Oxford: The Guild Bindery Press, 1901. Repr. Camden, South Carolina: J.J. Fox, 1991.

Horry Dispatch

Howard, Robert M. *Reminiscences.* Columbus, Georgia: Gilbert Printing Company, 1912.

Hoyt, James A. *The Palmetto Riflemen, Company B, 4th Regiment SCV and Company C, Palmetto Sharpshooters.* Greenville, South Carolina: Hoyt and Keys Printers, 1886.

Hudson, Joshua Hilary. *Sketches and Reminiscences.* Columbia, South Carolina: The State Company, 1903.

Inglesby, Charles. *Historical Sketch of the First Regiment of South Carolina Artillery (Regulars).* Charleston, South Carolina. Walker, Evans, and Cogswell, n.d.

Izlar, William Valmore. *A Sketch of the War Record of the Edisto Rifles, 1861–1865.* Columbia, South Carolina: The State Company, 1914.

Johnson, John. *The Defense of Charleston Harbor including Fort Sumter and the Adjacent Islands, 1863–1865.* Charleston, South Carolina: Walker, Evans, and Cogswell, 1890.

Jones, Eugene W. Jr. *Enlisted For The War, The Struggles of the Gallant 24th Regiment, South Carolina Volunteers, Infantry, 1861–1865.* Highstown, New Jersey: Longstreet House, 1997.

Jordan, Laylon Wayne, and Elizabeth H. Stringfellow. *A Place Called St. John's: The Story of John's Edisto, Wadmalaw, Kiawah, and Seabrook Islands of South Carolina.* Spartanburg, South Carolina: The Reprint Company, 2003.

Keowee Courier (Walhalla)

Kirkland, Randolph W., Jr. *Broken Fortunes—South Carolina Soldiers, Sailors and Citizens Who Died in the Service of Their Country and State in the War for Southern Independence, 1861–1865.* Charleston: The South Carolina Historical Society, 1995.

Krick, Robert K. *Lee's Colonels, A Biographical Register of the Field Officers of the Army of Northern Virginia.* 3d ed. rev. Dayton, Ohio: Morningside House, 1991.

Lancaster Ledger

Laurensville Herald

Lewis, Richard, Lieutenant. *Camp Life of a Confederate Boy.* Charleston, South Carolina: News and Courier Press, 1883.

Lexington Dispatch

Longacre, Edward G. *Gentleman and Soldier.* Nashville, Tennessee: Rutledge Hill Press, 2003.

Lynch. Harriet P. *Reminiscences and Sketches of Confederate Times.* Columbia, South Carolina: The R.L. Bryan Company, 1909.

Marion Star

McArthur, Judith N., and Orville Vernon Burton. *A Gentleman and An Officer-A Military and Social History of James B. Griffin's Civil War.* New York: Oxford University Press, 1996.

McDaniel, J.J. "Diary of the Battles, Marches, and Incidents of the 7th South Carolina Regiment." N.p., n.d. (Available from the Greenville County Public Library. Microfiche 973.7457, fiche 99.)

McSwain, Eleanor D., ed. *Crumbling Defenses or Memoirs and Reminiscences of John Logan Black, Colonel, C.S.A.* Macon, Georgia: J.W. Burke Company, 1960.

Melton, E. Frank. *War Between The States.* Hartsville: Old Darlington District, South Carolina Genealogical Society, 2002.

Mixson, Frank M. *Reminiscences Of A Private.* Columbia, South Carolina: The State Company, 1910.

Mulligan, A.B. *My Dear Mother and Sisters, The Civil War Letters of Captain A.B. Mulligan, Company B, 5th South Carolina Cavalry, Butler's Division, Hampton's Corps, 1861–1865.* Spartanburg, South Carolina: The Reprint Company, 1992.

Murray, J. Ogden. *The Immortal 600.* New York: The Neale Publishing Company, 1905.

National Archives and Records Administration. *Compiled Service Records of Confederate Soldiers Who Served in Organizations from the State of South Carolina* (CSR). Microcopy 267.

———. Register of Confederate Soldiers, Sailors, and Citizens Who Died in Federal Prisons and Military Hospitals in the North, 1861–1865. Microfilm publication. M918 (973.742).

Nichols, Wesley. *The Autobiography of Wesley Nichols.* N.p., n.d. (Available from the Greenville County Public Library. Microfiche SC 973.7457, Fiche 111.

Phelps, W. Chris. *Charlestonians in War: the Charleston Battalion.* Gretna, Louisiana: Pelican Publishing Company, 2004.

Reid, Jesse W. *History of the Fourth Regiment, S.C. Volunteers, from the Commencement of the War until Lee's Surrender.* Greenville, South Carolina: Shannon and Company, 1891. Repr. Dayton, Ohio: Morningside Bookshop, 1975.

Rhea, Gordon C. *Carrying the Flag.* New York: Basic Books, 2004.

Ripley, Warren. *The Battle of Chapman's Fort, May 26, 1864.* Green Pond: Ashepoo Plantation, 1978.

———. *Siege Train, The Journal of a Confederate Artilleryman in the Defense of Charleston.* Columbia: University of South Carolina Press, 1986.

Rivers, William J. *Rivers's Account of the Raising of Troops in South Carolina for State and Confederate Service 1861–1865.* Columbia, South Carolina: The Bryan Printing Company, State Printers, 1899.

Salley, Alexander S., comp. *South Carolina Troops in Confederate Service.* 3 vols. Columbia, South Carolina: The R.L. Bryan Company, 1913, 1914, 1930.

Sellers, William W. *A History of Marion County, South Carolina, from its earliest times to present—1901.* Columbia, SC: R.L. Bryan Company, 1902.

Sifakis, Stewart. *Compendium of the Confederate Armies—South Carolina and Georgia.* New York: Facts on File, 1995

Smith, C.F. *Jeremiah Smith and the Confederate War.* Spartanburg, South Carolina: The Reprint Company, 1993.

South Carolina Department of Archives and History.

———. Adjutant and Inspector General. "History of Charleston Zouave Cadets." 1904. 1 vol. N.d.

Roster of 14th South Carolina Infantry. 2 vols. N.d.

———. Comptroller General. Confederate Pension Applications Division, 1910–1926. Nos. 1941–2202 (Charleston-Cherokee). Microfilm Roll CW1231 (AD1149), No. 1995.

———. Confederate Historian.

"Annual Report For The Year 1899." *South Carolina Reports and Resolutions 1868–1900, regular session 1900.* Microcopy 13, Roll 29.

Memory Roll: Rolls of South Carolina Volunteers in the Confederate States Provisional Army. 5 vols. Microcopy 16, 1993.
Record and Roll of the German Fusiliers. 1 vol. 1904.
Record and Roll of the Washington Light Artillery, 1905. 1 vol.
Roster of Officers. N.d. 1 vol.
———. Miscellaneous Historical Sketches, 1866–1898. S108121.
Albergotti, W. Greer. "Sketch of Company F, 2nd Battalion, South Carolina State Troops." N.d.
Alston, Butler P. "Sketch of the 6th South Carolina Infantry." 1878.
Hammond, W.A. "Sketch of Company B, 37th Virginia Cavalry." 1898.
"Historical Sketch of the 5th South Carolina Cavalry." 1866. S108121.
James, A.A. "Brief History of the 18th. South Carolina Volunteers." N.d.
Lucas, J.J. "Sketch of Lucas's Battalion of Heavy Artillery." 1882.
Roll of Company G, 22nd South Carolina Infantry. 1884.
Roster of the 17th South Carolina Infantry (Partial). N.d.
Rion, J.H. "History of the 6th Regiment, South Carolina Infantry," n.d.
"Sketch of Company F, 21st South Carolina Infantry." N.d.
"Sketch of the 2nd South Carolina Artillery Regiment." N.d.
"Sketches of the 23rd South Carolina Infantry." 1891.
Stokes, William. "Sketch of Company G, 4th South Carolina Cavalry." N.d.
———. *Roll of the Dead, South Carolina Troops Confederate States Service*. 1994.

South Carolina Historical Magazine

Southern Historical Society. Southern Historical Society Papers. 52 vols. Richmond, Virginia, 1876–1959.

Starr, Linda Sparks. *W.R. Rankin, Manassas to Appomattox*. Norman, Oklahoma: Linda Sparks Starr, 1990.

The State

Stevens, Robert J. *Captain Bill, The Records and Writings of Captain William Henry Edwards (and others) Company A, 17th Regiment, South Carolina Volunteers, Confederate States of America.* 3 vols. Richburg, South Carolina: The Chester District Genealogical Society, 1985–1990.

Stone, DeWitt Boyd, Jr. *Wandering to Glory.* Columbia: University of South Carolina Press, 2002.

Sumter Watchman

Taylor, John S. *Sixteenth South Carolina Regiment CSA from Greenville County, South Carolina*. Private printing, 1964.

Thigpen, Allan D. *Recollections of Potter's Raid*. Sumter, South Carolina: Gamecock City Printing, 1999.

Thomas, John P. *Career and Character of General Micah Jenkins, C.S.A.* Columbia, South Carolina: The State Company, 1903.

Thomas, Samuel N., Jr., and Jason H. Silverman, eds. *A Rising Star of Promise: The Civil War Odyssey of David Jackson Logan, 17th South Carolina Volunteers, 1861–1864.* Campbell, California: Savas Publishing Company, 1998.

Tolar, J.R. "A History of Company B, 10th Regiment, SCV" (Available from the Greenville County Public Library. Microfiche 973.7457, fiche 101.)

Tompkins, D.A. *Company K, 14th SCV* Charlotte, North Carolina: Charlotte Observer Printing Publishing House, 1897. (Available from the Greenville County Public Library. Microfiche SC 973.7457, Fiche 110.)

Toole, Gasper Loren. *Ninety Years in Aiken County*. Private printing, 1961.

Tower, Lockwood, ed. *A Carolinian Goes To War, The Civil Narrative of Arthur Middleton Manigault, Brigadier General, C.S.A., R.* Columbia: University of South Carolina Press, 1983.

Triweekly Watchman

United Daughters of the Confederacy. South Carolina Division, *Recollections and Reminiscences 1861–1865 through World War I.* 9 vols.

United States War Department. *The War of the Rebellion: A Compilation of the Official Records of the Union and Confederate Armies.* 128 vols. Washington, DC.: Government Printing Office, 1891–1895. (It should be noted that some volumes in this series are broken into parts, while some are not. Entries for volumes with parts are listed in the endnotes with a series, a volume, a part, and a page number or numbers; entries for volumes without parts are listed only with a series, a volume, and a page number or numbers.)

Walker, C.I. *Rolls and Historical Sketch of the Tenth Regiment, So. Ca. Volunteers in the Army of the Confederate States by C.I. Walker, Late Lieut. Col. of the Regt. To which is added An Historical Sketch of the Georgetown Rifle Guards Company A, 10th South Carolina by Sol. Emanuel.* South Carolina: Walker, Evans, and Cogswell, 1881. Repr. Alexandria, Virginia: Stonewall House, 1985.

Warner, Ezra J. *Generals in Blue, Lives of the Union Commanders*. Baton Rouge: Louisiana State University Press, 1986.

———. *Generals in Gray, Lives of the Confederate Commanders*. Baton Rouge: Louisiana State University Press, 1986.

Welch, Spencer G. *A Confederate Surgeon's Letters to his Wife.* New York: Neale Publishing Company, 1911.

Wellman, Manly Wade. *Giant in Gray, A Biography of Wade Hampton of South Carolina*. New York: Charles Scribner's and Sons, 1949.

Wells, Edward L. *Hampton and His Cavalry in '64*. Richmond, Virginia: B.F. Johnson, 1899.

———. *A Sketch of the Charleston Light Dragoons, From the Earliest Formation of the Corps.* Charleston, South Carolina: Lucas, Richardson, and Company, 1888.

Wise, Stephen R. *Gate of Hell, Campaign for Charleston Harbor, 1863*. Columbia: University of South Carolina Press, 1994.

Woodward, C. Vann and Elisabeth Muhlenfeld. *The Private Mary Chesnut, The Unpublished Civil War Diaries*. New York: Oxford University Press, 1984.

Woodward, T.W. "History of the 6th Regiment, S.C. Volunteers." Speech. Columbia, South Carolina: Presbyterian Publishing House, 1883.

Wyckoff, Mac. *A History of the 2nd South Carolina Infantry 1861–1865*. Fredericksburg, Virginia: Sergeant Kirkland's Museum and Historical Society, 1994.

———. *A History of the 3rd South Carolina Infantry 1861–1865*. Fredericksburg, Virginia: Sergeant Kirkland's Museum and Historical Society, 1995.

———. Website on South Carolina in the Civil War. http://www.members.tripod.com/mwyckoff/.

Yorkville Enquirer

INDEX